BOUND FOR
FREEDOM

Douglas Flamming

BOUND FOR
FREEDOM

Black Los Angeles in
Jim Crow America

University of California Press

BERKELEY   LOS ANGELES   LONDON

Portions of this book draw upon ideas and prose previously published in William Deverell and Douglas Flamming, "Race, Rhetoric, and Regional Identity: Boosting Los Angeles, 1880–1930," in *Power and Place in the North American West*, edited by Richard White and John Findlay (Seattle: University of Washington Press, 1999); and Douglas Flamming, "Becoming Democrats: African American Politics in Los Angeles, 1920–1965," in *Seeking El Dorado: African Americans in California*, edited by Lawrence B. de Graaf, Kevin Mulroy, and Quintard Taylor (Seattle: University of Washington Press, 2001).

Arna Bontemps' poem "The Day-Breakers" reprinted by permission of Harold Ober Associates Incorporated. From *Personals*, © 1963 by Arna Bontemps. Langston Hughes' poem "History" from *The Collected Poems of Langston Hughes*, © 1994 by the estate of Langston Hughes, used by permission of Alfred A. Knopf.

University of California Press
Berkeley and Los Angeles, California

University of California Press, Ltd.
London, England

© 2005 by the Regents of the University of California

Library of Congress Cataloging-in-Publication Data

Flamming, Douglas.
    Bound for freedom : Black Los Angeles in Jim Crow America /
Douglas Flamming.
        p. cm.
    Includes bibliographical references and index.
    ISBN 0-520-23919-9 (cloth : alk. paper)
    1. African Americans—California—Los Angeles—History—
19th century.   2. African Americans—California—Los Angeles—
History—20th century.   3. African Americans—Civil rights—
California—Los Angeles—History.   4. Community life—
California—Los Angeles—History—19th century.   5. Community
life—California—Los Angeles—History—20th century.   6. Civil
rights movements—California—Los Angeles—History—19th
century.   7. Civil rights movements—California—Los Angeles—
History—20th century.   8. Los Angeles (Calif.)—Race relations.
I. Title.

F869.L89N4 2005
979.4'9400496073—dc22   2004018017

Manufactured in the United States of America
14   13   12   11   10   09   08   07   06   05   04
10   9   8   7   6   5   4   3   2   1

Printed on Ecobook 50 containing a minimum 50% post-consumer
waste, processed chlorine free. The balance contains virgin pulp, including 25% Forest Stewardship Council Certified for no old growth
tree cutting, processed either TCF or ECF. The sheet is acid-free and
meets the minimum requirements of ANSI/NISO Z39.48–1992 (R 1997)
(Permanence of Paper).

For Judith

Forever

The publisher gratefully acknowledges the generous contribution to this book provided by the African American Studies Endowment Fund of the University of California Press Associates, which is supported by a major gift from the George Gund Foundation.

Contents

Maps

Acknowledgments

When I began this project in 1990, I had no idea what a demanding and unpredictable journey I had begun—or how rewarding it would be. Part of the reward was meeting many wonderful people along the way. It is with great pleasure that I acknowledge the people and institutions whose kindnesses, great and small, have made this book possible. All have earned my gratitude; none are responsible for my shortcomings.

The John Randolph Haynes and Dora Haynes Foundation deserves my deepest appreciation. I am grateful to its administrative director, Diane Cornwell, and the board of trustees for their consistent support of this project. Through numerous grants and fellowships, the foundation has provided me with much needed resources and—that greatest of gifts—uninterrupted time for research and writing. The Haynes Foundation seeks a better, more equitable Los Angeles through its support of historical and social scientific research into the nature of the city and its people. In an age of cynicism, it optimistically seeks to fulfill the Haynes family's mission. I hope my book upholds its trust and makes some contribution to its worthy goals.

The William Andrews Clark Memorial Library of Los Angeles, in collaboration with UCLA's Center for Seventeenth- and Eighteenth-Century Studies, offered me an Ahmanson-Getty Fellowship in 1993 as part of its "American Dreams, Western Images" initiative. This placed me in a community of scholars, led by the historians Valerie Matsumoto and George Sanchez, with whom I enjoyed an enormously fruitful year of intellectual exchange. Heartfelt thanks to Valerie and George, and to Blake Allmendinger, Debbie Handren, Peter Reill, Marina Romani, and Lori Stein.

In 1994, John M. Findlay and Richard White invited me to participate in a stimulating conference hosted by the University of Washington's Center for the Study of the Pacific Northwest; that symposium, "Power and Place in the North American West," sharpened my vision of the region and its people.

The J. Paul Getty Center for the History of the Arts and the Humanities invited me to participate in a year of seminars and fellowship with other scholars and writers who were actively researching Los Angeles. My fellow Getty scholars broadened my understanding of the city and how we might study it. Special thanks to program coordinators Philip Roth and Sabine Schlosher, and to Dana Cuff, Robert Dawidoff, Biz Lopez, Becky Nicolaides, Samella Lewis, Carolyn See, and R. J. Smith.

Archival staffs around the country have been indispensable. I wish to thank Ann Allen Shockley of the Fisk University Library Special Collections; the expert librarians of the Sinclair Archive at Indiana University's Lilly Library; Everett Thomas of the African American Museum and Library at Oakland; Christie Hammond of the A. K. Smiley Public Library; and the expert librarians of the National Archives in Washington, D.C., and at the National Archives' southeastern branch in Georgia. The special collections librarians at the Stanford University Library and Stanford's Hoover Institute, as well as the Bancroft Library at the University of California, Berkeley, were invariably helpful. The staff of the California State Archives helped me locate elusive precinct-level election results. Maureen Harkey and James Dankey of the University of Wisconsin created the invaluable national database of African American newspapers. Jim H. Sakihara and Brenda J. Magee, of the Department of Registrar-Recorder of Los Angeles County, went out of their way to find historic precinct boundaries on microfilm. I appreciate the assistance of the Montana Historical Society and also the University Libraries of Iowa, where Jacque Roothler was tremomdously helpful. Hynda L. Rudd and Jay Jones of the Los Angeles City Archives were priceless. Carolyn Cole, head of the history department of the Los Angeles Public Library and founder, with Kathy Kobayashi, of the sensational Shades of L.A. photograph collection, has my eternal gratitude. Randy Boehm of the Library of Congress made it possible to copy the entire set of NAACP branch files for Los Angeles, which were inadvertently omitted from the microfilm set of branch-file records. Sarah Cooper, Mary Tyler, and the staff of the Southern California Library for Social Studies and Research were always helpful and kind. Jarvis DuBois at the California African American Museum of Los Angeles helped me navigate the Miriam Matthews photograph collection. Tom Sitton of the Los Angeles County Natural History Museum was, as always, terrifically helpful.

The California Institute of Technology was my home base when I started this book, and I wish to thank the leaders of the Humanities and Social Sciences Division—David Grether, John Ledyard, and Susan Davis—who supported me without fail. Former Caltech president Thomas Everhart always encouraged my work and funded Caltech's "Race, Politics, and Region" seminar series, which taught me much about Los Angeles race relations. Helga Galvan, my secretary and overall champion, made our seminar series a success and contributed greatly to this book. For their wise and gracious guidance over the years, I also wish to acknowledge Chris Brennan and Jerry Nunally. Thanks, too, to the Caltech media specialists who contributed to my work, especially Bob Turring and Richard Gomez. Hats off as well to Pamela Croomes for her Black History Month programs, which inspired and taught me. The staff of the Caltech Library was exceptionally helpful over the years. Thanks to countless other staff members, development officers, and administrators who made Caltech a productive and enjoyable place to be.

Many Caltech undergraduates were able research assistants. Eric Fung—long since an M.D.—was a terrific researcher and has waited longest for this acknowledgment. Alex Rosser did excellent work, as did Diana Watson, Andrea Mehea, and other Blacker House students. Edray Goins—now a mathematics Ph.D.—always supported the project. Jessica Barnett and Josh Prank were indispensable. Eric Hill, engineer, could have been an outstanding historian. His dedication to this topic and his extraordinary research greatly enhanced my work.

My colleagues at Caltech provided deep pools of ideas and encouragement. Dan Kevles's collegiality and professionalism were an inspiration. Morgan Kousser was enthusiastic about this project from the beginning and gave my early chapters on politics the grilling they deserved. I hope (very much) he finds my final versions more respectable. Over the years, Caltech's visiting scholars and postdocs brought new perspectives; thanks especially to Laird Boswell, Glen Bugos, Ruth Cowan, Jacquelyn Dowd Hall, Robert Korstad, Leonard Moore, Andrew Robertson, and Marlin Ross.

Kevin Gilmartin, an invaluable colleague and friend, made my years at Caltech all the more meaningful. I thank him and Susan, and young Raymond, for the joy they have given me and my family over the years. I met Bryant Simon at Caltech, and as a result, my outlook on the world has been expanding ever since. Bryant can do that for you. More important, his friendship has been priceless. I thank him and Anne Marie, and their sons Ben and Eli, for being so wonderful.

The Huntington Library has offered rich archival resources and spaces for quiet reflection. Robert C. Richie, the Huntington's director of reasearch, and administrative director Carolyn Powell have been unfailingly kind and supportive. Peter Blodgett and Susan Hudson are my heroes; they consistently discovered new materials for my work and made sure I found them. Bill Frank, Alan Jutzi, and Jennifer Watts all deserve medals for their deep knowledge of the collections. Innumerable colleagues at the Huntington offered encouragement and enriched my work with questions, suggestions, and the occasional raised eyebrow over lunch. To Charlie Royster: thanks for the letter. To Anne Scott: you're the best.

The Huntington also provided financial support for my research, with a Summer Fellowship in 1991 and a Haynes Fellow grant in 1996, and offered numerous venues for presenting my work as it progressed. I am especially grateful for the invitation to deliver the annual Haynes Foundation Lecture for 1999, and I am thankful to the Huntington's public relations staff for their assistance in that and other speaking engagements. The Huntington's Los Angeles History Research Group was a mainstay in my L.A. years. Thanks to all group members and leaders, who created a rich environment for the study of the city.

Fully deserving special mention is Bill Deverell, professor of history at the University of Southern California and the director of the Huntington-USC Institute for the Study of California and the West. He has been an invaluable colleague and cherished friend for many years, and I could not have written this book without his assistance and encouragement. To Bill, Jenny, and young Helen—thanks.

Bill was instrumental in getting me involved with the Western History Association, an organization that is unusually sane, slightly loopy, and invariably redeeming. Western history circles allowed me to meet Virginia Swift, singer-author and trail traveler; David Igler, the very embodiment of decency; and Janet Fireman, whose thoughtful creativity inspires me. Dave Gutierrez deserves a special word of thanks. When I stood at a critical fork in the road in writing this book, he gave my concerns a sympathetic hearing and offered the advice I needed to move forward with confidence.

Many other scholars have shared documents and suggestions that have shaped this book in ways large and small. Some have made formal comments on conference papers or draft essays. Here I want to recognize those not named elsewhere, realizing that merely naming them is too little praise for their contributions: Jane Apostle, Al Broussard, Robert Burke, Dan Cady, Al Camarillo, Gwendolyn Crenshaw, Mike Davis, Mike Engh, Miriam Feldblum, Philip Goff, Ronald Gottesman, Jim Gregory, Greg Hise, Dan Johnson, Marilynn Johnson, Robin Kelly, Kevin Leonard, George Lipsitz, Mary Odom, Judith Raftery, Andrew Rolle, Martin Schiesl, Ralph Shaffer, Howard Shorr, Doug Smith, and Mark Wild. For their helpful insights, I thank everyone in the Los Angeles Social History Group, especially Hal Barron and Steve Ross.

Many historians have examined black Los Angeles during the pre-1940 period, and I could not have written this book without their contributions. They include Patricia Rae Alder, Frederick E. Anderson, Lonnie G. Bunch III, Bette Yarbrough Cox, Thomas Cripps, DeEtta Demaritus, Jack D. Forbes, Lynell George, Dolores Hayden, Karen E. Hudson, Delores Nason McBroome, Jill Watts, and B. Gordon Wheeler. I have met few of these writers, but I want them to know how important their work has been to me.

The most influential historian of black Los Angeles has been Lawrence B. de Graaf, whose pioneering work inspired many historians. His recent work—on African American life in Southern California's suburbs—opens yet another new field for understanding the African American experience. I thank Larry for his very helpful comments on my manuscript and for his ongoing friendship and support for my work.

Larry also played a key role in the Autry Museum of Western History's 1994 Black History Month lectures, which served as the inspiration for a collection of essays, *Seeking El Dorado: African Americans in California*, which de Graaf coedited with the leading historian of African Americans in the West, Quintard Taylor, and the ever creative Kevin Mulroy. By inviting me to write an essay for that anthology, these historians presented me with a gift, for the project proved singularly beneficial to me; all three editors offered insightful readings of my work and forced me to think in new directions.

More recently, I have had the pleasure of working with Josh Sides, whose newly published book, *L.A. City Limits: African American Los Angeles from the Great Depression to the Present*, shares common interests with my own. Josh's work has greatly enriched my understanding of black Los Angeles during and after the Second World War. His generous sharing of research and his thoughtful reading of my manuscript are deeply appreciated.

Much of what we know about the history of African Americans in Los Angeles stems from the priceless collection of photographs and documents saved by the city's first black librarian, the late Miriam Matthews, who, along with her parents and siblings, appears briefly as an actor in this book. I am grateful for her foresight and persistence. I also wish to thank her nephew, Charles H. Matthews, who has graciously allowed me to publish photographs from her collection and who corrected some of my information about the Matthews's family history.

For sharing their personal histories with me on tape, I am indebted to Congressman Augustus Freeman Hawkins and the late L.A. County supervisor Kenneth Hahn. Marilyn White provided not only an interview but also a delightful afternoon of fellowship. Thanks also to George and Judie

White, who graciously invited me into their home to talk about their family's history; although I made no tape of that conversation, I learned much. Many other historians have conducted oral history interviews over the years, and these were invaluable to me. Special thanks to the oral history programs at UCLA and California State Fullerton.

In 1997, my family and I left Southern California for Atlanta, where I took a position at the Georgia Institute of Technology. Abandoning the scholastic repose of Caltech for Georgia Tech's buzzing classrooms was a positive experience for me, reminding me that I was an educator, not just a scholar. This shift transformed my vision of what my book needed to be and whom it should reach. The result is that I took a nearly completed book and completely rewrote it, causing a substantial delay in publication that I do not regret. The School of History, Technology, and Society (HTS), my home department, provided an exceptional environment for reworking and completing my book. I wish to thank Bob McMath, my friend and mentor in the profession and now vice provost for academic affairs at Georgia Tech, and Greg Nobles, my former chair and valued colleague, who helped me make the move to Atlanta.

I want to offer a special word of thanks to my colleagues in HTS for making me feel welcome from the beginning and for helping me bring this book to fruition. For their ideas about race relations in America, for their suggestions for the book, and for the research documents they have shared with me, I extend special notes of appreciation to Eleanor Alexander, Ron Bayor, Gus Giebelhaus, Bob McMath, Andrea Tone, John Tone, Steve Vallas, and Bill Winders. I also want to thank Sue Rosser, the dean of the Ivan Allen College of Liberal Arts; Richard Barke, associate dean of the college; and Willie Pearson, chair of HTS, for enthusiastically supporting my work.

Once in Atlanta, I needed to get back to California for more research. A travel grant from the Historical Society for Southern California helped. I also found a splendid long-distance researcher in Sarah Roggero. Sarah's work was exceptional in every way, and it came at an especially critical time in my writing; I am grateful for her hard work and congenial spirit.

Several Georgia Tech students contributed directly to this book. LeeAnn Lands, now a professor at Kennesaw State University, helped me understand the history of black Atlanta. Matt Hild, now a Ph.D. in history, undertook indispensable census work for me. Former undergraduates Andre Baron and Megan Murray conducted helpful research, as did George P. Burdell.

The staff at the Georgia Tech Library has been very helpful. Special thanks to Bruce Henson, for building the collection on race relations, and to the interlibrary loan department, headed by Katharine Calhoun.

One of the foremost blessings of my move to Atlanta has been the friendship and intellectual companionship I have found in Steve Usselman, a native of Los Angeles and now my colleague in HTS. Steve read every word of my manuscript with a level of care and thoughtfulness that has proved invaluable, instilling confidence and raising concerns as the situation warranted. Most of all, he has believed in this project, and in me. I am grateful to him and to his family more than they can know.

Back in the 1970s, Elliott West's history lectures lured me into the profession, and for that I am eternally grateful. It has been my privilege to know Elliott as teacher, mentor, and friend. The jaw-dropping originality of his work and his ability to reach a wide audience are an inspiration to me. I also want to thank John Kushma and Leslie Moch for their inspired teaching during my college days; their influence on my thinking endures. The older I get, the more I realize that a few childhood teachers also continue to influence what I do. Among these, I wish to acknowledge two from Madison Junior High: Lamar Anderson, who gloried in punishing me for dress-code violations but taught an excellent history course; and Jeannie Pfeifer, who insisted that her students follow their hearts and seek to attain a higher level of creativity.

Monica McCormick, my editor at U.C. Press, has been unfailingly enthusiastic about this project for many years, and she patiently awaited the final product, offering sage advice along the way. To me and countless others in the profession, she is a wonder—the consummate professional who, despite the intense pressures of her job, calmly handles frantic historians and remains, without fail, a friend to all. I was honored that Walter Nugent and Vicki Ruiz would read my manuscript for the University of California Press, and I am grateful for their generous assessments and helpful suggestions. Special thanks to Randy Heyman for his invaluable assistance and to Mary Severance for her skillful production of the book. My copy editor, Jacqueline Volin, was thorough and brilliant, and I will always be grateful for her contributions to this book.

The late Martin Ridge, former director of research at the Huntington Library and professor emeritus at Caltech, went above and beyond in shaping this book. He offered to read the full draft of the manuscript, and I later sent it to him from Atlanta, not knowing he had just undergone major surgery. He read the entire thing flat on his back—stitches tied in, half a lung missing—and marked up virtually every page with his notoriously sharp editorial pencil. He could do that because he was a tough old cuss. But I also know that he did it because he cared—about the issues this book raises, and about its author.

A final word about one of my dearest friends and colleagues. Like many people listed in these acknowledgements, I sorely miss Clark Davis. Clark was my Great Encourager, and even now his unfailing optimism brings a smile and keeps me going. My family and I hold cherished memories of time spent with Clark and his wife, Cheryl Koos. Our wish for their young son, Jackson, is that he grow strong and true, filled with the easy grace of his father and mother.

- - - -

I want to thank my own mother and father for everything they have done for me and everything they mean to me. I am continually inspired by their ongoing growth and creativity, and by their willingness to accept new challenges and move in new directions. My brother, J. Dee, continues to be a wonderful friend. I am honored to be his brother, and I thank him and his family, Teri, Lea, and Jessie. We all miss Dave, and I think of him often as I work, drawing inspiration from the memories. In the course of writing this book, his daughters—Anna, Cathey, and Sarah—have grown from wonderful little girls into wonderful young women, and they are a blessing to our lives. I am grateful to Betsy and P. J. for creating a loving home. My Colorado family—the Lacys—has always been kind and supportive. My Aunt Ann married Bob Cook, and he has been one of *those* uncles; I thank them both for all the fun.

I had scarcely started this book when my son, Peter, was born. As an infant, he filled my days with wonder and joy and love. He still does. Elizabeth, my beloved daughter, arrived next and began to sprinkle magic on the world. She has introduced a new sense of vitality and excitement to my life— and to our home—that I would not now live without. I am blessed to have Peter for my son, blessed to have Elizabeth for my daughter. They give me hope for the future.

The most important decision I ever made was also the best—to spend my life with Judith Crothers. The miracle was that she wanted to spend her life with me, too. By the time this appears in print, we will be nearing our twentieth anniversary, and during these years she has made my life immeasurably richer. For that and much more, I dedicate this book to her, with all my love.

INTRODUCTION

Think about American freedom. What does freedom mean? Who gets to be free, and why? When people are not free, how do they get free? When they are free, how do they stay that way? For centuries, Americans from all walks of life have debated and fought over the answers to these questions, and the results of those conflicts have shaped who we are, as a people and a nation. Long after you finish reading this book, I hope you will continue to think about freedom in the United States. That, in the largest sense, has been my aim in writing it.

But sweeping questions do not make the best starting point for a study of freedom, for the very notion of freedom is a topic of enormous breadth and complexity, encompassing an entire universe of theoretical conundrums. Somehow, I can't get at it by starting with the big picture. I get lost in the abstractions. My historical research has always gravitated toward what is local and concrete. I've been drawn to the neighborhood, the corner store, the church pew, the city council. I have always wanted to understand how real people at the corner of First and Main saw their world. In my approach to this book, then, I almost instinctively looked away from the universe of ideas inherent to "freedom" and tried to see how one group of people tried to get free in a particular place and time: the African American community of Los Angeles, California, in the half century before World War II—a period of vital importance to American race relations and the urban West.[1]

The story of this community is fascinating in its own right, but I would suggest that it also sheds light on the continuing dilemmas about race and freedom in America. It is fascinating because the city and its people were, in the first half of the twentieth century, caught up in a unique drama. It is instructive because Los Angeles *then* was what most cities in the United States are *now:* a sprawling, multiracial place where the rules of the game and the hierarchies of power seemed always in flux. When boosters in the early twentieth century insisted that Los Angeles was "the city of the future," they were speaking more truly than they knew. Looking back, we see ourselves.

Although black people—Afro-Spaniards—founded the city in 1781, the community I examine here arose along with modern Los Angeles, whose official birth was the real estate boom of the late 1880s. Most African Americans in the city were migrants from the American South, where Jim Crow had black people by the throat. What they found in Los Angeles was an oddly half-free environment. Racial conditions were far better there than in the South, and preferable also to what most blacks discovered in the cities of the North. Opportunities for economic advancement, home ownership, and social freedom were readily apparent, but so too were patterns of everyday racism that blocked African Americans every step of the way. Knowing they were not free enough, black Angelenos set out to change that, and therein lies the tale.

The African American community in Los Angeles has naturally captured the attention of many historians, who have explored various aspects of its past. Oversimplifying these studies a bit, I would say that their primary theme may be summarized in the words "Paradise Lost." Their basic conclusion is that there was, if not a Golden Age, a time when conditions for black Angelenos were relatively good. Then, over time, conditions worsened: white racism grew as the black population increased; an embryonic ghetto that had developed before 1940 reached maturity during the massive black migration of the Second World War; for a while, the jazz scene on Central Avenue kept spirits up, but eventually even that went downhill; living conditions deteriorated; police brutality continued; frustrations festered. The story of decline is compelling—a halcyon era fading ever deeper into disillusionment, ultimately fueling the Watts rebellion of 1965.[2]

I have come to distrust the Paradise Lost narrative. For one thing, neither the black Angelenos who lived through this era, nor the historians who have studied it, agree on just when the conditions were good. The Golden Age was the late nineteenth century, or perhaps the early twentieth century, or maybe the 1920s, or possibly the 1940s and early 1950s. Anyone who has lived in Los Angeles for any length of time will hear an older resident talk about what a great town L.A. used to be. The Paradise Lost ideal seems to be part of the city's essential culture: once-contented residents eventually come to see their town moving further and further from Eden.

What's more, the evidence suggests a more complicated pattern of racial conditions than that of steady decline. Regardless of time period, the basic rights of black Angelenos always faced attack from some quarter. And, just

as consistently, African American leaders in the city always found themselves vying to preserve rights they already possessed and to win rights they
had not yet gained. At any given moment, the community was only half-
free and locked in struggle—fighting to maintain and extend basic human
rights. Sometimes it witnessed tremendous victories, only to find that the
gains were not permanent. In some battles it suffered galling defeats, only
to see those losses reversed in the next engagement. To complicate the story
further, victories and defeats sometimes occurred simultaneously. As I see
it, the evidence reveals that racial conditions for black Angelenos usually
got better and worse *at the same time.*

Questions of decline and progress remain critical, but they are not the
focus of this book. Instead, I tell a story that speaks to our current state of
affairs, in which Americans are still deeply uncertain about the meaning of
freedom and the state of race relations. The main actors in this book are the
community leaders who kept fighting for equal opportunity and basic civil
rights. Their sheer tenacity was their most striking characteristic. For them,
the quest for civil rights was not a "movement" or a set of dramatic moments; it was a way of life. Indeed, that is the central theme of the book:
civil rights as a way of life.

Whatever their individual characteristics, black Angelenos were defined,
by law and by custom, as a group. That group designation denied them the
privileges of first-class citizenship, but not necessarily indefinitely. They
could, and did, draw upon their shared past and their "group" institutions
to challenge the status quo. In short, as a group they chose to get free and
stay free—and their struggle became a central focus in their lives.

On Los Angeles and "the West"

When I arrived in Southern California, in 1988, I already had an ethical and
scholarly interest in race relations, and, having grown up in West Texas,
where the South meets the West, I had an interest in both regions. I had
written a book on southern history, and I was eager to push my research
westward, with a focus on race. Los Angeles beckoned, big and mysterious.

Apart from my own fascination with the city, however, race relations in
Los Angeles command attention. With good reason, historians of American
race relations have usually focused on the nation's gravest racial tragedies—
slavery, the Jim Crow South, the ghetto North—and it may well be that
Americans have yet to come to grips with those traumas. But race relations
in America today have shifted into a new and unfamiliar phase. Never be-

fore have African Americans been so powerful and influential. The black middle class has grown significantly, and our nation now boasts a substantial black upper class. Many obvious barriers to equal opportunity have been dismantled. Yet all is not well. The black poor seem increasingly alienated and hopeless and are largely ignored or feared. Many affluent blacks, having "made it" economically, feel a deep sense of rage over America's color-bound sensibilities—the still widespread assumptions of black criminality and inferiority that slap them in the face every day.[3] Adding to the angst and confusion is the nationwide realization that race relations are no longer black-white. Latino and Asian populations, which have long been central to life in the Far West, are now sweeping across all parts of the country, introducing a new and sometimes turbulent dynamic throughout the nation.

During the first half of the twentieth century, black Angelenos confronted a similar world, one in which racism was more subtle than blatant, more unpredictable than not, and more diverse than black-white. Rachel Robinson, the wife of Jackie Robinson, grew up in Los Angeles in the 1920s and 1930s and recalled that "incidents of discrimination were often unexpected and inexplicable—you never knew when they would happen."[4] And because the racial mix in Los Angeles was also yellow and brown, the relationships among racial and ethnic groups proved persistently uncertain. Present-day Americans think, not inaccurately, that the nation has entered a brave new world of race relations, a multiracial situation in which the trends and problems are difficult to pin down and gains and losses are hard to calculate. The people in this book faced that kind of world, too, and perhaps by studying their lives we can gain a better perspective on our own world.

Throughout the book I emphasize "the West," which may seem puzzling, because today's L.A. is a global metropolis that seems detached from the "real" West. The historian Virginia Scharff calls modern-day Los Angeles a "post-western" city, and I think she is right. But during the half century studied here, Los Angeles styled itself a western city, and its black leaders identified both the city and their community with "the West." They spoke of themselves as westerners and insisted that racial prejudice was incompatible with western ideals.

At the same time, black Angelenos always had another region in view—the South. When Afro-southerners left Dixie and moved west, the South remained lodged in their consciousness. They feared the "southernization" of Los Angeles, and they had some cause for concern, because white southerners were also moving to Los Angeles, and though they were small in number compared to the flood of white midwesterners moving in, many of them were aggressive advocates of Jim Crow. They complained that blacks were too free in Los Angeles, that the city should adopt the South's model of segregation. Thus the two sections of the country—South and West—defined one another in a complicated interregional tussle, and again the question arose: whose freedom, on whose terms?

When contrasted with the Jim Crow South and the ghetto North, black life in the West seemed quiet and relatively nice. During the first Great Migration of World War I, far fewer blacks moved west than north, so most African American communities out West remained small. World War II and the second Great Migration would bring hundreds of thousands of blacks to the West Coast, but until then most western cities had only a few thousand African American residents. Among cities of the Far West, only Los Angeles had lured large numbers of black migrants. Perhaps for that reason, the fields of black history and western history took little notice of each other for many decades. Fortunately, studies of the African American experience in the West are now abundant. Pioneering historians of blacks in the urban West, such as Lawrence B. de Graaf, have at last seen their seeds bear fruit in the many available books, articles, dissertations, videos, and museum exhibits on the black West. Quintard Taylor's *In Search of the Racial Frontier*, a synthesis of African American history in the region, and Walter Nugent's *Into the West*, a demographic study of the region's diverse peoples, have placed the history of race in the West at the center of the American historical enterprise.

Many social and scholarly trends explain the recent ascent of black western history, but one fundamental reason for its rise is that the question of freedom is so clearly posed when we bring together African Americans and the West. That vast expanse of American dreams, "the West" loomed large for many African Americans. It drew blacks from back East—and especially from the South—who embraced the ideal of western freedom. But as Taylor observes, the "central paradigm" in the history of the black West is really a series of questions: "Did the west represent the last best hope for . . . African Americans? Was it a racial frontier beyond which lay the potential for an egalitarian society?"[5] If it was going to happen anywhere, Los Angeles was probably the place.

On Terminology

For all their personal differences, African Americans were "a people," collectively defined by outside forces and called together by the internal voices of history and culture. Like all social groups, they had names other people called them, and names they called themselves. Americans today seem to think the battle over group names is a recent phenomenon, a symptom of "political correctness." But even a casual reading of American history reveals that conflicts over naming have been going on for centuries, and because names often reflect respect or denigration, these questions have been a constant ingredient in race relations.

During the half century I study here, African Americans used many names to identify themselves and their group: African-American, Afro-American, Negro, colored, black, and more. Beyond these familiar terms were less frequent variations: Aframerican, Afric-American, Africo-American. Sometimes blacks used *Ethiopia* as shorthand for their group, as in "sons and daughters of Ethiopia." Through the years, blacks debated which term was most appropriate, and the disagreements could get heated, but in black publications these terms were used interchangeably. Frederick Roberts, the African American editor of the Los Angeles newspaper *New Age*, preferred the phrase *Americans of African descent* to the term *Negro*. As his wife, Pearl Roberts, recalled: "He wanted to stress the fact that we are Americans, too. Whereas most newspapers would say, 'Another Negro lynched,' my husband's newspaper would say, 'Another American lynched.'" But even Roberts's paper used a variety of terms interchangeably, including one of his own invention: Afro-Angelenos. In this book, following black writers of the era, I use all these terms interchangeably.[6]

In the late nineteenth century, white newspapers sometimes used cutting terms to identify blacks, including *nigger, darkie,* and *coon.* By the early twentieth century, most of the white daily newspapers were slightly more professional and used the word *negro* instead. That was term black leaders asked white newspapers to use, but African Americans insisted on the uppercase version that they themselves used: *Negro.* For many years, white publications would not agree to that, even though they did use the uppercase form for the word *Caucasian.* The term *Negro,* used with dignity during the civil rights movement of the 1950s and 1960s, was buried almost overnight by the "Black Power" movement of the late 1960s, which insisted on the use of the term *black,* but it now seems to be making a comeback within the African American community. Whether *Negro* will ever again be widely accepted we can't know, but we can at least be certain that the terms in use today will be altered in the future, for that is the nature of language—and perhaps of freedom.

Adopting a group name and having white people respect it was serious business, but among themselves at least, African Americans allowed for playfulness. Frederick Roberts offered his readers "Brother of More Color."

And as Hollywood swept the United States with its sepia-toned black-and-white movies, black stars opted for "Sepia Stars," and the term *sepia* came to include black entertainers generally, including jazz musicians and chorus girls. In 1938, Roberts's *New Age* reported that at a music awards program in Paris, the honors "happily went to artists of the sepia group." The headline read, "France Lauds Sepia Swing." When jazz great Cab Calloway took Harlem by storm with his tune "Copper Color Gal," the black newspapers announced, in fun, "'Copper Color' supplants 'Sepia.'" A black radio show in Los Angeles in the late 1930s offered a "Sepia Sportscast." Among local writers the euphonic couplings with *Angelenos* became something of an art form. Charlotta Bass, the black owner and editor of the *California Eagle*, came up with "Angelenos of Negro extraction." The local black writer Harold Bruce Forsythe, in a bit of inspired irreverence, topped them all with "Amerafrics of the Angeleno denomination."[7]

On the more meaningful side, some terms that blacks used for themselves were so common they escaped notice and debate, most notably *the Race*, with the word *Race* usually capitalized. A civic activist was a "Race man" or "Race woman." Black newspapers were "Race papers." A black person's success meant "progress for the Race." The middle class aimed its programs at "Race uplift." A black-owned business was a "Race enterprise." The phrases "our group" and "our people" were equally common. Used more personally, they became "my group" or "my people"—the final phrase recalling the concluding chapter title of Zora Neale Hurston's autobiography, a phrase that signaled, more clearly than the terms *Negro* or *African American*, the deeply felt connections fostered by a tragic past, a shared experience, and a collective hope for the future.

Americans classified as "white" (and *white* was a legal term, used in federal law) were also a diverse lot, but *white*, as a key identifier in American life, was used throughout the nation to refer to all people of European ancestry, so long as they did not have "one drop" of African, Asian, or American Indian blood. In recent years, the creation of whiteness—that is, how the many peoples of Europe morphed into a group called "whites" and how they used that designation to empower themselves at the expense of nonwhites—has become an important area of historical investigation, although not one I deal with in this book. Whites of the northwestern European stripe, along with wanna-be melting-pot types who knew where the power lay, often called themselves "Anglos" (or even "Anglo-Saxons," which was code for really-really white). However inaccurate the term *Anglo* may have been for many European groups, it filtered into the American language as a synonym for *white*.

Following the historian David G. Gutierrez, I use the term *ethnic Mexicans* to refer to all people of Mexican ancestry, whether they were American citizens or not. *Mexican Americans* refers to ethnic Mexicans who were American citizens. *Mexican immigrants* refers to those who crossed the border without becoming American citizens.[8] In the period covered here, there were no "illegal" Mexican immigrants; the borders were open. I apply the term *Asian* to both the Chinese and Japanese who appear in this story, even though they, like many Europeans, were separated by custom, language, history, and a certain amount of animosity.

Throughout the book I discuss the "black middle class" and insist that black Los Angeles was predominantly "middle class." The term may cause confusion, because it suggests a level of material comfort that black Angelenos did not enjoy and an access to white-collar work that they did not have. Most of the city's black middle class worked in blue-collar occupations, and most of those who held white-collar jobs knew the stitching on those collars was noticeably weak. In other words, they were "middle class" less in wealth than in values, lifestyle, and aspirations. They believed in the sanctity of home, family, and church; placed a premium on self-discipline and education; and had a penchant for thrift, savings, and acquiring real estate. They were strivers and joiners. Economic racism blunted their financial ambitions, but they had faith in the promise of upward mobility for themselves and their children. They were also the civil rights leaders of their era. They themselves seldom used the term *middle class,* which had not become an everyday term in America. Instead they spoke of themselves as the "better class of Negroes," or as "the educated class," or "the right sort."

The black middle class contrasted itself with blacks who, for whatever reason, did not share its faith in progress, its insistence on "proper home training," or its dedication to righteous living. The black middle class had a variety of terms for "lower-class" sorts, ranging from polite put-downs, such as "don't-care Negroes" and "sports," to stinging indictments, such as "the vicious element." My use of *middle class* in this book identifies a more broad-based crowd than that indicated by W. E. B. Du Bois's famous formulation of the black "Talented Tenth" (the college-educated professionals whom Du Bois hoped would lead the African American masses toward fuller civil rights), or that suggested by the historian William Gatewood in his study of "aristocrats of color." There were economic divisions among blacks in Los Angeles, as elsewhere, but I see the black middle class of this period as a large and inexactly defined group.[9]

The rise of this black middle class was a national phenomenon, and not everyone bought into it. The black middle class could be prudish and snobbish, but it is difficult to explain why later generations of black scholars and leaders spoke of it so harshly. The sociologist E. Franklin Frazier offered a famously scathing indictment of the black middle class in his late-1950s book *The Black Bourgeoisie*, which portrayed middle-class African Americans as a people living in a dream world of false pretensions and escapist black-society banquets. In his mid-1960s autobiography, Malcolm X recalled the members of Boston's black middle class, circa 1940, and condemned them for "breaking their backs trying to act like white people." In the late 1960s and early 1970s, young and radical Black Power advocates effectively caricatured their elders as Uncle Toms.[10] *Bound for Freedom* is part of a growing body of literature that takes a fresh look at the strivers of the black middle class in the years before World War II. What can be confidently said is this: They were not soft-spoken in their demands for equal rights or their denunciation of racism, and they were anything but escapists.[11]

I use *race* and *ethnicity* throughout the book as well, although both are slippery terms. Usually, I use *race* to specify the divisions that were socially constructed between the peoples of European, African, and Asian lineage. I normally use *ethnicity* to mean subgroups within the larger crowd of Euro-Americans, but also, where appropriate, as shorthand for "race and ethnicity." We cannot get too precise and remain historically accurate, for in the period from 1890 to 1940, the term *race* was unmanageable. Writers, scholars, and government agents used it to distinguish groups by skin color and other perceived biological features, but they also sometimes used it as we might use the term *ethnic* (i.e., the Mexican race, the Jewish race) and also as shorthand for nationality groups (the Japanese race, the Swedish race). To make matters more confusing, when government agencies conducted surveys on different nationality groups, they invariably included a category for Americans and a category for Negroes (a policy that angered black leaders) and, sometimes, another category for Mexicans that did not distinguish between Mexican Americans and Mexican immigrants. The term *race*, then, was all over the conceptual map. The term *ethnic* is more a contemporary term than one used during the period I examine. "Ethnicity" was seldom referred to prior to the 1940s. Instead, people spoke of "ancestry" or "nationality."[12]

In briefly discussing such terminology, I am merely setting the stage. But there is another word used throughout this book—*racism*—which is especially important and warrants fuller discussion.

On Racism

In the half century I cover, African Americans were not free, because the government and the economy, both controlled by whites, kept them down. This process is what we generally mean today when we speak of racism. One problem with that term, from an analytical perspective, is that Americans today use it with a notable lack of precision. Ask any group of people what racism is, and you will get a wide range of answers.

The people in this book did not use the term *racism* for the simple reason that it did not then exist. What we call racism they called "race prejudice," and they used that term with no greater specificity than we use the word *racism*. They also used the words *race hatred* and *bigotry* as broad equivalents of *race prejudice*. As the twentieth century progressed, and especially during the 1930s, Americans began to use the word *discrimination* in its negative sense, so the term *racial discrimination* naturally followed, and it, too, was often used interchangeably with *race prejudice*.

I want to dissect these terms a little, so as to have a clearer understanding of what race prejudice was—and what racism still is. First, I think it useful to distinguish between *bigotry* (a personally held prejudice) and *racism* (a public act of discrimination). The biases that people hold in their hearts need not result in hostile public behavior. We cannot seriously expect the people of one social group to appreciate and respect all those of other groups, but we might hope, in the real world, for people to respect and uphold equal rights among groups. When one racial group's biases find public and political expression and serve to keep another racial group down, then we have racism. A useful definition of racism, then, is *racial bigotry in action.*

Where did racism come from in the first place? Why did white peoples of diverse backgrounds accept and promote it? Why did it grow stronger at some times and weaker at others? One might suppose, in a commonsense way, that discrimination is a reflection of people's attitudes, that personal prejudices spark racist behavior. But that is by no means clear. Several generations of social psychologists and political scientists have struggled valiantly to determine the relationship between attitudes and behavior, the net result being that they cannot agree how that relationship works. Some argue that people's thoughts shape their actions; others argue that repeated actions shape ways of thinking; and still others see a complicated interplay between what individuals think and do.[13]

These are not merely academic questions. Americans have a long history of debating them. Do laws that force people to change their behavior ultimately change their attitudes, or are attitudes impervious to legislation? Do attitudes even matter when law boils down to force? Can values and behavior really change, and if so, how? Our nation's furious debates over slavery, Reconstruction, and Jim Crow boiled with these questions. The same questions pressed upon black leaders in Los Angeles, for they were looking for ways to keep good conditions good and make bad conditions better. As it happened, black Angelenos never formulated a precise model for how race prejudice operated or how it might be eradicated.

What you and I can do is to sort out the different types of racism that created problems for Afro-Angelenos and think about how those trends shed light on our own world. In my view, there were three general problems. The first—an explosive problem, but ultimately the least important of the three—was public insult: racial slurs intended to denigrate black people. America was rife with ethnic and racial insults—dago, kraut, paddy, chink, spick, peckerwood, the list goes on, depressingly, forever—so it wasn't that blacks were singled out. What mattered was the real power behind the insults. Slurs hurt in direct proportion to the degree of one's subordination. "Greaser" and "nigger" were not just insults; they were a reflection of broader discrimination against ethnic Mexicans and African Americans, a way for white people to say, "We're on top and there's nothing you can do about it."

Then there were structural, or institutional, inequalities—the second problem, and the one most often targeted by civil rights activists. What most blacks wanted was *equal opportunity*—an equal chance to live life to the fullest of one's ambitions and abilities. As one Race paper in Southern California put it, African Americans wanted "a square deal and a fair chance— no more, no less."[14] No black American had equal opportunity. Every aspect of the game was stacked against blacks. Jim Crow segregation, the one-party South, lynchings, ghetto poverty—these were the most visible signs of structural inequality. But less visible barriers ran far deeper. Most white-owned businesses would not hire colored people, and that was perfectly legal and would remain so, in most states, until passage of the Civil Rights Act of 1964. Where blacks were employed, they were usually hired last, fired first, and paid less than their white counterparts—and all this, too, was a legal institutional barrier to black advancement. When, in the 1910s, the Los Angeles County Hospital opened a training school for nurses, the administrators ruled that black women would not be admitted, and Afro-Angelenos had to engage in years of slow, frustrating legal work and politicking just to unlock that door. That kind of discrimination is what I mean by structural racism.

The third problem was the white presumption of black inferiority. It sounds relatively uncomplicated and redeemable, but it has proved monstrously difficult to eradicate. Even today, when public slurs are taboo and most of the obvious structural barriers to racial equality have come down, white assumptions of black inferiority lie at the root of many racial injustices. These assumptions scar the lives of even the most economically successful African Americans and are the spark that ignites what the journalist Ellis Cose has called "the rage of a privileged class." The Los Angeles writer Lynell George, who is part of that privileged class, put it this way: "Though giving up has never been an option, sometimes I can't help but feel that I will always be stretching for something that will remain forever out of reach."[15]

When white people looked at other white people, they saw individuals, but when they looked at black people, they went into group-think mode, imposing blanket characterizations on any Negro in front of them. The assumptions were that blacks, as an undifferentiated group, were criminal, violent, dirty, ignorant, lazy, loud, unsanitary, oversexed, carefree, and unambitious. Middle-class blacks spent most of their lives trying to dispel those assumptions. That is why they tried to be Super Citizens. But somehow whites could not—or would not—get the message. When they met blacks who obviously did not fit the stereotype, they classified those blacks as "exceptional"—the exception that proved the rule—thereby preserving their presumption of black inferiority.

Negative assumptions and structural racism fed each other. White policemen often stopped black people for no reason other than that they "looked like" criminals; when blacks were arrested, often on flimsy evidence, the same racial assumptions made white judges quick to order jail time. Because blacks were so frequently arrested and sentenced, whites continued to think of blacks as potential criminals, and the cycle continued. Individuals from all groups committed crimes, of course, including African Americans. But that was not the problem. The problem was the color-bound supposition that told white Americans that a white criminal was an exception but a black criminal was to be expected.

When black Angelenos spoke of "race prejudice" they meant all of this—assumptions, structures, insults. They did not overanalyze. They just went to work, chipping away at the mountain of race prejudice with whatever tools were at hand. Through exemplary behavior, well-phrased exhortations, and strident demands, they sought to change white minds about black people, and they sometimes succeeded. When they could alter the law so that African Americans could get a square deal and a fair chance, they did so. When whites shut them out, they formed their own institutions and businesses, looking after their own and sending the message that white assumptions of black ineptitude were false. Black leaders understood that bigotry in action was a complex, multidimensional problem, and they fought it on every front.

- - - -

When I began this project around 1990, it never occurred to me that I—a white American—could not understand the African American experience. After all, I was a trained historian, whose craft supplies keys for all doors to the past. But as the years progressed and my knowledge deepened, it gradually became clear to me that something intangible about the black American past was beyond my understanding. In one sense, such a gap is a normal part of historical research. When historians journey to the past, they arrive as outsiders—as pilgrims, if you will—seeking paths into places that can no longer receive them. Although years of research and contemplation give historians intimate familiarity with lost worlds, some separation between past and present invariably remains. But the intangible I am talking about here is something different, something linked to centuries of American slavery, to the trauma of Jim Crow, to the historical disconnect between the ideal of freedom and the realities of racism. In the America we live in, I have come to doubt that any white person, or any nonblack person for that matter, can fully understand the African American experience. Some doors cannot be opened. As the author DeEtta Demaratus recently wrote, after struggling unsuccessfully to imagine the feelings of a slave woman seeing her husband auctioned off to another white family, "There are places of pain I cannot enter."[16] But if I cannot fully comprehend what it means to have been—or to be—a black person seeking freedom in America, I feel a strong obligation to try, for our pasts are of a piece. And if only African Americans can fathom what antiblack racism has done to the soul, it is also true that most Americans, at some point in their lives, have felt only half free and have wanted to get freer. That is another way of saying that this story of black Los Angeles transcends what is local and what is black. It is a slice of American history for all Americans.

The protagonists in my story were bound for freedom because most of them were leaving a dangerously unequal South for a potentially equal West. They understood that movement itself was a way to find liberty. But because Los Angeles offered better racial conditions but not equality of opportunity, black Angelenos were not fully free to pursue their ultimate dreams and develop the fullness of their abilities. What's more, the freedoms they did have in California were constantly under attack from whites who preferred a Jim Crow racial order. Black Angelenos thus fought a double battle, laboring to attain those rights they did not yet enjoy while seeking to protect the rights they already had. To be bound for freedom, then, implied more than just a decision to leave the South for the West. It also meant that black Angelenos were *bound and determined* to keep Jim Crow out of their new home and to make Los Angeles and the West a shining example of what America might yet become. Their efforts did not follow the usual script of the classic American "western," but black Angelenos were indeed westerners who believed in the transformative power of the West. So perhaps it is fitting that our tale, like so many westerns before it, begins with a stranger riding into town.

PART ONE

Staking a Claim
in the West

Looking westward had changed the life outlook for "L. G." [Robinson] and his family. It gave indications of new and greater differences. . . . The difference between southern lawlessness and western law; of modified peonage and some freedom of opportunity; of an old world of oppressiveness and a new world of hope. Indeed, he had truly discovered a land where he, too, might make for himself a place in its warm sun.

BAXTER SCRUGGS, *A Man in Our Community*

Arrival

On September 10, 1910, Charlotta A. Spear rode into town on a train. No one met her at the Southern Pacific depot. She was just another sickly easterner who had come to Los Angeles seeking sunshine. She came from Providence, Rhode Island, a lone woman on a long, exhausting trip. The Pullman car porters—the black attendants who staffed the nation's passenger trains—must have wondered about her. As the unofficial guardians of African American passengers, they would have looked after her, quietly dispensing helpful tips and subtle warnings along the way. Spear was short and full bodied, with a handsome face, a light-brown complexion, black hair, and dark eyes. When she exited the bustling station, she would have found herself standing at 5th Street and South Central Avenue, where automobiles, horse-drawn wagons, and pedestrians jostled in the street and real estate hawkers offered wagon rides to the best slice of paradise.[1]

She had disembarked in a city exploding with growth. All about were carpenters framing bungalows, crane operators hoisting beams, teamsters hauling brick, laborers mixing mortar. From crude oil to citrus fruits, the city's diverse industries were producing vast quantities of goods for national and international markets. The spirit of the place could be seen in the way that city leaders, lacking a natural seaport and an adequate supply of freshwater, were able to wrangle both. They built an artificial port at San Pedro, well south of the city, and then annexed a "shoestring" addition—a strip of land only a half mile wide but sixteen miles long—to connect Los Angeles with the man-made harbor. Even as Charlotta arrived, they were reaching even farther—more than two hundred miles northward—to obtain Owens River water via an astonishing aqueduct, which would bring its precious contents to the vast, dry San Fernando Valley north of the city. Before long, Los Angeles would annex San Fernando as well. Overarching these manufactured advantages was the city's greatest asset: its climate—warm, dry air, mild winters, and brilliant sunshine.[2]

Charlotta Spear herself had come for "a two-year health-recuperation stay," as she later wrote. That was not unusual in Los Angeles. Doctors in the cold, consumptive East packed many a westbound train with ailing patients. Spear's physician in Rhode Island had "recommended that she spend

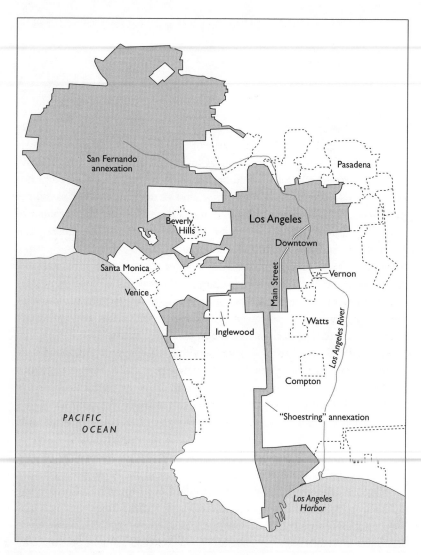

Map 1.   Los Angeles and surrounding cities, ca. 1918.

as much time in the sunshine as possible." What her ailment was, and whether she knew much about Los Angeles before she arrived, remains unknown. Her autobiography, written after a half century of highly public political activism in Los Angeles, reveals virtually nothing about her early years. Historians still know very little about her life before she reached Los

Angeles, and much of what has been written, and what can be found in public records, amounts to contradictory tidbits.

Depending on the source one examines, Charlotta was born in South Carolina, or maybe Rhode Island, or maybe Ohio. She was born in 1874, 1880, 1882, 1884, or 1890. Her parents were Hiram and Kate Spears (with an *s*), both of Sumter County, South Carolina, or they were Joseph and Catherine Spear (née Durant), she from South Carolina, he from Massachusetts. At a young age, and for reasons unknown, Charlotta went to live either with her older brother or with the family of her uncle, Ellis Spears, who lived in a two-story wooden home in the town of East Providence. She seems to have attended public schools around Providence. A class photo taken in her early teenage years shows her to be one of a handful of African American students. She may have attended college: sources provide scattered references to Penbroke College and Brown. She claimed to have worked for the *Providence Watchman*, a local Race paper. Beneath such shards of information lie mysteries yet to be discovered.[3]

Not that Charlotta Spear had anything to hide, or a tragic past to overcome. The point is, she let her past go, as if her early years had never happened. From Charlotta's point of view, her life began when she reached Los Angeles. Easterners who moved west could be that way. They claimed it as a special privilege to leave the past behind and start anew. Of Charlotta Spear's early life, this alone is certain: in September 1910 she arrived in Los Angeles and started getting well.

The City's African Roots

On another September day, 130 years earlier, forty-four settlers gathered on the open plain west of the Los Angeles River, about a mile north of where Charlotta Spear would disembark in 1910. Citizens of New Spain, they had been recruited from the colony's lower provinces to help populate Alta California, which stretched northward from San Diego. Felipe de Neve, the governor of Baja and Alta California, had picked this site for an agricultural settlement and had enticed settlers with promises of land, livestock, and other inducements. The governor had wanted young families, with husbands accustomed to hard labor, and for the most part he got them. Eleven families with young children made the arduous overland trip, and some of the colonists contracted smallpox along the way. None died, however, and when all had arrived and regained their health, they met to start something new.

In the name of God and the king of Spain, and with one ceremonial cannon shot, the governor officially founded *el pueblo de nuestra Señora la Reina de los Angeles*. The village of Our Lady the Queen of the Angels was usually called simply the pueblo and, later, Los Angeles.[4]

For black Angelenos in Charlotta Spear's day, the most important aspects of the city's origins were the racial characteristics of its founders. Virtually all of the first settlers were "colored," in the European sense of the word. The majority were of Negro heritage, although not purely so. Most were of mixed heritage—the offspring of African, Indian, and Spanish unions. In New Spain such mixing was not unusual, especially in the more isolated settlements, where one's choice of partners was limited and the Spanish desire for racial purity was diluted. The purely "Negro" presence in the pueblo soon subsided, when the two families headed by Negro men, the Mesa and Quintero families, were dropped from the colonial program along with one other family, apparently because they proved themselves of no use to the settlement. Where the Mesas and Quinteros went after their banishment is unknown. The mulatto trend in Los Angeles was more persistent. In 1792, as the historian Jack Forbes has shown, residents who were partly African constituted nearly 40 percent of the pueblo's population.[5]

Over time, as more Spaniards arrived and intermarriage continued, a kind of racial blending occurred, and the descendants of the colored founders came to be known simply as Spaniards. When Mexico won its independence from Spain in 1821, those descendants became Mexican citizens, or "Californios." Some residents whose lineage stretched back to the colored founders became Californios of wealth and power, including the last governor of Mexican California, Pío Pico. Black Angelenos of the twentieth century would herald the African roots of Governor Pico and other members of the Mexican elite, but white Angelenos of the early nineteenth century were fixated on the city's "Spanish" origins. Charlotta Spear herself would become a crusader for the inclusion of the Negro founders in the story of Los Angeles's history. When she wrote her autobiography in 1960, she began by condemning the white establishment—the Los Angeles school superintendent, the city's white journalists, and the white directors of the annual "Birthday Fiesta"—for whitewashing all colored people out of the story of the city's founding.

Charlotta was right about that; throughout most of the twentieth century, the city's white leaders did whitewash the founding and the Spanish era, turning both into romanticized, colorless periods and failing to acknowledge the role Afro-Spaniards had played in the creation of Los Angeles. That said—and with Charlotta's protest noted—it is also true that the black community she joined in 1910 traced its roots not to the Spanish or

Mexican era but to the early American period. The American era officially began at the close of the Mexican War with the 1848 Treaty of Guadalupe Hidalgo, in which the United States required Mexico to surrender the vast expanse of land that now comprises California and much of the American Southwest.

When California became a state—a free state—in 1850, Los Angeles was home to fewer than two thousand residents, including about a dozen African Americans. California's free-state status notwithstanding, the majority of white Angelenos had migrated from slave states; most supported slavery and did not welcome black residents. Even so, the decade marked the arrival of three African American families whose shared experiences, intermarriages, real estate investments, and support for Negro churches would provide a small but sturdy foundation for community building.

The Owens family came from Texas in 1853. All had been slaves. Robert Owens had purchased his own freedom and then earned enough to buy his wife, Winnie, and their three children out of bondage. They pushed west to Los Angeles, and despite the town's proslavery majority, Owens prospered, winning a U.S. government contract to supply wood, horses, and beef for military outposts and establishing a livery stable and cattle operation. Helping to run the business were his son, Charles, and a young black man who had become a friend of the family, Manuel Pepper. Robert purchased inexpensive land in Los Angeles, and by 1860 his real estate holdings were valued at five thousand dollars.[6]

After they settled in, the Owens family met a group of black women and children who were still enslaved—Biddy Mason, Hannah (who took no last name), and their children and grandchildren. They were the property of Robert and Rebecca Smith, a hard-luck white couple from Mississippi who had converted to Mormonism and, in the mid-1840s, with financial help from family or fellow church members, acquired Biddy Mason and her two young children; a third child, perhaps sired by Robert Smith, followed. Hannah was acquired later, in 1846, when Rebecca's father died and his slaves were auctioned to the highest bidder. With Rebecca's inheritance, and at her insistence, Robert purchased Hannah (Rebecca's childhood favorite) and her three children. The father of Hannah's children, a slave named Frank, was sold to a different family. In 1848, the Smith household left Mississippi to join the Mormons in Salt Lake City; en route, Hannah gave birth to another child, whose paternity was uncertain. During two difficult years in Utah, Hannah fell in love with another slave, Toby Embers, and the two had a son named Charles. In 1850, the Smiths and their slaves joined a mission to establish a Mormon colony in the hills of San Bernardino, some sixty miles east of

Los Angeles. Toby Ember's master also joined the mission. The travelers arrived at their destination in 1851.[7]

In San Bernardino, Robert Smith established a cattle ranch outside the
Mormon colony and was soon prosperous, but in the mid-1850s he had a
falling-out with church leaders, who, in a legal tangle, seized his land. In
1856, the defeated Smith decided to move to Texas. He sold his cattle and
moved his household to a camp outside Los Angeles, where he began to procure supplies for the journey ahead. Toby, not wanting to lose Hannah and
their two children (she was pregnant at the time, apparently by him), visited the camp. He urged Hannah to stay with him in California, insisting
they were free there and that he would soon have enough money to buy
them a home. She balked, uncertain of her freedom and fearing that if she
stayed, Smith would nonetheless take her children to Texas. Apparently in
an effort to buy time and to change Hannah's mind, Toby took their son
Charles back to San Bernardino. News of the Smiths' departure was equally
alarming to the Owens household, not only because they once had been
slaves in Texas but also because the young men of the household, Charles
Owens and Manuel Pepper, had developed romantic attachments with two
of the Smiths' slaves. Charles was in love with Biddy's oldest child, Ellen.
Manuel was attached to Hannah's oldest child, Ann.

Whether Toby Embers or Robert Owens or someone else alerted authorities about the situation developing outside Los Angeles, it is clear that
the San Bernardino county sheriff, Robert Clift, and Los Angeles county
sheriff, David Alexander, acted together to prevent Smith from leaving California before the status of his slaves was clarified. Were Biddy, Hannah, and
the children free people in a free state? Did Smith have the right to take
them out of California if they did not want to leave? These questions would
be answered in court. The sheriffs rode to Los Angeles and stopped at the
home of Benjamin Hayes, judge of the District Court—a southerner and
former slave owner. They showed Hayes a petition for habeas corpus,
which, by California law, would have been signed by a white person, not
one of Hannah or Biddy's black friends. The identity of that person is still
a mystery. Hayes signed the writ, empowering the sheriffs to take the
Smiths' slaves into custody until he could look into the case. Late that night,
the sheriffs and their deputies rode into the Smiths' camp, served their writ,
and took Biddy, Hannah, and their children back to Los Angeles, where they
were placed in protective custody.

Robert Smith contested the writ, arguing that his slaves had lived as
freely as his own family members and that they would be accorded that
same paternal guidance in Texas. A brief but tension-filled trial ensued; large

crowds—including the Owens family—packed the courtroom. After day one of the trial, the proceedings took a twist. The white man who had signed the habeas corpus petition and hired the slaves' attorney, and who had also appeared in the courtroom that day, suddenly disappeared from town, apparently under threat of bodily harm. What's more, the slaves' attorney was paid a hundred dollars to quit the case, and he did. Furious, Judge Hayes forced the attorney back on the case and grew increasingly suspicious of Robert Smith. By the end of the trial, he had come to believe that Smith was taking his slaves back to Texas so he could sell them and thereby recoup his recent financial losses. On January 19, 1856, the southerner and former slaveholder ruled that the Smiths' slaves were "entitled to their freedom and are free forever."[8] Hayes's stunning ruling, loudly condemned by most local whites as abolitionism gone wild, freed fourteen people at a stroke.

Charles Owens married Ellen, Manuel Pepper married Ann, and children followed, including Charles and Ellen's firstborn, Robert, who would later be heralded as the richest Negro in the west. Hannah moved to San Bernardino to live with Toby, who was able to buy her a home—and as a result almost got killed by local racists. Hannah continued to visit her children and grandchildren who lived in Los Angeles. (On one occasion in town, she rushed under a wagon to save Judge Hayes's only son, who had fallen out and was about to be run over. Hayes considered this rescue providential proof that he had made the correct ruling in the trial.) By 1860, some of Hannah's teenage children, including Charles, were living with Manuel and Ann Pepper, who had themselves brought two children into the world.[9]

And so the families of Robert and Winnie Owens, Biddy Mason, and Hannah—all recently liberated from bondage—formed a growing network of friends and relations that presaged the larger black community that would develop. Fortunately for Los Angeles's black residents, racial conditions improved during the 1860s, first because many of the white southerners went back East to fight for the Confederacy, and second because Lincoln Republicans took control of local politics after the war. Biddy Mason in particular emerged as a popular resident of Los Angeles, serving as a midwife and nurse. Accumulating a little savings, she purchased inexpensive real estate on the edge of town, land that would became the heart of downtown and thus bring her and her descendants a small fortune. One white pioneer resident, Joseph Mesmer, later wrote that these Negro families "were good neighbors and honest, upright Christian people." Of Biddy Mason he added that she "left to her family and heirs, a handsome fortune. But greater than this, she left behind her the life of a splendid, God-fearing, Christian woman, doing His work in deeds of relieving and aiding the poor, particularly those of her own color."[10]

In 1872, a small group of black Methodists organized the First African Methodist Episcopal Church in Biddy Mason's home. Almost simultaneously, the city's black Baptists organized the Second Baptist Church. These two congregations remained very small until the late 1880s, but they proved vitally important to community development. Black newcomers began to filter in at a steady rate. Charles C. Flint left the silver mines in Northern California for Los Angeles and established a general store. The town's first black attorney, R. C. O. Benjamin, arrived on the scene. John J. Neimore, a former slave from Texas, showed up in 1879 and established the first black-owned newspaper; it was short-lived, but other Race papers followed, signaling that Los Angeles's African American residents—numbering a hundred in 1880—were no longer simply a population of families and individuals but a growing community that shared a heritage and common interests.

The Community Takes Shape

The black community began to grow in earnest during the famous "Boom of the 1880s," which marked the origins of modern Los Angeles. Between 1876 and 1885, the Southern Pacific Railroad and its competitor, the Santa Fe, had linked Los Angeles to all parts of the nation. Seeing more profit in real estate development and urban growth than in fares, the two companies in 1886 reduced their excursion fares to virtually nothing, and small-town Los Angeles suddenly found itself swamped with wide-eyed visitors. Feverish boosters and realtors took it from there, prompting a manic two-year real estate spree and population surge. The predictable bust that followed bankrupted those who had speculated in real estate with borrowed money, and the Boom came to symbolize the essential madness of the place. But the bust proved surprisingly short-lived; even during the economic depression of the 1890s, the city grew rapidly, its population topping a hundred thousand by century's end. An unsurpassed warm climate year-round continued to attract snowbirds from the Midwest, tourists, and health seekers. An oil strike in 1892 energized the local economy. City builders created far-flung systems of streetcar travel and electric lighting. Local boosters kept crowing, and the railroads kept their fares relatively low. Between 1900 and 1920 the city's growth rate was simply ridiculous—an average of 23,710 newcomers *every year*—which raised its population to more than a half million by 1920.[11]

Between the Boom and 1920, the black community's growth rate equaled that of the city as a whole. Afro-Angelenos, who numbered only 100 in 1880, exceeded 2,000 by 1900. In the year Charlotta Spear arrived, the census counted 7,600 black residents in the city. By 1920, the Negro population was 15,500. By then, the direction of neighborhood development for black Angelenos had been determined. Racist exclusion barred African Americans from virtually all housing west of Main Street—the "Westside," in local parlance. On the "Eastside" (everything east of Main Street), black Angelenos would draw on racial pride and their desire for community cohesion to wield a political and social influence that far exceeded their proportion of the Eastside population, which consisted mostly of white peoples from all over the nation and the world, with pockets of ethnic Mexicans and Asians.

A black neighborhood of sorts had grown up in downtown after the Boom not far from where Biddy Mason had purchased her lots. As more black migrants moved into this area, they pushed southward a block or two and established a small business block. Unfortunately for these strivers, their "Brick Block" soon ran up against the southern edge of downtown, which was, as Charlotta Bass recalled, "a type of skid row that defied the imagination."[12] After 1900, this ugly "Drunks Paradise," as Charlotta called it, blocked neighborhood growth and created problems for the black families who lived nearby and for the black entrepreneurs who were trying to build up the area.

In response, blacks with middle-class sensibilities moved out of downtown. In effect, they leapfrogged over the skid row at 5th Street and pushed south down San Pedro Street. As their numbers increased, they pushed eastward from San Pedro to Central Avenue and continued moving south on both sides of Central, buying homes, building churches and lodge buildings, and setting up businesses. Thus began a historic, vitally important trend that was already evident by the time Charlotta Spear joined the community.

Some key institutions had already been established as well. The Los Angeles Sunday Forum, for example—usually known simply as "the Forum"—had been organized in 1903 by the First African Methodist Episcopal Church. Despite its church ties, meetings were held outside the church, and the Forum was explicitly open to everyone in the community regardless of religion, income, gender, politics, or social status. The Forum was just what its name implied: an open meeting for anyone to speak out on any subject. Dr. Ruth Temple, the first black female physician in Los Angeles (whose medical training was financed by Forum scholarships), recalled that "it gave a place for communication because it *was* actually an open Forum. Anybody could say whatever he chose in whatever way he chose to say it. And there was no restriction and no desire or attempt to muzzle a person. You were just free to talk."[13]

The Forum met every Sunday afternoon at Odd Fellows Hall, a two-story wooden building on 8th Street, between Maple Avenue and San Pedro Street. It met at 4:30, which gave churchgoers time to get home and have a good dinner before attending the meeting. Membership was free, and members elected the officers, whose jobs were to maintain open discussion and occasionally raise funds to support local charities and scholarships. One person was designated to collect Race news from across the country and read the clippings aloud each week.

As even sympathetic observers pointed out, some black Angelenos expended a bit too much hot air at those afternoon meetings, but that was not such a bad thing. The Forum was a kind of regularly scheduled town-hall meeting for the city's black community, an open space for debate, indignation, and organization and an important venue for black activism.[14]

In addition to the Forum, Charlotta discovered that the black community had a substantial number of churches (she would join Second Baptist), a growing number of Colored Women's Clubs, home-state social clubs such as the "Texas club," Race papers, and a civil-rights organization, the Afro-American Council. She was joining a community that was well established. In fact, all black migrants to Los Angeles after the Boom arrived to find a drama in progress. Black Los Angeles was well past adolescence and into young adulthood. Yet it was still small enough that a newcomer could find a niche and get to know almost everyone in the community. And Charlotta, though a newcomer, would quickly find herself presented with an unusual opportunity—and responsibility—to shape that community's future.

The Newcomer Arrives

The process began after she had benefited from several months of sunshine and rest. Charlotta needed money and found a part-time job at a little newspaper called the *Eagle*, which was John Neimore's latest and last attempt to establish a Race paper in Los Angeles. His enterprise consisted of a small printing shop—Charlotta called it a "shack"—on Central Avenue. Neimore paid Charlotta five dollars per week to solicit subscriptions, collect money, and handle odd jobs. By the time he hired Charlotta, Neimore had been a struggling newspaperman for several decades. He had seen at least three of his papers fail. As an outspoken editor, Neimore had made some enemies in black Los Angeles, but he had also earned the respect and friendship of many. His *Eagle* was the oldest black newspaper in town.

African American Race papers were published once a week, in contrast to the white-owned dailies. By the turn of the twentieth century, Race papers could be found in any town with a few hundred African American residents; large cities usually supported two or more. The papers varied in quality (excellent to fluff) and in length (four to eight pages), but most followed a similar structure, covering local doings and Race news from around the country. Newsworthy items included anything that affected African Americans: black accomplishments, civil rights campaigns, racist incidents, lynchings, political developments. Editorials, often focusing on abuses of racial equality, raged with indignation. News stories themselves often read like editorials, and their authorship was seldom clear. Pullman porters carried Race papers to every little depot in the North, South, and West. Few whites besides white politicians knew about these newspapers, but for African Americans they were the vital element connecting the national black network.

In the printing shack on Central Avenue, John Neimore preached to Charlotta a gospel of political activism, and she embraced the message. Race papers in the West, Neimore said, were the new Underground Railroad, guiding blacks from bondage to freedom. But that was not enough, for freedom in the West was becoming, for blacks, increasingly tenuous. The constitutional rights guaranteed in the Thirteenth, Fourteenth, and Fifteenth Amendments—freedom, citizenship, the vote—had to be defended at all costs. By the 1910s, Neimore's mission was to safeguard and expand black civil rights in California and the West. When Charlotta met him, however, Neimore was "a sick and discouraged man," suffering from poor heath and depleted finances. To recuperate, he took a trip to Northern California, leaving Charlotta and the paper's small staff to publish the *Eagle*.

Neimore returned to Los Angeles in early 1912, but his health continued to decline. In February he summoned Charlotta to his deathbed and said, "I don't want the *Eagle* to die. You are the one in whom I have confidence. Will you promise to keep it alive?" Overwhelmed and uncertain, she managed to answer, "I promise I will do my best." Then Neimore touched her hand and passed away. Barely a year and a half had passed since Charlotta Spear had traveled three thousand miles to relax in Los Angeles. Now, standing silently beside Neimore's lifeless body, she made another long journey, this time of the spirit. In the quiet of the moment, she took upon herself the responsibility of fulfilling Neimore's last request. Her "health-recuperation stay" had ended. Another sort of stay had begun.[15]

"I matured overnight," Charlotta later wrote. Her efforts to save the *Eagle* began awkwardly when Neimore's daughter apologetically declined her offer to take it over. Spear went to work on her own, only to learn that Neimore did not own the *Eagle*'s office. A wealthy white man—whom she later refused to name—held the mortgage. Not long after Neimore's death, he stopped by the office and found Spear alone. He looked her over with what Charlotta considered "a lascivious look," then made her a proposition: he would set her up in a nice apartment and let her use the printing shop free, in exchange for sexual favors. Furious, Spear called him a "dirty low-down dog" and shouted him out of his own building. In response, he put the shop up for sale by public auction. On the day of the auction, though, no one seemed to want the building. A few piddling bids were made. Charlotta watched despondently. She wanted to bid, but she had little money and so remained uncertain and silent.

Then a quiet miracle happened. Captain G. W. Hawkins, a leading black citizen who had known Neimore, was watching the proceedings and noticed Spear's "anxious, disturbed look." He asked her if she wanted to keep the *Eagle* going. She nodded. He offered to buy it for her if she would repay him when her finances allowed. They shook hands, and Hawkins bought Neimore's shop for fifty dollars and gave Charlotta the deed. Just like that, Charlotta Spear owned a newspaper. As she later recalled, "The sale transaction was very unbusiness-like. Captain Hawkins purchased the paper and handed it over to [me]. The entire transaction was done orally. There were no legal papers signed, no red tape involved. Los Angeles, in those days, was the center of the wild and wooly West. Things like buying a newspaper for an unknown person, free from any legal hullabaloo, or red tape, [were] all part of the uninhibited life that prevailed in those days." It was not much of a business—a run-down office with secondhand machinery, $10 in assets, and $150 in overdue bills. But it was hers.

That night, sitting in Miss Tiggs's Cafe, a black-owned diner near the shop, Charlotta was eating soup and reading a newspaper when she overheard two women discussing the *Eagle*. They did not like its chances with Neimore gone. There was "that young girl who came here recently," one suggested hopefully. Yes, said the other doubtfully, but "nobody seems to know her, and they say she will not be able to go it alone." Charlotta herself probably wondered whether she could make it run, but the amazing thing was that the question even existed. "Seemingly overnight," she later wrote, "this newcomer to a new frontier became owner, editor and publisher of a defunct newspaper." She was a topic of conversation—an item. The stranger had joined the community. But before long she realized she really could use a business partner.

Big Joe Bass

When Joseph Blackburn Bass arrived in 1911, black Los Angeles knew it. He was hard to miss—nearly six feet tall, barrel chested, well over two hundred pounds, with a large head, dark complexion, thick mustache, and powerful eyes. Forty-four years old and a veteran of decades of newspaper work and backroom politics, Bass looked tough and distinguished, self-confident and imposing. He was commonly known as Joe or J. B., but if the situation so dictated, "Mister Bass" would have been a good idea. A local minister later recalled Bass's "calm, dignified, and well balanced bearing," adding, "you cannot in thought couple him with anything silly or frivolous."[16]

Born in 1868 to Preston and Susan Bass, of Missouri, Joe Bass grew up in Topeka, Kansas, which had a vibrant black community, and where his father worked as a laborer. When he was ten years old, Joe served as a page in the Kansas statehouse. From then on, he was active in Republican Party politics. After a brief and unhappy stint teaching school, he gravitated toward journalism and became coeditor of the *Topeka Call,* which ceased publication in 1897. The following year, at age thirty, he took on a high-profile campaign when the Spanish-American War broke out and a peculiar crisis developed: Some white volunteers who wanted commissions as officers had been denied them in Kansas's white regiments; so they sought commissions as officers in the all-black Twenty-third Regiment instead. Bass, who wanted to see black officers leading black soldiers, "raised so much hell" that the governor of Kansas blocked the white appointments and ensured that African Americans received the officers' commissions.[17]

After the war, Bass worked for a new Race paper, the *Topeka Plaindealer,* and continued his work in the Republican Party. He also read law for a time, but his love was backroom politics. He helped reunite Topeka's black leadership, which had split into quarreling factions. He organized the Kansas Lincoln Day Club and forged connections to the state's Republican leaders. Bass secured patronage positions for Topeka's black leaders and engineered the election of an African American to Topeka's city council. By the time he left Topeka, at the end of 1905, he had a reputation as an effective political lieutenant—the man who could maintain black unity, get out the vote, and secure patronage positions for the Race.

Joe's decision to leave Topeka is a curious one, given his status in the community and in the state Republican Party. He was nearing middle age; perhaps he just needed a change in his life. More likely, his departure had to do with a failed marriage. Bass had married in 1901, when he was thirty-three. Details about that marriage—even his wife's name—are unknown, but he had no wife with him at his next locale. If his spouse had died, it seems unlikely that Bass would have felt a need to leave or a reluctance to speak about her; since he did make a permanent exit from Topeka, and since he never mentioned his first marriage in print, the marriage may well have fallen apart, prompting his desire to get out of town.[18]

In any event, Bass landed in Helena, Montana, a booming mining town with a few hundred African American residents. He quickly founded the *Montana Plaindealer,* whose goal was "the progress and uplifting of a race with which our destiny is forever linked." Bass promised readers that he would rather "pour oil on troubled waters" than "stir up strife," but would also "stand up for right and denounce the wrong." Bass published his paper for five years, fighting for equal rights, denouncing racial prejudice, and not worrying much about troubled waters. He found contacts within Montana's Republican Party and was appointed sergeant-at-arms of the state legislature.

Bass's views on civil rights blended those of the nation's two most influential black leaders of the time, Booker T. Washington and W. E. B. Du Bois. Washington gained national recognition with his "Atlanta Compromise" speech, delivered at the Atlanta Exposition of 1895. His aim that day was to calm the bitter racial hostilities (especially lynchings) that were destroying black civil rights in the 1890s. In the speech, Washington assured southern whites that black southerners would willingly sacrifice social and political equality in return for a fair and equal chance for economic opportunity. Some blacks lambasted Washington as a sellout, but few of those critics were standing in the midst of the bloodbath that was the South in 1895. For blacks, Washington's "accomodationist" approach came to mean an emphasis on racially separate economic development as a means of attaining full racial equality. In Washington's view, when African Americans became wealthy enough, whites would no longer be able to denigrate them as an inferior race. Then, with their newly won white respect, blacks could regain their political and social rights. To further these ends, Washington organized the National Negro Business League.[19]

W. E. B. Du Bois opposed Washington's accomodationism. He emerged as the nation's leading black intellectual and its most outspoken advocate of fully equal rights, regardless of race. Du Bois wanted racially integrated classical schools, not the racially segregated industrial education that Washington advocated. He urged the rise of an African American "Talented Tenth," a small group of intellectuals who would lead the Race in attaining full equality. After earning his Ph.D. from Harvard, Du Bois taught at Atlanta University, where he wrote *The Souls of Black Folk* (1903), which included an attack on Washington's accomodationism and became the "bible" of the black intelligentsia. A few years later, Du Bois helped organize the Niagara Movement, which brought together black leaders who opposed Washington's philosophy and leadership. In 1909, Niagara leaders joined with white reformers seeking to fight racial prejudice in America. Subsequent meetings led to the creation of the foremost civil rights organization of the twentieth century, the National Association for the Advancement of Colored People (NAACP). Du Bois soon moved to New York to become editor of the NAACP's monthly journal, the *Crisis,* which became the most influential and widely read magazine in black America.[20]

These two schools of thought were never completely incompatible, of course. Most black leaders in the North and West subscribed to both without concern for their contradictions. Joe Bass's *Montana Plaindealer* reflected both, an approach that presaged his Los Angeles editorial work. It praised Washington's ideas and the school for blacks Washington had founded, the Tuskegee Normal and Industrial Institute. Bass organized a local branch of the National Negro Business League and promoted the Afro-American Building Association, which operated as a black bank. Sometimes, however, the *Montana Plaindealer* highlighted Du Bois's activism and sounded as if it were written by Du Bois himself. Bass published fiery denunciations of inequality and segregation. When the state in 1909 passed an antimiscegenation law, Bass thundered: "Montana has joined the Jim Crow Colony alongside of Mississippi, South Carolina, Texas, and Arkansas. God help us!" He excoriated the Democrat who had introduced the bill as "the Ben Tillman of the Northwest." Bass, who never lived in the South, often used Dixie's foremost white-supremacy demagogues—Tillman of South Carolina and James Vardaman of Mississippi—as symbols of race prejudice at its worst.[21] To safeguard black rights in Montana, he helped organize the Afro-American Protective League and, later, the Colored Protective League.

In mid-1911, Bass told his readers that changes were in the offing. He was now on firm financial footing, he wrote, and planned to purchase new and better printing equipment for a bigger, better *Plaindealer.* That autumn he spelled out his plans to take a few months off to tour the West by rail with an old friend from Kansas. He promised a full account of his travels when he returned. Bass called in all outstanding subscription payments and left suddenly in late fall. The *Plaindealer* ceased publication. And Joe Bass never returned to Helena.

He may have intended to continue his work in Montana, but Helena had lost its economic vitality and was clearly declining. More important, when Bass arrived in Los Angeles, he fell for the city immediately. His friend suggested they return to Kansas, but Bass decided to stay. In his view, Los Angeles "was indeed Beulah Land and just what I had been looking for." Charlotta hired him as a news reporter. She was taken with Joe Bass—"the big man from Kansas," she called him—and apparently, he was equally impressed with her. Of their courtship nothing is known, except the end result: in August 1914, Joe Bass and Charlotta Spear were married during a getaway to San Diego. As Charlotta later put it, they "formed a life partnership." Charlotta A. Spear changed her name to Charlotta A. Bass, although she would use different derivations over the years.[22]

Joe and Charlotta returned to run the *Eagle* together. He became the "editor," in charge of content, and she the "managing editor," in charge of running the business. The separate professional titles probably helped prevent friction. In this arrangement, Joe showed remarkable respect for Charlotta. This was 1914, he was her elder, and the newspaper business was a man's world. It was Joe who had the credentials—several Race papers to his credit and Republican Party connections throughout the West. But he never shouldered Charlotta aside. At no time during their marriage, which lasted until his death in 1934, did he undermine her authority, censor her views, or check her ambition. That bespoke an open-mindedness on Joe's part, but it is also difficult to imagine Charlotta accepting any other arrangement. Even in her 1960 autobiography, published nearly thirty years after his death, the caption under Joe's photograph reads, "second in editorial command."[23]

It helped that Joe and Charlotta had shared views about Race papers and politics. Both thought it a good idea to spice up each issue of the paper with social news and a bit of gossip, but both also insisted on highlighting the larger issues of politics, economics, and civil rights.[24] They were loyal Baptists, with notable moral scruples. They were joiners, active and visible at their church and in the community. They prized Race unity. Both of them preferred to run the *Eagle* free of outside entanglements—they operated a printing business to keep the paper solvent, and the paper seems not to have been financed by any political group. They were Lincoln Republicans and doubtless received money from the party to run political advertisements at election time or simply to keep the paper going in times of financial crisis; but they were unafraid of voicing political independence when they felt their party was in the wrong, or another party was in the right. Perhaps most important, neither of them considered the *Eagle* to be merely an occupation. They believed Race papers were inseparable from black freedom. The *Eagle* was not their job—it was their calling.

To underscore their new partnership, Joe and Charlotta Bass changed the name of the paper to the *California Eagle*. It was a subtle change but one with appropriate symbolic implications. They were starting new lives, putting down roots in a new place. And that place was important. California had everything to do with who they were becoming. They were partners in marriage and in business, but as they saw it, the partnership was even larger: they were partners with California itself.

On the Margins of Freedom

In 1920, the federal government turned Charlotta and Joe Bass into white people—statistically speaking. It happened when the Census Bureau undertook its decennial tally of the population. Throughout Los Angeles, census agents carried ledger books door to door, gathering information on the members of every household: name, race, sex, age, marital status, occupation, and the like. In the 800 block of South Central Avenue, a census taker came to the Basses' apartment. The neighborhood was racially mixed, with about as many blacks as whites, and a smaller number of ethnic Mexicans and Asians. The census form asked about race, and the agent who visited the Basses filled in that column with a *B*, which stood for "black." The census taker also recorded their occupations, listing Charlotta as the managing editor of a newspaper, and Joe as the editor of a newspaper.

Later, probably after the local agents had returned their ledgers to the bureau in Washington, D.C., an office clerk apparently decided there had been some mistake. Perhaps the clerk could not reconcile the Basses' race with their occupations. Who had ever heard of a black person being the managing editor of a newspaper? So the clerk corrected the mistake by changing their racial designation. The *B*s in the race column were changed to *W*s, a change still clearly visible on the census form.[25]

This change caused no harm to the Basses or black Los Angeles. There were no federal funds at stake, no political or economic consequences. The Basses themselves never knew about it, and so could have felt no insult. But the change highlights the barriers facing black strivers in the early twentieth century. The clerk who made the change probably had intended no malice. To his way of thinking, black people could not possibly hold such prestigious positions. The white assumption that black people were naturally subordinate and inferior ran deep in America. For blacks in Los Angeles, as everywhere else, there was no dodging the issue. White people, astonishingly diverse themselves, simply could not, or would not, think of black Angelenos as equal players in their city or their nation.

Fortunately for the Basses and other African American migrants, racial conditions were better in Los Angeles than in most places. Race hatred was worst in the South, of course, and it was Dixie's Jim Crow system that had prompted black southerners to move to the West Coast. In the black community that formed in Los Angeles, Joe and Charlotta were atypical in one respect: they were not from the South. But as the content of the *California Eagle* would show, they knew full well what was happening to blacks in the former Confederacy, and they were dedicated to the proposition that their newly adopted home must never become like the South. Los Angeles had to be something different, something western, something free.

1

Southern Roots,
Western Dreams

One way to get free is to get gone. Move. Leave someplace bad for someplace better. Americans have always moved incessantly, looking for greener pastures, better jobs, broader opportunities, freer conditions, a place in the sun, a new start. At the turn of the twentieth century, Los Angeles offered all of that, which explains why it lured dream chasers from all over the nation and, indeed, the world. For white midwesterners—the majority of the newcomers during and after the real estate boom of the 1880s—Los Angeles promised freedom from harsh winters and the latest best bet for the big break. For Mexican exiles who surged north during the Mexican Revolution of the 1910s, Los Angeles offered escape from political violence and economic dislocation. For Japanese immigrants crossing the Pacific, Los Angeles meant opportunities for status and wealth that seemed no longer available in their homeland.

For African Americans, moving to Los Angeles had an even deeper meaning, one rooted in black history. Only free people can move freely, and no one understood this better than slaves and their descendants. Slaves had no legal right to free movement—no right to go where they pleased, when they pleased; no right to stay with family if a master said "sold." Slaves had to carry coinlike metal "passes" from their masters just to walk the roads. Running away from slavery—by law, illegal movement—was usually their only hope for freedom. The Underground Railroad thus attained immense cultural significance for black Americans. So too did the Exodus story. The old

Hebrew texts were fundamental to the slaves' outlook on the world: Genesis and Exodus—life, exile, bondage, deliverance.

Freedom from slavery came partly because of the slaves' own mass movement during the Civil War. When the Union Army entered the South, slaves by the tens of thousands flocked to their military camps. This movement prompted a crisis within the army and ultimately prodded white Republicans into thinking that the war might in fact lead to the destruction of slavery in the South. When emancipation became reality in 1865, slaves took to the roads, demonstrating their freedom in the most basic way—they walked the roads to find a better place to live, to search for lost family, or just to stroll down a road because a free person can choose to do that.

After the war, virtually all former slaves remained in the South, because the South, exorcized of slavery, was their promised land. Instead of taking the Red Sea out, they sought to remake Egypt. Dixie was a land they knew. Their roots there stretched back for centuries. Their loved ones lay buried in that earth. The land was good, and they understood how to work it. During Reconstruction, southern blacks became voters and elected officials, and, with their white Republican allies, they sought to turn a land of bondage into a land of freedom. It was an astonishing quest for redemption.

But it did not work out. Reconstruction officially ended in 1877, a half-finished thing, and through the 1880s, black Republicans struggled to maintain a semblance of racial equality. Then, in the 1890s, conditions grew far worse. Through unchecked political violence, southern white Democrats disfranchised black voters. Jim Crow segregation became entrenched in southern life and law. White southerners lynched African Americans to show who was really in control, to show that blacks had no rights that whites were obligated to respect. By the mid-1890s, many Afro-southerners had decided a new Exodus was needed. Concerted out-migration began in a quiet, persistent procession.

Black Los Angeles traces its thickest roots to this unreconstructed South. For Afro-Angelenos, "the South" was more than a place on a map. It represented their history, the essential tragedy of their people. It served as their negative reference point, the ultimate example of what America should not be. With a common heritage encompassing slavery, the failure of Reconstruction, and the rise of Jim Crow, black Angelenos viewed their departure from Dixie as an escape from bondage.

"The West," too, occupied a meaningful place in black Americans' hearts and minds. Through newspapers, magazines, art, political speeches, and dime novels, the Western Ideal had already assumed a powerful position in mainstream American mythology. The ideal held that the American West was a singularly egalitarian place, where opportunity was open to all citizens, regardless of background, lineage, or wealth. The West was the freest part of free America—pure democracy. Naturally, the ideal was largely bunk, but it was widely embraced, and it shaped the behavior and expectations of millions. The Western Ideal inspired many African American dreamers because it promised the equal opportunity they had never found in the East—whether they were in the North or the South. Interesting things were happening for blacks in the West during the late nineteenth and early twentieth centuries. Out West, and only out West, African American soldiers manned United States forts—armed black men were protecting the interests of the nation. There were dozens of all-black towns in the West, from Oklahoma to California—tangible symbols of civic freedom and Race enterprise. And finally, blacks were discovering an unusual amount of social and political freedom in the region's growing cities. Denver, San Francisco, Seattle, and Los Angeles had only tiny black communities, but the word was that racial conditions there were notably better than they were back East.

Black Los Angeles always had in view both the South and the West. Even those Angelenos who had not moved from Dixie, including the Basses, spoke the language of southern tyranny and western freedom. When Joe Bass, still in Helena, blasted the Montana legislature for turning his state into a colony of the Jim Crow South, he was expressing three fundamental views held by black westerners: that southern race relations were evil; that the Western Ideal promised a better life; and—critically important—that the West was in danger of becoming another South.

At the turn of the century, however, African Americans in Dixie did not know that black westerners were beginning to worry about the southernization of the West. They saw only the opportunity for a kind of freedom that the South refused to offer them. For many, there came a point when their southern dream died and a western one took its place. For three African American families in three southern cities, the choice was not an easy one. They had fared rather well in the New South, but as their hopes for Reconstruction fell to Jim Crow, they began to consider a move to the Far West.

Out of Texas

William Edgar Easton believed that salvation for blacks lay in the Republican Party. This idea was common among black southerners, for the Republican Party—the party of Lincoln and emancipation—advocated a social order based on the principle of equality for all American citizens. It was biracial party, although its northern wing was predominantly white and its southern predominantly black. It stood in opposition to the Democratic Party, which openly advocated a social order based on white supremacy: whites could be free individuals, Democrats insisted, only if all blacks were subservient to all whites—a caste system. Other issues divided Republicans and Democrats, but for Afro-Texans and other black southerners, the battle between racial equality and white supremacy dominated the agenda.[1]

William Easton was born in 1861, the second son of Charles F. Easton, a New Yorker with family ties to both New England and the West Indies, and Marie Antoinette Leggett-Easton, a native of Louisiana whose roots stretched to Haiti. Charles was a barber by trade, and Marie kept house. By 1870, the family had moved to Saint Louis; but when Marie died shortly thereafter, Charles and his sons moved to New Bedford, Massachusetts, where Charles, Jr., followed his father into the barbering trade. William, however, was often away from home, attending school at a French Canadian seminary, a New England academy, and a Catholic university. By his early twenties, Easton was a well-educated college graduate with a broad view of the world. In 1883, at the age of twenty-two, he moved south to take a teaching position in Texas. There he was married, and between 1890 and 1899, his wife, Mary, a native Texan, would give birth to four children.[2]

In Texas, Easton entered the rugged terrain of post-Reconstruction politics. Charlotta Bass, never one to understate a compliment, later wrote that "white politicians feared him because he was a master mind in political strategy." White Democrats probably did fear him, because he was everything they insisted blacks could never be—highly intelligent, politically astute, unmistakably urbane. Easton's complexion was virtually white, and he could have passed as white, but he embraced his African lineage and fought for black civil rights. Gradually his star began to rise in the Republican Party. In the 1880s he was elected commissioner of Fort Bend County, served as a political linchpin in Houston, became secretary of the state's Executive Committee for the Republican Party, and moved to Austin, where he chaired the county Executive Committee. In the mid-1890s he received two patronage positions, the first as a clerk in Galveston's customhouse, the second as a police clerk in San Antonio. By this time he had become a partner in a printing venture and editor of a Race paper, the *Texas Blade*. He wrote a historical drama, *Dessalines: A Dramatic Tale: A Single Chapter from Haiti's History* (1893), whose dual themes of racial pride and liberty were intended, as he wrote in the preface, to counter the image of Negro "buffoonery" presented in American theater. As editor of the *Blade*, Easton was "a fearless advocate and defender" of the Race.[3]

But as Easton's star was rising, the curtain was falling on black leaders and the Republican Party in Dixie. During the 1890s, Democrats used fraud, intimidation, and disfranchisement laws to rob virtually all blacks of the right to vote. When the U.S. Supreme Court ruled unanimously—in *Williams v. Mississippi* (1898)—that poll taxes and literacy tests did not violate the Constitution, the southern GOP was doomed. Northern Republicans had their own crises at home—massive immigration, urban-industrial chaos, labor unrest—and the Radical Republican bloc, which had supported black civil rights, was dying out. A new breed of northern Republicans sought to meet the needs of big business, rather than of southern blacks, and in Congress they found useful allies among southern Democrats. Seizing the moment, Dixie's conservatives wiped out all their opponents. Before 1890, only two of eleven southern states had disfranchisement laws; by 1903, all southern states had them. In a remarkably short period, the black vote in the South went from healthy to dead. The one-party South was born.[4]

By this time, life had become not just difficult, but dangerous for Texas Republicans. In 1902 and 1903, Texas Democrats passed their state's disfranchisement law, and in 1904 a Republican leader near San Antonio was murdered by Democrats. But by then, the Eastons had gone. William Easton believed that only through electoral politics could Afro-Texans win "freedom from the tyranny imposed upon them by the state." But he saw that "the Lone Star State . . . held the Negro in virtual bondage," so in 1901 he and his family had left San Antonio for Los Angeles. Their new home offered fresh political opportunities, because Southern California was a Republican stronghold. And if William Easton could not save Texas, perhaps he could defend and extend equal rights in California.[5]

Out of Georgia

George and Annie Beavers had a little home on Humphreys Street in a section of south Atlanta called Mechanicsville. George worked as a laborer at a grocery store for a dollar a day, and Annie took in laundry. They supplemented this with a little backyard economy, growing vegetables and raising chickens. They had three young children: George, Jr., the oldest, born in 1892, and Mary Elmyra and Leroy. George and Annie Beavers believed strongly in education, racial progress, Christian living, and upward mobility for their children. They were members of St. Paul's First African Methodist Episcopal Church, and they taught their children the values of learning and leadership. George Beavers, Jr., later recalled that "my father always took me to . . . any big gathering where there was a discussion of conditions involving our race, and when there [were] noted speakers, bishops, and such characters as Booker T. Washington, and other leaders at the time. My father wanted me to get every benefit possible from hearing inspirational speakers and leaders." The Beavers family might not have been middle class in terms of wealth (George, Jr., later described the family as "poor"), but like many blue-collar African Americans, they were strivers, middle class in spirit and outlook.[6]

In some ways, Atlanta was right for the Beavers family. Racial conditions were better there than in most southern cities. The economy was growing, and so was the city's black middle class, led by educators and business leaders. Black churches were well established. Several black colleges were clustered near the Beavers home, including Morehouse, Spelman, and Atlanta University, where W. E. B. Du Bois was then teaching. The colleges offered private grade schools, and George Beavers, Jr., attended them. White boosters emphasized the city's business mind-set—"the city too busy to hate"—and promoted a paternalistic approach to race relations in hopes of curbing racial violence.[7]

Yet the New South was still the South. Public schools were segregated and badly unequal. The state's cumulative poll tax, passed in 1877 (the first in the South), had driven most blacks out of the electorate. Economic constraints were suffocating the black poor. And, in the end, New South boosterism could not stave off racial violence. Lynching, the scourge of the 1890s, hit Atlanta in 1899 with the killing and dismembering of Sam Hose, whose alleged murder of a white neighbor had resulted in mob retaliation. Afterward, Hose's charred hand was hung for display in a downtown store window. Tensions escalated in the early years of the twentieth century and finally exploded in the Atlanta race riot of 1906. During four searing days, white mobs torched black neighborhoods and businesses and murdered more than a dozen African Americans.[8]

The Beavers family was already in Los Angeles by then, but their exodus from Atlanta three years earlier had been prompted by the "Pittsburgh riot" of 1902. In that case, a black man tried to kill an ex-policeman who had once arrested him, and when he failed, he barricaded himself inside a store in the south Atlanta neighborhood of Pittsburgh, which was only blocks from the Beavers home. Heavily armed, the man shot and killed several of the policemen and bystanders who had surrounded the building. Mobs then descended in force, passing the Beavers house as they went. Finally, the building was burned with the man inside it; but it was difficult for local authorities to stop the violence there. The mob went on to set fire to other black sections of south Atlanta. Late in his life, George, Jr., remembered the scene and how it had prompted his parents to leave. "The excitement of the [white] patrols going back and forth to the site of that incident made quite an impression," he recalled. George and Annie Beavers had seen enough. They decided to leave.[9]

At the time, black southerners had a tendency to move due north from where they lived: Those who left Florida, the Carolinas, and Virginia usually pushed up the eastern seaboard to New York, Philadelphia, and Pittsburgh. Black Cleveland became "Alabama North." Blacks near the Mississippi River found a convenient connection to Chicago on the famous Illinois Central Railroad. When Texans moved north they did not go far, migrating in huge numbers to Oklahoma; otherwise, they headed West. But black Georgians moved in all directions and could be found in substantial numbers in almost every large black community, North or West. Part of the reason for this trend lies in Georgia's exceptional railroad connections; rail lines spread from Atlanta in all directions. Relative affluence explains it as well. Black Georgians who were middle class (mostly in Atlanta), and those who were relatively poor but had accumulated some savings, such as the Beavers family, had money enough for tickets, and a wide range of destinations to choose from. Some of them could afford to be selective.[10]

George and Annie Beavers decided on Los Angeles, one of the most expensive and difficult places to go. The route from Atlanta to the West Coast was not a direct one, train tickets were expensive—train fare for a family of five would have cost about two hundred dollars at the time—and the distance of two thousand miles was daunting. From what George and Annie had heard, however, the move would be worth the effort and expense. Some of their friends had already moved to Los Angeles, and the letters they sent back described the "splendid conditions that existed" in Southern California. Los Angeles, they said, was like a "new heaven to the people, particularly our people." If you feel "burdened from racial segregation and discrimination," their friends said, then Los Angeles was the place to live. George and Annie Beavers believed it, and that is the message they passed on to their children. As George, Jr., later recalled, his family moved to Los Angeles "in quest of full citizenship rights and better living conditions."[11]

Out of Louisiana

The Atlanta riot of 1906 stunned the black South and hastened the exodus of the middle class. If it could happen in Atlanta, it could happen anywhere—

and signs of black affluence only seemed to incite a deeper hatred among rioting whites. The long arm of anxiety reached all the way from Atlanta to Alexandria, Louisiana, and into the home of Paul and Maria Bontemps. Even before the riot, Maria Bontemps wanted out of Louisiana. With increasing frequency, she and her mother, Sarah Pembrooke, had tried to convince Paul to leave Dixie. The Bontempses and Pembrookes were well-established Creole families that had long been prosperous in central Louisiana. Paul earned a good living as a brick mason and, on occasion, as a trumpet player in a New Orleans band. He had married well: the Pembrookes were successful in business and had status in the community; Maria had been a schoolteacher. In Alexandria, Paul had built a spacious two-story home off of Lee Street, a desirable thoroughfare. When Atlanta burned in 1906, Paul was building another home on a newly acquired lot. He was settling in.[12]

Creoles were an important group in Louisiana. Historically, they were neither white nor black, but something in between. Creoles were light-skinned descendants of long-ago unions among French, Spanish, Native Americans, and African people. They had a language of their own, a French derivation called *patois*, which they spoke in addition to English. No one could say for certain what the exact formula for a Creole was, but they were a group set apart. In the antebellum era, Creoles had seldom been enslaved. They were free people of color—*hommes de couleur libre*—well educated and known for their skills in the building trades. They were also Catholic, which further distanced them from dark-skinned Louisianans, who were usually Protestant.

By the time the plagues of the 1890s had passed, however, Creole status had changed for the worse. Racial configurations that had always been subtle and complex grew increasingly stark. Whites now dictated that all people of color, regardless of complexion or heritage, were, by law, black people. And all blacks were now subject to segregation laws. The goal was to create a caste system in which blacks might rise a little, but never to the level of whites. Successful Creoles, resistant to Jim Crow treatment, were becoming targets of violence. That was what worried Maria Bontemps. She and Paul had two children, a son named Arna, who was four years old in 1906, and a younger daughter, Ruby. Maria wanted them to receive a good education, but they would not get one in Alexandria. And what would happen to her and the children if her proud and prosperous husband fell into the hands of jealous whites? If Paul were killed, would Arna be next?

Paul Bontemps changed his mind about the merits of Alexandria almost overnight. The Atlanta riot had planted a seed of doubt in his mind, and Maria cultivated it. But what finally moved him—quickly—was a chance encounter on a sidewalk. One night, while he was walking home along the storefronts downtown, two drunk white men came stumbling out of a bar and almost bumped into him. One of them said, "Let's run over the nigger!" In that moment, what Paul Bontemps wanted to do clashed with what he did. What he wanted to do was teach those men a lesson. What he did was to keep his mouth shut, lower his eyes, and step off of the sidewalk. For a black man to hit a white man—or even to speak harshly to white men— was to invite a lynch mob or a house burning. Paul Bontemps made it home that night in one piece, but he knew there would be a next time, and he could not live with that kind of subordination.

In the South, informal racial mores were enforced with deadly seriousness. These customs demanded that blacks step off the sidewalk when a white person approached, look at the ground when they talked to a white person, and hold their tongue when insulted by a white person. Then there was language. Whites, regardless of age, called black adults "boy" or "girl," or, more generously, "uncle" or "aunt." White folks never called blacks by their last name—this was a privilege granted to whites only—and never afforded blacks the title of "Mr." or "Mrs." Black adults had to call white boys "Mr." and white girls "Miss." Affluent blacks knew their homes were at risk, and that fire departments would be unavailable to them in moments of crisis. All levels of government accepted or cultivated this culture of caste. For Paul Bontemps, it was not formal segregation laws but this larger culture of subordination that severed his ties with the South. He had bowed to white supremacy for the sake of himself and his family. Leaving a widow with children to raise was no kind of valor. But what kind of life would it be if a respectable, affluent citizen had to shuffle aside for drunken antagonists just to stay alive? Maria's view suddenly made sense.

They had heard good things about California from people they trusted. Sarah Pembrooke had received a letter from a friend who had moved to Los Angeles. Her friend referred to it as "a city called heaven." Paul had family and friends there, too. They sent him letters, extolling the virtues of Los Angeles, as well as San Francisco and Oakland, and praising the weather and the wages. He received a letter from a relative who was making good as a musician on the West Coast, and who urged him to come join the band. All of the letters emphasized California's good schools, which were open to all. Paul bought a ticket that would take him first to Los Angeles, then on to San Francisco. He intended to scout out the West Coast, but he never made it to the Bay Area.

Los Angeles captured him immediately. The climate, the openness, the demand for brick masons, the inexpensive real estate. He sent for his extended family: Maria and the children, Maria's parents, and Maria's sister. They met him in Los Angeles at the Southern Pacific depot. By the time they arrived, Paul had already purchased a home. Young Arna, who would become one the most talented writers of his generation, grew up in a household devoted to the idea that moving west was the key to black freedom. "My parents," he wrote later in life, "were always anxious to put the South (and the past) as far behind as possible."[13]

Migration Stories

In these three migration stories—typical enough for black Los Angeles—the families were city people, and they were middle class in outlook and ambition. They could afford to take their entire families on a long, expensive journey to California. And the journey was long. Even for the Eastons, living in the middle of Texas, it was slightly farther to Los Angeles than to Chicago. From Atlanta the distance to Los Angeles was three times that to Chicago, and from New Orleans, the distance to Chicago—920 miles—would leave westbound travelers still east of El Paso, not even halfway to L.A. And of course, train rides of this duration cost more. But perhaps the extra distance and expense were a blessing. Considering the circumstances, it probably was best to put the South as far behind as possible.

If Jim Crow had given these families a sinister push, Los Angeles provided a hopeful pull. Letters describing the city as "heaven" sent the essential, trustworthy message about the place. Los Angeles Race papers did their share as well: John Neimore's *Eagle* encouraged black emigration from the South; Jefferson Lewis Edmonds's *Liberator* said that southern blacks "will find no race problem in Los Angeles, only prosperity"; and Frederick Madison Roberts's *New Age* heralded the city's opportunities for African Americans, insisting that "this is the city after all." White Los Angeles also helped some. The *Los Angeles Times* occasionally encouraged black migration from Dixie, and the Southern Pacific Railroad recruited some black workers in Texas, some of whom probably relocated to Los Angeles. But most southern blacks who moved to the city, like the Beavers and Bontemps families, relied on information from friends and family.[14]

There is one final, important point regarding these migration stories. Consider how each was preserved: William Easton's story comes from his friend Charlotta Bass, who related it in her 1960 autobiography. The next was related by George Beavers, Jr., in an oral history he gave in 1982, at age ninety-one, having lived a successful life as a businessman and civic leader in Los

Angeles. The story of the Bontemps family found its way into print many decades later in the writings of Arna Bontemps. These stories had staying power. They were told and retold over the decades, handed down like heirlooms. People who move to seek freedom keep their stories alive: the Hebrews who left Egypt, the Irish who left the famine, the African Americans who left Dixie. Such stories link older tragedies and dashed hopes with the promise and vision of a new life. Most Americans have similar stories, imprinted in their memories by family and community. These migration narratives place individual and family lives in context and often connect them to a broader story—the story of a people.

Black Migrations Great and Small, North and West

The history of black migration in the United States embodies vivid and familiar images. Harriet Tubman and the Underground Railroad. The slaves' rush to the Union Army camps. The "Exodusters" of 1877 building communities in Kansas. The recurrent "Back to Africa" movements. And, most of all, the Great Migration of World War I. Less familiar is the quieter migration that took place between roughly 1890 and 1915. The emigration of black southerners during this period is usually referred to, following Du Bois's idea about Race leaders, as the migration of the Talented Tenth—the more educated, ambitious, and affluent African Americans. Emigrants were the teachers, newspaper editors, ministers, businesspeople, and other professionals who constituted the upper echelons of black society, as well as those with less social status who had upward mobility in mind, such as the Beavers family. The Talented Tenth migration did not have the look or feel of a mass movement. There was a certain urgency in each departure, but the out-migration proceeded without fanfare.

During this migration, blacks who moved North filtered into small, loosely knit communities that were, in large part, middle class. A small number of northern blacks were professionals, and some others owned businesses (which, in contrast to those of a later era, catered mostly to white customers), but most worked in the usual urban service jobs open to them: as porters, domestics, and custodians. Northern blacks could vote. There was some racial segregation, but there were no black ghettos to speak of, and white bigotry appeared muted, partly because blacks constituted such a small percentage of the population and were not really competitors for "white" jobs. Northern whites were more concerned about the new immigrants from southern and eastern Europe. White fear of black people, and the discrimination against blacks that stemmed from it, has often been correlated with the number of black people in the vicinity. Before 1915, black northerners were not numerous enough to set off white alarms. Black communities were small and orderly, and the Talented Tenth migration simply blended into them.

In the West, the Talented Tenth migration created black communities where they had scarcely existed before. In 1900, not a single city in the trans-Missouri West (excluding Texas) had a black population exceeding four thousand. The black populations of Denver, Los Angeles, Oakland, Omaha, Portland, San Francisco, Seattle, and Spokane *combined* barely topped ten thousand. Blacks were scattered into neighborhoods of whites and, sometimes, ethnic Mexicans and Asians. Blacks in the West could vote, and schools were usually integrated. There was racial prejudice, but the worst aspects of Jim Crow were largely absent. Home ownership was generally higher in the West than in the North, but black communities in the North and West were similar before the First World War. Then they went separate ways.

When war erupted in Europe in 1914, it created an enormous demand for American industrial goods, even as it cut off the usual supply of European immigrant labor. Northern factories faced a drastic labor shortage. Desperate for workers, northern industrialists opened their doors to blacks. Companies recruited in Dixie, Race papers such as the *Chicago Defender* implored southern blacks to move north, and African Americans everywhere exchanged letters and gossip to sort things out. By war's end in 1918, an estimated five hundred thousand black southerners had flocked to the nation's industrial heartland—to Cleveland, Detroit, Pittsburgh, and Chicago. The sheer number of blacks on the move, and the visibility of so much dark skin in what had been overwhelmingly white cities, stunned the people of the urban North, white and black alike.[15]

Whites panicked at the sight of so many blacks on the streets and in the factories. They erected residential boundaries, through violence and law, to keep blacks out of their neighborhoods, thereby penning the migrants into black-only districts that proved to be embryonic ghettos. Immigrant workers resisted the intrusion of blacks into workplaces and unions. Deadly race riots in East Saint Louis, Illinois, in 1917 and Chicago in 1919 were the worst manifestations of the North's racial tensions. Older black residents in these cities also resented the newcomers who had, from the "old settlers'" point of view, wrecked a good thing. They had overwhelmed the region's small, stable black communities, and their very presence had sparked a white backlash. Yet they large numbers of blacks meant something new and good as well: political clout. And now there existed a black clientele large enough to support black-owned businesses. The black communities of Chicago and Cleveland, despite the overcrowding and attendant poverty, offered the newcomers better jobs, better schools, and greater safety than they had ever had down South. And a certain pride emerged from living in a community that was virtually a city within a city.

This Great Migration bypassed the American West. In wartime Los Angeles, the black population grew at the same rate as it had been growing since the late 1880s—steady and sure. Even in places where labor shortages opened industrial jobs to newcomers, there was no obvious surge in black migration. In the urban West, a quieter "Modest Migration" continued.

Ralph Bunche, who would one day become one of Los Angeles's most famous African Americans, arrived as a teenager in 1917, just as the United States was entering the war. His arrival had nothing to do with a wartime boom; nor was he from the South. Bunche was born in Detroit in 1904, but his family moved to Albuquerque, New Mexico, in 1915, hoping that the dry climate would help his ailing mother regain her health. It did not, and by 1917 both his mother and father had died. Instead of going back to Detroit, Ralph's grandmother took him to Los Angeles. She had sisters there who told her it was a good place, where her grandson could get a good education. So, at the very moment that the Great Migration was creating a large black community in Ralph's hometown, Lucy Taylor Johnson took him to Los Angeles. She moved into a mostly white neighborhood, where Ralph entered the public schools and the black community. In 1922 he graduated as valedictorian from Jefferson High School, which was then predominantly white, and later began his studies at the Southern Branch of the University of California, which soon became UCLA. He went on to earn his Ph.D. at Harvard.[16]

Enola L. Atterway, a Texan who graduated from Texas College in Tyler in 1907 and shortly thereafter married Albert Chism, left Texas for Phoenix, Arizona, with her husband, where she became a leader in the black community, helping to organize a Colored Methodist Episcopal church and serving in the State Federation of Colored Women's Clubs. She and Albert moved to Los Angeles in 1918, apparently attracted by the prosperity of the city and its growing black population. Enola Chism immersed herself in community service and politics and also succeeded in the food-service business, becoming, according to one account, "one of the most efficient cateresses in the west."[17]

In Shreveport, Louisiana, Nyanza and Hattie Helena Hawkins were as affluent as a black family could be in northern Louisiana in the late 1910s.

They had a fine two-story home. Nyanza owned a successful pharmacy, invested widely in real estate, and bought two large touring cars—sleek, six-seat convertibles—with which he operated a shuttle service in northern Louisiana. Shreveport had a reputation as a tough town for blacks, but the Hawkins family, like others who were part of Shreveport's black middle class, had carved out a bit of prosperity.[18]

Increasingly, however, local whites came to resent Nyanza's wealth. What's more, he had a reputation for being outspoken about his rights, and as one black resident of Shreveport later recalled, "Old whitey didn't like that. And that is the reason Nyanza Hawkins is no longer a resident of this town." There were other concerns. Hattie wanted their children to receive a good education, but there were no good schools for them in Shreveport. And the very light complexion of their youngest son, Augustus ("Gus"), became problematic. For example, Gus was sometimes mistaken for white on streetcars. As he later recalled, "The streetcar that we used had signs that separated the blacks from the whites, and invariably when I would get on a streetcar and sit in the seat, they would move the signs so that I would be in the white section so as to protect me as a white child. But it caused me a problem, because one might have thought that I had deliberately adjusted to this in defiance of the law, and many times little incidents would occur." His parents feared that, as Gus grew older, such incidents "might lead to more serious problems." For all these reasons, they left Shreveport.[19]

On the advice of an old Shreveport friend who had moved to Denver, they moved to Colorado. But one frigid winter was enough to send them looking for warmth. Hattie, the more outgoing and perhaps more influential of the parents, had earlier taken a trip to Los Angeles to visit some of her friends who had moved there from Shreveport. A "little Shreveport" community was developing in Los Angeles. So the Hawkins family moved to Los Angeles, arriving shortly after the war. Nyanza set up a little shop near the corner of 12th Street and Central Avenue, selling cigarettes, soft drinks, and sundries, and Hattie became a fixture in the local community. Gus settled in to school, made friends, and did well.[20]

These wartime stories differ from the standard Great Migration narratives: The newcomers were not poor, and the wartime rush to the North did not directly affect their decisions to move. They were very much like the Beavers and Bontemps families. The Chism and Hawkins families never even considered moving north. They went west to Phoenix and Denver before settling in Los Angeles. Lucy Taylor Johnson was in Albuquerque when the Great Migration began. Many blacks back East would have said that Detroit in 1917 was offering the sort of economic opportunities young Ralph

Bunche would soon need. But in her view, Ralph's future was to be different, and African Americans in Southern California would not have questioned her judgment.

Black migration to Los Angeles was a selective process. Industrial jobs were not the magnet. Nor did Race papers such as the *Eagle* encourage black southerners to move west with the same urgency that the *Chicago Defender* advised them to move north. Black migrants to Los Angeles were less interested in the factory wages available in the North than in the generally good conditions in Southern California. Most of the migrants were city people, by birth and upbringing, and most arrived with some savings. They even took pride in their decision. As George Beavers, Jr., later recalled, "When people were ready to move from the South to come out West, we were getting the best of the lot, because it took a certain amount of income and vision to be able to do that, to be able to move so far West and start over again."[21]

City People

In the traditional Great Migration narrative, the "rural southerner" arrives in Chicago utterly unprepared for the maw of the industrial city. Observers at the time of the migration, and many historians since, have highlighted this farm-to-factory scenario. Whether or not it has been overblown—and it probably has—it is true that black southerners were overwhelmingly rural. As late as 1910, fully 75 percent lived in the countryside, so in a random exodus three in four would have been from farms and rural hamlets. But the migrations were not random, as the narratives for Los Angeles indicate. Most black migrants to Los Angeles hailed from the urban South. The trend highlights the selective nature of the westward migration, as well as the chain-migration links between Los Angeles and several key southern cities.

Statistics culled from the federal government's draft registration records for World War I strengthen this point. When the United States entered the war in 1917, the government required men between the ages of twenty-one and thirty-one to register for the draft; the men who registered had to list their *exact* place of birth. The records for Los Angeles indicate that, at the time, the black community was still overwhelmingly a migrant one: more than 90 percent of the black Angelenos who registered had been born elsewhere. A hefty majority—73 percent—had been born in the South. Two-thirds of these southern migrants—66 percent—had been born in towns or cities.[22]

Of these, Texans represented the largest group—no surprise. The surprise is how "urban" the Texas migrants were: more than three quarters of them—76 percent—were city born. San Antonio was the main contributor, but other cities stood out as well: Austin, Galveston, Beaumont, and Dallas. (Houston scarcely made the list in the draft-registration data, even though it would later develop a strong connection to black Los Angeles.)

Two other big cities besides San Antonio dominated the overall sample: New Orleans and Atlanta. Among the black men who had arrived in Los Angeles between the late 1880s and the First World War, one in five—fully 21 percent—had been born in Atlanta, New Orleans, or San Antonio. About 15 percent of the men from Louisiana were born in Shreveport, which helps explain the Hawkinses' connections in Los Angeles. The point of embarkation for the Bontemps family, Alexandria, also popped up in the data. In Georgia, Atlanta was almost the whole story.

So black Los Angeles grew steadily, a community filled largely with middle-class families from the urban South. Most newcomers were already accustomed to the rhythms and demands urban life and to the service jobs available to them in the city. If they faced a new challenge, it was demographic: the populations of Asians, ethnic Mexicans, European immigrants, and rural whites from the Midwest were larger than they were accustomed to. But black southerners seemed rather pleased with the diversity, perhaps because it offered a welcome relief from the stark racial lines of the Jim Crow South. Without much difficulty or conflict, then, black migrants filtered into Los Angeles.

God's Country

When the newly minted Harvard Law School graduate Hugh Macbeth visited Los Angeles in 1913, he wrote to his wife back East: "Come and dwell in God's country." In both his language and enthusiasm, Macbeth was only echoing sentiments that had been voiced by black newcomers since the Boom. A "city called heaven." "God's country." These were words that spoke to the history and longings of an oppressed people, and at the turn of the twentieth century, such optimism was neither inappropriate nor misleading.

Parents who desired good schools for their children generally found them in Los Angeles. There were the painful experiences one might expect: middle-class black children learning what the word *nigger* meant; white playmates sadly saying their parents would no longer allow them to be friends with colored kids; dark-complexioned African Americans jousting with lighter-complexioned ones; occasional race prejudice from a classmate or teacher. But the migration narratives that mention these problems do not dwell on them, emphasizing instead the generally favorable environment—good teachers and warm friendships, or at least tolerance, among the different racial and ethnic groups. The student bodies of all schools were mostly white, simply because of the city's demographics, but no school barred colored students. The local school board was slow to hire African American teachers, but as the new century progressed, it did, and these instructors, who taught mixed-race, majority-white classes, were important role models.

Arna Bontemps recalled that white teachers initially viewed him skeptically, assuming his skin color reflected a certain slowness, but that they soon saw the light and pushed his progress. Laura Elizabeth Adams, born in Los Angeles, found that white teachers appreciated her writing skills and encouraged her to excel. Nelson White, whose father had narrowly escaped lynching in Texas, won a high school architectural contest. The Matthews family, having arrived with small children from Pensacola in 1907, saw son Charles become a lawyer and daughter Miriam become the city's first black librarian. Hattie and Nyanza Hawkins's oldest son received his M.D. from the University of California at Berkeley.[23]

Opportunities for home ownership also were ample. In 1910, a striking 36 percent of Los Angeles's black families owned their homes. Few cities in the North or Midwest had black home-ownership rates of even 10 percent, and none exceeded 15 percent. Most southern states had rates similar to the North, perhaps slightly higher. Even in the West, where rates of black home ownership were higher, not all cities rated well: only one of five blacks in Denver owned a home, and San Francisco scarcely had a percentage for this at all. In Los Angeles, the middle-class nature of black migration underlay its home-ownership trend. As one local resident recalled, "Many had come to Los Angeles with ready cash."[24]

Housing stock in Los Angeles was not just plentiful; it was nice. After W. E. B. Du Bois toured the city in 1913, he told readers of the *Crisis* that black Angelenos were "without doubt the most beautifully housed group of colored people in the United States." As proof, Du Bois blanketed the *Crisis* with photographs of Los Angeles homes. Many homes *were* lovely, especially compared with what blacks were accustomed to back East. The city's bungalows and Spanish-style stuccos fit nicely with the climate, which made just about any house look good. And the lawns were an embarrassment of green, studded with palm trees, yuccas, jacarandas, and an endless variety of flowering plants and vines.[25]

Jobs, although not particularly good ones, were also plentiful. The black community, like the city itself, witnessed painful bouts of unemployment between the Boom and World War I, but these were few and brief. The city's economy was able to absorb hundreds of thousands of new workers, including most blacks. Wages were better than in the South, too. All told, then, the structure of opportunities fit what most black migrants to Los Angeles were looking for: good schools, nice homes, tolerable work at decent wages, and a more tolerant racial climate.

General Otis and the *Times*

Another thing black Angelenos liked about their new home was the *Los Angeles Times* and its owner, General Harrison Gray Otis, an aggressive Lincoln Republican and vicious opponent of organized labor.[26] Vilified by labor and Democrats—both advocates of white supremacy—Otis was popular among African Americans. Like most turn-of-the-century Republicans, he supported big business and limited government, but in racial matters he remained an old-school Reconstruction Republican. His *Times* blasted southern Democrats, criticized local racists, and insisted that American freedom must be color blind.[27] In 1903, John Neimore's *Eagle* said of Otis, "He has treated the Brother in Black with considerate judgment, moderation and even handed justice, his contention being that all men are created equal and that no man should be discriminated against because of his color or previous condition."[28]

Otis's views were evident in 1901, when President Theodore Roosevelt invited Booker T. Washington to dine with him in the White House—an event that ignited a firestorm of protest among white southerners, including charges of treason by the *Atlanta Constitution*. A *Times* editorial denounced these "fits of apoplexy" in the South:

> As to the action of the President in inviting an intelligent and cultured man, with negro blood in his veins, to sit as a guest at his table, it is really absurd to see the amount of 'tommy-rot' that has been belched forth on the subject by some of the fire-eating southern editors. The act was simply one of courtesy, paid by one distinguished gentleman to another, in which the question of the color of either one's skin did not enter. . . . Which is the truer gentleman, Booker T. Washington . . . or the overwrought southern editor who makes a swaggering and brutal attack upon Mr. Washington and his race because they are "niggers"? Can any sensible, unprejudiced, fair-minded man find more than one candid answer to this question?[29]

More broadly, the *Times* asked,

> Is it not about time that this absurd, illogical, unreasonable and unjust discrimination against a man because he happens to have a dark skin should be dropped? Such a sentiment might be explicable, and to a certain extent excusable, in an old-fashioned empire, where class distinctions are strictly drawn, and where the population is homogeneous; but here, in this land of liberty and equality, with a population composed of people from every corner of the globe, with skins varying in color from that of the fair-haired Scandinavians to the coal-black negro, how preposterous it is to ostracize a man simply because his hide happens to be of a different color from ours. It would be about as reasonable to boycott a girl because she has red hair.[30]

Touching on the biggest racial bugaboo of all, the *Times* added, "As to the fearful danger of miscegenation, regarding which the southern papers give vent to such terrible howls, we might suggest that some white women— even southern women—might do much worse than to have Booker Washington for a spouse."[31]

An editorial against "Race Prejudice" in 1905 continued to advocate for equal rights, for Jews as well as blacks. "One of the leading social clubs" had divided over the acceptance of Jewish members, the editorial reported, and then added, "One may expect sentiments of this kind among the ignorant peasants of Russia and other European countries, but it is certainly strange to find them cropping out in a cosmopolitan and cultured city like Los Angeles, the population of which is drawn from every State in the Union, and from almost every political subdivision of the world." As to bigotry against blacks, "We find there prevails in Los Angeles, to an unexpectedly large extent, a feeling against the negro race." Instead of race prejudice, the *Times* concluded, "we should be willing and happy to welcome all sorts and conditions of men, so that they are men, not mongrels. . . . The axiom should not need stating that there are good, bad, and indifferent Jews and negroes, as well as white men, in some of whom the whiteness is a very thin coat of whitewash."[32]

In 1909, the *Times* celebrated the hundredth anniversary of the "Great Emancipator's" birth with a special "Lincoln Centenary Number," which, in addition to its tributes to Lincoln, highlighted "Negro achievement in this Southland." It was loaded with photos of black homes and businesses, as well as favorable biographical sketches, and the *Times* allowed black leaders to write their own articles about their community. Afro-Angelenos offered glowing accounts of their financial, institutional, and spiritual progress and linked their success with that of the city itself. In effect, black Angelenos wrote the first brief history of African Americans in Los Angeles. It was a tale of finding opportunities and overcoming obstacles, a tale of a people on the rise in the West.[33]

The introduction to the section on black Los Angeles was penned by John Steven McGroarty. Editorialist for the *Times*, McGroarty would soon gain fame through his *Mission Play*, which was long performed annually at the San Gabriel Mission. But in 1909 he was not widely known. After he orchestrated the paper's Lincoln centenary edition, however, he became a beloved figure in black Los Angeles. McGroarty introduced the edition with a question: Would Negroes vanish the same way American Indians were vanishing? White Americans, he said, were discussing this question even though they really knew nothing about blacks. "No one seems to think it worth while to ask the negro himself for an answer," he wrote. "The *Times*, however, does think it worthwhile, and has, accordingly, invited the negro people of Los Angeles and Southern California to speak for themselves." He hoped the edition would bring the races together. Too many whites, he said, saw blacks as "a problem"—a "worse problem" than ever. He urged whites to reconsider their view in light of the local African American community. "If the negroes of Los Angeles and Southern California can be seen as an example of the race," he concluded, "it would seem from their own indisputable facts that the 'negro problem' is a thing that has no existence."[34]

There was no "negro problem": McGroarty stated it bluntly at a time when scientists were claiming that people of African descent were biologically inferior; when the federal government was ignoring lynching; when African Americans were portrayed in most newspapers only as criminals. From this perspective McGroarty's sentiments were broad minded, and black Angelenos read them that way. But, when read another way, McGroarty's words reflected the depth of race prejudice in Los Angeles. White readers had to be told that black voices were worth listening to. They equated Negroes with poverty, crime, and social unrest. In having to correct them at such an elementary level, McGroarty spoke volumes about white racial attitudes.

The *Times* itself could be unfaithful to the cause, offering the occasional "darkie" cartoon, as well as articles, letters, and poetry demeaning to the Race. Otis's calls for equality sometimes smacked of political self-interest; whenever black leaders explored political options outside the Republican fold, or voiced pro-union sentiments, they took a hit from the *Times*. But Race editors could give as good as they got. Angry at the *Times*, Joe Bass once roared, "The white man's paper cannot be depended upon, from Gen. Otis down." Still, Otis's *Times* and political agenda were a breath of fresh air to black Angelenos, who were keenly aware of the editorial policies of the southern dailies. As a *Times* editorial proclaimed in 1901, "Here in California there is little . . . antipathy to the negro, except among some of the old-time southerners who have settled here. In fact, California may be regarded as the paradise of the colored man, both climatically and socially."[35]

The Western Ideal

At the turn of the twentieth century, blacks in Los Angeles spoke of the South as a kind of anti-America—the ultimate example of what the rest of the nation should not become—and idealized the West as both a place and a metaphor. They rapidly adopted the region's booster rhetoric and sought to use mainstream notions of western opportunity to promote their civil rights campaigns. Editors of the Los Angeles Race papers trumpeted the West—*their* West, *their* California—as a unique place in which equal opportunity for black Americans really stood a chance. California and the West represented an ideal diametrically opposed to Jim Crow. Optimistic but not naive, black leaders understood the difference between rhetoric and reality. They pushed the Western Ideal because they saw in it the best opportunity for their own freedom, and because they saw that creeping southernism could undermine it. From their perspective, blacks had to be vigilant: the free West had to be protected from the precedent of the South.[36]

The earliest black newspapers in Los Angeles—published during the Boom—had already begun to draw regional distinctions. In 1888, the *Weekly Observer* expressed its mission of "conveying reliable information of the resources of Southern California to the people of the East." The *Observer* claimed, "With regard to Los Angeles and the condition of its colored citizens, there is no place in the United States where moral and intelligent colored people are treated with more respect than they are in Los Angeles, by all classes." In 1889, the local *Western News* continued the theme when it highlighted "the amazing progress of the Negro in the Western country."[37]

By the early years of the new century, the Los Angeles community had begun to attract the attention of national black journals, and whenever they had the chance, local Race leaders offered their versions of the Western Ideal for a national audience. Robert C. Owens, wealthy descendant of Ellen Mason and Charles Owens, had his moment in 1905 when the *Colored American Magazine* profiled him as "the richest Negro west of Chicago." In an article he wrote for the magazine, Owens, like so many boosters before and after him, urged sluggards to stay away: "It is truly hoped that no colored man who does not want to pursue an industrious life will come to California, for they are as undesired here as they are anywhere in this great nation." The migrants whom Owens had in mind would be the beneficiaries of a western political system far removed from the realities of the South. "Colored men . . . who want to better their condition and enjoy every political right as American citizens should come to the golden West."[38]

In his article "California for Colored Folks," published in the same magazine two years later, E. H. Rydall wrote, "Southern California is more adapted for the colored man than any other part of the United States." His reasoning: "The climate of Southern California is distinctively African. . . . this is the sunny southland in which the African thrives." Perhaps Rydall's geographical determinism was a playful twisting of white racial stereotypes about blacks, or perhaps he was completely in earnest, but in either case, his emphasis on the climate and black progress emerged as something of a rhetorical set piece for the city's black journalists. Southerners had long called Dixie "the southland," but here in the Far West was a "sunny southland" of a different order.[39]

The *New Age* and *Eagle* embraced the Western Ideal and saw Los Angeles as its fullest expression. The Basses trumpeted "the mighty march of progress on these Western shores."[40] Frederick Roberts's 1915 editorial "For the West" reflected his regional mind-set. That year, both San Francisco and San Diego would hold expositions to commemorate the opening of the Panama Canal, and Roberts expected Los Angeles to get its share of tourists as well. He urged his readers to spread the word about their city and region. After all, he said, "A real Westerner, whether by birth or residence, is loyal above all other things, and the expression of Western loyalty has been the making of our fine Western country. This spirit has been so typical of Los Angeles and her people that 'Boosting' has come to be our characteristic." He continued:

> [It is] time to renew our Western covenant, to get our Western and
> civic pride aglow. We are going to be hospitable to the visitors, . . .
> but we are also going to impress them with our absolute satisfaction
> with our Western home, our Western people and our Western ways.
> There will be nothing apologetic about us. There isn't anything South
> or North or East which we can't duplicate or excel here. . . . Individually and collectively we are doing better than any other equal number
> of a class of people in the country and there is nothing boastful in
> saying so, often and loud.

Any black Angeleno, Roberts added, should recognize that "he is living in the best part of the world and that his Race in this section is behind no one else." His concluding proclamation: "California for ours, Los Angeles and Southern California always, and our people here, the best forevermore." The basic creed of any Los Angeles journalist—overdo it—was evident in Roberts's prose, and there was in his "glory of the West" rhetoric a conventional regional defensiveness that placed "Western ways" over "anything South or North or East." But the important point was that local Race editors identified themselves and their community with the region itself.[41]

Black migrants who arrived unaware of the Western Ideal soon got schooled. Louis G. Robinson, for example, left Georgia for Los Angeles in 1903, carrying only a vague notion that he could improve his situation. Within a short time, "L. G.," as he was commonly known, had become a leader in the community, a home owner, and a proponent of the Western Ideal. In turn-of-the-century Georgia, he had been young and ambitious—the son of a landowning farmer—with a little college education and an entrepreneurial bent. But like many other ambitious black men in the South, his dreams crashed into Jim Crow. Then by chance he met a visitor from the West Coast, a white man, who told him that Los Angeles offered "excellent prospects for young people." Before long, he was on the train west. His biographer later wrote that "no well formulated set of dreams accompanied [Robinson] to California." He became active in politics, soon securing a patronage job as a custodial supervisor, which in turn led to his becoming one of the most prominent men in the black community. In the process, he absorbed the ideal and emphasized the contrast between "southern lawlessness" and "western law," between southern "oppressiveness" and western "hope." Not blind to the race prejudice that existed in Los Angeles, he spoke of "some freedom of opportunity" in the West, which was preferable to the "modified peonage" of the South.[42]

In 1912, after Robinson had begun to prosper, he returned to Georgia to visit his family. Tellingly, his Georgia-born wife refused to return to the South, not even for a brief visit. L. G. arrived at his parents' home sharply dressed, his pockets filled with money, his talk filled with the Western Ideal. He convinced his family—his parents and all his siblings remaining in Georgia—to leave the South for the West. Without doubt, they were well versed in the ideal before they set foot in Los Angeles.[43]

Giving voice to the ideal became something of a habit for all black Angelenos. In a 1915 obituary for Dr. Melvin E. Sykes, the city's first African American physician, black attorney G. W. Wickliffe wrote:

> Dr Sykes took to himself the advice of a sage who told young men to "go west and grow up with the country." He came west and grew up with Los Angeles, and as Los Angeles grew, he grew; as it acquired,

he acquired, until he had accumulated real estate of some proportions and had gained eminence as a physician. When a history is written of the part that colored men took in building up this western country, Dr. Sykes' struggles will stand out to encourage young men of the Race to go as pioneers into a country where they can by their own efforts build a foundation upon which will arise a condition that will be a hope and fulfillment to us all.[44]

Some years later, Senola Maxwell Reeves wrote the "Schools" column for the *Western Dispatch*, one of the city's new Race papers. Outlining a plan for "progressive" education in the state, she felt compelled to add, offhandedly, that "as Californians, we indulge ourselves in the thought that California, a state with a splendid history, a great people, magnificent resources; our California, will set the American standard; and therefore that of the world."[45] Noah D. Thompson, a black journalist in Los Angeles, raised western black boosterism to new heights and sewed together the fabric of California history, the Western Ideal, and Race progress in a 1924 article titled "California: The Horn of Plenty," published in the *Messenger*, a national Race journal. In his view, California's admission as a free state in 1850 "was the morning star appearing at the dawn of a new day in the Western Empire, marking the beginning of the end of slavery on this troubled continent." California statehood "precipitated the great Civil War. With the flow of gold and silver from her rich mines, she gave the Union its financial strength to carry on the battle of freedom to a glorious and successful conclusion." To Thompson, the relationship between black freedom and California glory was a lasting one. In Los Angeles and other California cities, he said, "the very stars of heaven spell Opportunity! Opportunity!! for all who care to come and work and work and then work some more to achieve the success that is the reward for efficient work."[46]

Black leaders in Los Angeles viewed their lives through a regional prism. Promoters in black Los Angeles repeatedly identified their community—and their freedom—with the West. From Robert Owens's "golden West" to Noah Thompson's "new day in the Western Empire," Afro-Angelenos promoted the idea that black freedom hinged on the promise of the region itself. If only the South would leave the West alone.

Postcards

In 1915, a large mob of white people lynched Will Stanley, a black man, in Temple, Texas. Accused of murder, Stanley was being held by local authorities when the mob assembled and demanded that he be released to them. When local authorities complied, the mob dragged Stanley down the street to a tall, thick pole, hanged him by a chain, and set him on fire. In accordance with lynching tradition in America, the local photographer rushed out to take some pictures. Acting fast, or tipped off in advance, the photographer in Temple set up in time to take two pictures of the mob gathering before the murder—hundreds of white folks pressed together in the street, waiting for the prisoner. Later he shot a more conventional photo of the aftermath—the charred semblance of a body, still hanging from the chain, surrounded by people milling about, inspecting their handiwork. As was customary, the photographer turned his negatives into picture postcards, which were sold on the street, locally and in neighboring towns, for a dime a card. Someone in Texas sent the postcards to W. E. B. Du Bois, who published them in the *Crisis* with the caption, "The crucifixion, at Temple, Texas."[47]

Hundreds of miles west of Temple, in a community outside of Phoenix, Arizona, lived a young black couple who had also gotten hold of those three postcards. George O. Paris White was a Pullman car porter; his wife, Ella Sarah, had been active in organizing the State Federation of Colored Women's Clubs (and therefore would have known Enola Chism). They were the sort of people who regularly read the *Crisis*. But they did not need a Race journal to know about this lynching. George White had been in Temple that day, perhaps on his Pullman route, perhaps visiting a friend. He was standing on the street when the mob boiled up, and some whites tried to seize him as an added victim. He fled, narrowly escaping.[48]

Ella Sarah took a plain white envelope, and, in neatly penciled script, she wrote, "Temple Texas Mob Pictures, Aug 1915." She tucked the postcards inside. Before too long, she and George would feel compelled to move farther west. In Arizona, antiblack sentiment was on the rise; whites in the state were adopting a more southern outlook. When George and Ella White considered their situation, it seemed to them that the distance between Phoenix and Temple was steadily closing. So they moved to Los Angeles. George gave up his job on the Pullman line and took a custodial job, not wanting to journey back East anymore, even as an employee. Along with their two young children and their belongings, Ella and George White carried with them the postcards of the Texas lynching. Those haunting images would serve as a reminder of what the South could be and what their new home must never become.[49]

2

The Conditions
of Heaven

African Americans moved to Los Angeles because they believed racial conditions were better in this "new heaven." Compared to the South, conditions *were* better. California law outlawed segregation, African Americans could vote, and the Republican Party dominated state and local politics. But how free were African Americans in Los Angeles? Did California law actually *prevent* the practice of racial segregation? To what extent were opportunities equal, regardless of race? In the decades before 1920, Afro-Angelenos pondered these very questions. They watched closely, swapped stories, weighed things in the balance. Eventually they developed a general consensus about local conditions: things had started out good but deteriorated as time went on.

Charlotta Bass wrote that the "new Angelenos of Negro extraction thought they had at least partially escaped from racial discrimination." Initially, blacks "ate, slept, and enjoyed all types of recreation provided by the new city, as did all other citizens. But the freedom-killers they hoped they had left behind in Texas followed close in their footsteps to California. Discrimination soon arose in restaurants, cafes, and other public places."[1] George Beavers, Jr., thinking back on his family's move to the city in 1903, recalled: "You have to understand that it was a very small Negro population in California at that time. And [whites] couldn't follow the patterns of segregation as . . . had been done in the South, because there just were not enough black Americans here. . . . That was to come later when they learned, learned from the South how to promote segregation."[2] To black Angelenos, the decline was obvious and so was its source: the white southerners who moved in and taught other whites how to promote segregation.

But the reality of racial conditions in Los Angeles was more complex than these recollections suggest. Historical records reveal little evidence of a golden age in local race relations. From the early years of the modern black community, racism was apparent in housing, jobs, and mainstream society. And however well things started off for black Angelenos, their notion of decline is open to question as well. A more accurate assessment would be that the city's racial conditions both improved and declined over time. To complicate matters further, black individuals and families did not, of course, always share the same experiences. Although they all sought freedom in the West, and all faced similar obstacles to racial equality in Los Angeles, Afro-Angelenos faced specific circumstances and made personal choices that sometimes set their lives on different paths. The three families whose stories launched the discussion of black migration in chapter 1 provide an instructive contrast between personal experiences and the city's overall racial conditions.

Easton, Beavers, and Bontemps Families Revisited

After he moved his family to Los Angeles, William Easton nearly drank himself to death. The specific reason for his descent is not known, but we may speculate. Perhaps he tried to become involved in local Republican politics and, for whatever reason, was not welcomed into party circles. More likely, the triumph of the Democrats in Texas had so badly injured his spirit that Southern California could not heal him. Maybe the entire situation was too much to bear: here was a bilingual college graduate in his prime, a man with white skin who identified himself as a Negro, experiencing the limitations imposed by racism, even in the Far West. Charlotta Bass said that race prejudice had destroyed his morale, and that, as she later wrote, he found it "impossible for his qualities of personality to flower and develop as they should have in a casteless society." In his despair Easton had written another drama, a tragedy titled *Christophe*, which chronicled the rise and fall of Henri Christophe, Haiti's black emancipator and subsequent king. The emperor built an impregnable fortress to keep enemies out, only to face betrayal within its walls, which led to his suicide. Charlotta saw Easton's own internal tragedy reflected in Christophe's demise. Easton was not a victim of palace intrigue but "of a society riddled through with the disease of white supremacy"—one that, in her view, had eroded Easton's will to fight for civil rights.[3]

But Easton did not stay down. His story in Los Angeles became one of redemption, as he regained his dignity and his status as a Race man. In the early 1910s, community leaders encouraged him to rekindle his interest in politics. Easton joined California's Progressive Party in the early 1910s. Dominated by restless Republicans who felt alienated by party conservatism, the Progressives won a large number of seats in the California legislature and elected Hiram Johnson governor. Easton rallied surprisingly strong black support for the Progressives, and he received due patronage. In 1915 he was made the custodian of the subcapitol building in Los Angeles, a kind of Southern California branch of the statehouse. His appointment received mention in the *Crisis,* and the Basses staged a banquet in his honor, to which Governor Johnson sent regards. For a man of Easton's education and abilities the appointment was not much, but for a black man in 1915 it was. He became supervisor of a crew of white janitors, and he began to hire black janitors as well, to a job that, at the subcapitol, paid ninety dollars per month. Shortly thereafter, the civil service system went into effect in California, and Easton, competing against sixteen white men, scored highest on the exam, thereby re-earning his custodial post without patronage strings. At age fifty-six, Easton had made it back from the depths. Ultimately, politics had put him back on track as a civic leader.[4]

Unlike Easton, the Beavers family got off to a good start in Los Angeles. They moved into a home on East Washington Street, near Central Avenue, where the black business and social district would soon emerge.[5] Their first Sunday in town, they became members of the First African Methodist Episcopal Church, a thriving, well-connected congregation. George landed a steady, long-term job as a track layer with the Pacific Electric Railway Company, which was then expanding its lines. He worked with an integrated crew—white, black, and probably ethnic Mexican, too—and this mixing on the job caused no problems. By southern standards, the wages he earned were more than decent. In fact, his school-age son, George, Jr., worked for the Pacific Electric Railway during the summer as a "water boy," bringing drinks to the men who were laying track, and he received one dollar a day—the same amount his father had earned as a day laborer in Atlanta. In Los Angeles, Annie Beavers did not have to take in laundry to make ends meet, and before long she and George were blessed with their fourth child, a daughter, Helen.[6]

Then came a series of personal hardships. George, Jr.'s teenage years got off to a rocky start when an accident left him blind in one eye. Then his high school sweetheart, Willie Mae Hutcherson, also a native of Atlanta, lost her mother to illness, leaving her orphaned. She and George, Jr., had planned to marry after his graduation, but under the circumstances he decided to marry her straight away, which required him to quit school and get a job. They moved into the home next door to his parents and were, he later recalled, "a happy couple." But in 1913 fire destroyed their home, and his parents' house, too. Shortly thereafter, Annie Beavers contracted cancer and died.

The family persevered, and even prospered. George, Jr., found steady, successively better-paying jobs. First he worked at a bank as an elevator operator, stock clerk, and messenger. Then, when the World War I defense industries heated up (he could not join the army for want of one eye), he got a job in the Los Angeles Foundry "molding iron—hot iron . . . into equipment for defense industries." He and Willie Mae, barely in their twenties, became leaders in the First AME Church. But the church split when the district bishop abruptly removed the congregation's popular pastor, the Reverend Napoleon P. Greggs, after an apparent falling-out. Greggs's supporters bolted, George and Willie Mae among them. They formed a new church, which they named the Independent Church of Christ (later People's Independent Church) and invited Greggs to be their pastor. Thus an important new church was born, and George, Jr., was at the center of the action. He served as secretary of the group that organized the new congregation and was elected to serve as church clerk. Willie Mae organized and ran a youth group.[7]

Like his father, George Beavers, Jr., became a Race man. Although the Beavers' story was one of good times, followed by hardship, followed by advance, George, Jr., still spoke of declining conditions, of a good city gone bad, and he felt increasingly constrained by race prejudice. But waking up every day as a black man in a racist world energized him and gave him a sense of purpose, even a sense of destiny. The same reality had temporarily driven William Easton into the abyss. But it inspired George, Jr., and Willie Mae to join Race organizations and fight for equality. They concentrated their efforts on making things better for their people, and in the process, the Beavers family became deeply respected leaders in the black community of Los Angeles.[8]

Becoming enmeshed in the black community was not everyone's dream, though. Paul Bontemps had bought a home for Maria and the children in Watts, then a new, racially diverse town seven miles south of the city, away from the stronghold of the black community. Arna, an impressionable four-year-old, had been sad to leave Alexandria, but his initial response to Watts was positive and lasting. Decades later he recalled, "We moved into a house in a neighborhood where we were the only colored family. The people next door and up and down the block were friendly and talkative, the weather was perfect, there wasn't a mud puddle anywhere, and my mother seemed to float about on the clean air." Watts was a blue-collar town; its boosters advertised it as a workingman's dream, where one could buy a home for one dollar down and one dollar per week. Paul found steady work as a brick mason, Maria kept house, and Arna started school—exactly what the family had hoped for.[9]

The Pembrookes, Maria's family, bought several acres between Watts and downtown Los Angeles, in an odd pocket of the city that local residents called the "Furlough Track" (officially the "Furlong Tract"). It was an ethnically diverse area, a patchwork of black, white, and ethnic Mexican homes, varying widely in size and quality. The Pembrookes built a large house there and settled in for a slow-paced retirement. But tragedy struck in 1908 when Maria became ill and died. Paul moved into the Pembrookes' home, where Maria's mother, Sarah, could take care of his young children. In their new neighborhood, the Bontemps children had black, white, and Mexican playmates. Arna learned Spanish as he grew up, and although he was usually the only black person in his class—the "lone wolf," as he put it—he found that his white teachers quickly discovered he was smart and encouraged his intellectual development. Education had been a priority for Maria, and Paul remained committed to that goal.[10]

Paul underwent profound personal changes in Southern California. He made a conscious break from the past, from the South, and even, so far as he could, from the Race. He gave up playing jazz and left the Catholic Church. He led his entire family into the Seventh-Day Adventist Church, which at the time had few black members. When his work as a mason declined in the face of pressure from white-only unions, Paul abandoned construction work altogether and became an Adventist minister. All the while, he kept a distance from the basic institutions of the black community—the traditional black churches, the lodges and clubs, the civil rights organizations. Sometimes he claimed to be of Malaysian heritage. By choice, Paul was no Race man, and the Pembrookes sought no connection with the community either.[11]

Arna and Ruby Bontemps were thus raised on the fringe of Los Angeles's African American community. To the white world, they were black children; but within the parameters of the black community, they were outsiders. They were middle class in both income and outlook, but they were not part of the black middle class that was trying to remake the city. When Arna was ready for high school, Paul arranged for him to attend an Adventist boarding school in San Fernando. Arna, and later Ruby, would be the only black children there.

Paul Bontemps's California dream was to live comfortably as an American man, pure and simple, without any racial qualifier attached to his identity. It was the ultimate dream of most black Americans—to live in a color-blind society, to be accepted, naturally and without hesitation, as citizens who had the full range of options all Americans should have. Paul's view, in direct conflict with that held by the city's Race leaders, was that an emphasis on race solidarity actually undermined the possibility of living in a color-blind society. Naturally, he could not actually live simply as an American—race shaped much of what he could and could not do in the West—but he acted on his ideals just as consistently as George Beavers, Sr., acted on his, and their difference in outlook was one of tactics, not of ends.

In a paradoxical way, the influence of these very different fathers would lead their sons to similar places in the world. George Beavers, Jr., became a Race leader at an early age and would eventually emerge as a prominent civic leader not just in black Los Angeles but in the larger circles of local influence. Arna Bontemps soon rejected his father's views about racial identity and tried to write his way back into black America. Yet his Race literature would ultimately reach such a high level of distinction that his influence, like that of George Beavers, Jr., would transcend the African American community.

The stories of the Easton, Beavers, and Bontemps families remind us that the experiences of black individuals and families were complicated and distinctive, that their collective identity—"the black community"—obscured the diversity of American Americans living in Los Angeles. The death of a parent, the helpful intervention of a friend, a curious turn of fate: personal experiences ensured that the "community" was never uniform. And yet, there was no way around the fact that black Angelenos were viewed, by whites and other nonblacks, as a separate group in society, as Negroes first and Americans second. When it came to housing and jobs, and to mainstream views about colored people, widespread race prejudice fostered common outlooks and concerns amid the diverse population of black Angelenos.

Housing Uncertainties

When they considered local conditions, black Angelenos often focused on housing, and Los Angeles scored well on this point. Suitable and affordable homes, for purchase or rent, were available to most newcomers. There was a wide range of options, from the cheaper homes in Watts to the open spaces of the Furlong Tract to the nicer Eastside bungalows. In the mid-1910s, a six-room home on a large lot in the Central Avenue district cost less than two thousand dollars, with monthly payments under ten dollars. Many newcomers could swing that. But there was a catch. The balance sheet on housing conditions was always qualified by the question of *where* African American were allowed to purchase homes in Los Angeles.[12]

Black housing in turn-of-the-century Los Angeles has been studied for a long time, beginning with J. Max Bond's 1936 sociology dissertation, "The Negro in Los Angeles," and continuing in more recent decades with analyses by historians and social scientists.[13] The now classic view holds that from the late 1880s to about 1910, African Americans found Los Angeles to be a fairly open city, residentially speaking, but after 1910, real estate restrictions on blacks increased and were difficult to surmount. As the historian Lawrence de Graaf wrote, African Americans "could and did live throughout the city and were much less concentrated in any one area in 1890 and 1900 than they would be after 1910." In the words of Charlotta Bass, "The Negro settlers who were the first arrivals . . . bought land and built beautiful homes in all sections of the city, free from restrictions." But then came the southern whites, and blacks "faced the old terror of racial hatred they had tried to forget."[14]

Testimonials from residents of the era seem to support this classic view. An old-timer who was born in Los Angeles in the 1860s and grew up in the city recalled that blacks "lived everywhere, as there were no special districts then, as there are now." Another pioneer resident said, "Negroes . . . were scattered; there were no restrictions." A migrant who arrived in the early 1880s stated, "When I came to Los Angeles, Negroes lived anywhere they could afford to live." As late as 1904, a local black realtor, J. B. Loving, wrote an article for the *Liberator*, an early Race paper, stating, "The Negroes of this city have prudently refused to segregate themselves into any locality, but have scattered and purchased homes in sections occupied by wealthy, cultured white people, thus not only securing the best fire, water and police protection, but also the more important benefits that accrue from refined and cultured surroundings."[15]

But the same old-timers who said they could live anywhere also offered unflattering descriptions of their early neighborhoods. Lots in the West Jefferson area, recalled one resident, were "swampy and 'fever-ridden,'" a "low rent, undesirable land area." Eventually that neighborhood became pricey and exclusive, but in the early days after the Boom it had a rough reputation. The neighborhoods where blacks lived in Boyle Heights were "originally undesirable territory, a cheap land area, located near the downtown business district and surrounded at the time of its origin by brick yards, railroad yards, and manufacturing plants." Land around the West Temple area was "knee deep" in mud to start with and soon was forested with oil wells. As one who lived there recalled, "When I came to this place, it was perhaps the filthiest, the most barren, the most disagreeable spot on God's earth; but it suited our pocket-book, so we stayed, built our homes, and reared our children. The city came to us and surrounded us. Then the wealthy people bought near us and soon began to buy us out, offering good prices for our land." In other words, it would be more accurate to say that housing in Los Angeles was once unrestricted, but only in the less desirable areas.[16]

Equally significant, incidents of white resistance to black neighbors actually occurred fairly regularly from the turn of the century onward. In 1902, when a black person moved into a home at Hooper Avenue and 33rd Street, then an all-white area, the neighbors paid an unfriendly visit, insisting that he leave. They dispersed when the owner pointed a gun at the crowd; he stayed, and more blacks moved into the area. In 1905, after two white neighbors had engaged in a long and bitter feud, one man sold his home to an African American, George Lawrence, apparently to "spite" the other; the house then burned down, with each neighbor accusing the other of arson. The *Los Angeles Express* in 1906 noted that black realtors were making money through what we would now call blockbusting, a sure sign of racial tensions. In 1907 a black family received threats when it tried to move into Glendale. The following year, when an African American family moved into another all-white neighborhood, vandals wrecked the home. In 1912, the *Crisis* reported that a black couple, Mr. and Mrs. C. A. Bywater, had moved into an affluent area—Kingsley Drive, in the East Hollywood area. But when they settled in, "twelve prominent residents" paid a visit; the leader said, "I come from Texas . . . where the Niggers have no rights. You've got to get out." When Dr. A. C. Garrott, a dentist, moved his family to Glendale in 1916, they received death threats. Judging from this evidence, there was continuity over time, not decline after 1910.[17]

But such resistance did little to quell black enthusiasm about Los Angeles. The 1902 incident occurred at the same time that George and Annie Beavers, still in Atlanta, were receiving glowing reports about the conditions in Los Angeles; they arrived the next year, fully expecting equal rights. The 1905 house burning occurred the year before the Bontemps family headed for Los Angeles, in part because they had heard it was "heaven." Hugh Macbeth told his wife that Los Angeles was "God's country" the year after the Bywaters' experience was reported nationally in the *Crisis*. Optimism remained, because black Angelenos kept on moving into all-white neighborhoods. They were never confined to a "black" section, or even a multiracial "colored" section of town. Most African Americans, Asians, and ethnic Mexicans lived on the Eastside (that is, east of Main Street), but the Eastside was still predominantly white. Colored people *were* shut out of some districts (virtually all the Westside), but when they encountered resistance on the Eastside neighborhoods, they usually moved in anyway—and then stayed put.

Black residents increasingly lived along Central Avenue, south of downtown, but the district was neither ghetto nor slum. It was mostly white, with significant numbers of nonwhites. Neither rich nor poor, it was a sort of middling area that represented some of the best property on the Eastside. The Central Avenue district was on high, flat ground, neither swampy nor prone to floods. Some homes in the district were shacks and housed the very poor, who at the time were mostly ethnic Mexicans. Most houses were nice, however, and some were excellent. The Central Avenue area also had convenient streetcar lines and plenty of stores, restaurants, churches, theaters, and nightclubs. One black woman later recalled that she wanted to live in the Central Avenue district but simply could not afford it. Central Avenue was no paradise—racially or residentially—but to imagine it as a cruel choice forced upon Afro-Angelenos misrepresents the essence of the place.

What infuriated black residents was not that they were restricted to poor locations, but that race played such a persistent and negative role at all. Why shouldn't they be allowed to live where they pleased, in accordance with their pocketbooks, aspirations, and tastes? That is what free people did. Yet for all black residents, even the wealthiest, the prospect was always in doubt. Whites who openly accepted one black neighbor might become angry when other blacks started moving in. In other instances, whites who were at first stridently opposed to having black neighbors later became friends with them. One white man in West Jefferson confessed, "Yes, I was one of the leaders in the fight against the Negroes. I reared my family in this community. In this house I have experienced the sweets and the bitters of life. This was a good home. Then the Negroes came! I had never known any Negro people, but I had read about them, their horrible crimes, how they steal, how shiftless they are. I thought that when they came our community would go to pieces." But he continued: "But now they are here and I have found them to be fine people. Sometimes I take my family next door and we eat supper with the Negroes whom I once fought. They come over to our house and eat with us, in return." This man changed his attitudes and behavior, but those changes angered one of his neighbors, who condemned him as "a traitor to the white race." "He himself is a nigger, I do believe," the neighbor said. "Once he led the fight against them, and now he eats with them, sings with them, and has the nigger next door come over to his house. . . . Yes, he stopped fighting the niggers and began to love them; but I'll never give up."[18]

By the late 1910s, white home owners were increasingly adopting a new strategy for maintaining all-white neighborhoods: the restrictive covenant, a legal device that proved more effective than threats. A restrictive covenant was jargon added to the title of a piece of real estate, dictating that the property could only be sold to or rented by whites. One typical covenant read, "At no time shall said premises or any part thereof or any building erected thereon be sold, occupied, let or leased, or given to any one of any race other than the Caucasian, except that this covenant shall not prevent occupancy by domestic servants of a different race domiciled with an owner."[19] Covenants sometimes specifically excluded ethnic Mexicans, Asians, and Jews, too. For legal reasons, covenants expired after a certain period of time, but for twenty, thirty, or even fifty years, they kept their white-owned property locked up.

In order for covenants to be effective, every household in an exclusively Caucasian neighborhood had to cooperate. But not all white home owners wished to. And so, the neighborhood association was born, to rally and cajole these stubborn residents into cooperating. Working closely with lawyers and real estate agents, the associations sought to have restrictive covenants added to all property titles in their own and surrounding neighborhoods. White housing developers had an even easier time restricting their houses to whites. They simply added covenants to all their property before they sold it, often using the "whites only" provision as a selling point. Some developers added an additional clause stating that, in the event a white person in the development sold to a non-Caucasian buyer (knowingly or not), the colored buyer forfeited the property, which then reverted to the developer.

White reaction to black neighbors remained unpredictable, and on the Eastside at least, Afro-Angelenos generally overcame informal resistance and lived where they wanted. But in one important respect, housing opportunities did decline in the 1910s. Restrictive covenants definitely made life more difficult for black Angelenos. Blacks fought against them in the courts as early as 1915, and for many years thereafter. Covenants did not absolutely hem in black residents, who continued to move into all-white areas, but they did severely curtail the directions in which blacks could move. And they proved a more effective roadblock than simple harassment, for covenants were clean, bureaucratic, and legal.

Working for a Living

From the 1890s through the 1910s, job options for black Angelenos were limited, though usually plentiful. Black Angelenos worked. Hard. They put in the hours, day after day, week after week. They dug ditches, cleaned toilets, laid brick, washed dishes, hauled lumber, scrubbed laundry, swept warehouses, handled luggage, shined shoes. Some were scrappy entrepreneurs, running mom-and-pop enterprises on a shoestring, walking the thin line between opportunity and disaster. Most jobs were difficult in their way, but everyone knew that some were better than others. Jobs combining higher pay with cleaner, safer conditions and greater personal autonomy almost never went to dark-skinned people. White Angelenos also held so-called menial jobs—most female maids and servants in Los Angeles were white, for example—but most whites had an opportunity to move up the ladder, whereas African Americans looked up at broken rungs or none at all.

White people did almost all of the hiring in the United States, and it went without saying that they would not offer the better jobs to black people, much less place them as bosses over whites. Even those African Americans with college degrees found most avenues of employment blocked, which meant that many a black man with a bachelor's degree worked as a redcap, and that many a college-educated black woman worked as a domestic. As Baxter Scruggs, a community leader in Los Angeles, would later write, "Occupation is not always synonymous with one's real capabilities . . . with minority group workers who have such limited opportunities for both qualitative and quantitative employment."[20]

Racial discrimination in hiring was legal. No federal statute addressed the issue, and state civil rights laws, such as California's, did not deal with hiring. Want ads printed in the newspaper often specified race as a qualification: "Wanted, secretary—whites only"; "Wanted, colored waiters." Want ads that did not specify race generally meant "for whites only." Black applicants could be turned down simply because they were black. They could voice indignation, but do little else.

Still, Los Angeles was a good place to find work, because the city's phenomenal growth generated so much employment, including many of the service and labor jobs that black urban southerners were accustomed to. (Black Angelenos experienced no "proletarianization"—no shift from farmwork to factory labor—such as that experienced by many blacks who followed the Great Migration north.) Employment patterns for Afro-Angelenos remained mostly static, but there were subtle changes, for better and worse. Some occupations that had been good bets for blacks, such as laundress and drayman, were eventually rendered obsolete. Others, such as skilled construction work, became increasingly unavailable to blacks. But new employment opportunities did arise: women moved into some professional and clerical fields, men into chauffeuring, metal trades, and professions. Changing employment trends thus cut both ways.

Opportunities for Women

Between 1900 and 1920, black women in Los Angeles had few options. About 70 percent of the wage-earning women in the black community were employed as domestics, or maids, by private families or hotels, or took in laundry. Around 5 percent were employed by commercial laundries, and another 5 percent were seamstresses, plying the needle trades in their homes. A smaller group worked as hairdressers. Scant opportunities and lots of hard work at the bottom of the ladder—in that sense, Los Angeles was not much different from the South.[21]

But there was something different for women out West: a smaller number of them *had to* work for wages. From 1900 to 1920, in Atlanta, New Orleans, and San Antonio, women constituted about half of the black workforce. In major western cities, women made up only 20 to 40 percent of the black labor force. In Los Angeles, women represented less than one-third of the black workforce in 1900, and slightly more than one-third in 1920. These figures reflect the middle-class nature of black migration to Los Angeles, as well as the higher wages that black husbands could earn out West.[22]

Among African Americans, little stigma was attached to domestic service, although men occasionally spoke against it, emphasizing that married women should stay at home. Domestics for private white families worked six days a week, and sometimes Sundays. In Los Angeles, some of the wealthier African American families also hired black domestic help, but that was rare. Domestic work was neither dangerous nor hectic, but the hours could be long, the commute tiresome, the environment isolating. The relationship between white employers and black domestics, ambiguously cordial, could be filled with vague suspicions and lingering resentments. Perhaps the worst indignity was the white assumption that domestics were poor people who had nothing going for them, even though many maids were home owners, real estate investors, leaders in their churches and women's clubs, and fully "middle class" within their community. Some black women were also shocked by white people's behavior. As Elizabeth Laura Adams would later write about her first experiences working as a domestic, "My home-training stood me in hand. I was courteous, obedient. I anticipated people's wishes. But I was not accustomed to the obscene talk I heard at some parties nor the wild life. . . . I had never realized that the conduct of white people could be so revolting."[23] Although some domestics were live-in servants, most black women preferred to commute, because living at home offered greater autonomy and a chance to retain one's sense of personal significance.

Taking in laundry was one way to work without having to leave home. The work was harder than domestic service and the pay was minimal, but the schedule was more flexible and other family members could help. Between 1910 and 1920, however, commercial laundries boomed, and the home-laundry trade declined. Worse, the number of white women working in the laundries soared, leaving black women in Los Angeles largely excluded from these jobs. As a result, they were increasingly channeled into domestic work.

There was one positive trend in the 1910s for black women: broadening opportunities in the professions. The number of black schoolteachers, which was zero in 1900 and eight in 1910, had reached twenty-five by 1920. These teachers were hired into Eastside schools, but because all schools were still predominantly white, these women taught mostly white children. Nursing proved more difficult. Around 1910, Los Angeles County opened a training school for nurses but refused to admit black women to the program. Only after a decade of struggle did the school agree to admit African Americans, over white-student protests. Even with these obstacles, by 1920 black Los Angeles boasted nineteen trained nurses employed in hospitals.[24] Taken together, the schoolteachers, nurses, private music teachers, and actresses exceeded one hundred by 1920. Compared to nearly two thousand black women servants, a hundred women in professional positions was not much, but compared with the number of black female professionals in the city twenty years earlier—all four of them—it was significant.

To be a female entertainer—even a relatively well-known one, such as the local musician and choral director A. C. Bilbrew—was no guarantee of glamour or income. According to the 1920 census records, Bilbrew lived with her husband, Ralph, and their eleven-year-old daughter in a rental house on East 14th Street, just east of Central Avenue. The head of the household was A. C.'s sister, Clara Simpson, a thirty-seven-year-old widow who took in laundry. Another sister, a domestic, lived there, too, as did a brother, who worked for the city. Rounding out the crowd was a male boarder who worked as a laborer at a garage. A. C. Bilbrew—listed as an "Entertainer" for "Private Families"—was a product of Tyler, Texas, who had come to Los Angeles in 1910. Both of her sisters were singers as well, on the side, and so was her husband, who worked days as a school janitor; but only A. C. worked solely as an entertainer. The Bilbrews' fortunes would improve in the decades ahead, as Hollywood tapped A. C.'s talents, but their beginnings were certainly humble.[25]

Opportunities for Men

African American men had broader job options than black women, but only barely. Low-end jobs, white-only unions, and competition with Asians and ethnic Mexicans crimped the economic possibilities of black men. A cluster of occupations accounted for most black-male employment. In any given year from 1900 to 1920, for example, some 20 percent of the black men working in Los Angeles earned wages as general laborers. These men did the heavy lifting in construction, manufacturing, and transportation—think of George Beavers, Sr., laying track for Pacific Electric—and performed a variety of tasks for retail stores, warehouses, and the city government. Porters comprised nearly 15 percent of the black male workforce in Los Angeles. The job took various forms; most famously, there were Pullman car porters.[26]

The Pullman company, a Chicago-based firm that outfitted the passenger coaches on America's railroads, had decided in 1867 that black men, and only black men, would serve as stewards on its cars. The job required porters to be away from home for long stretches, and it was hard duty: porters assisted passengers with luggage, shined shoes, cleaned berths, made beds, provided information, and did whatever it took to keep passengers comfortable—all with a smile and virtually no sleep. Pay was modest ($27.50 per month in 1915), so tips were essential, but within the community Pullman porters carried status. Men with lighter complexions could get jobs as Pullman cooks and waiters, positions that paid more than standard porter duty. By 1920, Pullman employed 12,000 black men nationwide, 275 of them in Los Angeles. Other porters were employed by local retail establishments to help customers with packages and work in the stockrooms. Then, of course, there were the redcaps at the railway stations and hotels, handling luggage for passengers and guests.[27]

Janitors represented between 5 and 10 percent of the black male workforce in Los Angeles during any given year. In some instances, custodial jobs derived from politics. Elected officials had control of public buildings throughout the city and county, and one way they attracted and held the loyalty of black voters was through patronage. If a black man could deliver the vote, he would be rewarded with a janitorial job—or, better yet, a job supervising a crew of custodians in a government building. In turn-of-the-century Los Angeles, however, this system was rife with corruption; janitors had to pay a twenty-five-dollar "tribute" to get their jobs, plus the occasional ten-spot to keep them. The Progressive Party eventually abolished all that—with the help of its leading custodial appointments, William Easton and L. G. Robinson. Even though they helped wipe out the tribute system, Easton and Robinson remained powerful figures in the community, because they controlled employment for hundreds of other African Americans in county and state buildings. To most whites, men like Easton and Robinson were invisible—just black janitors. But by the 1920s, Robinson supervised a cleaning crew of nearly 150 black men and women in the Los Angeles County Hall of Records, and some considered him the most powerful black man in the city.[28]

Cleaning buildings could also be an entrepreneurial venture. More than a few black Angelenos ran small-scale cleaning businesses, including, during his years at UCLA, an enterprising Ralph Bunche. Arthur L. Reese, a Louisianan who arrived in Los Angeles as a Pullman porter in 1902, is another example. Reese looked for economic opportunities in Venice-of-America, the developer Abbot Kinney's ambitious re-creation of Venice, Italy, on Santa Monica Bay (complete with canals, a pier, and an amusement park). He first ran a shoeshine operation, then started a janitorial service, which quickly took off. Needing more workers, he recruited family members from Louisiana. Then Kinney hired Reese as the "maintenance supervisor" of his Venice properties, and Reese found himself atop an enterprise that employed two dozen people.[29]

Black waiters accounted for about 5 percent of the city's black male workers. There were few black waitresses; serving food was for men in suits. Food service crews were just that—"crews"—and they were race specific. Restaurants hired white crews or black crews, supervised by a head waiter of the same race as his crew. Elizabeth Laura Adams, who grew up in Los Angeles during these decades, recalled in her autobiography, *Dark Symphony,* that her father got his start as a Pullman waiter and became head waiter at a fashionable hotel in town. He ran his crew with the severity of a military general, and within the black community he had status. He also made good money and purchased two homes, one in Los Angeles and one in Santa Barbara.[30]

White and black crews guarded their turf jealously (at one point the *Southern California Guide,* an early Race paper, happily reported the rumor that "the Steward hotel will put on a colored crew in a short time"), and competition among them carried racial overtones. The all-white waiters' unions exacerbated these tensions, as illustrated in a complicated struggle for jobs at McKee's Cafe in 1915. McKee's was a big place, and owner Samuel A. McKee employed white crews. But when his waiters organized and went on strike, he replaced them with a black crew. Pleased, Frederick

Roberts interviewed McKee, who told Roberts that his white patrons had opposed the change, but that he would stick with the black waiters. Less than two months later, however, McKee switched back to a white union crew. Roberts blamed the "liquor trust," saying this pro-union association had forced McKee to oust the blacks. He urged a strong vote for prohibition in the next election, and not only because he was a teetotaler: "Let's line up now and help throttle the cowards," he wrote. He added that "pioneers in this city can remember the time when the leading hotels in the city gave employment to colored waiters, but unionism has raised a great barrier in later years and there are very few places open to our men." His anger at the unions was justified, but in this case misplaced; between 1900 and 1920, black waiters held their own in the local economy.[31]

Male servants constituted between 5 and 10 percent of the Afro-male workforce. Most worked for wealthy whites as butlers and gardeners. In 1910, less than 10 percent of the city's male servants were African American, compared to the 38 percent who were Asian. Nearly a third were American-born white men, and 24 percent were foreign-born whites. By 1920, black servants had held their own, Asian servants had declined markedly, and the new dominant group was native-born whites, who held 38 percent of the city's male servant positions.

Such service jobs were competitive positions in Los Angeles, sought by people from all racial and ethnic groups. This was also true of an occupation that skyrocketed in Los Angeles after 1910: driving automobiles for wealthy people. In 1910 there were 590 chauffeurs in the city; by 1920 there were nearly 3,000. Competition was intense. It was a new kind of job, and there were no traditions to determine which group should dominate it. Being a chauffeur required a man to obey the wishes of a private patron, but it was not a particularly low-status or undesirable job. There were worse ways to make a living than by taking care of a fine automobile and driving it around Los Angeles. The proportion of chauffeuring jobs for different ethnic groups remained basically unchanged from 1910 to 1920. American-born whites of American-born parents—the whitest of the white folk—took most of the chauffeuring jobs early on (57 percent in 1910), and they kept them (54 percent in 1920). American-born whites of foreign or mixed parentage were behind the wheel about 20 percent of the time, followed by foreign-born whites (14 percent), African Americans (9 percent), and Asians (mostly Japanese, 2 percent). By 1920, blacks represented about 3 percent of the city's population, so their 9 percent share of the chauffeuring jobs was not bad, given the competition.

Irving Tabor, who had moved from Louisiana to Venice to work for his cousin, Arthur Reese, was sweeping the pier one morning when Kinney stopped by and asked if Tabor could drive an automobile. The eighteen-year-old Tabor had never been in a car, much less driven one, but he had the good sense to say yes. Kinney said he had purchased a Ford, that it would arrive from Detroit soon, and that he wanted Tabor to be his chauffeur. Tabor quickly learned to drive and never swept another pier. Eventually, he became "a second son" to Kinney, who bequeathed to Tabor his stately home on Grand Canal Street. This generosity clashed with the wishes of Grand Canal's white elite, who would not let Tabor occupy the house. So Tabor had it cut into sections and hauled to a less prestigious section of Venice, where he had it reassembled.[32]

By 1920 there were more black chauffeurs than black draymen, reflecting the rise of the automobile and the decline of the horse and wagon. That was a big change for African American men, because hauling goods by wagon had been an important avenue of black employment—a form of petty entrepreneurship that was open to men of little means. A. J. Roberts, a migrant from Ohio and father of Frederick Roberts, started out as a drayman; money saved from that venture underwrote his successful move into the mortuary business. As late as 1910, there had been some 270 black draymen rolling through the city, accounting for 12 percent of the black male workforce. But with the rise of automobile and truck transport, the horse-powered hauler declined.

In the decade after 1900, the numbers of black carpenters, masons, plasterers, painters, and plumbers increased, and by 1910 skilled construction workers represented 13 percent of the black male workforce. But the trend did not last. Between 1910 and 1920, the portion of black men working thic these jobs fell to 5 percent, not least because the white trade unions had squeezed them out.

The number of black professional men increased in these years, however. In 1900, there were few black professionals of any kind, excepting ministers. In 1910, there were forty-seven and still the majority were clergymen. By 1920, there were two hundred professional men, and only 25 percent were ministers. There were six dentists, ten lawyers, sixteen physicians, seven photographers, seven welfare workers, and four schoolteachers, as well as a smattering of loners in the fields of architecture, chemistry, and drafting. There were also forty-nine music teachers and twenty-one actors. Along with their female counterparts, these men represented the makings of an identifiable professional class in black Los Angeles, something that had been entirely lacking twenty years earlier.

During World War I, black men gained access to better jobs in the city's iron and steel mills and saw their numbers increase significantly in skilled and semiskilled metalworking positions: they became molders, machinists, mechanics, tinsmiths, and steelworkers. Semiskilled men also got work in the shipyards and in automobile manufacturing. These shifts resulted partly from a white-union strike at the Llewellen Iron Works, during which some blacks were brought in as strikebreakers, and partly from the general wartime labor shortages. The shifts were not overwhelming, but they were an improvement in local job prospects, and they held even after the war.[33]

Los Angeles was ahead of most American cities in the hiring of African Americans as policemen and firemen. At least since the Boom, there had been blacks wearing police badges. Their numbers were small, but so was the police department. Three black men served in 1907 in a force of two hundred. African American police officers were respected in the pages of the *Los Angeles Times*, and they were honored in the black community as representatives of equal opportunity. In time, the force would hire a small number of black women, too. Black and white officers usually worked together through the 1910s without much tension.

White firemen, however, rebelled when the city hired black firefighters and tried to integrate the crews. "The entire department has been stirred over the color line," wrote the *Times* in 1904. Observing that "there is nothing to prevent a bright colored girl from securing a place on the library staff and educated negroes can enter any branch of the [civil] service," the *Times* opined that as long as the Civil Service Commission operated honestly, "the [fire] department cannot refuse to accept negroes, however much they object." The fire department responded by accepting blacks and then segregating them in designated firehouses. Eventually the department hired enough African Americans to fill two stations. When, in the 1910s, the department was about to double in size (so that there would be a day crew and a night crew at each station), blacks expected that this change would double the number of black firemen. In a sleight of hand, though, the department placed both black companies in the same station, reassigning one as the night crew. Race leaders cried foul, but to no avail. Segregated firehouses remained in place for decades, and despite the insult, the Negro firehouse became a point of pride for black Angelenos.[34]

In the early years of the twentieth century, then, the black middle class of Los Angeles stood on a brittle economic foundation. Changing employment trends forced some into new, and sometimes lesser, occupations. Others found new opportunities, but few of these were secure. In truth, there was only a short distance between the income of a steadily employed domestic and that of a bootstrapping professional. But black social status was

not defined so much by income or occupation as it was by values and behavior. Most of the city's black middle class held "menial" jobs. They were
a blue-collar bourgeoisie, earning working-class wages but holding middle-
class aspirations.

Real Estate

Somewhere between home ownership and employment lay real estate investment, which was a path to better housing *and* a way to offset poor job
prospects. Blacks in Los Angeles showed an ongoing commitment to speculation, purchasing and reselling open lots, building on lots and selling
the homes, and acquiring rental properties. For a people who were shut
out of the best jobs, real estate offered an alternative means of getting
ahead. It was risky, but often rewarding. Dozens of Afro-Angelenos, men
and women, became licensed real estate agents. Many others in the community bought and sold on the side. As one man put it, "My hobby was dealing
in real estate."[35]

The trend was evident as early as the Boom. One of the city's earliest
Race papers, the *Western News,* ran an advertisement in 1889 announcing,
"The Western News can Procure Homes for the Colored Men and Women
of Los Angeles, On Long Term Payments." In other words, the newspaper
was acting as broker and bank: "As we have established a General Real Estate and Collecting Agency, special attention is given to Sales and Investments." The paper reported that its property lists included "excellent City
Residence Property, Vacant Lots, Ranches, Etc. Also choice business blocks
for sale."[36]

When the Boom went bust, land values tanked and people who had speculated with borrowed money lost their land. But black Angelenos emerged
in good shape, because they were cautious investors who seldom overex-
tended themselves. Many benefited from the real estate depression of the
1890s. They sensed that the lull was temporary and bought as much as possible at low prices. A prime example, later praised by the *Los Angeles Times*
for his savvy, was Hilliard Stricklin, who arrived from Chattanooga in 1892.
He had "a small amount of capital, saved from his earnings as a laborer"
and made "judicious investments in realty," the *Times* noted in 1905.
"Through the sales of various properties he has become possessed of considerable wealth." The small black community in Riverside, a town east of
Los Angeles, organized the Colored Land Association, which, after the bust,
purchased 160 acres of land for sale and development. When the next boom

hit in the late 1890s, real estate prices soared and black investors reaped the rewards.[37]

In understanding how blacks negotiated the local real estate market, L. G. Robinson's story is once again illustrative. His father in Georgia was a landowner, and Robinson had not been in town long before he developed an urge to purchase local real estate. For a while the Robinson family rented a home from a black landlady who owned a grocery store and several rental houses surrounding it. She demanded that her tenants purchase their food from her store, which irked the Robinsons. Then, too, it was a crowded house, for L. G.'s sister-in-law, her husband, and their two children also lived there. When L. G. had saved enough to buy a home for his own small family, he asked a real estate agent, a friend and fellow Georgian, Will Oakman, to help him find something suitable.[38]

Oakman first showed Robinson some Eastside homes in the $2,500-to-$3,500 range. Too expensive, Robinson said. His father's Georgia farm—two hundred acres—would not cost that much; he was not going to pay that much for a home on a hundred-by-forty-foot lot. Oakman then took him to an undeveloped section of town, where slightly larger lots, sporting head-high weeds, were selling for less than $200, at $25 down and $11 per month. Robinson bought three adjoining lots (total cost: $567), on which he built a five-room house. Once the area around him had been built up, he sold the land and the house for $6,500. He used that money to invest in another property on East Adams Boulevard and to purchase a home for his family in Pasadena, where he established a mortuary business while keeping his position as county custodian. Not all of Robinson's investments worked out so well. He and his friend T. B. Walker, an African American who owned a grocery store on Pasadena's Colorado Avenue, became real estate partners in an investment in obscure Hinckley, California. The deal washed out, but that did not sour Robinson on real estate. He scorned "aggressiveless men."[39]

Black women invested aggressively in real estate, too. California was a common-law state, so any property a husband purchased was also the property of the wife. But women who were independent could and did own property on their own, as the Robinsons' landlady demonstrated. In 1913, the *Los Angeles Times* ran a wide-eyed story about another black woman, a preacher named "Sister Smith," described as "an intelligent looking mulatto about 50 years old," whose healing powers were attracting a large following, black and white, rich and poor. Noting that she accepted no money for her services, the story added that she owned a good deal of real estate throughout Los Angeles.[40]

The 1920 census manuscripts for Los Angeles show that black women ran boardinghouses, rented out rooms, and owned rental properties. The Basses' neighbors on Central Avenue were, like Joe and Charlotta themselves, renters; but though Lulu Dobbs and her husband, Eugene, were renters, Lulu's occupation was listed in the census as "Landlady" of a "Rooming House." Two doors down was Roma Caulsberry, a single, middle-aged renter, who was also listed as a "Landlady."[41]

The number of black realtors increased with the population. Most of the leading agents were also speculators who bought and sold land as part of their business. Many black realtors were also engaged in other entrepreneurial ventures. John Wesley Coleman, a Texan who moved to Los Angeles with his extended family during the Boom, became a player in real estate even as he ran a well-known employment service. Real estate agent Hilliard Stricklin got his start in the late 1890s running a small market on Santa Fe Street; by the mid-1910s he was a full-time realtor and owned a business block on Santa Fe. Sidney P. Dones loaned money and sold insurance; he also constantly bought and sold land, eventually playing an instrumental role in the development of a successful black business district. Black journalist Noah Thompson used the *Eagle* to advertise the apartments and office space he had for let.[42]

In odd ways, racial tensions helped black realtors' business. For example, when whites wanted to sell out, they often employed black realtors because they were the ones most likely to find black buyers, who would pay more for a home in a good neighborhood. In fact, in what amounted to a game of racial payback, some black realtors profited handsomely from white fears of racial invasion. As one realtor told sociologist J. Max Bond, "One of my white friends would tip me off, and I would give him the money to buy a choice lot in a white community. The next day I would go out to look over my property. Whenever a white person seemed curious, I would inform him that I was planning to build soon. On the next day the whites would be after me to sell. I would buy the [lot] sometimes for $200 and sell it for $800 or $900. The white people would pay any price to keep the colored folks out of their communities." Another realtor told Bond, "One day I bought a piece of land in the Adams Street district. The next day I filled a wagon full of Negro children and took them out to my property. The whites wanted to know what I was doing there. I told them that I was going to build an orphan's home for Negro children. I made a new profit of $2,000 on my investment."[43]

Over time, as black investors had more money to work with, their real estate ventures grew larger. L. G. Robinson took part in an endeavor in which nine men from Pasadena collectively sank about six thousand dollars into "a large tract of land on East Colorado Street, with the idea of establishing a community of colored citizens, together with the usual business concerns," including a grocery. Their investment was only a down payment; the total cost of the property was forty thousand dollars, requiring a sizable mortgage. The project failed, but Robinson weathered it, apparently without significant difficulty. In 1914, some artistically minded entrepreneurs developed the Dunbar Park Tract (named after the black poet Paul Lawrence Dunbar), a suburban residential area on the Long Beach streetcar line. The two developers—a "Mr. W. M. Kinard" and a "Mrs. J. A. Fingers," offered, as inducement, a bit of verse: "When you speak of Paul Lawrence Dunbar / It fills our hearts with glee / For we have a fine tract by that name / Between the city and the sea."[44]

Whether real estate investment brought financial angst or filled hearts with glee, black Angelenos were committed to it. Because of the racist job market, towering barriers separated black strivers from their loftiest goals. Land speculation was one of their few legal ways to get ahead, and that is another reason why racially restrictive real estate covenants hit them so hard. The covenants not only wounded their sense of justice, but also scored a direct hit on their pocketbooks.

Jim Crow, West Coast–Style

In the early summer of 1912, Louise McDonald, an African American woman in Los Angeles fed up with racial conditions in her city, penned a letter of indignation and sent it to the *Crisis*, which published it in the July issue. "We suffer almost anything (except lynching) right here in the beautiful land of sunshine," she wrote. "Civil privileges are here unknown. You can't bathe at the beaches, eat in any first-class place, nor will the street car and sight-seeing companies sell us tickets if they can possibly help it. I am speaking from experience."[45]

That very month—July 1912—A. J. Davis, a white Angeleno with southern roots, also found himself fed up with racial conditions in the city. He typed up an urgent and angry political flyer, apparently intended for public distribution, and sent a copy to Meyer Lissner, one of the city's leading Progressives, insisting that he do something about it. Lissner filed the flyer, with no indication that he responded.

In the flyer, Davis urged white Angelenos to "DRAW THE COLOR LINE BEFORE IT IS TOO LATE. . . . NIGGERS ARE FLOCKING INTO LOS ANGELES, AT AN ALARMING RATE." He proposed that whites establish an "ANTI-COLOR

LEAGUE," which would "boycott every Bank, Firm or Restaurant who employ [blacks]" and to "discourage their imigration [sic] into Beautiful Los Angeles." No master of spelling or grammar, Davis pushed his point with sheer emotion:

[T]hink of it Los Angeles, has more niggers within its City Limits, than any other city on the Coast, while twelve years ago there was only sixty two, today you will find them on every block of our thoroughfares, in millinery stors trying on hats that the white ladies later may purchase.

Look at the Banks, employing niggers for janitors and messengers, while poor willing white men with families would be glad to do the work of janitor, our young men who are out of employment and discouraged would be glad to have the position of Bank messenger.

The Niggers are invading every possible avenue that they can, they crowd into our street cars, plant themselves next to some neatly dressed white maiden, they infest our amusement places and are a nuisance on our streets, Louisana, Texas, Alabama and Florida, in fact all the Southern States have separate appartments for them with this inscription, "THIS END FOR NIGGERS." Here the whites lower themselves to their equal and other employ them.

The sooner there is a move made to arrest this rapidly growing condition of contamination and stop the evil, the better it will be for our beautiful city, our homes and our families, especially our daughters, see! what the South has suffered by the BLACK MONSTERS!—who are a menace to any locality, they are different from any other race for they insist in mingling with the white population, so let us start at once to better conditions, BEFORE IT IS TOO LATE.[46]

Two letters, both highly critical of Los Angeles. Reading them, one could question whether McDonald and Davis were talking about the same city. But they were, and they had something in common: both writers represented marginalized groups in Los Angeles, groups that were trying to steer the city in different directions. Race women like McDonald were not going to sit idly by and have their civil rights trampled. White men like Davis were equally determined to "stop the evil" of equal rights. Here was a classic case of the South versus the West. McDonald and Davis actually agreed on what the South was like, and their different judgments about the virtue of Dixie informed their different disappointments about Los Angeles. For McDonald, the city was too southern. For Davis, it was not southern enough.

Race prejudice of a less outwardly hostile type had been blocking black Angelenos since the turn of the century. At the University of Southern California in 1903, a talented black student named Vada Watson sought admission to a women's literary club. A brouhaha ensued, with the *Los Angeles*

Times chastising the white students for their prejudice. Adult women's clubs confronted the same issue. In 1902 and 1906, white women's clubs hotly debated the issue of Negro inclusion. Daily newspapers covered these controversies and offered opinions—the *Times* opposed racial restrictions—but the clubs voted for whites-only policies.[47]

Local hotels and restaurants faced the question in 1904, when the Methodist Episcopal Church held its national convention in Los Angeles. Most black Methodists were part of all-black denominations, but some were part of the MEC (although not the Southern MEC, which was a separate body). The hotels and restaurants catering to the convention had not expected black delegates, and they responded by barring the blacks, a direct violation of state law. This racial exclusion shocked many of the MEC's white delegates, some of whom protested. But local proprietors refused to budge, and they got away with it.[48]

During the early 1910s, established black Angelenos perceived a rising tide of pro-segregation sentiment. In 1913, Frederick Roberts wrote that "proper steps have been taken in calling to the attention of the Mayor and Police Commission and Council, the growing discrimination against the Race. Insulting signs and other more direct methods of denying equal privileges to Race members have been on the increase for the last few months. So pronounced is the desire to brand Race patrons as undesirable that certain keepers of public places, even of picture theaters, have been going out of their way to insult the Race."[49]

That same year, Titus Alexander, a Race man and attorney who could pass as white, conducted his own survey of the city's saloons, theaters, and nickelodeons to determine their policies on serving African Americans. He reported that only three of the city's two hundred saloons would serve black customers and that some theaters charged whites a dime and blacks a dollar. "Discrimination in Los Angeles," he concluded, was "more widespread than many people suspect." Brandishing these findings, Alexander led a protest march to a city council meeting, demanding that the council pass a local ordinance prohibiting exclusion and unequal prices. When the council refused, an enraged Alexander threatened to blow up any saloon that refused to serve blacks. Some black leaders, especially ministers, publicly denounced Alexander's threats of violence. Joe Bass distanced himself from Alexander's threats as well, but he added, "We are not going to crucify him for thinking and having the courage to speak."[50]

In 1914 an incident at the Hippodrome theater further outraged black Angelenos. When community leader S. B. Battey accompanied two women to see a show there, they purchased full-price tickets without incident. But as they looked for floor-level seats, the manager ordered them to sit in the balcony. When Battey refused, a group of employees forcefully handcuffed him and dragged him outside. The manager called the police, who arrested Battey for disturbing the peace. He spent two days in jail without bail before the police let him go. Black leaders now openly feared "that a precedent has been established under which any theater in Los Angeles might 'pick a row' with colored men seeking certain seats and after violently ejecting them from the theater, lodge criminal complaints charging them with 'disturbing the peace.'" Under California law, African Americans could bring suit against establishments for practicing such discrimination, and if they did, they usually won. But the recompense, a small cash payment and a moral victory, was seldom worth the effort and expense.[51]

A. J. Davis's political flyer heralded a crusade to make the West more like the South, and, from Louise McDonald's vantage point, he and his cohort were winning. But Davis's words also revealed him to be a frustrated outsider. He was furious not simply because blacks were acting free, but also because so few whites seemed to care. Many white Angelenos *did* care, but in their sprawling, multiracial city, color lines were sometimes blurry.

John Somerville, DDS

White resistance to black progress sometimes proved surprisingly fragile. John Alexander Somerville, an immigrant from Jamaica who eventually became an American citizen, won his fight for admission to the dental school at the University of Southern California without breaking a sweat. He became the first black person to earn a DDS from USC; the second would be his wife, Vada Watson Somerville, who had been at the center of the USC literary-club debate well before she met her husband. When John Somerville enrolled in the dental school, the white students protested and held a meeting with the college dean, insisting they would all leave school if Somerville was allowed to attend. The dean asked Somerville to join the meeting and to speak to his classmates, a request that brought some laughter from the protesters. But, being from an affluent and well-educated family in Jamaica, Somerville spoke eloquently, with a Caribbean-English accent, and quickly hushed the crowd. "I would hardly expect to encounter race prejudice and intolerance in an institution of higher learning," he began. His friends from Jamaica had enrolled in "the great universities of England—Cambridge, Oxford, and London"—without confronting any racial barriers. "I have chosen an American college, and this is what I find—race prejudice and bigotry." The dean then said that Somerville would remain in the program and that any student who wanted to could resign. None did.[52]

Somerville had stunned and shamed his fellow students, many of whom became his friends. But one student in particular remained hostile. He was from Kentucky and spoke with a heavy drawl. Turning racial prejudice on its head, Somerville's classmates joked that the Kentucky student spoke "the Negro language," and they gave him the nickname "Nigger." Somerville later wrote, "I have heard that name applied to many individuals many times, but that was the only time I ever heard it applied so appropriately." In his autobiography Somerville says nothing about his own accent, but it probably influenced how the white students reacted to his speech. It is worth asking whether the students would have been swayed by a black person who spoke with a distinctly southern accent. And it is also worth asking, with A. J. Davis in mind, how the student from Kentucky liked his new western home.[53]

Somerville prevailed over the Kentuckian, but white southerners troubled him. "One of the characteristics of most southern white people is that they carry their prejudices wherever they go, and insist upon establishing them in any community where they live," he wrote. "The northerner goes south and quietly conforms to the customs there. The southerner trys [sic] to make Dixie out of the North or West."[54]

The Birth of a Problem

One white southerner intent on spreading the gospel of Jim Crow was the writer Thomas Dixon, whose novels *The Leopard's Spots* and *The Clansman* glorified the Ku Klux Klan, insisting that the group was necessary to protect white women from black rapists. The *Los Angeles Times* had warned readers about Dixon in 1903, lamenting that *The Leopard's Spots* had become a best seller and reporting Dixon's predictions that, unless blacks were reenslaved, there would be a race war in which "the Anglo-Saxon people will sweep the negro people off the face of the continent." A few years later, Dixon took material from both books and created a play, titled *The Clansman.* "My object," Dixon said, "is to teach the north, the young north, what it has never known—the awful suffering of the white man during the dreadful reconstruction period. . . . To demonstrate to the world that the white man must and shall be supreme." Opening in 1906, the drama received mixed reviews in the South but found responsive audiences in the "young north," where it inspired some whites to racial violence.[55]

When Dixon's play arrived in Los Angeles in late 1908, the Negro churches signed a petition warning Mayor Arthur C. Harper that the *Clansman* would provoke a race riot. Stating that Dixon's production "proclaims outlawry as a virtue, and under the hypocritical mask of chivalry puts a premium upon mob law," local ministers urged Harper to "use all the means in your power to prevent the presentation of the drama." Harper promised only "a careful inquiry," and the show ran for several weeks. Near the end of its run, a white mob nearly lynched a black man who had been convicted of rape. The police put down the mob, but the *Los Angeles Times*, which had treated the *Clansman* petition lightly, now issued an editorial that condemned lynching, dismissed the black-rapist myth, and bemoaned the "volcano of race hatred . . . smoldering under this city."[56]

The *Times* editorial warned that the lynching spirit was "no longer far off somewhere—at a comfortable distance. It's right here in our back yards. We've got to face it. I wouldn't have believed that these savage mobs could have been gathered in this city." What was the cause of this "hate wave"? "Of course, we tell ourselves that is because of the danger to our women. Rubbish! All the negro rape cases ever committed since the world began are not a lower-case letter compared to the wrongs done to young girls by white men in a single year—white men who have not been lynched." The writer, identified as "The Lancer" (probably John McGroarty) noted that this may have been the first rape case in Los Angeles involving an African American and asked, "How many men in that idiotic Police Court mob, eager to defend womanhood in such knightly fashion—Huh—have since abused their own wives?"[57]

Whether Dixon's play and the mob scene were connected, his influence on Los Angeles did not end in 1908, for his work caught the attention of D. W. Griffith, a rising filmmaker. Eventually, Griffith bought the film rights for *The Clansman* and collaborated with Dixon on the screenplay. By early 1914, Griffith and Dixon had come to Los Angeles to shoot the film. Southern California was gaining a reputation as a fine place to shoot motion pictures, and Griffith aimed to revolutionize the industry with new and improved cinematic techniques. He would succeed, pushing the art of motion pictures to a new level. The birth of the Hollywood aesthetic was thus linked with Dixon's white-supremacy message.[58]

When Griffith began production, Charlotta Bass, Frederick Roberts, and other Race leaders launched protests, urging the filmmakers to halt the project. The protests were unsuccessful, but Charlotta claimed that they forced Griffith "to cut some of the most vicious" scenes from the film; if so, those scenes must have been vicious indeed.[59] Released in early 1915, *The*

Clansman was a savage portrait of African Americans. In the film, happy slaves inhabit an idyllic Old South that is aglow with white chivalry. The Union Army ultimately unleashes black soldiers (looking and moving like apes in uniform) on the flower of the Confederacy. The soldiers loot homes and hunt white women. Reconstruction legislators—one of them ravishing a piece of chicken on the statehouse floor—cheer as they legalize interracial marriage, with their lecherous eyes trained on white women in the gallery. A former slave reveals his desires to his former mistress, sending her fleeing in terror to the edge of a cliff. When he pursues, she leaps off and hits the rocks below, choosing virtuous suicide. In her dying breath, she identifies her assailant. Heroic white men then form the Ku Klux Klan to protect white womanhood.

When the film was released, it met opposition in black Los Angeles, notably from the Los Angeles Race papers, the local branch of the NAACP (chartered in 1914), the Los Angeles Sunday Forum, and the Ministers' Alliance. All of these groups petitioned the city council to ban it from being screened.[60] The Interdenominational Association of Colored Ministers argued that *The Clansman* was "a peace-breaker" whose "message is debasing and immoral, its lesson infamous and sinful, and its affects [*sic*] damaging." The Los Angeles Forum feared that "the Clansman will awaken bitter and dangerous antagonism between the Caucasian and Negro citizens of this section. In every locality of the South where this play has appeared so much trouble and rioting has occurred that the Clansman has been prohibited throughout that section. . . . In Los Angeles today are several Negroes who fled their former Southern homes because of practical reigns of terror incited by the production." Concluding with a plea to keep the Western Ideal alive, Forum leader J. R. Scott wrote: "Thus far amicable relations have existed between the races here. The West is developing friendliness and co-operation. Should not everything be done to conserve the present conditions? The appearance of the Clansman will destroy them."[61]

The local NAACP had been given an advance screening of the film, and in its petition to the city council the group detailed specific outrages: the opening scene, in which a kindly abolitionist woman suddenly drops a black slave boy because he smells so bad, made the "sacred cause of Liberty" seem "ridiculous and repulsive"; Lincoln and the North were "belittled," while "the deeds of the South are glorified, its crimes and atrocities excused and justified"; the ugly portrayal of the black politician, named Lynch, was "an unwarrantable, unjust and unprovoked attack upon one of the ablest and most honored members of our race"—Major John Lynch, a Reconstruction-era congressman who was well known in black Los Angeles. The worst scenes would be "injurious to the public mind and calculated to excite feelings of animosity between the races." The film was "historically inaccurate and, with subtle genius, designed to palliate and excuse the lynchings and other deeds of violence committed against the Negro and to make of him in the public mind a hideous monster." It was "an attempt to commercialize the evil passions of men."[62]

When the city council met on February 3, 1915, it waded through the usual morass of building inspections and the like and finally heard the anti-*Clansman* petitions. Council members favored a ban, and when one moved that the city's "Board of Motion Picture Censors be requested not to allow the motion picture known as the 'Clansman' to be shown in the city," the vote in favor was unanimous. Uncertain whether the board actually had the power to stop a screening, the council instructed the city attorney to draft "the necessary ordinance" granting such power.[63] The next day, the city attorney addressed the council, insisting that the Board of Censors did have the power to prohibit screenings, and that the police were bound to follow the board's rulings. The chief of police then moved to prohibit the film from showing at Clune's Theater. But a California Supreme Court judge quickly issued an injunction blocking the chief's action. Saying that he personally felt the film should be banned, the judge claimed nevertheless that he could find no legal means for blocking it. His advice to blacks was to "go home and forget it." A despondent Frederick Roberts responded that African Americans were trying to forget, but that "Authorities and Caucasians must aid in the work of forgetting." Ultimately, he thought, "money rather than morality will rule the situation."[64]

The first showing of the film was in Los Angeles on February 8, with a screening in New York a few days later. The film electrified its audiences and won instant critical acclaim, whereupon Dixon and Griffith changed the title to *The Birth of a Nation*. African Americans continued to call it *The Clansman*. President Woodrow Wilson, a classmate of Dixon's at Princeton, agreed to a screening at the White House and offered his famous assessment: "It is like writing history with lightning. And my only regret is that it is all so terribly true." Twenty-five million Americans saw the film in 1915, and Clune's Theater in Los Angeles ran it for a full year. The Los Angeles Board of Censors soon called in the city council to rule against the screening of a copycat film, titled *The Nigger*.[65]

Not all Afro-Angelenos had opposed Griffith's film, however. Black actors had a stake in it and an eye on future roles: Many of the film's "Negro" characters were whites in blackface, but Griffith also had hired dozens of African Americans. Most were bit players, but a few had important roles, and all supported Griffith and defended their participation in the film, creating a rift within the black community. When the *Eagle* called upon "all civic, political, and religious organizations to join in stopping the production," Charlotta Bass wrote, it "unexpectedly found a road-block set up by Negroes themselves—that is, those who had parts in the picture and were getting what they considered good salaries from Producer Griffith."[66]

Frederick Roberts feared the film would destroy "the best feeling . . . in the West." If *Birth of a Nation* had its anticipated effect, racial conditions in Los Angeles might fall to the level of "other sections"—that is, the South. The white southern view of things did seem to spread as the film roared to box-office success. But the film's relationship to racial conditions was paradoxical. The controversy had fostered unprecedented unified action among the city's black leaders. It also had created a closer relationship between black Los Angeles and City Hall. The city council, city attorney, and police department had all joined forces with black leaders to prevent the screening. Their efforts had failed, but they made clear that Afro-Angelenos had friends in power. This was not enough to solve the immediate problem, but perhaps it was not coincidental that, two years later, Estelle Lawton Lindsey would become the first woman elected to the city council, having campaigned that she would "use all her voting power in the Council to discourage racial and religious discrimination."[67]

Another way for blacks to fight the influence of *Birth of a Nation* was to produce films themselves that counterbalanced it. Organized in 1915, the Lincoln Motion Picture Company aimed to do just that, producing three shorts and two feature-length films during the late 1910s and early 1920s. The company's inspiration and main actor was thirty-four-year-old Noble Johnson, a Colorado cowboy who already had motion-picture experience when he arrived in Los Angeles around the time *Birth of a Nation* hit the screen. Johnson landed a rare contract with Universal Studios, for whom he mostly played bad guys and Indians. After the success of Griffith's picture, Johnson and a white friend from Universal decided to produce their own Negro film—one with a positive message about the Race. They found several financial backers in the black community, who joined with them to form the Lincoln Motion Picture Company. Johnson kept his job at Universal and operated Lincoln on the side. *The Realization of a Negro's Ambition*, Lincoln's first effort, was a short film about a Tuskegee Institute graduate who goes to California and, through heroism and strong middle-class virtues, acquires wealth and gets the girl.

Thanks to Noble's brother, George, the brains behind the business, *Ambition* found wide distribution throughout black America. Before long, however, Universal decided Noble's Lincoln movies were stealing black customers from its own films. Forced to fish or cut bait, he stayed with Universal and left Lincoln. The company persevered on a shoestring, relying on local actors Beula Hall and Jimmy Smith and on George's determination to make it last. But the company's financial straits forced it to close shop in 1923. Although Lincoln's 1921 film, *By Right of Birth*, would resurface in Central Avenue theaters even after the company closed down, and other Negro film companies would try their hand, it proved impossible for black independents to compete with Hollywood's financial empire.[68]

Not Too Bad

Racial conditions in Los Angeles were complicated. Between the Boom and the 1920s, decline, progress, and continuity were all in evidence. As the black population grew visibly larger, white Angelenos paid closer attention to the color line. As the numbers of white southern migrants increased, demands for Jim Crow legislation grew louder. Free spaces contained hidden pockets of race prejudice. One could never quite be sure who or where the racists were. Countless whites accepted blacks as fellow residents with smiles or shrugs. A small group—the McGroartys and Lindseys—actively aided black Angelenos in their pursuit of equality. Others burnt crosses on lawns. The city was a difficult place to comprehend or explain. Arna Bontemps, who would make words his life and who would become singularly adept at finding the fitting phrase, tried, later in life, to describe the conditions in Los Angeles. If anyone could have done it, he was probably the one. The closest he came was "not-too-bad."[69]

The paradox was that things got better and worse at the same time, and for the same reasons. As more African Americans arrived, their community grew more vibrant and prosperous. Its visible growth set off racial alarms among local whites, especially those accustomed to the Jim Crow South. As blacks sensed the rise in race prejudice and felt the tide turning against them, they began to organize to demand their rights. By the mid-1910s, the African American population in Los Angeles had become a rooted "community," with a full array of Race organizations and a collective identity. Their efforts to live as equals in the West, and to protect their new western home from the South, created a deeper hatred among A. J. Davis and company, which required a stronger black reaction.

A stronger black response was possible because migrants such as the Beavers family joined with other community activists to promote equal rights in Los Angeles. As they saw things, the city was not free enough—not yet, anyway. It could be changed for the better, and they were committed to the task. But not all black migrants joined the fight, at least not within the bounds of the community. The experience of Paul Bontemps suggests an alternative outlook, one in which personal aspirations—however constrained by race prejudice—were best attained through individual strivings outside the African American mainstream. And because racial conditions in the city were not too bad—because their new home compared so favorably with the one they had abandoned—many black Angelenos were willing to accept existing racial conditions.

The decline felt by Charlotta Bass and George Beavers, Jr., stemmed not from a dramatic deterioration of conditions but from the fact that blacks in Los Angeles had to fight increasingly hard just to keep the rights they had. Instead of advancing to higher ground, they were forced to fight a rear-guard action. Despite what established settlers said, the golden age was not so golden, and the decline was not so sharp. Their sinking feeling was rooted in that gnawing fear that the South was closing in, and that black opportunities in the West were dwindling rather than expanding. That perception proved vital to civil rights activism in Los Angeles, for among those committed to the community it sparked a stronger spirit of purpose and a sense of urgency.

The clearest example of the city's racial paradox was the Central Avenue district, which emerged as the heart of black life in Los Angeles in the 1910s. Central Avenue became the center of the community partly because racially restrictive covenants locked African Americans out of Westside real estate, which pushed African American home buyers down the Central Avenue corridor. But neighborhoods along Central were mostly respectable, and the concentration of Negro residences, partly a matter of choice, had its own rewards—a flowering of community life and the rise of a black business district. For reasons that were equal parts bitter and grand, Central Avenue became the glory of black Los Angeles. No one ever claimed that the conditions of heaven would be uncomplicated.

3

Claiming
Central Avenue

In early 1915, in a casual aside to an upbeat story, the *Eagle* proudly referred to the Central Avenue district as the "Black belt of the city." About a year later, Joe Bass called Central Avenue "one of the most remarkable Negro business sections anywhere in the country." In 1918, voters in the 74th Assembly District, the political equivalent of the Central Avenue district, sent Frederick Roberts to the statehouse in Sacramento as California's first African American legislator. A few years later, on a tour of Los Angeles, the nationally known black journalist Chandler Owen, editor of the *Messenger,* expressed delight at the black community he discovered on Central Avenue. The homes, churches, nightclubs, and businesses reminded him of his own community in New York City. Here on Central Avenue, he told his *Messenger* readers, he had found "a veritable little Harlem, in Los Angeles."[1]

In the 1910s, Central Avenue emerged as the place to be for black Angelenos. More than six thousand blacks lived in the district by 1920. Joe and Charlotta Bass lived and worked on the avenue itself. Frederick Roberts's *New Age* was a few blocks west, next door to the Colored YMCA, at 8th and San Pedro streets. By the late 1910s, a black business center had grown up around the Booker T. Washington Building, built at the corner of 10th Street and Central Avenue. All of the major black congregations built impressive church buildings in the district. No wonder Central Avenue seemed to be a vibrant city within a city.

But it was not Harlem. Not even close. Like the South Side of Chicago,

Harlem had emerged as a virtually all-black section—and a large section at that—in Manhattan. The Central Avenue district, by contrast, was mostly white, with large numbers of Asians and ethnic Mexicans as well. Although a good portion of the city's black residents did live in the district by 1920, Afro-Angelenos made up only a small percentage of the district's overall population. As late as 1920, the 74th Assembly District was less than 20 percent black.[2] That was the little Harlem that inspired Chandler Owen; that was Joe Bass's Black belt; that was the district that elected Frederick Roberts.

White Los Angeles, however, made the same "black belt" association. When Anglo politicians courted black votes, they invariably campaigned along Central Avenue. When Westside whites wanted to go "slumming," they went to the nightclubs on "The Avenue." Indeed, Eastside neighborhoods were racially diverse *because* Westside whites barred African Americans and other ethnic minorities from living elsewhere. But if Westside antagonism kept most blacks on the Eastside, there was also a related dynamic at work within the black community itself. During the 1910s, Afro-Angelenos claimed Central Avenue as their own. With their churches, newspapers, lodge meetings, restaurants, nightclubs, and black-owned shops, they literally built themselves into it. The Eastside whites were a disparate collection of folks who lacked the unity and purpose necessary to lay claim to the area; ethnic Mexicans and Japanese were equal to Negroes in number, but Central Avenue was not theirs, either. Culturally and politically, black Angelenos placed their stamp upon the district. Central Avenue may not have been a little Harlem in fact, but it certainly was in spirit.

Eastside, Westside

By 1900, the landscape of the city had already been divided, socially and economically, into the Eastside and the Westside. In broadest strokes, "Westside" meant wealthier and whiter; "Eastside" meant poorer and ethnically diverse. The Central Avenue community lay squarely in the Eastside. (Although the district was directly south of downtown, no one spoke of the "Southside." As late as 1938, the *New Age* would reflexively write about "the Eastside, that is, Central Avenue.")[3] The city's population doubled between 1890 and 1900 (50,000 to 100,000) and tripled between 1900 and 1910 (to 320,000), but the basic Eastside-Westside divide held firm. The designations were not always precise, and some places were not included in the Eastside-Westside equation at all (the harbor at San Pedro and the San Fernando

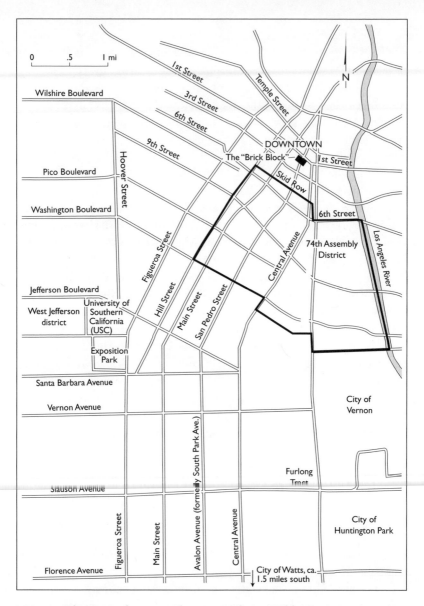

Map 2.　The Central Avenue district (74th Assembly District) and its surroundings, ca. 1920.

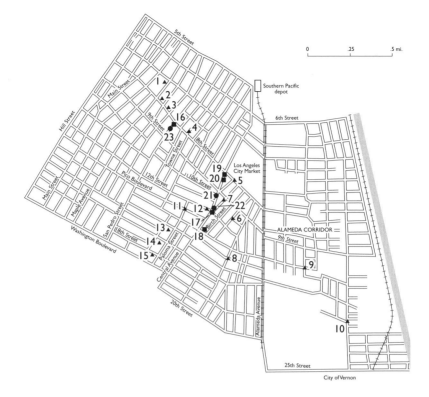

Churches

1. Mount Zion Baptist
2. Second Baptist
3. Wesley Chapel Methodist Episcopal
4. First African Methodist Episcopal ("Eighth and Towne")
5. Christian Church
6. First Holiness
7. Tabernacle Baptist
8. Colored Methodist Episcopal
9. Mason Chapel Methodist Episcopal
10. St. Paul Institutional Baptist
11. Elon Methodist Episcopal (meeting at Masonic Hall in 1919)
12. African Methodist Episcopal–Zion
13. Saint Philips Episcopal
14. New Hope Baptist
15. People's Independent

Newspaper offices

16. Roberts's original *New Age*
17. Roberts's second *New Age*
18. Neimore's *Eagle*
19. Charlotta and Joe Bass's first *Eag*
20. The Basses' second *Eagle*

Other familiar sites

21. Booker T. Washington Building
22. Angelus Theater
23. Colored YWCA

Map 3.   The Central Avenue district, ca. 1920. The boundaries shown here are those of the 74th Assembly District, which existed in this form from 1911 through 1929.

Valley, for example), but in general everyone recognized the basic divide. All but a few black Angelenos lived in Eastside neighborhoods.

The dividing line was Main Street, where the city's "east" streets became "west" streets. Main Street ran mostly north-south. From the city-center intersection of Main and 1st streets, it ran in a southwesterly direction for about thirty blocks, after which it turned directly south and continued for miles. Northward from 1st Street, Main ran northeast to the Los Angeles River; from there, it ran due east, "North Main" street signs notwithstanding.

The Eastside actually included three subsections. The Central Avenue district proper sprawled across flat real estate between two major north-south roads, Main Street and Alameda Avenue. Central Avenue, the main north-south thoroughfare on the Eastside, bisected this section, and the streets on either side were filled with bungalows and corner stores. The second subsection, the "Alameda corridor," was a grittier mix of small homes, rail yards, and manufacturing plants occupying the land between Alameda Avenue and the Los Angeles River. Across the river rose the gentle uplift of Boyle Heights, the third subsection of the Eastside. In the 1880s boom, wealthy white newcomers built stately homes there, but by the turn of the century Boyle Heights had become more economically (and ethnically) diverse.

Economically speaking, most Eastsiders were what Americans now would think of as lower-middle class. They worked blue-collar jobs, operated cash-in-the-pocket businesses, lived in relatively small homes, rented crowded apartments. They were, for the most part, scrappers and strivers. Among the nonwhites, African Americans were probably the most affluent group. Collectively, they also were probably more prosperous than Eastside whites, because prosperous blacks were basically prohibited from moving to Westside homes, whereas the district's upwardly mobile whites could relocate.

The Westside, which included everything west and north of Main Street, consisted of flat land that stretched toward hills and beaches. Westsiders included a broad range of the middle class as well as the seriously rich. After 1900, the Westside extended out along the Wilshire Boulevard corridor and into the hills well north and west of downtown. The farther south one went on the Westside, the less affluent the neighborhoods became. People in the southernmost reaches of the Westside dwelt in neighborhoods that were scarcely better, and sometimes not as fine, as the nicer Central Avenue neighborhoods; but they clung to their Westside identity all the more vigilantly and remained virtually all white.

Small numbers of blacks lived on the Westside. After the Boom, some of them settled in the Temple Street section, originally a not-so-desirable area that later became increasingly white and affluent. (As it did so, the African American presence there would decrease.) Then there were the blacks who worked as live-in servants and chauffeurs who resided in garage apartments—Westsiders in the most indirect sense. A more affluent group of Afro-Angelenos—true Westsiders, and influential in the city's long-run residential patterns—were the upper-middle-class families who were able to buy homes just west of the University of Southern California campus, in the West Jefferson district—one or two miles southwest of the 74th Assembly district. This district was a sandwich of streets bordered by Vermont Avenue, West Jefferson Boulevard, Western Avenue, and West Santa Monica Boulevard (later Exposition). An address in the West Jefferson district meant high status in the black community.

Downtown itself was home to thousands of Angelenos who roomed in the tight mass of boardinghouses and apartment buildings that rimmed the business district. The lodging complexes on the western edge of downtown were home primarily (but not exclusively) to an eclectic collection of white people—many young families and single men, a cross-class jumble of blue-collar and lower-paid white-collar workers.[4] On downtown's eastern and southern rim, people lived harder lives. The Mexican Plaza, Chinatown, and Little Tokyo lent an ethnic twist to this rougher area of the city. The lodging houses south and east of downtown were crammed with blue-collar workers and shopkeepers, representing virtually any ethnic group and nationality one might imagine.

Moving Down Central

Because it ran south of 1st Street, Central Avenue was named "South Central" Avenue. But there was no "North Central" to speak of, because the avenue basically dead-ended at 1st Street. The name "South Central" was accurate, if redundant, but other terms would catch on: "Central Avenue" or simply "The Avenue." Some seven miles south of 1st Street, Central formed the western boundary of the city of Watts, which, by 1910, already had black residents but was still far from the black belt.

White home owners sometimes resisted black movement down Central Avenue, but at every point they failed. Between 1900 and 1905, when African Americans began filtering south from downtown, white residents south of 7th Street declared, "They shall not pass!" But blacks passed 7th Street without difficulty. After that, whites drew the line at 9th Street, but the result was the same. It was not as if a wall of black people were pushing southward against a resistant wall of white people, however. For one thing, blacks moving southward were always leaving majority-white, mixed-race neighborhoods. For another, blacks spread south in a scattershot, happenstance way. They simply paid attention to good neighborhoods and took advantage of any opportunity to move into them. Negro movement down Central Avenue was less like a wave than an erratic advance that just kept going.

The range of black settlement on the Eastside expanded in the 1910s. Although a few black families had lived around Central Avenue and 33rd Street since the early twentieth century, black-owned homes in 1910 were largely limited to the neighborhoods north of Washington Boulevard. By 1920, black-owned homes could be found on either side of Central all the way to Jefferson Boulevard (or 35th Street), about twenty blocks south of Washington. This movement was happening during the same time that restrictive real estate covenants were sweeping Los Angeles, but neither they nor any other form of white resistance checked black movement southward on Central Avenue.

Nevertheless, there were some impassable racial lines in the district, particularly at the western edge, where Eastside neared Westside. From downtown south to Jefferson, San Pedro Street was that line. It lay only a few blocks west of Central, but it marked a rigid racial boundary, beyond which potential black residents were met with implacable resistance. Where San Pedro intersected with Jefferson, a new street began—Avalon Avenue—which paralleled Central Avenue southward. From that point, Avalon became the impassable line. Not until the 1940s would Afro Angelenos be able to push beyond this border.[5] The Eastside whites living in the San Pedro–Avalon sections were blue-collar types, but they had plenty of support from wealthier and more influential Westsiders, who wanted an all-white buffer zone between themselves and the Eastside. These same Westsiders never helped the white working classes resist black movement *southward,* however. Indeed, they were doubtless pleased to see blacks move south along Central Avenue, because that movement muted the urge for blacks to push west.

Black Angelenos thus moved down Central Avenue partly because Westside racism pushed them southward and partly because this corridor was a desirable, less-expensive location, much preferable to the rough downtown area where the Eastside community got its start. What distinguished Central Avenue was not the area's Negro-ness, though, but rather the stunning ethnic and racial diversity of the place.

Multicolored Los Angeles

The city's Afro-Spanish origins foreshadowed its complicated history of nationality, ancestry, and race. During the Boom, white midwesterners flooded the town, which suddenly acquired the cultural flavor of an "Anglo-Saxon" city. In fact, when the Los Angeles Area Chamber of Commerce was not heralding its quaint "Spanish" past to court the tourist trade, it was advertising the city as a haven for "Anglo-Saxons." And as that term began to mean anyone whose family tree was fully rooted in northwest Europe, there was some accuracy to the claim. Los Angeles was not a popular destination for the new immigrants from southern and eastern Europe who upset the ethnic establishments in northern cities. White Angelenos were overwhelmingly native-born Americans.[6] Moreover, unlike most cities in the American South, Los Angeles had only a small proportion of African Americans. Observers accustomed to the ethnic diversity of northern cities, or the black-white dichotomy of southern cities, were struck by the overall whiteness of Los Angeles—if, that is, their gaze remained fixed on the Westside.

The Eastside, on the other hand, was quite possibly the most ethnically and racially diverse urban area in America. In addition to its complicated mix of white folks, many of whom did not fit the Anglo-Saxon mold, it gained, between 1890 and 1920, a steady stream of Japanese immigrants and African American migrants. By 1920, even after the Great Migration had created huge black communities in Chicago and New York, the city of Los Angeles had a greater proportion of nonwhite residents (5.2 percent) than either of those cities. And ethnic Mexicans were not included in the "nonwhite" mix.[7]

As the Chinese Exclusion Act of 1882 gradually reduced the city's Chinese population,[8] four other ethnic or racial groups increased their numbers: African Americans, Japanese, Jews, and Mexicans. The Negroes, Japanese, and Jews arrived in roughly the same numbers at roughly the same time. They were also, generally speaking, of similar economic standing—neither rich nor poor—and drawn not by specific job prospects but by the overall climate of possibility. By 1920, more than eighty-five hundred Japanese lived in the city of Los Angeles, with another ten thousand or more living elsewhere in the county. They specialized in urban agriculture, growing fruits, vegetables, and flowers for local markets. Some were commercial fishermen. Others were merchants who marketed these goods.[9] Earlier Jewish migrants, with roots in western Europe, had filtered into the city's social system without much resistance, but around the turn of the twentieth century, an influx of Jews from eastern Europe arrived. "White" by law, they nevertheless were often treated as second-class citizens by Westsiders. By one estimate, there were two thousand Jews in Los Angeles in 1900, and about twenty thousand in 1917—very similar to the number of African Americans. Eastside Jews rarely competed with blacks for wage-paying jobs, but they were competitors in the development of small businesses.[10]

Mexican immigrants arrived in massive numbers, mostly as exiles of the Mexican Revolution, which lasted from 1910 to 1920. Havoc wrought by civil unrest pushed hundreds of thousands northward over the border, which was open. Estimates vary widely, but by 1920 the ethnic-Mexican population of Los Angeles County may have been fifty thousand—ten times what it had been in 1900. Although the Eastside included ethnic Mexicans who were among the poorest of the poor, the revolution also sent more-affluent Mexican families to Los Angeles, where they bought homes throughout the Eastside neighborhoods.[11] The striking thing about the Eastside was not simply its ethnic diversity but also that the racial and ethnic groups lived interspersed with one another. Despite references to the Mexican Plaza, Little Tokyo and the black belt, these ethnic groups lived side by side throughout the Eastside.

The 74th Assembly District

One way to see the diversity that surrounded black Angelenos is to examine the 74th Assembly District—the district that sent Frederick Roberts to the state legislature in 1918 and continued to reelect him for more than a decade. A plurality of local blacks lived in this district, and Central Avenue ran right down its middle. It might be said that the 74th Assembly District and the African American community grew up together.

The boundaries of the 74th district were determined by the state legislature and remained in place from 1911 until 1930. The northwest corner of the district was the intersection of Hill and 5th streets. From there, the district's northern boundary jogged eastward to the Los Angeles River. South from there, the district's eastern boundary followed the riverbed until it bumped into to the city of Vernon. From there, the district's southern boundary stair-stepped westward to Hill Street. Hill Street and Washington Boulevard formed the southwest corner of the district; from that intersection, the district line followed Hill Street back up to 5th Street, forming the district's western boundary.[12] U.S. Census Bureau manuscripts, whose information was compiled by district, are a mainstay for genealogists and social historians. They open doors to the past like few other sources do. Following the manuscripts from the 1920 census, we can step back in time and stroll through the 74th district, taking in the neighborhood.

Central Avenue was principally a thoroughfare of storefront businesses and apartment buildings. In 1920, Joe and Charlotta Bass rented an apartment at 820 Central Avenue, next door to their *Eagle* office and printing shop. All of the Basses' neighbors on their side of the street were African Americans: Eugene and Lulu Dobbs, a middle-aged couple without children (he a shoeshine man, she a "landlady"); William and Lulu Minor (he a school janitor, she the owner of a "cleaning and dyeing shop"), a younger couple whose household included their two school-age children and Lulu's parents, Nannie and Hamp Doyle (she a janitor, he a Pullman cook); and Roma Caulsberry, a middle-age single woman who, although renting her home here, owned property over which she was landlady.[13] Here was a classic slice of black Los Angeles in 1920—respectable people with blue-collar jobs or small entrepreneurial ventures, living in the heart of the community.

Right across the street, all the residents on Central Avenue were white, mostly midwesterners and native Californians. The even-numbered addresses between 818 and 836 Central Avenue, the Basses' block, were occupied by African Americans; the odd-numbered addresses between 817 and 845 were occupied by whites. Just north of these white residents there was a large all-black rooming house at 803 Central; just north of that, in the 700 block, there was a rooming house that was virtually all white, with a few ethnic Mexicans and Japanese renters.[14]

In the bungalows on either side of Central Avenue, the district's mix of black, white, ethnic Mexican, and Japanese is clearly shown by a list, taken from the 1920 census manuscripts, of the people who rented homes on the 800 block of Gladys Avenue, only a few blocks west of the *Eagle,* and the 800 block of Birch Street, a stone's throw from the Booker T. Washington Building. On Gladys Avenue:

No. 814—a black family, Tom and Frances Marsh, Tennesseans in their thirties, parents of a toddler daughter, he a chauffeur, she a housewife.

No. 828—a Mexican immigrant family, Trinidad and Gertrude Espinoza, parents of six children ages 3 to 28; they had immigrated in 1915.

No. 830—a white family, William and Alice Luckie, middle-age Georgians (he a brick mason, she a housewife) who had living with them one divorced daughter (a hotel maid) and a young white couple from Arkansas.

No. 834—a black couple, Allen and Annie Jefferson, both in their forties (he a musician, she a laundress), who housed as lodgers a young black couple from Louisiana, Walter and Lena Mavor (he a porter at a drugstore, she a housewife).

No. 840—an Italian couple, not U.S. citizens, he a laborer, she a laundress.

No. 848—a white widow from Kansas.

The house around the corner from no. 848 was home to a Japanese family.[15] And on Birch Street:

No. 816A—a Mexican American couple native to California with one child at home, he a cement laborer, she a housewife.

No. 816B—a Mexican American couple from Arizona with three children, he a warehouse laborer, she a housewife.

No. 818—a Japanese couple with three California-born children, he the proprietor of a produce market, she a housewife.

No. 820—a couple from Mexico with one California-born child, he a driver for a dairy business, she a housewife.

No. 822A—an African American couple, one from Kansas, the other from Tennessee, with no children, he a porter, she a housewife.

No. 822B—an African American couple, one from Oklahoma, one from Arkansas, with no children, he a Pullman cook, she an ironer at a laundry.

No. 824—a Japanese couple, one of whom immigrated in 1899, the other in 1916, with no children, he a worker at a produce market, she a housewife.

No. 832—an African American couple, one from South Carolina, the other from Georgia, he a janitor, she a housewife, with one brother-in-law, a night watchman, living with them.

No. 836—an African American couple, one from Tennessee, the other from Texas, he a machinist in a garage, she a housewife, with two Texas-born children at school and a black roomer (a porter).[16]

Birch Street below 9th Street became predominantly black, as did most of the streets that ran off of Central Avenue between 9th and 18th streets, but the multiracial mix is clear enough.

Amid all this diversity, interracial marriages were rare. Marriage between whites and nonwhites, including Asians, had been outlawed by California's miscegenation statute—a nineteenth-century law that would stand until the early 1940s. Black Angelenos chafed more at the racist implications of the ban than the limitations it placed on their choice of partners. Later in his life John Somerville would write, "In the State of California, before its intermarriage ban was lifted, it took only a few hours' ride to Mexico and a two-dollar fee to have a marriage performed. I have motored to Tijuana several times and have yet to find traffic jammed with white and colored couples hurrying to get married across the border."[17] Census takers in the 74th district did list a few black-white marriages, accurately or not. Edward and Ella Clements, both in their mid-forties and both from Alabama, lived at 1520 East 14th Street. Census agents usually made the call on the race of any given individual and sometimes mistook light-skinned blacks for whites. In this case, the agent listed Edward as white, Ella as black, and their eight-year-old son as black.[18] On East 17th Street lived Robert and Audie Young, both from Georgia. Robert was listed as black, Audie as white, and their five-year-old daughter as mulatto. Most likely, Audie was actually a light-complexioned Negro, not a Caucasian. Either way, Robert lived a precarious life, because black men escorting white-looking women were bound for trouble—dead in Georgia, beaten in Los Angeles.[19] Interracial marriages among different colored groups, which was legal, proved equally rare. There were almost no marriages between African Americans and Japanese. A very infrequent exception was the household of Meline Kusada, a black woman from Georgia, who was married to Kimi Kusada, a Japanese hotel keeper.[20] Only a tiny number of African Americans were married to American Indians (who were rare in Los Angeles anyway), and these couples, not surprisingly, had roots in Oklahoma, where blacks and Native Americans had lived together in Indian country.[21] Vaughn and Sallie Ellis—he a recent immigrant from Mexico, she a Negro from Alabama—were one of the few couples to emerge from these two communities.[22]

In short, people from different racial and ethnic groups married within their own groups. In the shadowed alleyways and brothels of the district, cross-racial sex with exotic "others" heated up Central Avenue. But when it came to settling down and raising children, people looked to their own for partners. Thus, there was a kind of racial separateness within the 74th Assembly District, its stunning heterogeneity notwithstanding. But separateness was one thing; claiming the district was another. Black Los Angeles gained cultural and political dominance in the 74th district because blacks, unlike the other racial or ethnic groups in the district, actively built the organizations and institutions necessary for staking their claim. And the three most potent of these institutions were Race papers, black churches, and black businesses.

Race Papers and the Community

"The press and the pulpit," wrote Charlotta Bass, "are the two main centers for the development of community consciousness."[23] For black Angelenos that was certainly true, and it is an important point, because the African American community could not have claimed Central Avenue without consciously seeking to do so. And the necessary consciousness was rooted in the local Race papers and Negro churches.

Virtually all Race organizations and civil rights campaigns depended on the black newspapers and churches, although the editors and the preachers did not themselves always foster unity. Newspaper editors fought over ideology, politics, and readers. Black churches split over governance and doctrine. Yet those conflicts and divisions helped define and sustain the community. People who think of themselves as a community do not always love or even agree with one another. Indeed, the constant give-and-take between shared interests and contested turf formed a vital component of black community life. It allowed Afro-Angelenos to express their individuality without surrendering their identification with the group.

John J. Neimore, Charlotta Bass's mentor, established the city's first black-owned newspaper, the *Owl*, shortly after he arrived from Texas in 1879. He must have had a tough go of it. No issues of the *Owl* survive, but it is clear that when the Boom hit it was already out of business. The *Weekly Observer* ("Our Liberty We Prize, Our Rights We Will Maintain"), the first Race paper of the Boom era, began publication in March 1888.[24] This paper brought three newspapermen together: Thomas Pearson, William Sampson, and John Neimore. Thomas Pearson was editor of the paper. Newly arrived from San Francisco, he was a Seventh-Day Adventist and a political independent.[25] William Sampson, a native of New Orleans, was the *Observer's* "local editor," making him second in charge. Sampson had worked his way around the West as a railroad hand, a miner, and finally as the founder and agent of the Kentucky Jubilee Singers, who sang their way from San Francisco to Southern California and arrived in Los Angeles in the late 1880s. "When the boom exploded," he said, "we exploded with the boom."[26] John Neimore had no official title at the *Observer;* he worked there merely as an employee, but not for long.

The *Weekly Observer* fell apart before the year was out. Neimore either quit or was fired and started a rival newspaper, the *Advocate.*[27] The *Observer* denounced him as an "ugly cornfield upstart" and "a smut-rag," "the boss idiot of all the idiots." And that was just for starters. The paper pointed to Neimore as an example of the principle that "the blacker and more ignorant the man the more he feels his capability of leading," and added that Neimore "was such a savage that the humane society of Texas sent him to Los Angeles to be civilized."[28] Even by nineteenth-century newspaper standards, that was harsh. Sampson, who probably wrote the tirade against Neimore, didn't get along well with Pearson, either. He wrested full control of the paper from Pearson, renamed it the *Western News,* and used it to scandalize Pearson with charges of adultery.[29] For his part, Pearson blasted Sampson in a piece published in a white-owned daily.[30]

Behind all this personal venom lay party politics, for nineteenth-century journalism amounted to no-holds-barred partisanship laced with slander and sensationalism. Pearson, insisting on political independence, openly condemned what he perceived to be black America's slavish devotion to the Party of Lincoln. He had approvingly printed a letter that stated, "The war is over, and the old fogy Republicans who try to whip the colored man in line on that issue should be set down on with a heavy hand."[31] In the local elections of 1888, he supported the Prohibition Party candidate for constable, S. B. Bows. Bows, the first African American to run for political office in Los Angeles, had not simply decided to throw his hat in the ring; running for office in those days required a man to receive the formal nomination of a bona fide political party. Pearson respected the local Prohibition Party not only because he was a teetotaler, but also because the party, which was virtually all white, had nominated a black man for office. Local Republicans, for all their talk of Lincoln, had never done that.

Stung by the Prohibitionist move and threatened by any effort to weaken black loyalty to the GOP, the *Los Angeles Times* accused the local Prohibitionists of being southern Democrats in disguise. It also condemned Pearson as a traitor.[32] Neimore was a regular Republican, and his falling-out with Pearson and Sampson may have stemmed from this dispute. Local Republicans probably put the money behind Neimore's *Advocate* to encourage him to smear the *Observer.* Working in concert with the *Advocate,* the Republican county committee brought its full weight down upon the *Observer,* hastening its demise.[33]

These early Race papers did nothing to build community. Black Angelenos recognized that a little conflict and competition within a group could be a good thing, but these ugly episodes had crossed the line. Even if these attacks were rooted in political differences, their vindictiveness showed poor leadership and served the Race poorly. By the end of the 1880s, the *Observer*, *Western News*, and *Advocate* were dead and gone.

But local Race papers soon improved. By the turn of the century there were two respectable black newspapers, the *Eagle* and the *Liberator*. Sampson and Pearson never reappeared in the local newspaper game, but Neimore persevered. Beginning in 1892, he began publishing the *Southern California Guide*, which folded in 1895, perhaps because, as the few surviving issues show, it was largely lacking in meaningful content.[34] Not long after that, however, he established *The Eagle*, which had both content and staying power.[35] Officially, the *Eagle* was published by the California Publishing Bureau and Investment Company, of which Neimore was president and John Wesley Coleman, the real estate player and labor agent, was acting secretary. Neimore was both editor and general manager of the *Eagle*. It was a Race paper in the truest sense of the word, informing readers of African American–related news on the national, state, and local levels and offering tough-minded editorials on race relations and politics. Neimore set up shop at 1306 Central Avenue, which was then a good distance from where most blacks lived. The *Eagle*'s location cast the Afro-Angeleno gaze southward along Central Avenue, setting an important precedent.[36]

If Neimore's *Eagle* continued to uphold the banner of regular Republicans, Jefferson Lewis Edmonds's *Liberator* offered a progressive-Republican counterpart. Born a slave and educated in Freedmen's Bureau schools in Mississippi, Edmonds brought his family to Southern California around the time of the Boom. In 1900 he established the *Liberator*, a monthly Race magazine affiliated with the "good government" movement—the emergent Progressive Party. In 1911, by which time the *Liberator* was a weekly, Edmonds strongly endorsed women's suffrage in California. Edmonds was not always the most popular man in the black community, probably because he often questioned the judgment of the regular Republicans and also because he pulled no punches in his columns. He felt free to blast anyone, from the *Los Angeles Times* to the most well-respected black minister. But at the time of his death in 1914, even his political opponents, including the editors of the *Times*, praised him as an honorable man and fearless proponent of equal rights. Unlike earlier disputes between Race papers, the Neimore-Edmonds divide did not split the community. This time, competition begat unity.[37]

In 1907 a third Race paper appeared in Los Angeles—the *New Age*, originally published by Oscar Hudson, a Missourian who had overcome severe childhood hardships to attain a position of educated respectability. During the Spanish-American War, Hudson worked for the federal government as a Spanish translator in Cuba. Later, he moved to Albuquerque, New Mexico, where he published a Race paper also titled the *New Age*. A desire to study law drew him to Los Angeles in 1907, and he brought his *New Age* with him. Hudson earned his law degree, became the first African American elected to a bar association in California, and served as U.S. consul to Liberia from 1917 to 1925. No issues from his Los Angeles *New Age* survive, but it seemed to be on solid ground when he sold it to Frederick Roberts in 1912.[38]

Smart, confident, righteous, and handsome, Roberts was a Race man among Race men. He touted the *New Age* as a "Journal for Community Interests and Race Welfare," and as an editor he proved outspoken, sometimes fierce, in his denunciation of race prejudice. In January 1915 the *New Age* sported a revealing new masthead—a detailed etching of Lady Liberty, standing tall, one hand holding the scroll of wisdom, the other the flame of justice. Classic Los Angeles scenes surround her: an orange grove, a bustling harbor, a Spanish mission, an airplane flying over rugged mountains, a magnificent sunset. It could have been the masthead of any Los Angeles daily, or an offprint crafted by the Los Angeles Chamber of Commerce, except for one significant thing: Roberts's Lady Liberty was black.[39]

Edmonds's *Liberator* died with him, but by 1915 the black community had its two solidly established weeklies, both of which had their offices near the heart of the 74th Assembly District. Neither the *New Age* nor the *Eagle* paid much attention to punctuation or proofreading, but they were owned and operated by first-rate leaders. Both papers supplied just enough sensationalism and gossip to keep readers coming back, and both offered a full plate of Race news (local, state, national, international), civil rights advocacy, and serious discussion of politics and economics. Each paper gave the churches, clubs, and black-owned businesses plenty of press. Both boosted Los Angeles as a haven for blacks while, at the same time, criticizing the city's bigotry and race prejudice. Neither sugarcoated disputes within the black community, but they were seldom antagonistic toward each other. In short, the Basses and Fred Roberts offered the community two fine newspapers. Black Angelenos read the white dailies, usually the *Times,* but they also read the black weeklies. The local Race papers—and their offices on Central Avenue and San Pedro Street—became anchors of the community.

After mid-1915, the *New Age* lost some steam, because Roberts left Los Angeles to head an all-black school in Mound Bayou, Mississippi. During his absence, the *New Age* stumbled and, in an odd turn of events in late 1915, seems to have been taken over by E. T. Earl, the millionaire white publisher and progressive Republican who owned two leading dailies, the *Los Angeles Evening Express* and *Los Angeles Tribune.*[40] Local black leaders occasionally wrote stories for this new version of the *New Age*, but essentially the paper turned to fluff. Beginning in September, it even ran a serialized version of Edgar Rice Burroughs's *Tarzan*. Roberts returned from Mississippi after about a year and regained control of the *New Age*. After his election to the state legislature in 1918, his editorial rhetoric cooled a bit and his attention was usually directed elsewhere, but his paper remained an important institution in the community.

The *Eagle* became the leading Race paper in the city and a vital source of community news, politics, and civil rights activism. In 1915, the Basses moved it to a newer, larger office building—a "new and more pretentious home," they humorously called it—the office at 814 Central Avenue.[41] Black Angelenos read other Race papers published in California as well—the *Oakland Sunshine*, which began publication in 1907; the *Western Outlook*, established in 1911; and a monthly magazine called the *Colored Citizen* ("A square deal and a fair chance—No more, no Less"), which appeared in Redlands, a town east of Los Angeles, in 1905–6.[42] The Race papers exchanged news, black readers swapped Race papers, and the Los Angeles papers had "stringers" throughout Southern California who kept the community apprised of conditions in Pasadena, San Bernardino, Venice, Watts, and San Diego. By the mid-1910s, the *Eagle* listed its location not as "Los Angeles" but as "Los Angeles, San Diego, San Francisco, Oakland"—an exaggeration with a grain of truth to it.

The Basses reached readers throughout California, but one of the *Eagle's* underappreciated roles was to anchor the black community on Central Avenue. The printing office on Central became an unofficial community center, a place where Race men and women dropped in to discuss the issues of the day. It was frequented by political lieutenants, Club women, striving businesspeople, and visitors to the community. It was a place to see and be seen. The same was true of Roberts's *New Age* office on San Pedro Street, only a few blocks away.

The dean of Los Angeles black history, the late Miriam Matthews, saved a photograph that shows what the *New Age* office looked like around 1908. On a storefront window, in the corner shop of a large brick building, bold painted letters announce the "NEW AGE PUBLISHING CO." and, painted on the adjacent storefront window: "Y.M.C.A." Both the newspaper and the Colored YMCA looked like small, unglamorous, street-side operations, because that is what they were. But there is something more important in the photo. Standing in front of the *New Age* are thirteen African American men. Arranged in two carefully spaced lines, they wear dark uniforms and hats, and they hold musical instruments at the ready—trumpets, trombones, horns, a snare drum. The man in the middle carries a big bass drum, which advertises to all that they are the "CITIZENS BAND—L.A., CAL."[43]

Ethnic communities are complicated, but they begin with *place*—with locations and addresses. They take root when bands give concerts in front of little ethnic enterprises, when the Colored Ministers' Federation meets weekly at the YMCA, next door to the *New Age*.[44] The newspaper offices at 829 San Pedro Street and 814 Central Avenue were more than printing shops. They marked important spaces on the Eastside, outposts of Race identity and progress, places in which black Angelenos had a stake. In their own secular way, Race papers reflected sacred territory and faith in the future. In that sense, they were much like black churches.

The Churches and the Community

Black Americans thought of themselves as a Christian people, but not just any Christian people. They were a chosen people—the new Hebrews, a people delivered from bondage. In slavery they sang: "Didn't my Lord deliver Daniel / Then why not every man? / He delivered Daniel from the lion's den / Jonah from the belly of the whale / the Hebrew children from the fiery furnace / Then why not every man?" These were the words of a people who knew deliverance would come, and who felt justified in asking why God tarried. Emancipation brought the long-prayed-for deliverance, but somehow, even after emancipation, the old spiritual rang true, because Jim Crow seemed to place Afro-southerners back into bondage. So they continued to sing, "Why not every man?"[45]

Christianity in the American South has a tortured history, for the simple reason that both the slaveholders and the slaves embraced the same God. White slaveholders often quoted scripture to defend the slave system, effectively saying not only that slavery was ordained by God, but also that white Christians carried the added responsibility of converting black Africans to the true faith. Slaves did convert, but the Christianity they embraced was about deliverance, about the priesthood of *all* believers. In their version of Christianity, slavery was an abomination and white masters were Christians gone astray, Satan's playthings. White masters understood that biblical messages could cut both ways, which is why, their duty to convert the Africans notwithstanding, they worried about slaves reading the Bible and punished slaves for singing spirituals that smacked of Exodus.

In the Old South, southern slaves and slaveholders had often worshiped together, the manner of fellowship inconsistent, the spiritual dynamic strained. After emancipation, the freed people established their own churches almost immediately. Sometimes they were assisted financially by northern missionaries, black and white alike, who came south after the war to help the former slaves. There were already longstanding all-black denominations in the North, most prominently the African Methodist Episcopal Church, and these quickly moved into the South after the Civil War. But mostly, black congregations came together independent of outside intervention. Southern blacks—overwhelmingly Protestant, usually some version of Baptist or Methodist—formed congregations, built places to worship, and created new denominational organizations, such as the National Baptist Convention, established at a meeting in Atlanta in 1895.

In their churches, African Americans separated themselves from white people by design. They did not see separate churches as a form of racial segregation; they did not protest all-white churches, and they almost never attempted to become part of white congregations. They made a clear distinction between separation by choice and segregation by force. Black churches were their pride and joy, their haven in a racist America. Race, obviously, had everything to do with the creation of black churches, but it was only in these churches that African Americans could truly act as individual Americans, without having to strain their lives through the filter of race. Among their own, black Christians could love, fight, rejoice, get jealous, make amends, whisper in prayer, or shout Amen. The choices were unburdened by racial considerations.

But separation from the outside was never absolute, because black churches were not just Sunday meeting places. Congregations had to consider the difficulties and responsibilities of black life during the week. Even in the most affluent black churches, those with the most formal Sunday services, ministers and lay leaders regularly addressed issues ranging from black employment needs to politics. And though whites seldom appeared in the pews, a few always appeared at the podium as election time approached. Any white politician who wanted Negro votes had to make an appearance at the leading black churches. The interracial dynamics of daily life were tightly entwined with Race-specific worship services. The secular blended with the sacred. That was the nature of the black church.

Until the boom of the 1880s, Negro churches in Los Angeles had been barely hanging on. By the time the Boom was in full swing, Los Angeles had several black churches, including the two leading congregations from which many others would spring: the First African Methodist Episcopal Church and the Second Baptist Church. There were also two smaller congregations that would become mainstays in the community: the Wesley

Chapel Methodist Episcopal Church and the African Methodist Episcopal Church–Zion.[46] A few black Angelenos, Paul Bontemps for example, became Seventh-Day Adventists, but they did not have their own meetinghouse.[47] Catholics from Louisiana were numerous; those who practiced took the sacraments with other, nonblack Catholics at the Cathedral of St. Vibiana, downtown.[48]

The Second Baptist Church was organized in the early 1870s and so named to distinguish itself from the all-white "First" Baptist Church. Before the boom it had just over twenty members, only five of whom were men (including a zealous John Neimore). But it flourished with the Boom, and membership soon exceeded two hundred. Its new members were solidly middle class. They built a two-story brick church at 740 Maple Avenue, near the corner of Maple and 8th Street, south of downtown, a little east of Main Street. Second Baptist offered both centrality and variety to local Baptists. It anchored many families in a historic congregation, but it also was torn by frequent internal disputes, which led to the formation of new congregations. Nothing in America splits like a Baptist church. The autonomy of each congregation, combined with the Baptist sense of urgency in spreading the gospel *correctly*, provides fertile ground for schisms. Black Baptists in Los Angeles followed this trend, and it was one of the few things they had in common with white Baptists. As Second Baptist grew and disagreements arose, dissident groups left to form their own congregations. By 1920, Second Baptist had given birth to the New Hope Baptist, Mount Zion Baptist, St. Paul Institutional Baptist, and Tabernacle Baptist churches.[49]

Schisms notwithstanding, Second Baptist remained strong and became a fixture not only in Los Angeles but also throughout California and the West. Charlotta and Joe Bass were members, and the church was a player in local politics. With its reputation as a popular, influential, and relatively affluent congregation, the Los Angeles Second Baptist Church could recruit nationally prominent black ministers, who had impressive connections around the country. The church's pastor from 1915 to 1920, the Reverend H. D. Prowd, had roots in New York and Cincinnati, and his daughter was married to B. G. Brawley, dean of Morehouse College in Atlanta. Second Baptist was fully part of the black national network.[50]

The city's black Baptists were affiliated with the National Baptist Convention, and they dominated the denomination's western branch. The Western Baptist Association (WBA) was established in 1891 and began holding annual meetings in 1908. Because most blacks in the West lived in Southern California, meetings were often held in or near Los Angeles. The 1914 annual convention, held in Riverside, showed Angelenos in the lead. The

Reverend Chester H. Anderson, formerly pastor of Second Baptist and at that point pastor of New Hope Baptist, was completing his second consecutive term as WBA moderator (or president). The newly elected moderator was the Reverend Joseph McCoy, the pastor who had succeeded Anderson at Second Baptist. Delegates also elected the Reverend J. T. Hill, pastor of Mount Zion Baptist, to be the chair of the WBA's executive committee, and they elected the Reverend A. C. Williams, head of the Los Angeles–based Providence Baptist Institute, as their new recording secretary.[51]

The black Methodists in Los Angeles had more members than the Baptists, and several of their larger congregations rivaled or surpassed Second Baptist in influence. By the late nineteenth century, African Americans could choose among three major African Methodist denominations: the AME Church, the AME-Zion Church, and the Colored Methodist Episcopal Church (CME). The AME and AME-Zion had been born in the North (Philadelphia and New York, respectively) during the late eighteenth and early nineteenth centuries, as black Methodists responded to white Methodist discrimination. In doctrine and structure, the two were largely indistinguishable. The CME branch of black Methodism had its roots in the postbellum South—after the Civil War, white and black Southern Methodists quickly went their separate ways. In the South, these were the primary Methodist denominations. Outside the South, blacks could be Methodist and yet not affiliated with any of them, because the Methodist Episcopal Church (MEC; i.e., the Northern Methodists) allowed African Americans to form all-black churches within their otherwise white denomination. Generally—but only generally—it might be said that the Methodists were a more affluent group than the Baptists, and that within black Methodism, the AME, MEC, and AME-Zion congregations were more affluent and more formal than their CME brethren.[52]

Black Methodism officially arrived in Los Angeles when a dozen residents organized the First AME Church in Biddy Mason's home in 1872. Mason continued to attend an integrated MEC congregation, but she basically funded First AME through its lean years. Like Second Baptist, First AME swelled with the Boom and soon became the congregation of choice for many middle-class blacks, such as the Beavers family. By the turn of the century, black Methodists in Los Angeles could also attend AME-Zion, Stevens AME, or Wesley Chapel ME. By the mid-1910s, the list of black Methodist churches had grown considerably, to include several more AME and MEC churches and a CME congregation.[53]

First AME built the most impressive black building in town, a church at 8th and Towne streets, two blocks east of the *New Age* and YMCA. In the community's early years, it stood as a magnificent architectural landmark. From the street, a broad sweep of steps climbed to three large doorways, which lead into an expansive sanctuary four stories high, with a slanting A-frame ceiling and an elegant bank of stained-glass windows on the street side. Adjacent to the main foyer, a commanding bell tower reached even higher, capped by four dramatic spires. In back of all that were the offices, Sunday-school rooms, and other departments of the church, all topped by yet another towering steeple. This was an important place in black Los Angeles. Most Afro-Angelenos called it "Eighth and Towne" church, rather than First AME. The building itself and the space it occupied—8th and Towne—stood for something more than just another church.[54]

One of the community's most influential churches, the Independent Church of Christ (later the People's Independent Church of Christ) resulted from the controversial 1915 schism within First AME in which pastor Napoleon Greggs was removed by the district bishop—"the abuse of the authority by the bishop," George Beavers, Jr., called it. After their dispute, the bishop ordered Greggs to leave Los Angeles for a church in San Diego. When Greggs refused, a portion of the congregation that supported him held a meeting in the Christian Church a few blocks over and formed a church outside the AME fold, with Greggs as their pastor. First AME survived: plenty of members remained, newcomers kept joining, and the congregation continued to be a force in the community. Meanwhile, Greggs and his relatively affluent People's Independent Church bought a piece of land at 18th and Paloma streets, just west of Central Avenue. There they built a twenty-five-thousand-dollar building, and the congregation continued to grow.[55]

A plot of the locations of the city's black churches in 1916, the year that People's Independent moved into its sanctuary on Paloma Street, indicates that church buildings helped Afro-Angelenos lay claim to the Central Avenue district. At that time there were seventeen Negro churches in the city. All but two—Harmony Baptist and Second AME, in the Furlong Tract—were in the 74th Assembly District. Fifteen black-owned church buildings dotted the Central Avenue district, almost all of them clustered within one square mile of urban space, between Main Street and Alameda Avenue. The people of Second Baptist, worshiping on Maple Avenue, had neighbors up the street at Mount Zion Baptist and Wesley Chapel ME. On Paloma Street, barely one-third of a mile long, there were five African American congregations: Elon ME, AME Zion, St. Philips Episcopal, New Hope Baptist, and People's Independent. Only blocks away, on the other side of Central Avenue, were Tabernacle Baptist, First Holiness, the Christian Church, and the

CME Church. It was a remarkable concentration, and these houses of worship were elegant buildings, not grim reflections of racial segregation but celebrations of black Christianity and Race pride.

First AME, Second Baptist, and other big churches held formal services, but not "white" services. They nurtured their own unique worship culture. Pastors from the leading black seminaries in America vied for pastorates in these churches, and when they got behind the pulpit they had the difficult task of showing both intellectual prowess and the ability to *preach*. (It didn't hurt, Charlotta Bass said, if they were handsome, too.) The big congregations demanded decorum and sang and played high-church music, but they blended in spirituals with a verve and resonance that would stop white Presbyterians in their tracks. It was not entirely taboo to shout out, or even fall out, if the spirit so moved. Large choirs were accompanied by small orchestras. At First AME, for example, the choir was fifty voices strong and backed by piano, organ, strings, and brass. Poorer people, or just those with less ornate sensibilities, could find these big churches intimidating and a little snooty. But for those whom they suited, Los Angeles's large African American churches were a taste of heaven on earth.

There were some racially integrated alternatives to the all-black churches, the most important being the black-led Azusa Street Mission, which launched a revival that began in 1906 and continued for three years, bringing together people of all racial backgrounds and marking the birth of modern Pentecostalism.[56] It was led by William J. Seymour, a middle-age minister who had recently arrived from Texas. Seymour belonged to the Holiness movement, an offshoot of the Methodist Episcopal Church. Black and white Holiness groups worshiped separately but embraced the same doctrine, which emphasized a "second" religious experience—sanctification—beyond the initial experience of salvation. In practice the differences between the ME Church and the Holiness Church involved worship styles, with the Holiness group giving such full emotional expression of sanctification that critics labeled them "Holy Rollers." While Seymour was pastoring a Holiness church in Houston, he heard about a new doctrine, that of a "third" religious experience—speaking in tongues. A woman who spoke in tongues, for example, would speak in a foreign language that she did not actually know—as Jesus's disciples did on the day of Pentecost. For those who accepted the "third experience" view of things, this "baptism of the Holy Spirit"—speaking in tongues—was the necessary condition of salvation.

Initially skeptical, Seymour ultimately embraced the idea, though he had not spoken in tongues himself. This got him fired by his Houston congregation. In 1906, Seymour was invited to lead a Holiness church in Los An-

geles, but he did not last long. He was fired again—after his first sermon—
because he preached the doctrine of tongues. But some of the members accepted his message, and he began holding Bible studies in a home in the West
Temple district. One night at dinner, the third religious experience broke
upon Los Angeles: Seymour's hosts began speaking in tongues. Crowds
gathered, and Seymour preached from the porch. Onlookers began speaking in tongues, and so, finally, did Seymour himself. Police cleared the growing throng from the West Temple residential area. Seymour and his followers
procured an abandoned warehouse on Azusa Street, a tiny road wedged into
the downtown area, where the Pentecost could flow loudly and continuously
without concern for neighbors or police. The setting was austere; Seymour
wanted no pulpit and himself did more praying than preaching. He took no
collections, but people left money voluntarily. Crowds soon reached the hundreds. The *Los Angeles Times* investigated and ridiculed the hoopla. Crowds
then grew to the thousands.

The revival was noticeably multiracial. As one scholar wrote, "Blacks still
predominated, [but] there were whites, Mexicans, Jews, Chinese, Germans,
and Russians noted in attendance." Participants gloried in the breaking down
of racial and language barriers, while critics fumed that people of different
races were kissing and hugging one another. Seymour himself may have
been ambivalent about this racial mixing. He never excluded anyone, but
he had been through some bad experiences with white Holiness leaders in
Texas, and that made him skeptical of white people. Indeed, in his statement
of doctrine and discipline, published after the revival, he insisted that all
church leaders be African American, even if the congregation was mixed.[57]

By 1909, the influence of the Azusa Street revival had spread across the
country and fostered the creation of several Pentecostal denominations, but
Seymour joined none of them. Instead, he formed the Apostolic Faith Gospel
Mission at the Azusa Street location. This multiracial congregation survived
his death, as his wife became head of the mission.[58] One all-black Pentecostal denomination that arose from the Azusa revival was the Church of
Christ (Holiness) U.S.A., a black organization from Arkansas that embraced
Pentecostalism. Although the denomination remained relatively small, it
gained a place in black Los Angeles and established its national publishing
house in the city.[59]

The Azusa phenomenon, compared with the mainstream Negro churches,
raises interesting questions. At Azusa, all races and nationalities were
welcome—tangible proof that a common religious experience could render
the color line meaningless. There is no evidence, however, that Seymour or
his followers ever took a stand for civil rights. In one sense, the congrega-

tion undermined racial prejudice simply by worshiping together year after year. But this was not the lesson drawn by mainstream culture. Pentecostalism was often dismissed as a fraudulent, low-class cult regardless of racial considerations, and the racial inclusiveness of Seymour's Pentecostalism may have caused people to view it even more suspiciously. Mainstream black churches were models of voluntary racial separation and exclusion and were proof positive to some white people that African American people did not really want any involvement with the white world. Yet it was these churches that formed the backbone of the city's civil rights campaigns. From a home base of racial separation came the drive to create a world of equal rights, equal access, and equal opportunity.

The Azusa revival notwithstanding, the Baptist and Methodist churches dominated the city's black religious landscape, and despite the schisms they experienced, these churches brought Afro-Angelenos together like nothing else could. Loyalties always went to one's home congregation, but blacks attended the local churches interchangeably—to visit friends, to attend social events and political rallies, and to hear different preachers. There were also larger evangelical efforts, such as the massive Union Revival of 1915, in which all of the city's major black churches joined together, erected a revival tent near the Colored YMCA, and sparked what the *Eagle* called "the Greatest Soul Winning Campaign Ever Witnessed Among Colored Churches in The Great West."[60] Like the competition between the *Eagle* and the *New Age,* the friendly rivalries among the local black churches allowed Afro-Angelenos to differentiate themselves as individuals while remaining connected to the broader community.

However important the spiritual aspects of church life were, the social and political aspects were equally so. Charlotta Bass recalled, "church was not only a place of worship; it was likewise the social, civic, and political headquarters where the people assembled for spiritual guidance, *and* civic analyses, political discussions, and social welfare talks and lectures." It was also something of an employment agency. "It was not uncommon at a Sunday morning service," Bass wrote, "for the church clerk to announce that a brother who was an experienced plasterer had just arrived in the city and needed employment; or that a woman, a good cook, would like a job." Churches sometimes acted as banks for aspiring entrepreneurs who had been denied funding by white banks. The broader cultural mission of the church found expression in the Mount Zion Baptist Church's "Get Acquainted Club," which set out to welcome strangers to the city, to promote literary work, to set high standards for public behavior, and to provide wholesome entertainment for Christian Los Angeles, especially for young people.[61]

Young people were critical to church culture, and most of the leaders of black community traced their engagement in local affairs to the churches' youth programs. The Baptists offered the Baptists Youth People's Union (called the BYPU or simply "the union"), whose many activities not only kept kids out of trouble and attuned to Christian messages but also served as a kind of school for responsible civic leadership. At People's Independent Church, Willie Mae Beavers organized the Young People's Lyceum, a popular social, religious, and entertainment organization that brought together teens from all denominations. Leon Whitaker (later the city's first black deputy district attorney) was its first president; Ralph Bunche was active; Louise Beavers (George, Jr.'s cousin), who became a successful Hollywood actress, participated in the Lyceum's elaborate theater productions. The BYPU, the Lyceum, and other similar church programs served, in effect, as the training ground for the black middle class.[62]

Charlotta Bass was right. Community consciousness was grounded in the press and pulpit, and the ideas expressed in Race newspapers and black pulpits left a powerful imprint on community identity and action. Place played a part, too. With each short trip from home to church and back, the people of the Central Avenue community notched deeper grooves into their collective identity. They grew accustomed to patterns of movement, to the feel of the neighborhoods. They could see, quite visibly, their own imprint there. Church buildings were particularly important in this regard, and, for the same reason that churches were noticeable and impressive, they were also difficult to move or abandon. One reason Chandler Owen thought he'd found "a veritable little Harlem" in the early 1920s was that the black churches had firmly grounded the community in the district. The same could be said of the black businesses along Central Avenue.

Race Enterprise and The Avenue

African American entrepreneurship stretches far into the nation's past. It clearly increased during Reconstruction, when most black business ventures—barbering, catering, entertaining, and hauling were common—catered to a white clientele. But from roughly 1890 to 1920, black business took a historic turn. Not only did the number of Race enterprises increase dramatically, but there also emerged a new sort of African American entrepreneur—one who catered to the needs and desires of black customers. The idea behind Race enterprises was simple: take care of your own. That was the course many new immigrant groups took, and as Jim Crow tightened its hold in the urban South, and as black communities grew in the urban North and West, the group-economy ideal became firmly entrenched in African American life. According to this ideal, black businesses would create a thriving class of economic leaders, employ large numbers of Negro workers, and offer first-rate, prejudice-free services to the black masses. Black money would no longer be siphoned off to white-owned businesses, many of which would not even employ black workers. It would circulate within the African American community, enriching the community economically and psychologically.[63]

During the Boom, these ideas began filtering through the tiny but growing black population in Los Angeles. In the earliest surviving issue of a local Race paper, the *Weekly Observer* of October 1888, editors plugged Frank Blackburn's newly opened "coffee and chop house" at 1st and Los Angeles streets and added, in what would become an endless refrain in the local Race papers: "If our people would only learn to patronize each other we could do a great deal of good."[64] A year later, the *Western News* listed a handful of local Race enterprises, including G. W. Hawkins's furniture store (the same G. W. Hawkins who would later buy the *Eagle* for Charlotta Spear), Reeves and McLaughlin's furniture store, Clisby and Henderson's grocery, and J. R. Walker's restaurant. The editors also printed a letter from "Freeman," which insisted, "Just as long as Negroes spend all their money with white merchants they will never have colored merchants to spend it with. Just as long as Negroes submit to buying goods from white clerks who refuse to work with colored clerks, just so long will colored boys and girls be kept in hotels, livery stables, barber shops and kitchens. . . . The Negro is too well known in politics and church circles and not well enough known in the banks and business marts."[65]

By the early 1890s, black enterprises were beginning to cluster on San Pedro Street between 1st and 2nd streets, where Walker's restaurant was. According to Neimore's *Southern California Guide,* San Pedro was "being made a popular business street." Hawkins's furniture store had moved there, and Myers's restaurant had added a club room. New establishments opened, including Ramsey's barber shop, a tent and awning shop, and a printing shop. This little hub of black businesses survived, and in 1903, A. J. Jones built a two-story hotel and restaurant there valued at twenty-three thousand dollars. Neimore's *Eagle* called Jones "one of the most successful restaurant men in this city" (and added that Jones's "faithful wife" was also responsible for that success). "One of the most important features that marks the progress of the Afro-American in this city," Neimore wrote, "is the brick building now being constructed at the junction of San Pedro and First Streets."[66]

But there was trouble on the "Brick Block," mostly in the form of be-sotted men. Two black-owned "private clubs," which stood nearly next door to A. J. Jones's establishment, formed the heart of what the *Los Angeles Times* called the "negro tenderloin." In 1904, the *Times* launched a scathing attack on the clubs, neither of which was licensed to sell alcohol but sold it anyway, and both of which were wide open for gambling and prostitution. Razor fights spilled blood every night, the police reported. The focus of the *Times*'s exposé was Ben's Place, where "Hell begins cooking at dark and boils on until dawn." The story described Ben as a "tall sharp-looking mulatto," who consorted "with a French woman degraded beyond all mention." Tamale stands, open all night in the street outside the clubs, fed a host of wild and drunken gamblers. Just around the corner on 2nd Street, the story continued, "is the 'Colored Republican Club,' which has nothing to do with politics. Across the street from Ben's is a Japanese dive not much better." A witness from the Salvation Army added that "pretty young white women" frequented the clubs at all hours of the night.[67]

At first glance, this seems like the standard fare that white dailies offered from time to time—stories about black-owned clubs in a state of lawless debauchery, with plenty of white women around, a sure formula to arouse the anger of white male readers and create momentum to get the black clubs shut down, which would allow white clubs to move in and monopolize the club-room trade. But for more than a year, the *Eagle* had been calling for city authorities to crack down on the clubs. Long before the *Times* ran its articles, Neimore had asked his readers: "Is it not about time that the busi-ness people along San Pedro street between First and Second received some protection from the ugly display of the club room hang on? There is no need of these dives, they promote neither happiness nor wealth; they produce sin and only sin." Neimore was a righteous Baptist, but there was more to it than that. He wrote this in the very same issue in which he promoted the construction of A. J. Jones's new establishment on San Pedro Street. He and other black middle-class leaders wanted the clubs shut down so that re-spectable black businesses could prosper in a better environment. "The way is open and the call is daily for industrious and self respecting men to come and labor," he wrote. He believed that "the sport and gambling element . . . produces nothing but crime." In fact, Neimoremay may well have asked Har-rison Gray Otis to run the *Times*'s condemnation of the "tinhorn sports."[68]

This fight between respectable black business and the club-room economy—the middle class versus the sporting set—was a classic conflict within the black community.[69] Leaders from both groups based arguments for their own type of business on the principles of Race enterprise. Both claimed they employed large numbers of blacks and kept African American dollars within the community. But from the point of view of an A. J. Jones or a G. W. Hawkins, the clubs were a liability. The problem of public drunkenness, for example, extended beyond the black clubs, because the city's skid row lay close at hand and effectively hemmed in the black business block to the west and south.

When problems surrounding the Brick Block became insurmountable, the Race enterprises relocated. Black home buyers abandoned downtown for neighborhoods to the south, and for the same reasons, black businesses leapfrogged over skid row and transplanted themselves along Central Avenue. A few enterprises first moved down San Pedro Street—Porter and Roberts undertakers, for example.[70] But Central Avenue soon became the main thoroughfare for Race enterprise. Black proprietors did not have the avenue to themselves, however. They struggled against white competitors, as George Beavers, Jr., recalled: "That . . . seemed to be the regular order of things," he said. "The Jewish people and the Caucasians going into the Negro community to benefit from their trade. They wanted Negro trade. They were not interested in developing any Negroes to be their competitors, naturally."[71]

Because the "Negro district" itself was still largely white, it was not that white entrepreneurs were pushing black businesses out of an all-black section, but that the competition for black dollars became intense. In the mid-1910s, the push for Race enterprise and a group economy reached a fever pitch in black Los Angeles. Both the *Eagle* and *New Age* filled their pages with success stories even as they admonished readers to support Race enterprises. In 1915, Fred Roberts reported that the Chinese people of California were boycotting Japanese produce because Japanese merchants were discriminating against Chinese buyers. Roberts approved of this tactic and added that any retailers who discriminated should be punished through boycotts. From there he easily moved the discussion to the question of black support for their own merchants. "Even in the West," he wrote, "the Race is learning that the need of Race enterprise and the patronage of those established are becoming the rule for preservation." Roberts, Joe Bass, and other middle-class leaders formed a local branch of the National Negro Business League to promote the cause. Too often, they thought, black buyers believed that white services were somehow superior. "Race organizations must demand that Race money shall be spent within the Race," Roberts insisted.[72]

If there was one individual who personified what Bass and Roberts wanted in a black entrepreneur, it was Sidney P. Dones, who promoted Race enterprise and himself with equal vigor. Born in Marshall, Texas, in 1888, Dones graduated from his hometown's Wiley College before moving to Los Angeles in 1905. The following year, he moved to back to Texas—this time to El Paso, where he made an unsuccessful attempt to establish a colored colony in Mexico. Returning to California, he prospered in the classic Los Angeles manner: by buying and selling real estate. He also became a money lender, an insurance agent, a music dealer, and ultimately, a filmmaker and actor. Dones was an entrepreneurial engine running full throttle without a governor. His primary clientele was African American, but the *Eagle* noted that his success stemmed from his ability to "win the confidence and respect of the better class whites of this section." If so, he was doubly beautiful for the Negro Business League set, for he fueled the group economy *and* turned the tables on white businesses that made money off blacks. "Dones has won the title of Los Angeles' most popular young businessman," the *New Age* noted in 1915. "[He] is enjoying the greatest real estate and insurance business of any race man in the West."[73]

When W. E. B. Du Bois visited Los Angeles in 1913 he was struck by the Race enterprises and the entrepreneurial mind-set of their owners. In the *Crisis* he trumpeted the "snap and ambition" of the city's "new blood." Dones had the most snap, and he was largely responsible for solidifying black enterprise on Central Avenue. He began in 1914, when he organized the Sidney P. Dones Company and set up shop at 8th and Central, next door to the *Eagle*. The company dealt mainly in real estate but also offered insurance and legal services, courtesy of the black attorney C. A. Jones. The Basses boosted Dones's business—"Owned and Conducted by Race Men"—and devoted an entire front page to the enterprise.[74]

Older black businesses around Central Avenue began to spruce up, and new ones appeared. J. H. Shackleford, a longtime furniture dealer, set up "a good business on Central Avenue." The Dreamland Rink, a roller skating "dream come true" that employed twenty black Angelenos, opened at 15th Street and Central Avenue. The grand opening, with entertainment by the Citizens Band, attracted seven hundred customers. Nollie B. Murray, an Atlantan who moved to Los Angeles around 1910 and became "King of the Bootblacks," gave up his string of shoeshine stands in 1915 and opened the Murray Pocket Billiard Emporium and Cigar Stand near the corner of 9th Street and Central Avenue. The *Eagle* trumpeted Murray as "A Strong Booster for Race Enterprise" and emphasized the emporium's success, which, the Basses insisted, made clear "the possibilities in store for a young man who sticks to bustle."[75] Other bustlers—not all young, and not all men—opened shops on or near Central Avenue, between 8th and 12th streets. Near Murray's place, Bessie Prentice established a dry goods store. "Just look at those attractive and clean windows and you will go in," wrote one booster. Rose's Variety Store, near 12th Street and Central Avenue, offered general household goods and specialized items, from china to tinware. Robinson's Empress Ice Cream Parlor opened near 8th and Central.[76]

Something approximating an official birth of the Central Avenue business district occurred in early 1916, when Sidney Dones opened the Booker T. Washington Building at 10th Street and Central Avenue. Two blocks south of the *Eagle*'s office, the Washington Building was a handsome three-story affair, with shops on the sidewalk level and offices and apartments above that. Joe Bass called it the "Largest and Best Appointed Edifice on Central Avenue" and added that it was "Procured for Colored Business Men." The headline boomed: "Central Avenue Assumes Gigantic Proportion as Business Section For Colored Men."[77]

Other entrepreneurial landmarks soon appeared on or near The Avenue. Ida Wills opened the Southern Hotel on Central between 12th and Pico streets in February 1916—a real estate deal financed by Dones.[78] One month later F. A. Williams of Los Angeles, in partnership with a business associate from San Diego, purchased the Angelus Theater at 932 Central Avenue. A "moving picture and vaudeville" house, the Angelus had previously been owned by whites, but it now proudly advertised itself as the "Only Show House owned by Colored Men in the Entire West." Dones also swung the Angelus deal. In the Race papers, the Angelus's advertisements gave its location as simply "Central Avenue, Between 9th and 12th."[79] Everyone in black Los Angeles knew where that was.

Ecstatic over these new trends, Joe Bass called Central Avenue from 8th to 20th streets "one of the most remarkable Negro business sections anywhere in the country." He gave the *Eagle* credit for promoting the theme of Race enterprise, but he placed the laurels on Sidney Dones. "It was not until a few months ago," he wrote, "that Central Avenue in the Negro section took on this spirit of 'Must Do' when Sidney P. Dones, the hustling young Race man . . . entered into its business life." Dones, wrote Bass, "has said by his action no obstacle is too great for me to surmount on my way to success."[80] Bass's chronology was off a bit, forgetting as it did the long-term trends in Race enterprise that he himself had reported in earlier years, but he nonetheless caught the spirit of the current trend. Race enterprise in Los Angeles had turned a corner and would continue to grow.

A change could be seen in advertisements placed in the Race papers. The city's nineteenth-century black newspapers rarely identified black proprietors, and indeed rarely advertised black enterprises. The surviving issues

of Neimore's *Eagle* were not much different, although occasionally a photograph of a proprietor made it clear that an establishment was black-
owned),[81] nor were early issues of Charlotta Bass's paper. But in the late
1910s, the *Eagle* and *New Age* ran more photographs of black proprietors,
and more slogans indicating African American ownership. A systematic ex-
amination of the advertisements that were placed in the *Eagle* in a given
year, starting in 1915 and repeating at five year intervals until 1940, indicates that between 1915 and 1920 Race ads increased dramatically. In the
first year, the very year the Basses were pushing so hard for Race enterprises, only 5 percent of all *Eagle* ads designated firms as black-owned. Five
years later, 19 percent did so—a dramatic increase.[82]

Amid the flurry of those years, the Progressive Business League of Los
Angeles (PBL) replaced the Negro Business League, but the emphasis on
boosting Race enterprises remained unchanged. Indeed, the ideals had been
constant in Los Angeles since the Boom. When in 1919 the PBL published
a list of all its members (185 black-owned enterprises in the Los Angeles
area) and implored readers to "get in the habit of spending your money with
your own people," it was only echoing what the *Weekly Observer* had said
thirty years earlier. What had changed was the level of black economic power
and the sheer number of African American–owned enterprises. While the
Boom-year editors called on several hundred black residents to patronize
Frank Blackburn's coffee and chop house, the PBL encouraged fifteen thousand Afro-Angelenos to get behind nearly two hundred enterprises, ranging in scope from hairdressers to attorneys to auto mechanics to paper hang-
ers to morticians to cement contractors.[83]

The PBL roster of 1919 lists the addresses of each firm, and they were
located overwhelmingly along Central Avenue, within the 74th Assembly
District. Fully one-fourth were *on* Central Avenue. Others were within
blocks of it. The league had a few members whose firms were in the West
Jefferson district, including Anjetta Breedlove's hairdressing salon, and a few
whose businesses were in the beach communities of Venice and Santa Monica, but the Central Avenue magnet was obvious. The early movement down
San Pedro Street had stopped. By 1920 the Colored YMCA had moved from
San Pedro to a building near Central. More revealing, Fred Roberts had
moved his *New Age* to an office at 1203 Central Avenue, right in the heart
of things. Finally, the PBL list showed a small number of businesses clustered along Central Avenue *south* of Washington Boulevard—that is, south
of the 74th district. One in particular foreshadowed the future. A very long
way to the south, near the intersection of 37th Street and Central Avenue,
a Race man had opened a real estate office.[84]

Central Avenue as a Group Project

Race enterprises were surging in Los Angeles at the time Jim Crow feelings were rising, and the two trends were surely related. As more African American newcomers settled in and assumed a more visible presence, Jim Crow attitudes gained a firmer foothold. White anxiety rose in proportion to the black population. Initially, the white backlash remained moderate, because black migration remained moderate. But as the African American population grew, and racial tensions grew with it, a kind of separation cycle developed. As white prejudice increased, it made all self-help ideas, including the idea of a group economy, sound better to blacks. And the same black population growth that sparked white discrimination also provided black entrepreneurs with an attractively large pool of customers. The rising number of black businesses on Central Avenue made whites in the district uncomfortable. Psychologically and institutionally, if not residentially, many whites began to abandon the district—to give up on it, so to speak. In the meantime, Afro-Angelenos felt increasingly at home there and moved decisively to stake their claim to it. The complicated dance of race and space continued.

Taken together, black residences, Race papers, black churches, and black-owned businesses served to root the black community in the Central Avenue district. Except for a few streets and neighborhoods that were predominantly black, most neighborhoods in the 74th Assembly District remained majority white, and the large number of Japanese and ethnic-Mexican residents further complicated any notion of a "black belt." But the black-belt ideal transcended population trends, arising more from strength of will and depth of vision than from strength in numbers and depth of power. Afro-Angelenos made Central Avenue into a veritable little Harlem in spite of, not because of, their numbers within the 74th district.

Their achievement was possible partly because there were still open spaces for development on the Eastside; but that was not the key. To move into those spaces and claim them, black Angelenos had to work effectively as a group, and they did. They became community builders. Not everyone joined in, of course. There were those like Paul Bontemps who avoided what they saw as an unnecessary obsession with race. And there were the "sports," whose illegal rackets—small and large, innocuous and evil—gave Central Avenue a hint of danger. But it was the middle-class blacks who took charge of Central Avenue. They viewed it as a group project, as an ongoing endeavor in their search for free and meaningful lives.

In a better world, they might not have relied so heavily on group consciousness. If their African heritage had not closed so many doors to their individual ambitions, the emphasis on Race progress might have been less important to them. But the world that confronted them day to day was not that better world, so they had to do something about it. How could they get the dominant white society—that vague and shifting phalanx of power—to pay attention, to change its collective mind, to create a world of equal opportunity? As individuals, blacks could be superachievers and stellar examples, proof positive that white people had no good reason to hold on to their race prejudice. But individual efforts only went so far. Blacks had no choice but to launch group-oriented campaigns. To live free as individuals in a world of equal rights and equal opportunity, they first had to become an effectively politicized group. Race papers could inspire action, and black church buildings could suggest the glories of group effort, but somebody had to rally the masses for civil rights, to get people engaged and keep them engaged. In the half-free environment of Los Angeles, that was the only way to remake the world.

4

A Civic
Engagement

At some point, people who want to be free must take a stand. Exodus has its limits. Finding a promised land ultimately means settling down and living free. Historically, Americans have understood this, for if they have been a nation of movers, they have also been a nation of fighters, ill-content to wander forever. Time and again, hard-pressed groups in America have found themselves standing at the walls of Jericho, determined to win a place in the land of milk and honey. But how to bring down the walls? That was the question facing black leaders in early twentieth-century Los Angeles, for the issue was never *whether* they would battle for civil rights, but, rather, *how* they should fight the good fight.

It was a trickier question than might be supposed, for the matter of tactics raised difficult questions about the nature of race prejudice in a half-free city. Who, or what, was the real enemy? What were the most pressing problems? Should the focus be on local concerns or national problems? Were solutions to be found through legislation, through the courts, or through moral suasion? Which tactics were most likely to yield positive results? When would controversial tactics have a beneficial effect, and when would they make matters worse? How could blacks negotiate the tension between their need for group solidarity and their ultimate goal of individual liberty? How could whites of goodwill be persuaded that there was a real problem, and that they should join black people in the fight for equality? Were Asians and ethnic Mexicans possible allies, or were they part of the problem? Might

126

they join with African Americans to fight the white establishment? Or were they stealing black jobs and trying to push Afro-Angelenos down to the bottom of the city's racial hierarchy?

If black leaders had waited until they had all the answers before taking action, they never would have acted at all. But they did not wait. Basing their actions on a few broad principles, they developed an approach to civil rights activism that is best described as pragmatic. They believed, first, that group solidarity was good and necessary, and to that end they established organizations that expressed the views of the Race and that engaged in cooperative efforts to promote change. Race leaders believed they had to fight on every front—at the local, state, and national levels—addressing a wide spectrum of issues, ranging from disrespect on the city's streetcars to deadly race riots in Illinois. They thought it best to remain flexible, to be experimental. Occasionally, they debated the two "great schools" of civil rights thought, but mostly they avoided the restrictive snares of the Washington–Du Bois debate. They believed that trying something was preferable to doing nothing. If a tactic worked, they used it again. If not, they tried something else.

The people who took action were "Race men" and "Race women"—or "Club women," because women's activism often operated through women's clubs. Race men and Club women ensured that there was a black *community*, not just a black population, and that Afro-Angelenos kept group welfare in view. Leaders clashed over tactics, and there were times when personal animosities, generation gaps, and conflicting ambitions led to nasty infighting. But Race men and women always held one thing in common: hope. They believed that things could get better if people would join together and try to remake society. They saw Los Angeles as an unfinished project, or, better yet, as an ongoing one. They remained consistently involved in city affairs. Charlotta Bass, over the course of her long life, probably had more harsh words to say about Los Angeles than any other Angeleno, but it was equally true—and an absolutely vital point—that she loved the city and believed in its possibilities. For Charlotta Bass and thousands of other local blacks, Los Angeles was worth fighting for.

Freedom, they believed, could be attained and preserved only through civic engagement. Their basic creed was simple: Get involved, stay involved. Black middle-class leaders tried, consistently and with enormous effort, to make their city a better place and, in so doing, to set an example the rest of the nation might follow. Through organizations such as the Afro-American Council, the Colored Women's Clubs, and the NAACP, they fought for racial equality. In ways quiet and loud, in churches and courtrooms and city council meetings, they made it clear to all who would listen that equal opportunity did not exist, even in the West, and that fundamental changes were necessary to make it a reality. This kind of civil rights activism was a slow-going, mostly frustrating process. That the city's black leadership stuck to the task speaks to their hunger for equality and to their commitment to civic engagement.

Black Boosterism, Black Activism

The Afro-Angelenos who spearheaded the local civil rights movement were also some of the black community's leading boosters. That is, the very boosters who lavished praise on their great western city would, almost in the same breath, lambaste Los Angeles for its race prejudice. This seeming contradiction was no contradiction at all. As black leaders saw it, the Western Ideal could be wielded as a weapon in the cause of black civil rights. They trumpeted the notion that the West was a land of rare opportunities, open to those with talent and verve. Simultaneously, however, they noted that white racism was undermining black advancement in the West. This repeated juxtaposition of the idealized West and the racist West created a distinctly African American vision of the urban West, somewhere between an endorsement and an indictment.[1]

Throughout the early twentieth century, black newspaper editors in Los Angeles masterfully contrasted the idealized West with the racial discrimination blacks experienced there. As editor of the *Liberator,* Jefferson Edmonds was an early booster. He insisted that California offered the best opportunities for blacks in America and wrote that "the law-abiding Christian people of this state, by their humane treatment of their colored citizens, are doing great work not only for them, but for humanity." He approvingly quoted the daily *Herald,* which wrote that southern blacks would find "no race problem in Los Angeles, only prosperity." But at precisely that time, Edmonds was a vocal critic of race prejudice in Los Angeles and helped found the Los Angeles Sunday Forum, in which black Angelenos voiced indignation over local conditions.[2]

Every editor of a local Race paper followed this tradition. The *Eagle* boosted and condemned Los Angeles in every issue. The Basses repeatedly compared the opportunity-filled West to the discrimination-riddled East. But no sooner did they write about "the mighty march of progress on these Western shores" then they would castigate white Los Angeles for its racism and hypocrisy. In 1915, Fred Roberts's *New Age* offered his beaming "For the West" editorial, which all but told critics of Los Angeles to leave.[3] And yet, as his *New Age* shows, in the mid-1910s the city probably had no harsher critic of local racism than Roberts himself. In the inaugural issue of the Los Angeles *Western Dispatch*, a Race paper launched in 1921, the editors gushed that Los Angeles was the "industrial center of the North American continent." Just below this unfettered boosterism, the *Dispatch* ran a story about an NAACP fight against local segregation. Readers in the Central Avenue district would have found nothing unusual in this.[4]

By simultaneously holding up the ideal of western opportunity and the realities of western discrimination, black boosters in Los Angeles fostered a regionally distinct language of civil rights activism. Blacks deserved full equal rights not simply because they were American citizens, but also because this was the West, and the West stood for unparalleled opportunity. Black boosters thus aimed their exuberant prose at Race uplift, hoping that their words would spur white leaders to initiate reforms and also that their rhetoric would encourage blacks to become involved in civil rights campaigns.

The Afro-American Council

The first long-standing civil rights organization in Los Angeles was the Afro-American Council (AAC). Initially known as the Afro-American League, the AAC was a national federation of state and local branches that existed—off and on—from the late 1880s into the early twentieth century.[5] The state AAC was not the first black civil rights organization in California, but it was the first that was more than transitory and the first to involve Southern California in any meaningful way.[6] The California branch organized in 1895 and remained active until 1915, playing a key role in creating standards for black activism in progressive-era California.[7]

T. Thomas Fortune of New York, a Race man and newspaper editor, sparked formation of the national organization in 1887. Increasingly alarmed by the denigration of the Fourteenth and Fifteenth Amendments, he issued a call to black leaders across the United States, insisting that a nationwide organization was needed to oppose the rise of Jim Crow in the South. The result was the short-lived Afro-American League. Black leaders in Los Angeles first formed a local branch of the league in the late 1880s. Initially wary of the league—fearing it was some kind of political front for the Democratic Party—Race papers such as the *Western News* soon supported the organization. The local league agreed to meet with Bay Area Race men to establish a statewide organization; although the national league quickly evaporated, the California groups survived.[8]

In 1895, California's local leagues gathered in San Francisco to form the statewide Afro-American League. More than a hundred delegates attended and were welcomed by the mayor. For the next three years, the California league met annually, discussing economic and political issues and voicing calls for black unity throughout the state. When Fortune revived the national effort and changed the name in 1898, California's league became an affiliate and acquired its new appellation, the Afro-American Council. What followed were years of contradictory efforts as the California AAC tried to define its goals and hold itself together. At different points in time, it seemed to be a GOP patronage machine, an economic self-help organization, or a seedbed for civil rights activism. What mattered, in the end, was that it survived, providing a training ground for black leaders and serving as a laboratory for working out the logistics of running a statewide organization.[9]

Local branches of the AAC, called "subcouncils," were set up in most of the state's major towns and cities. By the turn of the twentieth century there were subcouncils in Marysville, Oakland (actually the Alameda County Council), Sacramento, San Francisco, San Jose, Stockton, Bakersfield, Fresno, Los Angeles, Monrovia, Pasadena, and Riverside. The AAC was a black-only group, but white allies sometimes gave moral or financial support; Harrison Gray Otis was an early supporter of the Los Angeles group. For most of its history, California's AAC maintained a males-only membership policy. Wives formed auxiliaries, which engaged in cooking and sewing activities and helped arrange the annual banquet, but they took no part in the political activities.[10]

Subcouncils met monthly, and each August they sent delegates to the annual state convention, which by the early years of the twentieth century was always dominated by the Los Angeles subcouncil. The number of delegates each subcouncil sent depended on its size; representation at the state convention was in direct proportion to local membership. That mattered because convention delegates comprised the state executive council, which elected the state officers and executive committee. When the rules were set in 1895, they favored the Bay Area crowd, but the rapid growth of black Los Angeles turned the tables, ensuring that a plurality of delegates would be Angelenos and that most state officers would be Southern Californians. Delegates at the 1905 convention, for example, elected eight officers: seven were from Southern California cities, five from Los Angeles alone. The Southland's unexpected numerical superiority bruised Bay Area egos and prompted a new organizational scheme: the state executive committee was divided into two branches, north and south. Because state officers were still elected collectively, the president was always from Southern California, but Bay Area blacks had their own executive committee. This division of authority maintained interest in both parts of the state and gave each one autonomy to pursue local goals.[11]

The men who led the Los Angeles subcouncil were mostly blue-collar workers and shoestring entrepreneurs who had middle-class attitudes and ambitions. The membership also included a few ministers. Over the years, the elected officials of the Los Angeles subcouncil included Race men such as John Neimore, G. W. Hawkins, John Wesley Coleman, and T. A. Greene, who was then editing a small Race paper. The first Southern Californian elected state president was William Prince, of Pasadena, who took the post in 1902. Prince, thirty-three years old, had brought his family west during the 1890s. He worked as a janitor, and he seems to have gotten his custodial position through political patronage. He quickly emerged as a respected Race leader within the local community and then, by virtue of the AAC, throughout the state. His position atop the AAC showed just how open the black community in Southern California was at the turn of the twentieth century. Prince arrived in town, found a leadership vacuum, and filled it.[12]

In 1903, delegates to the annual meeting convened in Prince's home city. The mayor addressed the meeting, and the white Pasadena newspaper gave the affair a glowing report. The paper also listed the delegates from Los Angeles, thirty in all, most of whom were much like William Prince: They were young and new to the area—only four in ten of them had lived in Los Angeles in 1900. Their average age at the time of the Pasadena convention was only forty-one. Almost all had been born in the South, and fully half were from Texas. All were literate. Most held blue-collar jobs. Six in ten owned their own homes.[13]

Information from the Los Angeles City Directory further confirms that the AAC was a mostly blue-collar group. Three quarters of the delegates could be positively identified in the directory. There were four ministers, as well as editors Edmonds and Neimore. Besides the ministers and newspapermen, only one delegate could be considered a professional man: a mail carrier. The rest were small-time proprietors and blue-collar workers. The businessmen included Charles C. Flint, who ran a grocery and dry goods store. He was active in Republican politics and was friends with General Otis. His business was more secure than that of any other delegate in 1903, but Flint was no man of wealth; his grocery was a modest storefront operation catering to Eastside working people. John H. Jamison was a more representative entrepreneur. The 1903 city directory lists Jamison as a "metal broker" (that is, a scrap-iron dealer), but a later directory lists him as a "junk" dealer. Eugene Walker ran a tailor shop out of his home (although in time he became quite successful).[14]

The rest of the delegates were basically laborers. Four were porters, including James M. Alexander. Five were janitors, a significant group, often backed by political patronage. Custodians who owed their jobs to patronage had an extra incentive to remain active in civic affairs. Often they were persons of high visibility, influence, and prestige within the community. William Prince was the best example of that at the 1903 convention, but his path to power was hardly unique. Edmonds had been a janitor before he became editor of the *Liberator*. The Bay Area delegates had similar connections. John Wilds became the first African American in Oakland to win a patronage post when he was appointed janitor at City Hall in 1889. He went on to establish the *Oakland Sunshine*. Becoming a janitor, then, provided ambitious black men one of the few avenues of upward mobility in turn-of-the-century California, and becoming active in the AAC could further contribute to one's personal status, as Prince's own experience showed.[15]

Over time, the black leadership in Los Angeles came to include fewer blue-collar workers, in some cases because blue-collar men at the 1903 convention later moved into white-collar jobs. James Alexander, a porter at the time of the 1903 convention, was given a white-collar patronage position by the Republican Party. T. A. Greene became an assistant journal clerk in the California Senate (a patronage post), and then the executive secretary of the Colored YMCA. Edward Akers, a common laborer in 1903, later established a billiard parlor. Other men just held steady: George Warner was still working as janitor in 1922; Henry Posey was still a "floor polisher" in 1910 and worked as an "elevator starter" a decade later; Edward Wells went from one small business (a delivery service) to another (meat cutting). At the turn of the century, though, new men in town could land a blue-collar job, make a few connections, and rise to the top of the black community.[16]

The AAC flew its banner in state political battles, pushing for acceptable candidates and patronage positions. In 1904, when a black man was lynched in the California town of Mojave, the AAC joined the Race papers in blasting Governor George Pardee for not publicly condemning the mob violence. Pardee made amends in 1905; after the Los Angeles AAC petitioned him for the release of a black man arrested on false charges, he pardoned the prisoner. An AAC report in 1909 stated that "through the influence of our Council we secured one pardon, saved one life, and secured from prison on account of false arrest thirty-eight persons."[17]

Through the AAC, Texas-born James Alexander emerged as a Race leader in the state, gaining a reputation as "a manly man" who "lives a clean, home-centered life." One African American journal called him "a bright example of our young western manhood. . . . [He is] one of the foremost Negroes of the West." To hear Charlotta Bass tell it, women fairly swooned in his presence. After high school, Alexander attended business school, studied law a bit, and got his job as a porter. In 1905 he was elected president of the state AAC, a post he held until it disbanded in 1915. Alexander won a federal patronage post when President William Howard Taft's administration made him a collector of internal revenue in Los Angeles.[18]

In 1906, as AAC president, Alexander published a statement of principles, "Appeal to Reason," which was written as an open letter to Afro-Californians. "Appeal" encouraged civil rights activism and electoral pragmatism, especially at the local level: "What President Roosevelt may say in praise of us at the nation's capital, or what [Senator] Ben Tillman of South Carolina, or Gov. [James] Vardaman of Mississippi may say in abuse of us does not [affect] like local conditions." Municipal officials "are of the greatest importance to us," for they are "the main artery for the building up of a city of contented, happy homes, the establishment of water, sanitary, fire and police departments, the enforcement of law and order without prejudice." Equally important, the wise "use of our ballot" would result in elected officials who would "[give] us a chance to earn a livelihood by giving us positions." Alexander wanted patronage, but he extolled the virtues of good government. He supported "men who believe in municipal ownership of public utilities" and looked for candidates "who will not favor corporations as against the people, or unwisely oppress concentration of capital and its beneficence"—classic rhetoric of the California Progressives.[19]

Alexander's "Appeal" also blasted Japanese immigrants and the whites who employed them. "In the labor field where so many of us are engaged," he wrote, "we are competing with the Asiatic emigrants who contribute but little to the advancement of the country." The AAC, he wrote, advocates "America for Americans." Asians had not fought for American independence, or for the Union, or "for the supremacy of the United States in Cuba or the Philippines." Black Americans *had* spilled their blood for the nation time and again, yet white businessmen hired Asians over "brave black men who have marched upon every battlefield and who have suffered and died for the nation's good." He could not fathom why "in many places we are discriminated against simply because we are Negroes," while these "foreigners" get the jobs.[20]

At the state convention in 1906, Alexander outlined nine objectives for the AAC. The first was "to maintain a strong political organization in order to make secure our civil rights." The second was "to support the best material for public office and to condemn and oppose those who dare close the door of hope against us." Priorities three through nine all underscored the importance of attaining equal opportunities through political activism. Alexander believed that blacks in the West should seize upon the relative political freedom of the region and use it to confront discrimination head on. He sought alliances with "neighbors" who understood the meaning of true American principles—with "manly" whites who would "open the door of hope to us." Only then could California be what it needed to be.[21]

By 1908, the national organization was defunct, but California's AAC continued to promote the twin themes of political action and economic opportunity until it, too, was played out in 1915. When President Taft visited Los Angeles in 1911, he met briefly with the Los Angeles AAC, which presented him with an "engraved gold card" of appreciation.[22] In 1912, the AAC men invited women to join, perhaps to pad its thinning membership rolls or perhaps because, after 1911, California women could vote. Alexander was still president in 1914, when the AAC issued a twenty-three-point "Declaration of Principles" demanding equal rights and urging blacks to be active citizens. By this time, though, the Los Angeles branch of the NAACP had been established and Race papers talked openly of the council's decline. Quietly, California's AAC and its local branches disbanded.[23]

Although it did not endure in the long run, the AAC established a pattern of pragmatic activism that would long characterize civil rights efforts in Los Angeles. It had created a cadre of black leaders where none had existed before. Ambitious newcomers with little money or political experience could, partly through AAC activism, become respected Race men. A viable leadership class was established, providing role models and a sense of stability in the community. Given its limited financial resources and numbers, the AAC could do little more than monitor conditions, voice indignation, and lobby politicians—although setting free nearly forty men who had been falsely arrested was no small achievement. From the time blacks established the state Afro-American League in 1895, however, there would always be statewide black activism in California. By the time California's AAC evaporated, in 1915, the California Association of Colored Women's Clubs was firmly established and the NAACP branches had been organized in Los Angeles and the Bay Area. The leaders who headed these organizations would wield more clout and win greater recognition than the leaders of the AAC had, but they owed much to this earlier organization. Their middle-class outlook and political pragmatism were partly an inheritance from the Afro-American Council.

Women's Clubs

The most important organization for black women in the state was the California Association of Colored Women's Clubs, a branch of the National Association of Colored Women. The NACW was established in 1896. Its inaugural meeting included seventy-three delegates representing eighty-two clubs from fifty cities in twenty-five states.[24] The NACW's motto, "Lifting as We Climb," meant that the women of the clubs should not only strive to move up in the world but also lend a hand to uplift women who were not as fortunate. Club women were status-minded, and their work provided a means for gaining status, but their guiding ethos transcended individualism. Clubs functioned as hubs for community improvement and civil rights activism. If the notion of "Lifting as We Climb" carried overtones of condescension, it was also true that Club women were not operating in rarified air. Many of them worked as domestics and laundresses, and they knew well, often from the calluses on their own hands, what ordinary black women were up against.[25]

Although white and black women's clubs, like black and white churches, ran on separate tracks, racial issues exposed fissures within white women's clubs in the early years of the twentieth century. The issue was not the integration of individual clubs but rather the question of African American attendance at national and state conventions of the all-white National Federation of Women's Clubs. At the biannual convention in 1900, after federation officials discovered they had inadvertently chartered a black club from Massachusetts, they quickly withdrew the charter to appease southern delegates who were outraged at black participation. In 1902 the convention would meet in Los Angeles, and more than a year in advance, white clubs in the city—indeed, the nation—were debating whether the federation convention should admit delegates from colored women's clubs, as the NACW was urging them to do. A *Los Angeles Times* editorial scoffed that "to the outsider, who has not been brought up in the Southern states, it appears strange and somewhat incomprehensible that a body of women who are professedly devoted to the dissemination of intelligence and liberality should make such a fuss over the question of the color of a person's skin." Insisting that character, manners, and intelligence should trump race, the editorial added that it should not matter "whether the person happened to be endowed by nature with a complexion of peaches and cream, or one of ebony, or of any of the intermediate shades that go between."[26]

But it mattered to many white club women from the South. During a discussion at the Friday Morning Club, one of the more influential white clubs in Los Angeles, Mrs. W. L. Graves held for "the Southern point of view" by contrasting the white and black races: "The one of that blood which has for centuries ruled the world, the other a slave for over three thousand years; the one vested with every mark of authority, the other with every badge of inferiority; the one which has pushed forward the civilization of the world, the other, which has never civilized itself in any country, the one ever dominant, the other ever subservient." She added that blacks were criminals and rapists, and that admitting colored clubs into the federation would lead to social equality. "It is but a step from the club to the home. . . . Are we to admit the black race to our drawing rooms?" Caroline Severance, a prominent member of the club and a progressive who leaned toward racial liberalism, disapprovingly questioned Graves's facts. The *Los Angeles Times,* recalling the Teddy Roosevelt–Booker T. Washington dinner, suggested that "if the President of the United States thinks it proper to entertain an educated colored man at his table, the members of the women's clubs need not fear that they will sacrifice their dignity by sitting for a few hours under the same roof with an educated colored woman."[27]

Trying to make a case for admitting black women, Severance stated that she could not understand "the philosophy which causes [white] Americans to receive with honors Italians, Spaniards and representatives of other dark-skinned races, while the natives of Africa are debarred socially." When her comments hit the newspapers, the "Spanish-American Ladies" of Los Angeles were outraged that they had been characterized as a "dark-skinned" race; in protest, they refused to participate in the city's biggest booster event, the Los Angeles Fiesta, leading the *Times* to rebuke Severance and, for damage control, to add that Spanish Americans "may feel assured that the people of this city do not indorse [*sic*] the insinuations made by Mrs. Severance."[28]

The convention came, the debate continued without resolution, and in the midst of it all, black women in Los Angeles organized a new club—the Progressive Club, whose officers included Mrs. William Prince and Lula Greene, wives of AAC leaders. Among white club women the issue would not die. When Margaret (Mrs. Booker T.) Washington arrived for a three-week visit in 1906, the Friday Morning Club and Ebell Club were forced to decide whether to invite her to visit their clubs. The *Times* quipped, "To entertain or not to entertain, that is the question." Severance, having arranged Booker's engagement at the Friday Morning Club in 1903, was now eager to have Margaret Washington as a guest of honor. As for the opposition, the *Times* noted that "in Los Angeles there are scores of southern ladies who are prominent in women's clubs." One of them, a leader in the United Daughters of the Confederacy, stated, "I presume they can invite this woman to come and speak before our club, if they wish to; but if they do, I can tell you they won't see me there for a good long time—and as to asking that nigger to come and sit down to lunch with us . . . that is certainly the limit!"[29]

About six months later, the California Association of Colored Women's Clubs (CWC) was organized. On the surface there seemed to be no relation between the two events. Indeed, while questions of race continued to divide white clubs, California's colored clubs moved ahead without apparent interest in the debate. But events happen in time for a reason, and the club question had exposed large deposits of race hatred in California, much of it expressed by "southern" women who sounded like crusaders for the Jim Crow ideal. Another event that paralleled the establishment of the CWC was the publication of James Alexander's "Appeal to Reason." In each case, the combination of a growing black population and a growing sense of western racism seemed to be the catalyst.

The prime mover of the CWC was Eliza Warner of Los Angeles, the wife of AAC member George Warner. She was described by peers as "a little dynamic woman . . . with a clear vision into the future." Warner traveled up the coast to Oakland, where she met with Race women in the Bay Area, and at Oakland's 15th Street AME Church, the women established a state organization. For about two years the CWC operated independently of the NACW, but in 1908 it became an affiliate of the national organization. As members of a state federation, local clubs pursued separate aims but joined together in annual conventions to elect statewide officers, exchange information, attend seminars and lectures, and support statewide causes. Because delegates from Los Angeles dominated the conventions—in 1908, every state officer elected at the convention was from Southern California—the CWC followed the AAC's strategy and divided the state organization into separate Northern and Southern Divisions (and beginning in 1912 a Central Division as well), allowing for a more even distribution of leadership positions and greater autonomy at the local level. Statewide projects were run through "departments," which mirrored those of the NACW: the Departments of Domestic Science, Mothers' Work, and Juvenile Work, for example, with each department headed by a "superintendent."[30]

Women's clubs of the CWC stripe were different from the fraternal organizations to which so many women belonged—the women's branches of secret societies, such as the Knights and Daughters of Africa and the Masons. Those "fraternal circles" or "societies," as African Americans called them, sometimes designed service campaigns and supported local charities, but they were mostly social outlets. Many Club women were active in the societies, but the CWC-affiliated clubs were open and public and had a civic mission. Their leaders were church women and strivers, such as Eliza Warner, who served as state president the first three years. In 1908, officers included Mrs. James M. Alexander (whose husband was president of the AAC); Mrs. Etta V. Moxley of Santa Monica (prominent in church circles, later CWC president); and, as "state organizer," the Reverend Ida Ford of Pasadena, who was a minister and a mother of five. By the early 1910s, the women elected as state officers and department leaders were usually more affluent than the rest, but as late as 1920 the rank-and-file members who shouldered responsibilities at the local level were a middle-class group, residing in the Central Avenue district and keeping the CWC grounded in the community.[31]

Club women wrote and published a great deal, for their clubs and for the public, and much of what they wrote concerned morality and motherhood. America's mainstream culture maligned black women as ignorant, immoral, and incapable. Club women spent endless hours defending themselves against that blanket slander. They felt compelled to trumpet their chastity and fidelity, their devotion to Christian living, and their attentiveness to their children. But if Club women sounded prudish in one sentence—lambasting "rag time music and vaudeville tendencies"—they might sound like radical feminists and civil rights crusaders the next, looking toward the glories of woman suffrage and vigorously demanding a national anti-lynching law. Their writings wove together cultural conservatism and women's rights activism in ways that are still slightly disarming, but which made perfect sense given their precarious position in society.[32]

Inspirational verse filled their publications. One woman's poem, reprinted in the *Eagle,* caught the spirit of enthusiasm and high duty that drove Club women everywhere:

> O, women of the Colored race!
> Be earnest, prayerful, brave and wise,
> O, leave upon this age, your trace
> Of noble deeds and sacrifice.[33]

Katherine D. Tillman, second president of the CWC, wrote a Club song— "Keep on Striving"—for her Pasadena group. Published in the NACW's national journal, the final verse and chorus reflected the essence of Club ideals:

> For the Church, the Home, the Race
> Bravely every trial face,
> Do each duty well that comes unto hand

And the God who over all
Watches every sparrow's fall,
Will raise you up a power in the land.

Keep on striving, keep on climbing
Lifting others as you climb from day to day,
Keep on striving, keep on climbing
For the God we love and trust,
Shall the mountains move away![34]

The motto of the CWC was "Deeds Not Words," and one of its activities was to sponsor "Monuments"—institutions that met special needs at the local level. Two of the CWC's early Monuments were in Los Angeles: the Sojourner Truth Industrial Home and the Day Nursery of Los Angeles (later known as the Eastside Settlement House). The Day Nursery was a day care center that served working mothers and thus met a pressing need in the community. The woman who first envisioned a club geared toward day care was Mrs. L. V. Steward ("its inspiring genius," as the *New Age* put it). The first president of the Day Nursery Club was Vada Somerville. The club's philosophy was that there were "no bad boys or girls except as we make them bad. . . . [E]nvironment is stronger than heredity." White civic leaders and politicians admired the institution; Superior Court Judge Frank W. Willis referred to it as "that very excellent institution." By the 1920s, the Day Nursery was serving 260 children each month.[35]

The Sojourner Truth Club, one of the early women's clubs in town and an early affiliate of the CWC, completed the Sojourner Truth Home in 1914. It was the first major "institutional" project undertaken by local Club women. Envisioned by Mrs. M. D. Scott and supported by CWC president Etta Moxley, the home initially provided living quarters and job training for unmarried women and single mothers; ultimately it expanded its services, lectures, and training programs to all "busy women." Construction of the home, which began in 1913, received a lift from the churches. Every black congregation in the city took a special offering for the home on March 9. When finished, the home was a handsome two-story building, Spanish style, with a domed bell tower on one corner and an arched portico entry. An enthusiastic *New Age* stated that the home was "filling a long felt need in Los Angeles. Giving a protecting shelter to self-supporting women and girls in the city and to strangers." Under the care of "a capable matron," women would learn "how to be more efficient, to earn more, to be healthier and to realize the ever present love of God." Some of the available courses were "Domestic Science," "Bible Studies," and "Physical Culture." The home would continue as a flagship Monument for the CWC and would move to expanded quarters in the early 1920s.[36]

The number of black women's clubs in Los Angeles increased over time. By the end of the 1910s, some twenty clubs had been organized, most of them affiliated with the CWC. These clubs interacted with those from Pasadena and other Southern California towns, sharing facilities, meeting jointly, and keeping tabs on the larger doings of the Southern Division. Some clubs were more civic-minded than others. While the Eastside Mother's Club focused its efforts on establishing "a home for friendless girls," the Kensington Art Club had as its "prime object" the "art [of] needle work."[37] Because the CWC was trying to change negative perceptions of black women, issues of refinement were critical to the cause, and artistic guilds qualified as legitimate efforts within the state organization.

Not all women's clubs joined the CWC, but those that remained independent still imbibed its spirit. The Women's Business Club, for example, was organized in 1912 by Mary L. Motley, who, according to the *Eagle*, was "prominent in church, fraternal and club circles." She decided that women should contribute "to the success of the Race along business lines" and called together some neighbors in the West Jefferson district. Eight women formed the club and coined a classic women's-club slogan: "Be Something, Have Something, Do Something." What they did was accumulate cash. Membership required money—dues paid on a regular basis, all of which went to the treasury. By 1918 the Women's Business Club had eight thousand dollars, and, with Sidney Dones handling the transaction, the club purchased a two-story, ten-room house on East Adams Boulevard, just south of the 74th Assembly District. The plan was to rent the rooms and possibly build a larger apartment building on the property. The *Eagle* stated that "these women are of the plain, common, every day people, . . . and our men will do well to emulate their example."[38]

That Club women were not merely socialites was evident in the way they responded to a home-buying conflict in 1914. That spring Mary Johnson, an African American woman, purchased a home on 18th Street near Central Avenue. At the time, East 18th was an all-white street, and Johnson's arrival sparked a hostile response. While she was away from home, neighbors broke in, ransacked the place, threw her furniture and possessions onto the front lawn, nailed boards over the windows and doors, and painted a warning: "Nigger if you value your hide don't let night catch you here." When Johnson returned home and saw the scene, she went to find Charlotta Bass, who quickly met with other Club women to discuss strategies. That evening, as Bass herself later related the story, "a brigade of a hundred women marched to the Johnson home." Unarmed, they surrounded the premises and called the sheriff's department, which failed to respond. About midnight, the women finally succeeded in getting authorities to the scene— two motorcycle cops. The officers removed the offending sign, pried the boards off the windows and doors, and told Johnson she could move back in. She kept her home, apparently without further incident.[39]

Club women encouraged one another to achieve economic independence. The Women's Business Club exemplified their desire to "Have Something." Increasingly, women of the clubs moved out of blue-collar employment and into entrepreneurial and professional niches, a trend favored by the NACW. Describing the NACW and its programs in 1912, Margaret Washington spoke pointedly of "the professional and business women whose interests are being pushed so that the woman who is inclined to be independent of her father and brothers in her struggle for a living, may not be swallowed up." She added, "The National [organization] knows these women, where they are located, what they are doing." It "distributes literature bearing upon their work; presents them to the public, and in every way holds them together and so adds to their strength and usefulness."[40]

The CWC pushed beyond social work and economics into electoral politics, especially after California granted women the franchise in 1911. At the national level, the NACW kept suffrage closely in view. Margaret Washington wrote that "our attitude toward suffrage is of the conservative kind. We have not blown up any houses with dynamite." But, she added, "we are reading and studying the great questions which are to make for the good of the country, and when the vote is given to women as it surely will be where it is not already done, we shall be ready to cast our votes intelligently." Because it was "already done" in California, the CWC set an example for the national organization and reported on its efforts. In 1913, a California report printed in the *National Association Notes* told of the CWC's efforts to "assist our women to use the ballot in an intelligent manner." In the state capital, the Sacramento Monday Club was "keeping a close eye on the legislature to see that no bill which is detrimental to race progress is passed without earnest protest from our men and women, as a bill for the segregation of our children in the public schools is pending."[41]

During the mid-1910s, when California's AAC was dying, the CWC was growing and becoming more active in civic affairs. The clubs would support the NAACP, and some Club women would be leaders in it, but the CWC was never subsumed by the NAACP or any other civil rights organization. The CWC offered women a source of power, and an arena for service, that was unmatched by mixed-gender organizations. Women's clubs were a source of upward mobility for middle-class women, one of the few places men could not hold the top spots. As they grew, the clubs became more aggressive in trying to influence civic affairs. During World War I, they forsook artistic endeavors and focused on home-front needs. After the war, the clubs of Los Angeles held a "Mammoth Mass Meeting" to "educate women in social and economic conditions"—an indication of the CWC's future direction.[42]

The NAACP

The NAACP, a biracial organization open to women and men, had its immediate roots in the Springfield, Illinois, race riot of summer 1908. This deadly assault on black citizens within sight of Abraham Lincoln's grave prompted a group of white northerners to confront America's racial hostility. Mostly wealthy, mostly from the Northeast, these "new abolitionists" held a National Negro Conference in 1909 to address the issue. The parlor socialist William Walling expressed their fundamental premise: "Either the spirit of the abolitionists . . . must be revived and we must come to treat the negro on a plane of absolute political and social equality, or [Mississippi governor James] Vardaman and [South Carolina senator Benjamin] Tillman will soon have transferred the race war to the North."[43]

Wanting a biracial conference, the white leaders invited black civil rights leaders, including W. E. B. Du Bois and others from his Niagara Movement. After some useful discussion and awkward clashes, the National Negro Conference adjourned with plans to continue the effort. When participants convened again in New York in May 1910, they organized the National Association for the Advancement of Colored People. One year later, their organization was incorporated under New York law, making 1911 the NAACP's "official" birth date. White leaders wanted Du Bois's talents and needed his validation. He accepted their offer to become director of publicity and research and made his own exodus out of Atlanta to work in the NAACP's national office in New York.[44]

Within the NAACP, Du Bois proved himself a royal pain—bureaucratically ruthless, sometimes petty and defensive—but he was indispensable. Without him and his monthly news journal, *The Crisis: A Record of the Darker Races*, the NAACP might have failed. Du Bois quickly made the *Crisis* a national phenomenon—the first successful nationwide Race journal, capstone of the black national network. Du Bois wrote most of it and controlled the rest, filling its pages with Race news and photos from around the nation.

His goal was to mobilize mass consciousness among African American readers. His commanding indignation and searing satire made the *Crisis* an immediate success. It became a standard in black middle-class households. Parents read it aloud to their children. A subscription cost one dollar per year, and the journal's circulation rose steadily, reaching more than fifty thousand households by 1918.[45]

In Los Angeles, people were reading the *Crisis* before there was a local branch of the NAACP. Du Bois arrived for his famous first visit in July 1913. His report on that trip—"Colored California"—focused on his own doings with nary a word on the NAACP or its aims; but black Angelenos naturally linked Du Bois with the NAACP, and they were predisposed to organized effort. By the time Du Bois arrived, the state AAC had been operating for nearly twenty years, and the CWC was growing steadily. The city's black leaders understood what the NAACP was about, and some were eager to organize a local branch.[46]

The exact events leading to the formation of the local branch of the NAACP remain somewhat obscure, but the two major proponents were the attorney E. Burton Ceruti and the dentist John Alexander Somerville, Race men with impeccable credentials. The earliest document in the Los Angeles branch files, kept by the national office in New York, is a letter from Ceruti to Du Bois in September 1913. Ceruti began his letter with a rebuke: "In response to the request usually found in the legal directory of the Crisis, I forwarded to you my professional card in connection with my subscription to the Crises [*sic*] with the request that you use the same. No reference was made to it in your reply, and the card has not been entered." In other words, Why hasn't my name been printed in the legal section of the *Crisis*? It was a small matter—a touch of prestige and free advertising—but Ceruti had a habit of voicing complaints before saying hello. Still, he followed with a paragraph more worthy of posterity. He was considering "the advisability and necessity of organizing a local branch." Would Du Bois send the requisite materials and "suggestions for organization"? "Problems and grievances arise constantly demanding attention and action by someone on behalf of the race," he continued. "No one is charged with this responsibility or duty and few can afford to take it singly. Many fail to see the necessity and conditions gradually grow worse. We begin to feel the necessity, of an organization such as yours, supported by public spirited citizens and charged with this duty."[47]

Probably following Du Bois's advice, the national office bypassed Ceruti and contacted John Somerville instead.[48] Du Bois had stayed with the Somervilles when he visited Los Angeles. Newlyweds, John and Vada Somerville had never entertained a guest in their home, and they were anxious, know-ing Du Bois's reputation for being "cold, reserved and aloof." Upon arrival at their home, Du Bois looked around the house coolly, excused himself, and went out for a walk. Vada, hoping to impress with dinner, roasted a whole chicken but "neglected to fold the legs and wings under," so that the "legs stood straight up in the air and the wings stuck out on the sides." Awkward silence filled the dining room for a moment as Du Bois stared at the chicken and John tried to carve it. Then Du Bois said, "You had better hold that chicken before it runs away." The three of them burst out laughing, and in some strange way that quirky incident brought down the social barriers that separated Du Bois from most people. After that, the three of them were al-ways close friends.[49]

In late October 1913, John Somerville received materials from the na-tional office, asking if he would be interested in starting a branch and who, locally, might support the new organization. He replied, "I am interested in the National [Association], and have always thought Los Angeles would be a good place in which to start a branch." He listed twenty contacts: Mrs. Nellie M. Reed, Mr. and Mrs. Morgan E. Robinson, Mr. and Mrs. Eugene Walker, Mr. and Mrs. L. M. Blodgett, Burton Ceruti, Dr. Wilbur C. Gordon, Titus Alexander, Frederick M. Roberts, J. H. Shackleford, Dr. James J. Leggett, the Reverend E. W. Kinchen, Dr. Thomas J. Nelson, James M. Vena, attor-ney P. M. Nash, Charles Alexander, and Mr. Alvin Hill and his activist wife, Betty Hill. These names indicated that the NAACP would be established and led by a more affluent, professional group than the men who had organized the AAC. Nellie Reed was a probation officer for the city, and Somerville's list included doctors, dentists, attorneys, and well-established business lead-ers. Still, the difference ought not be emphasized, for the list included three men who had been leaders in the AAC: James Vena (a postal clerk), Charles Alexander (a teacher and newspaperman), and the tailor Eugene Walker. Others were classic Race men and women of the early twentieth century, and it could hardly be said that any of the professionals on the list were truly wealthy. Somerville closed his letter by volunteering to "do anything I can to forward this movement," and the wheels began to turn.[50]

In spring 1914, Ceruti sent the national office $22.50 in membership fees, and that August the national office issued the Los Angeles branch a char-ter. Membership cost one dollar, and if one wanted a subscription to the *Cri-sis*, that was another dollar. The branch kept fifty cents of each membership dollar for its treasury. No original membership list survives, but the $22.50 is evidence enough that the founding members were few in number. Ceruti was elected executive secretary of the branch, and the Reverend Charles Edward Locke, a white Methodist minister, was selected as the first president.[51] The branch's second president, the Right Reverend Joseph H. Johnson, bishop of the Episcopal Diocese of Los Angeles, was also white.[52] No evidence survives to explain why the branch elected white presidents, but both the national office and the local Race leaders doubtless thought it wise. A principal aim of the organization was to demonstrate that blacks and whites *together* were willing to fight for racial equality. Because most of the leaders and members of the local branch were black, everyone understood that it was important to put a well-respected white person in a visible position.

At the national level, whites were decisive in founding and running the organization. At the local level, race played out differently. In Los Angeles, white members were scarcely visible. Not that white support was entirely lacking. When Du Bois arrived in 1913, he noted considerable enthusiasm among white Angelenos, and John Somerville later recalled that the first meeting brought together "a militant group of white and colored people." But in the branch correspondence and in the local Race papers, white Angelenos almost never appear. Locke spoke out against the race riots that followed the First World War, but he had no real influence within the branch. There is no mention of him in the branch records during his presidency, except for a passing reference in what seems to be a white daily newspaper clipping. In a 1917 yearbook of the Los Angeles branch, put together by Ceruti, Johnson is shown in a full-page photograph striking a heavily jowled, liturgical pose. Other than that, he received no mention in the yearbook or, indeed, in any letter to the national office.[53]

Burton Ceruti carried the load in the branch's early years. In 1917 he gave up the executive secretary post and became the branch "attorney," an official—and, because the NAACP relied heavily on legal campaigns to protect and extend black civil rights, critically important—position. John Somerville was the "first vice president" for many years. Leading ministers embraced the organization from the beginning; in 1917, four of the nine members of the executive board were men of the cloth. The leading black churches hosted the branch's quarterly and annual meetings on a rotating basis. Professionals, business leaders, ministers, Club women—the higher echelon of the black middle class—took charge of the local NAACP. There were no janitors in the lead, not even politically powerful ones, such as William Easton and L. G. Robinson. James Alexander, longtime president of the AAC, also did not appear on the NAACP's leadership lists, even after his organization folded in 1915. Somerville's 1913 list had not included many women, but by the late 1910s, female leadership in the local branch was much in evidence. Mrs. Morgan Robinson, Eva Carter Buckner, Mrs.

Nellie M. Reed, and Mrs. E. R. Baldwin all held posts on the executive board. By 1920, Mrs. J. M. Scott, a leading Club woman, was second vice president. Most important, in 1917, Beatrice S. Thompson became the organization's executive secretary.[54]

It is not too much to say that the Los Angeles branch became Beatrice Thompson's organization. She served as executive secretary for a decade. Ceruti and John Somerville wielded considerable clout and shouldered much of the responsibility for the organization, but Thompson was no wallflower. An elegant, middle-age woman with a penchant for efficiency, she ran a tight ship, and she proved a forceful leader in her own reserved, insistent way.[55] Unlike Ceruti, whose letters to the national office habitually included opening barbs at New York's officials, Thompson had people skills and a diplomatic touch. Introducing herself by mail to Roy Nash, the national executive secretary, she praised Nash's work effusively. Nash marked her letter with a giant check mark. Thompson's relations with the New York office would not always be free of tension, but she worked cooperatively with national officials, who doubtless found her letters easier to open than Ceruti's.[56]

The Los Angeles branch's first controversy came from an unexpected source: Allensworth, a rural all-black town in California's Central Valley. Allensworth had petitioned the state legislature to build a Tuskegee-like industrial school for blacks, funded by the state, in the town. That petition divided California's African American communities. Joined by the Race papers, the Los Angeles NAACP assailed Allensworth's idea as southernism run amok: state-sponsored Jim Crow at the request of African American citizens. Allensworth defended the idea on practical grounds—the school would be useful to black Californians and would help ensure a prosperous future for the Allensworth community. But few black Angelenos embraced the black-town dream; their vision of freedom was equal rights within mainstream society. The plan eventually was abandoned, but not without high emotion, and not without tragedy, as Colonel Allen Allensworth, the town's founder, was killed on the streets of Los Angeles in the midst of the controversy. It was an accident, not an assassination—he was hit by a motorcycle as he was stepping off a streetcar. But the Allensworth conflict festered, and several years later, when Ceruti complained of opposition from the local "Tuskegee element," he was doubtless referring to residual ill will.[57]

The NAACP's fight over *The Clansman* in 1915 also divided black Angelenos, but overall it had an edifying effect on the local branch. It brought positive and much-needed attention to the NAACP locally and nationally, and it strengthened the branch's ties to the city government.[58] And *Birth of a Nation* was hardly the last film of its kind. In January 1918, Ceruti warned the New York office about a new film titled *Free and Equal*. He noted that the Los Angeles branch, by virtue of its location, had "the opportunity of detecting and reporting many of the pictures which by design or otherwise, would injure our interests." In December, an advertisement in the local dailies had announced a showing of *Free and Equal,* and the wording of the ad "aroused suspicion." A one-week "tryout" for the film was scheduled to begin on Sunday, December 23. The local branch persuaded the mayor and city council to join the NAACP in attending that screening. The film shocked Ceruti and city officials.

Ceruti described it as "the most vicious picture I have ever seen." The problem was how to stop it, especially given the results of the council's efforts to stop *Birth* from being shown three years earlier. The next day, Ceruti worked with local officials to "drive through the City Council a special ordinance, No. 37778, which enabled the city officials to forbid the production"—that is, to prevent its screening. In order for an ordinance to go into effect immediately, an "emergency clause" was needed, and that required a unanimous vote by the council. "This was quite a feat," Ceruti wrote, "but it was accomplished"—and all in one day. *Free and Equal* thus showed once and was shut down. Ceruti urged the national office to alert all of the branches. "If the matter can be handled through the National Board of Censors, it would be a better way," he said, "but, personally, I have little confidence in a Board consisting of representatives of the manufacturing interests." The national office sent warnings to branch secretaries throughout the country and thanked Ceruti for his "prompt activity in this matter."[59]

Ordinance 37778 made it easier to stop offensive films from being shown in the future as well. It created an official and salaried position—the commissioner of films—who would be appointed by the mayor and who could not be affiliated with the motion picture industry or the theaters. Before any film could be screened in Los Angeles, it had to be previewed and approved by the commissioner of films, who alone judged whether it included scenes of an "indecent, immoral, revolting or gruesome nature . . . offensive to the moral sense." If denied a permit by the commissioner, the producer's only appeal was to the board of police commissioners, an unlikely sympathizer. The film commissioner had power to seize films that were screened illegally and to arrest those who showed them—up to a five-hundred-dollar fine, or six months in jail, or both.[60]

There were other issues, of course, and in its first six years of operation, the Los Angeles branch addressed a wide-ranging set of local and national problems. Like the AAC and the CWC, the NAACP campaigned against lynching, holding rallies to denounce mob rule, sending petitions to President Woodrow Wilson, and urging their congressmen and senators to pass federal antilynching legislation. As race riots moved north, the local branch lent both moral and financial support to the victims of the East Saint Louis, Illinois, riot of 1917 and the Chicago riot of 1919. And, as a telling indication of the local branch's increasing respect and visibility in the community, Afro-Angelenos not affiliated with the NAACP sent contributions to riot victims through the local branch. At the prompting of national officials, the branch also urged California's congressional representatives to help strike down segregation in Washington, D.C., a new and galling result of Woodrow Wilson's Democratic administration.[61]

Closer to home, the branch fought hard for black women to gain admission to the county hospital's nursing school, which openly excluded all African American applicants on the grounds that white students would object. This campaign absorbed most of the branch's legal energies and monies. The fight lasted through most of the 1910s, with numerous advances and setbacks. Finally the branch won, and black nursing students were admitted in 1919, despite the objections of the white students, who threatened to quit. The local branch also tackled employment issues, investigating hiring discrimination at the Los Angeles post office and at retail stores and advocating that African American women be hired as elevator operators during the labor shortage caused by World War I. Eva Carter Buckner, executive board member and head of the branch's school committee, investigated incidents of race prejudice in the public schools, with good results, so that Beatrice Thompson could report in 1917 that "nothing of that nature is tolerated."[62]

Curiously absent in the branch's early correspondence is any mention of the multiracial dynamics confronting black Los Angeles. James Alexander had addressed the Asian question in his "Appeal," and the ethnic Mexicans and Japanese living in the "black belt" were daily reminders of the Eastside's complicated demographic. Du Bois noticed this during his 1913 visit and mentioned the city's Asian population twice in his "Colored California" piece. When he spoke at a large theater, he reported, the hall was "filled with 2,300 people from the white, yellow, and black races." Who these Asians were, or how many, cannot be determined, and although Du Bois seemed to suggest that those in attendance were possible allies—another group of colored people interested in advancement—he also voiced ambivalence. Du Bois failed to mention ethnic Mexicans, who far outnumbered the Japanese and who would have seemed, to his eastern eyes, equally exotic.[63]

Du Bois's curiosity quickly fell away, and the Los Angeles branch said nothing about the Japanese and ethnic Mexicans until the end of the decade—and then expressed uncertainty. In 1920, when Beatrice Thompson wrote to Mary White Ovington, who chaired the national board of directors, she noted that she had recently delivered a paper at the California State Conference of Social Agencies, an overwhelmingly white gathering led by Los Angeles progressives and educators such as the reformer Dr. John Randolph Haynes and the USC sociologist Emory Bogardus. The topic of Thompson's panel had been education, and her paper, "Education of the Colored People," elicited little comment. But the talk "Special Schools for Mexicans," presented by San Bernardino's superintendent of schools, who apparently favored the idea, created a stir. Ethel Richardson, California's assistant superintendent of public instruction, impressed Thompson by taking "a noble stand against segregation in the schools." Voicing her own views to Ovington, Thompson thought separate schools for Mexicans would be "merely another angle of the color question" and added that "separate schools for Japanese have been discussed at other meetings and the sentiment for both is increasing." This, she said, "will eventually affect us."[64]

"The Mexican and Japanese questions are getting very acute in this State," Thompson continued, "and while they have tended to divert the public mind from us temporarily, we know that the source of the attacks is racial prejudice." Here was a critical observation and one perhaps widely held among the city's black middle class: that the white backlash against the Japanese and Mexicans had taken the heat off the black community—a welcome relief, but probably a temporary one. Ultimately, white bigotry directed at Asians and Latinos would find fresh targets in the African American community. There was, however, another point of view, which was that African *Americans* should stand above the immigrant groups, especially Asians ineligible for citizenship. Alexander's "Appeal" had pressed the point, hoping to use white anti-Asian sentiment as a means of forming a stronger, more equal bond between whites and blacks.[65]

Could the various nonwhite groups become partners in the struggle against white racism, somehow transcending barriers of language and culture to fight a common foe? Or would the realities of everyday life make African Americans, Asians, and Latinos competitors at the bottom of the racial hierarchy? During these years, the city's Japanese and ethnic-Mexican civic leaders showed no apparent interest in the NAACP, and the local branch seldom indicated an interest in those communities. The eastern civil-rights establishment ignored multiracialism in the West. Thompson knew there was no way to predict how the situation would evolve. In her letter to Ovington, she concluded her discussion with appropriate understatement: "The outcome is apt to be somewhat complicated."[66]

If eastern leaders failed to appreciate Los Angeles's multiracial dynamic, it might further be said that they gave the West Coast little consideration at all. Ceruti complained that the Los Angeles branch received little support from New York, yet the national office consistently asked Los Angeles for money. In 1918, Thompson sent a testy missive after the national NAACP leader Oswald Villard came to California but failed to visit the Los Angeles branch. Worse, she complained, New York had failed to inform the Los Angeles branch of Du Bois's fiftieth birthday party, which turned out to be the civil rights gala of the year; the long list of well wishers, published in the *Crisis*, therefore failed to include the Los Angeles branch. The national office replied that Villard had been in California for his health (even though he had given two speeches) and that the announcement for the Du Bois testimonial must have gotten lost in the mail. When the Los Angeles leaders asked New York to send a representative to revive enthusiasm, the national office begged off, citing constraints of time and money. Ceruti grumbled that the local officers were working "unaided" and "surrounded by hostile sentiment." Thompson took it one step further, calling it "hostile sentiment from both races." In reality, membership in the local branch was growing, reaching about 350 by the end of 1918. But Ceruti and Thompson felt frustrated and isolated, partly because national officials had done little to bridge the distance.[67]

The East-West regional divide—or more accurately, the angst felt by black westerners at what they perceived to be northeastern arrogance—sparked a letter from Ceruti to the national office in early 1919. Having learned a little diplomacy, he opened his letter to Secretary John R. Shillady with praise for the national office's work. Then, getting to the point, he wanted to know why, in the recent selection of new members to the national board of directors, he had been snubbed. The New York office had asked each branch to submit a nominee for the board. The California branches, in a significant feat of unity, had all nominated Ceruti. But, as Ceruti put it to Shillady, "to our surprise and chagrin, the committee ignored the unanimous choice of the Branches of the State and, in fact, in all their selections ignored the entire West."

"The people of the West have labored hard against very heavy odds and much opposition from the Tuskegee element to make the National Association popular in this part of the Country," Ceruti fumed. "You will never know the sacrifices that have been made to this end. Some of us have unlimited faith in the integrity and efficiency of the organization, but others will be greatly discouraged by the apparent discrimination." There was no regional balance on the board of directors, he added. "For example: California has more Branches and more members than either New York or Massachusetts. Massachusetts received three prizes in the drawing while New York exceeded that number; neither California nor any other state in the West is represented on the Board. I think this is a mistake which will make more difficult the work of those who seek to keep alive the interest and enthusiasm for the Cause."[68]

Ceruti was lobbying for a position on the national board, but he was also voicing the sentiments of black westerners who felt marginalized by the East Coast civil rights establishment. Booker T. Washington had visited Los Angeles several times before his death in 1915, sometimes staying in Southern California for weeks on end; Margaret Washington made trips to Los Angeles in her work with the women's clubs.[69] By contrast, the NAACP staff only reluctantly visited the West, and not very often. Du Bois made his whirlwind visit in 1913, before a local branch even existed, and from then until after Ceruti's angry letter of 1919, the national office sent no one west, despite the repeated urging of Afro-Angelenos. Even after every branch in California had rallied behind a single nominee to the board, the national office had given seats mostly to New Yorkers, who joined a board already thick with New Yorkers.

Shillady responded to Ceruti with a defensive but ultimately redeeming letter. "I have noticed your work in my more or less casual reading of the California papers and have appreciated it," he wrote. But the national office was overworked—"I do not know how much the branch officers appreciate the fact"—and the board of directors situation was more complicated than Ceruti knew. Nominations were many but vacant seats few. Ignoring the issue of vacant seats given to northeasterners, Shillady noted instead that one vacancy on the board had been given to "a representative from the South," because "the South is after all our battle ground," and the branches from that troubled region deserved at least one representative.

He then confided that the national office had petitioned the state of New York to increase the size of its directorship from thirty to forty. And in what amounted to a secret handshake, he added, "I can say to you that the members of the Board are fully appreciative of the desirability of having a representative from the [West] Coast elected and that this matter has been discussed by the executive officers." Ten new directors would soon be elected, and Ceruti's nomination would be revisited at that time. "More than this I cannot say as you, as a man of experience, can well appreciate."

Having all but said "you'll be in," Shillady still flung a final barb, stating that a seat on the board was real work, not an honorary position, and adding that "it is fair to say that we cannot expect anyone as far away as California to be able to attend many meetings of the Board." At the next annual meeting, later in 1919, Ceruti would in fact be elected to the NAACP board of directors, the first westerner to hold an official position in the national organization.[70]

It did not hurt Ceruti's case that the Los Angeles branch boomed in 1919. It boomed in part because New York had finally sent out a representative to help the cause, and they had sent the right person—James Weldon Johnson. By the time Johnson became field secretary for the NAACP in late 1916, he was in his mid-forties and already one of the best-known black leaders in the country. A lawyer, educator, and publisher, Johnson was also a successful lyricist who had teamed up with his brother, the composer Rosamond Johnson, to write a long list of hit songs (as well as the Negro National Anthem, "Lift Ev'ry Voice and Sing," which was then beginning to circulate through black America). He also was a novelist and poet and an international statesman (U.S. consul to Venezuela and Nicaragua under presidents Roosevelt and Taft). His job with the NAACP was to build up the branches, and he succeeded. Nationwide, membership soared. Hiring Johnson as field secretary was probably the best thing the early NAACP did, other than giving Du Bois the *Crisis*. Johnson may have been even more valuable than Du Bois in the long run, for he had the qualities of a diplomat. African Americans may have admired Du Bois, but they loved Johnson.[71]

Thompson and Ceruti had been lobbying for a visit from Johnson for some time, and when it finally came to pass, the results were stunning. Johnson stayed in town a week. He gave two talks in Los Angeles and another in Pasadena, all of them well attended. In one fell swoop, the Los Angeles branch doubled in size, from about 350 members to 700. By 1920, the NAACP had solidified its position as America's foremost proponent of black civil rights, and Los Angeles had one of the largest branches in the nation.[72]

Fighting Restrictive Covenants

Not all efforts for civil rights and community uplift came through the AAC, the women's clubs, or the NAACP. Individuals fought for freedom too—usually by getting a lawyer and bringing suit against Jim Crow. But the connection between individual action and community well-being was always clear. For example, the early legal battles against restrictive covenants were fought by individuals but had obvious implications for all Afro-Angelenos. These court cases resulted in several important legal decisions in California—all of them uncomfortably ambiguous.

Fights over covenants were entwined with American real estate law, which had been shaped by English traditions. Since at least the thirteenth century, Anglo-Saxon common law had held that people who owned property should enjoy the free and unrestrained use of that property; they could sell it or dispose of it any way they saw fit. In legal terms, the disposal of land was called "alienation." The freedom to sell or give away property in any way one wished was known as the "unencumbered alienation" of land. In the United States, the tradition of unencumbered alienation became an essential element of property law. By the turn of the twentieth century, however, unencumbered alienation had come under attack from whites who feared the growing presence of blacks and new immigrants. Seeking to preserve all-white housing areas, they adopted the restrictive real estate covenant.[73]

In Los Angeles, blacks were fighting restrictive covenants in court as early as 1915. Homer L. Garrott, a black police officer, had purchased a home in the Angeles Park subdivision, developed by the Title Guarantee Company. Angeles Park lots were covered by restrictive covenants, which prohibited their sale or rental to people of African, Japanese, or Chinese decent. When an owner sold to Garrott, the Title Guarantee Company sued to have Garrott removed and to regain ownership of the property. Black attorney Charles S. Darden defended Garrott's right to the property. The ensuing case, *Title Guarantee & Trust Co. v. Garrott*, landed in the Superior Court of Los Angeles County, presided over by Judge John W. Shenk (later a chief justice of the California Supreme Court). In 1916, Shenk ruled in Garrott's favor. As the *New Age* put it, he "declared absolutely null and void Race restrictions so commonly found in deeds and conveyance against Negroes holding title to real estate in California." But the legal battle was not over. That spring the *Eagle* warned that "the white people of these tracts have organized, are holding mass meetings and are raising funds." Title Guarantee and the Angeles Park residents soon appealed.[74]

Outside the courtroom, a battle over public opinion began. White organizers for Title Guarantee issued a statement in the *Los Angeles Times* saying, in effect, that black Angelenos preferred segregation. They claimed that racial tensions between whites and blacks made it necessary to segregate in order to prevent violence and that African Americans were more comfortable living among their own. The *Eagle* countered that "the two Races are living side by side in almost every section of the city and nothing but a friendly feeling exists between them. No self-respecting Negro could ever sanction segregating the Negro because it would mean a sacrifice of our integrity and threaten the very foundation of our freedom."[75]

Both groups in this struggle believed freedom was at stake. The Angeles Park residents held to the notion—rooted in American slavery—that white people could be free only if blacks were not. African Americans proposed a model of freedom based on equal rights regardless of race. Everyone came to Los Angeles looking for a better life. For many whites, the good life meant living in neighborhoods that excluded colored people. For blacks, the desire was not simply to live among whites—they had done that in Dixie, to little edifying effect. It was to take advantage of one's financial successes without being stigmatized by race. "All of us are not content at living in the Los Angeles river bed," insisted the *Eagle*, "but are seeking to purchase real estate that is saleable and will have the advantage of civic improvements." Moreover, as the *Eagle* insisted, if the courts gave their blessing to restrictive covenants, it would be "a preliminary step to more degrading humiliation." It "is not for himself but his Race that [Garrott] is so ardently demanding justice," claimed the *Eagle*.[76]

As the *Garrott* case wound through the California courts, a residential-segregation conflict back East catapulted the national NAACP into the legal arena. City officials in Louisville, Kentucky, had passed an ordinance that divided the residential areas of the city into "white" and "colored" sections. The NAACP's national leaders took aim at the ordinance, and their efforts to kill it became the organization's first major legal battle, *Buchanan v. Warley*, which went all the way to the United States Supreme Court. Mindful of the court's enduring support for the "separate but equal" doctrine it had codified in its *Plessy v. Ferguson* ruling (1896), NAACP president Moorfield Storey, a "new abolitionist" from Boston, based his case on the individual's right to unencumbered alienation irrespective of race. In November 1917, the justices ruled in favor of the NAACP, striking down the Louisville ordinance. Their decision carefully upheld the separate-but-equal dictum but protected alienation from state intervention: "The right which the ordinance annulled was the civil right of a white man to dispose of his property if he saw fit to do so to a person of color and of a colored person to make such disposition to a white person." That, the justices insisted, violated the due-process clause of the Fourteenth Amendment and "was not a legitimate exercise of the police power of the state." In Los Angeles, Ceruti loudly trumpeted the ruling.[77]

But the unintended result of *Buchanan* was a surge in restrictive covenants throughout northern and western cities. The Supreme Court had ruled that "the state" could not violate property rights on account of race. Because the NAACP had sidestepped *Plessy*, the key issue for the justices was not racial equality but government infringement on alienation. Their ruling left open a critical question: Was it constitutional for individuals and private organizations to violate the principle of unencumbered alienation on account of race? Restrictive covenants were private arrangements, not state edicts. Whites who wanted whites-only housing therefore placed their faith in covenants, which might stand up in court and, in any case, bought time. Covenants, already present in many Los Angeles deeds, began to cover the city's all-white neighborhoods. The outcome of *Garrott* was therefore critical. If Judge Shenk's decision was upheld, covenants in California would be dealt a serious blow. If not, most of the city could become legally off limits to colored citizens virtually overnight.

Garrott went to the California Supreme Court, which rendered its decision in July 1919, three and a half years after Shenk's initial ruling. The court ruled for Garrott. Citing the California Civil Code (section 711), which states that "conditions restraining alienation . . . are void," the justices avoided distinctions between "state" and "private" restraints and ruled that restrictive covenants violated California law. In their last-ditch effort to win, lawyers for the Title Guarantee Company countered that since the racial restrictions in the deed were only temporary, they did not, in any fundamental sense, restrain alienation of the property. The lawyers pointed to precedents in other states, where courts had made distinctions between "partial restraints" on alienation (meaning temporary restrictions of, say, fifty years) and "general restraints" (meaning permanent restrictions); in those states where "partial" was legal, "general" was not. But in the *Garrott* case, California ruled that there was no distinction between partial and general. In the eyes of the court, both were unlawful restraints on the unencumbered alienation of land.[78]

Inevitably, the fight was not over. A slightly different covenant case also was nearing closure in the California courts, and no one was quite sure how it would go. This second case, *Los Angeles Investment Co. v. Gary*, was in many respects similar to *Garrott*. Alfred Gary, an African American resident of the city, had purchased a home in a new subdivision only to find that the property was restricted by covenant. The Los Angeles Investment Company, owners of the subdivision, sued Gary, demanding his eviction and claiming that, in accordance with the covenant, ownership of the property must revert to the company. And there was a twist, for this covenant also included an occupancy clause. The deed not only restricted sales but also stated, " . . . nor shall any person or persons other than of Caucasian race be permitted to occupy said lot or lots." In short, there were two big issues to be decided: whether restrictive covenants were valid, and whether occupancy clauses were valid.

The case went to the California Supreme Court, which ruled on *Gary* in December 1919. In one of the most curious decisions in American property law, the court made the following four rulings: First, it was against the California Civil Code to place a restraint on alienation; racially restrictive real estate covenants were a restraint, and therefore they were invalid. Second, there was no distinction between partial and general restrictions. Citing the initial decision in *Garrott,* which had long been rattling through the system, the judge in *Gary* ruled that restrictive covenants could not be sustained on the ground that they were only temporary; whether temporary or permanent, racially restrictive covenants violated the law of alienation and were invalid. This was wonderful news for Alfred Gary and the black community.

Then came the kicker, the third ruling, which dealt with the occupancy clause. To quote the language of the court: "[T]he provision in a deed that no person or persons other than of the Caucasian race shall be permitted to occupy the property, is not a restraint upon alienation, but upon the use of the property, and is valid." In other words, restrictive covenants could not prevent black people from buying a home, but they could prevent the black owners from living in it. Buy it, possess the deed for it, pay taxes on it—just don't live in it. The fourth ruling stated that occupancy clauses were not a violation of the Fourteenth Amendment, and that occupancy clauses imposed by individuals were legal, because they were private, not public, edicts.[79]

Alfred Gary had won and he had lost. The courts reaffirmed *Garrott,* striking down the validity of restrictive covenants—a major victory. Gary could keep his property, and the Westside could potentially be open to black buyers. But because the court upheld the legality of the occupancy clause, the law now barred Gary from living in his home—a stunning defeat. Residency clauses were now legally valid and enforceable, which meant, inevitably, that they would quickly spread over Southern California. The *Gary* decision rippled out of California through America's legal system as well, influencing restrictive covenant decisions nationwide. As a legal precedent, it both helped and hurt black Americans. Some state courts cited it in an effort to strike down restrictive covenants; others used it to validate restrictions on occupancy. Locally, the *Gary* decision did nothing to end the legal wrangling. It symbolized the half-free conditions black Californians faced and, by its very nature, ensured that the struggle over real estate would continue.

Listening Deeper

To be black and middle class and a Race leader meant carrying the everyday burden of being viewed as an inferior being while acting always as a superior citizen. After John Somerville had joined the Los Angeles Area Chamber of Commerce, he arrived early for one of the chamber's black-tie events and proceeded to the empty dining room, where he stood by his chair waiting for others to arrive. Soon another member walked up to Somerville and asked, "Are you going to serve us any wine tonight?" He assumed Somerville, a black man in a tuxedo, was the waiter. Somerville quipped, "I hope they at least serve us a good highball because I need a good appetizer."[80]

L. G. Robinson, head custodian at the county courthouse, once found a woman's purse that had been left in a courtroom and returned it to the main desk. When the woman came to claim it and discovered that its contents, a hundred dollars, had not been stolen by the black man who found it, she told the white clerk that she was amazed that a black person would not steal the money. The clerk said her reaction was inappropriate. The woman then found Robinson and offered him a five-dollar tip for his assistance; he simply declined. She went back to the white clerk once again, raving about what a "queer colored man" Robinson was—he would not steal or take a tip.[81]

It was difficult not to grow weary and bitter about such incidents, which piled up over the years. Robinson and Somerville were able to rise above the gall in these two cases, but it is also significant that Robinson's story appeared in his as-told-to biography, and that Somerville related the chamber of commerce story in his own autobiography, writing, with a noticeable effort at restraint many years after the event, "Quite often a person of color is confronted with situations that require patience and tact to prevent clashes and harsh words when dealing with Caucasians."[82]

There was weight also in shouldering the load in the community's Race organizations. The tasks involved could be long and lonely: the tired rustle of papers being filed late at night; the endless correspondence and record keeping; the criticism leveled by people who never lifted a finger to help; the banal points of order at stale meetings—not to mention the nail-biting delays in the legal system, or the empty feeling that followed a losing battle. It must have hurt sometimes. That the city's black leaders persevered means that they were listening deeper, that they were able to consider the humanity behind all their bureaucratic work.

Perhaps we, too, can transport ourselves to Central Avenue and listen deeper. We can hear the muted voices of the Afro-American Council as they walk into the police station to challenge a false arrest; we can hear the key in the lock as the jail cell swings open. We can hear children saying prayers over breakfast at the Sojourner Truth Home. And over on 18th Street, we can hear the stern determination of high heels, one hundred women surrounding Mary Johnson's vandalized home; we can hear the cracking sound as the sheriff's officers pry the wood from the doors and windows. It is easy to imagine the highbrow tones of Burton Ceruti as he marshals Ordinance 37778 through the emergency city council meeting of December 24, 1917. With more effort, we might imagine the commencement exercises at the county hospital's nursing school, or even hear the sound of a black woman's heart, beating fast, as she prepares to cross the stage and receive her diploma.

Such sounds, surely, were what kept Race men and Club women going, month in, month out, year after year. Yet the community's civic leaders could hear other sounds as well. They could hear African Americans such as Paul Bontemps, who, for whatever reason, were counseling their friends and family to steer clear of the Race organizations. On the residential streets on either side of Central Avenue, they could hear a chorus of voices going their own way—including the 90 percent of black Angelenos who would not pay a dollar to join the NAACP. They could hear quiet voices in uptown law offices, as white lawyers and real estate developers added occupancy clauses to their restrictive covenants. And beyond that, in the vast ocean of whiteness that was the Westside, they could hear an oddly detached population, living in blissful ignorance of black people and their struggles to live free in Los Angeles. African Americans almost never found an entrance into Westside consciousness, but on those rare occasions that they did, white racial assumptions often flared.

What blacks needed were ways to gain full access to American life without having white people respond with shock, fear, or condescension. How could African Americans live a normal life in a race-conscious, bigoted world? How could they break through? How could they convince white people that black people were fully human, fully American? How could they ensure themselves equality under the law? The Race organizations helped, but they had not yet turned the tide, and in many ways they themselves were driven by increasing white hostility toward colored people. One thing black Angelenos needed was greater political influence; another was to win the hearts and minds of white Angelenos, to convince a broad section of white residents to view Negroes as normal, full-fledged Americans, not some kind of enduring "other." As it happened, the First World War brought the opportunity—but not the certainty—of political empowerment and white respect.

Above: Charlotta A. Spear (center) poses with friends, probably in Providence before she left for Los Angeles in 1910. *Right:* Joseph B. Bass had this portrait taken in Helena, Montana, about 1911, the year he moved to Los Angeles. The two were married in 1914, and as owners and editors of the *California Eagle* they quickly became a pair to be reckoned with in black Los Angeles. Spear's photo: Security Pacific Collection / Los Angeles Public Library; Bass's photo: *Montana Plaindealer,* January 1911, Montana Historical Society.

Symbols of the South and West: George O. Paris White and his wife, Ella Sarah White, who moved to Los Angeles with their two children in 1917, saved photos of a 1915 Texas lynching as a reminder of what the South could be. *Right:* In Los Angeles, their son, Ela Nelson White, won a student architecture contest. He poses with the champion's cup. Shades of L.A. Archives / Los Angeles Public Library.

In what became a familiar Los Angeles pose, the Rozier family gathers on the lawn in front of their bungalow in 1910, amid palm trees and hydrangea bushes. African Americans in the West, and especially Los Angeles, enjoyed higher rates of home ownership than blacks in other parts of the country. The more affluent blacks from the South could afford to move west, where, in open-space cities such as Los Angeles, they found inexpensive real estate and newly built homes. Shades of L.A. Archives / Los Angeles Public Library.

Even during the Great Migration of World War I, Los Angeles experienced only a modestly paced middle-class migration of blacks to the city. Before moving west, Nyanza and Hattie Hawkins had prospered in Shreveport, Louisiana, as their home and touring car demonstrate. Their youngest son, Augustus Freeman Hawkins, was destined to become California's second black state legislator (1934) and its first black congressman (1962). Courtesy of Special Collections, Young Research Library, University of California, Los Angeles.

Most Afro-Angelenos lived in the Central Avenue district in what was then called the city's Eastside (not to be confused with what is now known as East L.A.). White antagonism to black neighbors and racially restrictive real estate covenants fostered that trend. But a small number of blacks, including Evelyn Turner Lofton, whose home on West 37th Street is pictured here with a toddler on the lawn (ca. 1930), were able to purchase homes in the West Jefferson district, a small oasis for affluent blacks on the Westside. Shades of L.A. Archives / Los Angeles Public Library.

Unlike many American cities, Los Angeles hired blacks as policemen as
early as the 1880s and continued to do so, although in small numbers.
Officer William Pipkins is pictured here wearing his uniform in 1915.
Afro-Angelenos who wore the badge seldom got good beats or promotions,
but by the early twentieth century the police force was at least integrated.
The city hired black firefighters as well, but segregated them into a single
firehouse—Station No. 30—which still stands on Central Avenue and
houses a small museum. Shades of L.A. Archives / Los Angeles Public
Library.

In 1915, the black-owned Lincoln Motion Picture Company was formed, in part to counter D. W. Griffith's infamously racist portrayal of blacks in *The Birth of a Nation*. Its key players are shown here, including the company's usual heroine, Beula Hall, and the founder and leading man, Noble Johnson (center). Johnson's obligations as a bit player for Universal Studios, along with overwhelming financial difficulties, forced Lincoln to shut down after it produced a few short but successful films. Courtesy of the African American Museum and Library of Oakland, the Miriam Matthews Collection.

Signs of a community in the making are evident in this photograph, taken near the corner of 8th and San Pedro Streets in ca. 1908. The Citizens Band poses in front of two small but important institutions: The *New Age* newspaper office and the Colored YMCA. Courtesy of the African American Museum and Library of Oakland, the Miriam Matthews Collection.

In keeping with national trends, the city's black businesses in the twentieth century catered to African Americans, although in the racially diverse Central Avenue district black businesses often had Asian, ethnic Mexican, and white customers, too. Most Race enterprises were mom-and-pop stores, such as E. G. Johnson's drugstore and soda shop, pictured here. Shades of L.A. Archives / Los Angeles Public Library.

Vital to the black community and its pursuit of civil rights were the Negro churches, whose faithful members built gracious sanctuaries throughout the Central Avenue district. The First AME Church, better known in the community by its address, "Eighth and Towne," had one of the finest choirs in the city. Its members pose on the front steps, ca. 1910. Shades of L.A. Archives / Los Angeles Public Library.

Left: James Alexander was a longtime president of California's first statewide civil rights organization, the Afro-American Council. The AAC was eclipsed by the local branch of the NAACP which was chartered in 1914. *Bottom:* Some of the NAACP's early leaders are shown in this 1923 photo, including the two who shouldered most of the work during the branch's infancy: the attorney Burton Ceruti (far left) and executive secretary Beatrice S. Thompson (front row, third from left). Also pictured are Frederick Roberts (back row, second from right) and his wife, Pearl Hines Roberts (front row, second from right). Courtesy of the Miriam Matthews Collection (California Afro-American Museum).

The Party of Lincoln—and the culture of Lincoln Republicanism—was strong in Los Angeles County, as this Lincoln Day production (ca. 1920s) suggests. An annual commemoration of Abraham Lincoln's birthday, Lincoln Day was to the early twentieth century what Martin Luther King Day is now—a day to reflect on oppression, liberation, and the ongoing fight for equal rights. Security Pacific Collection / Los Angeles Public Library.

As editor of the *New Age* and a popular Race man in the community, Frederick Roberts (shown here in 1925) cut a dignified figure and had the connections necessary for political success. He leaned toward the progressive-Republican camp and penned scathing editorials against white supremacy. In 1918 he became the first African American elected to the state legislature, creating a biracial Republican coalition that would keep him in office for sixteen years. Courtesy of the African American Museum and Library of Oakland, the Roberts Family Collection.

When W. E. B. Du Bois first visited Los Angeles in 1913, the community welcomed him with automobiles—the standard greeting for celebrities. This photo shows Du Bois standing next to the taller John Somerville in the auto at left. The location of the photo is significant: the community welcomed Du Bois in front of the Colored YMCA and Fred Roberts's *New Age* office, on San Pedro Street. Courtesy of the Miriam Matthews Collection (California Afro-American Museum).

Black Americans fervently supported the World War I effort, hoping their sacrifices to "make the world safe for democracy" would result in democracy in the United States itself. This group of Red Cross volunteers and two men in uniform—one from the army, one from the navy—exemplifies the breadth of African American participation during the war. But black war service, far from convincing white America to abandon race prejudice, seemed only to infuriate racist whites. The backlash was most severe in 1919, when white riots against black communities left deep scars across the nation. Shades of L.A. Archives / Los Angeles Public Library.

One of the few wartime civil rights victories Afro-Angelenos could claim was the admission of black women to the nursing school at the Los Angeles County Hospital. After years of litigation and protest, and over the vociferous objection of the white nursing students, the NAACP finally broke the barrier. The victory proved a lasting one and led to the tradition of a banquet for African American graduates—this one held at the Memo Club, at 42nd Street and Central Avenue, in 1940. Shades of L.A. Archives / Los Angeles Public Library.

5

Politics
and Patriotism

In spring 1918, the Reverend Benjamin C. Robeson of Los Angeles joined the United States Army and marched off to war in France. A popular minister in the AME-Zion Church and a contributing editor for the *Eagle*, Robeson enlisted as a chaplain, not a soldier, but his support for the American military campaign rang with the tones of a true believer. "Let us rally around Uncle Sam," he wrote in early 1918, "and help to whip the Kaiser." For the past four years, while the nations of Europe had slaughtered their sons in the Great War, America had tried to stay out of the bloodbath. Indeed, President Woodrow Wilson had won reelection in 1916 on a peace platform. But tensions between the United States and Germany escalated, and in April 1917 Wilson asked Congress for a declaration of war. Voicing his instantly famous justification, the president insisted that "the world must be made safe for democracy." America must fight for the "foundations of political liberty" and "the rights of mankind."[1]

For black Americans, this war for democracy recharged an old hope—that their patriotic support of the nation would result in racial equality within America itself. Military service to their country and patriotic campaigns on the home front were duties they would eagerly shoulder. In turn, they expected white America to grant them the respect, honor, and rights that they still longed for. How could America fight for liberty and democracy in Europe and not bestow basic liberties and democratic freedoms on its own citizens, especially loyal citizens who were willing to fight and die for their country? For years, black leaders had been fighting for "democracy," "political liberty," and the "rights of mankind"—exactly the things that Wilson now urged Americans to defend. Many black Americans believed that their wartime patriotism would win them those freedoms at home.

Robeson embraced the idea. "What have I to fight for?" he editorialized in the *Eagle*. "I was born here, lived here all my days and intend to die here. . . . Shall I be ungrateful to the land of my adoption because she has sinned? . . . I must fight to keep untarnished the glorious record of the gallant ones who tasted death that I might enjoy the prescribed privileges of today. The blood of Christopher [*sic*] Attucks, the martyr of '76, shouts from the Commons of Boston. . . . The fight may be hard, but the victory draweth nearer." Even though the government of the United States had treated African Americans first as chattel and then as second-class citizens, most Negroes expressed a fervent desire to back the nation in its hour of crisis. But for black Americans, there was always that second, equally important goal: black freedom at home. As Joe Bass wrote in the *Eagle*, it was also time for the government to make "California safe for the Negro."[2]

Even as Robeson mustered into the chaplain's corps, Fred Roberts heard a different call to arms—state politics. The editor of the *New Age*, a leading figure in his family's mortuary business, and a popular Race man of unimpeachable character, Roberts was perfectly suited for public service. As American troops began their fight in France, he quietly decided to run for the California state assembly in the 74th Assembly District. No Afro-Californian had ever held state office, though several had run on various tickets. In early 1918, Roberts sensed the time was ripe. Thanks to electoral reforms put in place by California's progressives, primary elections were now open to all comers. Scarcely a month before the 1918 primary, to be held in late August, Roberts surprised everyone by announcing his candidacy for the Republican nomination in the 74th district. Fewer than 20 percent of the district's voters were black, and Roberts faced several white candidates, but he gained steady support, even among white voters. In keeping with the spirit of the age, he ran not as a Race man but as an "American, on American principles." When the votes were tallied, Roberts had won the primary. In the 74th, winning the Republican primary usually was tantamount to winning the seat. In this case, though, Roberts faced stiff opposition in the general election: a white independent candidate whose campaign slogan was "My opponent is a nigger." November's results would amount to a referendum on racism in the Central Avenue district.

Robeson and Roberts were seeking the same goal in different ways. Robeson was praying in the trenches, trying somehow to steer the wildfire of war across the forest of American racism. Roberts was campaigning on Central Avenue, hoping to channel the steady flow of state policy toward equal rights. What would be the outcome of their efforts? Would black participation in the war for democracy yield greater racial democracy in the United States? Could a black man win state office in California, even at the district level, and if so, what difference could he make in the statehouse? As summer turned to fall in 1918, the answers to these questions remained altogether uncertain.

The Promise of Patriotism

The NAACP's annual report for 1917 stated, "If thousands of American black men do fight in this war, joining hands with the hundred thousand or more colored troops [from French Africa] that are fighting for the Allies in Europe, then who can hold from them the freedom that should be theirs in the end?" Black leaders had voiced similar sentiments in every American conflict, from the War of Independence through the Spanish-American War. As recently as 1916, during a series of firefights in Mexico, the all-black Tenth Cavalry had fought for the United States, thereby priming the African American patriot ideal for the World War. The Lincoln Motion Picture Company of Los Angeles quickly produced a movie based on the battle of Carrizal, *The Trooper of Troop K*, which highlighted African American heroism.[3]

The Tenth Cavalry's battles in Mexico actually stemmed from the European conflict. Hoping to divert America's attention away from Europe, and to tie up the United States Army with a conflict in its own backyard, Germany began covert operations to stir up trouble between the United States and Mexico. Those efforts and Mexico's political instability provoked border skirmishes between the U.S. Army and various Mexican forces, including Pancho Villa's bandits and Mexico's regular army. The black soldiers of the Tenth Cavalry fought the pivotal battle—the "Carrizal incident" in June 1916. Seeking Pancho Villa in the town of Carrizal, the Tenth found its way blocked by government *federales*, who were also seeking Villa. Mexican troops outnumbered the Americans five to one. Frustrated, the Tenth provoked a battle, killing thirty Mexican soldiers and suffering fourteen dead and ten wounded. In the course of the battle, the Mexicans took twenty-four African American soldiers prisoner. The diplomatic crisis that followed nearly led to war between the United States and Mexico, but what resulted instead was an uneasy peace and the return of the black American prisoners.[4]

Upon their return to El Paso, the blacks who had been held prisoner received a hero's welcome. The city's white newspaper noted that "though the captured men were negroes, they were United States soldiers and had gallantly upheld the honor of their nation on a foreign battlefield." That kind of response—from white Texans no less—was what Race leaders hoped for: whites giving blacks their due, perhaps even abandoning their assumptions about Negro inferiority. The Mexico campaign thus strengthened black America's faith that the Race might gain respect through military service. But El Paso's enthusiasm for black patriotism proved the exception, not the rule.[5]

As the United States mobilized for the World War in 1917, many blacks who sought to enlist in the Army found themselves turned away for spurious reasons. John Somerville tried twice to join the Army medical corps but was refused. The Army was top-heavy with officers from the South, men who had no desire to see blacks in uniform, holding guns. In Washington, D.C., Senator James Vardaman of Mississippi, a perennial villain for black Los Angeles, raged against putting African Americans in uniform. Such a policy, Vardaman said, would lead to the presence of "arrogant, strutting representatives of black soldiery in every community."[6]

Most blacks who served during the war entered the army through the draft. It stung that draft registration cards required blacks, and only blacks, to tear off the corner of their card—this so that draft boards could easily see that their card was that of a black person. The goal of this "tear off" system was to simplify the creation of segregated Negro units. American Indians, by contrast, found themselves eagerly recruited into the white man's army; Caucasian men openly voiced their desire to fight with the "warrior race." In the end, black men would be drafted in proportions slightly higher (about 13 percent of American draftees) than their proportion of the national population (about 10 percent). Most were slated for labor duty, not armed conflict. Blacks were not permitted in the whites-only officer-training camps, but African Americans wanted black officers to command black soldiers. Opting for segregation over exclusion (and only after much vocal insistence), blacks were granted a Negro-officers training camp in Des Moines, Iowa. Few black officers saw France, however, and white superiors quickly demoted most of them who made it overseas, replacing them with white officers.[7]

· Black hopes for democracy at home fell that July, when a white-on-black race riot in East Saint Louis, Illinois, turned into a virtual pogrom, resulting in nearly forty deaths; most of the remaining blacks were run out of town. In response, the NAACP's national office in New York organized its first mass demonstration—the "Silent Parade" against mob violence and lynching. Thousands of smartly dressed Negroes marched silently through the streets of Harlem, accompanied only by snare drums and the sound of marching feet. Two men carried a large banner on which was printed Thomas Jefferson's famous opening lines from the Declaration of Independence. Under that were the words "If of African Descent Tear Off This Corner."[8]

Things got worse, one month later, in Houston, Texas. Racial tensions rose wherever black troops were stationed during the war, but Houston topped everything. Here the Twenty-fourth Infantry, part of the all-black Tenth Cavalry, was briefly stationed prior to its expected departure for France. These men were accustomed to the relative racial openness of the West, but Houston's police force, disturbed by the sight of black men in uniforms, harassed and assaulted the soldiers when they came to town. Fresh from the border wars, many buffalo soldiers could not abide such racism, and some stopped trying. "To hell with going to France," one yelled, "get to work right here." One hundred infantrymen formed an unofficial unit and made an armed march on the police station. A firefight erupted, with black troops engaged against the police, who were aided by white citizens. Five policemen and ten white civilians died and a dozen or more were wounded. The black soldiers carried four dead and six wounded back to camp. Soon after the shooting stopped, white mobs descended on the black section of Houston, beating men and women indiscriminately, even though none had taken part in the uprising.[9]

Federal retribution against the soldiers was swift and severe: twenty-nine were hanged; fifty-three received life terms; and the remaining men found guilty by court martial received prison terms ranging from two to fifteen years. One famous branch of black military men vanished virtually overnight, and the rest of the Tenth Cavalry was not allowed to go to France. Most Race leaders made it clear that they did not condone the rebellion, but many openly questioned why federal force had never been used to stop a single lynching or any white mob that attacked black people.[10]

Charlotta Bass went to Houston to investigate the riot and its aftermath for the *Eagle*. It was a dangerous trip to take. Why she went, rather than Joe or some other reporter, we do not know, but her decision to make the journey was certainly in character with the political person she was becoming. She arrived two weeks after the riot to find most black Houstonians terrified and locked inside their homes. Many would not open their doors to her, for fear of white reprisals. Others voiced surprise at a female newspaper editor. Her reports focused on white violence during and after the insurrection, and she noted that eyewitness accounts were "gruesome beyond words." She did not hesitate to support the troops' uprising, regardless of the political costs. She acknowledged that some Race leaders thought that the black soldiers had made "a colossal mistake," but she disagreed. In her view, the soldiers "had a single thought that prompted their action. That thought was a united demonstration to show that they would not continue to bleed and die for this nation and not fight back to defend their own lives and honor against mob violence."[11]

Despite East Saint Louis and Houston—or perhaps because of them—blacks throughout the nation promoted wartime patriotism with exceptional vigor. When the first group of African American draftees departed Los Angeles, a large crowd from the community gathered at the train station to see them off in style, waving a large silk American flag, hand-sewn for the occasion. The black churches and women's clubs plunged into Liberty Loan campaigns, Red Cross drives, and other displays of home-front support.[12] Race papers, even the post-Houston *Eagle,* fervently pushed patriotism and printed patriotic verse submitted by local writers. A poem titled "Equal Rights," if not exactly elegant, caught the spirit of the hour, reading, in part:

> Just because we are not the wealthiest,
>   With resources of power and might
> Think what our boys have accomplished
>   For the cause of "Equal Rights."
>
> With our boys fighting so bravely
>   And the "Red Cross" doing their might
> All Striving for one great victory,
>   A flag called "Equal Rights."
>
> The great tidings that are coming,
>   Since the Kaiser has taken flight,
> Berlin or bust, with a bayonet thrust,
>   And then our "Equal Rights."[13]

Bayonet thrusts in Europe, then equal rights at home: that was the formula, and black Angelenos stuck with it. The local NAACP's quarterly meeting in October 1917 featured speeches on American patriotism. The Race papers published upbeat letters from local servicemen who were stationed across the country and in France. Delilah Beasley, the Bay Area Race woman and journalist who was doggedly compiling historical materials for her pioneering book, *The Negro Trail Blazers of California,* gathered biographical sketches, photographs, and poetry commemorating black sacrifices for the war effort.[14] The Lincoln Motion Picture Company bought French newsreel footage showing African American soldiers in France and distributed it throughout the country; Lincoln also shot its own newsreel footage of the Tenth Cavalry, stationed in Arizona and engaged in military training, restrictions on its participation in the war notwithstanding. And the film company sought a contract from the federal government that would have underwritten Lincoln-made patriotic films to entertain the black troops in France. The deal never materialized, but it was another example of how Afro-Angelenos threw themselves into home-front work, their aims ranging from profits to patriotism.[15]

William Easton exemplified how Race men became Super Patriots. Through a series of government appointments during the war, he became a spokesman for the patriotic ideal. The War Department's Bureau of Public Information selected him as a public speaker to boost black morale, and he enthralled audiences with his insistence that "there [can] be no World Democracy that [fails] to affect favorably the present status of the Negro in the American sun." The state of California commissioned him as the official historian of black California's wartime experience. Easton was also one of six black men in Los Angeles who were designated as "Four-Minute Men." This honor and duty was bestowed by Marshal Stimson, the local Progressive Party leader, who orchestrated the government's propaganda program in Los Angeles during the war. Four-Minute Men delivered orations in movie houses during the four minutes it took to change reels. Stimson selected about 120 Four-Minute Men from throughout the city. Other Afro-Angelenos chosen were John Somerville, Hugh Macbeth, Charles Alexander, businessman Hugh Gordon, music instructor H. Douglass Greer, and journalist and real estate man Noah Thompson.[16]

The critical question was whether white Americans were paying any attention. Black Four-Minute Men spoke to mostly black audiences, because the theaters to which they were assigned catered largely to African Americans. Liberty Loan and Red Cross drives usually operated out of the black churches and clubs, which were out of sight of white citizens. Did any of this black patriotic fervor register among white people? Black leaders knew they were preaching to the choir, so they made broader efforts to reach white audiences. Eloise Bibb Thompson, for example, published a long and elegantly crafted article on black patriotism in the *Tidings,* the monthly journal of the Catholic Archdiocese of Los Angeles, whose readership was overwhelmingly white. Thompson was a local Race woman of high stature. The wife of Noah Thompson, she was a journalist and a devout Catholic. In her essay "The Loyalty of the Negro," Thompson first voiced her regret that white Americans knew so little about African Americans. Whites too often accepted stereotypes and rumors, she said, without trying to get to know black people or reading Race literature. Even her white Catholic friends admitted that they "never read the Negro articles" in the *Tidings*, and many simply parroted white mainstream racial conventions without questioning them. She recalled how "an estimable Catholic lady, one of the dearest I have ever met," had recently suggested to her that segregation in the South was "absolutely necessary for the safety of the white people"—especially white women—because of the Negro's "unbridled moral appetite." "In other words," wrote Thompson, "she thought the Negro a moral leper who must be kept in his own colony. . . . She had let other people do her thinking for her, instead of acquainting herself with the truth regarding the Negro and then arriving at her own conclusion."[17]

It was regrettable, Thompson continued, that some white Americans were questioning black loyalty, believing, for example, that blacks in the South were working with the Germans to undermine the United States government. To help white readers reach different conclusions, Thompson quoted Race leaders who heralded Negro patriotism. She offered the full text of the "Oath of Afro-American Youth," which had been recently penned by Dr. Kelly Miller, the dean of Howard University, which Miller had distributed to black public-school children in the nation's capital:

> I will never bring disgrace upon my race by any unworthy deed or dishonorable act; I will live a clean, decent, manly life and I will ever respect and defend the virtue of womanhood; I will uphold and obey the just laws of my country and of the community in which I live and will encourage others to do likewise; I will not allow prejudice, injustice, insult or outrage to cower my spirit or sour my soul, but will ever preserve the inner freedom of heart and conscience; I will not allow myself to be overcome of evil, but will strive to overcome evil with good; I will endeavor to develop and exert the best powers within me for my own personal improvement and will strive unceasingly to quicken the sense of racial duty and respectability; I will in all these ways aim to uplift my race so that, to everyone bound to it by ties of blood, it will become a bond of ennoblement, and not a byword of reproach.

What both Miller and Thompson were doing with the "Oath" was less about wartime loyalty than about everyday Race values. The oath was an elaborate statement of the black middle-class ethos. "Note," Thompson insisted, "the high standard of morals."[18]

Race literature of this sort transcended the war effort. It was about gaining democracy at home. By linking black patriotism with black-middle class ideals, African American leaders tried to jar the racial assumptions of white Americans. Thompson urged white readers to change their minds about black people, to question the justifications proffered for Jim Crow and race prejudice. The moment seemed right. As Burton Ceruti wrote to James Weldon Johnson in the midst of the war, "The hour is psychological, and all peoples of the globe are taking advantage of it."[19]

By mid-1918, when Du Bois wrote his famous "Close Ranks" editorial in the *Crisis*, urging African Americans to lay aside their domestic grievances until the war in Europe was won, black leaders in Los Angeles were getting increasingly restless; their ranks were beginning to split.[20] Joe Bass thundered, "The loyal Negroes in this country who have contributed their mite to the Liberty Loan, the Red Cross, [and the] Thrift Stamp, and are sending their sons many thousand strong across the briny deep to England and France to help to oust the Kaiser and make the world a decent place to live in are wondering if at this time Uncle Sam has any little word to offer in defense of her black sons in those states where the lynching of black men is a pastime." Angry that white nurses continued to protest against the admission of black nurses in the county hospital nursing school, and that qualified black nurses were being turned away by the Red Cross, Bass concluded that "these people . . . are tearing down democracy at home faster than the boys who are fighting for it in the trenches can build it up." In an editorial titled "Want More Democracy Here," Bass wrote, "unlike Mr. Dubois [sic], we are not keeping this grievance in cold storage until after the war; we are complaining now, and yearning for at least some . . . democracy."[21]

But again, did white people get the message? Late in the war, the *Los Angeles Times* ran "The Negro in the War," a series of stories supposedly from the front lines intended to amuse a white audience. Noting that "the black soldiers. . . . are among the bravest of the brave," the writer suggested those soldiers, "like our Irish friends," were "relied on to provide a good deal of the amusement" at the front. The articles included anecdotes, mostly about southern blacks speaking in thick dialect: a black sentry demands of a white general, "Who is you?"; another, when given the incorrect password replies, "Why, hell, dat ain't it, is it?"; a soldier from Georgia, meeting a black soldier from French Africa, says, "Can't you all talk plain nigger talk?"[22]

Yet one Los Angeles County supervisor did get the message and capture the spirit of black patriotism. While the local NAACP was fighting to get black women admitted to the county hospital nurse-training facility, the supervisor exclaimed: "We are waging a war for democracy—the principle that all men are created equal. Colored men are laying down their lives in France for the protection of our homes, our women and our children. There is a crying need for nurses both at home and abroad. Our high schools are graduating numbers of colored girls who are in every way fitted for this self-sacrificing service. It would be undemocratic and unpatriotic, not to say unchristian, to deny them equality of opportunity in this field."[23]

Frederick Madison Roberts

While women were seeking admission to the county nursing school, another black Angeleno was seeking a seat in the California statehouse. Born in 1879 in Harris Station, Ohio, an all-black community near Chillicothe, Frederick Roberts was the oldest son of A. J. Roberts and Ellen Wayles Hemmings. Ellen and A. J. moved to Los Angeles when Frederick was six; their arrival in the mid-1880s ensured them "pioneer" status. A. J. became a drayman; Ellen gave birth to two more children: Estelle, the middle child, and William, the youngest. A. J.'s business succeeded, and he moved into the mortuary business, first in partnership, then on his own. His funeral home prospered.[24]

An 1894 photograph shows Ellen, Frederick, Estelle, and William in front of their home at 606 East 5th Street. It is a small, simple, but solid-looking place, bathed in sunlight and surrounded by palms, eucalyptus trees, a white picket fence, and an explosion of climbing vines and small cedar bushes— all the essentials of a Southern California yard. Frederick dominates the photograph, at once casual and confident. His head is tilted slightly back, his chin up (this would become a characteristic pose)—a fourteen-year-old assured of his abilities and his future. At that time, other black families lived in the area, just south of downtown. But it was this neighborhood which, by the early years of the twentieth century, had turned into rougher turf— near the skid row and tenderloin. Like others in the emerging black middle class, the Roberts family moved southward to a bungalow at 1331 Wall Street, its front porch adorned with flowers and plants, its windows graced with lace curtains.[25]

Fred Roberts had a comfortable but not affluent upbringing, rather typical of the city's black middle class. A. J. and Ellen were well respected in the community, members of First AME. Frederick entered Republican politics even before he could vote, joining the Charles Sumner Marching Society, a political club, when he was seventeen. He was the first black person to graduate from Los Angeles High School, which was the only high school in town.

Afterward he enrolled at the University of Southern California, but didn't stay long. He enrolled in Colorado College, in Colorado Springs, where he excelled as both a football player and a student, graduating with honors. In 1907 he prospected briefly for gold in Nevada. Returning to Colorado Springs, he edited a Race paper, the *Colorado Springs Light,* and plunged into politics. He received a patronage position, deputy tax assessor of El Paso County, a post he held from 1907 to 1909. That year, in another abrupt change, he moved to Chicago, where he entered the Barnes School of Mortuary Science.[26]

Back in Los Angeles in early 1911, Fred soon established himself as an up-and-coming leader in the black community. A. J. Roberts and Sons now occupied a two-story Victorian home on Los Angeles Street and was a familiar institution for Afro-Angelenos. In 1911, Fred (unsuccessfully) sought a seat on the Los Angeles school board. In 1912 he purchased the *New Age.* Fred became active in First AME and in fraternal circles. In 1914, he was secretary of the local Dumas Lyceum Bureau, which was run by some of the city's top Race men and women, and whose mission was to bind "the East and West more closely by an exchange of noted Race talent." As a well-known mortician, newspaperman, and church leader, Roberts was perfectly suited to community politics.[27]

Roberts made the *New Age* a strong advocate of black civil rights. He was openly critical of Harrison Gray Otis's *Los Angeles Times,* once dismissing it as a racist rag. Roberts denounced the negative and stereotypical representations of dark-skinned peoples that he saw in white newspapers and advertisements. He took aim, for example, at the Anheuser Busch company for its "Race ridiculing ad posters" that were "plastered upon the city bill boards." He proposed boycotts and protests against the company. "If it were not for the possible lawlessness of such a course," he suggested, "the New Age would say that such advertising should be torn from the boards where ever Race men see it."[28]

In late 1914, as the ruthlessness of the European war was becoming evident, Roberts asked why the white press was portraying the war in Europe so differently from the recent U.S. battles with Mexico. During the Mexican Revolution, President Woodrow Wilson and the white dailies had condemned the "'Brutality of the Barbarous Mexicans.'" Now that the atrocities were taking place in Europe among white-skinned peoples, talk of savagery had all but vanished: "How odd there is not much said of this," Roberts wrote. For the white press, "the Mexican war was savage and uncivilized—European war is refined, a titanic struggle of enlightened nations. Such we would infer from expressions of the Press." War was always brutal, insisted Roberts, "be the scene Europe or Mexico." He was enraged by the double standard: "Oh, the consistency of the dominant, superior Race!"[29] Abruptly, Roberts's editorials ceased when an October 1915 issue of the *New Age* announced that he had accepted the presidency of the Mound Bayou Normal Institute—an all-black school in Mississippi. By the time the *New Age* reported the news, Roberts was already on the train heading east.

He appointed his sister, Estelle Roberts Sanders, as the new proprietor of the *New Age*. Estelle had married the son of William H. "Pop" Sanders, who was an influential black politico in the 74th Assembly District, an ally of Joe Bass. Estelle was a Race woman in her own right.[30] Somehow, though, the white progressive newspaperman E. T. Earl effectively took over the paper. This connection with Earl suggests that Fred Roberts had ties to the white progressive wing of the Republican Party; it certainly squares with his tendency to denounce Otis, who was Earl's political enemy. The connection to Earl did not help the *New Age* in Roberts's absence, however. The content turned to mush, and it became a Race paper in name only.[31]

Roberts's move to Mound Bayou had the effect of boosting his stock in the local community. A foreshadowing of his future could be seen in early 1916, when he returned to Los Angeles for a brief visit. Afro-Angelenos feted him as if he were a celebrity, escorting him on a whirlwind round of speaking engagements at churches and community organizations. He went back to Mississippi for only a year. When he returned to Los Angeles—this time permanently—Roberts restored the *New Age* to its former respectability and ascended to the top rung of community leadership. It was 1917, the war was on, and he was thirty-eight years old. He set his sights on the state legislature.

The Republican Primary

By the time Fred Roberts ran for the California assembly, Republicans in the 74th district had virtually no opposition. This was a recent development, however. From the early years of the twentieth century through the early 1910s, the city's Socialist Party, led by Westside intellectuals and professionals, grew increasingly popular in the working-class districts of the Eastside. The antilabor campaign led by Republican Harrison Gray Otis, as well as the antilabor stance of local Progressives, encouraged organized labor to join hands with the Socialists. The labor-socialists were overwhelmingly white, but some black leaders took an interest. In a move that stirred controversy within the black community, the Afro-American Council voted to stand with the left-labor coalition in the explosive mayoral election of 1911, which the Socialist Party had a chance to win. That election, captured by an alarmed and effectively mobilized Republican-Progressive coalition, would be the high point of Socialist politics in Los Angeles. In 1912, the Socialists split into warring factions and quickly their lost electoral potency. After that, Socialist candidates in the 74th Assembly District became also-rans. The Democrats were weaker still, having virtually no presence in the Central Avenue district and often failing to field a candidate for the assembly seat.

Because the Democrats and Socialists offered no real competition after 1912, only the Republican primary elections were of interest in the 74th district. And most voters were not interested even in those. Turnout was pitifully low. The district had some twenty thousand potential voters, but in the 1916 Republican primary, the incumbent won with only 948 votes. That incumbent was Frank Mouser, who held the 74th assembly seat from 1912 through 1918, but just barely. He owed his victory in the 1912 general election to the Socialist split. In the 1914 primary, he just squeaked by a black challenger. Two years later, William Greenwood, an up-and-coming white Republican, came very close to ousting the incumbent. In 1918, Mouser ran for state senate instead of the assembly. He did not endorse any of the candidates running for his vacant seat, so the Republican primary was wide open.[32]

The August primary became a free-for-all. Four white men filed for the Republican ticket, Greenwood being the acknowledged front-runner. The *Eagle* praised his concern for black constituents and noted that he was better than "a whole lot of them, who see us only about campaign times." But just when it seemed that Greenwood would be a shoo-in, everything changed.[33] In mid-July, Fred Roberts suddenly threw his hat into the ring. With the primary just over a month away, he announced his candidacy with little fanfare. The *New Age* offered only a simple political notice, positioned discreetly over an advertisement for Roberts and Sons Funeral Home. Roberts had kept his plans very close to the vest. The 74th Assembly District was a small world, and the *Eagle* habitually spread rumors about African American candidates, even if the source was casual street talk. Roberts's name had not been circulating. If it had, the Basses would have leaked it. Even Roberts's father-in-law, Pop Sanders, had no idea his son-in-law was going to run; he had committed himself to Greenwood's candidacy. Clumsily, Joe Bass reported that "the water has been [made] a little murky by the entry of Roberts."[34]

California politics could be that way because, in the early 1910s, insurgent progressive Republicans had taken over the state government and successfully broken up Southern Pacific Railroad's GOP machine. One result of this change was a new political structure for the state in which partisanship was weakened and traditional party organizations no longer had control over nominations. The progressives' "open primary" law allowed virtually anyone to enter an electoral contest, with or without the blessing of party leaders. Roberts himself had taken advantage of this system in the first open-primary election—in 1911—when, just back from mortuary school, he ran for the Los Angeles School Board. His campaign card sported a dignified photograph and his bold slogan: "Justice For All." He was bound to lose in the at-large election, but Roberts seems to have been announcing his return to town and testing the electoral waters at the same time.[35]

Roberts himself had been a Progressive, as had a notable core of other Race men, including Jefferson Edmonds, L. G. Robinson, John Somerville, and William Easton. The Basses had remained true to Otis and the Republican regulars, who disdained the Progressives, but even the *Eagle* got in the habit of placing issues over party allegiance. Once the Progressives had reshaped California's political system, the Republican factions more or less reconciled and continued their domination of the state, but not so monolithically. Shifting coalitions rose and fell with the political winds.[36] Roberts did not appear to be part of any coalition in 1918; he simply entered the race, apparently without backing from an outside interest.

It is worth speculating on Roberts's plan in 1918. Maybe he ran on a last-minute whim. Or maybe his late entry was a clever calculation: Since the rest of the Republican candidates were white, and for several months they had battled in the absence of a black contender, most white voters had probably committed to a candidate by the time Roberts entered the race. As the sole Race candidate, Roberts could expect strong black support, but he would need a divided white field. Had he filed early, a white backlash might have developed, and the weaker white candidates might have been urged to withdraw in favor of a single white candidate—probably Greenwood—who likely would have won. Instead, every white candidate stuck it out. Roberts made it a five-man contest: four whites, one black.

Joe Bass wrote appreciatively that Roberts "informs us that he will make a clean cut race on his merit as an American citizen."[37] Earlier in the decade, Roberts had focused his political articles in the *New Age* on "the Race vote" and the interests of "our group." But now he sought to transcend Race interests. In the spirit of wartime patriotism, he portrayed himself not as a leader for African Americans but as a candidate for all Americans. Joe Bass, too, had long been an advocate of Race-vote politics, but he now praised Roberts for promising to run "on the big and broad principle of American citizenship." Bass now insisted that neither white candidates nor black candidates should run on a platform that referred to skin color. "The time has come where running on your color should be cut out," he wrote. "Run as a man, and if there is a chance you have a much better show of getting that chance."[38]

The *Eagle* did not immediately fly to Roberts's camp. Joe Bass seems to have made an early pledge to Greenwood and sounded loath to break it. He tried to split the middle, praising Greenwood as an able candidate, and praising Roberts as the choice of "the plain every-day people." In the final weeks of the campaign, the *Eagle* cast the election as a battle between Greenwood and Roberts, the other Republican candidates being judged unfit because they had "absolutely ignored the colored press." Late in August, with the primary only a week away, the *Eagle*'s editorials still urged a careful consideration of both men—"Read their announcements, consider their claims, and vote your judgement."[39]

On the eve of the primary, the *Eagle* and the black community suddenly pulled out all the stops for Roberts. The Sunday before the election, Afro-Angelenos gathered at People's Independent Church to dedicate the silk flag that had been used to send off the city's black soldiers. Roberts was front and center at this "impressive and patriotic" event, the *Eagle* reported, and everyone had been impressed by his "inspiring remarks." That afternoon, the Sunday Forum held a special "Roberts Day" program, chaired by Joe Bass. The following Monday night, Charlotta Bass orchestrated a "Monster Mass Meeting" for Roberts at the Angelus Theater, which, again, was chaired by her husband. The *Eagle* proclaimed both events "a grand success."[40]

On election day, Roberts won a historic victory—by 173 votes. He collected a total of 651 ballots—34 percent of the Republican vote. The runner-up was Peter H. Muller, who tallied 478 votes, ten ahead of a disappointed Greenwood. The other two Republicans were far behind. The low turnout helped Roberts, who had the best-organized group. But for an off-year election, especially one in which the district's military men were absent, the turnout was greater than one might have expected. More than 2,100 Republicans cast votes in the 1918 primary; fewer than 1,500 had done so in the presidential-year primary in 1916. The black community's strong support for Roberts inflated the 1918 turnout, helping tilt the primary in his direction. Predictably, he ran strongest in the precincts clustered around Central Avenue, south of 7th Street, the most heavily black areas of the district.

But Roberts had white support, too. He was the top vote-getter in several precincts west of San Pedro Street, where virtually no African Americans lived. He did most poorly in the southwest quadrant of the district, where the runner-up, Muller, dominated the precinct totals. Those same precincts would deliver a strong anti-Roberts vote in the general election, which means that Muller probably played the race card for white support in the primary. Greenwood, the white Lincoln Republican who had courted biracial support, got caught in a grinder. Without Roberts in the race, Greenwood would have won the black vote, topped Muller, and gone to Sacramento. Without Muller in the race, Greenwood would probably have won the more bigoted ballots by default, and therefore beaten Roberts. But Muller drew away the party's white bigots, while Roberts siphoned off Greenwood's Negro votes, thereby pushing the early front-runner to third place.

Normally, the winner of the Republican primary would take the general election with little to no opposition. In 1918, the five non-Republican candidates in the primary—combined—won only 9 percent of the vote in the 74th district. Barring massive and unprecedented defections from the Republican camp in the general election, Roberts would win a seat in the statehouse. As the *Eagle* put it, "Heretofore this nomination has been the equivalent of an election; therefore there is no reason to say otherwise in this instance. The people, regardless of race or creed, gave to Roberts a most splendid support."[41]

"Simon Pure Democracy"

But there was a backlash. Frank E. Gayhart, an old-fashioned Democrat who ran a cigar stand, stepped up to challenge Roberts on racial grounds. Gayhart had run for the state legislature in 1916, but he had lost his own party primary to the Republican incumbent Frank Mouser, who had cross-filed as a Democrat. Gayhart refused to enter the 1918 primary; he won ten write-in votes anyway. Peter Muller, who had placed second to Roberts in the Republican primary, had cross-filed as a Democrat and won that primary with forty-one votes. It was as far as Muller could go. Because he was a registered Republican, and because he had lost his own party's primary, Muller was by law ineligible to stand in the general election under another party label. That meant that the members of the Democratic Party's County Central Committee could tap any Democrat they wanted to stand for election in November. They chose no one at all.

The Democrats' refusal to designate a candidate was a sign of weakness, to be sure, but it was also a bit of cunning. They apparently decided that their best chance of beating Roberts was with an "independent" candidate— a Democrat in disguise, whose party label would be palatable to any Re-

publican who wished to cast an antiblack vote. The law allowed independent
candidates to run in the general election as long as they had not run and
lost in any primary election. Because Frank Gayhart had not been a candidate in the Democratic primary, he was eligible to challenge Roberts as an
independent. Roberts's other challenger was the Socialist candidate, but the
Left would generate only its usual antiestablishment vote and have no real
impact. The contest, then, boiled down to Roberts versus Gayhart, party loyalty versus race.

Frank Gayhart's campaign message was simple: he was white, Roberts
was black. Hence the slogan written on his campaign cards: "My opponent
is a nigger."[42] When the *Eagle* got wind of Gayhart's tactic, Joe Bass branded
him a "cringing coward" and "the most despised man in this whole district."
Bass drew on wartime rhetoric to oppose Gayhart. Men of all colors had died
in Europe for "the great principle of democracy," Bass fumed, but Gayhart
was bringing "pro-Germanism" into the 74th district. Tapping into more
familiar political language, Bass condemned Gayhart's "Vardaman platform."[43] Vardaman had opposed the enlistment and draft of black soldiers;
he thought a Negro in uniform was a "darky" who had forgotten his place.
That, in essence, is what Gayhart and his followers thought about Roberts.
They could live with a Republican representative, but not a "nigger" representative. In their view, Roberts had gotten uppity. It was time for the white
men in the West to follow the example of the South; that was Gayhart's
campaign message.

In truth, there were plenty of ordinary, everyday Vardamans who had been
reared in the North and West, and black Angelenos knew that. Racism had
never been simply a southern import. It came at black Angelenos from all
corners of the city, from all types of people. Fighting race prejudice required
blacks to identify a foe, an enemy with a name or an ideal—Vardaman,
Germanism—a force of wrongdoing that whites of goodwill would readily reject. Politically speaking, however, white southerners were not the immediate problem, at least not in the 74th district, for they constituted only
a tiny portion of possible voters. The real question concerned the overwhelming majority of whites in the district. With party loyalties eroded
by progressive politics, would white Republicans stick with their party or
their race?

Despite Roberts's generally progressive-Republican past, the *Times* supported him, urging Republican voters in the 74th district to rebuff Gayhart.
A *Times* editorial insisted, "Mr. Roberts won on his merits and should be
elected for the same reason." Another article on the contest noted that
"someone tried to start something against a man because of his color, and

[the voters] declared against such sedition. As a matter of fact, the man of color no doubt was the strongest candidate in his Assembly district, and when elected may be expected to represent his bailiwick with honor."[44] "When elected" was a boast, not a confident prediction, given the unpredictable situation. But the *Times* turned out to be right.

Roberts won, although not overwhelmingly. His 2,261 votes just missed being a majority—49 percent. Gayhart collected 1,778 votes, the Socialist candidate nearly 550. Gayhart's campaign of bigotry had its effect at the polls, but in an unexpected way. The total of non-Republican ballots cast in 1918 was just about what it had been in each assembly election during the 1910s. There was no surge toward Gayhart; he simply earned the usual ineffective opposition vote. What changed in 1918—and what made the general election unusually close—was that Republican turnout dropped noticeably. Roberts's vote total fell several thousand ballots shy of Mouser's vote totals in 1914 and 1916. Apparently, Republican voters uncomfortable with a black nominee chose not to vote at all. The good news for the black community was that Roberts had enough support to triumph anyway.[45]

The number of whites who cast ballots for Roberts cannot be judged effectively, but local observers, including Pearl Roberts, Fred's wife, believed that white support had been essential to the victory. For most white Republican voters in the district, party meant more than race. That was a victory of no small proportions for Afro-Angelenos. To be sure, many white Republicans had refused to vote for Roberts, and some doubtless had cast ballots for Gayhart, but the undeniable fact was that Roberts had triumphed with biracial support.[46]

"Real simon pure democracy if you please reigns in the 74th," the *Eagle* crowed in its jubilant coverage of the victory. Roberts's election, wrote Joe Bass, was "a practical demonstration of real democracy, for be it known, without the support of a very considerable part of the White voters in this District the election of Mr. Roberts would have been impossible." To be sure, Bass added, the 74th had "a great big colored population," but "the same does not by any means exceed that of the White people, therefore the victory for democracy is clean cut and unquestioned." The *Times* added its own enthusiasm. Deeming Roberts "eminently qualified for the position," the daily insisted, "He is highly educated and no doubt will serve with honor to himself and the district. . . . Those who would inject race prejudice into the fight placed Gayhart in the race, but he was badly defeated." With unintentional irony, the *Times* concluded that "the election of Frederick M. Roberts, a colored man in the Seventy-fourth Assembly District, shows that the voters used no little discrimination."[47]

The Promise of Politics

When Frederick Roberts took office in January 1919, the obvious question was whether one black legislator could have any impact on California's racial polity. Roberts did not waste time wondering. He quickly brought civil rights to the fore, introducing Bill No. 693, which aimed to strengthen the state's nineteenth-century civil rights law. The old law allowed those convicted of racial discrimination in public places to escape with minor civil punishment. Expensive and time-consuming cases brought against white restaurant owners, shopkeepers, and theater owners would, if successful, produce only a slap on the wrist. No effective legal or financial incentives compelled whites to uphold the equal-accommodation statutes. Roberts sought to change that by mandating fines of not less than one hundred dollars, with no upper limit, for convicted offenders. The bill made it to the assembly floor, found plenty of support in both houses, and soon became law.[48]

Beyond civil rights, Roberts also proved a successful advocate on a broad range of issues affecting the average working family in his district. In the first month of the legislative session he introduced seventeen bills, most of them intended to provide better services for average citizens (better sanitation and schools, for example) and to protect ordinary people from government misdeeds (such as land seizures and overtaxation). This legislative agenda, as Hugh Macbeth pointed out in the local Race papers, "gives the lie to those white Americans who have contended that a Negro American could think only in terms of black." Roberts also got his chance to do something for prohibition other than editorialize. Almost as soon as he reached Sacramento, the national prohibition amendment came to a vote in the statehouse. He voted yea, despite the liquor interests in his district. Roberts thus proved himself an energetic, influential, and independent legislator in his first term. His civil rights law helped his black constituents, as indicated by the increasing number of convictions and fines handed to civil rights violators in the following decade, and his other legislative efforts targeted the needs of his broader constituency.[49]

Shortly after Roberts took office, Afro-Angelenos also witnessed some success in the realm of symbolic politics. When the war ended, Marshal Stimson held a "demobilization banquet" for his Four-Minute Men at the elite Hotel Alexandria. All were invited to feast and be honored for their patriotic service to the cause of liberty. Stimson was not the sort to think twice about inviting the African American patriots, but those Race men must have wondered, privately, whether there would be any incidents. By California law, no hotel could bar black people on account of race, but it was under-

stood that most white-owned hotels did just that, especially those establishments that catered to the elite. But there were no incidents. A photograph taken at the banquet shows several of the black Four-Minute Men
scattered throughout the crowd of white men. Douglass Greer sits at an otherwise all-white table, as does Charles Alexander. Hugh Macbeth is shown
next to Fred Roberts, who was attending in place of someone who could not,
and the rest of their table was white. Everyone at those tables—black and
white alike—looked as if they thought a mixed-race banquet was entirely
normal. It was not normal, of course, and that was the point. Here was a
small but not insignificant advance for Race leaders, one achieved through
the patriot ideal.[50]

A more public display of white respect for black citizenship occurred
after Theodore Roosevelt died in early 1919. His passing set off a flurry of
memorial services nationwide. In Los Angeles the warriors of 1912—
Stimson in the lead—organized a program at Exposition Park. Fifteen thousand people came to pay their respects. Black Angelenos were unusually
prominent on the program. The Reverend H. D. Prowd, pastor of Second
Baptist, read a formal resolution from the Interdenominational Colored
Ministers' Alliance on behalf of "all the Colored People of Los Angeles."
The resolution called Roosevelt God's "gift to the Nation" and described
him as "the strongest, most conscientious and fearless defender of human
rights and liberty."

The Reverend A. P. Shaw, pastor of Wesley Chapel ME, offered a stirring, long-remembered eulogy. Stimson kept a copy of Shaw's speech and
recalled, many years later, that it still brought tears to his eyes. "The world's
great men," said Shaw, "transcend the bounds of caste, class, race, and even
of time and space and become the common heritage of all men in all ages."
As examples, Shaw offered the Jewish patriarch, Abraham; Booker T. Washington; and Abraham Lincoln. Shaw saw in Roosevelt that kind of great-
ness. "When any race produces a man dedicated to that splendid democratic
doctrine and practice of 'All men up and no man Down,' you may rest assured
that the colored people delight to honor him, and when gone, to revere his
sainted memory. Such a man was Theodore Roosevelt."[51]

Like many other blacks at Exposition Park, Shaw knew well that Roosevelt had not always been a true ally of African Americans, but the memorial service was no time to dwell on that. His speech, viewed from a distance, suggests he had deeper goals in mind than merely paying respects to
an erratic political ally. Shaw's oration deftly recalled the history of black
patriotism. In the middle of his conventional eulogy, the minister shifted
seamlessly into a dramatic conversation between black America and the de-

parted president. "You tell us that our Black Boys saved your life in that wild charge up San Juan Hill," he said to Roosevelt. "We tell you that we would freely sacrifice ten thousand lives to save one life such as thine." More than that, Shaw drew attention to the potential of the moment—both in Los Angeles and around the globe. The first sentence of his speech noted that the memorial itself—visibly interracial—was "made possible by the true spirit of democracy among us." He referred to "these marvelous times," in which the Allied leaders—Wilson, Lloyd George, and Clemenceau—had met in Europe to create a new world. In this new world, humanity would be cast in new molds—molds, Shaw said, that are "larger than racial and even national" identities. Roosevelt, he suggested, would approve of this effort to create a new global order, in which racial molds were cast aside. Roosevelt was the kind of man who "rises above the narrow confines of race and class sympathies and breathes the pure atmosphere of equal justice and opportunity to all men."

Shaw's speech "electrified the vast throng," the *Eagle* proudly reported. Never before had so many white Angelenos heard a black man deliver an oration, and Shaw had crafted a singularly useful interpretation of Roosevelt's ideals and legacy, with clear implications for American race relations. In Shaw's telling, Roosevelt had always been a spirited leader for black civil rights. Shaw's final words, spoken as if to Roosevelt himself, were: "We are assured of the fact that your strenuous spirit so accustomed to activity cannot die; and that your soul so full of the love of God and humanity is still marching on and your illustrious works will ever follow you." Theodore Roosevelt was not all that, but Shaw's larger intent was to challenge white Los Angeles to live up to Roosevelt's higher ideals.[52]

The War Comes Home: 1919

Only days after Fred Roberts won the 74th's assembly seat in November 1918, Germany surrendered and signed the armistice that ended the war. The *Times*'s huge banner headline simply said: "PEACE." As the new year dawned, President Wilson sailed to France to begin the peace negotiations, accompanied by a small army of American journalists, including W. E. B. Du Bois, all anxious to watch the architectural work on the new, democratic world order. For Americans, including African Americans, it was a moment of such high purpose and high promise that, when the postwar promise quickly blew to bits, it left millions of Americans deflated and disillusioned. Suddenly, it seemed, the world had been made safe not for democracy but for squabbling European nations, most of them wretched in grief, churning with political and economic turmoil, and hungry for traditional revenge and imperial power. When Wilson returned home, the Senate refused to ratify the Versailles Treaty. The president, fervently crisscrossing the country to win public support for his peace plan, suffered a stroke. Less than two months later, the Senate rejected the treaty. More than fifty thousand American men had died in six months of fighting, for this.

For African Americans, the disillusionment ran even deeper. The federal government later mandated that the official name for the conflict would be the "World War," but for black Americans the war's legacy was less global than domestic. That black patriotism would not be rewarded with racial equality became painfully obvious, as black soldiers in France received the full Jim Crow treatment from the U.S. Army during the demobilization process. As early as February 1919, the *Eagle*'s front-page headline sought to enlist the community for the civil rights battle on the home front: "Volunteers Needed in the Army of Justice." An editorial insisted that black patriotism must now be channeled into fighting racism in their country.[53]

While black soldiers enjoyed warm welcomes in their own communities, they met hostile, sometimes deadly, receptions in white America, especially in Dixie. Throughout the South, whites murdered black veterans *because* they were black men in uniform, the "strutting Negroes" Vardaman had warned them about. The *Eagle* was particularly outraged by events in Texas, where white mobs lynched black men and women and burned them at the stake. It was, Joe Bass thundered, "a most damning conviction of the crackers and red necks of Texas." Virtual race war in Arkansas also seared the emotions of Afro Angelenos. "We can now understand," Bass said, "what a prominent statesman meant when he said that if he had to choose between living in Texas or Arkansas or 'Hell' that he would, without hesitancy choose 'Hell' to live in." President Wilson, traveling through Texas to win support for his League of Nations plan, refused even to mention the issue of lynching or race violence, even though it was happening all around him. E. L. Dorsey, a black writer in Los Angeles, later sent a piece to the *Eagle* sarcastically praising Wilson for finally speaking a word against race riots and in support of black veterans—while he was campaigning in *Billings, Montana!*[54]

The most alarming trend in 1919, especially for African Americans who had already fled Dixie, was the wave of antiblack violence outside the South. The East Saint Louis riot of 1917, it turned out, had been only a prelude. Race riots erupted in more than two dozen cities, including Chicago, Omaha, and Washington, D.C. The summer of 1919 came to be called the "Red Summer," because of the anticommunist Red Scare that swept the country. African Americans used "Red Summer" in a different sense, because the riots, lynchings, and murders spilled so much black American blood.

The most deadly and destructive riot hit Chicago, a city whose working-class neighborhoods had been transformed by the Great Migration. In the final week of July, after an unpremeditated incident at a segregated swimming area sparked smoldering racial tensions, mobs of white workers roared into black neighborhoods. They quickly discovered that the Negroes fought back with equal force. The result was a city virtually at war. Joe Bass, along with Race leaders throughout the nation, praised black Chicago for taking a stand. "All peoples have been schooled [by] . . . a world's war for Democracy, they expect it, they want it, they will fight for it and if necessary will die for it. . . . [T]he Negro has reached that stage where he will no longer submit to gross indignities without retaliating in kind." Bass also warned that Angelenos should not be smug about their own conditions; "Like Nero, who idly fiddled while Rome burned, many of us out here in the new West are feasting and dancing to the tune of the white man."[55]

Los Angeles escaped riot, but Afro-Angelenos had little need for Joe Bass's warning. They were shaken by the nationwide upsurge in racial hatred. Rumors circulated that a drunken off-duty police officer had threatened a black club owner, saying, "There will be a worse riot here than there was in Chicago." The local NAACP sent Beatrice Thompson on a fact-finding mission to Omaha and Chicago. The Reverend Charles Edward Locke, the white president of the NAACP's local branch, decried white racism in an essay on the riots published on the front page of the *Eagle*. "The underlying cause of race riots," he wrote, "is bitter and uncontrolled race prejudice." Black soldiers had fought nobly for the United States and still had not received their justly deserved rights of citizenship. "The white race, which so loudly proclaims freedom and democracy, and yet deprives the Negro of his political privileges, is largely to blame for race riots," he insisted. Local blacks eagerly bought up the October *Crisis*, in which Walter White, the black Atlantan who was rising quickly in the national NAACP, gave his report on the Chicago tragedy.[56]

The Reverend Benjamin C. Robeson, having served in the trenches with the 369th Infantry, returned to Los Angeles a bitter and disillusioned man. As early as March 1919, he grimly predicted race riots in the coming months. Of the returning black veteran, he wrote: "He returns with the gleam of victory in his eye, wanting his just reward. Contrary to his expectations he perceives no apparent change, but finds the murky waters of prejudice still stagnant, and [is] commanded, in ungrateful tones, to drink therefrom. The feeling engendered needs no description." In October, after his prediction came true, he wrote a long essay for the *Eagle* titled "Heaven, Hell, or Democracy," in which he reminded readers that "a more optimistic soul never went to war." He was optimistic no more, but he was determined. "Our concern now is democracy. We want America to give us a square deal, a chance to work out our destiny without fear or favor. We have helped to save Europe, we would now save the land we love. . . . We fought no sham battle," he insisted, "and we will have no sham democracy. . . . We have fought upon a foreign battlefield for the sake of others and buried our dead beneath the foreign soil. By the great Jehovah we will fight our own battles at home, and if necessary, bury our dead beneath America's upturned sod."[57]

That November, Robeson took a journalistic tour through the South, sending reports back to the *Eagle*. From Memphis, he wrote, "The white man in the south is still the same," but also that the new "do or die spirit on the part of the Negro makes [the white man] fearful, not only of his life, but the false civilization he has so bloodily built up." This new spirit among southern blacks, Robeson thought, would lead to a new "Reconstruction." Shortly thereafter Robeson found himself in Arkansas directly in the wake of the Elaine Riot, a lethal shooting war between rural blacks and whites. Still wearing his army uniform, Robeson immediately drew the attention of local whites but somehow escaped harm. As Robeson saw it, "Arkansas is simply trying to out-Germany Georgia. I must confess she is running well." But what really struck Robeson, and heartened his veteran's soul, was the sheer intensity of the black people who would literally fight and die rather than live in fear of southern whites. "The south today is trembling," he wrote, and he did not mean the black South. "The day may seem dark but not so," he reported the following week. "The Negro with a more determined spirit proudly lifts his head. . . . [T]his is really the dawn of a beautiful day."[58]

Whether or not the war had actually changed white racial attitudes or behavior, America's entire wartime experience—from the Great Migration to Red Summer—had clearly changed black America. It stripped away several thin layers of patience; it created a tangible restlessness among both black leaders and the ordinary rank-and-file; it deepened black distrust of white Americans, bolstering black nationalism and the group-economy idea. It made African Americans from all walks of life more outspoken about their rights, and less willing to suffer racial insult.

The Arthur Valentine Incident

On May 31, 1920, Arthur Valentine and his extended family decided to spend the Memorial Day holiday by the Santa Monica seaside. The city of Santa Monica planned a bonanza-size celebration of American patriotism that day, with flags flying, puffy speeches ringing, fireworks exploding. Arthur Valentine, a young black man, was a chauffeur by trade. He and his wife and children lived at 1546 East 23rd Street, a few blocks south of the 74th district, just west of San Pedro Street, in a mostly white neighborhood. There seemed to have been no racial conflict in that integrated neighborhood, but the beaches were another story.

At Santa Monica there was sign that bluntly asserted Negro exclusion. Maybe Arthur Valentine was tired of such signs. Maybe he believed that the patriotic fervor of the day would erase the color line, if only for that day. Maybe he just decided to take his own stand for democracy. One thing is certain: he and his family crossed the line in Santa Monica. They settled in for a picnic in the whites-only section.

What happened in the next violent moments is difficult to pin down, given the fragmentary evidence available. It is clear that three sheriff's deputies approached the Valentine group: Miller Cooper, his brother Archie M. Cooper, and Frank Dewar. They were heavily armed, as court records would later show, with "two loaded rifles, one loaded shotgun, one loaded revolver and one sap stick or police club." They demanded that Valentine's group leave immediately, stating that "niggers" were not allowed on Santa Monica beach. Valentine and his friend, Horace Walker, made it clear they were not leaving. One deputy picked up and tossed aside a small black child who got in their way. Valentine, according to the officers, "drew or attempted to draw his gun," whereupon the deputies began to beat him. Then one of the deputies shot him, apparently with the revolver. It was not a fatal wound. The deputies beat him some more.[59]

Valentine filed a complaint with the county's Civil Service Commission, which notified the sheriff's department of his charges. In response, the sheriff's department filed suit against Valentine, charging him with assault with a deadly weapon. At that point, the Civil Service Commission dropped its investigation of the officers. When the sheriff's department hauled Valentine before the bar that July, he pleaded not guilty. That August, the superior court judge, acting on the motion of the county district attorney, dismissed the case.[60]

Valentine then presented his side of the incident to the newly elected county district attorney, Thomas Lee Woolwine, who, having previously served as D.A. from 1916 to 1918, had become popular in the black community for his policy of equal treatment before the law, regardless of race. Woolwine collared the deputies for "assault with a deadly weapon to do great bodily harm" and presented Valentine's case to the county grand jury. On November 12, 1920, the grand jury indicted the officers, who now faced felony charges in *The People of the State of California v. Miller Cooper, A. M. Cooper, and Frank Dewar*. Black Los Angeles no doubt felt heartened by Woolwine's decisive action. A district attorney willing to slap felony charges on racist and abusive deputies was reason for optimism. But the violence behind those charges was part of a larger pattern that was making it increasingly difficult for African Americans to hold any hope for the future.[61]

The Election of 1920

The police assaulted Valentine just as Fred Roberts was preparing for his re-election campaign. Like the Red Summer of 1919, the Santa Monica attack boded ill for California's only black legislator. Despite his impressive first-term record, and despite the racial harmony at the memorial service for Theodore Roosevelt, he and his supporters doubtless expected a white backlash against him in the 74th district. The big question was whether he could win the Republican primary that August. He had captured the primary in 1918 partly because several white opponents had split the dominant white vote. Could he prevail in the 1920 primary if white leaders organized a campaign around a single white candidate, such as William Greenwood? How would Roberts approach the campaign? What would his platform be? Would he draw upon the now-weary Super Patriot line?

William Greenwood returned to challenge Roberts in the primary, and again, if he had been Roberts's only challenger, he might have won. But there was a second white candidate, one John Dormer. No black challengers emerged, so the Republican primary pitted the incumbent against the party stalwart Greenwood and the newcomer Dormer. It was a presidential election year, and the servicemen were back in town, so turnout was expected to be higher than in 1918; but it was impossible to predict how the increased numbers would affect the outcome.

As it happened, Greenwood won a few hundred more votes than he had in 1918, but his gains paled in comparison to Roberts's. The incumbent doubled the votes he had won in the 1918 primary. Dormer finished third, not far behind Greenwood. Once again, the combined total of votes for the white candidates exceeded the total for Roberts, so it might be argued that a white split had again given Roberts the edge. Dormer seems to have appealed mostly to the white Republicans who placed race over party. He did best in the district's southwestern precincts, where the Democrat, again Gayhart, was most popular. As a result, Greenwood and Roberts once again courted the same constituents—blacks and moderate to liberal whites. Dormer's campaign unintentionally helped undermine the racists' own goal, because his candidacy robbed Greenwood of white votes. Roberts won 1,310 votes to Greenwood's 782.[62]

In the November general election, Roberts faced the same two candidates he had faced in 1918. This time Frank Gayhart, having run unopposed in his party's primary, ran openly as a Democrat. The Socialist nominee was a non-factor, especially after the Red Scare. The critical question for Roberts was whether the racial violence of 1919 would tilt the scales toward Gayhart. It seemed incomprehensible that a Democrat could win in the 74th, but most things about the postwar racial fallout had been incomprehensible.

The general election proved oddly anticlimactic: Roberts won easily, with 56 percent of the vote. He collected 3,720 ballots, nearly 1,500 more than he had won two years earlier. And unlike 1918, the combined total for Gayhart and the Socialist candidate did not surpass the tally for Roberts. Viewing the results at the precinct level adds another layer of understanding. Although the precinct boundaries from 1920 and 1918 were different, preventing a direct comparison, a map of the precinct results shows that Roberts clearly expanded his base of support in 1920. Only the die-hard antiblack neighborhoods in the southwest part of the 74th gave majorities to Gayhart. Roberts not only enhanced his already strong support in the central and southern part of the district, he also won majorities in many more precincts in the northern tier of neighborhoods. And he did so despite no significant change in the racial compositions of those neighborhoods.

Roberts won more white votes in 1920 than he had in 1918. In the wake of 1919, that was no small feat, even in Los Angeles. Fred Roberts was a political marvel: an African American politician with an expanding biracial constituency.[63] But Roberts's reelection raised questions. If whites were so racist, why were so many willing to vote for a black man as their state representative? If whites were not so racist after all, why were they so unwilling to have a black family move in next door? If Roberts could sit next to whites in the statehouse, why couldn't Arthur Valentine and his family sit next to whites on the beach in Santa Monica? Few white people in Los Angeles, or anywhere else for that matter, seemed willing to face such questions. They were tired of social problems.

As Roberts won reelection, American voters elected a new president, the dull, do-nothing Republican Warren Harding. After two decades of progressive crusades, capped by a devastating war and bitter postwar fallout, Americans seemed numb. Most breathed a sigh of relief when Harding promised a return to "normalcy." But that was the last thing African Americans wanted. "Normalcy" meant that the government would continue to ignore lynchings. Normalcy meant that the Jim Crow South would continue to oppress blacks, and that racial equality would continue to decline in northern and western cities. It meant that white minds would hold the same negative assumptions about black people; that white immigrants could assimilate toward power and prestige in ways that black citizens could not; that the American caste system would remain firmly in place. Normalcy. Black Americans did not want that. In 1917, they had hoped the war would shove the nation away from what was normal toward a new social order of equal opportunity. But from the vantage point of 1920, it was difficult for American Negroes, perhaps even Fred Roberts, to remember what that hope had felt like.

- - - -

The war for democracy failed to improve the lives of black Angelenos, and in many respects it only made them worse. Negro soldiers in France, black patriotism on the home front, and African American calls for democracy at home had somehow elicited a deep resentment within white America. Rather than changing the hearts and minds of white America, black sacrifice for the nation seemed only to infuriate many white people. Black patriotism met blatant rejection from the American mainstream. Among African Americans, that hurt ran deep.

Whether Los Angeles still offered hope was unclear. California's political stream had been redirected a bit by Roberts's civil rights law. Then, too, modern Los Angeles was still an urban adolescent, still largely unformed. The boom of the 1880s had transformed the sleepy town only thirty years before. Southern California possessed a certain capacity to grow and change with stunning rapidity. The black community felt the effects. By 1920, Biddy Mason's Los Angeles seemed almost ancient. Black migrants who arrived before 1900 were "pioneers." Even the Afro-American Council, defunct only since 1915, seemed a little quaint by war's end, so thoroughly had it been replaced by the NAACP.

The question was, could rapid change be channeled toward better racial conditions for the black community, or would it cut the other way? Some Afro-Angelenos were already complaining about decline, and sometimes they were right. But at the same time, black newcomers kept disembarking at the Southern Pacific depot and discovering good schools open to all, a row of beautiful Negro churches on Paloma Street, and a Race man in the state-house. Conditions in Los Angeles were always difficult to figure. While some whites cast ballots for a black representative, others sought to keep black women out of the county nursing school. There stood Reverend Shaw, touch-ing the hearts of thousands of white people at the memorial service for Theodore Roosevelt. There lay Arthur Valentine, beaten and shot on the Santa Monica sand. Which scenes reflected the real Los Angeles?

Fred Roberts pondered the question, knowing there was no simple an-swer. Elated over his reelection, he also knew what the war had failed to accomplish—and what 1919 had done to black America. He had achieved a political miracle in his hometown, but even he was not fully free; much of Los Angeles was still closed to him. He had more in mind than individual advancement. He would work for his people. Pausing for reflection after his victory in 1920, he penned an editorial. His words carried a tone of un-yielding determination, rather than unbridled hope. He thanked his sup-porters, then pointed them toward the future: "Suppose we all pull together now, and help make the country safe for Democracy."[64]

PART TWO

Civil Rights as a Way of Life

THE DAY-BREAKERS

We are not come to wage a strife
with swords upon this hill:
it is not wise to waste the life
against a stubborn will.
Yet would we die as some have done:
beating a way for the rising sun.

Arna Bontemps, 1925

6

Fighting Spirit
in the 1920s

In November 1920, Charlotta Bass became one of the vice presidents of the Los Angeles NAACP. The branch membership elected her to one of the loftiest posts in the city's foremost civil rights organization. At the same time, Charlotta was helping to establish a local division of the Universal Negro Improvement Association, the black-nationalist organization headed by New York's charismatic Jamaican immigrant Marcus Garvey. When the Los Angeles UNIA received its charter and elected its officers in January 1921, the members chose Charlotta as their "Lady President." The *Eagle*'s managing editor had become a top leader, simultaneously, in the city's biracial-integrationist organization and its black-separatist organization.[1]

For Charlotta Spear Bass, these honors affirmed the past decade of her life and set her on a course for ongoing civic engagement. Only ten years before, she had arrived in Los Angeles alone, a health seeker from Providence. Then came her fateful meeting with John Neimore and her growing commitment to his *Eagle*. Standing beside his deathbed, she had embraced Neimore's final request—that she keep the newspaper running and serve as an ambassador for her people. Then she had met and married Joe Bass, and the two had become a pair to be reckoned with. Running their newspaper on Central Avenue, sitting in the pews of Second Baptist, and finding a place among the city's Republican leadership, Charlotta and Joseph Bass were physically, spiritually, and politically at the center of black Los Angeles. Charlotta had become a Race woman of singular visibility and dedication.

Nevertheless, the 1920s proved a curious decade for her. She could not quite decide on a name for herself: she used Charlotta Bass, Charlotta Spear Bass, and Charlotta Spear interchangeably in the *Eagle,* switching from one to the other without explanation and suggesting a growing independence from her husband. Yet Joe Bass clearly remained the couple's political guide. Charlotta's presidency of the "ladies" of the UNIA did not mask the fact that Joe was the more visible leader in the Los Angeles Garvey movement. And when he later turned against Garvey, she followed his lead without dissent. On the other hand, she, not Joe, was elected to top offices in the city's leading race organizations, and she remained a political force in her own right. When Joe ran for the state assembly in 1928, she was his campaign manager and thought she had put him over the top. Instead, Joe lost miserably to Fred Roberts. Oddly, that defeat hurt Joe's reputation but not Charlotta's. From that point on, he would fade and she would rise higher. The 1920s were, for the Basses, a decade of uncertainty and change.

That Los Angeles needed changing was clear to both of them. They and others had risen to the top of the black-activist community, and the urban West had offered freedom enough to live a good life. But race prejudice—which blacks increasingly called "discrimination"—placed restrictions on what they could do and be. The color of their skin barred them from all but a few hundred feet of Southern California's pristine beaches. It barred them from meaningful employment in white-owned business and excluded them from countless clubs, hotels, restaurants, and theaters. They could make their home in only a small part of Los Angeles's sprawling residential areas. Anytime Charlotta sat down on a streetcar she might be accosted by a white person who demanded Jim Crow seating. Joe was always at risk of being beaten or arrested by white policemen—anytime, anywhere, for no reason. Race dictated that they and their people were all in the same boat. White people assumed, without even thinking, that blacks were inferior, poor, and immoral; that their lives were not intended for the center stage of American life. Race prejudice in Los Angeles meant that the Basses felt what the historian David Levering Lewis has called the "soul-weariness of living always under a white microscope."[2]

But how to change things? Charlotta's answer, and that of the city's Race leaders generally, could be found in her simultaneous involvement in the NAACP and UNIA. It was odd, to say the least, that she held leadership roles in both organizations. In their aims and outlooks, the NAACP and the UNIA stood in opposition to one another. The NAACP was dedicated to erasing the color line in all aspects of American life. Garvey's UNIA promoted black nationalism. Insisting that the Race could never be free within the dominant white society, Garveyites advocated black separatism in America and a "Back to Africa" movement. In New York, where both the UNIA and NAACP had their national headquarters, Garvey and Du Bois and their followers were virtually at war. But Los Angeles was not New York.

In black Los Angeles, the guiding ideal was pragmatic activism. Middle-class leaders embraced whatever seemed likely to help blacks live better lives in their half-free environment. The *Eagle* insisted on full racial equality in mainstream society through interracial political contests, legal battles, and organized protests. It also championed the group-economy model, Race-specific uplift campaigns, and cooperative movements to retain black wealth and power among their own people. Fred Roberts's *New Age* did likewise, putting a bucket into any likely pool of opportunity.

The *Citizen Advocate*'s approach to Garvey and the NAACP followed the same path. The *Advocate*'s founder and editor, Charles Alexander, was an NAACP loyalist who had served on the local executive board from the beginning. Nevertheless, in December 1920 he trumpeted the UNIA message with a front-page splash headlined "Marcus Garvey—Negro Moses . . . The Rise in the World of a Great Negro." The story that followed, penned by the New York UNIA headquarters, heralded Garvey and his aims in heroic tones. Alexander prefaced this UNIA promotion with his own encouraging introduction. "The most striking new figure among American Negroes is Marcus Garvey," he insisted. "His significance lies in the fact that he embodies and directs a new spirit of independence among the Negroes." Two issues later, Alexander's paper offered readers another front-page splash—a glowing report on the local NAACP.[3]

The ease with which black equal-rights crusaders in Los Angeles initially embraced Garveyism offers a clue to their basic approach to Race progress in the 1920s. They experimented. They borrowed ideas from an eclectic array of doctrines. Most leaders would abandon Garvey's UNIA before the year was out. But that, too, was part of the pragmatic approach; if an effort was not working, local black leaders cut their losses and tried something else. Black leaders in Los Angeles admired, and sometimes envied, the eastern civil-rights establishment, but they had a certain western tendency to go their own way. Afro-Angelenos listened to what Du Bois, Garvey, and others were saying, but they looked to themselves for guiding principles and appropriate strategies.

Flexibility was a necessary strategy for civil rights leaders in the 1920s. The "Roaring Twenties" proved a difficult decade for Americans who wanted to solve social problems, including racism. The engine of progressive reform, which had powered the crusades of the past two decades, lost steam after World War I. In mainstream culture, serious issues were out. Shameless consumerism and scandalous spectacle were in. Prohibition brought bootlegging dens and violent crime. The conservative reaction against these trends was swift and loud. Hate took organized form, and it was difficult for progressive reformers to be heard—all the more so if they were black.

In the 1920s Angelenos began to call their city "L.A."—a new appellation for a unique metropolis. "L.A." became the American Babylon, a wide-open city given to big spending, elitist decadence, and grand-scale corruption. Hollywood perfected the art of over-the-top pageantry, college students partied hard with bootleg gin, and consumerism triumphed. Carey McWilliams, one of L.A.'s wisest observers, recalled that "for Southern California the decade was one long drunken orgy, one protracted debauch." At the opposite pole of local culture, organized intolerance surged to the fore. The newly revived Ku Klux Klan, which was witnessing startling growth nationwide, came to town with the help of L.A. radio phenomenon "Fighting Bob" Shuler, a fundamentalist with roots in Dixie. Shuler supported the KKK and reached millions of adoring listeners with his denunciations of African Americans, Jews, Catholics, immigrants, drinkers, radicals, moderate politicians, and similar "aliens." The militant Right also organized the Better America Foundation, which hounded local reformers and radicals.[4]

In some ways, black L.A. partook of, and contributed to, the free-wheeling spirit. Afro-Angelenos bought automobiles by the score and took to the byways and beaches. Their social clubs hosted elaborate soirees. The sporting class bootlegged gin and offered painted ladies, paying off local officials to look the other way. Churches, civil rights organizations, and women's clubs all went in for pageantry and the "monster event." And then there was jazz. Jelly Roll Morton perfected his "New Orleans Style" in L.A., playing for what he called the "movie star trade" at the Cadillac Cafe (at 5th Street and Central Avenue), and then heading to Watts—no closing time there—to swing the rest of the night. He also made money from pimping his "Pacific Coast Line" of black women. The Black and Tan Orchestra from Texas also lit up Central Avenue, along with Kid Ory's Original Creole Jazz Band. The clubs along The Avenue lured wealthy Westside whites, too; "slumming" made for a titillating evening at the Apex nightclub. The Lincoln Theater, a large black-owned theater that opened at 23rd and Central in 1926, offered stunning stage shows and packed in black audiences on Saturday and Sunday nights.[5]

Many Race leaders frowned on the jazz scene, which smacked too much of frivolity and illicit sex for their conventional mores. In 1923, Joe Bass editorialized that "the world is going crazy with jazz, the modern histerical [*sic*] music has given mankind the rickets. It cannot soothe or refresh by its figgety [*sic*] strains. Nobody is satisfied, but everybody is restless and discontent—Jazzy music makes them so." Race leaders in L.A. found themselves caught between extremes. Not given to wanton excess or mass intolerance, they found themselves surrounded by both. Their demands for racial equality often got lost in the hubbub.[6]

J. C. Banks, elected president of the local NAACP in 1920, voiced concerns in his inaugural address. Alluding to the bitter racial fallout from the World War and predicting turbulence ahead, Banks warned that "whoever undertakes the social and political uplift of the Colored Citizen of the United States undertakes a tremendous task. And if the morale of the Colored man, particularly, depends solely upon his ability to determine the exact measure of progress he makes from day to day, he will fail, for in the present state of society we cannot advance so rapidly as we wish." He called on his audience to face the harsh reality that black advances in the "present state" of things would be limited and uncertain.

Banks then asked the critical question: "How shall the fighting spirit of the Colored man be sustained?" There was a way, he answered. Each black person must keep "securely in his heart a large element of faith—faith in himself, faith in humanity, faith in God. The same sort of faith that sustained our fathers and our mothers during the long and cruel night of slavery." Faith, duty, and history—that was Banks's message, and it fell on receptive ears. It was the essential creed of the city's black leaders. Activism was not simply a means to an end. It was their essential reason for living. Banks closed his address with a poem: "Right is right since God is God, / And right the day must win. / To doubt would be disloyalty, / To falter would be sin."[7]

Race women and men shouldered a heavy burden. To bear up under it, they had to maintain "the fighting spirit," even if the most likely outcome of their efforts was defeat and fatigue. Race leaders had to choose their battles carefully. Every day, week after week, year after year, blacks confronted race prejudice in all its various forms. To confront every instance would be overwhelming. To accept too many slights would be humiliating. To be a lifelong Race leader therefore required careful judgment, an abundance of patience, and an appreciation that one must pace oneself in order to be prepared for the battles that mattered most.

For these Americans, civil rights activism was not a "movement." It was not an exceptional moment in time. It was instead a way of life, an act of faith, a lifelong mission. To embrace that calling was to lead an exhausting life, much of it spent recovering from defeat. When the dueling forces of decadence and intolerance swept across Los Angeles, the city's Race leaders saw their faith and determination sorely tested.

The Tumult of '21

In late January 1921, the *Citizen Advocate* shouted, "Danger! Danger! Great Danger Ahead for the Negro—Ku Klux Klan in the North." The article that followed insisted, "If we are going to maintain our citizenship we shall have to contend for it. . . . Our white friends are becoming fewer and fewer each year, and if we depend upon them alone we shall be pushed back into serfdom. We must organize, organize, organize."[8]

Late that May, local blacks learned that the KKK had moved not just into the North but into Southern California itself. The daily *Examiner* had uncovered the Klan's plans to organize Los Angeles and all of the Pacific Coast. Burton Ceruti quickly notified the NAACP's national office and asked for "all available data relating to Ku Klux Klan, particularly statutes designed to suppress them . . . [and] exclude or prohibit them within limited territory." Walter White, now assistant secretary in the New York office, sent Ceruti recent literature on the revived Klan, a brief history of federal action taken against the Klan since Reconstruction, and a summary of all state laws intended to curb lynching and mob violence. He was pleased that "the California branches are actively on the job in stamping out this movement of organized lynching at its inception."[9]

Before Ceruti and the local NAACP could take up the task, though, an explosive collision of events in early summer brought Los Angeles to the brink of race riot. In early June, a white mob in Tulsa, Oklahoma, torched the city's black community. In the initial white assault, blacks fought back and checked the advance. But then the police force arrived to reinforce the whites. Backed by the power of the state, the mob burned down the black business district, then the homes of the wealthiest blacks, and finally the rest of the black neighborhoods. More than fifty square blocks of black property lay in ashes. In the process, the white mob murdered three hundred black residents.

More so than the Chicago riot of 1919, the Tulsa riot sent shock waves through black Los Angeles. Unlike black Chicago, the Negro community of Tulsa resembled that of L.A. Black Tulsa was largely middle class and noticeably prosperous, with nice homes and successful businesses. The ostensible motive of the white mob was the usual one—rumor of rape—

but Fred Roberts was closer to the mark when he claimed that the "simple reason" for the riot was that black Tulsa's "prosperity and intelligent development were becoming too evident to suit the wishes of a certain element of whites." Black progress had wrought not simply white jealousy but a racial pogrom. Whites rioted because black Tulsa was doing very well for itself. Black Angelenos were also doing well for themselves, and they were facing their share of white Okies and Texans. The parallels were ominous.[10]

L.A.'s population boom of the 1920s accompanied these growing tensions. The city counted 580,000 residents in 1920. Ten years later, local residents numbered 1.2 million. Put another way, seven new people joined the local population every hour of every day for ten years. County residents numbered more than two million by decade's end. Migrants continued to arrive by train, but now they also rolled in by automobile. Southerners—especially Texans—were a growing presence, but they remained a small presence compared to midwestern newcomers. The Jewish population grew—both the Yiddish-speaking group on the Eastside and the more assimilated element in Hollywood. Ethnic Mexicans flooded the city's Eastside, and the Japanese, whose numbers were checked by immigration restrictions, nonetheless saw a steady natural increase. A new group of immigrants began to arrive from the South Pacific: Filipino men, who came for jobs and adventure. As residents of an American protectorate, they had the right to come and go as they pleased, and they were a growing presence on Central Avenue.[11]

The city's black population more than doubled, from nearly 16,000 to just shy of 39,000. This increase of almost 150 percent made black Los Angeles the third-fastest-growing Race community in urban America. By eastern standards, the community was small; by western standards, it was huge. The black community of L.A. fell somewhere between regional norms. Demographically and culturally, it stood somewhere between the ghettos of the East and the small outposts of the West.[12]

Black Los Angeles continued to be heavily Texan. Of the migrants who arrived in the 1920s, one in four were from the Lone Star State. The urban connections held true as well: San Antonio, Dallas, Marshall, Tyler, and, increasingly, Houston sent black Texans westward. The "Home State News" column of one local Race paper, the *Western Dispatch,* carried plenty of news about Texas. Other states on Dixie's western edge—Louisiana, Arkansas, and Oklahoma—were next in the procession. Tulsa's conflagration sparked a sudden influx from Oklahoma. People born in these four states constituted nearly half of all black newcomers during the 1920s.[13]

As it happened, the same four states also sent most southern-born whites to L.A., so the fight over Jim Crow in the West intensified. Many whites from Oklahoma, Arkansas, and Texas moved into the working-class towns east of Alameda Avenue, such as South Gate, where they landed jobs in the industrial corridor that was emerging east of the river. These towns courted less-affluent white families, offering inexpensive lots and racial restrictions. As one civic leader from Home Gardens stated in 1925, "Home Gardens is a town of, by, and for workingmen—and we want hundreds more of them. The only restrictions are racial—the white race only may own property here."[14]

In the *California Eagle*, Hugh Macbeth urged black Angelenos to "prevent and eradicate the growth of southern prejudice in our state."[15] The local population remained overwhelmingly white and midwestern, but black and white southerners had the clearest racial agendas. To black southerners, the West promised freedom from Jim Crow. To white southerners, it promised new prosperity without any disruption of white supremacy. The two groups were locked in a struggle for the racial soul of Southern California, which helps explain the racial tensions that swept the Eastside in the summer of 1921.

The shock of the Tulsa riot had barely set in when L.A.'s Garrick Theater suddenly brought *The Birth of a Nation* back to the screen. Fred Roberts thundered that "the Clansman" was "not an entertainment, it is un-American propaganda" and was creating "the possibility of race trouble in this, our city of Los Angeles." L.A., he warned, could be the next Tulsa. Roberts blamed the Klan for the screening. "Might its exhibition at this time have any connection with the organization of the Ku Klux Klan so recently given publicity in our daily papers?" He urged the city's outgoing mayor, Meredith Snyder, to stifle any chance of race riot.[16]

In the third week in June, the *New Age* reported that the black community was on the verge of hysteria. A local judge had ruled in favor of a black woman—against a white Texas woman—in a case involving streetcar altercation; a black-on-white murder had occurred near 12th Street, heightening racial tensions. For many black Angelenos, those two events, occurring concurrently with the Tulsa riot, the arrival of the KKK, and the reissue of *The Clansman*, clearly suggested one thing—the imminent formation of a white mob. Rumors flew that black L.A. would get the "Tulsa treatment" on the Fourth of July, beginning with the wealthier West Jefferson homes. Fred Roberts, whose editorial the previous week had sounded the alarm, now urged his readers to calm down: groundless fears would only heighten the chances of a riot. The *Eagle* sent the same message more pointedly, with Joe Bass scolding local blacks for what he perceived as lower-class behavior: "Take that handkerchief off your head and be sane." He insisted that "this rumor is born of iniquity and has no foundation in spirit or fact." Angelenos should "pay no mind to this silly twaddle."[17]

Silly twaddle or not, Joe Bass was worried, and he devoted the front page of that same issue to an open letter by Hugh Macbeth, warning of racial violence if local officials did not act quickly. Macbeth addressed his plea to the mayor-elect, George Cryer, who would shortly take office. Tensions between blacks and whites in Los Angeles had been rising for months, Macbeth wrote, and "the newspaper accounts of the organization of the Ku Klux Klan here in Los Angeles, and the press accounts of the unspeakable Tulsa slaughter have but accentuated a situation which . . . was [already] serious enough to be alarming." He also condemned the *Examiner*'s "screaming headlines" of June 18 about a black man allegedly assailing a white woman in Los Angeles and a "'citizen mob assisting the police in a man hunt.'" Macbeth added that "for the last week there has been circulated among the colored citizens of Los Angeles a well defined rumor that [the] Los Angeles local of the Ku Klux Klan intended a public parade on July 4th." According to the rumor, the parade would "be the signal of an attack upon the Negro population of Los Angeles similar to the attack made upon the colored citizens of Tulsa."

Macbeth insisted the rumors were unsubstantiated but reminded Cryer that "once this violence is started—and it matters not that it be started by ignorant people of both races—our entire populace suffers." He himself would not "stand idly by and see a race riot situation precipitated in Los Angeles without strenuous effort on my part to prevent such an occurrence." He asked Cryer to appoint a committee of the "best colored and white people of Los Angeles" to lay rumor to rest, and to encourage daily newspapers to avoid the sensationalism that fostered "the primitive racial passions of one racial group as against another."[18]

The Fourth of July passed without riot, but tensions persisted and rumors continued to fly. Urging racial harmony, Joe Bass wrote that "the riot scare that is rife among us in Los Angeles at this time shows that our boasts of Christian civilization as practiced in this age [are] all wrong; for religion is love not rivalry." He asked white Angelenos to stop seeing blacks as competitors; the black American "is only asking that his passage be not blocked; in other words that he may be granted a place in the sun." He insisted that black Angelenos do their part to lay rumors to rest and act as good citizens. Slowly, the sense of panic would recede and a normal public mood would return, but not without an undercurrent of tension that never quite disappeared.[19]

Amid the tension, Burton Ceruti took aim at *Birth of a Nation*. Acting under authority of the local NAACP, he moved to have the film put back in the vault. Ceruti wrote a letter of protest to Mayor Snyder, who then urged his city prosecutor, Edwin W. Widney, to stop the film. Widney quietly called a private meeting, bringing together two leaders of the Moving Picture Producers Association and the owner of the Garrick Theater, which was the only place showing the film. Widney was pleased with the outcome. As he told Ceruti, all three men "were convinced of the necessity of removing the film from exhibition at the Garrick Theater, and also from further circulation." James Weldon Johnson praised Ceruti.[20]

The NAACP's victory flushed out the local Klan, which had been operating under cover since spring. When the Garrick shelved *Birth*, Widney received a hostile visit from William S. Coburn, the Grand Goblin of the KKK's Pacific States Division. Coburn was something of a missionary from Dixie; an attorney from the Klan's national office in Atlanta, he had recently moved to L.A. to build the organization on the West Coast. He castigated Widney and insisted that the film be shown in L.A., or else. Widney stood firm, alerted federal authorities, and took his story to the *Los Angeles Times*. In the first of what would become a torrent of anti-Klan articles, the *Times* quoted Widney as saying, "The gist of [Coburn's] remarks was that he considered it essential for white supremacy to exhibit that picture."[21]

That *was* the gist of it: *The Clansman*, the KKK, white supremacy, Tulsa if necessary—an effort to southernize the West. For Afro-Angelenos, it was not that Los Angeles had really been heaven, or that white supremacy was strictly a southern ideal. The problem was that the black faith in a West of greater equality and opportunity seemed suddenly to have been a false one. Fred Roberts stiffened his resolve and doggedly held to the Western Ideal. He predicted that neither "Los Angeles nor California will grant any lasting place to this 'Klan.' It is too un-American and *too much out of step with the spirit of the West*."[22]

The Klan in L.A.

The original Klan, exclusively southern, had been crushed by the federal government during Reconstruction. But the screening of *The Birth of a Nation* in Atlanta in 1915 inspired a band of Georgians to revive the secret society. After World War I, the "Second" Klan, which dubbed itself the "Invisible Empire, Knights of the Ku Klux Klan," rapidly spread across the nation, drawing mass followings in the cities of the North and West. These Klansmen and Klanswomen were lower-middle-class evangelical Protestants who perceived themselves as an embattled minority fighting off evil influences. Members from across the country converged in Washington, D.C., for a massive parade down Pennsylvania Avenue, robes on, masks off, American flags flying—mass intolerance gone respectable. The Second Klan targeted not only African Americans but also Catholics, Jews, bootleggers, political radicals, new immigrants, and the elite power structure that allowed such "aliens" to secure a place in American society. Klan members defined *American* as "white," and they restricted the term *white* to mean Protestants of old-immigrant stock who espoused a creed of cultural conservatism.[23]

Fresh from Atlanta, Grand Goblin Coburn was unprepared for the attacks waged upon him and the KKK by L.A.'s white newspapers. Without prompting from the black community, the dailies flailed the Klan. *Times* editor John Steven McGroarty went further, taking a stand for equal rights: "No class nor race can maintain any personal superiority over any other under the institutions of our government. What a mockery it would be if men were to be born equal in the American republic only to be compelled to submit to some self-imposed racial superiority as soon as they came into the world!" On his popular editorial page in Sunday's *Times Illustrated Magazine*, McGroarty would write: "When you consider that, man for man, in every way—in thrift, in property, in education, in art, in literature and in the highest forms of culture, the American negro stands equal today with the American white man, how can you fail to honor and respect him?" And yet, he said, white Americans "sneer at the negro. We have been taught to do so. And for that reason we do not know him and have not taken the trouble to find out what he has been doing. . . . But it must be a heart-breaking thing to be all that the best men ever were, to have brains, hearts and souls equal to the best that God has created, and yet to be sneered at."[24]

The KKK denounced blacks as criminal and reprehensible by nature, but McGroarty responded that "Los Angeles has now a greater colored population than any other Pacific Coast city; but our court records show that our colored citizens are, as a rule, close observers of the written law. They have not made themselves obnoxious to other races and the sections of the city in which they reside are neither immoral nor unsanitary. Hundreds of them own their own homes. One district has elected a colored Representative for two successive terms to the State Legislature and he has filled the position with credit to his people and to the State." Whatever the Klan claimed about "defend[ing] the Constitution," he wrote, "the term Ku Klux is associated with mobs formed for the purpose of terrorizing colored districts." Black Angelenos were "not accustomed to intimidation and, if it were attempted, they would be likely to organize to defend their rights."[25]

Black Angelenos grown accustomed to McGroarty's support frequently sent him personal letters of gratitude. Some clipped his editorials and read them to others in the community. James Vena sent "a word of encouragement . . . [for] you have been our life-long friend—faithful & true—not only to us but to your fellow-man whenever you see he needs you." Crystal Albright Marshall—"a busy wife and mother"—told him of her friend who had said: "The first thing I read on Sunday Morning is John Steven McGroarty's page—and I trust & pray that my two boys will grow up to be, if not as great men, at least as good men, as he." Now that the Klan had arrived, the Forum passed a resolution expressing the community's appreciation for the *Times*'s fight against it. John Somerville's message to McGroarty: "Those of us who are daily striving to take our places as men among men feel greatly encouraged and the burden seems a little lighter when we know that we have true friends who believe in us . . . and are big enough to tell the world that they honor and respect us."[26]

It was one thing for Klan leaders to face opposition from a white establishment dedicated to social order; it was another to have someone in McGroarty's position openly insisting that blacks were equal to whites. The *Times* editor hardly ruled L.A., but he reflected the difficulties the KKK would have working in the open. Indeed, public denunciations, as well as investigations by both the U.S. Attorney's Office and the FBI, forced Coburn's Klan to go underground for the rest of 1921 and the early months of 1922.

Two Trials, Two Defeats

As the Klan was emerging in L.A., Arthur Valentine's case against the sheriff's deputies who shot and beat him on Santa Monica beach in 1920 finally came to trial. Actually, the legal proceedings had been going on, erratically and very slowly, since the deputies were arraigned on November 13, 1920. Before the officers could enter their pleas to the charges, the case was transferred from department 18 of the superior court to department 15. Then the deputies pleaded not guilty, and the case was set to begin in mid-February 1921. When the court date arrived, the defense attorneys were successful in getting the trial date reset for May 13. On that date, they successfully requested that the trial date pushed to September. In September, the case was transferred from department 15 to department 12, and a new trial date was set: December 14, 1921, at which point it was *again* delayed at the request of the defendants. Then, prior to the next trial date, which was scheduled for February 27, 1922, the defense attorney, one S. S. Hahn, was disbarred for a breach of ethics, and the deputies were instructed to find another attorney. Finally, the trial actually began on March 8, 1922, nearly two years after Valentine was accosted.[27]

By March 1922, black Los Angeles was clearly anxious about the case. The same group of African American residents—including Dr. Wilbur Gordon, who apparently had treated Valentine's wounds—had received subpoenas each time a trial date was set, and they had to appear each time, only to have the trial put off again. At least one year prior to the actual start of the trial in March 1922, the Forum had created a committee to "inquire into further developments" of the case; as the committee reported each delay, its news doubtless sent ripples of concern through the Forum crowd and thence to the community.[28] These delays occurred in the aftermath of the riot scare and the emergence of the local KKK. Perhaps that was why, when the trial was barely under way, Joe Bass predicted, "The odds are 100 to 1 that no conviction will obtain in the Valentine case even though the evidence is clear and plain, for the cards are stacked against such—justice sometimes goes on a vacation."[29]

During the first seven days in court, Thomas Woolwine's prosecution team presented Valentine's case, with the *Eagle* praising the effort as "strong." But then the judge became ill, causing a delay of about two weeks, and then, after a few more days back in the courtroom, a second recess was called, which lasted through most of April.[30] Meantime, the attorney S. S. Hahn was readmitted to the bar and returned to the case. When court reconvened, he voiced a defense of the deputies that Joe Bass condemned as a "Ben Tillman tirade." In Bass's account, Hahn told the jury that he "would not care to be close to any colored person and for that reason [the defendants were] justified in assaulting Valentine." Having injected race prejudice into the trial, he allowed his cocounsel to press the issue of the officers' right to self-defense.[31]

When the case came to a close in mid-May, the jury deadlocked. In early June, one of the officers, Frank Dewar, was, on motion of the D.A.'s office, exonerated on account of "insufficient evidence." The trial of the Cooper brothers was to continue in October; but when the parties convened at that time, the court date was once again postponed, this time until January 1923.

Meanwhile, the case was transferred from department 12 to department 14, the third shift in venue since the proceedings began on November 12, 1920. By the time the parties returned to court in January 1923, Thomas Woolwine was no longer district attorney of Los Angeles, and the new D.A. moved to dismiss the charges against the Coopers "on account of insufficient evidence." Thus the Valentine case ended after nearly three years in the courts.[32]

When Valentine's case was in its trial phase during the spring of 1922, another case—this one a high-profile courtroom drama—grabbed headlines in L.A., courtesy of the KKK. The local Klan had resurfaced explosively in April 1922 with the infamous "Inglewood Raid." In a bizarre affair, the Klan raided the home of alleged bootleggers (Spanish immigrants) in Inglewood, a small town southwest of the Central Avenue district. When an Inglewood police officer arrived, he got into a shoot-out with the Klansmen, wounding two and killing one. The man he killed turned out to be a fellow officer on the Inglewood force; the two he wounded were also law enforcement officers.[33]

Woolwine, the L.A. County district attorney, launched a grand jury investigation. The mayor, the L.A. County Board of Supervisors, the judge of the Superior Court, the secretary of the Civil Service Commission, the city prosecutor, the county sheriff, and the city's chief of police all condemned the Klan. The *Times* received a list of three hundred local Klansmen, which it immediately turned over to Woolwine and threatened to publish. Branding the KKK as "an un-American band of hooded cowards and outlaws," Woolwine obtained a warrant to search the local Klan headquarters and once inside seized the membership records. He launched a highly public effort to run the Klan out of town and, indeed, California.[34]

The membership list showed three thousand members in Los Angeles County, including one thousand in Los Angeles city, three on Woolwine's own staff. Woolwine gave the names to the city council and the L.A. County Board of Supervisors, who pledged to get rid of all Klan-member employees under its jurisdiction. Law enforcement leaders publicly sought to purge their ranks of Klansmen. William A. Traeger, the county sheriff, moved to fire any deputy whose name was on a Klan list. Chief of Police Louis Oats told his officers to quit the Klan or quit the police force. But then it turned out that both Traeger and Oats were themselves on the KKK membership lists. Embarrassed, both men scurried forth with explanations: They had joined under false pretenses, not understanding what the organization was, and had quickly abandoned it when they found out. Those clarifications only highlighted how difficult it was to fathom the depth of Klan influence. All three

Klansmen shot in Inglewood were police officers. The Klan's Los Angeles "Kleagle," Nathan A. Baker, who directed the Inglewood Raid, was a deputy sheriff for Los Angeles County. When another list was found, city council president Ralph L. Criswell was on it, and he did not deny membership.[35]

Woolwine's grand jury indicted thirty-seven "Inglewood Raiders," charging each one with two counts of false imprisonment, two counts of kidnapping, and assault with intent to murder. The trial was a circus. Paul Barksdale D'Orr, described by admirers as "the brilliant and fiery orator of the South," defended the accused Klansmen. D'Orr packed the courtroom with wives and children of the defendants and portrayed the dead Klansman as a martyr, who "died there defending your children and mine." The jury found the men innocent, and Klan leaders trumpeted their vindication. By then, however, the local organization was falling apart. Coburn had a nasty power struggle with G. W. Price, a fellow Atlantan, who was "Imperial Representative" of the California KKK. Klan officials in Atlanta recalled both of them, leaving L.A.'s KKK in the hands of Nathan Baker, who would shortly attempt suicide and be institutionalized. The city council passed an "anti-mask" ordinance to thwart further Klan activity. By the fall of 1922, white newspapers considered the Klan dead and gone.[36]

Black Angelenos had mixed emotions about the rise and fall of the local Klan. Attacks on the KKK by white dailies and government officials were encouraging. Yet many police officers had been implicated, and as Beatrice Thompson told the NAACP's national office, the Inglewood trial had been "a farce." Fred Roberts saw it all as part of a larger problem. "Never before have we heard so much talk about 'white supremacy' as we hear nowadays, and never before have we seen so much of white brutality, white inefficiency and white failure as we see today," he wrote in the *New Age*. "A look at German Militarism, Russian Bolshevism and American Ku Klux Klanism makes the eternal clatter for sustained white superiority sound like a swan song, and a mighty poor swan song at that."[37]

The Woolwine Democrats

If black Angelenos saw the Klan as the embodiment of southern imperialism, they viewed Thomas Woolwine as the Western Ideal come to life. Here was a white southern Democrat who had moved West and seen the light. As soon as Woolwine announced that he would run for governor in 1922, on the Democratic ticket, black political leaders began to consider the possibilities. When the Klan endorsed Republican front-runner Friend Richardson, the obvious question arose: Should colored voters abandon the Party of Lincoln?

Woolwine filed for the Democratic primary while the Inglewood trial was in progress, and his fight against the Klan inspired enthusiasm around the state. A leading Democrat in Bakersfield wrote, "I find that your quick stand on this K-K-K matter, by which many believe that [the] State was saved from a 'pestilence of dam foolism' has taken hold of the people." In Kern County, he continued, "men that are not of our political faith" were determined to vote Democrat if Woolwine made the general election. The conversion of moderate Republicans was Woolwine's only hope—and it was plausible, for as he reminded voters, he had always won in L.A. County, a "life-long Democrat . . . in the banner Republican county of the state."[38]

Black Angelenos knew Woolwine, having supported him in local non-partisan elections since the mid-1910s. Woolwine pledged that, under his administration, Negroes would "receive the same square treatment that any other class of citizens receive at my hands."[39] The Watts Community League, a black political group, gave its support.[40] So did Joe Bass's influential California State Colored Republican League, whose headquarters was on Central Avenue and whose guiding principle was to "stand for free, equal and un-trampled political rights for all American citizens." Republicans could not vote for Woolwine in the primary, but the candidate and his supporters were looking ahead. With the primary three weeks away, Bass's league pledged to Woolwine that the "Colored citizens of the County of Los Angeles, are standing ready to back you up, work for, and vote for you." League secretary C. H. Alston assured Woolwine, "We have carefully watched your past actions, your sincerity of purpose, your honesty in trying to deal fairly and justly with all man kind, . . . let it be the big man, or the little man, the rich man as well as the poor man, the white man as well as the black man." Alston emphasized that should Woolwine win his primary, "you will get every Negro vote in California, with but a few exception [sic]." The league would "work for you, and do all we can for you, and don't want a cent of your money." What's more, "Your party affiliation does not enter into the matter with us," Alston added. "If we as a people were ever indebted to the Republican Party for what they have done for us, we feel that we have long since paid that debt by our faithful service and loyalty with compound interest, long, long ago."[41]

Woolwine did win the Democratic primary, and his fight against the KKK became the lodestone of his campaign. His opponent, Friend Richardson, was a far-right Republican. The Klan supported Richardson. Rumors flew that he was a member. An aide denied it, but Richardson did not. Republican

newspapers that had opposed the Klan sidestepped their dilemma by declaring the Klan a dead letter. Richardson's strategy was to say little, to avoid
mistakes, and rely on the usual Republican majority. The Klan was aggressive, though, sabotaging Woolwine at virtually every campaign stop, a plan
that probably ended up helping the dramatic Democrat's campaign.[42]

But the bankable Republican vote proved too much for the hard-charg-
ing Woolwine. The KKK took credit for Richardson's victory, but nobody
important believed that. Richardson finally acknowledged that he had no
connection with the Klan. Once in office, though, he would prove Klanish
in spirit, attacking California progressivism and hindering racial equality.
Woolwine's defeat was nonetheless instructive. California's Democrats had
made their first serious bid for the governor's mansion in decades, and
African Americans had played a key role.[43]

Did Joe Bass's Republican League deliver the black vote for Woolwine in
the 74th Assembly District? The answer is a qualified yes. Out of the 5,506
gubernatorial votes cast in the 74th—a district that had few Democrats—
Woolwine narrowly edged Richardson. No issues of Fred Roberts's *New
Age* survive from those months, but as a GOP incumbent who needed to
work effectively within the Republican-controlled legislature, Roberts
surely muted his support for Woolwine. Without doubt, it was difficult for
many African Americans to vote for a Democrat, even Woolwine. Some of
Roberts's strongest precincts in the 74th actually gave slim majorities to
Richardson.[44]

The defection of black Republicans who had voted for Woolwine proved
temporary, the result of particular circumstances and candidates. Another
decade would pass before black Angelenos seriously considered the Democrats again. Thomas Woolwine himself was through with politics, and he would
not live to see a black-white Democratic Party. He died in 1925 at the age of
fifty. But the Woolwine Democrats of 1922 were a symbol of hope for black
Los Angeles, the hope that the Western Ideal could triumph over the white-
supremacy influence of the South. Woolwine's life and politics certainly
proved that the "spirit of the West" could be successful. But his final two
defeats—the Inglewood Raiders verdict and the election of 1922—showed,
among other things, that the Western Ideal might yet lose out.

Fred Roberts and the Klan

The KKK also tried to undermine Fred Roberts's campaign in 1922. Six candidates, white and black, had crowded into the Republican primary for the

74th's assembly seat. The campaign had already been rumbling with racial overtones when, shortly before the primary, the Klan publicly endorsed Roberts as its candidate of choice. This bit of dirty pool probably had the opposite effect of that intended, but an infuriated Roberts roared that "the idea of the K.K.K. endorsing a black man for anything but tar and feather or the rope is too ridiculous for consideration."[45]

Roberts won the primary impressively. His vote total was nearly double that of the second-place finisher, and he gathered 55 percent of the vote. He won solid support throughout the district, meaning that his white-black coalition had grown even stronger during the Klan crisis.[46]

In the general election, Roberts seemed to face a stiff challenge from the former Afro-American Council president, James Alexander, who ran as an independent. Alexander had recently resigned his federal patronage job in protest of his boss's prejudice; his principled action made him something of a hero in the community. He had long been a "good government" man, and he now ran on a 1920s-style progressive agenda: efficiency in government and proportionate representation. The incumbent had also been in the progressive camp, but because Alexander was in the race, Roberts was, for the first time in his career, criticized for being a "regular Republican." For the moment, it did not matter. Roberts won 61 percent of the vote.[47]

Fortunately for black California, Governor Richardson's reactionary administration was balanced by a state legislature packed with neoprogressives who opposed him and the Klan. Fred Roberts, having already strengthened the state civil rights law and outlawed racially insulting textbooks in public schools, now sought a state anti-mask law aimed at the Klan. Burton Ceruti served as his legal aide, gathering information from the NAACP's national office prior to drafting the legislation. Assembly Bill 1224 reflected typical anti-mask legislation of the day, making it a crime for people meeting in public places to conceal their identity with a mask or "other regalia" (with exceptions for "good faith" entertainment and amusement). The kicker in Roberts's bill was that it made violation of the mask law a felony. As written, AB 1224 zipped through the assembly; it slowed in the more conservative Senate, which often rejected progressive legislation. This time, a San Diego senator urged passage because the bill was "an act to prohibit, as far as we can by law, the activities of the organization called the Ku Klux Klan." The senate passed the bill only after reducing the penalty from a felony to a misdemeanor—a tough break for Roberts. Even so, the Assembly affirmed the revised legislation and Richardson—even he—signed it into law.[48]

Klansmen did not have to wear hoods to do damage, however, and by the end of 1922 it was difficult to say how strong the California Klan actually was. The white dailies dismissed the KKK, not without reason. But other signs suggested growth. That December, the Klan in Venice initiated five hundred new members. Shortly thereafter, Beatrice Thompson informed the national office of the NAACP that the Klan was "growing alarmingly strong in this community." The Klan threatened Ceruti, as well as a white southerner named Mrs. Branch, who worked closely with the NAACP. In November 1924, Thompson reported that "the local K.K.K.'s held an immense mass meeting here. . . . One of the features of the meeting was the public presentation of a grandson of the organizer of the *original* K.K.K. who was given a terrific ovation." The meeting disturbed Thompson, but so did the fact that some Afro-Angelenos no longer saw the Klan as a threat. Despite the mass meeting, she wrote, "there are colored persons in this city who argue that the Klan is not 'after us' and who refused to give a dollar [for NAACP membership] to protect themselves or anyone else."[49]

The question of Klan influence in politics and local governance remained unanswered. After laboring in the 1924 elections, Thompson told the national NAACP that she was "convinced of the power and influence of the local 'Ks'" in the political arena. "The tragedy of it is the fact that colored voters helped to elect them to office in many cases—thanks to the G.O.P." Statewide, the 1924 election results were not as bad as Thompson suggested, because neoprogressives generally won over GOP reactionaries. But Thompson had a point. In California's open-primary, weakly partisan political world, it was difficult to say who was pulling the strings behind any particular candidate.[50]

Klan attempts to take control over Watts in 1925 added to black suspicions. That April, the *Eagle* published a Klan letter that had been intercepted by the Watts Police Department and mysteriously forwarded to the Basses. The letter's contents caused Joe to mourn, "How long, Oh! how long, Lord, will the Negro suffer himself to be a political target!" The letter had been written by G. W. Price, who had returned to L.A. from Atlanta to continue his work as the Imperial Representative of the California KKK. Written to an unnamed member of the "Big Ten Campaign Committee" in Watts, the letter promised that "our [KKK] investigators are on the job 24 hours per day" to ensure that pro-Klan candidates would be elected to office in Watts. Because the Klan was working secretly, Price insisted that the other members of the committee must never know that the Invisible Empire was involved. Yes, the committee included "all races, creeds, etc," and such inclusiveness was advisable "on account of the fact that you have such a large Negro Population in Watts, and also a large Catholic vote." But this was no problem, Price said. "You can use these aliens to forward the ideals of Americanism and can consequently relegate them to the rear." Price had determined which black leaders the KKK could use as pawns—those with "very little brains" and little "racial pride." And he had also discovered those who stood against them and needed to be pushed out of the picture (he named, in particular, one Reverend Knox, a respected black minister in Watts). These enemies could be eliminated through frame-ups: "We could plant a bottle of booze in an enemy's car . . . [or] fall back on the old method of 'a woman.'" Price thought "the best way to get rid of" people like Knox was "to make them leave Watts in disgrace."[51]

When the Basses published the full text of the letter, it caused an uproar within the black community and a counterattack by the Klan. Those African Americans implicated as dupes of, or collaborators with, the KKK raised angry voices at the Sunday Forum, demanding Bass's head. Price charged the *Eagle*'s editors with libel, and the L.A. city prosecutor stated that the letter "was clearly libelous." Joe, Charlotta, and assistant editor Robert Anderson were therefore arraigned and taken to court. Price made two simple claims: that he did not write the letter, and that the defendants had published it with full knowledge that it was fabricated in order to ruin his reputation and "expose him . . . to public hatred and contempt." Couching his response in middle-class rhetoric, and throwing a familiar barb back at the Klan, Bass thundered that the KKK was un-American and "Red."[52]

The case came to court as *The People of the State of Calif. v. J. B. Bass, C. A. Spear Bass and Robt. T. Anderson*. Joe Bass saw the lawsuit as part of the Klan's campaign to wipe out Race publications that fought the KKK; for that reason, he wrote, "the result of this case promises to be far reaching indeed." Hugh Macbeth and Lewis K. Beeks represented the *Eagle*. James Alexander donated bond money. John Somerville wrote an open letter to the community: "The fight that they are waging is not a personal one. They are fighting for principles in which the Freedom and Welfare of every Negro is concerned." The Colored Minister's Alliance pledged full support and raised funds for the defense. The courts in Los Angeles County were an iffy proposition; so much depended on the judge assigned to the case. The Klan, in decline nationwide, needed a victory desperately, and the Basses feared that "all of the resources of this powerful organization will be massed to secure a conviction."[53]

The fear proved unwarranted: in a triumph for the black community and its Race papers, the *Eagle* won the case easily. The conflict was not quite finished, though. Late one night, while Charlotta was working alone in the *Eagle* office, several Klansmen in regalia appeared at the door. Charlotta, who did not know how to shoot a gun, pulled an unloaded pistol out of the desk drawer and pointed it toward them. The startled Klansmen bolted and never came back.

This showdown on Central Avenue had the feel of a classic happy ending. The brave heroine had a faster hand, and the cowardly bad guys lit out. But things were not so simple. Fear and apprehension festered. Black Angelenos would not forget that the KKK had infiltrated all of their law enforcement agencies, and that many public officials and judges had appeared on the membership lists Woolwine had uncovered. By mid-1925 the Klan had been disgraced, but among African Americans, a seed of suspicion had been planted. When they dealt with any white police officer, any judge, any council member, it was always possible they were facing a Klan member or sympathizer. Not without reason, uncertainties would linger. That, in the end, may have been the most destructive legacy of the 1920s Klan in L.A.

The NAACP in the 1920s

The Colored Women's Clubs, the Forum, the churches, the lodges all displayed the fighting spirit of the black community in the 1920s. So did black entrepreneurs, Garveyites, and the newly organized Los Angeles Urban League (see chapter 7). But the main engine of civil rights activism in 1920s L.A. was the NAACP, whose erratic journey through the decade demonstrated the challenges facing civil rights activists.

In 1921, the local branch of the NAACP nearly doubled in size, with membership topping 1,200. Branch attorney Burton Ceruti worked tirelessly to win justice in the courts and city council. He assembled the permanent Legal Redress Committee, which eventually included four black attorneys who assisted him in the work, among them the up-and-coming lawyer Bert McDonald. Executive secretary Beatrice Thompson remained at the helm, and the leadership seemed strong, with stalwarts such as Charlotta Bass and Fred Roberts joined by a full contingent of high-profile ministers.[54] City and county officials respected and listened to the local NAACP; Mayor Cryer joined the branch. The Klan's anti-Catholic crusade created a sturdy alliance between the local NAACP and the influential Catholic bishop of the Los Angeles Diocese, J. J. Cantwell. The local branch sent large amounts of money to the national office to aid victims of racial injustice around the country. In turn, the national office constantly praised the Los Angeles branch.[55]

But then the momentum stalled, and by the mid-1920s the local branch was in crisis. The tumult of 1921 had boosted membership to its highest level, but after 1923 membership fell sharply, and by the end of 1925 it had dropped to only 274. The new members who had swelled the ranks soon came to resent the hold the "old guard" had on the branch. For their part, Thompson and Ceruti both complained that they had to do all the work and got "no co-operation" from the membership. The new members, many of them potential leaders, felt the organization was run undemocratically and that the procedures for electing officers had been rigged by Thompson. In late 1922 and early 1923, controversy over local governance had reached the national office, which only waffled on the issue, thereby heightening tensions in the branch.[56]

In spring 1923, Du Bois arrived for a visit, but enthusiasm and unity were not restored. The branch took Du Bois to tour Hollywood, but given the racial realities of the place, the result was strained. The only real excitement took place behind closed doors, as Du Bois fell for the feminine graces of Anita Thompson, Beatrice's daughter. Anita, it turned out, was eager to do anything to make Du Bois's visit a memorable one. That tryst, unknown to Beatrice, may have had something to do with Anita's eagerness to visit New York later that year. Mother and daughter thus went on an extended trip to the East Coast. In Beatrice Thompson's absence, the local branch drifted. When she returned to L.A. in early 1924, she found, in her estimation, that next to nothing had been done while she was gone. The acting branch secretary, Lulu Slaughter, president of the Sojourner Truth Club and a writer of local repute, had kept the records while Beatrice was back East. Thompson claimed they were so badly garbled it took months to straighten them out. She said Slaughter was no help and had responded to her criticism with a "resentful . . . 'take it or leave it' air."[57]

Shortly thereafter, without Thompson's advice or consent, the local branch added a "Junior Branch." Thompson objected that these young members were not "Juniors" at all. Most of them, she told the national office, were "University of California students" and some were "over 21 years of age." She worried about this misuse of the Junior Branch program, which was supposed to be for teenagers. "But the climax came," she said, "when the young lady secretary of the Branch [Ella Matthews] made her report at our March public meeting and closed her remarks by saying that their members 'did not like to be called the Junior Branch.'" Matthews's comment blew the meeting open, president J. C. Banks struggled to maintain order, and nothing was resolved. "At present," Thompson told the national office, "we really have two adult Branches." The first major project of the Junior Branch would come the following year, when it sought to stage Du Bois's historical pageant, The Star of Ethiopia, at the Hollywood Bowl. This event led unexpectedly to a major power struggle within the branch—or branches—

and the fallout was intense. That partly explains why so few NAACP members remained on the rolls the following year.[58]

The turmoil continued at the November meeting held to elect new officers. The ticket of candidates submitted to members by the executive board—the normal procedure—met vigorous disapproval from some members, one of whom condemned the existing board as a "closed corporation." A nasty debate followed, and many members left the meeting before any votes were taken. In the end, those who remained passed a motion that write-in votes would count. Predictably, many incumbents found themselves voted out of office, and something like a changing of the guard took place.[59]

At the center of this furor stood an impressive newcomer, Dr. H. Claude Hudson, a dentist and Race man. Previously he had been a resident of Shreveport, Louisiana, where he had been friends with Nyanza Hawkins. Gus Hawkins later claimed that his father and mother had been instrumental in getting the Hudsons to leave the South and come west. In Shreveport, Hudson had been president of the local NAACP, a dangerous position in any southern city. He later said that he had run the Shreveport branch unilaterally, because all the other officials were so afraid of the white establishment they simply followed his lead. Hudson was fearless and outspoken almost to a fault, and in that respect he took after Du Bois. But he was equally urbane, diplomatic, and popular, and in that respect he resembled James Weldon Johnson. Not surprisingly, by the time he reached L.A., he had earned a favorable reputation in the NAACP's national office.[60]

Beatrice Thompson also knew and admired him, and she tried to draft him as the local branch's presidential candidate for 1924. Hudson declined, saying he was "too new" in the community. When the election meeting exploded, Thompson and the board were stunned when Hudson rose to support the malcontents and lambaste the current officials. His sentiments won him a groundswell of popular support from the discontented crowd. As Thompson saw it, Hudson had played a sly game, refusing to accept the nomination from her because he did not want to be associated with the longtime administration, which he knew would come under attack at the meeting. Then, once the rout was on, he had established himself as the outsiders' leader and ridden the momentum into office. From Hudson's point of view, however, the local branch was "a dead thing" that had not undertaken any meaningful civil rights campaigns in years. He therefore had voiced support for those who were calling for new and aggressive leadership, not realizing the members would draft him as their new leader. As he wrote to William Pickins, the national field secretary, "these people elected me against my will."[61]

To her surprise, an embittered Thompson was reelected as executive secretary, but leadership of the branch quickly shifted to Hudson. In the old dispensation, the executive secretary had run the local branch while the president served as a figurehead—as in the national office. In Hudson's administration, the president headed the branch in deed and truth, with assistance from the secretary, who was now just a secretary, without the executive prefix. Thompson grumbled that she would "blunder along" despite Hudson's meddling. She only hoped that "some day the intelligent group of our people will realize that in order to accomplish things thru organization, we must learn to transact business aristocratically and distribute the benefits democratically."[62] Her indignation notwithstanding, Hudson's populist approach was the order of the day.

One thing did not change during this transition—the branch's difficulty in securing nonblack support for the organization. There had always been white members, and the first two presidents had been leading white ministers, but in its everyday work the local NAACP was a black group. Visible white allies, such as Mrs. Branch, demonstrated the possibilities, but she was asked to speak at NAACP events so frequently she became a mascot. When high-profile white leaders took part in NAACP work, local Race papers cheered just a little too loudly. As president, J. C. Banks had urged members to find new ways to get local whites involved, because he thought it the only way for white people to learn what African Americans were really like and how race prejudice hurt their life chances, and because "our great problem, which is truly a national problem, can never be solved in its entirety by ourselves." Whites and blacks needed to share an interest in racial democracy; it was "therefore not only desirable but highly necessary that we bring together here in Los Angeles . . . the thoughtful people of both the Colored and the white races, as far as we find it possible to do so." But throughout the 1920s, whites remained on the periphery of the work.[63]

NAACP correspondence and the local Race papers confirm that black Angelenos of the 1920s thought of civil rights as a black-and-white matter. Black L.A. formed no alliances with the ethnic Mexicans, the Japanese, or the Jews. The idea of such alliances was virtually never discussed. Blacks routinely spoke of relations between "the two races"—meaning American blacks and American whites. The Mexican American community had a core of middle-class leaders with their own organizations and goals. The Japanese had theirs. The blacks had theirs. All three minority groups acted independently, focusing on their own relationship with the dominant white group. It was almost as if they could not see one another—or that they would not acknowledge one another. Language, culture, and political circumstances built walls between them. The Japanese could not vote; Latinos seldom did. African Americans, Japanese, and ethnic Mexicans all suffered from racial discrimination, but the possibility of strategic cooperation escaped them. In one of the most diverse places in America—the Eastside of Los Angeles—black civil rights leaders continued to see their struggle in black and white.[64]

Most African American problems did involve whites, not Asians or ethnic Mexicans. Two cases pursued by the local NAACP involved public confrontations between black and white women. One was the Helen Brown case. In spring 1921, Helen Brown and her sister Adelaide, young women who lived with their parents, got on a streetcar in the West Jefferson district. When Helen sat down, the white woman next to her (a Texan) slapped her in the face. Helen Brown slapped her back, the two exchanged glares, and the incident ended. That night, the white woman's sons tracked down where the Browns lived and accosted the Brown daughters at gunpoint. The ensuing ruckus brought the police, who arrested the white intruders.

When the Browns pressed charges against her sons, the white woman brought suit against Helen for assault on the streetcar. The NAACP took up Helen's defense, holding a fund-raising rally and putting Ceruti to work. Prosecutors offered to drop the case against Helen if the Browns would drop their case, but Ceruti refused. The hearing on June 15 was brief. The judge heard the evidence and promptly dismissed the suit against Helen Brown. He then castigated the woman who had brought the suit, stating that she had broken the law first by striking Helen and that, no matter where she had come from, on the streetcars of L.A., she had only the right to her own seat. As the *New Age* had it, the judge "read the complainant quite a lecture upon the rights and duties of citizenship."[65]

Five years later, the NAACP won a similar case for Evangeline Kenner, who lived with her husband and five children at 1325 West 92nd Street. In summer 1926, the Kenners moved into this otherwise all-white neighborhood several miles west of Watts. One of the Kenners' white neighbors, a thirteen-year-old named Roy Pickering, pushed the Kenners' four-year-old daughter to the ground and then ran over her with his bike. Seeing this, twelve-year-old Harold Kenner rushed to confront Roy, and the boys got in a scrap. Roy's mother then joined the fray and began beating Harold. Evangeline Kenner rushed outside, shouted off Mrs. Pickering and shook an indignant fist in the white woman's face. Mrs. Pickering called the police, who arrested Mrs. Kenner—the black mother—for "assault and battery." On July 6, the case was heard in the Justice's Court of Gardena, a small town south of the Kenner-Pickering neighborhood, Justice J. S. Crandall presiding. He sentenced Kenner to thirty days in jail. Then he offered to drop the sentence if the Kenners would agree to move out of the neighborhood.

The NAACP quickly dispatched attorney Bert McDonald to get Evangeline Kenner released. McDonald arranged a hearing with the parole board, with Justice Crandall in attendance. When one of the board members asked Judge Crandall why he had sent Kenner to jail rather than just issue her a fine, he flatly replied that the Pickerings and other white neighbors "wanted the Kenners to give up their property and move away." He had made his ruling hoping "to force her out of the neighborhood." McDonald then had his say, and the parole board sided with him. Overruling Crandall's judgment, the board had Evangeline Kenner released after she had served only two hours in jail. It was a quick, impressive victory for the local branch.[66]

Then there were swimming pools. In Pasadena, the public pools were open to colored people one day a week, "International Day," after which the water was drained; other towns in Southern California had similar restrictions. In the city of Los Angeles, the public swimming pools had generally been open to all as a matter of policy. On occasion, pool managers tried to segregate. In 1921, for example, the swimming instructor at Exposition Park pool decided to exclude Negro children from the pools except on a special day. He posted a sign reading, "Colored People Mondays Only." John Somerville protested. He received an apologetic letter from the superintendent of the Playground Commission, who claimed that the policy did not have the consent of the commission. Blacks, and everyone else, were welcome to use the facilities: "They are public pools, and open to the public use."[67]

But on July 30, 1925, the Playground Commission adopted a policy of racially segregated swimming pools. Three of the city's pools would follow the International Day formula: Exposition Park, heavily used by black Angelenos, would be open to "colored groups" on Monday afternoons; Arroyo Pool on Wednesday afternoons; North Broadway, also heavily used by blacks, on Friday afternoons. The newly built Vignes Pool, used by few blacks in its first month of operation, would be open to colored groups every day. The NAACP immediately filed a protest, and George Cushnie, acting in concert with Hudson, filed one for himself. Cushnie lived near the Exposition Park facility and had three children, all of whom used the pool regularly. On August 13, the commission heard both complaints and simply rejected them. There was no municipal process for appealing the decision, so the new swimming pool rules were upheld and the NAACP moved toward the courtroom. Using Cushnie's complaint, Ceruti brought suit against the Playground Commission.

The name of the case was *George Cushnie v. City of Los Angeles,* but the local branch called it the "Bath House Battle." Ceruti's prosecution rested on the state's civil rights laws, which outlawed racial discrimination at "bath houses," and also on the claim that such segregation violated the Fourteenth Amendment's equal-protection clause. Locally and nationally, African Americans followed the case throughout late 1925 and the first half of 1926. NAACP officials in New York issued a nationwide press release about the case. Afro-Angelenos supported the Bath House Battle, raising funds for legal defense and rallying community spirit. That summer, Hudson, whose administration was gaining momentum, informed Walter White that the branch had been in the "thick of [a] fight . . . and I am doing my darndest to make the fellow unpopular who fosters segregation."[68]

The case went from bad to worse for the local branch. The city attorney simply asked the judge to dismiss Cushnie's case, and the judge complied. When Ceruti appealed, the results were both odd and terrible. The appeals court ruled that the Ceruti had raised "important contentions" that should to be heard. Yes, the judge insisted, swimming pool segregation was in violation of California's civil rights statutes, but, he added, the city of Los Angeles was no longer bound to those laws. The new city charter, adopted in 1923, stated that L.A. had the power "to make and enforce all laws and regulations in respect to municipal affairs." Therefore, he concluded, "the general laws of the state did not apply to the city of Los Angeles."[69]

Moreover, the appeals judge ruled, Ceruti's complaint about due-process violations could not withstand *Plessy;* in swimming pools as with everything else, separate could be equal. A trial was needed, he concluded, but only to decide a single question: Did the city provide "equal accommodation for both races"? The trial was held in December 1926. As NAACP attorney Bert McDonald wrote in his summation of the outcome: "The trial court held that the Playground and Recreation Commission had provided . . . substantial accommodations for colored groups," enough "to comply with the 14th Amendment."[70]

This legal setback occurred just as the local NAACP published its annual report for 1926. Still smarting from the branch's collapse in 1925, Hudson and branch leaders hoped the nicely published report would restore the community's interest, and faith, in the local branch. The report insisted, "You Should Join—This Is Your Fight!" It touted the Bath House Battle: "The Branch started the year in a fight for full fledge Americanism, and opposed the play ground commission's order discriminating against Negro children in the Municipal swimming pools. Regardless of the gallant fight the courts sustained the commission. The branch, through its legal committee, motioned for a new trial and same was granted. The battle is still on. IT IS YOUR FIGHT." But by the time black Los Angeles read this report, the fight was over.[71]

Ceruti and other NAACP officials worried that an appeal to the state Supreme Court would result in failure and set a disastrous legal precedent for all Afro-Californians. "It is my candid opinion," Bert McDonald wrote to Hudson in early January, that an appeal would result in a decision that "would probably be in accord with the rule as laid down in the case of Plessy v. Ferguson."[72] Hudson asked the national office for advice, adding, "It is my opinion that the matter of swimming is such a delicate one in the eyes of the American white man that if we force a decision in the State Supreme Court, it will probably be an adverse one, which will set a precedent for all forms of segregation cases throughout California." The defeat affected the local community, not the entire state, so, Hudson reasoned, it was best left in Los Angeles, where it might be remedied through local politics. The National Legal Committee soon recommended against appeal, with chairman Arthur Spingarn deciding, "All things considered and giving particular attention to the statements made in the letters of Dr. Hudson and Mr. McDonald, I do not recommend that an appeal be taken herein." The local branch quietly abandoned the case.[73]

Fighting Restrictive Covenants

The local branch's legal battle against restrictive covenants—the case *George H. Letteau, et al. v. William A. Long, et al.*—paralleled the Bath House Battle. Commonly known as *Letteau v. Long* or "the Long Case," this fight was critical to the well-being of the community. In Los Angeles, black home ownership remained high, but racially restrictive real estate covenants had sprawled across the city, threatening to confine Afro-Angelenos to the Central Avenue district. "Residential segregation seems to be getting worse," Claude Hudson wrote to the national NAACP in 1925. The Long Case would receive strong support from the community, with good reason. The suit brought against William and Eunice Long, the African American home owners in question, threatened not only to thwart Negro home ownership opportunities but also to rob thousands of black Angelenos of their homes, with no remuneration.[74]

In California, the legal status of covenants had been a bit shaky since the state Supreme Court's 1919 ruling in *Los Angeles Investment Co. v. Gary.* That decision had pleased no one. By a 3–2 margin, the justices had ruled that restrictive covenants against purchase were void, but that restraints on occupancy were legal. White developers, home owners' associations, and realtors fumed over the first part of the ruling. Blacks fumed over the second. At the outset of the decade, both sides of this fight were waiting for an opportunity to win a more favorable ruling than *Gary* had afforded.[75]

In the meantime, occupancy clauses had spread across the white neighborhoods of California. The Realty Board of San Diego urged home owners and developers to adopt racial restrictions "carefully and properly drawn as to occupancy." The Pasadena Realty Board insisted that deeds for all new subdivisions in the 1920s include "a race restriction as to occupancy." At Laguna Beach, an exclusive Orange County seaside town, restrictive covenants written in the 1920s included no language limiting sales but clear restrictions on occupancy. A typical deed from the mid-1920s stated that "said premises shall not [be] . . . occupied or used by any person or persons other than those of the Caucasian race, provided, however, that the foregoing restriction shall not be construed to prohibit the keeping of domestic servants of any race."[76]

What white realtors thought about race and real estate is known because the California Real Estate Association (CREA, an all-white organization) conducted a statewide survey on the restrictive covenants in 1927. The surveys asked each local realty board whether a "color line" was maintained in their community, which methods were used to exclude Chinese, Japanese, Mexicans, and Negroes, and how "this important problem [could] be best handled by real estate interests." The survey responses are notable for their frankness and for their enthusiastic support of racial restrictions. The realty boards obviously never considered the possibility that their answers might be viewed in a negative light. On the contrary, they eagerly shared their race prejudice and their methods for restriction in much the same way an urban booster might advertise a pro-business climate. William McMillan, president of the Glendale Realty Board, reflected the general spirit of the group when he wrote, "The Glendale Realty Board, and the Glendale brokers, as a whole, cooperate in every way to keep Glendale an 'All American City,' and by enforcing the race restrictions, we have been able to keep our standard well up in the front ranks of 'All American.'"[77]

The CREA published the basic results of the survey in an article in its monthly journal, *California Real Estate.* The essential finding was that "it is apparent that the color question has not become a serious problem in the northern half of the state, but is being gravely considered in all large cities and many exclusive residential communities in the southern half of the state." In Los Angeles County, the cities of L.A., Pasadena, Santa Monica, and Monrovia were all struggling to maintain the color line. Others, such as Beverly Hills, excluded nonwhites with little difficulty. The L.A. Realty Board saw covenant restrictions as the city's only hope. Pasadena's board reported "a large number of negroes who are recently trying to move into desirable sections of the city," but the board was "attempting to hold them in check." The article drew a clear distinction between the behavior of ethnic Mexicans and that of African Americans, seeing the latter as a distinct threat. "Mexicans do not wish to force themselves into better districts," the CREA article stated, "and when improvements are made they usually leave for a poorer district. They do not try to force themselves where they are not wanted; but negroes, it is held, seem anxious to get into a white district to command a big price to leave."[78]

The surveys from in and around L.A. reflect a deep antagonism toward nonwhites. The more genteel answers came from high-rent districts—Beverly Hills and West Hollywood—where the only colored people were live-in servants. Of colored people in Beverly Hills, the secretary of the local realty board wrote simply, "none permitted," adding, "Our district is a great deal different than any other in that it is the height of beauty and culture with no poor section, occupied only by white people outside of the servants in the homes of owners." From the grittier environs of Compton, just south of Watts, the realty board stated, "All subdivisions . . . since 1921 have restrictions against any but the white race." The Compton survey noted a "few Mexicans and Japanese in the old part of the city," but no blacks to date. The local creed: "Never sell to an undesirable."[79]

The Santa Monica Realty Board president gave one of the most extensive answers, in which he expended considerable ink trashing what he called "the Latin races   the Spanish, French, Italian and the Grecians [sic]," who, he claimed, were responsible for most of the crime in America, and in whom "there is no such a thing as the finer qualities demanded by American citizenship." "Personally," he insisted, "I place the Latin races, in exactly the same category as the color line." Most people in Santa Monica were white, but "there are isolated cases where the Mexican or Colored people have got in." Fortunately, he said, the local realtors had "an understanding that color is confined to certain districts comprising an area of about 2 blocks long by about 10 blocks in width . . . not more than 20 blocks alto-gether [sic]." Peer pressure kept the local realtors in line: "Any broker who will place or encourage the placing of any of the objectionable races in a section, where they do not fit, is not of quality or has no integerity [sic] of purpose, or principle."[80]

In Los Angeles proper, the local realty board advocated covenants and urged its members not to "sell property to other than the Caucasian race in territories occupied by them." But, as their survey response admitted, they had little control over the situation, because there were so many independent realtors operating in the city. The real force behind housing segregation was real estate developers themselves, in collaboration with white home ownership associations. J. A. Burgan, president of the Federated Home Protective Leagues, penned his own answer to the survey: "This race question is fraught with social and economic peril, owing to the rabid propaganda of the negro race." The best way to maintain the color line, he argued, was to crack down on independent realtors. State law should revise "the scope of unethical practices, so that State licences may be revoked where brokers offer to sell or rent property in a neighborhood where the occupants are predominantly white to persons of African, Mongolian or Japanese blood. This conduct is frowned upon by the Realty Board of L.A. but the taboo reaches only its members, leaving the swarm of brokers, often unscrupulous people, outside its ranks, subject only to the limited discipline of the State R[eal] E[state] Commissioner."[81]

In one survey response, southern sentiments were explicit. Charles W. Stewart, one of the fourteen vice presidents of the California Real Estate Association, wrote, "Allow me to sat [sic] that the western negro is a menace to our western city development, unless the situation is wisely handled." As an example of unwise handling, he wrote: "Years ago when I was In [sic] Los Angeles operating—some one sold to a negro—in the S W part of the City—the next door neighbor then wanted to get away—and so the endless chain went one [sic], and the area—I'll say a mile suare [sic] is a blot to the S W part of LA. They should be over on the S E part where the section first started." He added that "the western negro does not know his place. In Mississippi where I was born—and other states there—they know their place and keep it, but not here." He advised that the CREA try to keep blacks in their place by working through the city planning department. "The Mexicans can be well handled, and are quite reliable," he concluded, "but not so with the negroes. A big question is ahead, so we just as well prepare for it."[82]

Like many restrictive covenant cases, the Long Case had a tangled pedigree. It began in 1905, when a woman named Letteau developed an early subdivision called the Entwistle Tract. It was well south of downtown, just east of Main Street, around 41st Street. It was an all-white, relatively undeveloped part of the city. The property deeds nonetheless contained restrictive covenants, which happened to include restrictions on occupancy. The covenants also stated that if the provision was violated, the property would revert back to the original owners, that is, the Letteau family. But the restrictions had failed to keep blacks out. As early as 1907, an African American family had moved into to one of the Entwistle homes, and they were able to stay put. Other blacks gradually moved to the area. By the mid-1920s, Negroes made up about half the neighborhood, and they lived there without incident.[83]

In early 1924, William H. Long and his wife, Eunice, an ordinary, hard-working couple, were finally able to buy a home in Los Angeles. They found a small bungalow they liked at 771 East 41st Street, in the old Entwistle Tract. It had been bought and sold several times since Mrs. Letteau had first sold it in 1905. In the house across the street from the Longs, a black family had lived peacefully for seventeen years; down the street, another had been in their home for five years. During escrow, the Longs were surprised to learn that the deed to the home contained a restrictive covenant. The Longs' real estate agent was Clarence C. Jones, who was an attorney and a member of the local NAACP's Legal Redress Committee. He advised the Longs to buy, because other black families had lived there in peace for so long. With a down payment of nearly two thousand dollars, the Longs made it home.

Days later, heirs of Mrs. Letteau brought suit against the Longs. Drawing on *Gary*, they insisted the occupancy clause had been violated and that title should revert to them. Whether the Letteau heirs were motivated by racial ideas or simple greed is unknown. But their lawsuit had enormous implications. If the Letteaus won, they could go after every other black-owned property in the original subdivision, as well as all of the white-owned homes that were rented to blacks. By the mid-1920s, Afro-Angelenos owned millions of dollars' worth of real estate that was covered by old and forgotten covenants. The *Gary* ruling made many covenants useless, but those that happened to include occupancy clauses were a different matter. A victory by the Letteaus could have a domino effect throughout the city. The children and grandchildren of early developers might clean up on title-reversion cases in neighborhoods that had long since turned from all-white to mixed. Clarence Jones rushed word of the threat to the local branch, and the organization agreed, as Eunice Long later said, "to take up the fight and make a test case of it."[84]

Ceruti saw an opportunity to reverse the occupancy side of *Gary*. In his opinion, the *Gary* case had been bungled by irresponsible counsel. For no good reason, the attorney representing Alfred Gary had not made an appearance before the California Supreme Court or even submitted a brief for the justices' consideration. The justices had made a point of that in their written decision. Ceruti felt that the overconfidence or irresponsibility of the defense attorney had led to the damnable ruling on occupancy. In his view, *Gary* could be overturned with strong financial support and expert counsel. And he was just the man for the job. In April he suggested as much to the national office. "It is important that the next case on appeal involving this question should be thoroughly prepared and presented; the best of counsel should be engaged, and neither money nor pains spared to overturn the rule declared in the Gary Case." He felt certain the Long Case would be appealed, because "neither party would be satisfied with a decision . . . rendered against it." If the Longs won, he was certain that "the powerful Title Companies and the many Realty Companies who seem to be intensely interested in the subject would urge and, very likely, finance the appeal in order to obtain a more satisfactory decision confirming the rule in the Gary Case." The bottom line was this: the NAACP and all of its allies "should join in one supreme effort to prevent the segregation of our people in property matters." The Long Case provided that opportunity.[85]

But NAACP officials in New York were conducting their own case against restrictive covenants—*Corrigan v. Buckley*, a case that NAACP attorneys had argued before the U.S. Supreme Court in January 1926; the justices' decision would be rendered soon. The case originated in Washington, D.C., when a white woman (Corrigan) sought to sell her home to a black woman and was prevented from doing so by the restrictive covenant on her property. After losing twice in Washington district courts, the second time in federal court, the plaintiff's attorney convinced the NAACP national office to pick up the case. Attorneys for Corrigan argued that court-mandated enforcement of restrictive covenants constituted state action and was therefore a violation of the Fourteenth Amendment. Believing it was on the cusp of a major victory, the national office urged Ceruti to delay the Long Case until the Supreme Court ruled on *Corrigan*. It insisted a win in *Corrigan* would make the case against the Longs moot; conversely, a defeat in *Letteau* might have a negative impact on *Corrigan*. But the national office miscalculated; *Corrigan* proved disastrous. That May, the Supreme Court dismissed the *Corrigan* case, citing lack of jurisdiction. Justice Edward T. Sanford stated that covenants were a private, not public, matter. The justices thus upheld the lower court's ruling in favor of enforcing covenants. More important, Sanford's written opinion leveled a broadside against the NAACP's constitutional claims. Inadvertently, the national office's case had assured a defeat in *Letteau*.[86]

On a personal level, the Longs had suffered badly during the extended legal proceedings. First, William Long had been hospitalized, delaying the initial hearing. Shortly thereafter, Eunice Long became ill, and her four-month hospital stay further postponed the trial. Meanwhile, as Eunice later wrote, "Mr. Long, through worrie [sic] over the possible loss of our home, and my physical condition, lost control of his mind and had to be taken to the State Hospital for the insane." His condition grew worse, and he soon died. Eunice, virtually an invalid, held on to what little she had left.[87]

In December 1926, the court ruled in favor of the Letteaus, upholding the occupancy clause. Eunice Long and dozens of other home owners in the old subdivision—white and black—now stood to lose their property. The NAACP's defeat in the Long Case occurred at nearly the same time that the Bath House Battle was lost. Claude Hudson had to report both defeats to the national office in the same letter. Unlike the swimming pool case, though, Hudson insisted the branch would push the Long Case to the end. "If we lose in [the] Supreme Court here I am depending on [the] National Office to take [it] to Washington. It probably involves [a] half million dollars worth of property in Los Angeles alone."[88]

Everything went wrong for Eunice Long and the local branch. On March 21, 1927, Burton Ceruti died suddenly of heart failure; he was fifty-three years old. Superior Court judge Albert L. Stephens, upon hearing the news, called for a moment of remembrance in his courtroom, adding, "Mr. Ceruti was my personal and good friend. As a lawyer he was able, painstaking and conscientious, and was in every way a high-minded citizen and a credit to the profession and to the better citizenry of this community." Black Los Angeles had lost its most effective legal guardian, and the national NAACP had lost the sole western representative on its executive board. Unfortunately for the NAACP, Judge Stephens did not handle Ceruti's appeal of the Long Case.[89]

Days after Ceruti's death, a different Superior Court judge denied Ceruti's appeal. When that happened, the Letteau heirs sued every black home owner in the Entwistle Tract, as well as the white owners who had been renting to African Americans. Here was the full-blown catastrophe. On top of that, *Corrigan* was on the books and Ceruti was gone. Eunice Long, now a widow, feared eviction. Clarence Jones and Willis O. Tyler, attorneys acting for the NAACP, assured her she would be able to remain in her home as long as they kept appealing her case, which they promised to do.[90]

But they failed Eunice Long. Her case work got lost on a cluttered desk, and the lawyers forgot to file for appeal. The court's deadline for appeal passed, and the case died. Neither Long nor Hudson knew about it. Long learned the news only when the sheriff served her an eviction notice. Stunned, she called Hudson, who had also assumed the case had been appealed. Long sent an anguished handwritten letter to the NAACP's national office, and New York demanded an explanation from the L.A. branch. Hudson investigated and replied somberly that the attorneys had failed. Nothing more could be done to save the home, but "since she is a semi-invalid, an effort is being made [by the local branch] and a Committee has been appointed to secure funds for her benefit." This crisis, he added, "naturally and very properly . . . [caused] dissatisfaction in the eyes of the public against the Association for its conduct of the case." Eunice Long was evicted.[91]

"Very Much Depressed"

By the mid-1920s, the community's middle-class leadership barely remained standing. The smoke from Tulsa; the reappearance of *The Clansman;* the rebirth of the KKK; the turmoil within the NAACP; the segregation of swimming pools; the disastrous results of *Letteau v. Long;* the loss of Ceruti—it was difficult to absorb all these blows. The "spirit of the West," as Roberts called it, was losing out to Jim Crow.

White racism was the main problem, but it was not the only difficulty facing black leaders. As the emerging metropolis continued to sprawl, the African American community became, like the city itself, increasingly scattered—not so much geographically as within its ranks. Rapid black population growth made it difficult to absorb so many newcomers into the community. There was also that Southern California problem of getting people involved in civic affairs. "The great out doors calls," lamented Claude Hudson, and the people of the black community "go in as many different directions as there are automobiles to carry them." Leadership divisions and community fragmentation had an impact. As Lulu Slaughter of the NAACP wrote to the national office in 1925, "I suppose you know Los Angeles is about the hardest town in the whole state to work."[92]

J. C. Banks's address to the local branch had been prophetic. These were difficult days in which to maintain "the fighting spirit." Even John Somerville—an optimistic fighter if there ever was one—was losing hope. Boarding a train in Los Angeles to attend the 1926 NAACP convention in Chicago, he admitted that he "was very much depressed because of the many adverse decisions rendered in the courts against our group in our fight for equality."[93] If the battle for freedom could demoralize John Somerville, then Afro-Angelenos were enduring one of the more trying moments in their history. In black Los Angeles, the fighting spirit was faltering. Whether it could be revived remained to be seen.

7

The Business
of Race

George Beavers, Jr., turned thirty-two in 1924. His parents, George and Annie, had brought the family to Los Angeles from Atlanta twenty years earlier to gain the "full citizenship rights and better living conditions" they wanted so badly. They found better conditions, but also hardship: George Jr.'s early exit from high school, their homes lost to fire, Annie's death. Nor did they enjoy "full" citizenship rights in Los Angeles, which was why George Jr., became active in the NAACP. For all this heartache and frustration, the Beavers family established a singularly active and fruitful lifestyle. George Jr. and his wife, Willie Mae, took full advantage of their opportunities and devoted themselves to community service. His jobs steadily improved—chauffeur, elevator operator, messenger, factory worker. After World War I, he exchanged his blue collar for a white one, taking on sales jobs and then starting his own small building-maintenance company. Along the way, he earned his high school equivalency diploma and took additional business courses. He and Willie Mae had helped found the People's Independent Church in 1915 and remained active spiritual leaders. Their church aided their material lives as well, for pastor Napoleon P. Greggs was, George recalled, "a man who was very much interested in business success as well as in religion."[1]

Everything in Beavers's life primed him for the opportunity that knocked in early 1922, when a sales agent for the American Mutual Benefit Association came to his door. American Mutual was a black-owned, Texas-based insurance firm that had recently sent a representative west to establish a branch office in Los Angeles, which had no black insurance company. That representative was William Nickerson, Jr., a native Texan and veteran insurance man, who arrived in L.A. in 1921. Nickerson soon met another newcomer to L.A., Norman O. Houston, a Bay Area man who had studied business at UC Berkeley before the World War. Houston became Nickerson's first sales agent and was soon superintendent of the L.A. branch. The man who called on George Beavers could not adequately answer Beavers's probing questions about the enterprise and so, at a later time, brought Norman Houston to meet him. Sensing Beavers's business acumen, Houston soon introduced him to Nickerson. The three men quickly became friends and associates, with Beavers hiring on as a salesman. In 1924, when American Mutual abandoned its West Coast office, this trio—Nickerson, Houston, and Beavers—decided to form their own insurance company, which would be headquartered on Central Avenue.[2]

Their dream was only the latest manifestation of the community's longstanding faith in Race enterprise. Barred from the top wage-earning jobs and blocked from managerial positions in the corporate world, ambitious African Americans gravitated toward entrepreneurial ventures, especially those that catered to the growing population of Afro-Angelenos. The nationalist surge of the early 1920s strengthened the trend: black-owned businesses would hire African Americans and provide useful services to black consumers. Race enterprises would keep money circulating within the black community, uplifting and enriching it. One way to get free of poverty and dependence was to build a thriving ethnic economy. Because Race pride and company profit would go hand in hand, people like George Beavers, Jr., felt both a duty and desire to create prosperous black-owned businesses. In the best-case scenario, all blacks would benefit. But it was one thing to envision success, another to achieve it.

The Black Business Ethos

The ethos of Race enterprise in the 1920s was an ongoing theme carried over from earlier decades. Black journalists, entrepreneurs, Club women, and ministers had preached the gospel of Race progress through Race enterprise for many years. The pastor of Second Baptist, Dr. T. L. Griffith, voiced the essential view in an *Eagle* editorial in early 1921: "Spend something with the Colored merchants. We will increase the aggregate of our wealth by trading. Give the Negro business men a chance." Insisting that "trade" was an honorable pursuit, he said, "Think of the Jewish people in contrast to our people. The Jews are traders and have been for ages. Very seldom do you see a Jew in search of a job. Labor produces wages. The Jew gets wealth." Offering the usual formula, Griffith argued that black wages spent in black-owned stores would create a broad foundation of wealth in the community; prosperous Race enterprises would then be able to expand and hire more black employees, and the upward spiral would continue.[3]

Prodding the black community with ethnic comparisons was not uncommon. "Take a trip to First St. and see what the Japanese are doing there," Joe Bass suggested; then "go out Central Ave. and see what's going on there. The comparison will make you sick, it will show you up."[4] In its inaugural issue, L.A.'s newest Race paper, the *Western Dispatch*, complained, "On Central Avenue between Ninth and Washington streets, there are a great many stores which we do not own, but whose trade is almost entirely colored." And yet those stores refused to hire blacks as employees—an enduring source of black indignation.[5]

Not all the news was bad. "The Colored people of this section," Bass wrote in 1922, "now reinforced by the people from the South and East, are lining up along business lines as never before. . . . Right here in Los Angeles the Race for the past year has made giant strides along business lines." He gave special commendation to the grocery stores, drugstores, building contractors, and realtors, whose total transactions for 1921 he estimated to be well into the millions. And despite the *Western Dispatch*'s jab about white-owned Central Avenue stores, Fred Roberts's *New Age* boasted that a new string of black enterprises at 12th Street and Central Avenue would "stir your pride, if you believe in Race boosting." "That's the spirit," Roberts added in a subsequent edition: Race merchants "propose to reap, for the benefit of the group, some of the many thousands being spent in their vicinity."[6]

Such rhetoric could be heard in any Afro-American community nationwide, but black Angelenos spiced theirs with western flavor. A telling example was the book *Western Progress: A Pictorial Story of Economic and Social Advancement in Los Angeles, California*, published in 1928 by Louis S. Tenette and B. B. Bratton, young African American entrepreneurs who had established a little publishing company in the Central Avenue district. Tenette and Bratton hired black photographer G. C. Ecton, who owned and operated the California Studio on Central Avenue, to take pictures of the black-owned businesses in town. *Western Progress* advertised some sixty black businesses and sprinkled in some pictures of Southern California homes owned by African Americans.[7]

"The phenomenal growth of Los Angeles and its environs during the last decade has attracted world-wide attention," Tenette and Bratton wrote in their preface. To picture all of the city's growth would have been too large a task, they explained. Therefore, they had "selected the progress of a group whose achievements economically and socially would furnish the most potent basis of reflection and the greatest inspiration." Despite this claim that *Western Progress* was a case study of Los Angeles's commercial success, presumably of interest to the entire citizenry, the book was obviously a publication by blacks, about blacks, and intended primarily to inspire entrepreneurship within the local black community and to capture the attention of those back East who were contemplating the business opportunities for blacks in the West.[8]

The "western" emphasis resurfaced continually in the book, which offered photos or sketches of black businesses described by short blurbs. The *Eagle* was the "most widely known publication in the West." Nickerson's Drug Store was heralded as "an excellent example of the new idea in western business." The Western Cosmetic Company sold its special brand of hair straighteners "throughout the west," and the Conner-Johnson funeral home "[typified] the progressive west." Naturally, too, there were businesses that found a ready association with the Southern California climate, such as Blodgett Motor Company, which sold Hudsons and Essex automobiles and stood "ready to satisfy your longing for California's open spaces and her matchless scenic beauties." Similarly, the Pansy Flower Shoppe entry noted that "flowers, beautiful blossoms kissed by the morning dew, caressed by magical sunshine, are always in season in Los Angeles"—"California's natural beauty on sale here!"[9]

To ensure that boosterism was always in season, too, black entrepreneurs established a variety of business associations during the 1920s. Early 1920 saw the creation of the Pacific Coast Industrial Federation, which promised to launch "its services and influences in the West, like the voluminous Sun that transplants its rays upon the great Rocky Mountains." "Each month," an early blurb said, ". . . the great West [is] luring hundreds of Negroes to our doors." The federation, with its headquarters at 824 Central Avenue, would help newcomers get started in Los Angeles and would coordinate and support new Race enterprises. Newspapers and organizations such as the YMCA held rallies for promising enterprises. The Commercial Council of Los Angeles, "devoted to the promotion of business, manufacturing, and immigration," officially incorporated in 1924. Its board of directors was a veritable who's who of local Race leaders, including (only a partial list) the attorney and entrepreneur Lewis K. Beeks, the businesswoman Bessie E. Prentice, Elks leader Percy D. Buck, Joe Bass, Noah Thompson, Titus Alexander, Paul Williams, Norman Houston, and attorney Charles Darden. In 1928, the same year Bratton and Tenette published *Western Progress,* the Western State Publishing Company touted a "Negro Business Guide" to highlight the city's Race enterprises.[10]

Organizations like these rose and fell erratically, however. Their ephemeral nature suggested that black entrepreneurs were an individualistic lot— strivers too busy and competitive for long-term cooperation. As always, it was easier for black boosters to exalt Race unity than it was to attain it. Then, too, some black leaders would only go so far down the separatist road. Afro-Angeleno business leaders never organized a Los Angeles Negro Chamber of Commerce, for example. That would have been a controversial move, because some local blacks, such as John Somerville, were already members of L.A.'s regular Chamber of Commerce. Perhaps the creation of a separate, Negro Chamber smacked too much of Jim Crow for the Central Avenue boosters. The ethos promised both individual advance as American citizens *and* group uplift; and in the racial climate of 1920s America, that made sense. But it was still a fine line to walk.

Ultimately, the realities of black business never matched the ideal of Race enterprise. The "protected" Negro businesses—funeral homes, barber shops, beauty salons, and insurance companies that catered to blacks—were usually a safe bet and sometimes made small fortunes. In the broader world of commerce, however, the risks were much greater. For one thing, tensions sometimes arose between black capitalists and black consumers. When it came to restaurants, grocery stores, and other retail outfits, African American buyers often patronized white-owned or Japanese-owned enterprises more frequently than those operated by blacks. Many in the community believed white stores offered lower prices (sometimes true, because whites had broader wholesale connections) and better service (a subjective call).[11] This attitude outraged local boosters. "There are those of the Race," thundered Joe Bass, "who are determined (if they can) to make the rich corporations richer by withholding their support from their own Race."[12]

When the Colored Citizens Civic and Commercial Club organized in 1921, the question demanded attention. In the midst of organizing a "Negro Trade Week," club leaders acknowledged that black consumers were angry at some Race businesses, especially the eating establishments. An investigation by the club found that "often these places charge twice as much as they should, and in many instances eating places operated by whites and Japanese [offer] better service at much less the cost." The club urged residents to shun unworthy restaurants, and even warned that it might bring charges of racial discrimination against these black-owned businesses, because "while this club is deeply interested in building up Negro enterprise, it also insists that Negro business must deal fair with the Negro."[13] Even a booster like Reverend Griffith felt inclined to warn that some Race enterprises "will give you a square deal, just as some of the others will take advantage of you."[14]

Still, the ethos had an enduring allure and grew stronger during the 1920s. The danger was that black Angelenos had placed Race enterprise on a pedestal and imbued commerce with an almost messianic power: the group economy would save their people. Such an ideal asked too much of an unpredictable business world, and boosters surely knew that. But amid the racial crises of the immediate postwar years, Race enterprise offered a ray of hope. This beam shone brightly on Marcus Garvey, who envisioned a Negro commercial empire.

Garveyism as Race Enterprise

The Universal Negro Improvement Association meant many things to many people, but in black Los Angeles it initially meant the promise of Race enterprise on a grand scale. The organization's Black Star Steamship Line promised lucrative trade links between New York, the West Indies, and West Africa. In so doing, it would bring the African diaspora full circle and spark a global rise in Negro wealth. Garveyism won many enthusiastic middle-class converts in L.A. at the outset of 1921. Less than a year later, many of those converts threw their Garvey buttons in the trash, largely because the Garveyites in New York proved to be inept businessmen. The rapid rise and fall of L.A.'s Garvey movement also stemmed from the context in which it occurred. It rose and crashed just as the black community faced the tumult of 1921. The local Garvey movement could not have taken shape at a more chaotic moment. The context made its ascent more emotional, its fall more severe.

Garvey was an enigmatic character. A native of the West Indies, he briefly visited the United States in the mid-1910s, then traveled in Africa and Europe, where he had a vision of a new Black Empire, complete with black royalty and riches. He returned to America to build a movement that would make this vision a reality. Garvey captured the imagination of black America as few had ever done. Small and slightly plump in stature, with an almost perfectly black complexion, Garvey had a soothing, high-pitched voice that enraptured his audiences. He paraded in a gaudy military-dress uniform, complete with plumed hat and white gloves. He surrounded himself with a manly entourage, on whom he bestowed military titles. By 1921, his UNIA claimed more than four million dues-paying members nationwide. The central themes of Garvey's organization—Race unity, Race economy, Pride in Africa—were nothing new among American Negroes. But he presented those ideas with an exuberance and ornate ceremony that matched the spirit of the early 1920s, and his emphasis on racial separatism sounded sensible to a people who had experienced the disastrous postwar fallout. For all the show, however, the heart of the UNIA program was the steamship line. With so many members, the UNIA supposedly had millions of dollars to work with, and blacks could also purchase stock in the Black Star Line, with promises of excellent returns on the investment.[15]

The UNIA's song of Race unity and commercial empire played well in black Los Angeles when its middle-class leaders finally picked up the tune. Oddly, Los Angeles was one of the last communities in California to organize a UNIA division. Many smaller Afro-Californian communities latched on to Garveyism earlier. The UNIA had sixteen divisions in California in 1921–22, from San Diego to Bakersfield to Oakland, including smaller outfits in Los Angeles County such as the divisions in Watts and Sawtelle. As early as January 1920, the *Eagle* brought word that "the now famous Black Star Line promoted from New York has successfully launched its gigantic undertaking . . . and given a practical demonstration of our capacity to do big things." Actually, it took a while longer for Afro-Angelenos to be convinced of the "practical" nature of the line. One reason many came to believe in it was that the Reverend John D. Gordon, a pillar in the Los Angeles community, had become a leading official in the UNIA's national office.[16]

Dr. John Dawson Gordon and his brother, Hugh Gordon, were both well known Race men in Los Angeles. Reared in Atlanta, the Gordon brothers came to Southern California in 1903, the same year the Beavers family made the trek west. The Gordon brothers were bookish, but Hugh, who described himself as a "student of sociology, history, and economics," had a mind for business. He promoted group economics and established the Pyramid Cooperative Grocery and Meat Market in Los Angeles. John, hearing a different call, became a minister. In 1904 he accepted the pulpit at Tabernacle Baptist, near the corner of 12th Street and Central Avenue. He helped Charlotta Spear keep the *Eagle* afloat in her early years as editor; he was instrumental in organizing the Colored YMCA; and he assisted in the creation of the Sojourner Truth Home. Fred Roberts counted him as a key political ally, and during the World War, Marshall Stimson chose him to be a Four-Minute Man.[17]

Unexpectedly, in the summer of 1919, Reverend Gordon decided to leave

Los Angeles. After an emotional farewell ceremony, at which Charlotta Bass testified to Gordon's encouragement and help over the years, the popular minister boarded a train for Chicago. Leaving his wife behind, he had no new church and no clear destination. He evangelized through the urban North—Chicago, Pittsburgh, Philadelphia, New York. He met Garvey and committed himself to the UNIA. In late 1919, Tabernacle Baptist voted to recall Gordon as its pastor, and he accepted, returning to his old flock that December. But his roving was not finished. Garvey called on him to serve as "assistant president general" in the UNIA national office, and Gordon took a leave of absence from Tabernacle Baptist, maintaining his close ties to the Los Angeles community. When Garveyism finally swept through black L.A., many of Gordon's associates were at the forefront. The charter ceremony was held at Tabernacle Baptist.[18]

The Afro-Angelenos who organized the local UNIA, and who received their charter as Division 156 in January 1921, were familiar community figures. Joe and Charlotta Bass were front and center. So was the journalist and realtor Noah D. Thompson, who was elected president of Division 156. Other prominent members were John W. Coleman, the well-known realtor and employment-service owner; "Pop" Sanders, a perennial boss in black Republican circles; Hugh Gordon; and Hugh Macbeth. A few marginal characters found their way in, notably "Luke" Luke, a smart fellow but also a grifter in L.A.'s political game, known for his suffocating speeches at the Sunday Forum. Other enthusiastic members, such as Eva Overr-Solomon, who published pro-Garvey pieces in the Race papers, had never been inside the circle of middle-class leadership. Even so, the typical charter member of Division 156 was a mainstream activist.[19]

Division president Noah D. Thompson had a full résumé of middle-class leadership. A native of Baltimore who studied business in Chicago, Thompson got his start working for eastern Race papers and by serving a two-year stint at the Tuskegee Institute. By the early twentieth century, he had moved to Los Angeles and into its journalistic circles. Thompson was a dashing sort, with a medium-brown complexion and a goatee. Delilah Beasley's 1919 *Negro Trail Blazers of California* claimed that he wrote for L.A.'s dailies and was even "on the editorial staff of the *Evening Express*." He also wrote for local and national Race papers, his 1924 "Horn of Plenty" article in the *Messenger* underscoring his booster spirit and his faith in the Western Ideal for African Americans. After his first wife died, Thompson met and wed the elegant Eloise Bibb, herself a journalist who wrote for various local publications, including the local Catholic magazine, *Tidings*. Noah and Eloise were devout Catholics who moved comfortably within the arenas of more-affluent white society. Each was a popular speaker among both blacks and whites, so it was not surprising when Marshall Stimson tapped Noah as a Four-Minute Man during the war. Of course, he also dealt in real estate. He was, in short, a classic Los Angeles Race man.[20]

Just as black business was more than an economic proposition, Garveyism involved more than Race enterprise. The movement packed a cultural punch. In the beginning, the UNIA drew its share of middle-class converts, but most dropped out soon enough: Garvey's garish uniform and the overblown titles of his lieutenants were a bit ostentatious for middle- and upper-class types. Loyalists tended to be poorer blacks who would never be, and perhaps had no desire to be, part of the black bourgeoisie. Then, too, Garveyism blew the lid off of the issue of skin color among African Americans. In fact, Garvey pointedly made it an issue. Because of his complexion, he had been put down by light-skinned mulattos in his native Jamaica, and, as he saw it, the same pattern held in the United States: lighter skin meant more opportunities; the Tans lorded it over the Blacks; the "blue-vein societies"—a reference to blacks whose skin was light enough to see the veins on their wrists—looked down on darker Negroes. So when Garvey faced attacks from Du Bois and his ilk, the UNIA leader shot back that they were not really Negro at all. Their African ancestry, he said, had been polluted by white blood; they were a mongrel group, neither black nor white.[21]

This issue hit a little too close to home in Los Angeles, because there were so many light-skinned people in the community—for example, the many whose roots lay in Creole Louisiana. And it was also true that many local Race leaders had noticeably light complexions and "good hair," including William Easton, Burton Ceruti, Beatrice Thompson, John Somerville, L. G. Robinson, Albert Baumann, J. H. Shackleford, and Hugh Macbeth. Fred Roberts was medium brown, but his wife, Pearl Hines Roberts, was virtually white. The trend was hardly absolute, of course. Most of the leading ministers were dark skinned; Joe Bass, Noah Thompson, James Vena, Pop Sanders, and Charles Darden all had deep-brown or black complexions, as did many leading Club women.

Still, every African American knew there was a painful grain of truth in Garvey's generalizations. The preference for naturally wavy (as opposed to kinky) hair and lighter skin was evident in the endless run of Race-paper advertisements whose products promised straight hair and whiter complexions. All the drugstores on Central Avenue had shelves full of Kashmir Preparations, such as "Famous Bleach," which promised to "cure ugly skin."[22] Ads for Excelento Quinnie Pomade promised that "long, straight, silky hair can be yours," and that Excelento Skin Beautifier would "act immediately and almost miraculously on dark and sallow skins, whitening and removing all pimples and blisters."[23] Some observers saw black self-hatred in all of this, including the novelist Wallace Thurman, who left L.A. for Harlem and whose 1928 novel, *The Blacker the Berry*, set partly in Los Angeles, hammered on the theme of self-loathing. But that was making too much of it. After all, white women were spending millions of dollars to have their straight hair curled and their light skin darkened, and no one said they hated themselves. However one viewed the skin and hair issue, Garvey put Negro leaders on the defensive and forced them to respond.[24]

Fred Roberts urged his readers to leave all theorizing about skin color to the white-supremacy crowd. The *Eagle* contended that the UNIA had wrongly fostered a greater sense of color consciousness among African Americans. John Somerville had a further gripe with Garvey, since Somerville was a Jamaican of the light-skinned sort. In an interview later in his life, he was asked whether "Garvey stirred any great interest among West Indian settlers" in Los Angeles. Somerville's curt answer: "No. They made fun of him." Vada Somerville, sitting in on the interview, interjected, "He was just a show-off." Garvey was not their sort, and their point of view was hardly unique. Initially, the Basses and others had celebrated the possibilities of the UNIA, but differences in style separated Garvey and L.A.'s black middle class.[25]

The romance between Garveyism and Los Angeles's middle-class leadership chilled quickly in August 1921, when Noah Thompson attended the national UNIA convention in New York. Division 156 members had raised a thousand dollars so their president could attend the monthlong enclave, and he attended with unmatched verve. Questions about the Black Star Line and UNIA finances troubled the Los Angeles group, and Thompson promised to convey "the real dope" about things in New York. He found the proceedings appalling and sent critical reports to L.A.'s Race papers. "Inefficiency is startlingly apparent throughout the organization," he wrote in a piece for the *New Age*. "Two days were spent in debating how many buttons should be worn on the robe of a certain official." Worse still, UNIA finances were a closed book. On the convention floor, Thompson hammered away at top officials, demanding that they open their records for inspection. When they finally did so, the treasury showed eight thousand dollars—despite official claims that the organization had more than four million dues-paying members.[26]

Thompson demanded that delegates get to see the Black Star ships, since African Americans had purchased more than $250,000 in Black Star stock issues. Day after day, UNIA officials stonewalled. "Tomorrow" they would see the ships. But by the end of the convention, not a ship had been seen. The delegates did not know that there were no ships worth seeing, but they began to suspect it. Thompson's demands created a firestorm that engulfed many UNIA officials, including his own friend, the Reverend Gordon, who, deservedly or not, took the fall for the mismanagement. Gordon resigned under duress, but not before issuing his own public demand for official accountability, from the top down—a swipe at Garvey. Gordon returned to L.A., where Tabernacle Baptist welcomed him back as minister.[27]

Gordon's resignation and Thompson's scathing report to the L.A. UNIA (Joe Bass called it "educating indeed") sent Division 156 into revolt against New York. Before the convention, the division had boasted one thousand members. Afterward, only about one hundred remained loyal to the national organization. Garvey sent out a representative who dogged Thompson and urged loyalists to supplant him. Followers of Thompson endorsed a resolution condemning the national office's "inexcusable interference with the purely local affairs of the division." Such action, they insisted, "threatens to destroy the work in the West, which is largely influenced by Los Angeles activities." The national office responded by officially removing Thompson, Charlotta Bass, and the rest of the officers from their posts.[28]

In what was either a case of poor judgment or a calculated slap at the pro-Thompson crowd, national UNIA officials named the flamboyant "Luke" Luke as chair of the newly reorganized board of trustees for UNIA Division 156. His appointment stung the city's middle class. Garvey then revoked the division's original charter—thereby purging any remaining malcontents—and rechartered a brand new Division 156. The new group had about a hundred members, who elected H. Douglas Greer as their president. He was a good choice. Unlike Luke, Greer was by rights a ranking member of the middle-class leadership. A popular voice and piano teacher, "Professor" Greer had a studio near 7th Street and Central Avenue and another in Pasadena. He had served as a Four-Minute Man during the war. A good writer, he penned thoughtful articles for the *Eagle*. He remained loyal to Garvey, rather than to Thompson and the Basses. Perhaps, as a musician, he preferred pageantry to business. Or maybe he fully believed in an African Republic. In any case, he proved himself a witty defender of Garveyism and enjoyed poking fun at what he considered the pretensions and confused racial identities of the city's mainstream Race leaders. Technically, L.A.'s UNIA survived under Greer, but, for all practical purposes, the *Eagle* had it right in November 1921 when its headline read, "U.N.I.A. Is No More."[29]

Thompson and associates organized a rival organization—the Pacific Coast Negro Improvement Association—and once again held an inaugural meeting in Tabernacle Baptist. Thompson became president; Joe Bass, secretary. While lauding "the Garvey spirit," PCNIA point man Hugh Macbeth insisted that "ignorance shall not be installed over and above intelligence." Black L.A. would rely on "sane business methods." Joe Bass lambasted national UNIA officials as a bunch of half-wits. The Reverend Gordon, making clear where his loyalties lay, publicly endorsed Thompson. "It takes the highest form of manhood to do what Mr. Thompson has done. Under his leadership the Race is safe. He is intelligent, bold, honest to a fault." Thompson stated that the purpose of the PCNIA was "to consolidate efforts for the civic and commercial betterment of the community," and raise funds to establish a new "business block" on Central Avenue.[30]

The PCNIA was not so much a rival to Garvey's organization as it was the traditional Central Avenue ethos in a new package. Los Angeles's "neo-Garveyites," as the historian Emory Tolbert has called them, advocated cooperative economics without endorsing a separatist ideology or a "Back to Africa" program. They never promised a Cal Star Line, even though they had their own international business ambitions south of the border. When Garvey's rival from Harlem, the *Messenger* editor Chandler Owen, paid a visit in 1922, he gushed about the economic possibilities of black Los Angeles: "Verily she is a queen!" he wrote in the *Messenger*. But Owen also noted important differences between East and West. In L.A., he found "a remarkable laying aside of petty prejudices [within the black community], such as we *seldom* find in the East." Quickly becoming friends with PCNIA president Noah Thompson, Owen joined with Thompson to organize the California Development Company, which bought and operated an apartment building in the heart of the Central Avenue district.[31]

The neo-Garveyites in Los Angeles had a western chip on their collective shoulder. They enjoyed entertaining eastern leaders, such as Owen and Du Bois, but they chafed at any hint of dependence on the East and continued to view the West as a region set apart. As Joe Bass would write, in reference to one of Marcus Garvey's visits to Los Angeles, "California seems—at the present—to be a mecca for every Negro who has some sort of propaganda. . . . If our perspective was not so close, we, in California, would observe that we are rapidly coordinating our efforts and laying a foundation [for] our future economic and political betterment." And the clincher: "We need no help from the outside."[32]

By the time Garvey finally came to town for the first time in the summer of 1922, he was an embattled crusader. With UNIA spiraling downward, he needed friends. In Los Angeles, he sought reconciliation with Noah Thompson and the Reverend Gordon, which he knew could be difficult, because the PCNIA was strong and the local UNIA weak. To complicate matters, Chandler Owen had just completed his winning tour of black Los Angeles and, in doing so, had taken every opportunity to thrash Garvey and promote the PCNIA.[33]

But Afro-Angelenos gave Garvey a hero's welcome anyway, beginning with a gala parade down Central Avenue. An estimated ten thousand black people crowded the sidewalks to get a glimpse of the UNIA leader. Garvey rode in a convertible with none other than Fred Roberts, as well as Professor Greer. Division 156 added a marching band and a "Republic of Africa" float. Mayor George Cryer sent a representative to welcome Garvey at the Trinity Auditorium, the parade's destination, where an audience of about a thousand people turned out to hear the Black Moses. One young man in the audience was Paul Bontemps's son, Arna, home from college in Northern California, who attended more out of curiosity than anything else, but whose own longing to explore his African roots was growing. As he later wrote, the "pudgy spellbinder" had an "oddly lyrical style. The audience swayed and was transported."[34]

This fine performance temporarily bolstered local Garveyites. Reverend Gordon returned to the UNIA fold like a mourner to the bench, following Garvey back to New York and once again leaving Tabernacle Baptist in other hands. Garvey handed Thompson an olive branch, and the PCNIA president responded by burying the hatchet. Indeed, the PCNIA quietly disbanded, making way for other business groups with less-complicated baggage. But Garvey's days as a Black Moses were numbered.[35]

For most black Americans, Garvey committed an unpardonable sin in late 1922 when, in an effort to promote racial separatism, he shook hands with the Ku Klux Klan. Black Los Angeles learned of this alliance in the wake of the Inglewood Raiders trial, and local leaders bitterly denounced Garvey. In New York, Chandler Owen claimed that he had received a black hand, cut from its limb, in the mail; the package, he said, included a letter from the KKK, which praised Marcus Garvey. Joe Bass thundered, "Mr. Garvey here is your hat and please be on your way. . . . We want you to distinctly understand that the Ku Klux Klan is strictly un-American and the Negro who stands for this dastardly institution stands as a traitor to his race." Bass later told Owen, in no uncertain terms, that he favored Garvey's deportation and that he "heartily approve[d] of the gallant fight which you are making against the pernicious propaganda of Garvey. The straw that broke the camel's back was his assimilation of the Ku Klux Klan. He has become a menace to the future of the Negro race." In 1923, shortly before he was deported,

Garvey returned to Los Angeles with words of encouragement to the small but loyal cadre in UNIA Division 156.[36]

Although it had been discredited, Garveyism left its mark on black Los Angeles. Division 156 hung together, quietly and with negligible membership, until about 1933, when it disappeared from the records of the UNIA headquarters in New York, which continued to function after Garvey's deportation. Some bad blood remained between the national office and Los Angeles's middle-class leadership; Garvey's wife, for example, publicly accused Joe Bass of bribing Noah Thompson to smear Garvey for federal authorities. The Reverend John Gordon once again abandoned Garvey in late 1923 and left New York to retake the reins of his twice-abandoned Tabernacle Baptist. This time his return sparked opposition from the two-time interim pastor, L. B. Brown, and a sizable number of members, who soon left to form the *New* Tabernacle Baptist Church. Locals who remained in the UNIA maintained their faith in the future of an African Republic, as well as their belief that all white Americans were, at heart, white supremacists who would never allow black people to live as their equals. In so doing, they carved their own niche of black leadership outside the boundaries of middle-class leadership and laid a foundation in the community for future movements that would blend religious fervor and racial separation with black progress.[37]

For the city's black middle-class activists, however, Garveyism left a different legacy. The financial mysteries of the Black Star Line, the UNIA-PCNIA split, and Garvey's pact with the Klan left mainstream Race leaders uneasy. They no longer trusted schemes that did not originate with their own kind of people. The western habit of pragmatic engagement held firm, but local leaders began to narrow the boundaries of what they considered acceptable activism. Too much style and not enough substance would hereafter be suspect. In their efforts to remake Los Angeles, middle-class Race leaders remained flexible. But schemes that smacked of Garveyism were marked off their list of options.

Gordon Manor

In 1925, Dr. Wilbur C. Gordon sought to create a subdivision for the black middle and upper class. "Gordon Manor," as the development came to be known, was a long way from the hub of the Central Avenue community, and that was largely the point. It represented an effort to break the Eastside residential pattern. Wilbur Gordon (no relation to Hugh and Reverend John) had combined professional success with community service. In 1924, he had founded the Liberty Building and Loan Association, which provided black strivers a place to secure funding for entrepreneurial ventures.[38] Now he aimed to created "a high class [and] restricted Negro residential sub-division."[39] Joined by nine black realtors, Gordon began negotiations to purchase 213 acres of undeveloped land that lay in the southwestern part of Los Angeles County, halfway between the Shoestring and Manhattan Beach, just north of the city of Torrance. The tract was a good seven miles from the corner of 12th and Central. "Why not make Gordon Manor our Wilshire or Hollywood," an *Eagle* advertisement ventured that December.[40]

The land was pricey. Liberty Building and Loan was not big enough to swing the deal on its own, so Gordon's group secured a loan from the white-owned Commercial National Bank—$575,046 total, with a $191,000 down payment. Then Gordon got white financiers involved. Together the two groups formed a seven-million-dollar syndicate to develop Gordon Manor. They quickly spent half a million dollars for streets, curbs, sidewalks, ornamental street lighting, water lines, and fire hydrants. Several black Angelenos drew up plans for luxury homes in Gordon Manor whose estimated prices were $22,000 to $36,000. More affordable homes were planned as well, to cost an average of $3,500, but from the beginning the manor gravitated toward posh.[41]

A group of very wealthy white people who owned lavish homes and sprawling ranches south of Gordon Manor quickly moved to stop the development. They did not want Negroes that close, even in $30,000 homes. This elite group included the influential attorney Henry O'Melveny and the renowned landscape architect Frederick Law Olmsted. Collectively the group owned five million dollars' worth of real estate—the mansions of Palos Verdes which lay between Gordon Manor and the ocean. In a campaign that proved as complicated as it was devious, the O'Melveny group pushed the L.A. County Board of Supervisors to condemn the Gordon Manor land in order to build a public park. In the spring of 1926, the issue came to a head.[42]

The strange thing, even then, was that Gordon Manor was not very close to the winding, elegant thoroughfares where the O'Melveny group lived. Gordon Manor was north of Torrance; they were south of it. About a mile south of the manor, in the middle of Torrance, was a large oil refinery. Driving south from the refinery, there were still a few miles yet to travel before reaching the chic hillside mansions. In short, Gordon Manor was a good distance—and one large refinery—removed from the Palos Verdes estates, and the salty swagger of Los Angeles Harbor lay closer than Gordon Manor did. The fierce reaction to "invading" blacks did not make much sense, geographically speaking. But the protest would get a hearing simply because the people behind it were rich and powerful.

Because O'Melveny's law offices were associated with the condemnation proceedings, he became, for Afro-Angelenos, the most visible villain in the power play. As entries in his private journal show, however, he was more an interested observer than an active antagonist. The battle fascinated him. And as he followed the twists and turns of the case, he voiced increasing disgust at the treachery of his white colleagues and increasing admiration for Gordon. "Great goings on at Supervisors between the negroes and our people," he wrote, as a first reference to the conflict, on May 10, 1926. "The negroes have filed a complaint—asking for an injunction to restrain supervisors from proceeding further. There are rumors of war, of Ku Klux—and all sorts of things. Becoming interesting."[43]

When one of the ringleaders in his group explained a secret plan to take over the property, O'Melveny was unamused. Writing in his journal that night, he noted that the plan "involved plain, downright fraud." According to O'Melveny's account, he had argued against the plan, saying that "we could not participate or continue in this line of deception." But the (unnamed) ringleader would not concede the point: "you could not budge him." Wilbur Gordon tried to circumvent this racist scheme by meeting personally with O'Melveny, who later confided to his journal: "We agreed on armistice until June 30—He sets out his case very ably. [His] is a hard job, to raise the money to buy the property, and in effect, to move a whole community. Dr. Gordon is a very intelligent man."[44] But however much O'Melveny came to admire Gordon, he made no serious effort to stop the scheme from going forward.

Armistice or not, behind-the-scenes negotiations continued, leading to a curious end for Gordon Manor. Leaders on both sides of the conflict continued to meet with O'Melveny. In mid-June, another white antagonist brought a new plan to O'Melveny, who, with some weariness, wrote in his journal, "It would seem as if the plan was to have us attack the rights of the negroes." Back and forth, in public and in private, the struggle over Gordon Manor continued. In late July, O'Melveny thought they were close to a concluding deal in which the whites would "buy out the negroes" for $500,000. But the controversy continued, messily, for the rest of the year. Ultimately, the county condemned the land and issued bonds in excess of one million dollars to pay off the Gordon Manor group. By one estimate, "the Gordon interests will receive close to $700,000 from the sale of bond issue as payment to them under the condemnation proceedings." Gordon's group had made a down payment of nearly $200,000 to begin with, and the syndicate had later invested another $500,000 in improvements, so a settlement of $700,000 would have covered only expenses.[45]

The county gave Gordon Manor a new name—Alondra Park, which today is the site of a public golf course and of El Camino College. The creation of Alondra Park was, as one black observer noted, "the most costly segregation measure ever passed in the West." But the park did not get built in the 1920s. For the rest of the decade, the land stood vacant. Once the Negroes were out of the picture, the "public" need for the park evaporated. The land became a thorn in the side of the elite who had undercut Gordon Manor. As part of the condemnation deal, their group was legally bound to a ten-thousand-acre assessment district, for which they were liable for taxes. In 1932, in the midst of the Great Depression, they could not pay and asked for help from the county supervisors. John Somerville, writing in the *Eagle,* commented that "there can be no logical reason why the people's money should be used to pay for a project which is un-American in its principle. The County Treasury built up from the hard earnings of taxpayers should not be made the dumping ground for the follies of any section or class of people, especially when the underlying motive is based on bigotry and race hatred."[46]

The Urban League

Race enterprise was not the only way to improve the economic condition of black Los Angeles. The business of race also included efforts to open new doors for African American employment in white-owned businesses. Discrimination in hiring—on account of race, ethnicity, sex, religion, appearance, or anything else—was still legal. In the 1920s, it was difficult to even imagine an equal-employment law in America. Instead, the immediate concern was breaking the employment color line through suasion and negotiation. In this effort, the Los Angeles branch of the National Urban League took the lead.

Apart from a recession in 1921, L.A.'s economy throughout the 1920s was robust enough to keep unemployment low, even though some twelve thousand black job seekers arrived during the decade. But the vast majority of Afro-Angelenos, including the middle class, held uncertain jobs near the bottom of the pay scale. The problem was not a lack of jobs, but the absence of good jobs. Race enterprise—paychecks for black workers signed by black capitalists—offered a long-run solution. In the short term, though, African Americans needed better jobs in the world of white-owned business.[47]

That was where the Urban League came in. A product of the progressive-era milieu of the urban North, the National Urban League organized in 1910 (incorporated 1913) in an effort to deal with a wide range of "economic, social, and spiritual conditions among Negroes." Like the NAACP, it was a biracial organization. Initially there was some friction between the two, because they emerged at the same time and because Du Bois found his place in the NAACP while Booker T. Washington supported the league. This tension subsided after Washington's death in 1915, especially because the two organizations began to focus on different issues and use different tactics: the NAACP concentrated its efforts on securing civil rights, its main tactics being propaganda, political lobbying, and legal activism; the Urban League sought to improve black employment and social welfare, its principal tactics being sociological research and negotiations with white business leaders.[48]

In its early years, the Urban League's efforts reflected classic social-welfare progressivism: the league established employment bureaus, playgrounds, and traveler's bureaus; organized outings for working women and children; and advocated for better housing, the rehabilitation of black prisoners, and better health and sanitation within the community. To find the right solutions, the Urban League encouraged the training of black social workers, who would undertake careful research into prevailing conditions and make well-grounded recommendations for uplift campaigns. For all of Booker T. Washington's early support, this was classic Talented Tenth turf, and it appealed broadly to the black middle class. During the Great Migration, the league recruited black workers for white companies and created new job opportunities for blacks. Although the league never lost its interest in social welfare, the Great Migration directed it permanently toward employment issues.

In the 1920s, the league inaugurated its own monthly publication—*Opportunity*—edited by the sociologist Charles S. Johnson, who became the league's chief researcher. *Opportunity*, though it lacked Du Bois's strident critiques, produced a steady stream of articles documenting race prejudice, offering practical examples of how it might be overcome. Johnson added upbeat success stories and enough poetry and literary pieces to draw a broad audience, and he published research results in language understandable to general readers. Soon, the journal found its place beside the *Crisis* on the coffee tables of America's black middle class.[49]

An L.A. branch of the Urban League was founded rather belatedly, mostly because there had been no Great Migration to prompt its organization any sooner. The timing of its appearance in L.A. during the summer of 1921 made sense—it was the summer of the Tulsa race riot, the unearthing of the local KKK, the L.A. riot scare, the increasing pace of black migration to the city, the economic slump. The local branch of the Urban League grew out of an existing women's club, the Tuskegee Industrial Welfare League. The Tuskegee group had been focused on employment for women and the day-care needs of working mothers. Three women led the club: Katherine Barr, Mrs. Ellis N. Warren, and Mrs. Louis S. Tenette. Barr and Warren were well-known Club women. Tenette, from New Orleans, was a more recent arrival but had risen fast. Her husband's reputation had preceded their arrival: Louis Tenette had been the instructor of printing at the Tuskegee Institute, then a newspaperman in New Orleans, and he came to Los Angeles to become the managing editor of the new *Western Dispatch*.[50]

In June 1921, Barr, Warren, and Tenette announced that their organization would become the Los Angeles branch of the Urban League, with its headquarters on Spring Street downtown. Their initial goals were the establishment of an employment service and a community center complete with day nursery. More immediately, they organized a beach outing. Actually, this "outing" was a weeklong, all-expenses-paid vacation in a hotel at Playa Del Rey "limited to working women and children who are not able to take a vacation upon their own expenses." In an advertisement in the local Race papers, the league asked "churches and other organizations . . . to send the names of women and children who will be guests of the Urban League for the week." They wanted sixty to a hundred people for the outing; the league would pay for it out of a newly created "Recreation Fund," to which Barr urged all readers to contribute. The cost of sending "a poor woman or unfortunate child to the beach for a week" was only $5.08, the advertisement said. "How much will you give?"[51]

By August, the L.A. Urban League had elected its first board of directors, which included blacks and whites. As with the NAACP, interracialism meant blacks and whites only, with no thought given to including the Japanese or ethnic Mexican communities. The board was also strangely lacking in black women. When the Tuskegee League announced it would become a branch of the Urban League, the women stated that they would continue as officers. But Mrs. Warren and Mrs. Tenette were replaced by their husbands, Ellis Warren becoming executive secretary and Louis Tenette becoming associate executive secretary. Race papers gave no explanation. Katherine Barr was chosen as executive secretary and became something akin to what Beatrice Thompson had been to the NAACP in its early years. Barr also served on the executive board, but she seems to have been the only black woman on it, although several white women had places on the board. The top officers were African American: the league's first vice president was the dentist A. C. Garrott; the second vice president was A. J. Roberts (Fred's father). Board members included five high-visibility men: Fred Roberts, the Reverend A. P. Shaw, J. H. Shackleford, Willis O. Tyler (all of whom were, or had been, officers or board members of the local NAACP), and T. A. Greene, executive secretary of the black YMCA.[52]

The beach outing marked a philanthropic beginning, but by fall 1921, the league had placed employment issues front and center. It announced a two-pronged campaign. First, the league would seek to boost "the employment of Race workers in the occupations now open to them." Simultaneously, it would "seek new avenues of employment." This was the classic Urban League approach: maintain steady paychecks where blacks were already working, and try to open doors where blacks were excluded. The league continued to advertise its social-welfare programs, but henceforth the "Employment Bureau" would receive top priority.[53]

Large segments of the Southern California economy were off-limits to blacks. The petroleum industry—from drilling to refining—hired virtually no African Americans. Very few blacks got jobs in the harbor, which became one of the world's busiest ports (and whose workforce was controlled by AFL unions that aimed to keep Negroes out). Hollywood, which grew into a huge industry, hired very few blacks, even for labor. Negro actors and actresses, who received plenty of ink in the Race papers, and even in the *Crisis* and *Opportunity*, were mostly bottom-scale bit players; even these Negro "stars" had little choice but to accept demeaning roles. Many large-scale factories that migrated from the east, such as Firestone and Ford, tapped the white working class and hired virtually no blacks. Knowingly or not, Firestone signaled its racial policies by building its giant new plant on the border of South Gate, a working-class town that pointedly excluded blacks. Dozens of other manufacturing plants opened in and around that Jim Crow town as well. In 1928, the factories clustered near South Gate paid out $4.7 million in wages—almost none of those dollars to black Angelenos.[54]

The question of black labor in industry was near the heart of the Urban League, and it followed that the L.A. branch would investigate. In 1926, the L.A. league, with cooperation from the local branch of the NAACP, sought ways to survey the racial policies and attitudes of the manufacturing plants of Southern California.[55] Under the auspices of the National Urban League's Department of Research and Investigations, Charles S. Johnson himself came to L.A. to conduct a far-ranging research project, "Negro Workers in Los Angeles Industries."[56] With the help of the Los Angeles Chamber of Commerce, Johnson surveyed 456 plants—large and small—in widely varied industries. He conducted personal interviews with management and workers at 104 of these plants, half of which employed blacks and half of which did not. His survey did include women workers, but it focused on plants employing men because so few manufacturing firms hired black women. Johnson recognized the unique character of L.A.'s multiracial workforce and made a special effort to understand what employers and white workers thought about the different racial groups—Mexicans, Japanese, and Negroes.[57]

The results stunned Johnson. Much of his original report, and the briefer published versions that followed, represented an exhausting attempt to make sense of L.A.'s puzzling employment data. Plant policies on race varied widely even within the same industry. Every plant manager claimed to base his racial policies on "natural" theories of race, but these theories varied from plant to plant. In different plants in the same industry, Johnson found some managers who claimed they employed blacks because the Negro race was "naturally suited" to that kind of work, and others who said Negroes were "naturally unsuited" to that same work. And although managers and workers in each plant seemed to have a clear idea as to whether Mexicans were "colored" or "white," the judgments were markedly different from plant to plant. In an extraordinary description of these conflicting views, Johnson wrote:

> In certain plants where Mexicans were regarded as white, Negroes were
> not allowed to "mix" with them; where Mexicans were classed as col-
> ored[,] Negroes not only worked with them but were given positions
> over them. In certain plants Mexicans and whites worked together, in
> some others white workers accepted Negroes and object[ed] to Mexi-
> cans; still in others white workers accepted Mexicans and object[ed]
> to Japanese. White women worked with Mexican and Italian women,
> but refused to work with Negroes. Mexicans and Negroes worked
> under a white foreman; Italians and Mexicans under a Negro foreman;
> and Mexicans in some places were refused entirely because of plant
> policies against "mixing." In a hospital Negro nurses attended white
> patients, but were segregated from white nurses in the dining halls;
> in a manufacturing plant white workers refused to work with Negroes,
> but worked under a Negro foreman. Brick manufacturing was declared
> to be too hot and dusty for Negroes, yet the Negroes were reputed to
> be the best brickworkers and were given a better scale of wages than
> Mexicans.[58]

To Johnson, these results underscored "the importance of plant policy in Negro industrial relations." Managers in each plant were defining the "natural" characteristics of racial groups and were doing so with no consistency whatsoever. With better education and understanding—enlightened by Urban League–type research—industrial managers who barred blacks as "unfit" for certain work might change their minds; views about what was "natural" for black workers might change; barriers to black workers in local industry might yet fall. "There is evidence," an optimistic Johnson suggested, "that the objection of white workers to Negro workers is not a permanent or deeply serious contingency, and further evidence that the objection has faded after a short period of contact." New doors might open. Racial barriers in industry were not as solid as they appeared.[59]

Organized Labor and the Race

When Charles Johnson conducted his survey in 1926, he looked into the question of black workers and the labor movement. Could unions help black workers? Most Afro-Angelenos thought the answer was no. Nationally, the only viable labor organization was the American Federation of Labor, an association of craft unions that had been openly racist. Almost all AFL unions excluded black workers (and ethnic Mexican and Asian workers) from their ranks. When colored competition or the threat of black strikebreakers made the concept of working-class "brotherhood" more appealing, AFL workers sometimes recruited African Americans to strengthen the union. And black workers sometimes joined. But even when that happened, AFL locals usually shunted blacks into Jim Crow auxiliaries and made sure that union membership did not mean equality on the job.

Besides, unions in L.A. were in sorry shape. Organized labor had always been on the defensive in General Otis's town, and the tradition was continued in the 1920s by a new generation of anti-union power brokers, including Otis's son-in-law and successor at the *Times*, Harry Chandler. A nationwide strike wave in 1919 had led to disastrous defeats for many AFL unions, leaving L.A.'s locals doubly handicapped. By the time Johnson conducted his survey in 1926, card-carrying members of all labor unions in Los Angeles numbered about forty thousand—only 8 percent of the local workforce. But one did not really need the numbers to know that L.A. was no union town.[60]

Johnson favored organized labor and urged the creation of a biracial working-class alliance; but his report on L.A. gave little evidence for optimism. Among the city's black workers, he counted a total of seven hundred union members. Generally, he found that whites made no bones about excluding blacks. A few unions which sensed they were in trouble and needed black support had reached across the color line. But even then, the union leaders created Jim Crow auxiliaries. Some white unionists told Johnson their locals did not practice racial discrimination, in clear defiance of the facts. The best-organized group of blacks and whites was the letter carriers. Post-office work was a federal civil service job (beyond the reach of Chandler's crowd) that, in effect, had a closed-shop arrangement; anyone who took a job automatically became a member of the integrated union. A small number of L.A.'s ditch diggers had organized a Hod Carriers union, which included about a hundred black men who represented about 17 percent of the membership but operated in a segregated auxiliary. Eighty black bricklayers signed union cards, but they represented less than 10 percent of the local and caught flack from hostile white members, who wanted to corral them more than to help them.[61]

Black wage earners also had their own separate organizations, usually sanctioned by the AFL and usually in jobs for which there was no white competition. These all-black locals were the Race-union equivalent of Race enterprise. The most famous and popular was Musicians Local 767, which had 150 members in 1926. It represented almost all the black musicians in town. The Negro musicians had a union hall in the Central Avenue district, and it became a lively community center. Black musicians knew the white musicians' local got better-paying gigs, and some chafed at the Jim Crow implications, but in jazz-era L.A. the demand for black bands at parties and in studios was at its peak and kept Local 767 hopping. The largest all-black union Charles Johnson found was the Waiters Union, Local 17, which had organized only a few months before he arrived; it had 250 members. The white waiters' union had about a thousand members. The musicians and waiters constituted about two-thirds of all unionized black workers in the city.[62]

The Brotherhood of Sleeping Car Porters, built by A. Philip Randolph, was the nation's best-known black union, but it was slow in coming to Los Angeles and made little noise when it arrived. In contrast, L.A.'s dining-car workers organized a strong union in 1926, sparking a national movement of dining-car unionization. Clarence R. Johnson (no relation to the Urban League sociologist) was the driving force behind the organization of the Dining Car Cooks and Waiters Union, Local 582.[63]

Clarence Johnson was born in 1899 in El Paso ("Well, I'm a Texan," he would begin his oral history in 1967), and was five years old when his mother moved her children to Arizona. "My mother was quite a rebel," he recalled. Whenever any community in Arizona Territory segregated its schools, she would move to another town, insisting on her children's right to an equal education. They moved many times until, in 1912, Arizona became a state and segregated its schools; then they moved to Los Angeles. When Clarence was fifteen his mother became ill, and he left school to support his family, attending night school when he could. He got a job at Western Farms Dairy at 30th and Grand, where the white owner took him under his wing and became, as Johnson later recalled, "like a father to me." He urged Clarence to get whatever education he could and to develop a sharp mind for business. This fond association, and a certain confidence in dealing with a white man in a powerful position, later aided Johnson, who became a masterful union negotiator.[64]

In 1920, the twenty-one-year-old got a dining car job on the Southern Pacific. For two years he was a chef's helper; then he became a full-fledged chef, the best job for blacks in the Pullman ranks. "Conditions were not the best in the world," he recalled, but he knew that this job was an outstanding break. As he recalled, "The railroad employees, whether they were Pullman porters or whether they were dining car employees, they, along with the postal employees, among the Negroes, are what you'd really call the cream of the crop." Before the union, dining car men earned fifty-nine dollars per month (before tips), which placed them among the leading wage earners of the black middle class. "You had a great number of people, workers, who were very substantial, in terms of even their low salaries, that were factors in the security and the stability of the community, because they were home owners."[65]

An incident in 1921 turned Johnson toward unionization. A white supervisor had made a costly mistake; instead of accepting blame himself, "he had to find a scape goat, so he gave this young man thirty days on the ground" (that is, a temporary layoff) as punishment. Johnson made a vow: "If I can ever do something about this, I'm going to." In 1924 Johnson made good on his pledge and began to organize—tentatively, understanding the risk. Besides working toward "job security, [and better] wages, hours, and working conditions," Johnson thought it essential that the black dining car workers gain "the right to be recognized . . . so that . . . a man could not treat you like dirt." It was critical, he thought, "that you have some rights, that you have some recourse." That was his ultimate goal for the union—to "give workers the dignity and the status that they ought to have to take their places in society."[66]

The Dining Car Cooks and Waiters Union, later known simply as the Dining Car Employees Union, represented the men who worked in the Pullman dining cars—chefs, waiters, and dining car porters. The local fell under the jurisdiction of the AFL's Hotel and Restaurant Workers union. The national AFL welcomed the Dining Car union because it threatened no white jobs, sent dues to the national organization, and allowed AFL officials to claim that African Americans were eager to join their ranks.[67]

Many black Angelenos questioned Clarence Johnson's judgment, especially his willingness to affiliate with the AFL. He described the local reception to his organizing campaign as "cold"—"not exactly hostility, but a lack of understanding." Some demanded to know how he could support unions, "knowing what the American Federation of Labor has done to black labor." Johnson responded that "you can't change anything on the outside, you can only change it when you are on the inside, influencing the whole thing." He believed, along with A. Philip Randolph (whom he called "the genius of the age"), that education from the inside, not separation on the outside, was what would ultimately change white attitudes. In a larger sense, he held that black union workers could ultimately empower the American labor movement by helping white workers lose their race prejudice, "because they can't go anywhere with these prejudices."[68]

As it turned out, the Southern Pacific recognized Local 582 without a fight, not because the company favored it but because management hoped to bog down negotiations until the rank-and-file dining car employees lost faith in the union. The railroad would use the complicated wage-tip issue to undermine the union's position and stall the proceedings. At the contract talks, management confidently took what Johnson called a "very hard-nosed position," especially on the wage issue. The Southern Pacific argued that current wages were adequate because the workers received good tips, and that tips were the equivalent of wages. Johnson responded, "If the person serving could reach into the man's pocket and take what he wanted, then it might be wages." Negotiations dragged on for more than a year, but the union hung together. Finally, the issue went to arbitration.

At the arbitration meeting, the Southern Pacific lawyers brought in "elaborate charts" to demonstrate that, with tips, the dining car employees actually earned $125 per month. The ploy backfired. Local 582 replied that the workers "would be perfectly willing to accept the facts that the company had so ably produced." They would gladly accept $125 as their basic wage and give all their tips to the company. Southern Pacific cried foul, but the arbitrators agreed with the union, telling the railroad executives, "They're completely correct, you introduced this." After that, all dining car tips went to the company, and the waiters took their nicely increased flat rate. And, as Johnson recalled, "the back pay ran into thousands of dollars." Even so, he added, "[w]e had an excellent relationship with the company. They came to respect us; we respected them."[69]

Before long, the black community respected Local 582 as well. The union built a family-oriented clubhouse near the corner of 12th and Central. It also established a credit union ("the first credit union among Negro workers in the West"), which invested its surplus funds with the black-owned Liberty Building and Loan. Membership reached 150 by decade's end, and the men added a women's auxiliary (for wives), which included fifty members who "created a commissary from which they take succor to needy applicants." Thus the Dining Car union became a notable Race organization in Los Angeles. In addition to Clarence Johnson, the local's officers—Arthur Binkley, Henry Bailer, James Cook, and Lubby Cook—as well as the women's auxiliary officers—Mrs. J. C. Williams and Mrs. Henry Bailey—were a new set of community leaders. In many respects, though, Local 582 was just as middle class as the NAACP, the leading congregations, and the women's clubs.[70]

Unionization helped the dining car waiters, but for most black workers organized labor remained more a problem than a solution. The *New Age* continued to view the AFL with deep skepticism, not because Fred Roberts was a conservative but because he was a black man who had seen what white unions had done to black workers.[71] When white labor leaders wanted to know what black Angelenos thought about organized labor, they asked Charlotta Bass to speak to them on the topic. Neither she nor Joe had warmed to organized labor, and they were furious that the typographers' union in L.A. had blocked the *Eagle's* typesetter from getting the training he needed to become a certified Linotypist; he had to go to the Bay Area to get trained and certified. Charlotta gave the labor crowd a cordial but cool report, insisting that white unions had to begin viewing black workers as allies, not enemies. She said African Americans would join the labor movement when the AFL was sincerely ready to welcome them.[72]

The Urban League proved more enthusiastic. By the 1930s, the executive director of the Los Angeles league was Floyd Covington, who was both Talented Tenth and pro-union. Charles Johnson called biracial unionism "the very essence of all inter-racial effort." Interaction between black leaders and "cultured" whites, he said, would not change anything. *Opportunity* trumpeted A. Philip Randolph's efforts and even gave William Green, the conservative head of the AFL, a chance to answer the perennial black question "Why Belong to a Union?" Green answered that "the union needs you and you need the union. Join the union of your trade and perform a constructive part within your group." Since most trade unions barred colored people, and since Green's answer hinted at Jim Crow within unions—stay within your group—his words may have unintentionally undermined *Opportunity's* efforts.[73]

What mattered was that pro-union sentiment was filtering through the black national network, and that its source was not so much the average worker but the bourgeoisie. The union ideal failed to take hold in the black mainstream, however, and Charles Johnson flirted with heresy when he stated that biracial unionism—not middle-class activism—was the only way to improve conditions. It would take the Great Depression, a new Democratic Party, and a new labor movement to channel biracial unionism into mainstream black activism. In the 1920s, black unionism remained esoteric and black wage earners were mostly stuck. That is one reason so many strivers tossed aside their brooms and mops and tried to start little businesses of their own along Central Avenue.

The Mom-and-Pop Economy

If advertisements published in the *Eagle* were any indication, small black businesses held steady during the early 1920s. In 1925, about 16 percent of all *Eagle* ads indicated that a particular business was owned by an African American. This percentage was down a bit from 1920 but far higher than it would be in subsequent years. Almost all "group" ads in 1925 came from black businesses; identifiably Asian enterprises accounted for only 2 percent of the ads, and "white" and Jewish ads constituted only another 2 percent. Black female advertising, which had risen sharply between 1915 and 1920, declined between 1920 and 1925, while ads placed by Negro men increased dramatically. Photographs of the owners signified the majority of black ads in 1920 and remained the most common way to indicate race in newspaper ads throughout the decade. But there also was a striking increase in the number of black ads that used Race slogans, not photos, to inspire customer loyalty. This trend mirrored the rhetoric of black nationalism and Race pride that saturated community affairs in the early 1920s.[74]

Race enterprises with Central Avenue addresses became more numerous, and a few moved farther south on The Avenue. The Terracotta Inn and the Thomas Hotel Apartments offered lodging. The Menelek Poultry Market, at 1537 Central Avenue, advertised heavily in the *Eagle*. Sidney Dones maintained a real estate office at 1720 Central; the Indiana Real Estate Company opened two blocks north of that, the A. J. Harris Real Estate Company one block south. The center of black business along Central Avenue continued to be the ten-block area between 9th Street and Washington (about 20th Street), with the hub around the Booker T. Washington Building. By 1925, some Race enterprises had pushed south of 20th Street. Bessie Prentice, whose New Idea Store on Central near 9th Street was a community institution, opened another dry goods store, dressmaking shop, and beauty parlor at 2703 Central. The Hefflin Manufacturing Company, which made furniture, opened a small plant as far south as 3429 Central. At the time, though, southward businesses were the exception.[75]

In the second half of the 1920s, Race advertisements declined sharply—by more than two-thirds. Black-owned businesses accounted for roughly 20 percent of the *Eagle*'s advertising in 1925, but less than 8 percent in 1930. The ethos of Race enterprise persisted, of course, but the trend in advertising meant a change was taking place. That change was the appearance of national chain stores. Safeway supermarkets came to Central Avenue in the late 1920s. In 1925, not a single Safeway existed near the black community. By 1930, there were six Safeway stores catering to L.A.'s African American population, and all of them advertised in the *Eagle*. Three of Safeway's supermarkets were on Central Avenue itself, at 1229 Central (near the Booker T. Washington building); 3427 Central (near Elks Hall); and 4401 Central (which was near a rising business center). Two other Safeway stores were just off of Central in predominantly African American neighborhoods. Safeway also placed two stores adjacent to the smaller, wealthier black community along West Jefferson Boulevard. These supermarkets hurt black-owned groceries and drugstores. Race markets could not compete with the prices or selection offered by Safeway, and apparently few of them tried to woo business through advertising or new appeals to Race pride.[76]

National chains thus were a blessing and curse to the community. They allowed consumers to partake in the process of American consumerism as never before. Safeway offered better grocery services than the community had ever had; good prices and selection were never far from home. But national chains seldom hired black Angelenos for any kind of job, and certainly not good jobs. They undercut many of the smaller mom-and-pop shops that had given hope to strivers, and they put a pervasive strain on the ideal of Race enterprise. Some black businesses were still safe from chain stores—for example, barber shops, beauty salons, and mortuaries—but most of these remained small. There was, however, one striking exception that affirmed the ideal of Race enterprise and grew far beyond anyone's expectations.

Golden State Life

By the 1920s, black-owned insurance companies had become the largest Race enterprises in the United States. Negroes needed good, inexpensive insurance policies, but white-owned companies charged them high prices for limited coverage. Nor would mainstream insurance firms issue loans to black subscribers. Few of them hired blacks, except to peddle inequitable policies to the Race. But African Americans had alternatives. Fraternal organizations offered policies on a limited basis. Then there were the large companies. Most black Americans knew about Alonzo Herndon, who founded the Atlanta Life Insurance Company and became a millionaire. By 1921, his company had one hundred branches, seven hundred black employees, and almost ten million dollars in assets.[77] North Carolina Mutual Life, also black owned, was even larger. These firms grew from a long tradition of small-scale benefit associations, rooted in the fraternal organizations, which offered ordinary African Americans some security in an insecure world. Long-standing tradition and viable examples of success made black insurance companies an alluring investment that benefited the Race. Enter Golden State.

William Nickerson, Jr., spearheaded the company. A native Texan born in 1879, Nickerson attended college and taught school before shifting to the insurance trade, selling policies to blacks for a white firm in Houston. He learned the ropes of the industry and realized how badly the white firms discriminated against black clients. In 1908 he and other Race leaders in Houston began offering Afro-Texans better policies by organizing the American Mutual Benefit Association, a black fraternal group. In the 1920s Nickerson and his partners decided that a California branch of American Mutual would benefit black Californians and the company, and in 1921 he headed for the West Coast.[78]

In Los Angeles, Nickerson met the dynamic Norman O. Houston, an Oakland native who had recently moved to Southern California. Houston's parents had sent him to the University of California at Berkeley, where he studied business. World War I interrupted his studies, and he served as an officer in France. Afterward he moved to Los Angeles and became an insurance agent for a white-owned company, selling policies to Pullman cooks and waiters. Nickerson hired Houston to be American Mutual's first California salesman and soon made him the branch superintendent.[79]

One spring day in 1922, a novice sales agent for American Mutual knocked on the door of George Beavers, Jr., who asked dozens of questions about the firm, stumping the agent. As Beavers later recalled, "most of his sales pitch focused on race pride, and he didn't satisfactorily answer my other questions" about the company's "stability, management, and . . . ability to pay." The salesman brought his superintendent to meet Beavers. That was the first meeting between Beavers and Houston, and the two liked each other immediately. Beavers remembered Houston as a "very affable person, very friendly, aggressive, and that's what I like[d] about him." Houston recognized Beavers's business sense and arranged for him to meet Nickerson. "I shall never forget the meeting with Mr. Nickerson," Beavers later recalled. "He had such a magnetic personality and an abundance of enthusiasm, and that enthusiasm was contagious. After talking with Mr. Nickerson, I not only paid the premium for an insurance policy, but I became an agent for the Association." Beavers sold his building-maintenance business and plunged into insurance, taking every possible opportunity for additional education and training in the industry.[80]

Nickerson, Houston, and Beavers quickly made American Mutual's West Coast branch a going concern. But they wanted more: a full-line black-owned insurance company in California, one that would employ African Americans and provide loans for black homes and businesses. Back in Texas, the directors of the American Mutual rejected Nickerson's plans for expansion in California; what's more, they refused to renew the company's California license. So, in 1924, Nickerson, Houston, and Beavers decided to establish their own insurance company. They met with insurance specialists and white attorneys. The lawyers made two key points: first, a full-line "mutual" insurance company required a $250,000 guarantee deposit to the state treasurer—up front; and second, their law firm would look into other options and handle the paperwork for $1,500. Nickerson huffed out of the meeting. As Beavers remembered, "We left the lawyers' office, and he said to me, 'Beavers, where can we get some law books?' And I took him to the law bookstore that I was familiar with, and there he purchased a copy of the Civil Code of California." "In other words," recalled Beavers, still laughing at Nickerson's stubborn determination decades later, "Mr. Nickerson would become his own lawyer."[81]

Nickerson discovered a way to operate their company on a smaller scale. They could get a state license to operate a "guarantee fund insurance company" if they met the following requirements: $15,000 deposited with the state treasurer in advance; five hundred applicants, with policies paid in advance; and bank deposits equaling $10,000 for operating money (which included the cash paid-in for policies). All told, then, they needed $25,000 cash and five hundred clients *before* they could actually begin operations. The three could invest a little, but most of the $25,000 would have to be raised from scratch. Black Angelenos had that kind of money, but they were cautious.[82]

In spring 1925, the trio made their pitch to the community, announcing plans to establish the Golden State Guarantee Fund Insurance Company. The clucking that followed on Central Avenue was not the sound of optimism. "We had to do a good selling job," Beavers recalled. "We had a lot of doubting Thomases to deal with." The *Eagle* tried to help. Congratulating Nickerson for launching the enterprise, it emphasized his experience in the insurance field. Joe Bass called Nickerson "an intelligent son of the South" and added, "Let him teach us, therefore, great sons of the West, to do something big by giving him a chance." After all, Bass concluded, "we have preached all along for economic enterprises as a vital means of our material salvation. Will our personal hates and petty prejudices be bigger than our own preachings? Brothers—one and all—this is our chance to show it!" Bass failed to elaborate on those hates and prejudices among the great sons of the West, but he seemed to be prodding reluctant investors. Regardless, he hardly sounded optimistic. Beavers later said he never doubted the company would fly, but in spring 1925 such confidence would have been difficult to maintain.[83]

The three men divided their tasks. Nickerson handled legal matters. Beavers sold five hundred applications. Houston raised the $15,000 "guarantee fund," which was the real kicker. He sold "certificates of contribution" at $1,000 apiece. If the company survived and prospered, investors would eventually get their money back, with interest. Otherwise, bust. "Some people would call it a gamble," said Beavers. "At least it took a lot of faith to put out a thousand dollars for something like that, in a nonexistent company, hoping it would succeed and you would get your money back."[84]

Momentum began to build. The organizers each bought a certificate. J. H. Shackleford, the furniture dealer and real estate man, invested; so did Wilbur Gordon, whose Gordon Manor was then in the works. A leading black physician, Dr. Henry H. Towles, invested heavily, as did the mortuary owner Simon P. Johnson. A. Hartley Jones, a leader in Liberty Building and Loan, as was Norman Houston himself, bought in. Others stepped up: E. L. Dorsey, F. G. Thornton, J. A. Evans, Edward T. Banks, R. A. Clark. "These men were of high caliber," Beavers said, "and they were concerned about building more businesses owned and controlled by black Americans." All of the investors were men; no women seem to have purchased certificates. These original contributors became the company's first board of directors. By summer 1925, it looked as if the Golden State dream would materialize.[85]

Then something fishy happened. Without warning, the state legislature changed the state insurance code, raising the requirements for getting a guarantee-fund license: a $25,000 deposit with the state treasurer (up from $15,000), and a thousand paid-in applicants (up from five hundred). The new law would go into effect on July 23, 1925. In Sacramento, an alarmed Fred Roberts could not stop the new law, but he alerted Beavers and other Race leaders. If July 23 arrived before Golden State reached the original requirements, the new law would kill the effort. Black leaders believed white insurance companies were behind the strange and sudden change in regulations. For white insurance companies, blacks were easy money. "There was no doubt in our mind," Beavers recalled, that the new law "was specifically aimed at stopping or blocking our success."[86]

But the legislature's plan backfired, for it caused black L.A. to rally around Golden State as it hadn't before. The company had been just another Race enterprise; now it was a *cause*. Memberships and investments quickened. Ministers urged support. In mid-July, with the final state inspection of Golden State's books only a day away, the company was still $1,800 short. Beavers described what happened next. "We gathered at the mortuary owned by S. P. Johnson, and we had a little meeting—the Directors—it reminded me something of a church in raising money. The pastor needs just a certain amount to round out the collection, and he makes a frantic call for additional contributions. At that meeting, though, in about twenty minutes, we raised that extra eighteen hundred dollars." On July 23, the very day the new law went into effect, Golden State received its license from the state of California. "That," Beavers said, "was a very happy and glorious time."[87]

In the beginning, the Golden State Guarantee Fund Insurance Company ran mostly on hope. "At that time," recalled Beavers, "we were operating in just one room in the building, a little . . . two-story frame building over on Central Avenue and Newton Street"—at 1435 Central. For all the excitement that attended Golden State's race against the legislative roadblock, it was still just another storefront enterprise in the Central Avenue district. But it did not stay that way. Blacks throughout California snatched up thousands of life- and health-insurance policies. Soon the company abandoned its tiny office for a large warehouse at Central Avenue and Jefferson Boulevard. Rapid growth continued. In 1928, Golden State built its own spacious headquarters at 4111 Central Avenue, a magnificent building designed by black architects and built by black contractors.[88]

By 1930, Golden State was bringing in $240,000 per year and hiring hundreds of blacks for white-collar positions. Initially, the company hired whites who knew the industry, but it also began training blacks for insurance careers. After five years in business, Golden State employed 130 people, most of them African Americans who worked at any number of jobs: "clerks, bookkeepers, stenographers, agents, officers, superintendents, inspectors, claim adjusters, medical examiners." The company owned its $50,000 headquarters free and clear. It had paid out $300,000 in benefits to its members. Equally important, it gave mortgage loans to black Angelenos at a rapid rate—mortgages large and small, for homes and businesses. One booster rightly called Golden State "The Growing Giant of the West."[89]

Beavers, Houston, and Nickerson were the right men in the right business at the right time. In building Golden State into a "Growing Giant" they offered black Californians excellent policies at reasonable rates, created hundreds of good jobs for the black middle class, and invested hundreds of thousands of dollars in home and business loans to black strivers. All the while, the company and its three leading men ardently supported the local NAACP and the Urban League. These were Race men in the fullest sense of the word, and their business kept growing, even during the Great Depression. In 1942, the company would plunk down the $250,000 necessary for turning their guarantee fund into a full-blown mutual life insurance company. By that time, they had made millions in loans to black Californians, experiencing few defaults and giving the lie to redliners in white-owned banks. Indeed, white insurance companies and white financial institutions began to compete aggressively for black dollars. This, in its fullness, was the promise of Race enterprise. Unfortunately for black businesses in Los Angeles, it was a rare exception to the mom-and-pop norm.

8

Surging Down
Central Avenue

In 1924, Verna Deckard drove into L.A. in a new Ford coupe, its smooth finish covered with seven days of dust and dirt. The car was her own, a gift from her father, Jule Deckard, an auto mechanic from Terrell, Texas, just east of Dallas. The dirt had accumulated during the Deckard family's two-car road trip from East Texas to Los Angeles. Verna's parents drove in her "Papa's" automobile, a Ford touring car that sported a sign: "Texas to Los Angeles." Papa had enlisted a young fellow to ride in Verna's car to share the driving, but his daughter would not give up the wheel. She thought, "Well, this is my car and I don't want anybody driving my car." Verna Deckard drove every mile herself. She was seventeen.[1]

Nearly seventy years later, when asked about that journey in 1924, Verna's recollections crackled with excitement. "We stopped every night and we camped along the way. See, [black people] couldn't stay in the motels and we couldn't eat anyplace you wanted to eat either. If you did, you had to go in the kitchen and eat. So Papa brought a little tent along, and we set up camp every night. And we slept in the tent, and if he'd see a rabbit on the way, he'd stop and kill the rabbit and Mama would cook the rabbit for dinner. . . . It was really fun. It was just like a camping trip." The highway into Los Angeles "brought you right through downtown," she remembered. The people on the street "saw this dusty car with the luggage on top and the sign, 'Texas to Los Angeles,' and they all hollered, 'Hello, Texas!' And we just felt we had a welcome committee waiting for us because the crowd was just hollering, 'Hello, Texas.' . . . So right away I fell in love with Los Angeles because everybody was so friendly."

Despite the race prejudice that was sapping the community's fighting spirit, black southerners, especially Texans, kept falling for Los Angeles. The Deckards' tale bears a little more telling, however. Jule and Eula Deckard intended only a summer's visit with their son and other relatives, who lived in L.A. Jule Deckard had once been a respected blacksmith in Tatum, Texas. There he taught himself to fix automobiles and made good money. But his affluence enraged jealous whites, who torched his shop. So Jule moved the family to Terrell, where he opened a garage and once again prospered. Eula's complexion was virtually white, but the white folks there knew she was colored, so Jule could escort her around town without incident. In 1922, however, a friend of the family visited, and she also was very light skinned; Jule showed her around Terrell before escorting her to the train for departure. Seeing this, some white men thought Jule was escorting a white woman in broad daylight—a lynchable offense. That night a carload of men drove to the house and asked Jule to check their battery.

When Jule bent over, one of the men hit him in the head with a sledgehammer. The blow knocked him down but not out, and he came up fighting. His teenage son plunged in to the fray. Father and son broke free and ran, their assailants shooting at them. Jule took a bullet in the arm—a flesh wound—but they got away. In the morning, a local doctor tended Jule's bullet wound and stitched up his head; then Papa and son left immediately for Los Angeles, believing a lynch mob would be next and guessing—correctly—that the whites who had attacked them would not bother Eula and Verna if the Deckard men had left town. In L.A., Jule Deckard did not send for his wife and daughter; instead, he sent word for a relative to run his shop in Terrell, while he worked as a mechanic on Central Avenue. After a year of this arrangement, Jule Deckard—astonishingly—moved back to Terrell. More understandably, his son refused to return to Texas, and Papa let him stay with relatives. A year later, in spring 1924, Jule bought Verna her car, and the family made its memorable caravan trip—not a relocation but a visit.

But when it was time to go home, Verna wanted to stay. With her car, good looks, and Texas ways, she made friends easily at summer school with kids from the local community, on trips to the beach, at church activities and weekend parties. She even had a nice boyfriend. It was a lot to like. Most of all, though, she "didn't want to go back to 'old bad Texas.'" As she later remembered, "I called it 'old bad Texas' then because [of] the way they treated us, you know. . . . I came out here and people were so nice that I decided I'm not going back to Texas." Her parents disagreed, insisting that she return with them. That evening, the night before their departure, Verna went out and married her boyfriend, a young Angeleno named Arthur Lewis. Jule and Eula were shocked, but their daughter was now eighteen and had a marriage certificate—and her own car—so there wasn't much they could do about it. Besides, they liked Arthur. Verna Deckard Lewis thus avoided returning to Texas. To celebrate their marriage, she and Arthur drove to the beach. Mama and Papa drove back to Terrell, having lost both of their children to L.A.

One year later, though, Eula and Jule finally gave up, sold their holdings, and moved to L.A. themselves. Jule opened a garage on Central Avenue. He also paid thirty-two hundred dollars in cash for a "cute little bungalow" on East 58th Place, a cul-de-sac between Hooper and Central. Most neighboring homes were restricted by covenants, but not this one. The house was some three miles south of the Booker T. Washington Building and about three miles north of Watts. European immigrants lived on either side and proved friendly, but whites from adjacent neighborhoods felt otherwise.

One day while Jule was at work, fifty men drove up, gathered on the lawn, and threatened Eula Deckard, saying, "Get out before daylight." The sheriff's department took two hours to respond to Eula's call. Friendly neighbors later said that the officers who finally responded had been part of the mob. When they arrived, Jule was there. He pulled out the Winchester he had from the World War and told the sheriff's officers he would gun down anyone else who threatened him or his family. Afterward, the officers went to the neighboring families and warned them, "He's a bad nigger, you'd better leave him alone." Wanting more protection, Jule drove up to 12th and Central and gathered a small army of street-corner men who willingly guarded the Deckard home each night for a month. Eula cooked for them, and Jule bought guns for those who had none. That show of force marked the end of it. The Deckards stayed put, without further incident.[2]

In the demographic history of black Los Angeles, the Deckards' move to L.A. revealed basic trends of the decade—newcomers flowing in to the Eastside, and a push southward along Central Avenue. While the Deckards showed careful deliberation and fighting spirit, other newcomers simply went with the flow. The Avenue remained the primary artery of black life, and the intersection with 12th Street remained the center of things, but late in the decade the community would make a decisive shift southward, to 41st Street, not far north of where the Deckards had settled in. With firm restrictive covenants covering the Westside and working-class whites east of Alameda Avenue, blacks congregated in the mixed-race neighborhoods on either side of Central, moving south in the same scattershot fashion they always had. By decade's end, black homes and businesses could be found in a much broader area of the Eastside—as far south as Slauson Avenue, more than forty blocks south of the Booker T. Washington building. This unprecedented geographical expansion—and its restricted borders to the east and west—resulted from both rapid black migration and rising white racism. But neither demography nor race restrictions quite explains the timing and speed of the southward shift.

The decisive catalyst for the surge down Central Avenue was the construction in 1928 of the Somerville Hotel at 41st and Central. A venture undertaken by the dentist and Race leader John Somerville, the hotel was part of L.A.'s robust campaign to host the national NAACP convention in 1928. Almost overnight, the convention's success ignited a movement that created a new and vibrant center of black life around the Somervilles' elegant establishment.

Central Avenue in the 1920s

In the mid-1920s the Central Avenue district was still a patchwork of ethnic groups living within erratic swatches of poverty and prosperity. The 74th Assembly District, which remained unchanged through the decade, was still represented by Fred Roberts, whose *New Age* office was just down the Avenue from the Basses' *Eagle*. Maple Avenue and Paloma Street still offered rows of handsome Negro churches, and First AME shone at 8th and Towne. Sweet bungalows lined most residential streets, but there were scraggly lots and ugly shacks, too. Big-city lights and dusty back roads both found a place in an urban space that defied easy description.

The novelist Gilmore Millen captured the diversity of the district in *Sweet Man*, in which the protagonist, the black newcomer John Henry, confronted the Eastside: Henry "idled along the hot street with strange men—down-and-outers, boys new from the middle western farms, Mexicans from the last revolutionary army below the border, ex-convicts from San Quentin and Folsom, cowboys from Utah and Wyoming, derbied old men who had sold their little businesses in Iowa to come west, only to lose their life savings in real estate investments, [N]egroes from Harlem and the Chicago Black Belt, bums, Chinese dishwashers, Filipino bus and elevator boys—the most heterogeneous crowds he had ever seen." John Henry had confronted "the blaring unreal newness of Los Angeles." The jazz musician Marshal Royal recalled the ethnic composition of Jefferson High when he attended in the late 1920s: "Very mixed. . . . There were about 20 percent blacks, 5 percent Espanol [sic], 2 percent Japanese, Italians would be 25 percent, the Jewish people would be 20 percent, and rest would be just regular Caucasians." He added, "They were all in the same room, and they got along very well."[3]

The intersection of 12th and Central remained the hub of black L.A., but there was a steady move southward, not just among black home owners but also among key Negro institutions. In the mid-1920s, the Colored YMCA, the Elks Hall, and the Second Baptist Church relocated south of the 74th district. Second Baptist bought land on 24th Street, just west of Central Avenue, and hired the black architect Paul Williams to design its stately new home. A big church had moved south; that was no small thing. The Elks pushed all the way to 33rd and Central, where they built their sharply designed and decorated meetinghouse. Elks Hall had two auditoriums, one on each floor, and became a center for civic meetings and weekend dances. The YMCA, still headed by T. A. Greene, desperately needed a new building to replace what one critic called the "shabby YMCA clubroom." The Y bought land at 28th and Central and hired Williams to design the facility; his striking four-story building featured relief sculptures of black American leaders such as Frederick Douglass and Booker T. Washington.[4]

Slowly, black-owned businesses moved down Central as well. The Golden State insurance company relocated to Central and Jefferson. Jule Deckard opened his automobile repair shop at 23rd and Central. In 1926, the sparkling new Lincoln Theater also opened at 23rd and Central, only a few blocks east of Second Baptist. Known as the "West Coast Apollo," the Lincoln was a grand movie palace, complete with an orchestra pit and a broad stage for concerts and theatrical productions. "The Lincoln Theater was a big-time place for the blacks in town," recalled Marshal Royal. "You couldn't get into that place on Saturdays and Sundays. Just loaded. On top of that, they had probably twelve of the most beautiful black girls in town as usherettes at the theater. A lot of men around the neighborhood just came to look at the usherettes."[5]

One young woman who worked at the Lincoln—as a cashier—was Verna Deckard Lewis. Her husband had died of tuberculosis in 1927, only three years after their marriage. Shortly thereafter, she got her first job, as cashier at the Gaiety Theater, a Japanese-owned establishment at 23rd and Central across the street from her father's garage. With that job she became, according to the *Eagle*, the first African American in L.A. to get work as a cashier in a nonblack establishment. The Gaiety operated at the same intersection as the Lincoln Theater, and in 1929 the Lincoln hired Verna away for higher pay.[6] None of these organizations or businesses moved dramatically from the community hub, yet together they pointed the future southward. Black residential movement, Race enterprises, and community organizations shifted in a three-partnered dance; racist barriers ensured the dance moved southward. Developments in the town of Watts, still several miles south of the Central Avenue community, helped foster this trend. The town's black population had grown steadily over the years, and by the mid-1920s African Americans constituted enough of Watts's voting population to be able, quite possibly, to elect a black mayor. As subsequent events would demonstrate, there was some strong white resistance to this kind of black empowerment, and, perhaps as a result, the city's white elected officials asked to be annexed by the city of Los Angeles. Advocates of annexation raised issues about Watts's inadequate water supply and other matters of civic services, but it was difficult to ignore the racial politics involved. In 1926, Los Angeles did annex Watts. The demographic result would be that the Central Avenue community and the black community in Watts would grow toward one another, which encouraged residential and business shifts in both directions.[7]

In practical terms, the bright new buildings of the Central Avenue community—Second Baptist, Elks Hall, the YMCA, the Lincoln—encouraged further movement south of Washington Boulevard. As signs of progress, they boosted the reputation of black L.A. and helped attract new migrants. Equally important, though, was what the buildings said about the spirit of Afro-Angelenos. They reflected rising expectations and deepening resources. They indicated a restless desire for bigger and better—for the full and equal right to pursue dreams and live well.

The New Negro Renaissance

The mid-1920s witnessed a flowering of black literature and art—the New Negro Arts Movement, more commonly known as the New Negro Renaissance, or the Harlem Renaissance, because it first blossomed in Manhattan. The movement's early momentum came from the officials of the national office of the NAACP—James Weldon Johnson, Walter White, W. E. B. Du Bois, and *Crisis* literary editor Jessie Fauset—who wrote and promoted literature from a distinctly Negro perspective. The Urban League's monthly, *Opportunity*, also published black literature, poetry, and art. As Du Bois and his crowd saw it, the arts movement was pointedly political. An outpouring of serious cultural production by African Americans would force white Americans to abandon their assumptions of Negro inferiority. For centuries, Europeans and their American descendants had argued that their own "civilized" art reflected their mental and moral superiority over dark-skinned peoples. The black middle class aimed to topple that pillar of race prejudice through Negro art. If civil rights activism was stalled, if black economic progress went unnoticed, then perhaps black art could turn the tide.[8]

Du Bois gave the movement its defining name—the "Renaissance"—in an article he wrote for the *Los Angeles Times* in 1925. On June 14, the Sunday Literary Page of the *Times* announced that W. E. B. Du Bois's theatrical extravaganza, *The Star of Ethiopia*, would play at the Hollywood Bowl on Monday and Wednesday of the coming week. Under a banner proclaiming "A Negro Art Renaissance," the paper ran a large photograph of Du Bois, accompanied by a laudatory introduction, probably written by John McGroarty, which praised Du Bois as "an educator of high standing and wide recognition." Du Bois insisted that New Negro Art was not strictly American in origin but actually a reemergence of black African artistry, an adaptation of deeply rooted traditions. He debunked the idea that African American art and literature had begun with emancipation. Although American slavery had caused "a vast hiatus in Negro development," ancient African artistry had never been completely destroyed or forgotten. Indeed, it was now reasserting itself with unprecedented force and power. Hence, "there is today a renaissance of Negro genius, linking the past and the present."[9]

This Renaissance ideal found voice in black L.A. in 1926, when community leaders sponsored a choir contest at the Hollywood Bowl. Ten choirs from Negro churches competed, drawing huge, integrated audiences. The *Pacific Defender* waxed ecstatic over the success of the event. It was not simply that First AME's famous Eighth and Towne Choir had won the competition or that a crowd of ten thousand had witnessed "this great musical treat." It was rather that "the beautiful voices [blending] together in harmonious expression, rolling up and out of the throats of bright-eyed, smiling artists, answering to the baton of their leaders, was an evidence of the Race's right to demand its place in the American citizenship."[10]

If the Harlem ideal energized Central Avenue, Arna Bontemps and other young Angelenos longed for the real Harlem. Paul Bontemps had sent Arna to the San Fernando Adventist Academy in 1917, and later to Pacific Union College, an isolated Adventist university fifty miles north of San Francisco. Paul encouraged his son to study medicine, but Arna majored in English. In L.A. during summer break, Arna attended classes at UCLA, discovered

Renaissance poetry, listened to jazz in Watts, and determined that his upbringing had robbed him of what he called "Negro-ness." In 1924, he left
for Harlem and loved it. He became best friends with Langston Hughes and
won poetry awards from the NAACP and the Urban League. He taught at
an Adventist school, married one of his students, Alberta Johnson, and published his first novel, *God Sends Sunday*, in 1931.[11]

L.A.'s Young Crowd

For Bontemps, raised on the fringes of L.A.'s black community, Central Avenue could never feel like home. But other "New Negroes" in L.A. wanted
a homegrown Renaissance. Most attended the University of Southern California or the University of California's "Southern Branch" (later UCLA),
which became a more popular option during the 1920s, when USC's environment became increasingly hostile to colored students. Some blacks went
to Pasadena City College or Compton City College, two-year schools that
were springboards to universities. The small Negro communities at UCLA
and USC became the core of young leadership in black Los Angeles. Race
and social position brought them together inside and outside the classroom.
Money was not the key to the college crowd, because all were broadly middle class and none were wealthy. Most worked evenings and weekends to
pay for their education.

Stylish, ambitious, and a bit cocky, they were the children of early-
twentieth-century migrants. Churchgoers and can-do optimists, they read the
Race papers and also wrote for them. They devoured the *Crisis* and *Opportunity* and felt free to criticize both. They were a generation of Race women
and men in the making. If this kind of black youth culture was not exactly
unique to the era, the temper of the 1920s set New Negroes apart and created
a generation gap within the community. Black college students—carrying
the hopes of their families, if not the Race itself—avoided the bathtub-gin
culture that made college life scandalous in the 1920s, but they did believe
their elders were stodgy and behind the times.[12]

The Matthews children—Ella, Charles, and Miriam—exemplified the
group. Reuben and Fannie Matthews had left Pensacola, Florida, for the West
Coast in 1907, when Ella and Miriam were toddlers and Charles was an infant. In the early 1920s, all three children graduated from Los Angeles High
School. They were smart, popular, and active in church. Ella went on to business school and became the first secretary of the NAACP's Junior Branch.
Miriam set her sights on becoming a librarian, enduring the blank stares

and obstacles along the way, graduating from the University of California at Berkeley with her librarian certificate in 1927. That same year she became the first African American librarian hired in the Los Angeles library system. Charles started college at UCLA but transferred to Berkeley, where he excelled in track and academics. He earned his law degree from Berkeley and passed the California bar in 1930.[13]

Ralph Bunche, one of Charles Matthews's closest friends, grew up in the same crowd of go-getters. Smart, handsome, likable, athletic, light-skinned, entrepreneurial—he had all the right stuff for black L.A. Valedictorian at Jefferson High in 1923, he attended UCLA, lettering in track and basketball and wowing everyone academically. He became the leading light of L.A.'s New Negro generation. To black teenagers with high ambitions, Bunche was a hero and role model. The Women's Auxiliary of the NAACP raised money for him to attend graduate school at Harvard.[14] There were other rising stars as well. The *Eagle* wrote that the Junior Branch president, James McGregor, "embodies the ideals and intellectual aspirations of the New Negro. . . . [H]e has implicit faith in the power of true education to surmount all obstacles and to solve the Negro's problems." And the *Eagle* deemed Naida Portia McCullough, also active in the Junior Branch, "a woman whose comprehensive culture and winning personality bespeaks eloquently of the entrance of the New Negro woman into a field of endeavor which is unquestionably for the good and ultimate liberation of the Race."[15]

But tensions emerged between the young and the middle-aged when the Junior Branch asserted itself. The young crowd chafed under the older leadership. Hence Ella Matthews's demand to the "Senior Branch": do not call us "Junior" anymore. That declaration of independence outraged some venerable NAACP leaders, especially Beatrice Thompson. Other adult members, including those who rallied around Claude Hudson's leadership, probably appreciated their spirit. Having taken a stand, however, the Junior Branch needed to prove its merit. In a move reflecting youthful race activism in the 1920s, the Juniors decided that the key to their ascent would be a grand theatrical pageant.

The Star of Ethiopia

The Juniors decided to stage W. E. B. Du Bois's historical pageant, *The Star of Ethiopia*. "To the white world," wrote one enthusiast, "the pageant will be a tremendous revelation. To the Black world its picture of our life will be a stirring inspiration. Its purpose is to educate each one of us—Black and

White alike." The leaders of the Junior Branch's production were James Mc-
Gregor, Naida Portia McCullough, and Fay Jackson. McGregor and Jackson
served as president and vice president of the Juniors. McGregor was a rising star in black Los Angeles. High-profile in church and social circles and
a senior at USC, he was national vice president of Alpha Phi Alpha, a leading black fraternity. In January 1925, McGregor made a tour of the East that
included a stop in New York, where he dined with Du Bois at the New York
City Club. Naida McCullough, also a USC student, took an eastern tour to
represent her sorority, Alpha Kappa Alpha, at its annual convention. A talented musician, McCullough also met with Du Bois and asked him about
the possibility of the Junior Branch producing his pageant.[16]

Du Bois had first staged *The Star of Ethiopia* in 1913 in New York. In
five acts, history in motion swept across the stage. To the accompaniment
of orchestral music, several hundred volunteer actors and dancers presented
an epic theatrical version of black history, personified in the beautiful
Ethiopia, carrying the story from African splendor through American slavery and finally to the rise of the New Negro in the 1920s. *Star* was a hit,
playing to some fourteen thousand blacks and whites. Ongoing demand for
the pageant led to two subsequent performances under Du Bois's direction—
in Washington, D.C., in 1915, and Philadelphia the following year—both
well attended. *Star* demanded a cast of hundreds, and the novelty was that
the host community supplied the actors, dancers, singers, and musicians. Du
Bois maintained full control, however. He selected the music, and Charles
Burroughs, his right-hand man from New York, directed each production
according to Du Bois's desires.[17]

In early February 1925, L.A.'s Junior Branch announced it would stage
Du Bois's pageant, perhaps at the Hollywood Bowl. The news "swept intelligent Los Angeles like wild fire," the *Eagle* reported: "The past week alone
witnessed an army of capable and enthusiastic workers who, after aligning
themselves together, are now out to ensure the successful enactment of the
story of their suffering, but nevertheless triumphant race." In late February, Fay Jackson issued "a call for talent," asking for one thousand participants for the stage production. McCullough estimated the music would require a fifty-piece orchestra and a two-thousand-voice chorus. The Avenue
buzzed. Organizations and individuals came together with unified purpose.[18]

But in late March the fabric of cooperation started unraveling. Du Bois
announced his intention to come to L.A. for the event, sparking a wave of
excitement and misunderstanding that created ugly tensions between the
Junior Branch and what the Race papers were now calling the "Senior"
Branch. Beatrice Thompson, still executive secretary, told the national office

that "our most active field workers are assisting the Junior Branch to stage 'The Star of Ethiopia' this summer. In fact, the entire program of the Juniors seems to parallel in many ways the work of the older Branch, which fact does not strengthen the efficiency of either." By early April, reports of the pageant preparations had become a bewildering mix of booster rhetoric, conflicting claims, and vague accusations.[19]

Du Bois and the Junior Branch reached an impasse over who would control the pageant. The Juniors had already been working on their version of the pageant when Charles Burroughs came to town to take charge. He was armed with a letter from Du Bois, which emphasized that "Mr. Burroughs is a director of dramatic action and knows exactly what he is doing." Burroughs called a casting meeting for May 18, stating he would "select the principal characters and groups."[20]

Outraged by this takeover, the Junior Branch boycotted the pageant. If they could not stage it on their own terms, they would not participate. As Du Bois later put it, "we ran afoul a strike of the young colored intellectuals." The boycott quickly spread among other young people, and Burroughs could not get enough musicians for the orchestra or actors for the drama. On the eve of the pageant, he was still several hundred actors short and was working with a skeletal orchestra. Du Bois later said the production "nearly floundered" because the young people simply would not participate. The older generation pushed on. Du Bois's promotional piece in the *Times* assured readers that *Star* would offer "a beautiful spectacle in brown and black skins." The *Eagle*, critical of the pageant when it splintered, now urged the community to fill the Hollywood Bowl.[21]

On opening night, the giant amphitheater was mostly empty. The Bowl had an estimated seating capacity of 10,000, and the premiere on Monday, June 15, drew a biracial audience of only 1,651. It was by far the lowest attendance for any of Du Bois's stagings of *Star*. The audience was scarcely larger than the number of people in the show itself. The second performance, on Wednesday, June 18, drew 1,763. Black Los Angeles was disgraced. Du Bois tried to put a good spin on it in his summary report to the local Race papers. Financially, the bottom line was a debt of $749, but he had heard that no pageant at the Bowl had ever made a profit: "So much for business." He suggested that "as a spectacle the pageant was a success. If we had a larger number of participants it would have equaled Washington in spectacular effect and Philadelphia in Artistry." He thought that Ada Gaines, who played the key role of Ethiopia, was "the best we ever had." But his prose carried notes of weariness: "The band was not so good as we could wish for, but Mr. John Spikes worked faithfully." In conclusion, he thanked Los Angeles "for loyal co-operation, and dogged grit in putting over a beautiful thing." He thought it "a fine adventure in souls."[22]

Black Los Angeles, however, was left with debt, humiliation, and a bitterly divided NAACP. A chagrined Burton Ceruti wrote to Walter White: "In spite of some embarrassing circumstances, the Pageant was 'put over.' Dr. Du Bois and Prof. Burroughs labored indefatigably, making it an artistic success, notwithstanding a small financial loss." What hurt the most were those "embarrassing circumstances." In the beginning, the community had thought the pageant would place black L.A. in the national spotlight. It did, but for the wrong reasons. The national office regretted the "rather unfortunate" episode, because it derailed the branch's regular work and "created some very serious problems."[23]

Established leaders took out their frustrations on the Junior Branch. When the Race papers printed commendations for *Star*, not a single member of the Junior Branch received mention. Only weeks before, the *Eagle* had lavished praise on the spunky Juniors, but after the boycott they disappeared from the news. The *Eagle* and Du Bois both praised Vada and John Somerville, who had "headed" the pageant. Frozen out, the Junior Branch disbanded. The "regular" executive board officially declared all Junior offices "vacant" and changed the name to the Junior *Division*. A national official wrote, "I trust now we may get a real Junior Division in Los Angeles, composed of adolescents. I think it is well that the others have drawn out."[24]

The financial debt remaining from *Star* was trivial, but no one would pay it. The national office suggested that a "citizens committee" might assume the pageant debt, but the local branch found no takers in the community. The Senior Branch felt no obligation to settle it, the Junior Branch was defunct, and the idea of Du Bois shelling out was beyond anyone's imagination. The debt had become linked to weightier issues—status, blame, responsibility, pride. It had become an explosive $749. Whoever was to blame, *Star* had poisoned the branch. In 1921, the local NAACP boasted more than 1,200 members. By the end of 1925, membership had fallen to 274.[25]

Hudson Rebuilds

The new local president, H. Claude Hudson, somehow stabilized the branch. By summer's end, he informed the national office that "most of the petty dickering has disappeared." For all his brashness, Hudson had a knack for calming troubled waters. With a combination of good humor and straight talk, he could take over contentious meetings and settle the quarrels. When it came time to elect new officers in late 1925, Hudson had the branch under control, and he handpicked them all. He made sure that Burton Ceruti remained at the center of power, that Beatrice Thompson was pushed out, and that newly elected officers were "regular" and "respected" team players. As he told the national office, "Today was election day and I set to work to clean house." It was, he confided, "a walk over." In the final months of 1925, Hudson kept the membership's focus on civil rights and launched an aggressive fund-raising drive. Membership leaped upward as black L.A. rallied behind him and money for national civil rights efforts rolled in, delighting national officials. "You will be pleased to know," Robert Bagnall wrote Hudson, "that the state of California led the entire country in total amounts contributed to National Work." L.A. was quickly regaining its reputation as a branch that strongly supported the national office where it mattered most.[26]

The 1926 national convention in Chicago reinvigorated Hudson and the Somervilles. John and Vada spent time with Du Bois; despite the *Star* fiasco in L.A., he warmed to their idea of holding a national convention there in the near future. Hudson became friends with Walter White, who told him that L.A. was "one of the branches of which we are most proud." Accolades for L.A. rolled in when Mrs. J. M. Scott, a vice president of the branch and leader of the Baby Contest fund-raising event, smashed the national NAACP Baby Contest record by raising four thousand dollars for the national treasury. (Baby Contests were NAACP fund-raising events, held by the local branches, in which babies were "entered" and people could "vote" for the baby of their choice by contributing a dime per vote. Babies with the most votes won and sometimes got their photos in the *Crisis*.) For this she won the Madam C. J. Walker Medal, awarded annually by the national office for the most outstanding individual achievement on behalf of the NAACP. With momentum building, Hudson launched attacks against segregated beaches and police brutality. Both campaigns provoked controversy within the branch but also energized it to counteract the race prejudice that had staggered black L.A. in the early 1920s.[27]

Desegregating the Beaches

With few exceptions, Southern California's publicly owned beaches were off limits to colored people, the state's civil rights laws notwithstanding. African Americans could enjoy only two small stretches of beach. One was the "Ink Well," a half-mile stretch between Pico and Ocean Park boulevards in the Ocean Park neighborhood in southern Santa Monica. There, a black-owned lodge and bathhouse, La Bonita, rented swimsuits to African Americans, who could walk a half mile down to their sliver of shore.

The other option, a popular one in the black community, lay a good nine miles south of Santa Monica, at the small coastal town of Manhattan Beach, where blacks could swim at "Bruce's Beach"—so named because Mrs. Willa Bruce, an African American who purchased frontage property in the early 1910s, had established a bathhouse and dining club there for blacks. The Bruce property lay between 25th and 26th Streets not far from the beachfront. A few other black families moved in nearby, apparently without molestation from whites in the area. By the mid-1920s, Charles A. Bruce had inherited the property, and he continued to run the bathhouse. To cross racial lines at any beach was to court certain conflict and possible arrest. "They made it miserable for you," recalled Charles Matthews. "Sand would get kicked over on your place and all the rest of it." And, as the assault on Arthur Valentine had demonstrated in 1920, blacks who transgressed racial boundaries at the beach risked violent assault.[28]

In the summer of 1922, whites in Santa Monica and Ocean Park sought to purge blacks from the Ink Well section. The cause of conflict was a new club opened by an African American, George Caldwell. His dance hall at 3rd Street and Pico Boulevard hosted parties each Sunday night. Neighborhood complaints convinced Santa Monica's commissioners to pass an ordinance prohibiting dancing on Sundays. Caldwell responded by shifting his dances to weekdays. The commission then adopted a blanket ban on dance halls in residential districts. Black protests were no match for the Santa Monica Bay Protective League—the white home-owners' association in the area—which claimed "the dance hall was conducted in a disorderly manner, and that it constituted a public nuisance." Hugh Macbeth urged Afro-Angelenos to fight this "discriminatory action taken against our people as a whole." Recent dances at Caldwell's hall had gotten out of hand, Macbeth agreed, but he was "firmly of the opinion that the most disgraceful conduct on the part of a few individuals does not warrant wholesale discrimination and limitation of a race of people." Concerted protest would be needed to "help prevent and eradicate the growth of southern prejudice in our state."[29]

The closing of Caldwell's Dance Hall was only part of it, however. In 1921, a group of black investors had arranged to purchase a large lot on Pico Boulevard, with plans for a first-class resort with beach access. The Santa Monica Bay Protective League sought to block that development as well. When the commissioners silenced Caldwell's club, they also denied a construction permit for the proposed Negro resort. The white owners of the property agreed to pull the plug on the sale. Then, as the *Times* reported, without apparent disapproval, "further steps toward barring negroes from the beach cities has [*sic*] been taken by large property owners of the district." Leading white owners were parceling and selling their beach property, but they had "placed a Caucasian restriction on their properties, barring negroes from ownership and occupation. Property owners throughout the district are being urged to follow suit."[30]

The Los Angeles Area Chamber of Commerce board of directors discussed the matter, and "southern prejudice" did in fact arise. At an August 1922 meeting, Sylvester Weaver urged his fellow directors to preserve the beaches for the public. They should stop the sale of private beach land at Santa Monica before the general public found "the ocean fenced off." He thought Santa Monica, or maybe Los Angeles city or county, should buy the land for public use. When pressed on the matter, Weaver blurted out, "In front of where I have a summer residence, . . . a piece of land has been fenced off and none but colored people allowed. I was born pretty far south to have that in front of my house." With such sentiments in the air, new struggles at the beach were bound to emerge.[31]

Hudson brought the NAACP into the beach wars when Bruce's Beach came under attack in 1927. The "beginning of the end of Bruce Beach," as attorney Willis O. Tyler wrote, was an eight-hundred-person party intended to impress a Race visitor from back East. The crowd "struck such alarm in the minds of the leaders of Manhattan Beach" that the city's board of trustees condemned the Bruce's Beach area for use as a public park, paying a total of seventy-five thousand dollars to compensate the property owners, black and white. The remaining question was: just how "public" would this new "city" beach be? Manhattan officials moved to make it a whites-only beach by leasing the entire park to a private individual, Oscar Bassonette, for the price of one dollar per year. With Bassonette in charge, the beach park excluded blacks. One female college student decided to test the waters. She went to the beach, and the local police asked her to leave. She refused and, after being charged with resisting arrest, was thrown in jail in her swimsuit.[32]

Acting unilaterally as branch president, Hudson organized about a half dozen people who wanted to press the issue and "who didn't mind going to jail." The participants in this, the branch's first act of civil disobedience, were not all young people but also included the venerable Race woman Mrs. Sadie Chandler Cole (mother of the famed soprano vocalist Florence Cole-Talbert), who was also a key figure in the local NAACP. Cole was both singularly refined and militant. A graduate of Fisk University, with a son who fought in the World War, a daughter who performed in an opera in Italy, and a husband—Thomas Cole—who was a deputy in the L.A. sheriff's department, Sadie Cole would not abide racial restrictions. Once, in the 1920s, when she was refused service in a soda shop, she began throwing cups and plates and trashing the place. The owner changed policies and served blacks after that. Hudson himself participated in the beach protest.[33]

The swim-in began quietly, but police soon arrived. When the Negroes refused to leave the beach, the police began to haul Sadie Cole off the beach. A white man on the beach—who was not involved with the NAACP—saw what was happening and tried to stop the police. He was arrested and taken away, and Cole escaped arrest. For a while, nothing else happened. The protesters split into groups, some remaining on the sand, others in the water, thereby testing both beach and ocean access. Five policemen arrived to remove them. Stories about what happened next are contradictory, but Hudson later told the national office that he had been watching from a distance when the officers arrived, and, seeing the officers' attitude as "belligerent" and fearing violence, he intervened.[34]

Hudson urged the officers to stop the "quarrel" and avoid violence. If they intended to make arrests, he said, they should just get on with it. The policemen then charged two men who were in the water, another who was sitting on the beach, and Hudson. The official charge was "resisting an officer." Thus was the president of the local NAACP arrested and jailed. The other men incarcerated were James Conley, Romulus Johnson, and John McCaskill. Hudson and two others got out on ten dollars' bail, but one stayed behind bars in ongoing protest. At a hearing held on August 2, Oscar Bassonette claimed that he merely had instructed local police to remove "undesirable characters" from the park; but the policemen testified that he said to remove "any colored person." Hudson and crew were found guilty and sentenced to a four-hundred-dollar fine or twenty days in jail. Hugh Macbeth appealed, and the men were released on five hundred dollars' bond.[35]

John Somerville and other black leaders thought Hudson's arrest brought disgrace to the branch, but Hudson's actions won adulation in the community and in the national office. National Field Secretary William Pickens wrote a nationally syndicated article for the Associated Negro Press that insisted the protestors were "more than right." In sentiments he would restate in a personal letter to Hudson, Pickens added, "If they mean to arrest colored folk for frequenting any part of the beaches or for bathing in any part of the ocean, then every colored person in Los Angeles should get himself and herself arrested."[36]

Hudson's stock skyrocketed when Manhattan Beach suddenly capitu-

lated. On August 15, 1927, the city's trustees announced that they had revoked the lease to Bassonette and had secured for their city a perpetual lease
on all of its beach frontage. Most important, as the *Pacific Defender* stated,
Manhattan Beach would "forever remain open and free of access to the general public without restrictions." Race papers were ecstatic, of course, but
so was the *Times*, which editorialized that the new Manhattan Beach policy "sets an example in public spirit for the older beach communities in
Southern California. . . . it has secured for the recreation and enjoyment of
all the people two miles of foreshore, free from private exploitation or the
erection of barriers, assuring residents and visitors an ocean playground in
keeping with the spirit of American democracy." The NAACP's New York
office quickly issued a national press release trumpeting Hudson's leadership and the L.A. branch's "militant stand in behalf of Civil Rights."[37]

After the victory at Manhattan Beach, racial restrictions on public
beaches generally disappeared. The timing of this victory was odd. Three
years earlier, L.A.'s public swimming pools had unexpectedly been Jim
Crowed; now, public beaches that had been segregated were suddenly open
to all. Racial conditions in Southern California thus continued to be unpredictable, if not downright incomprehensible. For the moment, though,
Hudson's swim-in, and its successful outcome, had energized the community. His fight against police brutality, which took place at the same time as
the beach fight, also spurred greater interest in civil rights efforts.[38]

Hudson vs. Davis

Police harassment was an old story for black Angelenos, but it seemed to
get worse in the late 1910s and early 1920s. Los Angeles Police Department
statistics from 1918, which analyzed the nativity of "foreigners" arrested
in Los Angeles, showed that the "Negro" and "Mexican" groups were arrested in numbers far higher than their proportion in the population would
warrant. The assault on Arthur Valentine at Santa Monica beach, and the
acquittal of the officers who beat and shot him, set the tone for the decade.
In 1921, the LAPD's vice squad decided to "clean up" the Eastside, and white
dailies ran banner headlines about black vice. The *Eagle* countered that "the
clean-up . . . demonstrated that the Colored people have no monopoly on
vice; to the contrary, the depravity of white women and men down in the
black belt is shown up in all of its loathsome and shameful conditions." The
LAPD's focus on *colored* vice nonetheless continued.[39]

In May 1925, the *Eagle* charged that the police had designated the Eastside as a "poaching reserve upon which to build a record of arrests." In a rare instance of trans-ethnic rhetoric in local Race papers, an *Eagle* editorial headlined "Police, Mexicans and Negroes" stated: "This week on Monday there were more than fifty offenders in the morals court and every one was either a colored person or a Mexican. Now it stands to reason that all of the moral infractions of the law are not committed by these two groups. . . . We do not object to law enforcement, but we cannot see any reason of enforcing it for a part of the people and letting the others slide."[40]

At the same time, the *Eagle* reported a string of injustices inflicted by the police department and condemned the "reign of terror that a few petty officers have been creating in the East side." An incident on May 10 turned deadly. A white officer, E. E. Jones, sought to arrest an unarmed black man, Christopher Malcolm—a city employee—for a minor crime. Malcolm ran. Instead of merely chasing him down, Jones jumped in his squad car and ran him over, killing him. The community protested and the district attorney, Asa Keyes, eventually charged the officer with murder. This action by Keyes, the *Eagle* said, showed Jones "that Los Angeles is far removed from Georgia."[41]

Maybe it was, but the police department was still a difficult agency to fight. The LAPD was governed by a civilian Police Commission, which was in charge of overall policy, and by the chief of police, who oversaw everyday operations. Both the commission and chief were appointed by the mayor. The progressives who put this dual system in place had hoped it would clean up departmental corruption, but it did not. The LAPD's "Red Squad," which cracked down on radicals, labor unions, and activists in general, continued to operate openly and unchecked. Department officials at all levels were enmeshed in racketeering networks, which lined their pockets from L.A. vice— bootlegging, prostitution, and gambling. In 1926, Mayor George Cryer, a decent fellow aligned with the progressive wing of the Republican Party, and controlled by 1920s kingmaker Kent Parrott, appointed James E. Davis as the new chief of police. Parrott encouraged this appointment as a sop to the city's conservative elite, whom Parrott's candidates had thrashed in recent city elections. But Davis proved a hard sop to control. His rhetoric suggested that the LAPD was now a modern, clean-cut department—orderly and efficient. Beneath the progressive facade lay an ugly world of bribes, spies, money handlers, and thuggery.[42]

On the Eastside, two of Davis's essential agents in the racketeering machine were black officers: Maceo B. Sheffield and his sidekick, Frank Randolph. Black Angelenos feared and resented these men. As early as 1924,

Sheffield was involved in shooting incidents in the community.[43] It remains unclear how Sheffield and Randolph came to occupy their beat or why they delighted in tormenting black Angelenos. What is clear is that Sheffield and Randolph were on the take. Sheffield controlled the vice operations in the district, usually acting on "uptown" or police department directives. If boot-leggers and pimps were paying off properly, Sheffield let them remain in business without hassle. But operators who would not pay up, or who tried to sneak past the system, were sure to receive a visit.

Jimmy Smith, a native Angeleno and black-entertainment agent on The Avenue, later described a typical raid. Sheffield would "get word from up-town to raid them. They hadn't paid off." He wore trademark boots, and "he used to come and kick the door." In he would come; "he could play the piano, and if there was a piano" he would sit and play awhile, with no one daring to stop him. The paddy wagon would come; anyone with a chance would make a break for it. Sheffield knew Jimmy Smith well enough to stop by his talent agency and share bootleg gin with him from time to time. If not exactly friends with Sheffield, Smith knew enough to placate him. Once when Sheffield raided a gin joint on Central Avenue, he found Smith inside and blurted out, "What are you doing in here?" Smith replied, "What do you think, I came in to say my prayers?" and bolted for the back door. But if Sheffield's raids sometimes had a comic angle, they more often revealed a ruthless side, for Sheffield and Randolph could raid whomever they pleased, at whomever's bidding—a situation ripe for foul play, vendettas, and innocent victims.[44]

A Sheffield raid in spring 1927—which involved the use of lethal force—threw Claude Hudson into battle with Chief Davis. Sheffield and Randolph raided the home of Clara Harnes, just east of Central Avenue.[45] Without a warrant, they burst into the house on the premise that Harnes and her brother, Sam Faulkner, were running a bootlegging operation there. What happened next became a source of controversy and conflict. Maybe, as Chief Davis insisted, Faulkner shot at Officer Randolph, wounding him in the arm, whereupon Sheffield shot and killed Faulkner in self-defense. Or maybe, as Sheffield's critics (and later Randolph) charged, Sheffield gunned down an unarmed Faulkner, wounded his partner in the process, and planted a gun on Faulkner's corpse. Whatever happened, the event infuriated black Angelenos, prompting Davis to undertake damage control. Hudson sent a let-ter of protest to the DA's Office, calling Faulkner's death "an unnecessary, brutal and ruthless murder." He also criticized Davis for allegedly saying that "only the negroes of the underworld are opposed to the conduct of

Officers Sheffield and Randolph"—Hudson's point being that many respectable blacks were also opposed to the conduct of the two colored officers.[46]

Chief Davis, getting hold of Hudson's letter, responded with a lengthy rebuttal to the NAACP branch leader, suggesting that no friend of civil rights and moral order could be opposed to Sheffield, Randolph, or the Los Angeles Police Department. "From the complete report that has been made in this case by officers assigned to investigate it from every angle," Davis chided, "it is difficult for me to understand how it is possible for any persons who have not been completely and deliberately misinformed to believe 'that this was an unnecessary, brutal and ruthless murder.'" He felt "confident that your national association would be the last group in the world to assert that officers engaged in the performance of their duties need not defend themselves when attacked with a deadly weapon." His "fixed policy" in the LAPD, he said, was "a law enforcement policy that takes no account of race or creed." The arrest record for Sheffield and Randolph "is one of which this department and every law abiding citizen may be proud." From January 1925 to May 1927, the two officers had "been responsible for 3,038 arrests" and had "secured convictions in 89.4% of these cases." Anticipating Hudson's rejoinder to those statistics, Davis added: "Unless you charge your courts with constant miscarriage of justice you cannot accuse these officers of making unwarranted arrests."[47]

Davis forwarded a copy of his letter to both James Weldon Johnson and William Pickens in the NAACP's New York office. The chief's cover letter to Johnson hinted that the national NAACP should help protect Sheffield and Randolph—"colored officers who have proved to be exceptionally efficient men." Painting Hudson into a corner, Davis added, "I am of the opinion that your group is particularly interested in good work done by colored men in responsible positions." Johnson responded vaguely, saying he had not heard of the case and thanking Davis for the information. But Pickens rose to Davis's bait, responding that "it is clear that officers who enter premises in the line of duty should defend themselves when attacked by a deadly weapon"—a line Davis would save for later use.[48]

Hudson answered Davis in a long, prudently worded letter, which he had printed in the local Race papers, and in which he spoke officially for the local branch. The relationship "between the Colored people and the Police Department" in L.A. had always been one of "heartiest co-operation," he wrote, and added that the thousands of officers "who do their duty in an orderly and humane manner" had the full respect and support of the black community. But Sheffield and Randolph were a different matter.[49]

Explaining that the main law-and-order concern for NAACP members had always been "mob violence," Hudson added that "we consider Sheffield and Randolph 'a mob' unto themselves." Moreover, he wrote, "it is an easy matter to create sentiment against what is called the 'underworld,' and it has been, from our way of looking at it, an extremely easy thing for these two officers to arrest people who because of poverty or lack of influence and standing, have stood practically helpless before their brutal assaults and ruthless attacks, and often unwarranted arrests."As a result, people who would not be enemies of the police were becoming bitter toward the LAPD—"needlessly so." Real criminals—whether "members of the 'underworld' or Sheffield and Randolph"—did not have the support of the NAACP. But, Hudson concluded, "it would seem that there remains some rights to the individual, both in his person and his home, and once Sheffield and Randolph have learned this, we are sure there will be no trouble between Colored people and the Police Department."[50]

Some members of the local NAACP were outraged at their president's brash and independent action, but Joe Bass voiced a more common sentiment when he supported Hudson's "fearless and courageous reply." It *was* courageous; anyone at odds with Davis put him- or herself in harm's way. Hudson's aggressive activism had already prompted death threats from the KKK. "The more we see of the intense interest which the doughty president of the N.A.A.C.P. displays for and on behalf of the people," Bass wrote, "the more we appreciate him for his real worth as a factor in this community."[51]

Ultimately, Sheffield and Randolph were indicted for murder, prompting a worried note from William Pickens to Hudson, admitting that he had sent approving words to Davis early on, and hinting that Hudson should send him assurances that an indictment was the right thing. Hudson did so. Of Davis's early letter to Pickens, Hudson wrote that the chief "knew his guilt and that is the reason he was trying to strengthen his position." As for the NAACP supporting a trial against black officers, Hudson said, "You know my loyalty to the group, and I hated to fight colored officers, but they are the tools of the system, and I had an opportunity to fight [the system] through the officers." He had taken special precautions with the district attorney, too. "When I took a committee to the District Attorney's office to urge him to go into this, I opened with the statement, 'I want it distinctly understood that we are not fighting Negro officers, but two policemen of the City of Los Angeles, who incidentally happened to be Negroes.'"[52]

A superior court jury acquitted the officers in late July, prompting Hudson to tell Pickens: "It made me sick. . . . It did 99% of all the people (both groups)." Hudson thought "too much higher up was involved and to cover their tracks Sheffield had to be turned free. . . . All agree however that Sheffield and Chief Davis will not get over the scare." He also noted that Faulkner's sister had been tried (apparently for resisting arrest) and acquitted. Hudson thundered, "Her home raided, her brother killed and she was *not guilty.*" Randolph had been dismissed from the police force, ostensibly on account of his injured arm; he had ultimately turned against Sheffield, testifying for the prosecution. But Sheffield went free and Randolph permanently lost his job and any possibility of a pension; plus, his arm was paralyzed from the shooting. At a subsequent branch meeting, Hudson asked the members to take up a collection for Randolph, but there was too much bitterness for that. One man at the meeting called out that Randolph "had done enough devilment to suffer."[53]

The LAPD issued a press release on the case. The language used and the arrest statistics wielded on behalf of Sheffield suggest Davis's authorship. The report emphasized the LAPD's victory over the "vice profiteers" who sought to undermine Chief Davis's legal authority to order "legitimate raids." It pulled out the supportive quote from William Pickens's letter to Davis: "It is evident that the jury agrees with William Pickens, Field Secretary of the National Association for the Advancement of Colored People, who said in a letter to Chief Davis discussing this case, 'It is clear that officers who enter premises in the line of duty should defend themselves when attacked by a deadly weapon.'" Hudson sent Pickens a copy of the report, adding a handwritten note: "This gives you an idea of how careful National officers should be in writing the enemy. I am sure you are disgusted."[54]

To Win a Convention

While Hudson was bringing the branch out of the doldrums, the Somervilles were trying to bring a national convention to Los Angeles. The NAACP's national conference, a seven-day event, was held each summer during the last week of June. It lured delegates from virtually every state, featured nationally and internationally renowned speakers, and was, without doubt, the most important civil rights conclave in America. The delegates at each convention chose the site of the next one, although there was plenty of behind-the-scenes influence from the national executive board. The NAACP had never held its convention in the West, partly because easterners worried about a low turnout. The Somervilles wanted to change that. The resurgence of the local branch made their job easier.

In spring 1926, Robert Bagnall visited the L.A. branch, found it a beehive of activity, and sent excited word back to New York: "They are going some!" The reorganized Junior Division filled with teenagers under Vada's leadership, and they gained publicity by selling Mayor Cryer an NAACP membership. When Hudson announced a drive to sign up five thousand members in L.A., Bagnall responded: "I have confidence in you and know something of the resources of your community, and have felt that all it needed was a dynamic personality like yours. Go to it, and add to the splendid record of your new state—that of leading the country."[55]

The local branch lobbied hard for the convention. Vada Somerville reported good news about the branch to New York officials—and closed her letters, "Yours for Los Angeles in 1928." Hudson's battles against beach segregation and police brutality and corruption, as well as his appointment to the Board of Education of the city's *white* YMCA, further enhanced his and the branch's national reputation. Meanwhile, Mattie Patton, a Texan and a dynamic lieutenant for Hudson, became president of the branch's new Women's Auxiliary, established as a standing committee for fund raising. Patton's Baby Contest exceeded the seemingly unbeatable record set by Mrs. J. M. Scott the previous year, meaning that L.A. was contributing big money to the national office. By the time the NAACP convention met in Indianapolis in June 1927, L.A.'s case was strong.[56]

John Somerville played the trump card when he pledged to build a convention hotel if the NAACP would come. His commitment impressed national officials, Du Bois praising it as a "gesture of faith in our cause." The L.A. branch chose Mrs. Scott and J. C. Banks as delegates to Indianapolis and instructed them to request the convention. Bagnall had already hinted to Hudson that the chances were good. Hudson could not attend the 1927 conference but sent an emphatic message: "Yes we want it in '28." Du Bois, Bagnall, and Pickens lined up behind Los Angeles. Bagnall would later write to Hudson, "You had two fine delegates there in Mrs. Scott and Mr. Banks. The rest was easy." L.A. won the convention. One week later, the national executive board elected John Somerville to replace the late Burton Ceruti on the NAACP's board of directors. The resurgence of the local branch was complete.[57]

Winning the convention was important for Afro-Angelenos and, in a larger sense, the black West. For decades, Race communities out West had operated as distant outposts of the national black network and the East Coast civil rights establishment. The NAACP's convention was the most important civil rights event in America. By choosing L.A. to host it, the national membership demonstrated its faith in a branch that had, only recently, been on shaky ground. The decision effectively forgave the branch for the pageant fiasco. It also validated Hudson's aggressive tactics, honored Somerville's faithful service, and rewarded the fund-raising prowess of the Women's Auxiliary. The decision to meet in L.A. in 1928 signaled that the NAACP's western membership had moved into the nation's civil rights mainstream. The South was still a different country, but the gap between North and West was beginning to close.

The Feud

It was all too much in too short a time: *The Star of Ethiopia*, Hudson's rise, Thompson's fall, Manhattan Beach, Sheffield, the convention. No sooner had the L.A. branch secured the convention than it exploded in a feud pitting John Somerville against Claude Hudson. Led by Somerville and J. C. Banks, a faction on the executive board coalesced in opposition to Hudson's aggressive— they would have said "reckless"—leadership. "I started a *'mess'* that will not down," Hudson told Pickens, reporting that his arrest and his attack on the LAPD had divided the branch. Bitterness simmered among the membership— and more broadly among L.A.'s black middle class—as the community grew polarized between supporters of Hudson's hard-hitting style and Somerville's opposition to it. To the majority of the community, Hudson was a hero, a Race man willing to risk his reputation and safety for racial equality. A minority, mostly among the well-established NAACP leaders, charged that Hudson's renegade actions were dictatorial and had disgraced the local branch. Hostility ran so high that Somerville and his clique insisted that the branch's legal committee *not* represent Hudson in court after his arrest on the beach. Hudson's supporters were vindicated when they won the Manhattan Beach struggle, but after Sheffield's acquittal bad feelings were bound to come out. Fortunately for the branch, they came out *after* L.A. won the convention.

The feud erupted at the monthly branch meeting that August. Upward of five hundred members crowded the pews of a tension-filled AME-Zion. As usual, the meeting opened with the Negro National Anthem, a bit of entertainment, and an outside speaker. Then came the fireworks. Hudson opened the business meeting by stating that he and the executive board "were at loggerheads, due to a difference in policies." He motioned for a vote to determine whether the general membership supported his actions. A flood of vocal support for Hudson followed, some of it from pioneer Race leaders, such as the entrepreneur J. H. Shackleford, but most of it from newcomers. When Somerville and Banks took up for the executive committee and moved to table Hudson's motion, all rules of order flew out the window. "For a time," the *Pacific Defender* reported, the meeting "threatened to become a free-for-all scrap." At a critical moment in the debate, a follower of Somerville rebuked Hudson for making the executive board look bad. To this Hudson responded, "THE BRANCH IS BIGGER THAN THE EXECUTIVE BOARD!"—earning thunderous applause from the crowd and effectively silencing the Somerville faction.[58]

After the meeting, John and Vada Somerville tendered their resignations from their NAACP offices. The new branch secretary, Emma Lou Sayers, told New York that their resignation would undermine preparations for the convention. "I do think it unnecessary and terrible to have to give the Somervilles up at this time because of the differences of opinion between TWO MEN—DR. HUDSON AND DR. SOMERVILLE! Dr. Hudson is a good president and he has put the Los Angeles Branch on the map as never before, I firmly believe. The Somervilles have LABORED with the Branch for thirteen years! . . . And with the national convention here next year WE NEED THEM as never before." She urged the national office to write to Hudson—"You know he is from Louisiana and his patience is sometimes too short"—asking him to work with the Somervilles.[59]

National officials panicked. They urged L.A.'s leadership to unite in common cause for the convention. Bagnall insisted that "personal differences" must not be allowed to undermine the branch's work, "especially in view of the coming conference." In an unprecedented move, he wrote an open letter to branch leaders and mailed a copy to *all* officers and executive board members of the branch, hoping it would "have the effect of causing the officers to get together so as to put united shoulders under the wheel of the Branch's success and to forget whatever differences that have existed in the past."[60]

Curiously, the Hudson-Somerville feud had the effect of invigorating the branch, not destroying it. After the initial eruption, tempers cooled a bit; membership grew and enthusiasm for the convention rose. Both men had spirited followings within the existing organization. Supporters embraced programs espoused by their champion, working hard to see *their* man succeed. Behind the scenes, the men distrusted each other, but they kept their personal antagonisms mostly private, seeking a public show of unity and avoiding open conflict. It was as if each man saw the advantages of having the other pull the branch's weight to a different arena of action. So the city's two leading Race men developed an unspoken truce, and the community appeared able to deal with the awkward situation. In late 1927, for example, an upbeat review of the local NAACP in the *Eagle* praised both men, without hint of dispute. That was fortunate, for as the convention neared there was much to do.[61]

The Hotel Somerville

Many branch members and local organizations, especially the churches, shouldered responsibilities for the conference—they planned the program, entertainment, and dinners; found venues; served as ushers; the works. Hudson's supporters in the branch handled most of this work. For his part, Somerville focused his efforts on the conference hotel, which, six months prior to the convention, was barely under construction. In December 1927, Vada had reassured William Pickens that they were "about to close a deal for a 150 room hotel and office building"; estimated completion date: June 1— "so don't let any body say that there is no place to stay in Los Angeles."[62] Her confidence notwithstanding, the conference was scheduled to begin on June 27, less than a month after the proposed opening. Any snag in financing, contracts, or construction would spell disaster. Then there was the matter of staffing the hotel—including kitchen and dinning room—and getting everything up and running smoothly in a matter of weeks.

Somerville found a good lot at the corner of 41st Street and Central Avenue. "The location was far removed from the center of Negro activity," he later wrote, "which at that time was around 12th and Central Avenue. Many people thought that we were going too far away."[63] The area was still overwhelmingly white, and it was still mostly undeveloped, with an almost rural look. But the 12th and Central district was too built up and too expensive. Somerville needed low-priced land and plenty of open space for a big hotel. The Westside was out of bounds, and east of Alameda Avenue was downright dangerous, so he headed southward and found what he was looking for.

But then there was the money. Fortunately for Somerville, he had recently tried his hand at this game. In 1925 he had decided to build a first-class apartment building for more-affluent blacks. Somerville recalled that he "approached the president of one of the financial institutions that was making large loans," but the president refused to lend him seventy-five thousand dollars because of the location; he thought the Eastside risky and doubted any tenants in that vicinity could pay high rents. Somerville then gathered signatures from people in the community who would pay such rents. The surprised president then partially financed the apartment building. La Vada apartments—a twenty-seven-unit building—arose on Vernon, quite a distance from the 12th Street hub. Somerville's positive experience in that "far removed" location encouraged him to look southward again when planning his hotel. His La Vada success allowed him to get financing for the hotel, because the same loan officer, having seen the apartment deal succeed, now swung Somerville one hundred thousand dollars for his new venture.[64]

The ground-breaking ceremony was captured in a photograph that shows dignitaries from the black community gathered on both sides of a bulky steam shovel—with Vada posed behind the controls of the dirt-moving machine. The Basses and some clergymen were there, as was the good Dr. Hudson, standing in a different group from the good Dr. Somerville. Behind the dirt lot stood a wooden home, like a farmhouse, with scrubby outbuildings in the back—and beyond that, trees. This place did not even look urban, much less like the site of a national convention. But that was 41st and Central in early 1928.[65]

Excitement swelled as the event neared and construction crews labored. In May and June, the Race papers filled their pages with conference news. The *Eagle* announced each major piece of the program as it fell into place ("Unusual Entertainment For Delegates," "Monster N.A.A.C.P. Parade"), making pleas for unity and keeping tabs on the Hotel Somerville's construction. Charlotta, writing what would become her long-standing weekly column, "On the Sidewalk," demanded a cleanup on The Avenue: "No, it is not New York's Seventh Avenue, or Chicago's State Street, that we are interested in just now—it is our Central Avenue, and the East Side of Los Angeles. . . . Let's not only make new frocks for the occasion but let's clean up Central Ave., our back yards, and our alleys, wash our windows and polish our fronts, and all together let us be ready to receive this great delegation of human rights activists. Also let us start a better behavior week, and demonstrate that we are ready to conform to a program of advancement along all lines."[66]

Charlotta's concern for the convention's success reflected a larger interest among the community's female leaders, who drove the event through early 1928. Betty Hill, a founding member of the branch and a longtime member on the executive board, took charge of the program. Mattie Patton, chair of the Women's Auxiliary, launched a statewide "Miss California Popularity" contest; any organization could nominate a candidate, and each vote cost a dime. The candidate who brought in the most votes (that is, money) would be crowned Miss California, receiving glory and a gown at the convention. More than two thousands dollars rolled in. The women of Friendship Baptist Church held a musical revue at the Rose Bowl and tapped Charlotta Bass as "Mistress of Ceremonies." The program featured performances by Florence Cole-Talbert and the NAACP Chorus, a five-hundred-voice choir created for the convention and directed by Elmer Bartlett, First AME's choral director. Fay Jackson (of Junior Branch notoriety) was now writing for the *Eagle*. She reminded readers that everyone in the community had a responsibility in making the convention a success. "In keeping with the West's reputation for hospitality, it is up to every Angeleno to consider himself a committee of one to put forth every effort to see that our visitors are properly received and entertained."[67]

A very popular committee of one—Carolynne Snowden, "California's Josephine Baker"—lent her more flamboyant gifts to the cause. Snowden got her start dancing in Central Avenue jazz clubs but had soon moved to the big time, appearing as the headliner at Sebastian's Cotton Club, the high-brow, whites-only jazz club in Culver City. In addition to her stage talents, Snowden was also known "for the gracious support she so freely contributes to various race organizations." In early May, she appeared at a "monster N.A.A.C.P. benefit show" at the Lincoln Theater, where, as the *New Age* had it, "East siders were given demonstration of just what the millionaires receive for their money in Culver city." She brought "her entire revue" of dancing girls for the show and "displayed her ability to stage the greatest show the West has ever seen." Shortly thereafter, Snowden agreed to stage a "Spirit of Jazz" revue for the convention—a show starring herself and "a fast moving chorus of forty beautiful bronze dancing girls." This performance, the *Pacific Defender* predicted, would "demonstrate to the East that Los Angeles knows how."[68]

Meanwhile, John Somerville showed that he "knew how" by getting his hotel finished—with no time to spare. Less than two weeks before the conference began, the *Eagle* announced that the building was ready. One week later, Somerville held a grand-opening bash for the general public. On Saturday and Sunday, June 23 and 24, anyone could drop by to tour the hotel and get a meal in the dining room for a dollar. Thousands of people streamed through the Somerville that weekend, and few could have been unimpressed.[69]

The Hotel Somerville was handsome on the outside and elegant on the inside. From the sidewalk, it appeared five stories tall; unseen were the basement level for storerooms and a rooftop garden. Nearly square, the Somerville fronted both Central Avenue and 41st Street, with the main entrance on Central and an entry into an artfully conceived Spanish-style patio from 41st. The hotel's first floor, framed by heavy stone blocks, was actually two stories high. The next three floors, occupied by the hotel's hundred-plus rooms, were red brick, with crafty features and balconies. Street-side, the ground floor sported tall archways for the hotel entrances and the shops that rimmed the hotel. Albert Baumann's newest drugstore occupied the corner; it was surrounded by a salon, barbershop, flower shop, and real estate office. Inside, the spacious lobby and dining room followed the classic Spanish style, with tile and wrought-iron staircases ascending to the mezzanine level, with its gracious lounge and decorative arches.[70]

"On the whole," John Somerville later recalled, "it was the finest hotel in America catering to colored people. There were others in the larger eastern cities, but they were old buildings vacated by white people." His hotel was "something new; something clean and fresh; something that made the guest feel happy that they did not have to wait for white people to wear off the newness, before they could clean up the place and move in." The *Eagle* called it "the beauty spot of Los Angeles, the monument to Negro enterprise," and predicted that "it is destined to be the gathering place of the best manhood and womanhood of the city as well as a restful haven for the stranger passing through our gates." In language reminiscent of his editorial praising Sidney Dones and the Booker T. Washington building twelve years earlier, Joe Bass congratulated Somerville on his "courage and genius" and voiced his hope that the hotel would "live forever and be the sign post of a renewed and successful effort for our group to assume the place it should occupy in the mighty march of progress."[71]

Du Bois's assessment was as poignant as it was enthusiastic. Somerville's hotel was "a jewel done with loving hands. . . . It was all full of sunshine and low voices and the sound of human laughter and running water." More than that, it was "an extraordinary surprise to people fed on ugliness—ugly schools, ugly churches, ugly streets, ugly insults. We were prepared for— well, something that didn't leak and was hastily clean and too new for vermin. And we entered a beautiful inn with soul." Unequal opportunities had led to unequal experiences and expectations. Where was American freedom in that? "Funny," he added, "that a hotel so impressed us—but it was so unexpected, so startling, so beautiful."[72]

The Convention of '28

Delegates from forty-four states met from Wednesday night, June 27, to Tuesday, July 3, and the program was packed. So were most of the venues. Opening night at the Philharmonic Hall, which held thirty-five hundred people, was filled to capacity, with that many or more turned away. Like every evening session, it began with thirty minutes of music from Elmer Bartlett's

NAACP Chorus. Then came welcoming speeches from Claude Hudson and Mayor George Cryer. Du Bois offered a powerful keynote address, "The Presidential Election, Black Votes and Democracy in the United States," which emphasized not only the injustice of black disfranchisement in the South but also the way in which it allowed an "oligarchy" of southern whites, elected by pitifully few voters, to be virtual dictators over the politicians from the North and West. "We must decide, and decide soon," Du Bois concluded, "what public opinion in the United States shall rule. Shall it be the public opinion of a small select group of persons of Nordic descent? Shall it be the public opinion of rich controllers of capital? Shall it be the public opinion of college graduates? Shall it be the public opinion of all adult Americans except Negroes, Asiatics, and Latins? Or Shall we try to make it the public opinion of all intelligent adults?" Joe Bass noted that of all the speeches he had heard the *Crisis* editor give, this "was the most splendid and wonderful."[73]

Daily sessions ran from 9:30 A.M. to 5:00 P.M. each weekday at Second Baptist Church. One session, for example, featured a talk by Mrs. A. C. Richardson, local NAACP stalwart, which addressed a perennial tough nut: "How to Keep the Branch Interested and Vigorous When There Is No Local Crisis." Second Baptist hosted three evening sessions as well. These offered a diverse array of speakers and topics: "The Superstition of Race Superiority," by a Hindu leader; "Negro Womanhood," by a black female lawyer; "The Rights of Minorities," by a rabbi; "Economic Interpretation of Race Problems," by William Pickens; "The Work of the N.A.A.C.P. as a Program of Practical Christian Ethics," by a local bishop; and "A Program for the Minority," by the famed progressive journalist Lincoln Steffens.

The weekend brought time to lighten up and step out a bit. Saturday offered sightseeing and entertainment. In the morning, delegates packed into automobiles and headed in all directions: Pasadena, the Westside, Hollywood, Mulholland Drive, the recently integrated beaches. That evening, locals and delegates alike jammed the Shrine Auditorium for a gala musical revue, which included Carolynne Snowden's "peacock dance." Dancing for all followed at the Shrine Pavilion. On Sunday, the local community held a giant parade that featured church groups, fraternal organizations, women's clubs, and businesses—on foot and in automobiles—floats blooming, banners flying, fraternal uniforms glittering. Afro-Angelenos by the thousands made their way from Washington Boulevard and Main Street to the Shrine Auditorium. There, the NAACP Chorus sang, and an impressive lineup of local, state, and national leaders held forth, including Fred Roberts, California governor C. C. Young, and James Weldon Johnson. After that crescendo, things slowly wound down until Tuesday night, when the conference concluded.[74]

By all accounts, the local branch had hosted one of the NAACP's finest conventions. Du Bois could scarcely contain himself in his *Crisis* recap. It was as if he had discovered L.A. all over again. Enlivened by the vitality of the host community and the Somerville Hotel, and by the sheer number of automobiles owned by Afro-Angelenos, Du Bois wrote that "we wise men of the East" seemed small and lost in that western city. "The boulevards of Los Angeles grip me with nameless ecstasy," he insisted. "To sing with the sun of a golden morning and dip, soar and roll over Wilshire or out to Pasadena where one of the Seven Streets of the World blooms; or out Washington to the sigh of the sound of the sea—this is Glory and Triumph and Life."[75]

After the Convention, or Betty Hill's Crusade

The local branch hoped to capitalize on the enthusiasm created by the conference and stave off postconference malaise. "Our group, you know," Bagnall told Hudson, "warms up quickly and cools off just as quickly." He suggested the branch launch a membership drive immediately after the conference. Thinking grandly, Hudson proposed a membership goal of ten thousand, but he later revised it to five thousand, which was still idealistic, given that his 1926 drive for five thousand had not come close to that. The Race papers announced the drive in the midst of the convention. Bagnall remained in town to direct it, but the real work was carried out by the ladies of the Women's Auxiliary, who were in charge of canvassing preassigned districts all over Los Angeles. The membership drive headquarters, fittingly, was the Hotel Somerville. The drive did boost membership, but not to the five-thousand mark.[76]

The branch also tried to regain momentum in the courts by reviving the battles against restrictive covenants and segregation in public swimming pools. *Letteau v. Long* had marked a disastrous setback. The branch now initiated a follow-up case in the Entwistle subdivision Eunice Long had lived in. The case, *Gilmer v. Letteau*, sought to avoid past missteps. Branch lawyers received assistance and approval from the national office's legal experts, and the branch went a step further in hiring two high-powered whites to lead the case: Robert P. Stewart (assistant attorney general under Presidents Wilson and Harding) and Robert Cordel, a respected local attorney. The branch made the *Gilmer* case a major part of its postconference membership drive, emphasizing the possibility of a major legal victory and urging Angelenos to join the organization that was waging the battle: "This Is Your Fight and You Must Recognize Your Responsibility!" In August the case suffered a negative decision in the L.A. County Superior Court. The branch announced its full intention to appeal all the way to the U.S. Supreme Court, if need be, but the case actually foundered in legal tangles.[77]

The fight against swimming pool segregation proved more successful. It was led not by the branch but by *one member* of the branch—Betty Hill. As Claude Hudson later wrote, this was a story "of a most remarkable fight of one woman when all the rest of us had lost hope." A native of Nashville, and the wife of an army officer, Hill was a well-respected Race woman in Los Angeles. Active in Colored Women's Clubs, she had been a founding member of the local NAACP and had always served as an officer in some capacity. An affluent "housewife" who lived in the West Jefferson district, she had helped organize the Westside Property Owners Association in 1920 (which protected black property against bigoted attacks) and had served as president of that association since 1925. In addition, she joined the board of directors of the local Urban League. Successfully shouldering the NAACP convention's program committee boosted her status even further.[78]

In 1929, Hill organized the Republican Women's Study Club of California, which analyzed policies and politicians, disseminated information, lobbied, and championed selected candidates, hoping to mobilize black voters, especially women. By the early 1930s, black women in L.A. County had organized more than twenty chapters of the club. In 1932, Claude Hudson wrote that the club's "significance is already demonstrated in the increased respect for the Negro's political support which recent office-seekers have manifested in many ways and for which potential office-seekers seasonably make their bid."

The city's swimming pool policies and the local NAACP's defeat in the Bath House Battle infuriated Hill. The Playground Commission sought to protect its racial restrictions by constructing the city's finest pool in the Central Avenue district. That pool admitted anyone in the community, including the white majority population. But pools in other parts of the city had only one "colored" day per week, or excluded colored people altogether. The local branch urged a boycott of the new Eastside swimming pool, but it was asking too much for families along Central Avenue to forgo the use of their sparkling new neighborhood facility. "It was with great difficulty," wrote Hudson, "that we held attendance at this pool below normal. Frankly, most members of the branch were discouraged."

Hill decided to test the policy again, but this time, in concert with branch officials, she launched a case outside of the NAACP. She thought a localized test case—in her own West Jefferson neighborhood—might be effective. As president of the Westside Property Owners Association, she took on the case under the auspices of that organization. One of Hill's neighbors—a "Mrs. Prioleau"—agreed to send her child to the Olympic Park pool on a "whites only" day. Her child was turned away, and Prioleau allowed Hill to file suit on the Prioleaus' behalf. Hugh Macbeth and Eugene C. Jennings served as Hill's attorneys, pro bono. The NAACP lent moral support, but Hill, Jennings, and Macbeth hauled the freight. Twenty-five court appearances followed—with Hill present at every one. Ultimately, in February 1931, superior court judge Walter S. Gates ruled that racial discrimination by the Playground Commission was illegal. He issued a writ of mandamus, ordering city pools to drop their segregation policies by June 16.

Hill now faced her most intense battle. By law, the Playground Commission had sixty days (after June 16) to appeal Gates's decision. But the city attorney refused to approve the commission's appeal, and it could not go forward. Only if a majority on the city council voted in favor of an appeal, he said, would he approve it. The commission thus "fought bitterly" (Hudson's words) to get the council to order an appeal. Hill fought just as hard to prevent one. The council took a vote in June, with Hill's supporters blocking an appeal. But the battle was not over, because Hill's supportive council was soon replaced by a newly elected one, which was more inclined to support the Playground Commission. When the new council voted on the appeal, it deadlocked, 6 to 6. The tenacious commission tried one more time, but the council's third vote on the case went 8 to 6 in Hill's favor. Time had run out on the commission.

Playground officials had no choice but to enforce the Judge Gates's writ. Commissioners therefore "instructed all superintendents or supervisors of parks and playgrounds that the swimming pools of the City of Los Angeles must be open to all races alike by order of a binding mandate of the Superior Court." The city's swimming pools dropped their racial restrictions that August. "The whole problem of racial contact and self respect was at stake here," wrote Hudson. "The humiliation of children daily does such harm, that it is impossible to calculate." He saw Hill's triumph as "one of the greatest victories in the history of the progress of the Race."

The Surge Down Central

The Somerville Hotel not only brought the NAACP convention to L.A., it also altered the geography of black Los Angeles with stunning rapidity. John

Somerville himself accurately gauged its influence: "Within six months after the opening of the hotel, capital began to flow into the neighborhood,
all the vacant property was bought, new buildings started, and before the
end of the year 41st Street and Central Avenue became the hub of the colored business section."[79] Indeed, almost overnight, the Somerville Hotel replaced the Booker T. Washington Building as the community's architectural
landmark, and although 12th and Central continued to be a dynamic space,
the intersection at 41st and Central soon gained the top spot. Twenty years
earlier, a similar shift had taken place when black entrepreneurs leapfrogged
over downtown's skid row to set up shop along 12th and Central. But the
relocation in 1928 was more dramatic.

The speed of the Hotel Somerville shift can be gauged by information
found in *Western Progress*, the booster publication that appeared late in
1928, less than six months after the convention. The business ventures featured in the book ranged from mom-and-pop shops to the Somerville Hotel. Most were clustered along the Avenue. Of those directly on Central, the
majority were located in the traditional business district. Others were already south of that, in the vicinity of Second Baptist, the Lincoln Theater,
and the YMCA. What is striking is the cluster of businesses that had already set up shop—or advertised their plans to do so—near the Somerville
Hotel.[80]

One pivotal but unfinished establishment featured in *Western Progress*
was Claude Hudson's new dental office, then being built at 4122 Central
Avenue, catty-corner from Somerville's hotel. Hudson's partner was the
physician E. B. Liddell. Paul Williams agreed to design their building, beginning a warm friendship between Hudson and Williams that would
deepen when two of their children exchanged wedding vows. The Hudson-
Liddell Medical Building was a Spanish stucco, with a tile roof and a second-
story balcony. Large pane windows at the sidewalk level and rows of second-
story windows let the light pour in. Hudson and Liddell held their open
house in April 1929, less than a year after the hotel opened. Hudson and
Somerville had built new buildings at 41st and Central within twelve
months of each other. That alone sent a powerful signal to the community:
This was the place.[81]

The Golden State Insurance Company's new headquarters sealed the deal.
Not long after Somerville began building, William Nickerson and company
purchased the corner lot across the street, at 4111 Central Avenue. Golden
State, too, hired black architects and contractors. One observer described the
finished building as "an architectural beauty, being a two story brick and concrete structure of Spanish design." The first floor was leased to shop own-

ers; Golden State's 130 employees worked on the second floor. Somerville, Hudson, and Golden State now occupied three of the four corners at 41st and Central.[82]

Thereafter, the momentum was unstoppable. Black-owned drugstore chains followed—and furthered—the trend. Albert Baumann built three stores in the 1920s: Baumann Drug no. 1 at 853 Central Avenue, no. 2 at 1301 Central Avenue, and no. 3 at the Somerville Hotel. Another drugstore developer built his first two stores on the edge of the traditional hub; his third was six blocks from the Somerville. Ritzy jazz clubs snuggled in, too. The black-owned Apex Club (which in the early 1930s gained its more famous appellation, Club Alabam), opened in November 1928 between 42nd and 43rd on Central, luring Westside limos to the Avenue. Club Memo and the Downbeat Club opened nearby; the *Eagle* dubbed this stretch of Central Avenue "Brown Broadway."[83]

The unprecedented black migration to L.A. in the 1920s; the growing affluence of the black middle class; and the racist barriers to residential movement west and east—all these factors ensured that Afro-Angelenos would push southward. When Jule Deckard bought his home in 1925, he and Eula moved in amid a sea of white folks. Only five years later, the center of the black community had come down to his neck of the Eastside. The "old" business center was not that old, and few neighborhoods anywhere on the Eastside were strictly black, but Afro-Angelenos continued to place their stamp on the Avenue—to invest themselves in it, to build it up. Even as they fought the restrictive covenants and segregation that hemmed them in, they claimed more of Central Avenue as their own. As half-free strivers trying to remake their world, that was their best option.

Flying High

On February, 12, 1929, the local branch held a banquet at the Somerville Hotel to celebrate Lincoln Day and the twentieth anniversary of the national NAACP. The *Eagle* judged the standing-room-only event a "Monster Success." Hudson—whom the *Eagle* called "the wonder president of the local branch"—opened the program, introducing the master of ceremonies, J. C. Banks, who was apparently no longer at war with Hudson. L. G. Robinson "invoked the devine [sic] blessing," music flowed, and John Somerville recounted the "past accomplishments" of the local branch. Then came John Brown's granddaughter, Adeline Clausen, whose mere appearance brought deafening applause. She spoke about her grandfather, and then everyone present sang "John Brown's Body." Frederick Warde, a white actor famous for Shakespearean drama, then took the stage for a one-man rendering of Lincoln's life—"This man who rose from obscurity and grasped 'Opportunity.'" Warde drew parallels between Lincoln and the NAACP, calling both a "great guiding force . . . for equal opportunity for all." Hudson made a plea for contributions to the legal defense fund, and "the responses were gratifying indeed." Clarence Muse, a rising Negro star in Hollywood, offered a "closing number" that "climaxed the most wonderful and history-making meeting of its kind ever held by the local branch of the N.A.A.C.P."[84]

Later that year, Joe and Charlotta Bass capped the surge down Central with a fiftieth anniversary party for the *Eagle,* also held at the Hotel Somerville. Neimore's newspaper had not actually run continuously between 1879 and 1912, but Charlotta may not have known that, and it did not matter anyway, for the *Eagle* celebration in 1929 highlighted the community's growth as much as the paper's longevity. The guest of honor was Chicago's Oscar DePriest, the nation's only black congressman. Enthusiastic onlookers crowded around the welcoming committee at the Southern Pacific depot. Amid hoopla, DePriest was guided to an automobile caravan, which traveled slowly down Central Avenue to the Somerville Hotel, where an eager crowd awaited.

En route, a single-engine airplane appeared above the caravan, making slow "S" turns to keep pace with DePriest's caravan. The pilots, Lieutenant William J. Powell and his flying companion, Herbert Banning, were hoping to inspire interest in their local airplane-building enterprise, Bessie Coleman Aero. They flew low enough for everyone to read the name of the plane, painted on the fuselage—the *Oscar DePriest.* Once the autos reached the Somerville, the pilots waved to the cheering crowd and flew off, signaling the start of the *Eagle*'s celebration party. The next day, DePriest, the *Eagle* entourage, and a crowd of spectators gathered at Lincoln Field airport, where Susie Hancock, Booker T. Washington's mother-in-law and an investor in Bessie Coleman Aero, christened the *Oscar DePriest.* Powell took the congressman for a plane ride—DePriest's first with an African American at the controls. DePriest urged the crowd to invest in Coleman Aero, which he saw as a fitting symbol of black Los Angeles.[85]

So, at the end of the 1920s, the community seemed to be flying high. The decade had begun in crisis—the Tulsa scare, the KKK. It brought the advent of swimming pool segregation and a restrictive-covenant disaster, not to mention the *Star of Ethiopia* debacle. But newcomers such as the Deckard family kept arriving with high hopes, and community leaders maintained the fighting spirit. The NAACP experienced a rebirth under Claude Hudson. Membership increased, beach segregation fell, police brutality was met head on. The Somervilles won the NAACP convention for L.A. in 1928 and built the finest black-owned hotel in the nation, thereby establishing a freshly polished center for the black community. The *Eagle*'s anniversary gala, enlivened with the flash of Bessie Coleman Aero, sent an uplifting message: Afro-Angelenos could claim a noble past, enjoy the prosperity of the present, and look forward to a bountiful future.

9

Responding to
the Depression

Shortly after the *Eagle's* anniversary celebration, the prosperity of black Los Angeles came crashing down. John Somerville went bankrupt. He lost his La Vada apartments and the Hotel Somerville. "The fate of my financial ventures could not withstand the crash of 1929," he later recalled. "Banks and mortgage companies in that year suddenly discovered the word 'Liquidation'; my equities were highly attenuated and frozen at that. I had no reserve to make them liquid, so I went down with millions of other Americans." In fact, he lost everything *before* the stock market's horrific crash—indicating just how fragile the community's prosperity had been. His losses frightened and exasperated black Angelenos. "Where is the Hotel Somerville now?" Mattie Patton of the NAACP lamented. "Lost! Lost!! Lost!!!" Black L.A.'s Great Depression began with the fall of Somerville.[1]

Southern California's diversified economy initially shielded much of L.A. from the economic crisis, but not the Eastside. At the outset of 1930, unemployment among black men was 8 percent; a year later it was 30 percent, and among women nearly 40 percent. By the time Herbert Hoover left the White House in 1933, nearly half of black L.A. was out of work.[2] Employers went bankrupt or cut back; private households eliminated maids, yard men, and chauffeurs. African Americans from the South continued to arrive, seeking work and often finding none. Some companies fired black employees in order to hire unemployed whites. Competition at the bottom of the ladder was especially fierce in L.A., because other "colored" workers were fighting for employment too.

Elizabeth Laura Adams, a young woman with an ailing mother to support, labored to find a job. A graduate of Santa Monica High School and a talented writer, Adams had worked mostly as a domestic. Never in good health, she had lived with a heart condition since contracting influenza during L.A.'s epidemic of 1918. During the Depression, she spent days in a crowded employment agency, eager to accept any position. Finally the exasperated employment agent insisted, "I've told you over and over again there's no work coming in for Colored!" Eventually she walked the streets of the city, going door to door, asking for any kind of work. Between rejections, she tried to keep her spirits up by reciting to herself the poetry of the Harlem Renaissance. Only when absolutely necessary would she stand in a breadline. She mowed a lawn for fifteen cents. She moved a heavy icebox for a quarter. Not long after that, her heart gave out, and she was hospitalized.[3]

Hunger gnawed at Ersey O'Brien's family. "I can remember as a young kid, walking from 49th and Hooper to 9th and San Pedro to the market, before school. Twice a week, sometimes three times a week, my mother and I would get up early in the morning, I'd take my little wagon, we'd go to the market and pick up spoiled fruit that they had discarded, cut the bad part off. . . . You got a wagon full of fruit or potatoes, maybe a little spoiled and you couldn't sell it in the market, but it was still good." He and his mother were not alone. O'Brien remembered the crowds; there would always be "25, 50 more kids" scavenging through the bins.[4]

Not everyone in black Los Angeles suffered in the 1930s. Verna Deckard Williams quit her job as a cashier and became a prosperous real estate agent. Minnie Lee and Roy L. Loggins started a catering business that quickly took off, finding a profitable niche in catering for the Hollywood studios. Paul Williams became the architect of choice among Hollywood stars, who could still afford to build sparkling mansions. The Golden State Insurance Company grew rapidly. Even John Somerville was able to recoup his losses. But success stories were exceptions and could not mask the suffering in the Central Avenue district.[5]

For many, the economic crisis shattered the ideal of middle-class living and upward mobility. Then, too, the community still had to deal with racism—restrictive covenants, segregation and exclusion in many public places, police brutality, and the daily burdens of race prejudice. Paul Williams could design homes for Hollywood, but he was not allowed to live there, even though he could afford it; and he was just as likely as any black man to be forced to leave a whites-only restaurant or be fraudulently accosted by the police. The struggle for black freedom remained, and community leaders continued the fight for equal opportunity. Now, on top of all that, a new question had to be dealt with: How should the community respond to the Great Depression?

Responses to the Crisis

The NAACP was poorly positioned to deal with the Depression, because it rarely dealt directly with economic matters, and because the national office was rocked by financial woes and internal divisions. As early as December 1929, Robert Bagnall wrote Claude Hudson, "The industrial depression and the stock market catastrophe [have] hit us quite hard, and we are very anxious that the branches shall make an extraordinary showing in December that the year might close without too large a deficit." The national's new executive secretary, Walter White, had an ego to match Du Bois's and the two quickly were at loggerheads. Du Bois's embarrassing lasciviousness, his inability to keep the *Crisis* out of debt, and his lack of diplomacy with the national board of directors finally led to his ouster in 1934. Under pressure, he resigned to accept a faculty position at Atlanta University. Shortly before he did so, the L.A. branch had held a public meeting to denounce Du Bois—"by unanimous vote"—for ignoring "far West workers" in the *Crisis.* Hudson privately expressed delight that Du Bois was gone. Du Bois, however, had been one of the few national officers to propose that the NAACP develop economic programs.[6]

In 1931, White established a legal defense team to defend the "Scottsboro Boys," the nine young black men who had been fraudulently charged with raping two white women on a freight train in Alabama. The NAACP was the first group to provide legal representation for the defendants, and White persuaded the famed attorney Clarence Darrow to take the case. However, the Communist Party's International Defense Fund soon took up the cause and convinced the defendants and their parents that only the IDF, not the NAACP, could secure their release. The IDF thus gained control of the defense, offering to let Darrow and other NAACP representatives remain on the case only if they would renounce their affiliation with the NAACP. Under these conditions, the NAACP withdrew from the case, and the Communist Party made the Scottsboro trial a cause célèbre. The NAACP national office then shifted its focus to getting a federal antilynching law through Congress.[7] Either way, the emphasis was not on the Great Depression.

The L.A. branch was no better prepared to meet the economic crisis. It sent money to support both the Scottsboro trial and the antilynching campaign, even though it was itself "greatly in need of funds."[8] To make matters worse, the branch became embroiled in an explosive community controversy over Hudson's involvement in a school board appointment. The board, seeking to add another African American teacher to the local schools, asked professors at the University of Southern California to suggest a candidate. The board also sought Hudson's advice. The USC candidate had not been involved in the NAACP or any community activism, so Hudson opposed him and pushed another candidate who was more of a Race man. Within the black community, factions rallied around both candidates, and tempers flared. The conflict involved just one teaching job yet sapped the branch's energies.[9] In the early years of the Depression, both the national office and local branch were criticized for their apparent insensitivity to the unemployed masses.

The Los Angeles Urban League, with its traditional focus on black employment and aid for the working poor, was better positioned to deal with economic problems. Floyd Covington, the executive secretary of the local league, quickly emerged as a key leader in black Los Angeles. His challenge, however, was overwhelming. Winning new job opportunities for African Americans was hard enough in a flush economy. A frustrated Covington wrote that "the day of the so-called traditional Negro job is over. The occupations once considered only fit for black men are now being competed for by an increasing number of whites, Mexicans, Filipinos, and European immigrants." The "good" white jobs remained firmly white, he discovered. But at the bottom of the ladder, interracial competition was fierce.[10]

If there were ever a time for working-class solidarity across racial and ethnic lines, the Great Depression was it. There was *some* solidarity. In L.A., for example, poor people of all nationalities and races formed multiracial "cooperatives," which amounted to elaborate bartering organizations. But the Depression also cut the other way, as workers at the bottom competed for jobs. Something of a litmus test for ethnic solidarity on the Eastside was the issue of ethnic Mexican "repatriation." Beginning in early 1931 (and for years thereafter), government injunctions forced nearly a hundred thousand ethnic Mexicans out of Southern California, sending them back to Mexico; tens of thousands were from L.A.'s Eastside. Repatriation roundups took place in full view of Afro-Angelenos. The black community, even the local branch of the NAACP, raised no word of protest on behalf of its Latino neighbors. During the height of the repatriation crisis, in February and March of 1931, the *Eagle* said absolutely nothing about it—a silence that spoke to tacit support for repatriation.[11]

For its part, organized labor did little to assist black workers or foster cross-racial solidarity in the early 1930s. Most local unions remained weak and lily-white. All-black unions, such as the Musicians Local and the Dining Car Employees, held their own, but there was nothing they could do to help absorb unemployed African Americans. The Brotherhood of Sleeping Car Porters, A. Philip Randolph's famous union, was still an underground organization in the early 1930s and had only a tiny following in Los Angeles. The Teamsters, although they were one of the only local unions to admit Afro-Angelenos, were not paragons of racial equality. When one black Teamster, Walter Williams, lost his job because fellow union members wanted a white man to have his position, white Teamsters silenced Williams's protest at gunpoint.[12]

The job crisis in black Los Angeles prompted Charlotta Bass to organize the Industrial Council in August 1930. In her words, the council's goal was "to see to it that Negro men and women were employed the same as white men and women; and that merit alone, not color, should count." She recalled that the founding group included "representatives of churches, clubs and various business groups" and that "the professional people present were urged to work closer with the laboring class." The group elected Charlotta president and launched letter-writing campaigns, legal proceedings, and boycotts to achieve broader and better Negro employment.[13]

One of the council's efforts—the "Don't Spend Your Money Where You Cannot Work" campaign—began in late 1930 and became a long-standing tradition in black Los Angeles. The council adopted the slogan from the *Chicago Whip* (a famed Race paper), believing the boycott idea well suited to the Central Avenue district, where white store owners seldom hired black help and, when they did so, hired blacks only at the menial level. The "Don't Spend" slogan could be heard in black communities throughout urban America, and coordinated boycott movements rose and fell through the decade. The main idea was to gain white-collar jobs for black people, especially the growing number of college and business school graduates who were badly underemployed.

The "Don't Spend" campaign caught on in Los Angeles. One local Race paper put the slogan on its masthead and kept the campaign going into the 1940s. Floyd Covington made the boycott an important part of the local Urban League's mission. Fred Roberts's *New Age* offered a spin-off—don't bank where you can't work—insisting that black money should be placed in the black-owned Liberty Building and Loan Association instead of the white-owned banks, which would not hire African Americans above the janitorial level. When a bus company in Watts refused to hire Negro drivers, the Industrial Council initiated a "Don't Ride if You Can't Drive" campaign. "Don't Spend" campaigns scored occasional victories, but as with similar programs nationwide, the boycotts proved more important in galvanizing the community for further activism than in gaining concessions from whites.[14]

Lieutenant William Powell's response to the Depression was to launch a Race enterprise that, in its fullest manifestation, would solve the problem of black unemployment. Bessie Coleman Aero, despite its successful *Oscar DePriest* stunt, soon fell flat amid a tragicomedy of mishaps and community indifference. Undeterred, Powell regrouped and established a new company—Black Wings. In 1934, he published his own book, *Black Wings*, which was equal parts autobiography and boosterism and served as a primer for aspiring pilots. In it, Powell also chastised the Race for not supporting black aviators and revealed his plans for a grand new economic venture.

Powell proposed that African Americans take the lead in developing the airplane industry, which he saw, rightly, as the next great breakthrough in transportation. Commercial and passenger service would become commonplace, and Powell wanted blacks to be a vital part of making it happen. He pointed to other transportation industries—railroad, steamship, automobile—and asked, "What position do blacks have in those industries?" Blacks were porters, stewards, and chauffeurs. This time, he insisted, they should be "in on the ground floor." They needed to develop the industry itself. Race men and women needed to create a company that would design and build aircraft, which would be flown and serviced by black pilots and mechanics. Black companies would build new airports and run them. The spin-off industries and jobs would banish unemployment from black America. Here was black nationalism on a grand scale—and with a twist, because the business would cater to all Americans, not just African Americans.[15]

This breathtaking vision was ahead of its time and exceeded the black community's immediate resources. It would take time to develop the company, time to overcome African American skepticism of black aviation. Unlike the Bessie Coleman Aero company, Black Wings survived more than a season. Powell's company built some planes and published a newspaper to promote the enterprise. But Black Wings could not stop the Depression; no single enterprise could have.[16]

From Powell's grand scheme to the enthusiastic cries of "Don't Spend," the established leaders of black Los Angeles envisioned a wide array of potential solutions to the economic crisis. None of those early ideas involved government action on the community's behalf. The community's first responses to the Depression amounted to traditional civic activism adapted to new circumstances. But changes were in the wind, not least because a new set of leaders and organizations was emerging on Central Avenue.

New Leaders, New Options

Leon Washington, Jr.—a Kansas man—came to L.A. in 1928 and quickly made an impact. Smooth and charismatic, Washington may have been the best salesman to hit Central Avenue since Sidney Dones. He came to take a job with a new Race paper, the *California News,* run by David Taylor. Taylor's abrasive, short-lived publication divided the community and took frequent shots at Claude Hudson in particular. Washington soon outgrew it and began his own venture, a free advertising news sheet called *Town Talk.* His business savvy attracted Charlotta Bass, and she hired him as the *Eagle's* advertising manager. He worked at the *Eagle* for a year and a half. Joining the Industrial Council, he championed the "Don't Spend" campaign and took it right to the storefronts, wielding signs advocating the boycott. On one occasion, he placed a sign on his car and parked it in front of Zerg's Furniture Store, at 42nd and Central, which got him thrown in jail, briefly, on trumped-up charges.[17]

At the *Eagle,* Leon Washington—known familiarly as "Wash"—joined two talented young journalists—Fay Jackson and Loren Miller, who was Washington's cousin. Jackson had been a leader of the NAACP's controversial Junior Branch. In the late 1920s and early 1930s, she worked as a staff writer for the short-lived news magazine *Flash.* She helped the *Eagle* cover the NAACP's 1928 convention, and she, among other staffers, sometimes ghostwrote Charlotta Bass's "On the Sidewalk" column.[18]

Loren Miller, a native Angeleno and the offspring of a black-white marriage, was a brilliant young lawyer-activist, a product of USC law school. When Wash joined the *Eagle,* Miller was already the Basses' city editor and a rising star in the community. When Langston Hughes moved to Los Angeles in the early 1930s, he and Miller became friends and political soul mates. Hughes moved into Miller's apartment and followed him into the John Reed Club, a racially integrated group committed to democratic socialism and filled largely with Communist Party members. In 1932 Miller and Hughes drove out of L.A. in Miller's automobile, speeding cross-country to New York to catch a boat to the Soviet Union. On board were other young leftists of the New Negro Renaissance. Their much publicized—and criticized—journey to the heart of communism came at the request of the Soviet state, which asked the Renaissance intellectuals to produce a film that reflected the realities of race relations in the American South. The film project floundered and failed, much to the delight of the hostile American press, including most Race papers. But Miller came back flush with enthusiasm, and before a full house at Second Baptist, he gave a speech extolling Soviet life.[19]

After eighteen months at the *Eagle,* Leon Washington struck out on his own, and in spring 1933 he founded the *Los Angeles Sentinel.* The *Sentinel* was free of charge, supported only by advertising dollars, and was heavy with real news presented in a professional format—easily the most sophisticated Race paper ever offered to the community. Washington's paper promised a "Fearless—Independent—Free" newspaper and used the "Don't Spend Where You Can't Work" slogan as its rallying cry. The paper thrived partly because of Washington's business acumen. He had a talent for landing large advertisements from Central Avenue supermarkets, such as the E. F. Smith Public Market at 43rd and Central. He soon lured Fay Jackson away from the *Eagle* and hired her as editor. Ultimately, Loren Miller joined the staff as well. Opening an office near 41st and Central, the trio made the *Sentinel* a strong new voice in the community.[20]

In a real sense, the *Sentinel* represented the continuation of the generation gap that had divided the NAACP, and the larger black community, when the Junior Branch demanded independence in 1925. Fay Jackson had been at the center of that controversy, and both Miller and Washington were part of the same cohort of African Americans—smart and restless intellectuals who had grown to young adulthood just as the New Negro movement of the 1920s reached its peak. Writing for the *Eagle* in 1932, Miller had editorialized that black Los Angeles was crippled by complacent middle-class leaders—charlatans who constituted, in his view, an "army of stuffed shirts."[21] For the younger activist crowd, it was easy to forget that only about five years earlier, Claude Hudson had been arrested on the beach and gone head-to-head with the chief of police. The *Sentinel*'s founders are best viewed not as radicals but as a younger version of the city's established black leadership.

There were other newcomers and organizations that were, in every sense, new in the community. One such group was the Utopian Society of America, a mostly white but emphatically biracial organization that emerged in L.A. in the early years of the Depression. Its goal was to break down barriers of class and race and to sponsor a political agenda that would facilitate brotherhood and equality. The foremost black Angeleno among the Utopians was Hugh Macbeth, who served as the organization's lawyer and who wrote editorials for its newsletter. The Utopian Society was a semisecret organization, with a full complement of rituals, codes, and greetings. But the group was decidedly political. Its newsletter assessed candidates for office, favoring left-liberal Democrats.[22]

The ideology of the Utopian Society, like the extent of its membership, was difficult to pin down. Openly patriotic, members of the society were nevertheless critical of American capitalism. They were left-leaning, but not communists. Their desire for a "cooperative" economy drew more from late-nineteenth-century populism than from radical socialism. The society favored racial equality but made economic equality its top priority. A secular organization, its membership was concerned with spiritual matters and public righteousness. Favorable to labor unions, Utopians were themselves middle-class types who feared they were slipping down the economic ladder. In the mid- to late 1930s, as the Utopian fire died, its loyal members would merge with another new group in town, the followers of Father Divine, or the Peace Mission Movement.

When the Peace Mission Movement arrived in L.A. sometime in the early 1930s, it marked an odd sort of homecoming. Father Divine was originally George Baker, a black man whose first trip to Los Angeles coincided with the Azusa Street revival of 1906. Caught up in the revival, Baker spoke in tongues and took his new religion back East. Eventually, he wound up in New York, not as Reverend Baker, but as the Father Divine, who claimed to be the incarnation of God on earth. Promising healing and earthly immortality, he gained a large group of followers, called "angels." Most of Divine's devotees were poor African Americans from Harlem, but he attracted an economically diverse following that also included Anglo Americans. Preaching righteous living and cooperative economics, he steered clear of politics, viewing sin, not flawed political systems, as the cause of human suffering. He himself did not suffer much—at least not financially. Peace Mission money allowed Divine to enjoy an opulent lifestyle, which proved to his critics that he was a fraud, and proved to his angels that he was indeed God.[23]

The Los Angeles Peace Mission Movement developed independently of New York's influence. Despite his messianic status, Father Divine wanted a decentralized movement, one without the trappings of organized churches. Converts had the freedom to organize Peace Mission groups anyplace they liked, and to maintain considerable autonomy. Some converts in L.A. were wealthy Westsiders, who fattened the local group's bank account and brought wealthy whites and poor blacks together in a uniquely mixed movement. Like the Utopians, the Peace Mission Movement in L.A. considered racial brotherhood in terms of blacks and whites, despite the multiracial environment in which the movement flourished. L.A.'s Peace Mission purchased property, provided meals for the hungry on Central Avenue, and published a newsletter, the *Spoken Word*. What set the L.A. group apart was its active involvement in politics. Unlike the movement back East, which felt Father Divine's presence more directly, the L.A. group plunged immediately into the electoral arena and used the *Spoken Word* as a means of supporting liberal candidates in the early 1930s. Before long, the L.A. group had changed the direction of the entire movement; Father Divine brought several L.A. leaders and the *Spoken Word* staff to New York, where he steered his followers toward electoral politics.

After the mid-1930s, L.A.'s Peace Mission Movement more or less absorbed the Utopians, many of whom became followers of Father Divine. Utopian attorney Hugh Macbeth, for example, became an ardent Peace Mission member and also one of its leading attorneys. The L.A. movement would begin to fade in the late 1930s, when one of its leaders, a Westside white man with substantial wealth but limited stability, became involved in a nationally embarrassing sex scandal. But in the early 1930s, both the Utopians and the Peace Mission were new and exciting organizations in L.A. Concentrated in the Central Avenue district, but also appealing to some Westsiders, both groups infused the Eastside with new energy and new visions of interracial possibilities, and they channeled their enthusiasm into the electoral arena, hoping to promote new possibilities through liberal politics.[24]

The Communist Party held some ideas in common with the Peace Mission Movement and the left-leaning Utopians, but it never allied with those groups. The party made fewer gains during the early Depression than one might expect, and its presence in Southern California would be lightly felt until the late 1930s, when the party began to support liberal Democrats in its famous "Popular Front" campaign. Even so, the Communist Party gained some ground in the Depression's early years. Loren Miller's active participation in party affairs and his influential positions at both the *Eagle* and the *Sentinel* assured a growing respect for, or at least increasing knowledge of, the far Left. Neither paper was pro-communist in tone or content, but Miller's views were well known and he was constantly in the public eye. Pettis Perry, a native Alabaman who moved to L.A. in 1920, became a deeply committed communist in 1932 and ultimately attracted considerable FBI surveillance. Local communists, including Miller, blasted the local NAACP for not supporting the Scottsboro Boys—a cheap shot, since the branch had made generous contributions to the Scottsboro defense and only ceased doing so after the Communist Party forced the NAACP off the case.[25]

If leftists found little enthusiasm for radical socialism on the Eastside, they nonetheless added to the cacophony of new political voices echoing through the district in the early 1930s. The *Sentinel*, the Utopians, the Peace Mission Movement, and the Communist Party all raised doubts about established leadership and political loyalties along Central Avenue. At the same time, the district itself was undergoing important social and political changes.

Continuity and Change in the Central Avenue District

In some ways, the Central Avenue district remained much the same as it had been in the late 1920s. The growing hub of activity around 41st and Central expanded as the community shifted southward. Lucius Lomax, a newcomer from Chicago, purchased the Somerville Hotel (which had been briefly owned by a white real estate syndicate) and renamed it the Dunbar Hotel, in honor of the poet Paul Laurence Dunbar. Lomax was a gambler who quickly established black L.A.'s first significant numbers game, but because he used some of his wealth to aid local Race papers—including the *Eagle* and *Sentinel*—and to keep the Dunbar in African American hands, he had high status. The debilitating impact of John Somerville's loss was reversed, and the hotel once again became the gem of black Los Angeles. Between the Booker T. Washington Building and the Dunbar Hotel, black neighborhoods and businesses spread out on both sides of Central Avenue, elongating the residential trends that had begun decades earlier. A 1935 survey of 12,142 African American households in L.A. gave evidence of an enduring middle-class environment. More then 30 percent of the households owned their homes, and 42 percent owned automobiles.[26] The multiracial character of the district also persisted. At the district high school, Ersey O'Brien recalled that blacks "were just about the minority" and that the Japanese, Chinese, African American, and white students got along fine.[27]

Assemblyman Fred Roberts and the Republicans still controlled the politics of the Central Avenue district in the early 1930s, but Roberts made sure that the boundaries of his political district expanded to embrace the black movement down The Avenue. In 1930, his 74th Assembly District became the 62nd. Roberts's new realm, like the black population itself, stretched southward from the old 74th district, keeping Central Avenue at its center. The new lines eliminated the least-black neighborhoods on the west, north, and east of the old 74th. The heart of the old black community was now the northernmost part of Roberts's territory. The rest of the 62nd district stretched southward to Slauson Avenue, comfortably encompassing the hub at 41st and Central.[28]

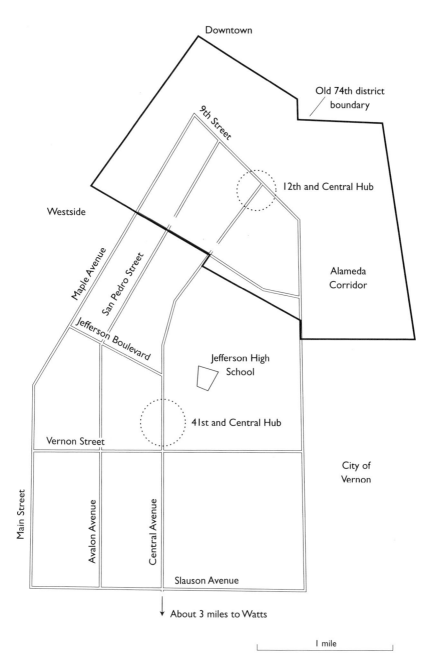

Map 4.   The 62nd Assembly District, 1930–1940.

During the 1930s, nearly 25,000 black migrants moved into the 62nd district. Most were from the urban South, especially Texas—Dallas and Houston primarily—and Louisiana, mostly New Orleans. By the end of the 1930s, the African American population in L.A. had reached 63,774. To appreciate the size of this community, consider other black communities in the West. By 1940, San Francisco had a black population of less than 5,000; Oakland, about 8,500; Seattle, less than 4,000; Denver, not quite 8,000. Even Dallas, a major southern city, had only 50,000 Negro residents. Black Los Angeles was big and getting bigger. How could all these newcomers fit into an already crowded Eastside?[29]

Fairly easily, it turned out, for as black migrants were moving into the district, other groups were moving out. Repatriation drained large numbers of ethnic Mexicans and Filipinos. Later in the decade, New Deal housing programs lured working-class whites to the new suburban developments, which were off-limits to blacks. Japanese immigration was still restricted, and some Japanese parents sent their teenagers back to Japan to learn homeland culture. European Jews fleeing Nazism arrived in L.A. in large numbers but settled mainly on the Westside. So, during a decade in which L.A.'s Westside and San Fernando Valley witnessed skyrocketing population growth, the Eastside neighborhoods grew little or even declined slightly. Lack of overall population growth did not mean lack of change, however. The demographic turnover in the Central Avenue district was striking. In 1930, black residents accounted for only 35 percent of the population in the 62nd district. By 1940, they accounted for 60 percent. In short, the Central Avenue district became larger and blacker, but not more crowded.[30]

But the black community began to change during the 1930s. As it grew larger, it also became less middle-class—in economic condition, in outlook, and in public behavior. Even though black newcomers were overwhelmingly urban in background, a larger number of arrivals were poor in the 1930s. Leaving behind an impoverished South, they landed in a community racked by unemployment. In the mid-1930s, the Eastside Shelter, a homeless shelter for women run by the Colored YWCA, was packed with hundreds of women in need. Storefront churches, which had always been rare in black L.A., now popped up all over the Central Avenue district. Small Baptist congregations, some meeting in tents and vacant buildings, became a large part of black L.A.'s churchgoing crowd. Their emotionally charged services ruffled the larger, more reserved, established churches in the community. The black sociologist Max Bond, reflecting the middle-class outlook he had become accustomed to, wrote of these churches that "the preacher is usually ignorant and insincere. His chief aim appears to be that of stirring the emotions of his listeners. The congregation represents the lowest group on the occupational scale, many members being not far removed from the rural South." They were not from rural places, by and large, but from the point of view of the entrenched middle class these newcomers were not quite the right sort.[31]

The local Peace Mission Movement, which drew largely from poorer African Americans, stunned black L.A. in the summer of 1934 by purchasing the Dunbar Hotel for its members. Lucius Lomax, Sr., the owner, was probably happy to sell it, because as his ex-daughter-in-law Almena Davis Lomax later recalled, he was more comfortable running the numbers and working within the sporting economy than he was with conventional investments, which usually lost him money. In May, the *Sentinel* had reported that the "Father Divine Cult" was growing rapidly and was planning to occupy the Dunbar. In late July, Father Divine's followers moved in. Sister Rebecca, leader of the group, discharged the staff and began to renovate the hotel, which would now serve as lodging for members of the Peace Mission. The dining hall, where the *Eagle*'s anniversary celebration had taken place five years earlier, was now used for the Peace Mission's holy communion banquets. Its political tilt notwithstanding, the *Sentinel* sounded rather aghast in its story reporting on the Dunbar's transformation. (Before decade's end, the Nelson family would purchase the Dunbar from the Peace Mission.)[32]

The rise of storefront churches and the Peace Mission movement was evidence of a growing class divide within the black community, but the internal divisions of the 1930s were as much cultural as economic, for among African Americans in L.A., the economic distance from middle class to lower class was usually not that far, and many of the sharpest divisions of the decade pitted one middle-class group against another. What actually came under fire in the 1930s was the middle-class establishment, which was criticized for being an exclusive clique and for being all talk and no action. Neither charge was true, but the perceptions sparked dissent. The Great Depression and New Deal gave rise to a new willingness to question the powers that be. The city's established black activists were not really powerful, but they were the closest thing to the "powers that be" that could be found in the Central Avenue district. Loren Miller and other critics in the community came to see their middle-aged leaders as entrenched failures who would never solve the community's problems. In their view, new approaches were essential.

As sharper divisions began to appear within the black community, the white working class in the 62nd district found a new sense of solidarity and political activism. Even though many whites left during the late 1930s, a solid core remained, especially in an all-white section on the west side of the district. This section lay west of San Pedro Street, or, in the southern part of the district, west of Avalon Avenue. Most workers in this area were high-wage blue-collar men. They were union workers, concentrated in the whites-only railroad brotherhoods. Blacks who tried to move into these neighborhoods met fierce opposition. Black leaders spoke of this part of the 62nd as the "west side" (not to be confused with the city's Westside). Within the district, "west side" was code for "white side." During the 1930s, this west side would play an important role in Central Avenue politics.[33]

Black Angelenos were especially troubled by a new group of white Angelenos—the "Okies," whose overloaded automobiles chugged into Los Angeles from Arkansas, Oklahoma, and Texas. Although most Okies migrated to California's agricultural camps, sizable numbers moved to L.A. Few actually settled in the 62nd district. Most moved to the industrial communities east of Alameda Avenue—Bell Gardens and South Gate—which were already home to thousands of white southerners who had been arriving since the 1920s. Okies were angry and hurt that California's white citizens viewed them as unwanted "foreigners," so they clung tenaciously to their home culture, including the culture of white supremacy. For black leaders, Okies represented the latest threat from Dixie.[34]

Floyd Covington of the Urban League bemoaned the "Southernizing of California" and explained that "by this I mean that California is becoming a state as southern in influence as the states largely contributing to its [white] population: Texas and Oklahoma. On all sides can one sense a general change of attitude toward the Negro, due to the impress of the southern influence on almost every activity within the community." It was by now a familiar refrain in black L.A.—the notion that conditions were declining because white southerners were spreading the germs of racism throughout the city. Southern whites constituted only a small part of the city's Caucasian population, but black Angelenos believed that Dixie's white migrants were undoing the tenuous freedoms Afro-Angelenos had won.[35]

As the 1930s progressed, however, the rhetoric of regional struggle—West versus South—was heard less frequently along Central Avenue. The reason was clear: the New Deal. Federal government programs suddenly became an everyday part of American life, including African American life. Slowly, Los Angeles began to lose its "western-ness" as its leaders and citizenry embraced the nationalizing influences of the era. Among American regions, only the South maintained its distinctiveness. White southerners vigorously defended Jim Crow, even as they embraced federal aid—knowing full well that their congressional bloc could kill any New Deal legislation that messed with segregation. Black Angelenos knew that the South remained their foremost opponent in the struggle for racial equality, but their view of the battleground began to change. They seldom touted the Western Ideal anymore. The new promised land for black Angelenos ceased to be the West, or even Los Angeles. In fact, the new land of opportunity was not a "place" at all. It was instead a political movement.

New Deal Liberalism

Everyone expected Franklin Roosevelt to defeat Herbert Hoover in 1932, but no one could have guessed the consequences. As soon as Roosevelt took office in March 1933, his vague campaign promise of a "New Deal" became a truckload of emergency legislation that his administration rolled through Congress. In the historic "First Hundred Days" of FDR's presidency, the federal government took unprecedented steps to control the economy and to provide direct relief to people in need. Almost overnight the federal government became a vital part of everyday life for ordinary Americans. Revitalization legislation such as the Agricultural Adjustment Act and the National Industrial Recovery Act, which created the better-known National Recovery Administration, became part of America's daily vocabulary. The Civil Works Administration and Works Progress Administration, the Civilian Conservation Corps, the Federal Emergency Relief Administration (which provided money to states and cities through State Emergency Relief Administrations)—these critical relief programs quickly became an accepted part of the age.[36]

In L.A., the traditionally pathetic Democratic Party surged into power. Party registration figures for Los Angeles County show that Republicans outnumbered Democrats by more than three to one in 1930. But the Depression mobilized hundreds of thousands of new Democrats and placed the parties near parity by 1932. New Deal legislation and faith in Roosevelt boosted the Democrats further and caused some defections from the GOP. By 1934, more than half of L.A. County's registered voters were card-carrying Democrats. The numbers were stunning. By 1940, the number of registered Democrats in L.A. County, fewer than 170,000 in 1930, had topped a million. Statewide trends were equally dramatic: in 1930, California's Republicans outnumbered Democrats 1,638,575 to 456,096; by 1940, the state's Republican membership had declined slightly, while the number of Democrats had skyrocketed to 2,419,629. Republican power in California did not suddenly dissipate, of course, and the new army of Democrats would be weakened by factionalism, but the rapidity and scope of partisan realignment permanently transformed city and state politics.[37]

For African Americans, the New Deal Democrats presented a dilemma. The Democrats had long been controlled by southerners dedicated to white supremacy. The Okies despised and feared by L.A.'s black community were, by upbringing, Democrats. New Deal liberals were a new breed of Democrat, however, and as they surged to power in the North and West, they created a powerful new wing in the party that looked alluring to many black Americans. New Deal liberals were not racial liberals, but their economic liberalism aimed to help ordinary working people, and for many blacks—younger ones in particular—the GOP's "Party of Lincoln" claim had worn thin.

But political loyalties are not easily changed, and blacks had powerful ties to the Republicans. In 1932, Frederick Roberts published a four-page pamphlet, *The Citizen of African Descent and the Federal Government*, which emphasized that history. "The Record of the Democratic party is plain—against the Negro," he stated. "The Record of the Republican party, and particularly the Hoover administration, is also plain—friendly to the Negro." Not all African American leaders shared his view in 1932. In New York and Pittsburgh, black leaders turned out large numbers of Democratic voters for Roosevelt. But most black voters either stuck with the GOP or stayed home. The predominantly black precincts along Central Avenue gave Hoover slim majorities over FDR. There was, in 1932, little reason for black Americans to trust Roosevelt and the Democrats. But after the New Deal took shape, the African American electorate began to reconsider.[38]

The Passing of the Old Guard

In 1930, Fred Roberts retained his assembly seat without significant opposition, but his reelection two years later was a different matter. In the spring of 1932, two African American candidates filed for the 62nd Assembly District race—as Democrats. Black Angelenos had challenged Roberts before, but always as Republicans or third-party candidates. Given the bitterness of the moment, a black Democrat stood a chance. Fortunately for Roberts, the surge in Democratic voters in the 62nd lay in the west side neighborhoods, not along Central Avenue. In an ugly campaign marred by racist overtones, a white candidate won the Democratic primary. That outcome should have ensured an easy victory for Roberts, but it proved a close call. In the general election, Roberts polled the highest total of his career yet captured only 55 percent of the vote. The stage was set for 1934, a year loaded with political significance for California and the 62nd district.[39]

In 1934, California witnessed a supercharged gubernatorial contest, which pitted a former Socialist, Upton Sinclair, against a staunchly conservative Republican candidate, Frank Merriam. Sinclair, the Pasadena author and perennial Socialist Party candidate for various statewide offices, had switched his party registration to Democrat in 1933. The following year, he shocked California's (and the nation's) political establishment by winning the Democratic gubernatorial primary. His cleverly titled booklet, *I, Governor of California, And How I Ended Poverty: A True Story of the Future*, and his "End Poverty in California" campaign, known as EPIC, ignited a grassroots upheaval throughout the state. The left wing of California's Democratic party swelled rapidly as the EPIC platform of aggressive, even radical, intervention in the economy promised jobs and a redistribution of wealth and political power. Old-school Democrats and moderate New Dealers viewed this populist surge uneasily, fearing they might lose control of their party. Not surprisingly, EPIC sparked a ferocious Republican counterattack in what came to be called the "Campaign of the Century."[40]

That campaign overshadowed—but also influenced—what happened in the 62nd Assembly District. Roberts mopped up in the Republican primary without incident, but the Democratic primary was a different story, as five black aspirants did battle. Unlike in 1932, there were no serious white competitors and no racist shenanigans in the Democratic primary. White Democratic leaders apparently accepted the fact that only a black Democrat could unseat Roberts. Moreover, a good candidate would not be hard to find, because the New Deal and the Roosevelts were beginning to win over African Americans. The question was, who would the candidate be?

John Somerville announced his candidacy early that summer. It made sense. He had been a Progressive Party loyalist in 1912, and his bankruptcy in 1929 may have inspired additional angst with regard to the traditional Republican Party. He and Vada had been active in New Deal circles since 1932, his finances had stabilized, and he was still a well-respected leader in the community. Somerville earned an impressive list of endorsements from local Democratic clubs and civic associations. The *Eagle* gave him so much favorable press that some black Democrats suspected he was a "fake" candidate running at the behest of Republicans who wanted him to win the Democratic primary and then throw the election to Roberts. The conspiracy theory lost credibility when national New Deal officials called Somerville to Washington, D.C., for a series of meetings in July. With Vada running the campaign in his absence, rumors flew on Central Avenue: John would meet with leading New Deal administrators, even FDR himself. Upon his return to L.A., Somerville assured the community that "a new day was dawning for the American Negro."[41]

But Somerville faced serious opposition from Fred Williams, who shocked everyone by throwing his hat in the ring. As publisher and editor of the *Pacific Defender*, Williams was a powerful and respected Republican handler. Since 1926 he had served on the Republicans' County Central Committee. In 1934 he left that position behind for the New Deal. Waiting until the very last day to file for the Democratic primary, Williams drew a large crowd at the post office, where he dramatically switched his party registration to Democrat and filed for the primary. The *Eagle* voiced astonishment that this "staunch Republican . . . renounces his party, his position, and accepts the [D]emocratic faith within the twinkling of an eye." Williams emphasized that he would join FDR's efforts "to alleviate depression, distress, racial animosity, and class antagonisms, and to promote peace, happiness, prosperity, and opportunities for all individuals." Like Somerville, Williams was a long-standing community leader, and he quickly garnered endorsements.[42]

Two other contestants were surefire losers. The flamboyant Sidney Dones, claiming to be "the man of the working people and the unemployed people's candidate," campaigned in a sixteen-cylinder Caddie, the *Eagle* said, "just to show the boys the sort of speed he intends to put into the race." Everyone liked Dones, but no one expected him to compete. One white candidate filed for the election from the EPIC camp, but he soon dropped out of the race.[43]

Somerville and Williams were old-guard leaders with Republican roots, but the two remaining candidates were young Afro-Angelenos—both in their twenties—who represented a challenge to the district's entrenched leadership. These challengers fit the profile of the emerging black Democratic leadership throughout the country. They were college graduates with professional ambitions and no real ties to the Republican Party. They came of voting age during the Depression and saw in the Republican Party not Lincoln, but Hoover.[44]

One was Sam Baumann. A product of New England, Baumann arrived in L.A. in 1923 with a Harvard business degree and an eye toward Central Avenue enterprise. He had family connections in L.A., too, being related to Albert Baumann, the revered Race man and owner of the popular Baumann Drug Store chain. Sam was a success in his own right, and his family name promised to help him that much more success in the political arena. He had run in the Democratic primary in 1932 and had nearly won it. In 1934, he once again entered the primary, but he got off to a slow start, winning little attention from either the *Eagle* or *Sentinel*.[45]

The other maverick was Augustus Freeman Hawkins, the Shreveport native whose parents had brought the family to L.A. shortly after World War I. At Jefferson High School, Gus Hawkins dreamed of studying engineering at Berkeley (his older brother was already pursuing an MD). When it came time for Gus to attend college in the mid-1920s, his parents could not quite afford to send him to Berkeley, so he stayed at home and enrolled at UCLA, majoring in economics as a prelude to graduate studies in engineering at Berkeley. But soon after he graduated, the stock market crashed, wrecking his father's finances and his own chances for graduate school. His generation of black college graduates found themselves adrift in a world without opportunity. Angry and restless, they blamed the Republicans and cast about for something that might improve things. For the first time in his life, Augustus Hawkins got political. He and a group of young black friends (mostly UCLA graduates like himself) set out to gain their own version of freedom through Democratic Party liberalism. Frustrated that more-established black leaders could not, or would not, unseat Roberts in 1932, the young Democrats decided to challenge him themselves. In 1934, Hawkins would vie for the 62nd district.[46]

With slogans promising a "New Day" and "Prosperity for the Masses," Hawkins came out swinging. His rhetoric sounded the most radical of the bunch, even though his relationship to the EPIC campaign remained questionable. The *Eagle* basically ignored him. The *Sentinel* gave him coverage, and doubtless appreciated his left-leaning liberalism, but noted less than a month before the primary that he was running third behind Williams and Somerville. But Hawkins proved tireless and, for a political novice, exceptionally savvy. Whereas Sam Baumann looked to be merely a younger version of John Somerville, Hawkins set himself completely apart from conventional black leadership.[47]

Alone among the black candidates, Hawkins sought the support of white voters on the west side of the 62nd district. His virtually white complexion helped him. Some voters on the west side probably thought he was white, and he did nothing to suggest otherwise. Hawkins later recalled the strategy: "We planned that we would probably not win the black community. One, my complexion was not identifiable with blacks, many of them didn't know I was black—so I lost votes. On the other side, on the white side, however, it was an asset, so it was a gamble as to which would be the greater loss." As for EPIC and Sinclair, they did not really understand race; they

saw all social problems as economic. Sinclair's editorial advice to EPIC supporters: "Do not discuss racial problems. Explain that we are going to End
Poverty for Jews, Japanese and Negroes, Portuguese, Hawaiians and Nordic
beings." Sinclair also flailed John Steven McGroarty, still much beloved in
black Los Angeles, for refusing to join EPIC. Sinclair and his handlers never
contacted the main political players on Central Avenue but corresponded
inconsistently with Afro-Angelenos of little to no influence. Sinclair therefore bungled the race issue and failed to win support among black Angelenos.
But he did whip the white working class into an electoral frenzy, including
those in the 62nd district, and Hawkins benefited greatly from those votes.[48]

Hawkins also sought west side votes through organized labor. The all-
white AFL unions, especially the railroad brotherhoods, were strong in these
neighborhoods, and they were fervent in their support of EPIC. They now
saw their chance to oust the anti-union Roberts; they would turn out in large
numbers. To be a New Dealer in 1934 was not necessarily to be a strong proponent of unions, but for Hawkins, Democratic liberalism was inseparable
from the labor movement. The white railroad brotherhoods were racist, but
according to Hawkins himself, they were critical to his success. Even if they
understood that he was African American, they worked for his election. They
wanted a pro-labor legislator, and, black or not, Hawkins was their only hope.
Hawkins courted AFL constituencies under the radar of the Race papers.
Central Avenue rumor mills failed to notice that he was amassing a substantial west-of-Avalon vote. His pro-union campaign lost him black votes,
but also won him some. Antilabor voters were not going to vote for him
anyway, and as the *Sentinel* noted, Hawkins was courting the young black
Democrats—those open to new directions, including labor alliances. Black
unions in L.A. were few and weak, but Hawkins gained campaign funds and
needed votes from the Sleeping Car Porters, Dining Car Employees, and Musicians unions.[49]

Hawkins also joined the Utopian Society of America, which strengthened his biracial coalition. Because the society was semisecret, there was little risk in alienating any voters and a nice chance to gain votes without much
effort. The society gave its members a code number, which they put on their
correspondence or advertisements to identify themselves as Utopians. Hawkins printed the code number on his campaign literature. Non-Utopians, not
knowing what it meant, simply ignored it, but, as Hawkins recalled, Utopian
members saw it and "they said 'Oh, he's one of our group.'" The result was
a stronger white vote for Hawkins, and a few more black votes. The Utopians would later claim Hawkins's victory as their own, and there was a grain
of truth in that exaggeration.[50]

Finally, Hawkins sought the votes of Father Divine's followers. The Peace Mission Movement in L.A. was still relatively new and largely unknown at the time of the 1934 primary, but Hawkins plugged into the growing organization. He recognized that the Peace Mission had some legitimacy in the district, especially among people who were already alienated from established black leaders. The mission's members in the 62nd district were mostly black and poor, and Hawkins found a favorable reception among them. On the advice of some local blacks, Upton Sinclair himself tried to connect with Divine's Southern California leadership, but his attempts were ineffective.[51]

When the primary ballots were counted, Hawkins had won 1,793 votes, 29 percent of the Democratic vote. That was enough for him to win the six-man race—only 232 votes ahead of Baumann. Hawkins won a little of the black vote and most of the west side vote; the other four black candidates split the remaining African American ballots. Bigoted white unionists, EPICs, Utopians, Pullman men, black college grads, and followers of Father Divine—such were the curious makings of Hawkins's emerging coalition. The most remarkable aspect of the election results was how poorly Somerville and Williams had fared; considering their credentials as Race men, their vote totals were humiliatingly low. The rise of black Democrats thus meant the rise of new, youthful leaders in the black community.[52]

Roberts, meanwhile, had cruised through his primary, winning more votes than all the Democrats combined. It was difficult to see how Hawkins could unseat a community legend in the general election. Some established leaders chastised him for even trying. But Hawkins and his peers were undaunted; indeed, they seemed almost hungry for a confrontation with Roberts and his generation. Between the primary and the November election, Hawkins campaigned nonstop, solidifying his white vote and hoping to somehow expand his black vote. Roberts appeared oddly detached, perhaps underestimating the challenge.

California's Democrats quickly divided into warring camps, leaving Hawkins to walk a fine line. Viewing EPIC as radicalism unleashed, old-line Democrats and moderate New Dealers were dismayed by Sinclair's victory in the gubernatorial primary. Many worked against their candidate, throwing their support to Republican Frank Merriam. Others did whatever they could to keep the EPIC forces at bay. The EPICs, meanwhile, felt the political millennium was at hand and campaigned with unprecedented enthusiasm. Hawkins avoided the fray, promising a broad pro-labor, pro-welfare platform. Shortly after his nomination, he attended the state Democratic convention and subsequently distributed a campaign letter outlining his votes at the convention, which even the *Eagle* published. He stood in favor of old-age pensions, an income tax on the rich, repeal of the sales tax, elim- ination of taxes on small property owners, and jobs for the unemployed as a substitute for charity. He carried endorsements from both Upton Sinclair and from California's mainstream New Deal senator, William McAdoo.[53]

Hawkins portrayed Fred Roberts as a puppet of corporate interests and therefore as part of the problem. He condemned Roberts as a watchdog for the utilities industries—the gas, electric, telephone, and streetcar compa- nies, who, he said, financed Roberts's campaigns and underwrote his *New Age*. Why were utility bills and streetcar fares high? Because Roberts and the Republicans kept them high. The New Deal was creating jobs, but the Republicans were fighting the New Deal. The message was simple and prac- tical: right versus wrong; benefits versus despair. Hawkins's biggest prob- lem was not the message but getting a chance to be heard in the traditional venues for black politics.[54]

All of the important African American ministers, still Republicans, re- fused to let Hawkins address their congregations. Undeterred, Hawkins and his supporters stood outside the churches and distributed their literature; as he later recalled, the people seemed to appreciate the effort. The Elks Club barred Hawkins from speaking in its hall until a Pullman porter and re- spected Elk, Percy Buck, led a rollicking in-house campaign to give Hawkins a hearing. The community's traditional Republican organizations would not allow Hawkins to address their meetings either, but he and his friends clev- erly infiltrated and disrupted the meetings until Hawkins gained a chance to speak. Openly tailed by the LAPD's Red Squad (and slightly shocked that he and his followers were never accosted by the squad), Hawkins found that black Angelenos increasingly admired his firebrand tactics. He delivered two speeches every night between the primary and the general election. Near the end, even the *Eagle* reported, with a hint of admiration, that "Hawkins is just gumshoeing right along and had better be watched."[55]

As election day neared, Hawkins's chances looked surprisingly good. Whereas Roberts lamely announced a last-minute endorsement by "the Affiliated Teachers Organization of Los Angeles, a non-political body," Hawkins boasted endorsements from every candidate who had lost in the 62nd district primary. Three days before the election, Hawkins prophesied an end to Roberts's career: "After 16 years, in campaigning on the basis of promises and empty phrases, the Assemblyman admits his weariness and inability to find a solution to our problems. . . . The little show is now over," Hawkins said. "The people have their own play to act."[56] His optimism proved justified.

On election day, the 62nd district chose Hawkins over Roberts. The young

Democrat amassed 11,199 votes, 53 percent of the ballots. Roberts polled well, considering the tidal wave of Democratic victories in 1934, but he won fewer votes than he had in 1932. The district's Democratic vote increased just enough to ensure his defeat. The key to Hawkins's victory lay in his biracial coalition. The district's white west side voters were effectively mobilized and turned out for him. In addition, a small but significant group of blacks joined them—just enough to tilt the majority from Roberts to Hawkins. Many other Democrats were elected to the California legislature, but in the explosive gubernatorial contest Merriam beat Sinclair. Hawkins was sure most black voters in the district had cast ballots for both Roberts and Merriam. Still, he had triumphed, and though the outcome stung the district's old guard, the *Eagle* offered Hawkins a gracious front page write-up.[57]

The Utopians celebrated Hawkins's triumph in a newspaper article that heralded the new biracial coalition and, more broadly, a new era in American race relations. Hawkins had "snapped his fingers at entrenched privilege and its money bags." He had won "against an arrogant hired hand of the special interests, a man who had held tight his grip on Los Angeles' Negro electorate for the past sixteen years." Offering a sweeping history lesson, probably written by Hugh Macbeth, the article chronicled the African American struggle for equality after slavery, a struggle that had led blacks and white workers to compete disastrously against one another. "But today, in 1934," the *Utopian News* insisted, "we are brothers in arms with our colored citizens, in an intelligent revolt against a continued form of slavery."[58]

Could black and white liberals be brothers in arms? Did black Democrats represent a passing fad, or would African American voters leave the Party of Lincoln for the Party of Roosevelt? Would the New Deal push for racial equality or lead to continued racism under a new party banner? Was the Democratic Party a viable avenue for black freedom? Hawkins's election—and more broadly the Democratic surge in 1934—put these questions on the table. No one could say. But Roberts's defeat portended greater changes. It felt something like a changing of the guard.

The GOP's feeling of loss was deepened by the death of Joe Bass, who passed away of natural causes just before election day. The very day the *Eagle* announced Roberts's defeat, it also announced Bass's death. In poor health for several years, the seventy-one-year old Bass died with Charlotta at his bedside. His funeral was large, orderly, serious—like the man himself. Joe Bass had helped put Roberts in power and worked to keep him there. It was difficult to think about Fred Roberts without also thinking about Joe Bass. The two editors had not always agreed, and Bass had tried to unseat Roberts in the election of 1928, but the two had been powerful allies, pillars of Central Avenue politics. Now Joe Bass was gone, and Roberts had lost his post. The old guard would not suddenly lose its power in the district, but Hawkins's triumph and Joe Bass's death would mark a turning point in black Los Angeles.[59]

Charlotta Bass remained to observe, and to take part in, the political transformation that was taking place. A generation earlier, at the deathbed of John J. Neimore, she had promised to sustain the *Eagle*. In keeping that vow, she had met Joe Bass, and they had become a power in the community. Now, at the deathbed of her husband, Charlotta once again committed herself to the *Eagle*, only this time, the choice was a given. She and the *Eagle* were virtually synonymous, and through the early 1930s, as Joe's health had deteriorated, she had basically run the paper independently. The bigger question, now that the political winds were shifting, was which side she would join in Joe's absence. For the time being, she held course and kept watch.

Black Democrats Rising

In 1935, while Hawkins was unpacking in Sacramento, an increasingly liberal Congress in Washington was pushing the New Deal to a higher level, passing the Social Security Act, which provided unemployment insurance and old-age pensions, and the Wagner Act, which provided federal protection for organized labor. This "Second New Deal" created an economic safety net for most Americans—most white Americans. The Social Security program excluded nearly all African Americans by excluding farm labor, city and county employees, and common laborers. The Wagner Act also failed to support domestic workers, which was why Hawkins would try—unsuccessfully—to win them that right in the state legislature. The Wagner Act did spark the rise of a major new labor organization in the United States, however: the Congress of Industrial Organizations, which sought to organize all industrial workers, regardless of race, and to make them a vital part of the New Deal coalition. Hawkins liked the CIO's vision of biracial working-class power; indeed, he joined the CIO and worked for it when the legislature was not in session. Being the only African American in the statehouse, he would need the help.[60]

Hawkins's first term went poorly. Unlike Fred Roberts, he did not "look" black. On opening day, an assemblyman introduced himself to Hawkins and confided: "I understand they elected another nigger to the Legislature. I'd sure like to meet him." Hawkins replied, "You already have. As a matter of fact, you are talking to him now." The white man sputtered an apology; remarkably, the two men would later become friends and political allies. Hawkins embraced the role of the white-looking African American. He shook up Sacramento's white politicians, who, simply because of Hawkins's presence and skin color, were forced to reconsider assumptions about race. Still, the "new nigger" incident suggested how difficult it would be for Hawkins to fight for civil rights, even among economic liberals.⁶¹

Worse, the Second New Deal in Washington did not translate into success in Sacramento. There were plenty of Democrats in 1935, but they broke into hostile camps—moderate New Dealers and left-leaning EPICs. Conflicting ideologies and petty politics undercut the Democrats' advantage and resulted in legislative gridlock. Hawkins hewed to the EPIC crowd, which suited his core voters. But the legislative zero pleased no one, and black Republicans in the 62nd district—including a newly energized Fred Roberts—condemned Hawkins as the kind of EPIC radical who had derailed practical New Deal programs in Sacramento. The black community's old guard eyed 1936 as the chance for Republican redemption and Roberts's return to power.

In the presidential campaign of 1936, Republicans nominated Alfred Landon of Kansas, who eagerly courted black votes. He needed those votes, because he offered nothing but a more efficient New Deal, and FDR was overwhelmingly popular. Landon won an important endorsement when the track star Jesse Owens, just returned from his gold-medal triumphs at the Berlin Olympics, threw his support to the GOP candidate and joined Landon's campaign entourage. (Pasadena's Mack Robinson had won Olympic silver in the two hundred meters, and L.A.'s Cornelius Johnson had broken the world record and won gold in the high jump, but the Republican Race papers devoted their space to Owens and his support for Landon.) Landon was more of a racial liberal than FDR, so GOP leaders hoped for black partisan loyalty.⁶²

African Americans were torn over the New Deal. Twisted by southern Democrats, federal programs sometimes hurt blacks more than they helped: the Agricultural Adjustment Act forced thousands of sharecroppers off the land in Dixie; blacks dubbed the National Recovery Administration the "Negro Removal Act" and "Negro Run Around." And most black workers were excluded from the provisions of the Social Security Act. But African Americans loved Franklin and Eleanor Roosevelt. Both spoke at historically black colleges, Eleanor became a political ally of the influential black educator Mary McLeod Bethune, and FDR established the "Black Cabinet," his unofficial cadre of African American advisors. More important, African Americans did receive emergency relief money to help them survive the crisis. So as the 1936 presidential campaign moved forward, reports of strong black support for Roosevelt could be heard across the North and West. Black voters in the South switched to FDR in their hearts, even though they were not yet able to vote.[63]

Hawkins rode FDR's coattails in 1936, seeking reelection as a "Rooseveltian Democrat" and steering wide of California's lingering EPIC controversy. Sidestepping the issue of legislative gridlock, he emphasized the stands he had taken in the legislature, not their results. He campaigned as "a militant fighter for increased benefits to the District in the form of Federal relief." He again supported repeal of the sales tax and the granting of old-age pensions, as well as better working conditions for domestics and railroad employees. He had fewer opponents in this election. Fred Williams did not run, and John Somerville, who had received a New Deal administrative appointment in the state's emergency relief agency, had neither time nor inclination to oppose Hawkins. Sam Baumann again challenged Hawkins in the primary, styling himself as the true New Dealer and winning the endorsement of John Somerville. And of course there was Fred Roberts, eager to regain his seat. Charlotta Bass kept the *Eagle* in the Republican camp, explicitly endorsing Roberts and ultimately turning her guns against the Democratic incumbent. Even before things heated up, the *Eagle* predicted that the "fight for Assemblyman, 62nd District, promises to be one of the most spectacular ever witnessed in the district."[64]

As Roberts began his spirited fight for "re-election" (his term), he shocked everyone by cross-filing for the Democratic Party primary. The strategy was simple. As the *New Age* put it: "nominate Roberts on both tickets." Even the *Eagle* had to raise an eyebrow at this move. "Just as well make it unanimous Fred," Charlotta quipped, "and include Townsendites, Epics, and Communists. . . . Just how the boys can stand on all these different platforms at one time is beyond our mathematical skill to figure out."[65]

In late July, "many representatives of some of the leading organizations of the community" held a "mass meeting and luncheon" to boost Roberts. There, endorsements rolled in from civic leaders such as Albert Baumann, who said, "We owe re-election to Roberts because of the manner in which he served us the last time," and Betty Hill, founder of the Women's Political Study Club (formerly the Republican Women's Study Club), who added that "few people know how many helpful bills Frederick M. Roberts is responsible for passing because he is such a modest person. He has an unequaled legislative record."[66]

The *New Age* detailed Roberts's legislative accomplishments and reminded readers of his strong record on "social welfare" and "humanitarian" legislation. In early July, Roberts took advantage of an opportunity to style himself as the workingman's candidate. A group of about thirty state employees in L.A. asked Roberts to speak on their behalf for a pay raise at a hearing of the State Personnel Board. Roberts appeared before the board, and the employees got their raise. "Fred Roberts Aids Labor," the *Eagle* proclaimed: "As a result of Mr. Roberts' efforts the minimum wage was raised from $90 to $100 and the maximum from $120 to $130 monthly."[67]

But even as Roberts was positioning himself as the workingman's liberal, his *New Age* was railing against FDR and the New Deal. The editorial page presented long attacks written by Captain W. W. Weston, a local Roberts supporter, who called Roosevelt's program "the Deal that is neither new, nor square," and whose columns continued from one issue to the next (each literally concluded with "to be continued") throughout the campaign. Lavishing praise on Landon, the *New Age* blasted what it perceived to be the empty promises, idiocy, and racism of FDR's New Deal. The paper placed a Landon plug in large print *above* the regular masthead, emphasizing Landon's commitment to equal rights. Somehow, Roberts expected to succeed in the Democratic primary even as he excoriated Roosevelt.[68]

Roberts's class identification did not help either. If there were ever an election to be affiliated with the "common" people and the "laboring class," 1936 was it. On this point, Gus Hawkins had every advantage. When, only ten days before the primary, the *Eagle* boasted that Roberts's political "corner is filled with the big shots of the district—men and women who rate high in the religious and civic life of Los Angeles," it unintentionally spelled out one of Roberts's fundamental problems. Hawkins was no commoner—his roots ran to the black upper class of Louisiana, his older brother was a physician, and he himself held a diploma from UCLA—but he was still considered a scrappy outsider among the "big shots" in black Los Angeles, and he had succeeded in 1934 by championing organized labor. If not by family lineage, then at least by political pedigree Hawkins could claim working-class credentials in a way that Roberts could not.[69]

Roberts *had* always been a humanitarian and a legislator with an eye toward blue-collar benefits. He had good reason to be an opponent of organized labor during his years in Sacramento. But the old progressive style of humanitarianism suddenly seemed outmoded. To be a candidate of the "little people" in 1936 was to be pro-union. Roberts really had not changed his ideals; nor was he a "conservative" in any meaningful sense. But America's political world had changed, and views that seemed perfectly acceptable in 1930 were now out of style and could not be peddled as Democratic liberalism.

On the eve of the primary, however, Roberts boldly predicted victory on both tickets. George Beavers, Jr., offered a last-minute endorsement in the *New Age* and *Eagle*, insisting that Roberts "fought all battles on the broad principle of Americanism. By avoiding special class or race legislation and consistently fighting on the broad platform of Humanitarianism and Americanism, Mr. Roberts maintained a strategic position that enabled him to do real constructive work while in the Assembly. As a result, he is recognized by those who know him, regardless of racial identity, as one of the most able legislators who has been in the Assembly in recent years." The election returns showed that Roberts's optimism was misplaced and Beavers's final pitch irrelevant.[70]

Hawkins easily won the Democratic primary, while Roberts placed dead last in the four-man field. Roberts's embarrassment was muted by his overwhelming victory in the Republican primary, and by the spin the *New Age* and *Eagle* put on the primary results. Roberts noted that "the three other candidates on the Democratic ticket polled a larger vote than [Hawkins]." In other words, Roberts would get the anti-Hawkins Democrats and win the general election. Charlotta Bass agreed, noting it was "common gossip on the avenue that Sam Baumann [has] moved bag and baggage into Fred Roberts's camp." The *Eagle* added that "we are preparing a welcome home for [John Somerville] before the close of the campaign." Such were the dreams of black Republicans in 1936—that prodigals would come home.[71]

Roberts campaigned energetically between August and November, emphasizing black progress within the Republican Party and Landon's racial liberalism. The *Eagle* reported that Sidney Dones had decided not to run for office this time around because he was too busy founding the suburban development of "Landon" in San Bernardino County, where he held a "Republican Day" rally. Trumpeting the Jesse Owens–Alfred Landon connection, the *New Age* wrote that Owens had seen the "misery of dictatorship" in Germany and would now "oppose New Deal dictatorship" at home. In late October, when the Landon campaign reached L.A., the *New Age* front page splashed a photo of him being greeted by an enthusiastic throng, including Roberts.[72]

Roberts objected to Hawkins's portrayal of him as a lame assemblyman and shot the charge back at the incumbent. At a mass meeting sponsored by the Progressive Business Women's Club (his wife was an officer), Roberts regained his old fire and pledged that he would "willingly resign from the present 62nd Assembly District race, if even the fruits of my first years as Assemblyman in Sacramento can be proven worthless to the citizens whom I was elected to represent." At high tea accompanied by poetry readings and musical performances by students of Gray's Conservatory, the

Republican congressional candidate, William D. Campbell, emphasized Roberts's legislative skills: "It is only through cooperation brought about by wide friendships [at the statehouse] that a man in that office can put over an effective program." In a series of meetings in October, Roberts reminded voters that Hawkins had failed "to live up to his platform promises of last term, namely: to secure more jobs for the Eastsiders and to lower the street car fare to five cents." In countless ways the Republicans repeated the theme: Roberts could get things done; his opponent could not. Hawkins had voted "all through the Legislative session with the destructive Epic block." Roberts's record in Sacramento, in contrast, "was that of a constructive Liberal."[73]

Roberts painted Hawkins as an irresponsible leftist—a pawn of the "Radical bloc" who had chosen the "Russian trained" Loren Miller as his campaign manager. Charlotta Bass also branded Miller a communist, and when Miller objected, the *Eagle* gleefully responded: "Our fellow countryman Loren Miller . . . slapped us on the wrist for saying he was a Communist. [We] heard Loren deliver an eloquent speech at the Second Baptist Church several months ago, in which he beautifully portrayed the glories of Red Russia. Pardon us, we thought you meant it." Days before the election, Bass pulled out the stops and fumed "there is no place in the scheme of our state government where a registered Socialist, backed by Epics, Communists, etc., can fit in."[74]

Finally, the Republicans played the other color card, charging that Hawkins was not just a red but also a "white." The *Eagle* claimed Hawkins was passing for white in the west side neighborhoods, repeating a rumor that "a certain candidate . . . denied his racial identity in a certain part of the city, saying he was an Italian." Roberts portrayed Hawkins as being too white to be a true Race candidate. Loren Miller cried foul, but the *New Age* countered that Hawkins had brought the issue on himself by passing for white to win west-side votes in 1934. Roberts said Miller wanted the color question silenced only because it was now backfiring. The *New Age* insisted that Roberts had "always stood as an American, but unafraid and unmasked in every campaign, as well as elsewhere, as an American of African descent."[75]

But all of the GOP's red-baiting and race-baiting proved for naught, because Hawkins demolished Roberts, racking up 17,548 votes to Roberts's 7,912. The Communist Party candidate gathered only 399 votes. After one ineffectual term, a Democratic incumbent had captured 68 percent of the ballots. In 1936, then, voters in the 62nd considered Hawkins the legitimate leftist, the legitimate liberal, and the legitimate Race man. Almost everyone fit into his big New Deal pocket.[76]

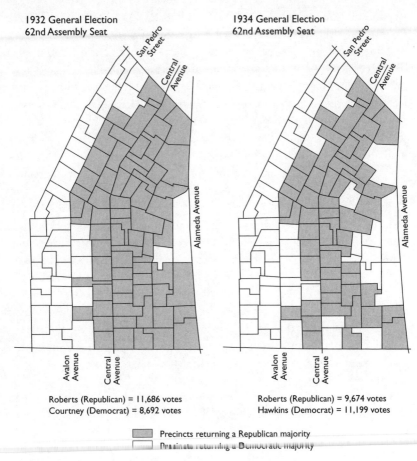

1932 General Election
62nd Assembly Seat

San Pedro Street
Central Avenue
Alameda Avenue
Avalon Avenue
Central Avenue

Roberts (Republican) = 11,686 votes
Courtney (Democrat) = 8,692 votes

1934 General Election
62nd Assembly Seat

San Pedro Street
Central Avenue
Alameda Avenue
Avalon Avenue
Central Avenue

Roberts (Republican) = 9,674 votes
Hawkins (Democrat) = 11,199 votes

Precincts returning a Republican majority
Precincts returning a Democratic majority

Map 5.   Voting trends in the Central Avenue district: from Republican to Democrat, 1932–1936. Source: California Secretary of State, *Statement of Vote*, 62nd Assembly District, 1932–1936; precinct boundaries from Department of Registrar-Recorder of Los Angeles County (maps on microfilm).

Roberts ascribed his defeat not to Hawkins but to FDR. "The Roosevelt Tide Carries All Before It," the *New Age* reported. Roberts's face-saving interpretation of the results, after "casual check of a few precincts," was that he himself had fared better than Landon in the 62nd, and that only the unprecedented Roosevelt landslide had saved Hawkins. "With the normal vote and except for the extraordinary outpouring of Roosevelt voters, keyed to the highest pitch of enthusiasm for the President and his ticket, the results would have been far different." Charlotta Bass also chalked up Roberts's defeat to "the Democratic landslide."[77]

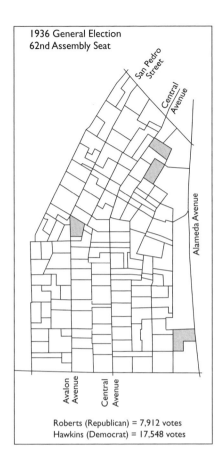

1936 General Election
62nd Assembly Seat

San Pedro Street

Central Avenue

Alameda Avenue

Avalon Avenue

Central Avenue

Roberts (Republican) = 7,912 votes
Hawkins (Democrat) = 17,548 votes

That landslide had transformed L.A. into a Democratic-majority town. Such a thing had been inconceivable only six years earlier. In 1930, every one of the city's twenty-two state assembly seats was held by a Republican. After the 1936 election, the Democrats held sixteen seats, the Republicans six. County-wide, voters registered as Democrats now outnumbered their Republican peers by more than 320,000. Only 22 percent of the county's voters were registered as Democrats in 1930. By FDR's reelection, more than 60 percent were Democrats. And black Angelenos were part of L.A.'s new Democratic Party, just as black voters everywhere had permanently shifted their party allegiance.[78]

As early as 1933, Claude Hudson estimated that 60 percent of black voters in L.A. had shifted from the Republican Party to the Democrats. He reasoned that the GOP had slapped black people one too many times, and the Depression was changing loyalties. Hudson's estimate was premature but prescient. In 1936, Afro-Angelenos voted overwhelmingly for Democrats, joining a nationwide trend in which black Americans left the Party of Lincoln for the Party of Roosevelt. Central Avenue gave FDR a huge margin over Landon, Jesse Owens notwithstanding. FDR did not need black votes in 1936, but that year's black vote marked a turning point in national politics. In California terms, these voters were not Woolwine Democrats. From 1936 onward, black voters would become an increasingly loyal, increasingly influential constituency within the Democratic Party, transforming the course of national and regional politics.[79]

Looking toward the future, the *New Age* predicted "the continued political activity of Mr. Roberts."[80] In a broad sense of the word *political*, this proved accurate. Roberts remained an active and revered Race man in the community, highly visible in civil rights activities. In 1937 he produced a weekly radio show, *The New Age Talent Hour*, which featured local black musical talent on KFVD. An overnight sensation, the *Talent Hour* ultimately reached some five hundred thousand listeners on Sunday afternoons.[81] In electoral terms, however, Roberts's political career had effectively ended. In 1938 he sought a higher level of service but failed to win the 14th district's congressional seat. Thereafter, he occasionally sought to regain the assembly seat, without success. He would run his last campaign in 1946, seeking a congressional seat but losing to the white Democrat, Helen Gahagan Douglas.[82]

No other Republican ever won the 62nd district—except, strange to say, Gus Hawkins himself. When Roberts opted out of the assembly race in 1938, several young men scrambled for his spot on the Republican ticket. But with the August primary still three months off, the *Eagle* said, "[We] wish we were as sure of a million dollars as Gus Hawkins is of his reelection. Unopposed for the Democratic nomination, his party is behind him to a man. Mr. Hawkins has many influential Republican friends also." With so many Republican friends, Hawkins cross-filed for the GOP primary. He won 62 percent of the vote in the Republican contest. Die-hard Republicans could stay true to Lincoln and vote for a New Deal liberal at the same time.[83]

Hawkins's reelection story repeated itself in 1940 and, with little variation, for years to come. In the 62nd district, Republicans and Democrats alike selected Hawkins as their party's candidate. In 1944, Fred Roberts ran again for the 62nd Assembly District seat and, in what was surely the most demoralizing defeat of his career, he lost to Hawkins in the *Republican* primary. Hawkins usually faced competition in the primaries, but it hardly mattered. He never lost the seat and did not give it up until 1962, when he won a seat in the U.S. House of Representatives, where he served until retirement decades later.

There would always be Republicans in the district, but their ranks steadily thinned. In order to cross-file, Hawkins had to petition for a place on the GOP ballot, which required that he get signatures from several dozen Republicans. That was no problem for a while. Eventually, though, Hawkins found that virtually all Republicans in the 62nd had changed their registration to Democrat. "It got to where I could hardly find enough Republicans in the District to fill my petition," he recalled. "They just sort of vanished."[84]

The Ultimate Response

Since the days when General Otis ruled the *Los Angeles Times* and African Americans began to arrive in earnest, black Los Angeles had maintained a political alliance with the white Republican elite. Despite mild shake-ups during the Progressive era, and during Woolwine's gubernatorial campaign of 1922, the coalition remained intact as Los Angeles grew from an aspiring town to a powerful city. Blacks held little power in this alliance, which often disappointed them but occasionally helped improve racial conditions. It did, however, ensure that black leaders had a voice in the halls of power, and it allowed Fred Roberts to pass some constructive laws for the Race in Sacramento. A firebrand editor in his early years, Roberts settled into a career as a pragmatic progressive. Given the political context in which he governed, there was actually little he could do to improve racial conditions in L.A.

Hawkins's sudden rise to power was altogether different, and not just because he was a Democrat. His biracial alliance included white voters who favored organized labor, a political block that General Otis, in his day, had despised and destroyed. Like Roberts, Hawkins was the only African American in the state legislature. But unlike Roberts, Hawkins found himself in the midst of a liberal coalition that was seeking to use state power to transform California's social and economic systems. Roberts had gained power when national progressivism was on its last legs, and most of his tenure in office occurred during the 1920s, a decade in which the dominant culture sought a retreat from serious issues. Hawkins gained power in a vastly different political environment.

The ultimate black response to the Great Depression was to tranfer partisan loyalty from the Republicans to the Democrats and to become, therefore, a significant component of the Democratic Party's liberal wing. In regional terms, this partisan realignment proved especially interesting. Instead of supporting a Republican Party that had no presence in the South and that largely approved of Dixie's social and economic conservatism, black voters in the West and North now joined the party of their political nemeses, the southern Democrats. Previously, black voters who were frustrated by GOP apathy had nowhere else to go. Now it was the southern Democrats—dismayed by the composition of its new liberal wing—who had nowhere to go. In the West and North, blacks now waged war on the Jim Crow South within their own political party. Black Democrats insisted that civil rights issues be part of the liberal agenda; and as their white allies sought to wrest party control from Dixie's demagogues, black Democrats became an increasingly important part of the plan. In this way, issues of racial equality would slowly filter into America's liberal agenda.

For black Angelenos, the key issues remained the same—full civil rights, equal access to jobs and housing, an end to police brutality. In a word, freedom. The NAACP, the Urban League, the leading churches, and the women's clubs would continue to be the major players in the community's civil rights activism. But the locus of their efforts was changing. Henceforth, the pursuit of equal rights would be linked to an unprecedented expansion of federal power and to the policies of the emerging welfare state.

10

Race and
New Deal Liberalism

On the morning after the 1936 election—and the reelection of both FDR and Gus Hawkins—two hundred women congregated in the basement of the Second Baptist Church. As the *New Age* reported, they were mostly "women of African and Mexican descent," mostly "mothers of dependent children." They were employees of a Works Progress Administration sewing project that operated out of Second Baptist, and they were "jubilant over the Roosevelt re-election." When they arrived at work that day, they "cheered for the President and sang patriotic airs for some time before settling down to work." Then they got laid off. That very morning, word came that the project had been scrapped. "I have orders to let you out," the supervisor said; "the federal government is transitioning projects to state control." Admitting that he himself did not know what to make of it, he said the women would be eligible for financial aid under the Social Security Act. He had no idea how soon or for how long they could get Social Security relief, but in the meantime, they were "to be taken care of" by the Los Angeles County Relief Agency.[1]

In this *New Age* account of the layoffs, Fred Roberts was obviously taking a partisan shot at New Dealers, but he also had a point. It was one thing for black voters to become Democrats and rejoice over their candidates' triumphs. It was quite another to make the New Deal meet the everyday needs of the Central Avenue district. Federal aid *did* help L.A.'s Eastside, and recipients sang praises, but Afro-Angelenos also found that the New Deal could be a cumbersome, sometimes capricious, bureaucratic system. It operated in mysterious ways, and its benefits were not always fairly or rationally distributed—especially when it came to race.

Among local Race leaders, however, Roberts's pessimistic view was rare. Indeed, most black activists saw the New Deal's bureaucratic nature as an advantage. They had long steered civil rights campaigns into the legal arena, and because the New Deal lent itself to litigation, black leaders were prepared for the ensuing struggle. So while the local NAACP had been poorly equipped to respond to the Depression, it was well positioned to challenge racial discrimination within New Deal programs. And while the Urban League's strategy of changing society through social-science research had seemed esoteric during the 1920s, its academic approach was now standard operating procedure in New Deal agencies. What's more, the new bureaucracy required an army of clerks and administrators, and black leaders in L.A. won some of those posts. The ongoing civil rights movement in L.A. now braided itself with the liberal wing of the Democratic Party, a process that was at once a logical evolution of black civic activism and a monumental shift in racial politics.

Among the city's black leaders, the Western Ideal gradually gave way to the Liberal Ideal—the idea that all levels of government, especially the federal government, should actively protect citizenship rights and use the power of the state to promote the general welfare of the people. Unlike most white liberals at the time, African Americans insisted that basic American rights must include black civil rights and that any notion of "general welfare" must be measured by equality of opportunity. In a sense, Afro-Angelenos were exchanging one dream for another. Their version of the Western Ideal had always included more than white boosters were willing or able to envision. The same could now be said about the Liberal Ideal. What black leaders hoped for in the New Deal transcended what FDR and most white liberals were able to see or support. But there was a key difference between the two ideas. Whereas the Western Ideal offered black leaders a rhetorical device of questionable effectiveness, the Liberal Ideal offered the possibility that state power—including unprecedented federal power—could bring about racial equality, that the liberal state could enforce black freedom wherever moral suasion failed to achieve it.

The collective fight against race prejudice in Los Angeles traced its roots at least to the formation of the Afro-American Council and Colored Women's Clubs of the 1890s. It had been sustained by the NAACP, the Urban League, and other Race organizations. Now that struggle became affiliated with powerful national forces. The quality of life on Central Avenue now depended largely on the community's success in using the New Deal to its own advantage, in using liberalism to attain its goals. The distance between the White House and the Dunbar Hotel was rapidly shrinking, and L.A.'s black activists found that they had access to a newly cut political trail. Whether they could remake their world by following that path remained uncertain. Once on that road, however, it was certain they would try.

Race and the New Deal in L.A.

Los Angeles received New Deal infusions from both Sacramento and Washington. The conservative governor, Frank Merriam, and his Republican allies ultimately joined with squabbling Democrats to pass New Deal legislation for the state: an emergency relief law, old-age pensions, and a liberal-oriented tax law to pay for the expanding state government. L.A.'s Republican mayor, Frank Shaw, was one of a new breed of American mayors who established a direct relationship between his city and the federal government; he aggressively and successfully sought federal funds for Los Angeles. The city council placed federal programs under the city engineer, whose office drafted the proposals Shaw peddled in Washington. Between 1933 and 1938, Shaw's administration oversaw 444 federal projects, which employed forty thousand people and infused fifty-four million dollars into the local economy. L.A.'s young people also found jobs in the Civilian Conservation Corps or received employment and college tuition through the National Youth Administration.[2]

Through these "alphabet agencies" and the Social Security Act, the New Deal created the American welfare state. The term *welfare state* was not intended to indicate that "the state"—that is, the federal government—was putting people "on welfare." Instead, *welfare state* meant that the general welfare of the American people was now the responsibility of the federal government.[3] State governments, charitable organizations, voluntary associations, labor unions, corporate welfare programs—all of these were still needed to help people live fuller, healthier, more secure lives; but after the "Second New Deal" of 1935, federal officials accepted the notion that the government is obligated to ensure the well-being of ordinary Americans—a tall order in a sprawling, diverse nation. Ordinary Americans loved the welfare state because it saved their lives, their homes, their families, their futures. But it could be devilishly hard to find out who was stringing the safety net, how strong it was, and why there were holes in it.

Almost from day one, race became a New Deal issue. Who would get New

Deal aid, and on what terms? Would black applicants receive the same aid as white applicants? Who would decide? Would jobs programs be segregated? Would colored workers earn equal wages? Most of FDR's liberal advisors were unprepared for such questions. From their experiences in the North and West, they did not understand the fullness of racism. They naively viewed the "Negro problem" as an economic one: because blacks were poor, they were looked down upon by whites; eradicate that poverty, and white race prejudice would vanish. These liberals quickly crashed against "the southern way of life," which was guarded with massive congressional fortresses. Beyond Dixie, racism was less conspicuous and more erratic, but economic liberals quickly learned that throughout America race was its own variable, quite apart from economic status. And of course, New Dealers in Southern California faced a relief line that included Japanese, Chinese, American Indians, and, repatriation notwithstanding, a huge population of ethnic Mexicans. Were Mexicans white or colored? Was the sewing project in the basement of Second Baptist integrated or segregated? In practice, classifications were made on the fly, and chaos ruled. Somehow, though, no matter how Southern California's white administrators categorized the Asian and Latino populations, they always considered African Americans to be the most basic nonwhite group, the nation's fundamental "other."

Unlike other "colored" Angelenos, however, blacks could and did vote, and they had long been active in civic affairs. Perhaps that is why local Race leaders were tapped as New Deal administrators at the state and local level. Floyd Covington was a caseworker for the State Emergency Relief Administration and was later promoted, becoming one of the directors of caseworkers in SERA's local offices. He was also appointed to L.A. County's National Youth Administration Executive Committee. Baxter Scruggs, having replaced T. A. Greene as executive secretary of the Colored YMCA, was an advisor for the Los Angeles District NYA. Jessie Terry, older sister of Emma Lou Sayers (the late NAACP branch secretary) became an increasingly influential figure in New Deal circles and was one of the few African Americans pictured in Who's Who in the New Deal. These and other appointments gave black Los Angeles visible representation in the liberal crusade.

John Somerville rose in California's Democratic ranks. Angry that African Americans were being discriminated against in the early days of SERA, Somerville sent a letter of protest to his contacts in Washington, D.C. In early 1934, he was summoned to Washington, where he had his say and found an ally in Aubrey Williams, the white racial liberal from Alabama who was assistant director of FERA. Williams hired Somerville as the "technical advisor" on Negro problems for California's SERA, empowering him with "full authority to work out a program for the integration of Negroes into the State Relief set up."[4]

With offices in San Francisco and L.A., Somerville succeeded, in his own estimation, in breaking down racial discrimination in SERA's work projects—despite the objections of the many department heads who told him, "'You cannot mix the races. There will be trouble if they work or live together.'" Wielding Aubrey Williams's authority, Somerville won out. "As a result," he wrote, "hundreds of [Negro] college and high school graduates were given work commensurate with their training. Many of them were employed as supervisors and foremen working with mixed crews. The whole program was carried on without incident. The depression had made them economically equal, and white people were glad to work alongside colored, often in subordinate positions."[5]

Floyd Covington had a more frustrating experience with the bureaucracy. In his 1936 article "Where the Color Line Chokes," Covington charged that "there is a type of social and economic choking by the administrators of this 'New-I-Deal,' who are tightening the color line around the multicolored throats of Uncle Sam's every tenth nephew." The immediate point of conflict involved the African American caseworkers who visited homes to investigate relief claims. A decision sent from above mandated that black caseworkers visit only black families, even in mixed neighborhoods where white or ethnic Mexican households also seeking relief were right next door. One administrator explained, "If a Negro investigator should enter the home of a non-Negro client, the 'poor relief subject' would expire saying 'Have I really come to this?'" Another said that many poor whites in Los Angeles were from the South and that "this group would simply tear up the place if a worker of color should be assigned them." At the same time, though, these officials deemed it perfectly acceptable for white caseworkers to visit black clients, insisting that Negroes were accustomed to looking to whites for help. Mexicans who applied for aid were classified as "white" regardless of skin color and therefore assigned only to white caseworkers.[6]

The insult and inefficiency of this policy galled Covington, who noted that wealthy whites would gladly pay blacks to come to their homes to provide numerous services (as domestics and chauffeurs), but "the administrators of our local county and federal relief program pay to prohibit the Negro from entering the homes of, and administering to, the new [white] poor." Using classic Urban League rhetoric, Covington insisted that cultural traditions, not solid evidence, were driving this policy. Offering counterevidence, he noted that in the frantic early period of the relief program, some white applications had been given accidentally to black caseworkers, who handled those requests. In virtually every instance, Covington reported, white applicants were cordial, invited the black caseworkers into their homes, and appreciated the services provided.[7]

Covington was also at the center of what he called "California's unusual racial experiment." The director of the Vernon District SERA office in L.A. appointed Covington as the director of caseworkers in his district. Covington trained and supervised all caseworkers, regardless of race; he was the boss. And though, as he wrote, "it had previously been maintained that persons of the lighter race would not work with or under persons of the darker race," he encountered no racial problems in his new position. If the whites were upset, they never showed it. Nevertheless, the notion that races should not mix in relief work persisted among top officials. "Thus," Covington wrote, ". . . the cultural lag of the aftermath of our American slavocracy completes its concentric circle and ends the possibility of a true democratic experiment under government supervision, and finance is shoved once more into the sand pits of fear."[8]

At the most obvious level, Covington's critique showed that the "true democratic experiment under government supervision" could be torturous for black Americans, even for those in relatively privileged positions. But at a deeper level, it demonstrated a fundamental change in the relationship between African Americans and the federal government, for Covington was criticizing the New Deal from the perspective of an insider. His article was not merely an angry denunciation. Underlying Covington's grievance was the hope that this matter would be resolved in his favor, that race discrimination would be eradicated from the operation of Democratic liberalism. The alternative outcome—that Jim Crow would be chiseled into New Deal stone—was also possible. To prevent that, Race leaders in L.A. would draw upon their tradition of civic activism and channel that tradition into the corridors of the welfare state. From the First Hundred Days to the outbreak of the Second World War, black Angelenos would fight for equal opportunity within a new arena. The results would be mixed, the legacy profound.

"Strategic Points of Control"

As the New Deal began to take shape, the NAACP in Los Angeles was gaining strength. The branch survived the shock of the Depression and the infighting that had exacerbated the crisis. By the mid-1930s, the Hudson-

Somerville feud had spent itself; Hudson had solidified his position in the local branch, and Somerville had transferred his energies elsewhere. In 1935, Hudson's handpicked successor, the attorney Thomas L. Griffith, Jr., easily won election as branch president.[9] The local also benefited from a very successful membership drive in 1934.[10] Actor Clarence Muse, the branch's self-styled "Hollywood Representative," boosted the membership campaign and brought influential whites, including Hollywood stars and members of Westside Jewish organizations, into the NAACP.[11] Within the black community itself, some old wounds were healed when the Junior Branch dissidents of 1925—James McGregor, Fay Jackson, and Naida McCullough—rejoined the organization. Jackson and McGregor were elected to the executive committee.[12] The Los Angeles Police Department's Red Squad placed the local branch on its "Reds" list and conspicuously attended the branch elections in 1935—a sure sign that the branch was gaining influence.[13] And in June 1935, Muse staged a star-studded fund-raiser at the Lincoln Theater to support the NAACP's campaign for passage of the Costigan-Wagner Anti-Lynching Bill. Jack Benny served as the master of ceremonies at the glittering event, whose other participants included Jimmy Cagney, Marlene Dietrich, Frank Capra, and Lionel Hampton's Orchestra.[14]

The New York office had begun its campaign to receive a fair share of federal aid even before Congress passed jobs legislation. The new assistant secretary, Roy Wilkins, launched a nationwide effort in 1933 to "secure a larger share of employment for colored women on federal, state and municipal building projects." As the year progressed and reports of discrimination rolled in, Walter White urged Claude Hudson and the L.A. branch to "be on the alert in the matter of the N.R.A. [National Recovery Administration] codes, watching out for instances of discrimination and particularly of wage differentials and of displacement of Negro workers by whites." NRA codes, one set for each major industry, were guidelines stipulating minimum wages, maximum hours, and other matters of operation that companies were supposed to adhere to. But there was no real penalty for violation, and violations were frequent. FERA was controlled at the state and local levels and therefore, as Covington discovered, was unpredictable. Throughout the mid- to late 1930s, the local NAACP branch would confront both exclusion and segregation in New Deal programs, especially jobs programs. Blacks working in California's Civilian Conservation Corps camps, for example, were virtually all placed on segregated "Negro" projects, a trend that angered the local branch and the national office.[15]

But the major fight for the L.A. branch began in late 1933, when the Civil Works Administration was created. The CWA was the brainchild of Harry

Hopkins, Roosevelt's hard-driving champion of public works and the director of FERA. Frustrated by the decentralization of FERA and the weakness of its jobs component, Hopkins campaigned successfully for a larger public-works program that was under federal control. Racial equality was not foremost on his mind, but Hopkins was an economic liberal who wanted to employ as many people as possible, and his FERA experience with white southerners had taught him to protect the interests of Negro workers from state and local racists. His CWA rules and regulations therefore contained a clause to prevent race discrimination. The final point under "Conditions of Employment" stated that "no person shall be discriminated against because of race, creed, or membership in any group or organization"—quite likely the first federal regulation explicitly requiring racial equality in hiring. But establishing the rule was one thing, implementing it another.[16]

Shortly after the CWA began distributing paychecks, in late November 1933, the local NAACP established a watchdog committee to make sure Central Avenue got its share of the jobs. Chaired by Baxter Scruggs, the committee consisted of Betty Hill, attorney Edwin L. Jefferson, Dr. Eldora Gibson, and Claude Hudson—all heavyweights in the black community. On December 12, they discovered that some six thousand unemployed blacks had registered for work projects at the Central Avenue district branch of the State Employment Office—and that zero had been placed on CWA jobs. The situation was especially critical because the Los Angeles CWA was supposed to fill its quota of fifty-eight thousand jobs by December 15. With only three days to secure jobs for blacks, Scruggs acted quickly. But he and the committee soon found themselves pinballing through a bureaucratic maze that would have tried the patience of Job and discovering, in the end, that one white bigot occupied a strategic point of control for all Los Angeles public-works employment.[17]

Scruggs's first move was to telephone Eugene Brown, the executive secretary of L.A.'s Emergency Relief Committee. Brown told him the CWA developed the work projects but that each project got its workers from the L.A. County office of the National Re-employment Service. Since December 1, the L.A. NRS had been headed by Roy C. Donnally, whose office was downtown in the Western Pacific Building, which was also headquarters for the larger NRS district. Three NAACP committee members—Scruggs, Hudson, and Jefferson—drove immediately to Donnally's office. There they "found a beehive-like atmosphere, with a large number of persons awaiting attention amid numerous telephone calls, conferences, dictations, etc." They arranged a meeting with Donnally that evening. In the meantime, they discovered that some of Donnally's job-placement supervisors had been able to place every unemployed person in their districts—making the Central Avenue numbers all the more troubling.

Later, at the meeting, Donnally acknowledged that his South Central office had six thousand registrants and that none of them had been placed. When the committee asked why, he responded that no "Negro projects" had been developed. Donnally then blamed the black community itself for not developing "special Negro projects" so that "Negroes could be given C.W.A. work." The astonished committee demanded to know why private citizens should develop public-works programs; Donnally said that was the way it worked. The committee demanded to know why there had to be "Negro projects" for blacks to be put to work; Donnally evaded the question and suggested that they talk with their county supervisor, Gordon McDonough, or one "Mr. Eaton" (whose position was not explained to the committee), or, perhaps the best bet, Major Jules Henique, who was responsible for CWA project development in Los Angeles. The committee immediately phoned Henique and got an appointment with him the following morning.

Early on December 13 the committee met with Henique, whose office was also in the Western Pacific Building. Henique, it turned out, did not create CWA projects for L.A.; he approved proposals sent to him by government agencies. As to Donnally's advice about "Negro projects" and the possibility that the NAACP might propose one, Henique told the committee that Donnally was wrong on both counts. Only government agencies, "such as the City Council [or] Board of Supervisors," could propose CWA projects. Private individuals and civic organizations could not. Henique picked up the phone and called Donnally to say that he was wrong about project development. When he hung up, Henique told the committee that his office was responsible only for approving government proposals; after that, things were out of his hands—the NRS supplied the labor for the projects he approved. He added that no project ever specified "the type of labor to be supplied as to color or creed." He suggested they meet with Donnally's boss, Henry Walker, who was the district director of the NRS and whose office was in the same building.

Leaving Henique's office, the committee decided it would be bad form to go over Donnally's head without first seeing him a second time. But the point was moot, for neither Donnally nor Walker had time to meet with them. Donnally said he could meet with them on December 16. The committee reminded him that such a meeting would take place after the L.A. quota had already been filled, but Donnally assured them it would be no problem. That afternoon, the committee met with Gordon McDonough, their county supervisor, who telephoned Donnally and leaned on him a bit to give "Negro workers . . . a larger opportunity," but Donnally offered only vague responses. Shortly after midnight—having in two days' time spoken to four different administrators for a total of nearly six hours, and having gotten nowhere—the committee sent wires to President Roosevelt, Walter White, and their congressman, Thomas Ford, urging each of them to take action. As Hudson telegraphed FDR: "Los Angeles Civil Works Administration ignores Negro workers. Situation distressing. White House action needed if Negro citizens are to be benefitted by C.W.A."

Whether or not FDR or Ford took any action, Walter White alerted Roy Wilkens, who dashed off a letter to Harry Hopkins, urging him to correct the situation in Los Angeles. He was surely disappointed to receive, more than a week later, a form letter from a Hopkins assistant, who stated, almost incomprehensibly, that "Civil Works projects in the various States are under the jurisdiction of the State Federal Civil Works Administration in each State." Wilkins was instructed to contact the California CWA office in San Francisco and told that the national office would forward his letter to that office, where "it will be given due consideration." At least the assistant had also sent Wilkins a copy of the CWA rules and regulations, which confirmed the agency's policy of racial equality in hiring.[18]

Meanwhile, the local branch's CWA committee once more entered the labyrinth, meeting with Donnally on December 16. Donnally had his wife and young daughter behind his desk (to protect himself against verbal assault, Scruggs thought). Things went from bad to worse. Sniffing corruption, the committee ask why Donnally was willing to work with them privately to establish "special projects for Negro workers" even though the law mandated that only government agencies could propose projects and even though the NRS was exclusively "a labor-placement bureau," not a project developer. Donnally replied that if they wanted a Negro project, it could be done—and added that he was willing to help them because that was the only way to get Negroes on the CWA payroll. The committee then demanded to know where race entered the picture, since Henique had made it clear that no CWA proposal contained racial specifications. Donnally claimed that Negro projects specify "black labor only," and projects that make no racial specifications mean "white labor only." Finally the committee ask him, point blank: "If you should receive a requisition from C.W.A. calling for one thousand workers, would you be willing to place unemployed Negro workers on these work projects without regard to color?" Donnally's reply: "I most certainly will not."[19]

Hudson and Scruggs pushed on, meeting with Charles Frye, the "engi-neer-in-charge" of the Los Angeles CWA. Harry Hopkins had created the engineer positions to weed out graft by having apolitical professionals make programmatic decisions. Henry Walker, Donnally's supervisor, joined the meeting with Frye. Both officials insisted that CWA projects were for *all* citizens. Afterward, though, Walker asked Hudson and Scruggs to speak with him privately in his office. Once there, he sounded less favorable to equal opportunity. He hemmed and hawed about population percentages and added that the county's CWA quotas had already been filled.[20]

On December 19, the committee members paused to review their amaz-ing week. They agreed that they would write a detailed report of their ac-tivities, further investigate the inner workings of the CWA and NRS, and call for Donnally's resignation. The day after Christmas, with 3.5 million Americans earning CWA paychecks nationwide, Hudson sent Walker a let-ter urging him to dismiss Donnally. Bristling at the idea, Walker penned a defensive response and met again with the NAACP group, emphasizing his support for Donnally and scarcely concealing his contempt for their de-mand. After that tense meeting, Scruggs responded with a terse letter, once again insisting on Donnally's ouster and adding new demands for repre-sentation in the CWA. Scruggs also took issue with Walker's rosy assess-ment of NRS practices, especially the idea that the NRS had "in the past" always been an equal-opportunity employer. "As to the future," Scruggs added, "we cannot speak, other than to say that the same official or officers, at whose hands, the Negro has suffered some inequalities, remain at strate-gic points of control."[21]

That was indeed the rub. Scruggs's report, finalized just before the New Year and sent to the NAACP's national office, concluded on that depressing point: "the Committee wishes to re-emphasize the fact that greater atten-tion must be paid to the general administration and functioning of all phases of the Federal Relief program, if Negroes are to enjoy an equitable portion of its benefits. The more extensive the program becomes, the more arduous the task of following its administration."[22]

Even in top-down programs such as the CWA; even when powerful New Dealers such as Harry Hopkins imposed written rules against racial dis-crimination in hiring; even in nonsouthern cities generally known for racial moderation, the Roy Donnallys of America occupied hidden points of racial control. Roy Wilkins, attuned to the national picture, could scarcely believe the Los Angeles situation. "The excuse which was offered, namely, that there were no Negro projects on which Negroes could be employed, is the first of its kind that has come to our attention in the United States. There is plenty of discrimination under the C.W.A., but no one, not even in Mississippi, has thought of this peculiar Los Angeles excuse."[23]

But it was not over. By late January 1934, the Los Angeles CWA had become a cauldron of political corruption and factionalism. The NAACP's local concerns thus became part of a larger problem for Washington to solve. In early February, Hopkins announced he was sending out a representative to "overhaul the entire set-up." Wilkins quickly informed Scruggs, making sure the local branch was ready to make its case to the new administrator. And the news got better. That June, a federal grand jury in Los Angeles issued indictments against several CWA and NRS administrators—including those who "discriminated against Negro workmen and conspired to administer the National employment act contrary to the intent of the law and in a discriminatory manner." The grand jury's assessment rested partly on the local branch's report and the committee members' testimony. Baxter Scruggs, understandably proud, wrote Roy Wilkins, "In all probability you will not run across a similar situation in the entire country where an indictment has been returned against government officials because they discriminated against Negro citizens in the administration of a Federal work relief project." The trials were scheduled to begin in late September.[24]

The bad news was that by the time the grand jury indicted Donnally in June, the CWA had been scrapped. FDR had qualms about long-term work relief and its impact on the federal budget, so he insisted that Hopkins terminate the CWA, and Hopkins had reluctantly complied that March. In the short term, then, there was nothing that local blacks could gain from the CWA, even if the feds and the NAACP emerged victorious.[25]

But if the program had vanished, the larger concern had not. Scruggs was right to see the federal indictments as an important turn of events. Regardless of the trial's outcome, the federal government had already made a significant statement. A New Deal agency had specifically outlawed racial discrimination in hiring; when administrators at the local level had casually ignored that regulation, they were investigated. The feds hauled them before a grand jury and pressed charges. So many explosive events rocked the nation in 1934 that this one got lost in the rubble. But the fact was, the federal government, acting on the concerns of black citizens, in 1934 took its timid first step toward racial equality in hiring. In the process, Democratic liberalism struck an inaugural blow against the thick roots of states' rights racism. It happened in Southern California, not the South, but the local NAACP could claim a victory for its version of the Liberal Ideal.

In 1925 the city suddenly instituted strict segregation at its public swimming
pools. In what came to be known as the "Bath House Battle," the local NAACP
tried—and failed—to get the courts to overturn the policy. Even if your father
was a member of the state legislature—as was the case with the daughters of Fred
Roberts, pictured in this group of young women—the racial regulations applied.
In the 1930s a legal crusade led by Betty Hill would once again open city pools
to all. Courtesy of the African American Museum and Library of Oakland, the
Roberts Family Collection.

An aggressive group of young "New Negro" leaders emerged in L.A. in the 1920s, challenging the community's old guard. The Junior Branch of the local NAACP consisted mostly of college students, whose self-assurance and style are evident in this 1925 photo, taken about the time that the Junior Branch's secretary, Ella Matthews (front row, fourth from the left), insisted that the older members of the local branch cease calling them the "Junior" branch. James McGregor, president of the Juniors, is front and center, with sideward gaze. Shades of L.A. Archives / Los Angeles Public Library.

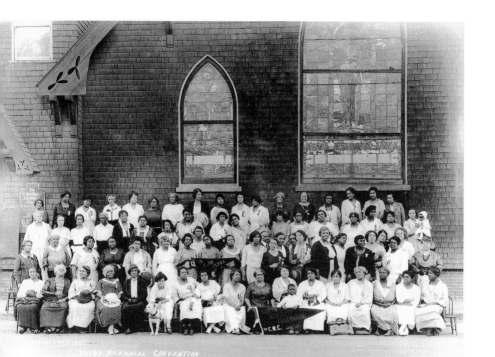

The old guard—not so old, really—maintained their civic activism throughout the 1920s, as suggested in this photo from the 1923 regional convention of the Colored Women's Clubs, held in L.A. Perhaps because the clubs were not as high-profile as the NAACP, and because there were so many of them (with meaningful leadership positions available at the local, sectional, state, and regional levels), the clubs did not experience the generation gap and internal strife that tore at the local NAACP. Shades of L.A. Archives / Los Angeles Public Library.

Race enterprises blossomed in the 1920s, and the local Race papers and Negro churches boosted them as enthusiastically as ever. Marcus Garvey's black nationalist movement of the early 1920s gave added inspiration to black entrepreneurs. Most bootstrappers ran mom-and-pop operations, such as Daddy Grant's barbecue on Washington Boulevard. Black Angelenos fought to keep Dixie's politics at bay, but southern cooking was another matter. Shades of L.A. Archives / Los Angeles Public Library.

Right and opposite page: In the 1930s, Fay Knott composed the autobiography of her life in L.A. with photographs. In the most compelling scene, she strikes a starlet pose (right down to the cigarette) in her maid's uniform outside the mansion where she worked. In her free time she took in the Central Avenue nightlife with friends and swam at Santa Monica's segregated Ink Well beach. Shades of L.A. Archives / Los Angeles Public Library.

Verna Deckard (top left), the seventeen-year-old Texan who in 1924 drove her car all the way to L.A. without giving up the wheel, poses on her car with the "Joy Girls"—the friends she made in L.A. that summer. Shortly after this photo was taken, Verna secretly married a young man she had met in L.A. so she would not have to return to Texas with her parents. She would remain in L.A. thereafter, eventually prospering in real estate. Security Pacific Collection / Los Angeles Public Library.

Ralph Bunche (left) and his lifelong friend Charles Matthews, posing here in 1923, represented the "New Negro" ideal of the decade. Matthews earned a law degree from UC Berkeley and became the first black prosecutor in the L.A. District Attorney's Office. Bunche earned his PhD in political science at Harvard; he would later become a leader in the United Nations and win the Nobel Peace Prize. *Below:* Because Bunche was an intellectual powerhouse, it is often forgotten that he was also a basketball player for UCLA (ca. 1926). Shades of L.A. Archives / Los Angeles Public Library.

Like the Cotton Club in Manhattan, Sebastian's Cotton Club, in Culver
City, was a 1920s hot spot where African American entertainers performed
for whites-only audiences. Sebastian's main attraction was Carolynne
Snowden, the "Josephine Baker of California" (the only woman standing
in this 1930 photo). Snowden lent her entertainment talents to community work. She performed to raise funds for the NAACP's 1928 national
convention, hosted by the L.A. branch, and then she wowed the convention
delegates with her famous "Peacock Dance." Jazz great Lionel Hampton
is at the drums, top. Shades of L.A. Archives / Los Angeles Public Library.

At the ground-breaking ceremony for the Hotel Somerville, which would house the NAACP's national convention delegates in 1928, Vada Somerville poses at the controls of the giant shovel. John Somerville and Claude Hudson were in mid-feud when this photo was taken and stood in different groups, Somerville in the right-hand group standing second from the left, and Hudson in the left-hand group fifth from the right. Joe and Charlotta Bass were also in attendance, both in the left-hand group—Joe third from left, Charlotta fourth from right. Note the rural-looking surroundings. Within a year, this area would become the vibrant new center of African American business and nightlife in L.A. Courtesy of the Miriam Matthews Collection (California Afro-American Museum).

Shortly after it opened in 1928, the Somerville Hotel raised a welcome banner for the delegates to the national convention of the NAACP. The hotel, and the 1928 convention, were both smash hits, but the euphoria would not last long. In 1929 John Somerville went bankrupt and lost his hotel. It remained in black hands and was renamed the Dunbar Hotel. Courtesy of the Miriam Matthews Collection (California Afro-American Museum).

Despite the Depression, the area around the Somerville Hotel continued to develop. Baumann's pharmacy No. 3—the third in his local chain—was established within the hotel. Claude Hudson built his new dental office across the street, and the Golden State insurance company did the same. Before long, the area around 41st and Central had eclipsed the 12th and Central hub as the center of black enterprise in Los Angeles. Courtesy of the Miriam Matthews Collection (California Afro-American Museum).

Walter White, executive secretary of the national NAACP, paid a visit to the city in 1935 and was met at the station by a veritable who's who of black Los Angeles. Notable figures include, from left: Betty Hill; Fred Roberts (next to Hill); John Somerville (tall man behind Roberts); Thomas Griffith, Jr., president of the local branch (front, dark suit, holding satchel); Clarence Muse, the unofficial "Hollywood Representative" for the local NAACP (front, smiling, with white hat); Walter White (between Griffith and Muse); Claude Hudson (taller man with light suit behind Muse); George Beavers, Jr. (black suit, white shoes); and L. G. Robinson (far right). Shades of L.A. Archives / Los Angeles Public Library.

Emma Adams smiles from her desk at the National Youth Administration. She is one of the few African Americans to have received a white-collar position through a New Deal jobs program. New Deal programs saved many black families from destitution but were always racially loaded. Well-educated African Americans seldom received white-collar jobs for which they were qualified. Shades of L.A. Archives / Los Angeles Public Library.

Betty Hill, shown here in a portrait taken in the 1910s, led the successful campaign against swimming pool segregation in the early 1930s. Courtesy of the Miriam Matthews Collection (California Afro-American Museum).

Above and opposite: Charlotta Bass was the Progressive Party's nominee for vice president in 1952, a first for African Americans and for women. Bass's transformation from Republican to Democrat to leftist was remarkable, but there was a striking consistency in her outlook over the decades: she placed civil rights at the top of the political agenda no matter which political party she supported. Here she speaks at a banquet during the campaign, joined by the Progressives' presidential candidate, Vincent Hallinan, and confers with campaign manager C. B. Baldwin on a train. Both photos, the C. B. Baldwin papers, University of Iowa Libraries, Iowa City.

Robert McNeal and his son, Robert, Jr., in Los Angeles, ca. 1939. The Second World War had begun in Europe and Asia, and no one in the city could then foresee the profound impact it would have on L.A., and especially black L.A., when the United States entered the conflict two years later. Shades of L.A. Archives / Los Angeles Public Library.

The NYA and "Negro Affairs"

Like the CWA, the National Youth Administration confronted Afro-Angelenos with a cruel choice between segregation or exclusion. Organized in 1935, the NYA was essentially the youth branch of the WPA. Its goal was to help young people (ages sixteen through twenty-five) survive the Depression and be prepared for jobs when the economy recovered. New Dealers feared this age group was, in the words of California NYA director Anne Treadwell, an "all but lost generation." Too few had money for college. Too many with high school diplomas were unemployed and yet too young to apply for WPA jobs. To address these problems, the NYA provided young people with scholarships, wage-earning jobs, and vocational-training programs.[26]

Black Americans had a special interest in the NYA, partly because FDR had placed the organization under the direction of their ally Aubrey Williams, and especially because Williams created a "Division of Negro Affairs" in the NYA and tapped Mary McLeod Bethune as its director. Bethune's appointment reflected both the promise and problems of New Deal liberalism. It was the highest federal position ever given to an African American woman, and it demonstrated the Roosevelt administration's growing awareness of racial issues, but the very need for a "Negro" division bothered many black leaders, who complained that it gave segregation a stamp of federal legitimacy. Actually, the Negro Division was not intended to develop "special Negro projects." Its job was to guard against discrimination in the program and identify the special needs of black youths. Aubrey Williams sought to combat racial exclusion in the NYA by demanding monthly "Negro Activities" reports for each state. Misunderstandings were almost unavoidable.[27]

Anne Treadwell ran California's NYA from her San Francisco office, but Los Angeles had the greatest needs and got most of the funding. The L.A. supervisor, Ruth Lockett, was a Stanford graduate who had been national vice president of the Young Democrats. Lockett's local advisory committee included Floyd Covington and Baxter Scruggs (not to mention film star Mary Pickford). Compared to the WPA, the NYA was tiny. Treadwell hoped the NYA could create sixty-eight hundred new jobs for California's youth, twenty-six hundred of which would be in the Los Angeles metropolitan area. Unlike most state NYA offices, which quickly established state branches of Bethune's Negro Division, California refused to create such an office until 1938, because Treadwell's black advisors, Covington and Scruggs, fresh from their meetings with Donnally, read "Negro Division" as code for segregation.[28]

Treadwell's monthly reports to Aubrey Williams reflected confusion and conflict over California's "Negro activities." Her office proudly noted a project for "Negro youths" in San Diego County: "This project will be operated in the colored people's Community Center and will be supervised by a trained colored person." The project would include "domestic and recreational activities, personal hygiene and cultural activities such as drama, music, art, and social development." In addition, "a survey will be made by members of the project of the number of young colored people in the community. It is hoped that a cooperative employment system will result from the survey." In San Francisco, NYA funds were used to hire "Negro leadership" at the Booker T. Washington Community Center. Black youths there had "been urged . . . to form a unit to meet their own needs." The Santa Barbara office, however, reported that "no definite plan has been made for any constructive program for Negro youths. . . . After projects have begun to operate, the supervisor will devote his attention to this problem."[29]

Covington and Scruggs chafed at these developments. Treadwell reported that neither of them "approves of the policy of developing projects especially for Negro youth. They feel it tends to intensify racial feeling to do so." At their suggestion, Treadwell sought to develop projects in Los Angeles "not . . . on a racial basis, but rather on the basis of districts where the Negro population is concentrated." This strategy would avoid segregation and address the multiracial needs of the Central Avenue district. Targeting neighborhoods on the Eastside would help black families without neglecting nonblack households. As the programs moved forward, however, black Angelenos found that although they were never fully excluded from NYA work projects, they remained underserved. In early 1936, Covington and Scruggs stood firm and gained a little ground, with Treadwell reporting that some "Negro youth have been assigned to several [non-Negro] projects."[30]

Meanwhile, the San Diego district had a highly successful "Negro project" up and running. It was "composed completely of Negro and Mexican youths." Blacks and ethnic Mexicans were "housed in a Negro community center and are engaged in such activities as minor repairing of the building, beautification of the grounds, and recreational work for young people in athletics, drama, and art. They are also compiling material pertinent to the entire Negro population in that section."[31] As the multiethnic dimensions of this "Negro" project suggest, the categorization of races and nationalities bedeviled California's NYA.

The state's NYA "Student Aid" reports carefully noted enrollment statistics for "White" and "Negro," without reference to Mexicans. But the "Unit Project" reports that detailed work relief and job training tallied employment figures for "White," "Negro," "Mexican," and sometimes for "Indian" and "Other" as well. As indicated in a report for 1937–38, racial categories were never quite sorted out. Explaining why the number of blacks enrolled in the Student Aid program had dropped markedly from the previous year, the report suggested that "figures for 1936–37 are not altogether reliable, as it is believed that some schools included other than the Negro race under the category of 'colored' on their reports."[32]

A table compiled in 1937 shows the race and nationality of California's NYA Work Project employees in three categories: White, Colored, and Oriental. Whites were further subdivided into American, British, Italian, Mexican, Portuguese, Spanish, Scandinavian, and Other. "Nationality," a footnote explained, "refers to a youth's extraction, not his place of birth." "Oriental" appeared to refer only to Chinese in northern California. The number of Orientals in the Southern California NYA equaled zero, meaning either that the Japanese and Chinese were excluded from the NYA or that they were lumped together with blacks under "Colored." The NYA's statistical reports reveal what had long been true in Southern California: beyond black and white, racial categorization was a tricky business.[33] But if nonblack populations could be lumped in with Negro or Colored, it was never the case that blacks were simply counted as Americans or tabulated under the category "American." What was unclear, then, was the status of the ethnic and racial groups that lay between white and black.

Through 1937 and most of 1938, black Angelenos remained underrepresented in NYA projects. Covington continued to oppose segregated projects, even as community pressure against his ideal began to grow. Treadwell sought middle ground, calling on traditional Race organizations, such as churches, to encourage Negro interest in the NYA.[34] The effort saw limited success but mostly resulted in continued black exclusion, usually to the benefit of ethnic Mexican youths.[35]

In April 1938, Bethune herself journeyed to California, promoting NYA activities and drawing enthusiastic crowds in Pasadena and L.A., where she spoke before a packed house at Second Baptist. Her visit seems to have changed the dynamics of the debate between Covington and his critics. That October, the California NYA created a separate Negro Division, which was placed under the direction of Vivian Osborne-Marsh, an African American woman from San Francisco. Covington and Scruggs may have gone down fighting or simply given in, but they apparently made no objections to the new division. The creation of a Negro Division was, theoretically, intended to ensure black inclusion in integrated projects, but it also cleared the way for official Negro projects in the Los Angeles area. Osborne-Marsh soon made a sweeping tour through Southern California's black communities, pinpointing problems and spurring enthusiasm for the Negro Division.[36]

Black participation in NYA projects increased noticeably. A tally in late 1939 revealed that the number of African Americans employed by the NYA in L.A. County had increased from 132 to 434. These jobs were divided equally between men and women, and they were not bad jobs. Nearly half the women were employed in clerical posts, and most of the others worked in nursery schools, the garment industry, "household demonstration," recreation projects, or medical-dental offices. Most young men were in gardening or agriculture, but substantial numbers found work as clerks, carpenters, and construction workers. Osborne-Marsh attributed the change not to all-black projects but to good public relations work in black communities, which, she added, had been "very favorable in their attitude to the program." Photographs she included in her report show integrated work projects—blacks and whites working side by side, as well as black teachers giving instruction to white students. Writing to Bethune, Osborne-Marsh noted that "harmony has been restored in those communities previously having difficulty over participation on the NYA programs. In almost every area a larger quota of Negro youths on the program has been obtained."[37]

Success stories publicized by California's Negro Division, even though they concealed the identity of the youths involved, revealed the human dimensions of NYA relief. A typical story for Southern California read:

> Robert B___ was seriously handicapped when he left high school
> and tried to get a job. His widowed mother had four younger children
> to worry about, and could do nothing for Robert. On the contrary,
> she needed his help. As the result of infantile paralysis, Robert had
> a twisted neck so that he carried his head at an awkward angle. His
> sense of physical and financial inferiority was further complicated
> by a vocational maladjustment. He had been advised at school to take
> a trade training course in sheet metal work, but he discovered when
> he left school that the sheet metal trade offered no employment for
> Negroes. Discouraged and resentful, he came to the NYA for help.

The NYA found him a construction job that taught him "pipe-fitting, welding, and pipe-laying," and he excelled. After eight months on this job, he quit the NYA "to do private contract work laying sprinkling systems for property owners in the district where he lives." The story concluded that "Robert has been so successful that he now employs five full-time assistants and has a profitable business, assuring him an excellent income."[38]

Then there was "E"—a young fatherless man whose mother and sisters survived on aid from SERA. The family was musically inclined and "showed more than normal aptitude and inherent capabilities in this line." "E" had no other skills and had done poorly in high school. NYA officials got him an audition with the Federal Music Project. Even though he could not read music, his solo impressed the judges, who "felt that because of this boy's natural aptitudes and voice that he should be accepted for immediate placement if for no other reason than to furnish the youth with the proper environment for a furtherance of his ability." Later, when he gave a performance for the Emergency Education Department's Music Division, "the faculty of a music institution in Redlands" was so impressed that they gave "E" a full scholarship to attend the Redlands conservatory. A choir in Redlands "which sings commercially in that area" then hired him as a member of its chorus.[39]

Ongoing difficulties nonetheless plagued California's Negro Division. San Diego's NYA officers insisted on Jim Crow operations. Elsewhere, Osborne-Marsh had difficulty turning all-black and all-white projects into "mixed" undertakings, because whites did not want to take jobs in "colored" programs and refused to accept blacks into white programs. Osborne-Marsh also notified Bethune about a discovery she made when going through the NYA application files throughout the state: the application card of each of "the Negro youths" included notations "as to his various shades of color, and his neatness." This kind of remark, she added, "is seldom found on the cards of other races."

Worse, private industry proved reluctant to hire NYA-trained blacks—because they were blacks. As a result, African Americans in the NYA programs had to stay on longer than whites, which in turn meant that other needy youths—especially colored ones—could not obtain positions with the NYA. Osborne-Marsh sent a letter to every chamber of commerce in the state, hoping to enlist their assistance in finding black NYA workers full-time jobs in the private sector. When the chamber leaders wrote back, Osborne-Marsh was shocked by their open hostility to the idea. As she confided to Bethune, her letters "bring forth remarkable replies. The writers do not know that they are writing to a Negro."[40]

The NYA thus revealed the best that the New Deal had to offer black youths, as well as the underside of the federal bureaucracy in a racist society. A white racial liberal was placed at the head of the NYA, and when it was clear that black youths were being slighted by the program, he created a Negro Division to try to redeem the program. The NYA helped real families, real individuals. It kept people in school, gave them jobs and hope for the future. But black leaders had to fight to place young people in jobs if those jobs were not segregated. And, once on work relief, these young people found reemployment in the private sector difficult. When it came to New Deal public works, blacks were often the last to get on and the least likely to get off.

Val Verde's New Deal

Not all New Deal aid was so freighted. The same NAACP activists who opposed "Negro projects" in the CWA and NYA proudly accepted aid in some Negro-only situations. The best example was the government-funded improvement to Val Verde, the black-owned mountain resort fifty miles north of L.A. This rustic black township had its origins in the goodwill of a wealthy white woman in Pasadena. Upset by Jim Crow in Southern California, especially the barriers that kept blacks out of many parks and recreation areas, she opened her family ranch—in Chiquito Canyon, in the far northwest corner of Los Angeles County—to African Americans. The area had once been a Mexican mining town called Val Verde, or Green Valley. After World War I, Val Verde became a "weekend picnic spot" for Afro-Angelenos.[41]

In 1924 Sidney Dones acquired the land, and he and Joe Bass became partners in developing a resort there called Eureka Villa. Dones and Bass did not intend to live there; they hoped to prosper from lot sales and to create a place where black Angelenos could relax without the threat of race prejudice. Dones reserved spaces for a clubhouse and community commons. Opening their Eureka Villa headquarters at 17th Street and Central Avenue, they insisted that Eureka offered "Industry, Education, Pleasure, Religion." To jump-start their real estate campaign, they announced a giveaway of a lot at Eureka Villa headquarters; three thousand people showed up on that Sunday afternoon for the chance to win it. Lots sold like hotcakes. A piece of Eureka Villa cost $125: only $10 down and $5 per month. The *Eagle* printed long lists of people who purchased lots, for investment or family fun. Bluster abounded for a while, but enthusiasm soon fizzled. Nevertheless, Eureka Villa survived. A few families lived there, renting cabins, running restaurants, and offering horseback riding to weekend visitors. In 1928 the development became an independent township, and residents changed the name back to Val Verde.[42]

The resort bloomed in the 1930s, thanks mostly to public initiatives. A group of black leaders organized the Val Verde Improvement Association and launched an improvement campaign that renewed community interest in the mountain town. Holiday celebrations were held, an AME church was built, and a Los Angeles Race leader, A. Ray Henderson, purchased an eighty-acre ranch. The *New Age* began a weekly "Val Verde" column, featuring chitchat about comings and goings at the resort. That momentum was soon channeled into positive government assistance. In 1937, after one resident agreed to donate fifty-three acres for the cause, the L.A. County Board of Supervisors created Val Verde County Park. The county commissioners approved funds for picnic tables, barbecue grills, ball fields, and what the *New Age* called a "fine recreational building."[43] In 1939, the WPA brought the biggest splash—a bathhouse and Olympic-size swimming pool. The pool was a county project, funded by a federal grant of thirty-nine thousand dollars.

That spring, as the facility neared completion, a gala was held to lay the cornerstone of the swimming pool. The Race leaders who planned this celebration included Charlotta Bass, Fred Roberts, Betty Hill, L. G. Robinson, Vada Somerville, George Beavers, Jr., and Fay Jackson—all leaders who consistently denounced segregated projects but apparently viewed Val Verde as a matter of separation, not segregation. The swimming pool celebration was a big event. The WPA sent a representative. Two L.A. County supervisors who had helped get federal funds for the Val Verde swimming pool, John Anson Ford and Gordon McDonough, were conspicuous at the photo sessions. The ceremony brought out a veritable who's who of black Los Angeles, including film stars Louise Beavers (George, Jr.'s cousin) and Hattie McDaniels, who was then shooting *Gone with the Wind* and would shortly make history by becoming the first African American to win an Oscar.[44]

Hollywood was still largely closed to Negroes, but the New Deal provided some relief for black entertainers. Those with stage talents were employed by the WPA in the Federal Theater Project. Like Val Verde, the all-black theater productions sparked pride, not resentment, among the city's black activists. Other black Angelenos were employed by the Federal Music Project, also a WPA program. As the historian Bette Yarbrough Cox has written, "Some church choirs simply became WPA choruses."[45]

As always, then, there were forms of racial separatism that Afro-Angelenos accepted without second thought. The development of Val Verde, like the attempt to build the Gordon Manor subdivision in the 1920s, was a response to the exclusion and humiliation blacks often experienced when trying to act as free people in an overwhelmingly white America. But those examples notwithstanding, black Angelenos consistently fought for an equal right to buy and occupy homes on the basis of pocketbook and preference, not on the basis of race. The New Deal, it turned out, would have a profound influence on black housing.

Race and Housing under the New Deal

Louise Beavers and Hattie McDaniels, among other film stars and wealthy blacks, lived in the West Jefferson enclave, but virtually all other African Americans lived along the Central Avenue corridor. The New Deal did not change that, and, indeed, federal housing policies under FDR actually increased residential segregation. Not all the news on housing was bad. African Americans began moving into previously whites-only neighborhoods in the western and southern sections of the 62nd Assembly District. These neighborhoods had good housing, and more-affluent blacks moved in as whites moved out. But less-affluent black migrants found themselves in coarser neighborhoods, which only went downhill during the Depression. Except in its poorest areas, the district had never really been a "slum," but in the 1930s slum housing became an issue. Gus Hawkins constantly fought to improve low-income housing in his district. Nationwide problems with urban blight and home foreclosures prompted New Deal housing programs.

Hawkins was deeply involved in housing issues, which to him reflected larger concerns. Neighborhood integration, he believed, would not merely give blacks a chance for better housing but would also erode white prejudice. To Hawkins, segregated housing meant segregated politics, which, in turn, translated into political powerlessness—the kind of black tokenism that he had perceived in Fred Roberts's rule. Hawkins's biracial, pro-labor coalition convinced him that integrated housing would mean integrated interests and therefore more power to push for civil rights and labor legislation. An aggressive opponent of restrictive covenants, he fought for fair-housing legislation in Sacramento but received little support. Restrictive covenants would be undone not by legislation but by the NAACP's dogged legal efforts, which finally resulted in favorable rulings in the U.S. Supreme Court during the late 1940s and early 1950s.

In the early 1930s, however, the immediate problem for home owners was simply holding on to their homes. L.A. remained a good home-owning town for blacks, but of course, most home owners were actually mortgage holders, and therein lay the problem. During the 1920s, some 70,000 urban Americans lost homes through foreclosure each year. In 1930 alone, banks repossessed 150,000 homes, not counting farms. By 1933 that figure had more than doubled, and 50 percent of all American homes were in default. At the time, mortgages ran for five to seven years. Home owners made regular payments on the interest and saved money to pay off the principal when the mortgage expired. Normally, a mortgage could be renewed if the owners had not saved enough to pay off the note. But during the Depression, fewer owners could pay off their notes, and fewer banks would renew mortgages.[46]

FDR's administration confronted this disaster almost immediately, creating the Home Owners Loan Corporation in 1933. The HOLC offered home owners low-interest, long-term (twenty-year), amortized mortgages, and it saved millions of homes across the country from foreclosure. In the process, though, the HOLC created "redlining," laying the foundation of another racial crisis. Redlining, as one definition has it, "refers to the arbitrary decisions of government and private financial institutions not to lend in certain neighborhoods because of general characteristics of the neighborhood rather than of the particular property to be mortgaged."[47] Race became the key ingredient in redlining blacks out of mortgage-assistance initiatives.

The HOLC put Washington, D.C., in the business of giving mortgages to millions of ordinary Americans, many of them poor. This financial gamble required some assessment of the risks involved. Nobody wanted to see tax-funded loans go belly up. In classic New Deal style, federal bureaucrats devised a standardized system for determining the level of risk for each loan. HOLC representatives visited major cities, where they met with real estate and financial leaders. Together, they mapped out distinct real-estate areas of the city. They first determined the boundaries of what they considered to be coherent "neighborhoods," and then they gave each neighborhood one of four grades—A through D, best to worst. Each grade corresponded to a color for use in color-coded maps, with green and blue for the top grades and red for D neighborhoods. According to this system, floating a loan in an A or B neighborhood was safe, but granting a mortgage in a red area was risky. These "Security Maps" were not available to the public; they were kept secret at HOLC and in every bank.[48]

Neighborhood grades usually hinged on what the HOLC called "racial elements." In this scheme, used nationwide, racial elements usually meant Jews and Negroes, with blacks being a riskier "element" than Jews. In L.A., racial elements also meant ethnic Mexicans and Asians. Neighborhoods with any ethnic minority presence were dropped to the C and D grades, and those with blacks almost automatically received a D ranking.

A late 1930s Security Map for the Central Avenue district assessed the area. The "Class and Occupation" of the district was "WPA workers, laborers, low scale clericals, factory workers, etc., income $500 to $1500." The terrain was "level," with "no flood or construction hazards." Standard "conveniences" in the district were "readily available." "Encroachment of industry" was "a threat" but it had not yet occurred, and the district was "largely single family dwellings." The average building was a five-room home built at the turn of the century, and virtually all homes were occupied. Housing and rental prices had increased since the mid-1930s, and HOLC-assisted homes had sold well. In other words, Central Avenue sounded like a decent place to live for working-class and lower-middle class families.[49]

But the HOLC gave the district the worst possible security rating—"low red." The reason was race. The survey noted that 40 percent of the residents were foreign-born and listed their "Nationalities" as "Mexicans, Japanese and low class Italians." Residents who were "Negro"—a standard part of the grading form—accounted for 50 percent of the population. "This is the 'melting pot' of Los Angeles," the reported concluded, "and has long been thoroughly blighted. The Negro concentration is largely in the eastern two thirds of the area. Original construction was evidently of fair quality but lack of proper maintenance is notable. Population is uniformly of poor quality." Many homes were "in a state of dilapidation." As a result, "this area is a fit location for a slum clearance project."[50]

The HOLC did grant mortgages to all areas, regardless of risk, but the grading system took on a life of its own. Banks had HOLC Security Maps in their files and proved reluctant to lend money in redlined neighborhoods. Worse, the Federal Housing Administration, created by the 1934 Housing Act, adopted the HOLC's grading system and used it in ways that doomed red districts to decline. Instead of lending money to home owners, the FHA insured the construction and real estate loans granted by banks—in an effort to boost the home-construction industry. The FHA guaranteed that banks would recoup their loans even if the contractors or home owners defaulted. Backed by a federal guarantee, banks could safely lend money to housing contractors and to buyers who wanted those homes. Banks reduced down payments to 10 percent (because the FHA insured up to 90 percent of the loan), reduced interest rates, and extended amortized mortgages to thirty years. It was a home-buyer's dream. Less-affluent families suddenly found it cheaper to buy a new home, especially in a suburban or newly developed area, than to rent in the city. As a result, the home construction industry started humming, and home-ownership rates soared nationwide.[51]

But the FHA was a godsend for whites only. The housing law that created the FHA in 1934 said nothing about race, but as the FHA bureaucracy standardized its system its policy tilted decidedly in favor of white Americans. Whereas the HOLC had granted loans to people in its redlined districts, the FHA would *not* insure bank loans for those areas—and the FHA would far outlast the HOLC. Developers who wanted to build new homes in redlined districts were turned down. Nor would the FHA underwrite a mortgage for a black American who wanted to buy a new home in a neighborhood that was mostly white. Without ever saying as much, the FHA's 1938 *Underwriting Manual* suggested that racially restrictive covenants in new housing developments were desirable. Beginning in the late 1930s, and accelerating in the 1940s and 1950s, working-class whites moved out of the inner cities and into the new outlying developments. Although this process opened up more space for African Americans on the Eastside, it also insured that suburban whites would be better housed, for the FHA would not underwrite renovations or new developments in the Central Avenue district.[52]

By 1938, news about this nationwide problem had begun to circulate in the local Race papers. A front-page story in the *New Age* noted that the national office of the NAACP "had received numerous complaints from over the country . . . that the FHA was assisting local banks and finance companies in the jim crowing of Negroes." For example, a white contractor in New York who applied for an FHA-insured loan to build "a housing development for Negroes" was turned down, he was told, because "this area was 'too white' to have a Negro settlement started in it." Affluent blacks were also "being turned down on FHA mortgages . . . if their homes are to be outside what is considered locally as the 'Negro district.'" Simultaneously, "Negroes who have the money and the steady employment to finance homes" were rejected even when they sought new homes in black neighborhoods.[53]

Blacks were thus stuck in districts that were, by federal housing law, destined to go downhill. African Americans and other ethnic minorities could not get FHA assistance to upgrade their older neighborhoods; nor could they get money to move out. The NAACP national office demanded to know whether the FHA was "pursuing any policy to 'regulate or restrict the purchase of homes by Negro Citizens.'" "We do not believe," the NAACP said, "that the Federal government, through one of its agencies, should use the public tax money to restrict, instead of extend, opportunities [or] to enforce patterns of racial segregation."[54]

The federal government did it anyway. Whites in the 62nd district traded their ethnically diverse neighborhoods for all-white suburban developments, the only kind the FHA would sponsor. Central Avenue became more uniformly black, while its housing stock, barred from FHA-renovation support, deteriorated. Here was one case in which federal insistence on racial equality could have overcome local resistance. The FHA was such a windfall for developers, the construction industry, and banks that officials in Washington could have demanded almost anything and local authorities would have complied. Federal officials could have stipulated that FHA backing would be given only to those developments that were open to all, regardless of race; virtually all developers outside of the South would have complied, and the history of American race relations might be very different. But the FHA did the opposite, cementing racial minorities into aging, increasingly colored city districts.

Another program that caught on during the New Deal was one that had been promoted by progressive reformers early in the century: the construction of publicly owned housing. Every city had slums, and welfare-state liberals wanted to guarantee decent housing for all. Established in 1934, the Housing Division of the Public Works Administration sought to solve the problem through slum removal and redevelopment, but obstacles loomed. Slum clearance meant, first, that privately owned real estate had to be acquired by the state through eminent domain, and it was not clear that any local or state government had the authority to do that. Alternatively, the state could purchase the real estate at market value, but the high costs would result in homes too expensive for poor tenants. Either way, troubling questions remained: When slums were razed, what would become of the people who lived there? Who would rebuild? What kind of housing would it be? For whom? At first, public housing languished.

After his reelection in 1936, Roosevelt pushed for legitimate public housing legislation, leading to the Housing Act of 1937. The law created the U.S. Housing Authority, which supported low-cost public housing projects by giving grants and generous loans to local housing agencies. Organized by municipal governments, housing agencies would plan the housing projects and supervise the work. The program, FDR boasted, "marks the beginning of a new era in the economic and social life of America. Today, we are launching an attack on the slums of this country which must go forward until every American family has a decent home."[55]

But the same sticky questions remained. The Housing Act mandated that local housing agencies would have the authority to provide answers. Although "projects" had to be approved in Washington and meet minimum criteria, the operating principle was local control. For Los Angeles, Sacramento had to first clear the way. In 1938, Gus Hawkins's slum-clearance bill became law, giving the state of California and its municipal governments the power to designate slum areas, to claim these areas through eminent domain, and to replace the slums with public housing. In Hawkins's view, the law involved "doing away with slums and giving the common people the benefit of modern homes at a cost that all can afford to meet."[56] Southern California's smaller, whiter towns simply refused to create housing authorities, which made them ineligible for Housing Authority funds, which ruled out public housing in those communities, which guaranteed that poor or minority populations would not move into town.

In the 62nd district, many residents wanted public housing. L.A.'s city council soon created the Housing Authority of the City of Los Angeles and named New Deal matron Jessie Terry as one of the five commissioners. If some racial conservatives reasoned that public housing would keep colored people on the Eastside, liberals had loftier goals. Hawkins's vision for low-income housing in his district began to bear fruit in 1940, when the Housing Authority approved construction of the four-hundred-unit Pueblo del Rio Housing Project, designed collectively by a stellar group of architects, including Paul Williams. Political controversies and the outbreak of World War II complicated matters, but Pueblo del Rio was completed in 1942, marking, at the time, a significant victory for New Deal liberals, black, white, and otherwise.[57]

Organized Labor

With the passage of the Wagner Act in 1935 and the rapid rise of the Congress of Industrial Organizations, "big labor" came of age in the United States. The CIO was not just a rival version of the American Federation of Labor. The AFL was officially nonpartisan; the CIO was aggressively liberal Democrat—and often left of that. The AFL still focused its efforts on shop-floor concerns; the CIO targeted not just economic issues but also social issues, including racial equality. The CIO thus became a player in the New Deal coalition and, potentially, a significant partner to big government in the creation and maintenance of the liberal welfare state. Blacks who held jobs in auto plants, steel mills, and other major industries—mainly a northern, not western, phenomenon—won CIO representation and entered a political alliance with working-class whites. That alliance was unstable and unequal, but some black leaders—including a Central Avenue favorite son, Ralph Bunche—saw organized labor as the salvation of black America.

Since graduating from UCLA in the late 1920s, Bunche had gone east, received his Ph.D. in political science from Harvard, and assumed the chairmanship of Howard University's political science department. While at Harvard, Bunche became friends with John P. Davis, who was en route to his law degree. Unlike most young black professionals, both men distrusted the Roosevelt administration, at least at that time. "For the Negro population," Bunche wrote, "the New Deal means the same thing, but more of it." FDR's administration was not friendly enough to organized labor to redistribute power to the working class, and it simultaneously failed to recognize that black citizens labored under special, deeply entrenched inequalities that existed independently of economic conditions. What African Americans needed was an umbrella organization that brought middle-class black leaders into an alliance with blacks and whites in the labor movement.[58]

In 1935 Bunche hosted a conference at Howard to address the New Deal's shortcomings and to create a new organization for black protest. The result, in 1936, was the National Negro Congress, a left-leaning, pro-labor organization that sought to connect the Left with middle-class civil rights organizations such as the NAACP and the Urban League. Although both he and Hawkins were products of L.A.'s black middle class, Bunche doubted the NAACP and the Urban League could—by themselves—effect changes that would aid the African American masses; traditional civil rights organizations must form alliances with organized labor, he argued. But Bunche also recognized barriers to that goal: most white workers would not accept blacks as equal partners in the struggle, and blacks remained divided on organized labor. Eventually, he would develop a more positive assessment of the New Deal, partly because the Wagner Act had launched the CIO, and partly because his enthusiasm for the Left had cooled by decade's end.[59]

The Los Angeles Council of the National Negro Congress was organized in 1936, and Gus Hawkins himself became its head. The Los Angeles NNC embraced organized labor, the local Urban League, and the NAACP and even had a voice in Sacramento. It also sponsored public meetings, rallies, and forums to address critical issues such as the extension of Social Security benefits to domestic workers. In 1938, when the federal government announced the creation of a Negro health program, the local NNC held a debate on socialized medicine. Unfortunately for Hawkins and his NNC, the 1930s labor movement in L.A. seldom reached out to African Americans, and black Angelenos remained wary of unions.[60]

Both the AFL and CIO achieved victories in Los Angeles during the 1930s, and, given the lingering ghost of the virulently anti-union General Otis, that was saying something. In a particularly stunning turn of events, women—especially Chicanas—won representation in the garment district, and the heavily Latino cannery industry recognized its workers' leftist union. But blacks were mostly shut out of the action. The black-only Musicians Local was still in good shape, and the Dining Car Employees remained strong; but most white unions remained exclusive. Whereas big auto, steel, and rubber plants in the North employed African Americans, big industry in L.A. rarely hired blacks, and much of it was still situated in the heavily southern-white neighborhoods east of Alameda Avenue. So white racism and the lay of the land had something to do with it. But it was also true that, through the 1930s, black Angelenos remained ambivalent about organized labor—CIO or AFL.

A case in point was the Pullman porters' union, the nation's largest and best-known all-black union. A. Philip Randolph had organized the Brotherhood of Sleeping Car Porters in the mid-1920s, but the organization remained underground for nearly a decade. Few porters in L.A. risked joining the BSCP; many of those who did, including union president Charles Upton, were found out and fired. As a local Urban League report noted, citing Upton himself, "Many of the Porters in Los Angeles were married, had responsibilities and were either buying or owned their homes; for those reasons they could not come out into the open with their union activities, and it was not until the national election in 1935 that they were entirely free from company persecution." That 1935 election resulted from New Deal railway legislation, which, in 1934, had given Pullman porters the right to organize and bargain collectively. Backed by a federal mediation board, Randolph engineered a nationwide election to be held in June 1935. By secret ballot, porters would choose between two possible labor representatives: the BSCP, or the Pullman Protective Association (the company union).[61]

As the election of 1935 neared, L.A.'s BSCP seemed apathetic and disorganized. Despite the 1934 legislation that allowed BSCP locals to go public, the union's national office could not discern much interest or commitment among the Pullman men in Southern California. The L.A. group infuriated C. L. Dellums, the BSCP supervisor for the West Coast Zone and a close ally of Randolph's. A dynamic Race man in Oakland, Dellums was also a tough-talking labor man. His aggressive machismo fit the Bay Area's hard-nosed labor scene, but it grated on the L.A. leaders, especially because they received the brunt of his frustration. The L.A. election was slated for May 27 through June 3, the week's duration necessary because Pullman workers were, of necessity, out of town part of that time. Responsible for turning out a winning vote in his zone, Dellums viewed the L.A. situation with alarm. In early April, the union's secretary-treasurer, W. B. Holland, was ill. Charles Upton, still president, was serving thirty days in jail. There had been a "steady decline in dues paying," along with bitter internal conflict over leadership.[62]

Dellums told Holland that L.A.'s Pullman men put too much faith in prayer and timid leaders. He deemed Henry Edward Washington—a venerable Race man and one of the most respected men in L.A.'s Pullman and fraternal circles—"weak-kneed." Listing other men who had influence in the Pullman community, Dellums huffed, "If the men of Los Angeles wish to be led by such weaklings as that, they are practically hopeless."[63] Dellums's insults misfired. If such assaults on manhood could fan the flames of union pride in the Bay Area, in L.A. they served as wet sand on dying embers. A community that had told Marcus Garvey where to get off; that had boycotted Du Bois's *Star of Ethiopia;* that had ignored Father Divine's injunction not to get into politics; that had chafed at the thought of an NYA Negro Division in California—this L.A. community, as self-confident and independent as any, was not about to let Randolph's right-hand man—a *northern* Californian at that—pound them into shape.

The Pullman Protective Association surged in L.A., and by mid-May, with the election nearing, Randolph sent word that he was "worried about Los Angeles." The entire West Coast was solid for the Brotherhood, but L.A. would have a very large vote, and its loyalty to the BSCP was still uncertain. "The boys of Los Angeles signed up with the Protective Association too strong," wrote a concerned (and now less hostile) Dellums to Holland; Holland could not "take any chances." Randolph urged Dellums to go down to L.A. at once; Dellums urged Holland to get the *Eagle* on board. In the end, the BSCP won nationwide, with California's porters voting four to one for the BSCP. Almost all of the dissenting votes came from Southern California, where Pullman's company union actually defeated the BSCP in several voting districts: "fools on the job," Dellums scoffed. Still, the Brotherhood was in, and union officials hoped L.A. would soon develop a strong local.[64]

That did not happen, at least not in the 1930s. By 1938, only half of the city's Pullman men had actually joined the union. Dellums's letters to the local sounded a constant refrain of complaints. L.A. was always behind in dues and kept sloppy financial records. The ladies' auxiliary was slow to evolve. "Petty fights" within the L.A. membership sapped the local's energies. Oakland's local was booming, but "things are not developing very favorably in Los Angeles." The union failed to develop steady relations with local Race editors, such as Fay Jackson, who were clearly sympathetic to the cause. There seemed to be a basic disconnect between the L.A. local and Dellums's Bay Area headquarters. When Dellums visited L.A. in late 1935, holding a campaign to promote local interest in the Brotherhood, no one in the local even bothered to follow up with him; after more than a month of silence, he wrote Holland in disgust, asking why he had heard nothing. Finally, there was the issue of communism, which apparently divided the L.A.

local. If Dellums originally thought L.A.'s Brotherhood was too conservative, he was equally concerned that the Left was trying to take it over. "We must be careful about the Communist organization because we want no part of them," he urged Holland in 1935. A year later, he wrote to Upton, emphasizing that "Los Angeles men have been complaining to me for quite some time about the Communists frequenting our headquarters there." When one of Dellums's friends visited the L.A. local in 1939, looking to develop new leaders for the national office, the report was pessimistic: "I have been very disappointed in the crop here in LA."[65]

On the eve of the Second World War, black Angelenos were not antagonistic toward organized labor so much as they were ambivalent about it. There were reasons. The AFL brought the BSCP into its fold because it threatened no white workers and made for good public relations, but most AFL unions remained exclusively white. Through the late 1930s, the CIO targeted industries in L.A. that hired virtually no black workers. Then there was the question of efficacy. After the BSCP won its historic election in 1935, two years passed before the Pullman company signed its first contract with the union. Among the Pullman porters in L.A., there remained no real barriers to membership in the BSCP: the company would not fire them for joining; after 1937 their wages went up (because of the union's contract), which helped them pay those mortgages; and the Brotherhood was a respected Race organization nationwide, one that campaigned as much for civil rights as for better wages and hours. Yet only half of the local porters joined the union. L.A. was not a labor town. Black L.A. was not a labor community.

A "Tri-Minority Relationship"?

In late April 1939, a new civil rights organization met in L.A. and outlined a list of fundamental grievances: "discrimination in the right of employment, differentials in wage payments, discrimination in relief, lack of cultural opportunities, lack of civil and political rights in many sections. . . . [These conditions] are completely at variance with American standards." Save for the reference to New Deal relief programs, such critiques of racial inequality and Jim Crow had been voiced in black Los Angeles for nearly half a century. But this new inventory of injuries was not voiced by African Americans. It was the opening foray of El Congreso de Pueblos de Habla Española—the Congress of Spanish-Speaking Peoples, which was holding its first national convention in Los Angeles.[66] The hope was to bring together ethnic Mexicans from across the nation, to forge alliances between rural and urban, middle class and working class, Mexican Americans and Mexican immigrants. In unity, ethnic Mexicans would find power. The organization was not strictly Latino, however. The Congreso also attracted a few Hollywood stars, some of L.A.'s liberal politicians, and at least one African American.

Floyd Covington chaired a session at the three-day convention. He was there because he had been building relationships with Mexican American leaders on the Eastside—a move probably born of both his work as a relief administrator and his position in the Urban League. The idea grew. A year after the convention he wrote: "There is the possibility of working toward a tri-minority relationship, comprising Mexicans, Orientals, and Negroes. These groups are very largely shunted together in the twilight zone areas and the problems of each [are] parallel, although they are not identical."[67]

In previous decades black leaders had grappled, at least a little, with L.A.'s multiracial conundrum: James Alexander's 1906 "Appeal to Reason" insisted that Afro-Americans should receive jobs before the alien Japanese; Beatrice Thompson admitted that the anti-Japanese movement took the heat off blacks temporarily, but feared that blacks might be next; W. E. B. Du Bois, upon his first visit in 1913, noted with fascination that Asians had come to hear him speak; in the 1920s, the *Eagle* argued that the police had it out for Negroes and Mexicans. But it was Covington who finally made it plain. Early in the Depression, he pointedly observed that L.A.'s racial minorities were locked in ugly combat over jobs. Now, at the close of the decade, he was thinking of an alliance. With the economy starting to heat up, with CIO leaders trumpeting interracial unionism, with Mexican Americans and, to a lesser extent, Japanese Americans finally moving into the electoral arena, who knew what was possible?

During World War II, tenuous cross-racial, cross-class alliances would offer a fleeting glimpse of the tri-minority vision. If Japanese internment initially won cheers from black leaders such as Charlotta Bass, they (Bass included) soon felt guilty about it and promoted interracial cooperation with their colored brethren, the Japanese. Anti-Mexican riots in 1943 inspired many black Angelenos to equate the plight of Latinos with that of African Americans. The result was movement toward interracialism along Central Avenue. This trend found support in the Race papers, the labor unions, the NAACP, and the Urban League.[68]

But it did not hold. The postwar housing crunch sparked residential conflicts between blacks and browns. The Congress of Spanish-Speaking Peoples proved short-lived. Although Negroes and Mexican Americans joined together in 1949 to elect the first minority member of the city council—the Mexican American Edward Roybal—that coalition proved fleeting. Then, when the Japanese returned to L.A., they joined hands not with African Americans and Latinos but with white leaders, whose guilt over internment caused them to lower the barriers to Japanese advancement. Several hundred years of black enslavement and Jim Crow had never inspired such an outpouring of white guilt and racial reconciliation.

What's more, many proponents of the tri-minority ideal had close ties to the Communist Party or the leftist wing of the CIO. That list of leaders included NAACP branch president Thomas Griffith, Jr., and Charlotta Bass. In the Red Scare atmosphere of the late 1940s and early 1950s, the interracial movement, frail to begin with and now tinged with communism, could not survive. Liberals and conservatives, blacks and whites and browns, labor unions and corporations—all hammered the Left into dust. As a result, the legitimacy of wartime interracialism was damaged beyond redemption. But that is a story for others to tell—an important story historians continue to explore.[69]

It is also a tale that moves beyond the 1930s and the boundaries of this study. Yet there is a necessary point to make here. Covington's "tri-minority" vision—and its fate in the 1940s and 1950s—provides an answer to the lingering question of Eastside heterogeneity and its effect on the black freedom movement in the West. Simply put, the multiracial mix of the Central Avenue district did little to alter the political views or alliances of Afro-Angelenos. That was true in 1900, and it remained so on the eve of World War II. Only for a fleeting moment during extraordinary circumstances did Covington's vision take any shape at all. Racial diversity made the West unique, but demographic chaos did not determine the course of black activism in the West. Instead, "the West"—as an ideal, as a symbol, as a rhetorical device—played a more important role in local civil rights efforts, which almost always adopted the traditional black-white dialogue, despite the racial complexity that marked everyday life on L.A.'s Eastside.

From New Deal to 8802

African American struggles to win equal participation in New Deal programs began to pay off at the end of the 1930s, and not just in terms of better representation in federal programs. Increasingly, the NAACP and the Urban League, as well as Randolph's BSCP, sharpened their ability to locate the

New Deal's strategic points of control, and they learned how to apply pressure at those points. By decade's end, these organizations had formed a loose but effective alliance that was lobbying hard for equal employment in federal and state jobs programs. These efforts placed Race leaders in a good position to demand black employment in the National Defense Program, which began to heat up after Europe went to war in 1939. In L.A., the NAACP and Gus Hawkins pushed for a state law demanding equal hiring in defense plants. The problem was basic: industrialists who won fat defense contracts from Washington were refusing to hire black workers. By this time, black leaders throughout the North and West had gained experience in seeking equal hiring in federally funded programs.

In the spring of 1941, black outrage at continued hiring discrimination culminated in Randolph's plan for a "March on Washington"—a mass protest in the nation's capital—if FDR would not issue an executive order banning racial discrimination in defense plants and federal agencies. The NAACP's Walter White quickly joined Randolph, as did the head of the national Urban League, T. Arnold Hill. Mary McLeod Bethune stood with them. L.A.'s BSCP local, if not particularly strong, jumped on board and organized a local March on Washington committee. Nationwide, black organizations formed something like a united front in support of the march. As the day of the march neared, Randolph and White won a meeting with FDR, at which they insisted that a hundred thousand African Americans were prepared to march. Seeking to avoid the protest in a time of international conflict, Roosevelt made a deal with Randolph: he would issue an executive order to address the problem if Randolph would cancel the march. Drafted by Randolph, White, and others, Executive Order 8802 banned racial discrimination in defense plants with federal contracts and created the President's Committee on Fair Employment Practice to oversee compliance. Roosevelt's language was significant: "I do hereby reaffirm the policy of the United States that there shall be no discrimination in the employment of workers in defense industries or government because of race, creed, color, or national origin." Reaffirming a policy that did not actually exist, FDR had, with a stroke, legitimized a policy that African Americans had been longing for since emancipation.[70]

By decree of the most popular and powerful president in American history, racial equality in hiring—in principle—was on the books. Upholding his part of the deal, Randolph called off the march. Lacking teeth for enforcement, 8802 had a limited impact at the hiring line, but FDR's response to the African American protest was symbolically monumental. In the long run, the planned march and its results proved vital to the postwar civil rights movement. And, as the historian Beth Tompkins Bates has stated, Executive Order 8802 "did not just put civil rights on the national agenda, it also introduced the idea at the national level that access to work was a civil right, giving legitimacy to the idea that the right to economic opportunity was embedded in citizenship." What followed was a long, bloody road to Section VII of the Civil Rights Act of 1964, which banned discrimination in hiring on account of both race and sex.[71]

Executive Order 8802 did not stem simply from the global crisis of 1941, or from the timely coalition formed between the BSCP and the NAACP. Its roots also stretched to the conflicts between all the Claude Hudsons and all the Roy Donnallys, between local-level black activists and lower-level New Deal administrators. In Los Angeles, the black civil rights movement—or, more accurately, civil rights activism as a way of life—had continued steadily since the turn of the century. But by the end of the 1930s, black activism in L.A., and in other major cities, had taken a significant turn. By joining hands with liberal Democrats and committing themselves to fight the old battles within a new political coalition, Race leaders carried their civil rights agenda into the New Deal. Negroes were not always welcomed at the Democratic feast; but they kept coming, refused to leave, and insisted on a seat at the table. Ultimately, they would push racial equality to the center of the liberal agenda. Over fierce objections from southern Democrats, liberals placed a civil rights plank on the Democratic platform in 1948—marking a revolution in party doctrine and a portent of Jim Crow's demise.

If African American leaders from Los Angeles and elsewhere had not pushed the matter, racial equality might never have become a viable part of the liberal agenda. And if that had been the case, the southern civil rights movement of the 1950s and 1960s might have gained little to nothing from Congress. Slowly—painfully slowly—but nonetheless surely, the black political realignment of the 1930s changed the United States. Black activism outside the South—in cities as diverse as Los Angeles, Seattle, Denver, Chicago, Philadelphia, and New York—eventually exerted a strong force on national politics and on the South itself.

Channeling traditional black activism into the new liberal state involved risks, of course. A sprawling Democratic Party advocating massive federal programs was, and continues to be, difficult for African Americans to influence, much less control. African American concerns about black dependence on the federal government were voiced in the 1930s and continue to smolder.[72] But perhaps the clearest lesson of the era is less about consequences than about process—about an ongoing commitment to get free. Floyd Covington, Fay Jackson, John Somerville, Vivian Osborne-Marsh, Gus Hawkins—they all lost more battles than they won. Their response was to regroup and fight again. If the new battleground for civil rights was the welfare state, so be it. Black leaders saw the pitfalls of the New Deal as clearly as anyone, but in the rising tide of Democratic liberalism they could also see, stretching off into the distance, rough and uphill, a new road to freedom.

Departure

On August, 27, 1952, Charlotta A. Bass again rode into town on a train. Forty-two years earlier she had arrived in Los Angeles unnoticed, a sickly woman disembarking at the Southern Pacific depot with no one to greet her. Now she arrived at L.A.'s Union Station to a cheering throng of admirers. Bass was no longer merely a local activist, no longer a Republican or Democrat. She was instead the national standard-bearer of the Progressive Party, the final haven for communists, socialists, and fellow travelers in cold-war America. Earlier that year she had been chosen as the party's candidate for vice president of the United States, a first for both women and African Americans.

It was a homecoming of sorts, for Charlotta had recently moved to Harlem. But that was not her real departure, for she would soon return to Southern California to live out her days. The real departure was political. After World War II, amid the Red Scare, her political allegiances moved to the left. In the process, Charlotta emerged as a nationally and even internationally known activist. She persistently addressed foreign policy issues, advocating a peaceful coexistence with communist nations and demanding the eradication of European colonialism. Along with W. E. B. Du Bois, now a crusty leftist, and the famed singer and actor Paul Robeson, she was a scandalous Black Red. Whether Charlotta actually joined the Communist Party was a secret she took to her grave. When asked by California's infamous Fact-Finding Committee on Un-American Activities, "Are you a Communist?" she replied, "If you will explain the meaning of 'Communist,' I shall, according to my understanding, answer your question." In 1950 she journeyed to the Soviet Union and wrote glowing reports of the country, declaring it utterly free of racial discrimination. Party member or not, she made no bones about where her sympathies lay. In 1952, *Time* magazine called her "shockingly pink."[1]

Charlotta's worldview had broadened and she had moved left, but from her point of view the rest of American politics had moved decisively to the right. Through the 1930s the *Eagle* had remained nominally Republican. Even after Joe's death in 1934, Charlotta maintained an official allegiance with the Republican Party. She may have privately crossed party lines to vote for Roosevelt in 1936, but the *Eagle* supported his opponent. In 1940, when the Republicans nominated civil rights advocate Wendell Wilkie for president, she accepted a job with the Republican National Committee to support his candidacy and served as a member of the California delegation to the Republican Convention in Chicago. Shocked to find that the seating in the convention hall was segregated—whites in one section, blacks in another—she decided "there was no future for my people in the Republican Party."[2]

During World War II, Charlotta officially joined the Democrats and became a supporter of organized labor, especially the CIO—all the while pushing unions to open their ranks to black workers on an equal basis with whites. She remained heavily involved with the NAACP and the interracial organizations that coalesced during the war. During the early years of the war she became increasingly enamored of her young nephew, John S. Kinloch, the son of her sister. Raised in Harlem, the left-leaning Kinloch moved to L.A. in the early 1940s to work for Charlotta's *Eagle*. He also became president of the local NAACP's Youth Division, proving himself an aggressive advocate for equal rights. During the early 1940s, Kinloch led a protest in the city council chambers, demanding racial equality in war-plant hiring. Like most black leaders young and old, Bass and Kinloch supported the "Double V" program, urging victory over fascism overseas and racism at home.

Charlotta's political star rose during the war, and she was given the honor of christening the U.S. Liberty Ship *James Weldon Johnson*. Flanked by dignitaries and black shipyard workers, Charlotta held the bottle of champagne and said: "You have heard the story of the memorable life of James Weldon Johnson. There is nothing I can add to that tribute. Speaking for my people, we thank the Maritime Commission for permitting another Liberty Ship to bear the name of another of our famous Negroes, and we thank the California Shipbuilding Corporation for its efforts to give recognition to all people. Truly it is a sign that slowly but surely the light of a better racial understanding and recognition is dawning, nearing the goal of true democracy."[3]

In 1944 Charlotta's nephew came of age, joined the army, and arrived in Europe just in time for the Battle of the Bulge, the first battle of the war in which black soldiers fought alongside white soldiers. There, Private John Kinloch was killed in action. Charlotta was crushed. She adored him and had already decided to place him in charge of the *Eagle* upon his return. When a wave of antiblack sentiment swept the nation after the war, not unlike the backlash of 1919, John's death seemed especially bitter. Charlotta determined that she would carry his fight forward, adopting his leftist views and promoting agendas that seemed increasingly progressive in the conformist post-war environment.[4]

By that time, black Los Angeles had been transformed by a massive wartime migration. This nationwide trend became known as the "Second" Great Migration. But for L.A., and for the Bay Area, it was really their first, paralleling what Chicago, Detroit, and other northern cities had experienced during World War I: intense overcrowding, deteriorating living conditions, a white backlash, political tensions. Black Angelenos who had been part of the community for decades had mixed feelings about the mass migration. On the one hand, it presaged greater political empowerment and provided new opportunities for black entrepreneurs. On the other, the community's traditional civil rights organizations and social institutions were over-whelmed, their members' quality of life was declining, and many newcom-ers were not quite "their type." Then again, old-timers and newcomers alike took advantage of war-production jobs when they were opened to African Americans late in the war. Black workers fought for and eventually won im-portant gains in the labor movement. In 1945, emboldened by the growing black electorate and new interracial interactions with Eastside Mexican Americans, community leaders urged Charlotta Bass to run for city coun-cil. It was a nonpartisan election, but she ran as a Democrat: a pro-labor lib-eral. She lost the election, and her days as a Democrat were numbered.

During the war, Charlotta had embraced FDR "and the brave course he led toward world peace and world brotherhood." But, as she later wrote, "with his death, I saw the Democratic party fall into the hands of lesser men. I saw a handful of southerners who have never risen above the thoughts of slaveholders, tighten their grip upon the party of Roosevelt." In an *Eagle* editorial in the summer of 1947, she publicly severed ties to both major par-ties and urged the creation of a new third party to challenge the status quo. That December her prayers were answered when Henry Wallace, the left-liberal Democrat who had been Roosevelt's vice president before Harry Tru-man, bolted from the party and announced he would run for president on a new Progressive Party ticket. Bass and other enthusiasts collected enough signatures to place the Progressive Party (officially named the "Indepen-dent Progressive Party" in California, a mere technicality) on the state bal-lot. Bass served as a California delegate to the Progressives' national con-vention and campaigned energetically for the ticket. When Wallace made a campaign stop in L.A., he sparked tumultuous enthusiasm along The Av-enue. The rest of the nation was less impressed. Wallace barely won a mil-lion votes nationwide, and when communist North Korea invaded South Korea in 1950, he sought to distance himself from the Left. Claiming that communists had taken over the Progressive Party, he returned to the Democratic Party.[5]

Bass remained an enthusiastic booster of the Progressive Party. In the summer of 1950, she traveled to Europe. The FBI had been spying on her for several years by then, with agents sending monthly reports on her activities, and on the *Eagle*, directly to J. Edgar Hoover. When she left California for New York, en route to Europe, the Los Angeles agent told eastern agents to be on the alert for a suspect who was "short, elderly, negro, female, gray hair, fat, wearing glasses, waddling walk." The CIA tailed her in Europe, but she still made it to political meetings in Czechoslovakia and toured the Soviet Union. That spring, at the urging of Progressive Party leaders in Southern California, she returned to L.A. to run for the congressional seat for the 14th district. The seat had been left vacant by the liberal Democrat Helen Douglas, who was running for the U.S. Senate (she lost to a rising Republican, Richard Nixon). Charlotta's opponent was also a liberal Democrat, Sam Yorty, who was destined to become one of L.A.'s most conservative mayors.[6]

Bass reminded voters of the 14th district that "I have not lived on the border of this cauldron of racial mixtures known as the Eastside, and only hurled my 'sympathy' at you in your pain and distress, in combating police brutality, in trying to secure jobs and find houses to live in. I have been a part of the struggle, and still am a fighting part. I feel that as your Congressional representative I can do more on the national front than on the home front to bring to fruition your desires for peace and security." In short, she was one of them, but her battle for freedom must now move to the national stage. Drawing on old-fashioned Lincolnesque rhetoric, she pledged her "sacred honor to aid in the task of bringing forth a new nation conceived in the hearts of the people, and really dedicated to the cause of freedom, liberty, and justice for all mankind." The ministers' alliance joined her campaign, so she got plenty of support from the Negro churches, based more on her credentials as a Race woman than as a radical. In the election, Bass won the Central Avenue vote but little more.[7]

Her defeat did not dent her faith in the Progressive Party, but she was worn down from three hectic years spent campaigning for Wallace, traveling in Europe, and running for Congress. In early 1951 she might have been sixty-one or seventy-seven or somewhere in between. Whatever her age, she decided to retire from the newspaper business. That April she sold the *Eagle* to the journalist and attorney Loren Miller. Any old-timer in the community would have seen the irony. Miller had gotten his journalistic start at the *Eagle* but then joined the Left and traveled to the Soviet Union; Joe and Charlotta's *Eagle* had given him plenty of grief about that, especially when Miller became Gus Hawkins's campaign manager and took aim at Fred Roberts. By 1951, however, Miller was a mainstream liberal Democrat and Charlotta was the fellow traveler just returned from the Soviet Union. Nevertheless, Miller's "Red" years would dog his legal career for the rest of his life, probably preventing him from receiving a federal judgeship.

In 1951 Miller was a legendary figure in black L.A., but not because of his 1930s radicalism. Rather, it was because of his unrelenting and successful legal assault on racially restrictive real estate covenants. Working with the NAACP and leading black attorneys throughout the nation, Miller helped bring the issue before the U.S. Supreme Court. Teamed with Thurgood Marshall, Miller presented part of the case *Shelley v. Kraemer* before the justices. The result was the court's 1948 decision ruling that restrictive covenants were unenforceable. The justices concluded that even though covenants were private matters outside the state's jurisdiction, the judicial actions necessary for upholding those covenants amounted to state action and were therefore a violation of the Fourteenth Amendment. That idea was not new (Burton Ceruti, among others, had made the point years earlier, to no avail), but times, and the Supreme Court, were changing. A subsequent case originating in Los Angeles, *Barrows v. Jackson* (1953), sealed loopholes in *Shelley* and served as the final legal blow against racially restrictive covenants.[8]

After selling the *Eagle,* Charlotta Bass rested—but not for long. After Wallace abandoned the Progressive Party, Vincent Hallinan of San Francisco emerged as the head of the party, and in early 1952 he was nominated to run for the presidency in the upcoming election. Not a communist, nor even particularly leftist in political orientation, Hallinan was a tough-talking, fearless attorney who was closely aligned with the city's Irish politicos. He enjoyed supporting underdogs, and he had become the darling of the Left by defending union activist Harry Bridges against charges of communism. His aggressive defense earned him a six-month jail term for contempt of court. Hallinan was rich, thanks to his brilliant and beautiful wife, Vivian, who had made a fortune in local real estate. Nominally a Democrat, Vivian Hallinan was the radical behind the throne, steering Vince's political course and urging him to accept the Progressive nomination in 1952. Her book, *My Wild Irish Rogues,* an insider's view of Irish American politics and labor in San Francisco, published early in the cold war, was a best seller, but FBI director J. Edgar Hoover condemned it as "a flagrant employment of the Communist Party line, including references to racial discrimination."[9]

The Progressive Party surprised everyone by nominating Charlotta Bass for vice president. Whether she moved to Harlem that year to be with her sister, or whether she relocated to ensure that the Progressives had a bicoastal ticket, she was introduced to mainstream American newspaper readers as a resident of New York City who had formerly published a Negro newspaper in Los Angeles. Progressives trumpeted her nomination as a stride toward equality, but the mainstream press presented a different view. *Time* magazine, for example, noted that the Progressives' "choice for vice-presidential candidate was dumpy, domineering Mrs. Charlotta Bass, Negro, former Los Angeles publisher and, until 1940, a power in California Republican ranks. Childless Mrs. Bass was steered left by a young nephew she adored, became bitterly radical when the nephew was killed in World War II. She visited Russia, dined . . . in Moscow"—a description curiously reminiscent of the FBI alerts in 1950.[10]

Charlotta campaigned vigorously, crossing the country by rail six times, handing out thousands of campaign cards to Pullman porters, and delivering hundreds of long, detailed, impassioned speeches. Indeed, she carried the Progressive load for most of the campaign, because Hallinan's six-month jail term began on April 1, and he did not get out on parole until September, leaving him little time to stump before election day. Vivian spoke on his behalf, but it was Charlotta who remained in constant motion, accompanied by campaign manager C. B. Baldwin and his wife, Lillian. Although the Progressive Party convention was held in Chicago in July, the party announced its Hallinan-Bass ticket that spring, and Charlotta began her nonstop efforts immediately.[11]

As a "peace candidate," she called for an end to "this senseless war in Korea" and insisted that the United States help to thaw the cold war. "We must insist that the President agree to a meeting of the great powers to settle outstanding issues, to end the bankrupting arms race, to stop the continued oppression of the colonial peoples," she told a group of labor leaders that April.[12] "We fought to end Hitlerism. But less than 7 years after the end of that war, I find men who lead my government paying out my money and your money to support the rebirth of Hitlerism in Germany to make it a willing partner in another war. We thought to destroy Hitlerism—but its germs took root right here." On European colonialism, she singled out England's continued violations in its colonies, especially Malaya, and France's increasingly bloody effort to control Vietnam. She also called attention to the repression of blacks in South Africa and demanded an end to apartheid.[13]

Bass linked women's equality in the United States to the broader theme of global freedom. Speaking before the Women's Committee of the Amer-

ican Labor Party at the Astor Hotel in New York, she told the story of a
young woman who, upon learning that a woman was running for vice president, replied, "We are not ready for this yet." Bass asked the women assembled, "How many times have these words barred the path to progress?
And how much longer shall we bear with them? For these are the words of
the oppressor—even when they are echoed by the oppressed. How often
have we heard these words—in many languages—in many lands—but always to delay the day of freedom, to prolong the days of bondage—for
women, for the Negro people, for all people who sought freedom." She recalled the history of women pioneers who *were* ready—Harriet Beecher
Stowe, Harriet Tubman, and those who gathered for the woman's rights convention in Seneca Falls in 1848. "I say we are ready now," she cried, "for
peace, for freedom, for progress."[14]

Bass's speeches emphasized freedom and equality for colored peoples in
the United States and globally. Domestically, she still saw southern Democrats as the main barrier to African American freedom. Federal laws were
needed to abolish Jim Crow segregation, reenfranchise southern blacks, and
ensure equal employment opportunities for Negroes and women nationwide. But those were not the only problems. Domestic inequality and cold-
war foreign policy were now entwined. "We may use the $65 Billion that
goes for death [in Korea] to build a new life. These billions could lift the
wages of all people, give them jobs, grant education and training and new
hope for our youth. Free share croppers from the endless toil without reward that is their lot. The billions now being spent to rearm Europe and
crush Asia could tear down the ghettos of America and provide homes for
all who live today in firetraps and tenements." Her rallying cry was "Let
my people go!" Her people were African Americans, of course, but now they
also included white steelworkers and Vietnamese peasants—she spoke for
"the Kingdom of all the people of all the world," which was not merely in
heaven "but right here at our feet. Acres of diamonds: Freedom—Peace—
Justice for all, if we will but stoop down and take them."[15]

The Progressives were bound to lose, badly, which was why Charlotta
often told her audiences, "Even if we lose, we win"—which, translated,
meant "Even though we are going to lose, we will keep our issues before the
American public, thereby winning a moral victory."[16] A vote for Hallinan-
Bass would be a protest vote. As it turned out, too many liberal Democrats
loved their candidate, Adlai Stevenson, and too many feared the Republican candidate, Dwight Eisenhower, to be willing to spend their vote on a
moral statement. Eisenhower still won in a romp, and the Hallinan-Bass
ticket earned embarrassingly few votes: only a few hundred thousand

nationwide. It was difficult to claim even a moral victory with those kinds of numbers.

But several months earlier, when Charlotta made her triumphant return to L.A., no one was worrying about a crushing defeat. Accompanied by Paul Robeson, Charlotta drew a wildly cheering crowd of ten thousand to Culver City stadium for what was one of the magical nights of her life. She and Robeson campaigned on the Eastside, with Robeson making his speeches in Spanish. Bass soon returned to Chicago, where, in the words of a Progressive Party press release, she "spoke to the largest audience any Negro woman has ever had when she appeared on a joint NBC-ABC radio and television coast to coast hook up." On September 6, 1952, almost forty-two years to the day after she had arrived alone in Los Angeles, Charlotta spoke for thirty minutes on national television. Her concluding line: "I make this pledge to the American people, to the dead and the living, to all Americans black and white, to every mother who waits for news of a loved one abroad and every son in uniform on alien soil: I will not retire nor will I retreat, not one inch, so long as God gives me vision to see what is happening and strength to fight for the things I know are right."[17]

Freedom's Uncertain Journey

In the America of 1952, Charlotta's platform was almost utopian. For Charlotta, that was part of the appeal. The Progressives had no chance to win, so she could air her political wish list without restraint. Powerful federal laws that would outlaw racial segregation, require equal employment opportunities for women and blacks, and ensure that black southerners could vote? An end to colonial rule? A cessation of the arms race? A policy of cooperation between the United States and the communist superpowers? The abolition of apartheid in South Africa? The political realities of the time made her demands seem like a pipe dream. And yet, before the century was out, every single item on Charlotta's list had come to pass. Indeed, each one had become a part of mainstream political opinion in the United States—the usual way of looking at things.

It was not Progressive Party radicalism that moved Bass's definition of freedom to the center of national politics. The key, rather, was the insistent activism of blacks and voters in the West and North after they joined Roosevelt's Democratic Party. When New Deal liberalism first blossomed, racial equality was not on the liberal agenda. Black activists such as those in L.A.

put racial liberalism on the Democratic table and made sure it stayed there. In 1948 the Democratic Party, despite its deep roots in white supremacy and southern conservatism, added a civil rights plank to its platform. That same year saw victory in *Shelley v. Kraemer*, followed in 1953 by the favorable ruling in *Barrows v. Jackson*. The next year, the Supreme Court's decision in *Brown v. Board of Education* electrified the nation and set in motion the wheels that would drive the southern civil rights movement, and its opponents.

Not without reason, most Americans view the civil rights movement as a southern phenomenon. The sit-ins, Bull Conner's Birmingham, Martin Luther King's speeches, the freedom riders, Bloody Sunday, the climactic March to Montgomery—all are rightly part of our national consciousness. Black southerners, and their white allies, literally put their lives on the line. Their commitment to the very basics of American freedom—equal citizenship rights, including the right to vote—and their strategy of nonviolent civil disobedience, roused the nation and reoriented its moral compass.

But it is often forgotten that the moral authority of the movement might well have resulted in nothing. African Americans won the struggle because the U.S. Congress passed the Civil Rights Act of 1964 and the Voting Rights Act of 1965. The first outlawed racial segregation and demanded equal employment opportunities for blacks and for all women. The second reenfranchised southern blacks. Both laws brought powerful federal force to bear on the South, and both would transform Dixie. Neither would have been passed without the heroism of the southern activists. Without that direct action, Congress would have done little or nothing to alter Dixie's Jim Crow system. It was also true, however, that the civil rights bills would not have prevailed in Congress without the support of racial liberals from the North and West. Members of the House and Senate from outside the South were prepared to vote "yea" in 1964 and 1965 only because black activists in their districts and states had been pushing the issue since the welfare state had been created in the 1930s. Floyd Covington, Claude Hudson, John and Vada Somerville, Jessie Terry, Betty Hill: these local activists from L.A. and the thousands of others like them in cities across the West and North played an essential role in the civil rights victories of the 1960s. Because they had gradually forced white liberals and Republican moderates to include racial equality as part of their agenda, both the U.S. Supreme Court and the Congress were open to positive action on civil rights issues.

Within California itself, racial liberals scored a remarkable string of victories in the late 1950s and early 1960s. Gus Hawkins was no longer the only black legislator in Sacramento—William Byron Rumford of Berkeley had been in office since 1948—and he also found influential allies in such white racial liberals as San Francisco's fiery Phillip Burton and Los Angeles's power broker, Jesse Unruh, who would become the Speaker of the assembly in 1961. What's more, in 1958, Hawkins helped engineer the election of a dynamic liberal governor, the San Francisco attorney Edmund "Pat" Brown. This often contentious circle of liberals united when it came to civil rights legislation. The 1959 legislative session saw passage of a fair-employment act, which established the California Fair Employment Practices Commission; a new and stronger civil rights act; and a modest fair-housing law, which would be upgraded four years later by the stronger Rumford Fair Housing Act. In 1962, black Angelenos sent two new black assemblymen to Sacramento—Mervyn M. Dymally and F. Douglas Ferrell—and elected Hawkins to Congress. In 1963, three African Americans were elected to the Los Angeles city council, including the city's future mayor, Tom Bradley.[18]

By the time Lyndon Johnson signed the Voting Rights Act in 1965, Democratic Party liberalism seemed invincible. Of course there would be problems and conflicts, but they could be resolved. The Republican Party was in shambles after Barry Goldwater's crushing defeat in 1964, and the liberal Democrats were about to gain millions of new voters and elected officials because southern blacks would be surging to the voting booths. Johnson pledged to use the nation's vast resources to build a "Great Society," one in which enlightened federal programs would lift all boats and leave no one behind. He would wage a war on poverty that would finally free all Americans from privation. When the Voting Rights Act became law on August 6, American liberals—including racial liberals—were confident that they could achieve anything. That certainty lasted five days.

On August 11, Watts exploded, sparking antiwhite ghetto riots throughout America. For their own part, whites proved more hostile toward civil rights legislation than liberals had expected, especially when it came to housing and schools. Simultaneously, the Vietnam war began to divide liberals into warring camps—Hawks versus Doves. Student radicalism and Black Power advocates denounced the liberal establishment and also weakened it. Then came 1968 and all the trauma that came with it, including the assassinations of Martin Luther King, Jr., and, in Los Angeles, Bobby Kennedy, the racial liberal and Democratic presidential hopeful. By the end of the riot-torn Democratic national convention in Chicago that summer, American liberalism—racial liberalism included—was nearly dead. What had seemed invincible in 1965 was politically crippled three years later.

Moving On

The Booker T. Washington Building still stands today, though few would know it. The bold lettering Sidney Dones put on the building in 1916— "BOOKER T. WASHINGTON BLDG."—is gone, as are the original sidewalk awnings. An old and unused neon sign on one corner of the building reads "Tokio Hotel." One street-level store sells cellular phones and pagers; the other sells "market equipment" for the hundreds of little Latino markets scattered throughout the old 74th district. The upper two floors are apartments. A brightly colored sign hanging out front marks the current flavor of the neighborhood: "Cuartos de renta precios bajos, Con muebles y cosina." Some brickwork has secured the top layer of bricks, and the sidewalk doors have iron bars, a protection once unknown and unneeded on Central Avenue. Otherwise, the building looks much the same as it did when Joe Bass trumpeted its completion with his typical booster style: "Central Avenue Assumes Gigantic Proportion as Business Section for Colored Men."[19]

Go to the McDonald's on the southeast corner of Central Avenue and Olympic Boulevard (formerly 9th Street) and you can find the building. Park in the lot facing Central Avenue and look across the street to the southwest— the old Booker T. is the three-story red brick building that fills the little block between 10th and 11th Streets. It looks much like any other aging, eclectic building in the neighborhood. The McDonald's is nice, with large historic photographs on the walls effectively wrapping each Big Mac with images of the community's past. The photos are of two locations: the big produce market that once operated on Central Avenue just north of Joe and Charlotta's apartment, and the architecturally famous Coca-Cola Bottling Plant, built in the 1930s, that stretches down Central from 12th to 14th Streets. Neither the market nor the bottling plant were vital parts of the black community, and none of the photos show any African Americans. The historical images add a smart touch, but customers would never know that they were standing near the heart of the city's first major African American community—once a multiracial, majority-white area of the Eastside, which Negro businesses, churches, organizations, and newspaper offices marked as an African American place.

One can hardly blame McDonald's, for virtually no vestiges of that black community survive. There are no obvious remains of the Angelus Theater, which once stood near the McDonald's lot. Walk a few blocks south from Olympic and you will be standing near the spot where Charlotta Spear first walked into John Neimore's shacklike *Eagle* office, now covered by part of the Coca-Cola plant. Look north from the McDonald's lot and you will be facing the block that once housed Joe and Charlotta's up-graded *Eagle* office, as well as their apartment building. There is no sign of either. The offices and apartments that ran along both sides of the 800 block have been razed: on the west side of Central Avenue, a Burger King rubs elbows with Casa Mexico and other ethnic Mexican wholesalers; on the east, an artfully designed trucking station occupies the space where the Basses lived.

Over on San Pedro Street, all signs of Fred Roberts's original *New Age* building, and its Colored YMCA neighbor, have been lost amid a tightly packed row of sweatshops, markets, and the occasional chic boutique. Vir-tually all of the black churches of the old 74th district are gone. The 8th and Towne sanctuary of First AME burned down in 1972, and there is no trace of it. All five black churches that graced Paloma Street's church row have disappeared, replaced by empty spaces and warehouses. Nearby, a road sign erected by the city identifies the area as the "Fashion District."

Interstate 10 is partly to blame for this erasure. Entering Los Angeles from the east, it curves southward around downtown, tracing most of what used to be the southern boundary of 74th Assembly District. The Somer-villes' home on San Pedro Street, where Du Bois stayed during his historic visit in 1913, may well have stood where the pylons now prop up the free-way. One of the few remnants of the early black community that remains is Fire Station No. 30—a small, beige-painted building at 14th and Central, across the street from the Coke building and oddly surrounded by vacant land. Here, the city's all-black firefighting crews pulled their shifts for decades. The station and its crews were a source of community pride, al-though that pride was always mixed with angst about the fire department's segregation policies. Today, Fire Station No. 30 is a museum dedicated to the history of African American firefighters. A hand-painted sign indicates the hours of operation. It is run by volunteers hoping to maintain what once was an important symbol of black Los Angeles.

By the time the freeway was built in the 1960s, however, most of the black community and its leading institutions had already moved out of the old 74th. Today, when people think about the historic heart of black Los Ange-les, they think of the Dunbar Hotel, and not without reason. The 1928 NAACP convention solidified L.A.'s status in black America, and the Hotel Somerville had acted as a magnet for Afro-Angelenos, quickly pulling homes and businesses southward to 41st and Central. The hotel's change in own-ership and name, and its brief occupation by Father Divine's followers, did nothing to stem the southward shift of Afro-Angelenos. Charlotta Bass herself eventually moved the *Eagle* from the old hub to the Dunbar area. In recent years, African American activists and local historians have worked to ensure that the Dunbar survives and that its importance to the history of black L.A. will not be lost. It is a protected historical site, and nicely refurbished. Leaders of the Dunbar Economic Development Corporation not only offer history programs to all; they also provide housing and social services to the mosaic of Spanish-speaking peoples who now surround the hotel.[20]

In the 1950s, black Los Angeles experienced its third major geographical shift, as middle-class residents moved to the Westside, into the West Adams district, which essentially became a broad northern and western extension of the West Jefferson neighborhood. Several dynamics were involved in the shift: Loren Miller's fight against restrictive covenants, which contributed to the Supreme Court decisions that made these covenants moot; the enormous population pressures and declining quality of life on the Eastside; the growth of white suburban developments outside the city; and the expansion of L.A.'s black middle class as white-collar service jobs were increasingly opened to African Americans. Critics later charged the Negro middle class with "black flight" from lower-class African Americans, but as jazz musician Marshal Royal said, "When I moved [west], I wasn't running from anyplace; I was just trying to find a better place to live. There was no flight. I just tried to better my condition and have a better condition for my wife to live in." Afro-Angelenos had been trying to break the Westside barrier for decades; finally they had won. The unintended consequence, however, was that many businesses and other community institutions also moved to West Adams. At the same time, the Los Angeles police, whose violence against black Angelenos was increasing, began an intimidation campaign in the Central Avenue jazz clubs, prompting the more affluent white and black club goers to stop coming. The Dunbar scene went downhill; or, as Royal said, "It just faded away. Nothing was happening. It just went kaput."[21]

West Adams did not have an easily identifiable "center"—no Angelus Theater, no Dunbar Hotel. If there was a community landmark, it was the new Golden State Mutual Life Insurance building, designed by Paul Williams in 1948 and built far to the west of any other black institution at that time. A tall, strong, elegant structure, the Golden State office had something of a Hotel Somerville effect, drawing middle-class businesses and home owners westward. Williams would later design the new First AME church (his home congregation), which arose very near the Golden State building. By 1960, the West Adams district was majority black. Even then, however, middle-class African Americans were moving southward into Inglewood, and moved those who could afford it westward into the more exclusive Baldwin Hills area, in part because Interstate 10 cut a wide swath through the loveliest neighborhoods of the West Adams district.

The Eastside, meanwhile, changed dramatically. Virtually all of the ethnic Mexicans, Asians, and whites, including Jews, moved out of the district. All of these groups found it relatively easy to find new and better housing elsewhere after World War II. Those who were middle class experienced surprisingly little resistance when they moved into white neighborhoods; by contrast, white resistance to black neighbors intensified in most areas of the city and county. The result, along Central Avenue, was the disappearance the multiracial Eastside; by 1960, the area was about 95 percent black. Watts, a city that was about one-third black when the war began, was by 1960 virtually all black. The Central Avenue district had pushed south and the black community in Watts had expanded northward until the two were effectively joined—a seven-mile stretch of African American neighborhoods locked between Main Street and Alameda.[22]

By 1960 Angelenos were pointing to a divide between middle-class blacks on the Westside and lower-class blacks on the Eastside, and the rise of Interstate 110—which, beginning in the 1950s, ran south from downtown parallel to Main Street—had created a massive structural and symbolic barrier between the Eastside and Westside communities. The point can be pushed too far, however. West Adams had its sore spots, and many neighborhoods along Central Avenue still offered nice, affordable bungalows to African Americans. Compton, south of Watts, had emerged as a little jewel for home-owning blacks. And Watts itself, so often scorned as the lowest place a Negro could land in Los Angeles, had plenty of residential neighborhoods that were, by national standards, almost lovely.

The divide among Afro-Angelenos involved more than income or even social status. When the established middle class left the Eastside for West Adams, it unintentionally created a leadership vacuum that was not easily filled. For L.A.'s black leaders not only moved their residences, they also moved their businesses, churches, newspapers, and clubs. When that happened, the Central Avenue district no longer served as the vital center of black Los Angeles. For a while the jazz clubs sufficed, but when these went kaput, what remained on the Eastside was not a community but merely another uncentered residential area in Los Angeles—one filled only with black people, living in neighborhoods that more successful people were leaving behind. Here, finally, was a "black belt" indeed, but it was not the kind Joe Bass had longed for. It was no longer a place to claim but a place to move out of. In 1928, L.A.'s black leaders rapidly shifted their community south-ward to the Somerville Hotel, and they were able to do so without disman-tling the older hub at 12th and Central. In the 1950s, the same generation of leaders moved to West Adams and again moved their enterprises and in-stitutions. But the miracle of 1928 was somehow not repeated. Perhaps in the postwar decades the city's African American population simply became too large to operate as a single community and instead evolved into a con-stellation of loosely associated groups that had different outlooks and op-portunities, different visions of how to get free.

Los Angeles demographics and neighborhoods have constantly shifted and continue to do so. West Adams is now majority Latino. After 1980, African American population growth in the city stalled and is now declin-ing; meanwhile, African immigrants have begun arriving in L.A. by the tens of thousands. The African American population dropped off because many families were leaving the city for outlying suburbs, especially in Orange and Riverside counties. Black newcomers to the West Coast flocked to San Diego, whose black population has boomed in recent decades. But these Southern California trends are only part of the reason the African American popula-tion in L.A. is shrinking. As recent census figures show, there is now under way a "Third" Great Migration, or, perhaps more accurately, a Return Mi-gration. During the 1990s, four million African Americans from the North and West moved *to* the South. Mostly composed of professionals, entre-preneurs, and the white-collar middle class, this new generation of black migrants comprises the children and grandchildren of those who had been fleeing Dixie since the 1890s. One popular destination is the burgeoning me-tropolis of Atlanta.

In 1903 George Beavers, Jr., and his parents left Atlanta for Los Angeles "in search of full citizenship rights and better living conditions."[23] One cen-tury later, boosters at the *Atlanta Journal-Constitution* trumpeted the re-sults of the 2000 census with a front-page headline: "Atlanta is top magnet for blacks." A subsequent issue bragged: "Atlanta No. 1 in Growth of Black Prosperity." Both articles offered maps and statistics to prove that more African Americans had moved to Atlanta during the 1990s—nearly half a million—than to any other American city. Why? The economy was boom-ing, the weather was nice, the children of the Great Migrations wanted to reconnect with their roots, and—the real kicker—African Americans be-lieved racial conditions were better in the South. Comments from recent arrivals to Atlanta have a curiously familiar ring. One woman came right out and said it: "Atlanta is a mecca for African-Americans."[24]

Tomorrow

In 1952, while Charlotta Bass was running for vice president, Fred and Pearl Roberts bought land in Malibu Canyon and had Paul Williams design a rustic but elegant home for them. Fred did not get to enjoy it, for he died that year from injuries suffered in an automobile accident. The way that historians have treated Fred Roberts and Charlotta Bass is an interesting study. Roberts has been generally dismissed as a conservative Republican, while Bass has become a larger-than-life legend for community activists and radicals of all stripes. Yet Roberts was never a "conservative" in any meaningful sense, and though he did remain with the Republican Party during the New Deal revolution, his principal criticism of New Deal liberalism was that it gave blacks short shrift and often supported Jim Crow more than it undermined it—the same critique being made by the Basses, Ralph Bunche, and Loren Miller. Long before Charlotta Bass found her political voice, Fred Roberts was hurling editorial lighting bolts at white supremacy.

Their paths parted during World War II. After several failed attempts to regain office, Roberts stopped running and settled into the traditional Race man role, supporting the NAACP, the Urban League, and the women's clubs. He enjoyed being the grand old man in Republican circles, and he had some friends—George Beavers, Jr., being one—who also stayed with the GOP. Charlotta, on the other hand, finally embraced organized labor and joined the Democrats during the war. The more politically independent she became, the more influence she commanded; the more radical she became, the more she rejected pragmatism for ideological visions. Late in their lives, the tenor and scope of their political activities diverged, but for most of their years in L.A., Roberts was a leading Race man, Bass was a leading Race woman, and the political differences between them were insignificant.

After the 1952 election Charlotta returned to L.A. and settled in the West Jefferson district. With little to lose and verve to spare, she continued to denounce racism in the United States and throughout the world and to promote the Left through speeches and articles. FBI agents continued to tail her. During 1959 she wrote her autobiography, flipping through old issues of the *Eagle* to jog her memory and to chronicle the history of race relations and civil rights struggles in Los Angeles. Of her personal life in L.A., Charlotta's book revealed very little, and of her life before then it offered next to nothing. The first half of the book is filled with the kind of stories any Race woman from her generation might write. The second half takes on the tone of a leftist political tract. No matter. Her basic demands remained constant from 1912 on: full civil rights for Afro-Americans and equal opportunity in all areas of life. Her strategies for achieving these ends—and the allies she deemed most helpful—did change over time. Her basic indignation and fighting spirit did not. For her, civil rights were a way of life, whether she sought to achieve them through the Party of Lincoln, the NAACP, the UNIA, the CIO, the Party of Roosevelt, or the Progressive Party. She herself published *Forty Years: Memoirs from the Pages of a Newspaper* in January 1960—or rather, she had Loren Miller publish it for her. By then, Charlotta was the grande dame in L.A.'s black community.[25]

Six years later, she suffered a stroke and was confined to a nursing home in L.A., where, according to the FBI agent still keeping tabs, she was still "potentially dangerous." She would have been amused and probably pleased by that. Perhaps, given her rising status among radical historical figures, she is still dangerous to the J. Edgar Hoovers of America. One recent scholar even proclaimed her to be a "Radical Precursor of the Black Power Movement." Her belated and sometimes misplaced recognition could not be foreseen, but she was certain of her next destination. Despite her glorification of the Soviet Union, and despite her call for people to stop looking to heaven and start building a heaven on earth, Charlotta Bass held firm to her Christian faith. As she suggested in a touching chapter tucked into the middle of her book, she hoped and fully expected to see Joe and many other old friends when she crossed into "the world beyond." If her hopes were not misplaced, the reunion took place on April 12, 1969, when a cerebral hemorrhage took her life.[26]

Considering the sum of her career as she was completing *Forty Years*, Charlotta wrote: "It has been a good life that I have had, though a very hard one, but I know the future will be even better. And as I think back I know this is the only kind of life: In serving one's fellow man one serves himself best. . . . Of course, the battle is not won, nor the struggle past. But the growth of Los Angeles and the development of the Negro people within its boundaries have been phenomenal. The end result is certain to be a source of real satisfaction to those of us who have believed, worked and fought for the dawn of Freedom's day in our beloved country."[27] Her words call to mind Langston Hughes's poem "History," which compels us once again to consider America's most basic and vital ideal:

The past has been a mint
of blood and sorrow.
That must not be
True of tomorrow.[28]

Notes

For sources cited frequently in the notes, I have used the briefest titles possible, even for first references. All brief titles are listed in the bibliography. The following abbreviations have been used throughout the notes.

AAHM	California Afro-American History Museum, Los Angeles
AAMLO	African American Museum and Library of Oakland, California
BC	United States Bureau of the Census
BF	Branch Files, Los Angeles branch, 1913–1940, National Association for the Advancement of Colored People collection, Library of Congress, Washington, D.C. (photocopy version, courtesy of the Library of Congress)
CE	*California Eagle* (Los Angeles)
Cit.	*Citizen Advocate* (Los Angeles)
Dir.	*Los Angeles Negro Directory and Who's Who, 1930–1931*
ED	Enumeration district
Fisk	Special Collections, Fisk University Library, Nashville, Tennessee
HEH	Henry E. Huntington Library, San Marino, California
LACA	Los Angeles City Archives, Records Management Division, City Clerk's Office, Los Angeles
LAT	*Los Angeles Times*
NA	*New Age* (later *New Age Dispatch*, Los Angeles)
PD	*Pacific Defender* (Los Angeles)
SCL	Southern California Library for Social Studies and Research, Los Angeles
SLA	Shades of L.A. Archives, History Department, Los Angeles Public Library
SV	California, Secretary of State, *Statement of Vote*
UCLA	Special Collections, Young Research Library, University of California, Los Angeles

WD   *Western Dispatch* (Los Angeles)
WW   *Negro Who's Who in California, 1948*

Introduction

1. Two recent essential works that examine the concept of freedom are Eric Foner, *The Story of American Freedom* (New York: Norton, 1999), and Gary Gerstle, *American Crucible: Race and Nation in the Twentieth Century* (Princeton, NJ: Princeton University Press, 2001).

2. Bass, *Forty*; Bond, "Negro"; Bryant, et al., *Central*; Bunch, "Past"; Cox, *Central*; de Graaf, "City"; Horne, *Fire*.

3. Cose, *Rage*.

4. Robinson, *Jackie*, 24.

5. Taylor, *Search*, 17; see also White, "Race."

6. Lerone Bennett, Jr., "What's in a Name?" *Ebony* 23 (Nov. 1967): 46–52, in Peter I. Rose, *Americans from Africa: Old Memories, New Moods* (New York: Atherton, 1970), 373–83. Debates in Los Angeles: *NA*, Oct. 22, 1915; *CE*, June 15, 1928; Pearl Roberts oral history, 13.

7. *NA*, Oct. 30, 1936, May 27 and July 8, 1938; Bass, *Forty*, 13; Forsythe Papers, HEH. See also Randall Kennedy, *Nigger: The Strange Career of a Troublesome Word* (New York: Vintage, 2003).

8. Gutierrez, *Walls*.

9. Gatewood, *Aristocrats*; Lewis, *Du Bois: Biography*. An ad in the black-owned *CE*, Jan. 2, 1915, stated, "This store was instituted to serve what is called the middle class."

10. A 1997 reprint of Frazier's controversial classic goes so far as to advertise it, in bold print on the front cover, as "The book that brought the shock of self-revelation to middle-class blacks in America", see E. Franklin Frazier, *Black Bourgeoisie* (1957; New York: Free Press, 1997). Malcolm X with Alex Haley, *The Autobiography of Malcolm X* (New York: Ballantine Books, 1965), 40–44, 59–60 (quote, 40).

11. Darlene Clark Hine has been a leader in the historical recovery of the black middle class. Her works include *Black Women in White: Racial Conflict and Cooperation in the Nursing Profession, 1890–1950* (Bloomington: Indiana University Press, 1989); "Black Professionals and Race Consciousness: Origins of the Civil Rights Movement, 1890–1950," *Journal of American History* 89 (March 2003): 1279–94; and "The Corporal and Ocular Veil: Dr. Matilda A. Evans (1872–1935) and the Complexity of Southern History," *Journal of Southern History* 70 (Feb. 2004): 3–34. Recent biographies of Langston Hughes and W. E. B. Du Bois have added greatly to our understanding of Race men and women during this period; see Rampersad, *Life*, and Lewis, *Du Bois: Biography* and *Du Bois: The Fight*. See also Cynthia Neverdon-Morton, *Afro-American Women of the South and the Advancement of the Race, 1895–1925* (Knoxville: University of Tennessee Press, 1989).

12. Harold Bruce Forsythe, a black writer in L.A., used the terms *ethnic* and *ethnic history* in 1933 the way we use them today; see Forsythe, "The Rising Sun," unpublished ms., first paragraph of full text, Forsythe collection, Box 3, HEH.

13. Among the many works dealing broadly with racism, see Joe Feagin and Hernan Vera, *White Racism: The Basics* (New York: Routledge, 1994); Debra Van Ausdale and Joe Feagin, *The First R: How Children Learn Race and Racism* (Lanham, MD: Rowman and Littlefield, 2000); Michael Omi and Howard Winant, *Racial Formation in the United States: From the 1960s to the 1990s*, 2nd ed. (New York: Routledge, 1994); Donald Noel, "A Theory of the Origin of Ethnic Stratification," *Social Problems* 16 (1968): 157–72. A useful review of the literature is J. Morgan Kousser, "Social Scientific and Historical Models of Race Relations," paper presented for the annual convention of the Organization of American Historians, Washington, D.C., April 1990 (copy in author's possession). I have benefited from these studies, but the authors listed here would not necessarily agree with my interpretation their work. My own schema about the three aspects of racism does not consciously follow any theoretical model, although I recognize that some theory is embedded in my ideas. Put simply, I have based my views about racism on the experiences of black Angelenos during the half century I have studied.

14. *The [Redlands] Colored Citizen*, July 1, 1905.

15. Cose, *Rage*; George, *Crystal*, 219.

16. Demaratus, *Force*, 106.

Arrival

Section epigraph: Scruggs, *Man*, 62.

1. Bass, *Forty*, 27.

2. Fogelson, *Fragmented*, pt. 1, provides a thorough discussion of the city's growth; Rolle, *Los Angeles*, a brief version. See also Deverell, *Railroad Crossing: Californians and the Railroad, 1850–1910* (Berkeley: University of California Press, 1994), chap. 4, and Kevin Starr, *Material Dreams: Southern California through the 1920s* (New York: Oxford University Press, 1990), pt. 1.

3. Because the information is scattered and contradictory, it will be helpful to identify my sources in some detail. When Charlotta worked for the Republican National Committee in 1940, she signed up for Social Security; the personal information on the application form was typewritten, but Charlotta signed it herself and added bits of extra information in her own handwriting. This document says she was born Feb. 14, 1890, in Little Compton (Newport County), Rhode Island. Her parents are listed as Joseph Spear and Catherine Durant. Charlotta A. Bass, Application for Social Security Account Number, Oct. 14, 1940, photocopy in author's possession. (Copies of Social Security applications are available from the federal government upon request; I used the request program provided through Ancestry.com.)

Cairns, *Front-Page*, 153–54, n. 16, reveals that Charlotta's Los Angeles County death certificate gives her birthplace as Ohio, and that her cemetery records (at Evergreen Cemetery in Los Angeles) also list her birthplace as Ohio and give her birth date as Feb. 14, 1874. Cairns (80) also notes the inconsistency of Spear and Spears.

Streitmatter, *Raising*, 96, gives the Feb. 14, 1874, birth date but says her place of birth was Sumter, South Carolina, and that her parents were Hiram and Kate Spear (no "s").

Sharynn Owens Etheridge's entry "Charlotta Spears Bass" in *Notable Black American Women*, ed. Jessie Carney Smith (Detroit: Gale Research, 1992), says she was born in Sumter, South Carolina, but gives her birth date as October 1880.

Marriage Record for Joseph B. Bass and "Charlotte A. Spearin" [*sic*], Aug. 1914, San Diego County, California, gives Charlotta's age as thirty-two, which would mean a birth year of 1882. I viewed this record online, Feb. 2, 2003, through RootsWeb.com, an Ancestry.com search engine.

U.S. Census ms., 1920, Los Angeles City, Assembly District 74, Precinct 75, ED 417, p. 1A, lists Charlotta's age as thirty-six (meaning a birth year of 1884), her state of birth as Rhode Island, and no knowledge of her parents' place of birth.

U.S. Census ms., 1930, Los Angeles City, Assembly District 60, [no precinct], ED 752, p. 10A, lists Charlotta's age as forty (meaning a birth year of 1890), her state of birth as Rhode Island, her father's state of birth as Massachusetts, and her mother's state of birth as simply "Carolina." It also says Charlotta was twenty-four years old when she was married; because we know she married Joe Bass in 1914, this information squares with an 1890 birth year.

Various online biographical sketches also disagree. For example: *Encarta Africana*, which basically reprints the entry for Charlotta Bass that was published in *Africana* (203–4), says she was born to Hiram and Kate Spears in South Carolina, and gives no birth date (http://africana.com/research/encarta/tt_602 .asp [May 2004]); *Britannica Online* gives the name as Spears and provides a birth date of 1880 in Sumter, South Carolina (http://britannica.com/women/ articles/ Bass_Charlotta.html [May 2004]); the *Online Archive of California*, drawing on the biographical sketch prepared for the Charlotta A. Bass Papers archived at the Southern California Library for Social Studies and Research in Los Angeles, claims that Charlotta Spears was born in Little Compton, Rhode Island, in 1874 (www.oac.cdlib.org/findaid/ark:/13030/tf6c60052d/bioghist/ 46603373 [May 2004]).

Charlotta saw and signed off on her Social Security information; we cannot be certain she actually gave information to the census takers and clerks. It is certain she did *not* give the information for the 1930 census, because that document lists Joe's occupation as "Proprietor, Printing Shop" and Charlotta's as "None"—and neither of them would have given such answers.

4. For this and the following paragraphs on the city's origins, I have drawn

from Forbes, "Early African Heritage," in de Graaf, Mulroy, and Taylor, *Seeking*, 73–97; Bass, *Forty*, 1–5 (and material following 198); Richard Griswold del Castillo, *The Los Angeles Barrio, 1850–1890: A Social History* (Berkeley and Los Angeles: University of California Press, 1979), chap. 1; McWilliams, *Southern*, chap. 3; Douglas Monroy, *Thrown among Strangers: The Making of Mexican Culture in Frontier California* (Berkeley and Los Angeles: University of California Press, 1990), pt. 2; Wheeler, *Black*, chaps. 1–2; John Caughey and La-Ree Caughey, *Los Angeles: Biography of a City* (Berkeley and Los Angeles: University of California Press, 1977), 63–78; and Nugent, *Into*, 39–40.

5. Forbes, "Early," 80. On the Mesas and Quinteros, I connected Forbes with Caughey and Caughey, *Los Angeles*, 71.

6. Pitt and Pitt, *Los Angeles*, 371–72; real estate value in U.S. Census ms., 1860, Los Angeles City, p. 72.

7. This paragraph and those that follow draw on Demaratus, *Force*, the definitive work on the lives of Hannah, Biddy Mason, and the trial discussed below; for these paragraphs, see esp. chaps. 1, 3, 5, and 7.

8. Demaratus, *Force*, 113.

9. U.S. Census ms., 1860, Los Angeles City, pp. 46, 68, 71–72.

10. Demaratus, *Force*, 185–93; Mesmer letter quoted in Bass, *Forty*, 114–17.

11. Dumke, *Boom*; Pitt and Pitt, *Los Angeles*, 53–54, 478; Fogelson, *Fragmented*, 66–67; Nugent, *Into*, 93–95.

12. Bass, *Forty*, 37.

13. Anderson, *Development*, ch. 4, largely informs this and the following paragraph. (Temple quote, 55, italics in the original.)

14. Anderson, *Development*, 54, seems to suggest that the Forum moved from Wall Street to Central Avenue around 1910, but as late as fall 1914, local Race papers still advertised the meetings at the Odd Fellows Hall; see, *New Age*, Oct. 16, 1914.

15. Here and the paragraphs following: Bass, *Forty*, 28–31.

16. *CE*, Nov. 9, 1934.

17. Information in this and following paragraphs: *CE*, July 13, Aug. 24, 1928, and Nov. 9, 1934; Lang, "Nearly," 50–57; Taylor, *Search*, 211–21; Bass, *Forty*, 32.

18. The date of Bass's first marriage is calculated from U.S. Census ms., 1930, Los Angeles City, Assembly District 60, ED 752, p. 10A, which states that he was first married at age thirty-three.

19. Louis R. Harlan, *Booker T. Washington: The Making of a Black Leader, 1856–1901* (New York: Oxford University Press, 1972), and *Booker T. Washington: The Wizard of Tuskegee, 1901–1915* (New York: Oxford University Press, 1983); and Booker T. Washington, *Up from Slavery: An Autobiography* (1901. Reprint, New York: Modern Library, 1999).

20. Lewis, *Du Bois: Biography*; Gatewood, *Aristocrats*, 309–13; Du Bois, *The Souls of Black Folk* (1903. Reprint, New York: Vintage, 1990), chap. 3.

21. Lang, "Nearly," 57.

22. "Beulah Land": Sides, *L.A. City*, 15, quoting *CE*, Nov. 24, 1933. "Big man": Bass, *Forty*. Marriage Record for Joseph B. Bass, San Diego County, California. "A life partnership": *CE*, Nov. 9, 1934 (Joe's obituary, probably written by Charlotta); *Montana Plaindealer*, 1911.

23. Bass, *Forty*, 32. One eulogy for Joe Bass praised him for his principled refusal to squelch Charlotta's work: *CE*, Nov. 9, 1934.

24. Lang, "Nearly," 53; Bass, *Forty*, 31.

25. U.S. Census ms., 1920, Los Angeles City, Assembly District 74, Precinct 75, ED 417, p. 1A.

1. Southern Roots, Western Dreams

1. Kousser, *Shaping*; Lewis, *Du Bois: Biography*, 373.

2. Beasley, *Negro*, 258–59; Vivian, "American Guide," 2–3; Bass, *Forty*, 33–35; U.S. Census ms., 1870, St. Louis [MO] City, subdivision II, p. 339; U.S. Census ms., 1880, New Bedford, Bristol County, MA, ED 111, p. 42; U.S. Census ms., 1920, Los Angeles City, Precinct 514, ED 341, p. 3A.

3. Rice, *Negro*, 93; Bass, *Forty*, 33; Beasley, *Negro*, 258–59; Vivian, "American Guide," 2 ("fearless"); Robert J. Fehrenbach, "William Edgar Easton's *Dessalines:* A Nineteenth-Century Drama of Black Pride," *CLA Journal* 19 (1975): 75–89.

4. Kousser, *Shaping*, chap. 1; Hall et al., *Oxford*, 932; C. Vann Woodward, *Origins of the New South, 1877–1913* (Baton Rouge: Louisiana State University Press, 1951), and *The Strange Career of Jim Crow* (New York: Oxford University Press, 1955).

5. Rice, *Negro*; Kousser, *Shaping*; Beasley, *Negro*, 258; Bass, *Forty*, 33 (quotes).

6. Beavers oral history (UCLA), 1–3.

7. Doyle, *New*; Ronald H. Bayor, *Race and the Shaping of Twentieth-Century Atlanta* (Chapel Hill: University of North Carolina Press, 1996); Hunter, *'Joy*; Gary M. Pomerantz, *Where Peachtree Meets Sweet Auburn: A Saga of Race and Family* (New York: Penguin Books, 1996).

8. Doyle, *New*; Bayor, *Race*; Jonathan W. McLeod, *Workers and Workplace Dynamics in Reconstruction-Era Atlanta: A Case Study* (Los Angeles: Center for Afro-American Studies, University of California, Los Angeles, 1989); Kousser, *Shaping*; Lewis, *Du Bois: Biography*, 226.

9. Beavers oral history (UCLA), 3; Franklin M. Garrett, *Atlanta and Environs: A Chronicle of Its People and Events*, vol. 2 (New York: Lewis Historical Publishing, 1954), 423–34; Hunter, *'Joy*, 47, 49.

10. Gottlieb, *Making*; Grossman, *Land*; Kimberley L. Phillips, *Alabama North: African-American Migrants, Community, and Working-Class Activism in Cleveland, 1915–45* (Champaign: University of Illinois Press, 2000).

11. Beavers oral history (UCLA), 1–3; *Atlanta Independent*, April 22, 1905.

12. This and subsequent paragraphs based on Bontemps, "Why I Returned,"

1–10; also see Bontemps, "The Awakening"; Jones, *Renaissance;* Flamming, "Westerner"; Bontemps oral history (Shockley).

13. Arna Bontemps to Verna Arvey, Dec. 29, 1941, Still-Arvey Collection, University of Arkansas, cited in Madison and Smith, "Introducing Harold Bruce Forsythe," 3, Forsythe Papers, HEH.

14. Bass, *Forty,* 12; *NA,* July 23, 1915; Fisher, "History," 174, citing *Liberator,* January 1904; *LAT,* Sept. 29, 1888; de Graaf, "City," 330; Taylor, *Search,* 207.

15. See, among many others, Grossman, *Land;* Spear, *Chicago;* Gottlieb, *Making;* Kusmer, *Ghetto;* Trotter, ed, *Great.*

16. Ralph Bunche obituary in the *New York Times Obituary Index,* vol. 2, 1969–78, (New York: New York Times, n.d.), 5–6; Charles Matthews oral history.

17. *Dir.,* 89.

18. Hawkins oral history (Vasquez), 1–8.

19. Ibid., 8–12. Shreveport resident quoted in unpublished ms., Hawkins collection, UCLA.

20. Hawkins oral history (Vasquez), 15–16.

21. Beavers oral history (UCLA).

22. The national conscription law passed for World War I required all males ages twenty-one to thirty-one—U.S. citizens or not—to register at their neighborhood draft board or face stiff penalties. Registrants wrote information about themselves on a thick, preprinted card, about the size of a large note card. If they were illiterate, a draft board volunteer asked them the questions and the registrants signed with an X. Besides the obvious information—name, age, address— the registration cards required information on exact place of birth. Only the cards used for the first draft registration (there were two later, smaller ones) asked this question.

This information on place of birth forms the basis of my migration analysis. Race was a question all registrants were asked about, but there was more. The bottom left corner of each card was set off by a diagonal dotted line, forming a triangle in the corner. Small print within the triangle instructed draft board clerks to tear off that corner if the registrant was "of African descent"—creating a simple method for the draft board to find, avoid, or segregate black registrants. The registration cards for every city or county in the United States are preserved in their original boxes at the National Archives, Southeastern branch, Carrollton, Georgia. The cards from all draft boards in Los Angeles were filed together alphabetically. Seeking a 5 percent sample of the entire city of Los Angeles, I estimated the number of cards per box and the number of boxes for the city and then calculated the number of cards I needed to use from each box, which equaled one card for each inch of cards packed in any given box. The number of cards in my sample—fifty-five hundred—did approximate a 5 percent sample and contained registration cards for nearly five hundred African Americans, a slight over sample. I defined "the South" as the former Confederate states and used 1890 census figures to determine if someone's birthplace was rural or urban. The cen-

sus definition for "urban" at that time was an incorporated place with a population of 2,500 or more; by that standard, most Americans lived in rural places
until 1920.

23. Bontemps oral history (Shockley); Adams, *Dark;* Charles Matthews oral
history; Miriam Matthews oral history; Hawkins interview (Flamming); on Nelson White, see SLA, photo S-000–339, and Marilyn White oral history.

24. Bond, "Negro," 77; BC, *Negro,* 473.

25. Du Bois, "Colored," 193; numerous photographs in SLA, and the Miriam
Matthews collection, AAHM.

26. Gottlieb and Wolt, *Thinking,* pt. 1; Pitt and Pitt, *Los Angeles,* 371; Stimson, *Rise.*

27. *LAT,* "The Constitutional Amendments," Oct. 31, 1886, "The Solid
South," Nov. 17, 1888, and "Colored Men for the Police Force," April 3, 1889.

28. *CE,* Sept. 5, 1903.

29. *LAT,* Oct. 21, 1901, sec. 1, p. 8.

30. Ibid.

31. Ibid.

32. *LAT,* April 30, 1905, sec. 2, p. 4.

33. *LAT,* Feb. 9, 1909, sec. 2 (advertisement promoting special edition); Feb.
12, 1909 (the Lincoln Centenary Number; section 3 covers black Los Angeles).

34. *LAT,* Feb. 12, 1909, sec. 3, p. 1. On extinction theories, see Frederickson,
Black, and Lewis, *Du Bois: Biography;* on the *Mission Play,* see Pitt and Pitt,
Los Angeles, 319, and Deverell and Flamming, "Race," 123–24.

35. *CE,* March 13, 1915. *LAT,* Oct. 21, 1901, sec. 1, p. 8.

36. Deverell and Flamming, "Race," 117–43.

37. *Weekly Observer,* Oct. 20, 1888; *Western News,* Nov. 16, 1889.

38. F. H. Crumbly, "A Los Angeles Citizen," *Colored American Magazine*
9 (Sept. 1905): 482–85.

39. E. H. Rydall, "California for Colored Folks," *Colored American Magazine* 12 (May 1907): 386.

40. *CE,* Dec. 17, 1921; see also Nov. 23, 1918.

41. *NA,* March 25, 1915; see also Oct. 9, 1914.

42. Scruggs, *Man,* 58, chaps. 4–5.

43. Ibid., 61–62.

44. *NA,* July 23, 1915.

45. *Western Dispatch,* Oct. 6, 1921.

46. Thompson, "Horn," 215, 220.

47. *Crisis,* Jan. 1916, 145.

48. Marilyn White oral history. The granddaughter of George and Ella, Marilyn White, found the lynching postcards in the top dresser drawer of her father when she was a young girl. When she asked her father, Ela Nelson White,
what they were, he could barely answer through tears. The photos had been
passed to him by his parents. If he knew the full story of his father's ordeal, he
spared Marilyn the details, which remain unknown.

49. Marilyn White oral history; original envelope and postcards of Temple

mob in Marilyn White's possession; lynching postcard in SLA photo no. A-006–826.1.

2. The Conditions of Heaven

1. Bass, *Forty*, 13.
2. Beavers oral history (UCLA), 9.
3. Vivian, "American Guide," 3; Bass, *Forty*, 34–35.
4. Bass, *Forty*, 34–35; *Crisis*, Dec. 1915; Beasley, *Negro*, 259.
5. Beavers oral history (UCLA), 1–2, 7.
6. Ibid., 4–6.
7. Ibid., 6–9, 14 (quote, 8).
8. Ibid., 1–35; Beasley, *Negro*, 168–69.
9. Adler, "Watts," 49–50, 101, table V.6, and chap. 4; Bontemps, "Why," 5–6.
10. For the Furlong Tract, see Adler, "Watts," 280, n. 24; Bontemps, "Why," 5–6.
11. Bontemps, *Black*, xxiii; Jones, *Renaissance*, 9, 36; Flamming, "Westerner."
12. *LAT*, June 18, 1906, sec. 1, p. 4, and June 24, 1906, sec. 2, pp. 1, 2; *NA*, ads during 1914.
13. Bond, "Negro"; de Graaf, "City"; Garcia, "Adaptation."
14. De Graaf, "City," 328–29; Bass, *Forty*, 33.
15. Bond, "Negro," 23–24 (n. 44), 26, 47; Bass, *Forty*, 13–14, citing *Liberator*, Jan.–Feb. 1904. "Residential intermingling," rather common in Dixie, was no guarantee of good conditions; see Kusmer, *Ghetto*, 173, and LeeAnn Bishop Lands, "Class, Race, and the Workers' City: Atlanta, 1880–1920" (Ph.D. diss., Georgia Institute of Technology, 2001), chap. 3.
16. Bond, "Negro," 68–69.
17. Ibid., 70; *LAT*, Aug. 3, 1905, sec. 2, p. 1; Rydall, "California," 387; *Los Angeles Record*, Jan. 15, 1908; *Los Angeles Express*, Jan. 15, 1908; *Crisis*, Oct. 1912; *CE*, July 27, 1952.
18. Bond, "Negro," 93. These comments are from ca. 1930; I use them here to convey the varied sentiments held by white home owners throughout the early twentieth century.
19. Vose, *Caucasians*, vii.
20. Scruggs, *Man*, 87.
21. The occupational figures that inform this section and the next section, "Opportunities for Men," are calculated from statistics presented in BC, *Occupations*, 590–93; BC, *Twelfth*, table 23; BC, *Thirteenth*, 560–61; BC, *Fourteenth*, 1129–32.
22. In 1900, the portion of the black workforce comprising women was 54 percent in Atlanta, 31 percent in Los Angeles. In 1920, that percentage had fallen to 44 percent in Atlanta, but was still lower—37 percent—in Los Angeles.
23. Adams, *Dark*, 165.
24. Helen Eastman Martin, *The History of the Los Angeles County Hospi-*

tal (1878–1968) and the Los Angeles County–USC Medical Center (1968–1975) (Los Angeles: USC Press, 1979), 220–22; *Crisis,* April and May 1912.

25. U.S. Census ms., 1920, Los Angeles City, Assembly District 74, Precinct 84, ED 420, p. 1B; Cox, *Central,* 50, 191–92, 304–7.

26. In the 1910s, the railroad companies operating in Los Angeles, which had previously hired very few black laborers, switched course and began to hire African Americans as general laborers. By 1920, nearly 130 black Angelenos were working on local tracks.

27. *Western News,* Dec. 7, 1889; Taylor, *Search,* 201; Bates, *Pullman,* chap. 1. It was understood that light-complexioned men would receive the dining car positions, and the U.S. Census manuscripts often show this correlation. For example, in the 1920 Census for Los Angeles, Fred Thornton is listed as a "mulatto" and a dining car waiter for Pullman; U.S. Census ms., Los Angeles City, 1920, Assembly District 74, Precinct 61–62, ED 411, p. 10B.

28. Scruggs, *Man,* 68, 76–77.

29. Alexander, *Abbot,* 215.

30. Adams, *Dark,* chap. 5.

31. *Southern California Guide,* Jan. 16, 1892; *CE,* June 20, 1914; *NA,* July 23, Sept. 17, 1915.

32. Alexander, *Abbot,* 216.

33. Anderson, *Development,* 62, n. 32; A similar shift occurred in wartime Seattle, but it did not hold; see Taylor, *Forging.*

34. *LAT* Jan., 20, 1904, sec. 2, p. 2; April 9, 1904, sec. 2, p. 2 (quote); May 1, 1907, sec. 2, pp. 1, 3.

35. Bond, "Negro," 67.

36. *Western News,* Dec. 7, 1889.

37. Garcia, "Adaptation," 63–66, chap. 3; *LAT,* Nov. 5, 1905, sec. 2, p. 1; *Southern California Guide,* Jan. 16, 1892.

38. Scruggs, *Man,* 70–72.

39. Ibid., 72–73, 81 (quote).

40. *LAT,* Sept. 24, 1913.

41. U.S. Census ms., 1920, Los Angeles City, Assembly District 74, Precinct 75, ED 417, p. 1A.

42. Garcia, "Adaptation," 61–66; *CE,* Jan. 31, June 20, and Dec. 19, 1914.

43. Beavers oral history (UCLA), 33–35; Bond, "Negro," 67.

44. Scruggs, *Man,* 74; *NA,* Sept. 4, 1914.

45. *Crisis,* July 1912.

46. A. J. Davis to Hon. Myer [*sic*] Lissner, Aug. 4, 1912, Meyer Lissner Papers.

47. *LAT,* Feb. 9, 16, and 22, April 20, 22, 24, 1902; Nov. 5, 1903, sec. 2, p. 1; Jan. 26, 1906, sec. 2, p. 1; *Los Angeles Herald,* March 13, 15, April 12, 29, 1902.

48. Robert Moats Miller, *Bishop G. Bromley Oxnam: Paladin of Liberal Protestantism* (Nashville, Tenn.: Abingdon Press, 1990), 456; *Los Angeles Express,* May 10, 1904 (concurrent incidents: Dec. 16, 1903, and Jan. 15, 1904).

49. *NA,* Oct. 24, 1913, cited in Fisher, "History," 191–92.

50. *CE*, Dec. 13, 1913 (for similar survey results, see *CE*, Sept. 12, 1914); Fisher, "History," 190–91.

51. *CE*, Oct. 3, 1914 (for similar cases before and after, see *LAT*, Jan. 14, 1904, sec. 1, p. 12; *CE*, March 31, 1923).

52. Somerville, *Man*, 65–66.

53. Ibid., 64–71.

54. Ibid., 157.

55. *LAT*, Feb. 24, 1903, sec. 1, p. 6, and Oct. 1, 1908, sec. 2, p. 2; Cripps, *Slow*, 44.

56. *LAT*, Oct. 1, 1908, sec. 2, p. 2; Oct. 25, 1908, sec. 2, p. 7.

57. *LAT*, Oct. 25, 1908, sec. 2, p. 7.

58. Cripps, *Slow*, 45–46, chap. 2; Michael Rogin, *Blackface, White Noise: Jewish Immigrants in the Hollywood Melting Pot* (Berkeley and Los Angeles: University of California Press, 1996), chap. 4; Steven J. Ross, "How Hollywood Became Hollywood: Money, Politics, and Movies," in *Metropolis*, ed. Sitton and Deverell, 255–76.

59. Bass, *Forty*, 35–36.

60. *NA*, Jan. 22, 1915; *CE*, Jan. 30, 1915.

61. City Council Petitions, 1915, new series, vol. 788, nos. 379 and 380, LACA.

62. Ibid., no. 381.

63. City Council Minutes, vol. 99, Wednesday, Feb. 3, 1915, 300–301, LACA. The Board of Censors had been created in 1913 "to inspect nickelodeons, arcades, etc., where pictures were displayed, [and] to examine motion picture films." In 1915, the board became the Municipal Picture Censorship Commission; in 1916, a single commissioner replaced the commission. See Hunter, *Evolution*, 142–43, 165.

64. City Council Minutes, vol. 99, Thursday, Feb. 4, 1915, 319, LACA; *NA*, Feb. 5, 12, 1915.

65. Taylor, *Search*, 238–39; Cripps, *Slow*, 52; City Council Minutes, vol. 102, Nov. 30, 1915, 600, LACA.

66. Bass, *Forty*, 35.

67. *NA*, Feb. 5, 1915; Bass, *Forty*, 42 (quote).

68. Johnson oral history (UCLA), 39–45, 108–36, 270–73; *CE*, June 13, 1924; Cripps, *Slow*, 75–89.

69. Bontemps and Conroy, *Anyplace*, 269.

3. Claiming Central Avenue

1. *CE*, Jan. 16, 1915, and April 8, 1916; Owen, "From," 409.

2. In an effort to analyze demographics and neighborhood development in the 74th Assembly District, I tabulated every individual in the district as listed in the U.S. Census manuscripts for 1920. Having done so, I discovered that the census enumerators who went door to door actually *failed to include* a large

cluster of precincts that were within the 74th district boundaries, and they inaccurately *included* fourteen precincts from adjoining districts. In short, the published census figures for the 74th district in 1920 were wrong, and they have never been corrected. Those figures show that African American residents constituted 14 percent of the district's population. I have not yet been able to determine the correct percentage, which could be higher or lower. (I hope to be able to determine the correct population figures and to make them available in a future publication.) Given the errors, I estimate that the black population could have ranged anywhere from 10 to 20 percent. In any case, African Americans made up a small portion of the district's population, which is the point I am emphasizing in this paragraph.

3. *NA*, March 4, 1938.

4. Davis, *Company*, 84–88.

5. Hawkins oral history (Vasquez), 26.

6. Fogelson, *Fragmented*, 80.

7. Ibid., 83.

8. Alexander Saxton, *The Indispensable Enemy: Labor and the Anti-Chinese Movement in California* (1971; reprint, Berkeley and Los Angeles: University of California Press, 1995); Nugent, *Into*, 167; Chinese Historical Society of Southern California, *Linking Our Lives: Chinese American Women of Los Angeles* (Los Angeles: CHSSC, 1984), pt. 1.

9. Modell, *Economics*, 18; Fogelson, *Fragmented*, 76; Nugent, *Into*, 165–70; Valerie Matsumoto, "Japanese American Women in the Creation of Urban Nisei Culture in the 1930s," in *Over*, ed. Matsumoto and Allmendinger, 291–306; Roger Daniels, *The Politics of Prejudice: The Anti-Japanese Movement and the Struggle for Japanese Exclusion* (Berkeley and Los Angeles: University of California Press, 1962).

10. Nugent, *Into*, 162, 210; Gabler, *Empire*; Vorspan, *History*.

11. Gutierrez, *Walls*, 57; Sanchez, *Becoming*, chap. 1, and 73–77; Nugent, *Into*, 202.

12. *The Statutes of California and Amendments to the Code, 1911*, Extra Session, p. 163; *The Statutes of California and Amendments to the Code, 1926–27*, p. 1780. On the process of reapportionment, see Don A. Allen, Sr., *Legislative Sourcebook: The California Legislature and Reapportionment, 1849–1965* (Sacramento: Assembly of the State of California, 1966).

13. U.S. Census ms., 1920, Los Angeles City, Assembly District 74, Precinct 75, ED 417, p. 1A.

14. Ibid., Precinct 74, ED 417, pp. 7A (white residents), and 8–11 (other rooming houses); Precinct 75, p. 1A (black residents, including the Basses).

15. Ibid., Precinct 73, ED 417, p. 14B.

16. Ibid., Precinct 75, ED 417, pp. 3A–3B.

17. Somerville, *Man*, in the chapter "Social Equality," 100–21, discusses the issue of intermarriage at some length (quote, 108).

18. U.S. Census ms., 1920, Los Angeles City, Assembly District 74, Precinct 84, ED 420, p. 1B.

19. Ibid., Precinct 83, ED 421, p. 13A.

20. Ibid., Precinct 86, ED 422, p. 2A.

21. Ibid., Precinct 75, ED 417, has examples.

22. Ibid., Precinct 80, ED 419, p. 18A; see also Walter and Isula Hudson in ibid., Assembly District 74, Precinct 75, ED 417, p. 4B.

23. Bass, *Forty,* 16.

24. There are two surviving issues of the *Weekly Observer,* dated Oct. 13 (issue no. 15) and Oct. 20, 1888.

25. *Weekly Observer,* Oct. 20, 1888.

26. *Western News,* Dec. 7, 1889.

27. The only reference to the *Advocate* is in "An Unwanted Assault," *Weekly Observer,* Oct. 20, 1888.

28. *Weekly Observer,* Oct. 13, 1888.

29. Sampson's *Western News* had the exact motto and format as the *Weekly Observer.* His co-owner and editor was a Republican Party leader from Texas, Monroe Majors; see the State Historical Society of Wisconsin's newspaper database, titled African-American Newspapers and Periodicals: A National Bibliography and Union List. On Majors, see Logan and Winston, *Dictionary,* 421.

30. *Western News,* Nov. 30 and Dec. 7, 1889.

31. *Weekly Observer,* Oct. 13, 1888.

32. *LAT,* April 15, 1888.

33. *Weekly Observer,* Oct. 20, 1888.

34. *Southern California Guide,* Jan. 16, 1892 (inaugural issue, which states, "There has been no paper published in Southern California to champion the colored man's cause since the latter days of the 'boom,' but the steady increase in population and business of the colored people the past two years justifies us to once more enter the field of journalism." The Wisconsin newspaper database says the *Guide* folded in 1895.

35. The earliest surviving issue of Neimore's *Eagle* is Sept. 3, 1903, which identifies itself as vol. 12, no. 23—meaning that Neimore was counting, as part of the *Eagle*'s run, the *Southern California Guide* of the early 1890s. The Wisconsin newspaper database offers conflicting information on this: it shows the *Eagle* dating from 1888 (clearly referring to Neimore's *Advocate*), and the Basses' *California Eagle* dating from 1879 (the year of Neimore's *Owl*).

36. *Eagle,* Sept 3, 1903, and Dec. 15, 1906; these are the only surviving issues from Neimore's *Eagle.*

37. Lonnie G. Bunch, "'The Greatest State for the Negro': Jefferson L. Edmonds, Black Propagandist of the California Dream," in *Seeking,* ed. de Graaf, Mulroy, and Taylor, 129–48; Vivian, "American Guide," 3–4. Obituaries and eulogies for Edmonds include *CE,* Jan. 31, 1914, and (a later memorial service) *CE,* Jan. 16, 1915. On support of women's suffrage, see Flamming, "African," 208. Edmonds's surname was spelled inconsistently, as Edmond or Edmonds; Bunch, who interviewed family members, uses Edmonds, and I follow his lead here.

38. Entry for "Oscar Hudson" in Vivian, "American Guide," 5–6.

39. *NA,* Jan. 8, 1915, is the first surviving issue with this masthead. The mast-

head in 1914 was simply an American flag. The black Lady Liberty masthead endured, with slight variations, through World War I; see, e.g., *NA*, March 10, 1916, August 2, 1918.

40. "Edwin T. Earl (1856–1919)," in Pitt and Pitt, *Los Angeles*, p. 127; for Earl's influence in the *NA*, see the issues for late 1915, asking readers to support his dailies.

41. *CE*, Jan. 16, 1915.

42. *Oakland Sunshine* and *Western Outlook* on microfilm at University of California, Berkeley, Library; the *Colored Citizen* archived at the A. K. Smiley Public Library, Redlands, CA.

43. Miriam Matthews Collection, Box 1, photo no. 93.019–058, AAMLO. The caption on the back of the photo reads: "Citizens Band, Los Angeles, Calif., playing on San Pedro St. (between 1906 and 1909) in front of the New Age Publishing Co. (829 San Pedro St.) and the YMCA next door to the New Age office."

44. *NA*, Oct. 16, 1914.

45. My general views on the black church, expressed in this paragraph and the ones that follow, have been informed by numerous works, including John Blassingame, *The Slave Community: Plantation Life in the Antebellum South* (New York: Oxford University Press, 1972); Drake and Cayton, *Black*; C. Eric Lincoln and Lawrence H. Mamiya, *The Black Church in the African American Experience* (Durham, NC: Duke University Press, 1990); Myrdal, *American*; and Albert Raboteau, *Slave Religion: The "Invisible Institution" in the Antebellum South* (New York: Oxford University Press, 1978).

46. *Weekly Observer*, Oct. 20, 1888; *Wilson's Official Guide* [for 1901], 51–52.

47. *Weekly Observer*, Oct. 20, 1888; *Wilson's Official Guide* [for 1901], 49, 53.

48. Bond, "Negro," 29.

49. Bass, *Forty*, 16–20; Goins, "Ol' Time"; *Wilson's Official Guide* [for 1901], 50; *NA*, Oct. 16, 1914.

50. *CE*, Sept. 27, 1919, cited in Goins, "Ol' Time," 9, n. 20.

51. *Encyclopedia of American Religions*, 525–26; *NA*, Aug. 28, 1914, and Aug. 12, 1921; *CE*, Aug. 22 and 29, 1914.

52. *Religions*, 362–66.

53. Bass, *Forty*, 20–25; *Wilson's Official Guide* [for 1901], 51–52; *NA*, Oct. 16, 1914.

54. A photograph of the Eighth and Towne church is in Anderson, *Development*, app. C.

55. Bass, *Forty*, 22–23; Beavers oral history (UCLA), 28–29; Goins, "Ol' Time," 8, n. 17.

56. Tinney, "William," 213–25; Bass, *Forty*, 25–26; Pasadena *Star News*, April 4, 1992, B-6; Cecil M. Roebeck, Jr., "William J. Seymour and the Bible Evidence," in *Initial Evidence: Historical and Biblical Perspectives on the Pentecostal Doctrine of Spirit Baptism*, ed. Gary B. McGee (Peabody, MA: Hendrickson Publishers, 1991), 72–95.

57. Tinney, "William," 220–22.

58. A racial split in the 1920s destroyed the mission; see Tinney, "William," 222; Bass, *Forty*, 25–26.

59. *Religions*, 392; SLA photo S-000–184 shows the publishing house and its staff as they appeared in 1932.

60. *CE*, May 8, 1915.

61. Bass, *Forty*, 21, 13 (italics in the original); *CE*, Dec. 13, 1913.

62. Miriam Mathews oral history; Charles Matthews oral history; Beavers oral history (UCLA), 35–36.

63. Meier, *Negro Thought*, chap. 3.

64. *Weekly Observer*, Oct. 20, 1888.

65. *Western News*, Nov. 9, 1889.

66. *Southern California Guide*, Jan. 16, 1892; *CE*, Sept. 3, 1903.

67. *LAT*, Dec. 22 and 23, 1904.

68. *CE*, Sept. 3, 1903; *LAT*, Dec. 22, 1904 ("tinhorn sports").

69. For a similar conflict, see *CE* Dec. 11 and 18, 1915.

70. *CE*, Dec. 15, 1906.

71. Beavers oral history (UCLA), 33.

72. *NA*, March 5, May 14 and 22, 1915.

73. *CE*, Dec. 5, 1914; *NA*, Nov. 12, 1915, and Feb. 11, 1916.

74. *CE*, Dec. 5, 1914; Du Bois, "Colored," 194.

75. Beavers oral history (UCLA), 31 ("good business"); *CE*, Jan. 16, 1915 ("King"); *NA*, Sept. 4, 1914 ("dream").

76. *CE*, Nov. 20, 1915, and March 10, 1916.

77. *CE*, Feb. 12, April 8, 1916.

78. *NA*, Feb. 18, 1916.

79. *CE*, March 10, 1916; *NA*, March 3, 1916.

80. *CE*, April 8, 1916.

81. *CE*, Dec. 15, 1906.

82. The purpose of the survey was to determine if the *Eagle*'s advertisements reflected a practical, as opposed to rhetorical, interest in Race enterprise. What were the long-term trends in racial advertising? The *Eagle*'s extended run of issues made it particularly attractive for this analysis. I chose five-year intervals to gain a more precise sense of change over time, using 1915, 1925, 1930, 1935, and 1940. Most of the *Eagle* for 1920 is lost; the figures I give in the text for 1920 actually came from October, April, and July 1919 and January 1920. For each year, I surveyed four months in quarterly fashion, recording and coding all advertisements appearing in the first issue for January, April, July, and October. The data for all years combined contains information on 1,349 advertisements. Race ads were those that identified a business as a Race enterprise by photo, slogan, affiliations, name of business, or the surname of a person widely known in the black community (e.g., Sidney Dones). The percentage of advertisements identified as Race ads in each survey year: 1915 (5 percent), 1919–1920 (19 percent), 1925 (16 percent), 1930 (8 percent), 1935 (5 percent), and 1940 (6 percent).

83. *CE*, Oct. 4, 1919.

84. Ibid.

4. A Civic Engagement

1. Deverell and Flamming, "Race," 124–33.

2. Fisher, "History," 174.

3. *CE*, Dec. 21, 1921; *NA*, March 26, 1915.

4. *WD*, Oct. 6, 1921.

5. On the AAC nationally, see Thornbrough, "National"; Gatewood, *Aristocrats*, 307; Meier and Rudwick, *Plantation*, 172, 182. On the AAC at local and state levels, see Katzman, *Before*, 188, 192; Cox, *Blacks*, 134–35; Trotter, *Black*, 26.

6. On earlier civil rights organizations, see de Graaf, et al., introduction to *Seeking*, ed. de Graaf, Mulroy, and Taylor, 3–18; Rudolph M. Lapp, *Blacks in Gold Rush California* (New Haven, CT.: Yale University Press, 1977), chaps. 8–9; Philip S. Foner and George E. Walker, eds., *Proceedings of the Black State Conventions, 1840–1865*, vol. 2 (Philadelphia: Temple University Press, 1980), 110–203.

7. Crouchett, et al., *History*, 31; Stimson, *Rise*, 336–37; Lapp, *Afro-Americans*, 32–35, 108 n. 1.

8. *Western News*, Nov. 30 and Dec. 14, 1889.

9. The best collection of California AAC materials is in the George C. Pardee Papers, "Incoming Correspondence" group, Box 37, "Afro-American Council" file, Bancroft Library, University of California, Berkeley (hereafter cited as AAC File). See also Fisher, "History," 162–66, 180–82.

10. "The Afro-American Congress. What It Accomplished," news clipping, ca. August 1905, AAC File; *LAT*, Aug. 13, 1904, sec. 2, p. 5, and March 15, 1908, sec. 2, p. 6; Lapp, *Afro-Americans*, 34; *Pasadena News*, Aug. 18, 1903.

11. J. B. Wilson and F. W. Moore, State Executive Council [AAC] to Pardee, Aug. 28, 1902; Floyd H. Crumbly to Pardee, Dec. 12, 1905; Wilson to Pardee, Nov. 9, 1905, all in AAC File; *Pasadena News*, Aug. 18, 1903.

12. "T. A. Greene," in *Dir.*, 80; Covington, "Greene." For Prince, see U.S. Census mss., Los Angeles County, Pasadena City, 1900, and *Pasadena News*, Aug. 18, 1903.

13. Delegates listed in the *Pasadena News*, Aug. 18, 1903, traced to the U.S. census schedules of 1900 and the Los Angeles City Directory for 1903.

14. Except for newspaper editors, occupations were determined by the 1903 Los Angeles City Directory. Names were also traced to the directories for 1910 and 1922.

15. On Wilds, see Crouchett, et al., *History*, 10–11, 13.

16. The 1903 delegates were traced to the Los Angeles City Directories of 1910 and 1922; one-third could still be found in *Dir.* in 1930.

17. The AAC File is filled with letters sent to Governor Pardee between 1902

and 1905; the 1909 report is in *Oakland Sunshine*, Sept. 11, 1909; see also Anderson, *Development*, 30–33; Fisher, "Political Development," 260; Fisher, "History," 18–85; and *LAT*, March 13, 1904, sec. 1, p. 4; March 14, 1904, sec. 1, p. 5; March 16, 1904, sec. 2, p. 4; March 17, 1904, sec. 2, p. 8; March 18, 1904, sec. 2, p. 3.

18. Quotes in Beasley, *Negro*, 134–35; Fisher, "History," 184–85; Bass, *Forty*, 9.

19. James M. Alexander, "Appeal to Reason," attached to J. B. Wilson to Hon. Geo. C. Pardee, June 25, 1906; Alexander, "Official Call of the Afro-American State Congress, to Convene at Riverside, California, August 27–29, 1906," both in AAC File.

20. Alexander, "Appeal." Another AAC official made similar contrasts between new European immigrants and "the ten million loyal, faithful, generous-hearted, patriotic Negroes": *CE*, Aug. 22, 1914.

21. Alexander, "Official Call," and "Appeal."

22. United States Secret Service, Daily Report of Agent, Office of Los Angeles District, Oct. 16, 1911 (quote). Beasley, *Negro*, 273, 299.

23. *CE*, Aug. 22, Oct. 3 and 17, 1914; Aug. 8, 1915; *Crisis*, Oct. 1911, Oct. 1912; *Oakland Sunshine*, March 27, issues from May through August, and Sept. 18 (last reference to the AAC), 1915.

24. [Iantha Villa Mays, State Historian of California CWC,] *History, California Association of Colored Women's Clubs, Inc., 1906–1955* (n.p., ca. 1955), p. 4, in Records of the NACW, microfilm version, pt. 1, frame 181 (hereafter cited as *CWC History*); *75 Years of Progress of the California State Association of Colored Women's Clubs, 1906–1981*, p. 50, in Records of the NACW, pt. 1, frame 227 (hereafter cited as *75 Years*). The acronyms for the state and national organizations changed over time or were simply used differently: Mays's 1955 history uses NACW for the national organization and CSACW for the California organization; *75 Years* uses NACW and CSACWC.

25. For larger trends in Colored Women's Clubs, see Cynthia Neverdon-Morton, *Afro-American Women of the South and the Advancement of the Race, 1895–1925* (Knoxville: University of Tennessee Press, 1989); Deborah Gray White, "The Cost of Club Work, the Price of Black Feminism," in *Visible Women: New Essays on American Activism*, ed. Nancy A. Hewitt and Suzanne Lebsock (Urbana: University of Illinois Press, 1993), 247–69; Taylor, *Search*, 219–21.

26. *LAT*, March 26, 1901, sec. 1, p. 11; Feb. 16, 1902, sec. 3, p. 8; Feb. 9, 1906, sec. 3, p. 4 (quote).

27. *LAT*, Feb. 22, 1902, sec. 1, p. 8 (Graves quote); April 20, 1902, sec. 3, p. 4 (*Times* quote).

28. *LAT*, April 21, 1902, sec. 1, p. 5; April 22, 1902, sec. 1, p. 6.

29. *LAT*, April 24, 1902, sec. 2, p. 7; Jan. 26, 1906, sec. 2, p. 1.

30. *CWC History*, 6–7 (frame 182); *75 Years*, 50 (frame 227); *National Association Notes*, Oct. 1908, Nov. 1911, Feb. 1912, June 1913 (Margaret Washington, "National Association of Colored Women's Clubs," quote p. 5). The *National Association Notes* provides information on clubs at the state and local

level; issues of the *Notes* are available in the microfilmed Records of the NACW, pt. 1, reel 23 (hereafter cited as *Notes*).

31. *Notes*, Feb. 1912 (list of state officers with addresses; most from Los Angeles lived in the West Jefferson district); *NA*, Nov. 12, 1920: of the ten women heading up "local units," nine lived in the 74th district, only one in the West Jefferson neighborhood.

32. *Notes*, June 1913, p. 7.

33. *CE*, June 20, 1914.

34. *Notes*, Feb. 1912.

35. *CE*, June 20, 1914 ("no bad boys"); *NA*, June 26, 1914 (all other quotes); *WD*, Oct. 6, 1921.

36. *LAT*, Jan. 26, 1906, sec. 2, p. 1; *CWC History*, pp. 8–9 (frames 183–84); *Notes*, May 1913; *CE*, June 20, 1914; *NA*, June 26, 1914. The name of the home varied in the press: Sojourner Truth Home, Sojourner Truth Industrial Home, Sojourner Industrial Home, Sojourner Truth Home for Working Girls. For expansion plans, see *WD*, Oct. 6, 1921. In 1939 the home hosted a CWC convention: see *CE*, May 25, 1939.

37. *WD*, Oct. 6, 1921.

38. *CE*, May 11, 1918.

39. Bass, *Forty*, 95.

40. *Notes*, June 1913, p. 7.

41. Ibid., May ("assist our women") and June ("our attitude") 1913; see also Lewis, *Du Bois: Biography*, 419.

42. *NA*, Nov. 12, 1920; *75 Years*, 51.

43. Lewis, *Du Bois: Biography*, chap. 14 (quote, 389).

44. Ibid., chap. 14, esp. 405–7.

45. Ibid., chaps. 15, 17; for subscription figures, see 416, 474, 514, 544.

46. *Crisis*, Aug. 1913; Lewis, *Du Bois: Biography*, 479.

47. Ceruti to Du Bois, Sept. 24, 1913, in BF Box 151 folder "1913–1917."

48. Somerville to [May Childs] Nerney [NAACP secretary], Dec. 8, 1913, in BF 15: 1913–1917.

49. Somerville, *Man*, 96–97.

50. Somerville to Nerney, Dec. 8, 1913, in BF 15: 1913–1917; Somerville, *Man*, 81.

51. Nerney to Ceruti, May 26, 1914; Nerney to Ceruti, June 13, 1914; "Constitution of the Los Angeles Branch of the National Association for the Advancement of Colored People," adopted [by the local branch] July 1, 1914 [and officially approved by the national board Aug. 31, 1914], all in BF 15: 1913–1917.

52. Somerville, *Man*, 81, gets the order backward, placing Johnson as the first president.

53. Du Bois, "Colored," 193; Somerville, *Man*, 81. There are no letters from, or any mention of, Locke or Johnson in the Los Angeles branch files from 1913 through 1919. References to Locke might have been lost, for the branch files for Los Angeles are empty from mid-1914 to mid-1917 (BF 15: 1913–1917, 1918–1919). *The Annual of the Los Angeles Branch of the National Association for*

the Advancement of Colored People, Year 1917 (Los Angeles: n.p. [Charles Alexander], 1918), in BF 15: Clippings, 1920 [which actually contains materials from ca. 1918 to 1922].

54. Local officers are listed on correspondence letterhead; see BF 15: 1913–1917, 1918–1919, 1920–1922; see also *Annual* for 1917, in BF: Clippings, 1920.

55. E. Burton Ceruti to Roy Nash, March 3, 1917; Roy Nash to Mr. E. Burton Ceruti, March 15, 1917, both in BF 15: 1913–1917.

56. Thompson to Nash, March 7, 1917, in BF 15: 1913–1917.

57. Fisher, "History," 193–97.

58. Lewis, *Du Bois: Biography,* 507.

59. Ceruti to James W. Johnson, Jan. 5, 1918 (Ceruti enclosed a description of the film, but none was found in the files); Acting Secretary to Ceruti, Jan. 16, 1918, both in BF 15: 1918–1919; undated news clipping titled "Ordinance Number 37778" in BF 15: Clippings, 1920.

60. Los Angeles City Council, Ordinance No. 37778 (New Series), Dec. 24, 1917, LACA.

61. For support sent to East St. Louis, see letters dated March 9, March 23, July 9, July 22, Aug. 9, Sept. 19, Oct. 4, and Oct. 18, 1918, all in BF 15: 1918–1919. For support to Chicago, see [Beatrice Thompson,] "Secretary's Report," Nov. 24, 1919, in BF 15: 1918–1919. For antilynching legislation, see the Branch Bulletin for Oct. 18, 1918 (attached to Thompson to Mary White Ovington, Oct. 18, 1918), in BF 15: 1918–1919, and various news items in BF 15: Clippings, 1920. For segregation in Washington, D.C., see Ceruti to Johnson, June 1917; Acting Secretary to Ceruti, June 25, 1917; and Ceruti to Johnson, July 17, 1917, all in BF 15: 1913–1917.

62. See letters dated March 7 and Oct. 7 1917, and Thompson to Nash, March 7, 1917, in BF 15: 1913–1917; see also Thompson's "Branch Bulletin" reports to the national office, Oct. 18, 1918, and Nov. 24, 1919, in BF 15: 1918–1919.

63. Du Bois, "Colored," 193.

64. Thompson to Ovington, May 10, 1920, in BF 15: 1920–1922.

65. Ibid.

66. Ibid.; Sanchez, *Becoming;* Model, *Economics;* and Gutierrez, *Walls,* show no connections between the Asian or ethnic Mexican communities and the NAACP in this era.

67. Ceruti to Johnson, June 18, 1917, BF 15: 1913–1917. Thompson to [John R.] Shillady, April 23, 1918; Assistant Secretary [Walter White] to Thompson, May 4, 1918; Ceruti to Johnson, April 25, 1918; Thompson to Ovington, Oct. 18, 1918, all in BF 15: 1918–1919. An increase of 115 new members is noted in Thompson to Shillady, Secy., June 22, 1918; the total figure for 1918 is an estimate based on Thompson's annual report, Nov. 24, 1919, both in BF 15: 1918–1919.

68. Ceruti to Shillady, Jan. 9, 1919, in BF 15: 1918–1919.

69. *CE,* Jan. 31, 1914; Bond, "Negro," 28; *Los Angeles Record,* Jan. 6, 1903 (Booker), and Feb. 1, 1906 (Margaret).

70. Shillady to Ceruti, Jan. 20, 1919, BF 15: 1918–1919.

71. Lewis, ed., *Portable*, 749–50; James Weldon Johnson, *Along This Way: The Autobiography of James Weldon Johnson* (New York: Penguin Books, 1990; originally published 1933).

72. Thompson, "Secretary's Report—December 1918–November 1919," Nov. 24, 1919, in BF 15: 1918–1919.

73. On covenants, see Nieman, *Promises*; Vose, *Caucasians*; Miller, *Petitioners*; Hall et al., eds., *Oxford*, 96.

74. *CE*, May 27, 1916, and July 19, 1919; *NA*, Jan. 7, 1916.

75. *CE*, May 27, 1916.

76. Ibid.

77. *Annual*, 1917, 10–12, in BF 15: Clippings, 1920.

78. *Title Guarantee & Trust v. Garrott* (1919) 42 Cal. App. 152, 183 Pac. 470. *CE*, July 19, 1919, lauded the ruling in general terms.

79. *Los Angeles Investment Co. v. Gary* (1919) 181 Cal. 680, 186 Pac. 596, 9 A.L.R. 115.

80. Somerville, *Man*, 74–75.

81. Scruggs, *Man*, 90–94.

82. Somerville, *Man*, 74.

5. Politics and Patriotism

1. *CE*, Jan. 12, 1918; Keene, *United*, 92–93 (Wilson's speech). In 1918, Robeson's younger brother, Paul, was known as an All-American football player at Rutgers University, not yet as an actor and singer or political radical (George P. Johnson oral history, 295; Duberman, *Paul*).

2. *CE*, June 9, 1917 (reprinted, June 4, 1937), May 18, 1918.

3. *NAACP Annual Report, 1917*, Du Bois Papers, Box 11, Fisk; George P. Johnson oral history, 52–54; Cripps, *Slow*, 78–79.

4. Taylor, *Search*, 189–90.

5. Ibid., 190.

6. James Clyde Sellman, "World War I and African Americans," in *Africana*, 2027; Somerville, *Man*, 109.

7. Keene, *United*, 60–63 ("warrior race," 61).

8. *Africana*, 923.

9. Taylor, *Search*, 179–81; Bass, *Forty*, 43–46.

10. Taylor, *Search*, 181; Lewis, *Du Bois: Biography*, 540–42.

11. Bass, *Forty*, 45.

12. *CE*, April 13, June 1, Sept. 28, and Oct. 5, 1918.

13. *CE*, Sept. 7, 1918; see also July 20 and Aug. 2, 1918.

14. The NAACP meeting also included a talk on the "conscientious objector"(Branch Report, Oct. 7, 1917, in BF 15: 1913–1917); *CE*, Jan. 26, March 2 and 16, Nov. 23, 1918; Beasley, *Negro*, has material on World War I scattered throughout; her chapter devoted to military service contains little on this war.

15. Slightly different accounts of Lincoln's activities during the war appear in Cripps, *Slow*, 81–82, and George P. Johnson interview, 125–30.

16. *CE*, July 13, 1918 ("no World Democracy"); Oct. 12 and Dec. 14, 1918; NAACP letters dated Jan. 23 and Feb. 3, 1919, in BF 15: 1918–1919; Beasley, *Negro*, 259, 273–74; McBroome, "Harvest," 9, 35 n. 22; M. Guy Bishop, "'Strong Voices and 100 Percent Patriotism': The Four-Minute Men of Los Angeles County, 1917–1918," paper delivered to the Los Angeles History Research Group, HEH, May 21, 1992, copy in author's possession; Marshal Stimson Scrapbook, vol. 3, 136 (banquet photo) 140 (list of all the men), Stimson Papers, HEH.

17. The *Tidings*, May 11, 1917, in BF 15: 1913–1917.

18. Ibid.

19. E. Burton Ceruti to James W. Johnson, July 17, 1917, in BF 15: 1913–1917.

20. Lewis, *Du Bois: Biography*, 555–59.

21. *CE*, July 27 ("loyal Negroes"), Aug. 31 ("unlike Mr. Dubois"), Sept. 7 ("these people"), 1918.

22. *LAT*, Sept. 20, 1918, sec. 2. The *Times* also praised local black soldiers; see "Negro Soldier Wins Laurels," Nov. 1, 1918, sec. 2.

23. *NA*, Aug. 2, 1918.

24. *CE*, Dec. 3, 1921, July 24, 1952 (Frederick's obituary); Fisher, "History," 203; Logan and Winston, *Dictionary of American Negro Biography*, 526–27; one-page typed biography in Roberts Papers, Box 1, folder 1, Roberts collection, AAMLO.

25. Photos in Roberts collection, Box 4, AAMLO. The 1894 photo: 92.021—021A; Wall Street home: 92.021.086.

26. *Sacramento Bee* news clipping c. 1924, Roberts collection, Box 1, folder 4, AAMLO; Fisher, "History," 203; Beasley, *Negro*, 255–56; *Dir.*, 87.

27. Photo of A. J. Roberts and Sons: Roberts collection, Box 4 (92.021–072), AAMLO; *Dir.*, 87; *CE*, Dec. 5, 1914.

28. *NA*, Oct. 8, 1915; June 4, 1915, Sept. 25, 1914 (quotes). I could not find the advertisements Roberts was denouncing.

29. *NA*, Sept. 11, 1914.

30. *NA*, Oct. 8, 1915. Over the years, the *Eagle* spelled the Sanders name inconsistently—as both "Saunders" and "Sanders," sometimes within the same article (e.g., May 18, 1918). *Dir.*, 73, uses "Sanders."

31. See discussion of this in chapter 3.

32. *SV*, primary and general elections, 1912, 1914, 1916; *NA*, Sept. 25, 1914; Flamming, "African-Americans," 208–9.

33. *SV*, 1918 primary election; *CE*, March 16, 1918, and April 29, 1922.

34. *CE*, July 20, 1918.

35. Campaign card, Roberts collection, AAMLO.

36. Flamming, "African-Americans," explores this period.

37. *CE*, July 13, 1918.

38. *CE*, July 20, 1918; *NA*, June 26, Sept. 4, and Aug. 28, 1914.

39. *CE*, July 20, Aug. 17, and Aug. 24, 1918.

40. *CE*, Aug. 24 and 31, 1918.

41. *SV*, 1918 primary election; *CE*, Aug. 31, 1918.
42. Beasley, *Negro*, 255.
43. *CE*, Oct. 5, Nov. 1, 1918.
44. *LAT*, Sept. 22, 1918.
45. *SV*, 1914, 1916, 1918 general elections.
46. Pearl Roberts oral history.
47. *CE*, Nov. 9, 1918; *LAT*, Nov. 8, 1918.
48. *CE*, Feb. 1 and 15, Mar. 8, April 12 and 19, 1919. There was another "first" in the 1919 legislative session: the first four women elected to the California legislature took office; see Karen Stapf Walters, "Works in Progress: California's First Women Legislators," *California Studies* 6 (Spring 1996): 3.
49. *CE*, Feb. 15, 1919; Aug. 12, 1922.
50. Photo in Marshal Stimson scrapbook, vol. 3, 136, Stimson Papers, HEH.
51. Marshal Stimson, *Fun, Fights, and Fiestas in Old Los Angeles: An Autobiography* (n.p.: ca. 1966), chap. 26, and p. 229; news clippings in Stimson scrapbook, vol. 3, 156–57, Stimson Papers, HEH; *CE*, Feb. 15, 1919, reprints Prowd's resolution and Shaw's speech.
52. *CE*, Feb. 15, 1919.
53. *CE*, June 14, Sept. 13, Feb. 1, and Dec. 20, 1919.
54. *CE*, Sept. 2 and 20, 1919.
55. *CE*, Aug. 2, 1919.
56. *CE*, Aug. 23, Oct. 18, 1919.
57. *CE*, Oct. 21, 1919 (which reprints Robeson's words from March 1919).
58. *CE*, Nov. 29, 1919; Jan. 3, 1920 ("day may seem dark").
59. Los Angeles County Superior Court, Case No. 15807, *The People of the State of California v. Miller Cooper, A. M. Cooper, and Frank Dewar*, first page of the indictment ("two loaded"); *CE*, March 11, 1922 ("nigger"). The *Eagle* was recalling the incident, which had occurred nearly two years earlier; the issues that originally reported the event have not survived.
60. *CE*, May 13, 1922; Los Angeles Superior Court records, *The People of the State of California v. Arthur Valentine*, Case No. 15417.
61. *People v. Cooper et al.*
62. *SV*, 1920 primary election.
63. *SV*, 1920 primary and general elections.
64. *NA*, Nov. 19, 1920.

6. Fighting Spirit in the 1920s

Section epigraph: Arna Bontemps, "The Day Breakers," originally in Allen Locke, ed., *The New Negro* (New York: Albert and Charles Boni, Inc., 1925), 145; the version printed here (modified structurally) is in Arna Bontemps, *Personals*, 2nd ed. (London: Paul Breman Limited, 1973), 35.
1. NAACP records contain no election report for November 1920; Bass's

name and title first appear on branch stationary in 1921; see BF 15: 1920–1922. See also Tolbert, *UNIA*, 51–63.

2. Lewis, *Du Bois: Fight*, 31.

3. *Cit.*, Dec. 18, 1920, Jan. 1, 1921.

4. McWilliams, *Southern*, 136; William Deverell, "My America or Yours? Americanization and the Battle for the Youth of Los Angeles," in *Metropolis*, ed. Sitton and Deverell.

5. Bryant et al., *Central*, 4–7, 32–33; Cox, *Central*.

6. *CE*, March 31, 1923.

7. *Cit.*, Jan. 1, 1921.

8. *Cit.*, Jan. 29, 1921.

9. E. Burton Ceruti to James Weldon Johnson, May 23, 1921; Assistant Secretary [White] to Ceruti, May 31, 1921, in BF 15: 1920–22.

10. *NA*, June 10, 1921; no other local Race papers survive from early June; *CE* issues are missing from Jan. 7 to June 24, 1921.

11. Nugent, *Into*, 219; Vorspan, *History*.

12. Bond, "Negro," 40; growth rate for cities with at least 20,000 black residents calculated from BC, *Negro*, 55, table 10.

13. Calculations from BC, *Negro*, 34–39, table 16. The census counted 31,668 migrants from other states; percentages for the top nine states were: Texas (25 percent), Louisiana (14), Georgia (9), Mississippi (5), Arkansas (5), Missouri (5), Alabama (5), Tennessee (4), Oklahoma (4). *WD*, Oct. 27, 1921; see also Texas-style Juneteenth celebration in *NA*, June 10, 1921.

14. Becky M. Nicolaides, "The Quest for Independence: Workers in the Suburbs," 87, in *Metropolis*, ed. Sitton and Deverell; Nicolaides, *My Blue Heaven*, chap. 2, esp. 39–44.

15. *CE*, Aug. 5, 1922.

16. *NA*, June 17, 1921.

17. *NA*, June 24, 1921; *CE*, June 24, 1921.

18. *CE*, June 24, 1921.

19. *CE*, July 2, 9 (quote), and 23, 1921; *WD*, Oct. 6, 1921.

20. *Cit.*, June 25, 1921. Interestingly, Ceruti did not seek to employ City Ordinance 37778, which suggests that he had no faith in the film commissioner to find the film objectionable. Secretary [James W. Johnson] to Ceruti, July 8, 1921, in BF 15: 1920–1922.

21. Von Brauchitsch, "Ku Klux," 10–12.

22. *NA*, July 22, 1921; italics mine.

23. Jackson, *Ku Klux*; Moore, *Citizen*. See also Christopher Cocothchos, "The Invisible Government and the Viable Community: The Ku Klux Klan in Orange County, California, during the 1920s" (Ph.D. diss., University of California at Los Angeles, 1979).

24. *LAT*, July 23, 1921, sec. 2, p. 4; McGroarty, "The Negro," in *LAT Illustrated Magazine*, June 4, 1922, 1.

25. *LAT*, July 23, 1921, sec. 2, p. 4.

26. Vena to McGroarty, Dec. 24, 1924; Marshall to McGroarty, Dec. 26, 1922; Somerville to McGroarty, June 5, 1922; Mrs. Richard Winter to J. S. McGroarty, Jan. 31, 1923; all in Scrapbook, vol. 1, McGroarty Collection, San Fernando Mission, San Fernando, California. Forum recognition: *Cit.*, July 30, 1921.

27. Los Angeles County Superior Court, Case No. 15807, *The People of the State of California v. Miller Cooper, A. M. Cooper, and Frank Dewar.*

28. *Cit.*, March 5, 1921 (quote); see also *NA*, Sept. 23, 1921.

29. *CE*, 18 March 1922.

30. *People v. Cooper et al.; CE*, March 18, May 13 ("strong") 1922.

31. *CE*, May 13, 1922.

32. *People v. Cooper et al.*

33. Von Brauchitsch, "Ku Klux," 12–22; an account favorable to the raiders is *The Inglewood Raiders: Story of the Celebrated Ku Klux Case at Los Angeles and Speeches to the Jury* (n.p.: Published by L. L. Bryson, 1923). On KKK attempts to enforce prohibition, see Leonard Moore, "Prohibition and American Society during the 1920s: Observations on Ohio and California," paper presented at the Eighty-sixth Annual Meeting of the Organization of American Historians, Anaheim, CA, April 1993 (paper in author's possession).

34. *LAT*, May, 17, sec. 2, pp. 1, 10; May 18, sec. 2, p. 1; May 20, sec. 2, p. 1; May 28, sec. 1, p. 1, and sec. 2, p. 1; June 3, sec. 2, pp. 1, 3; June 4, sec. 1, p. 1, 1922. Von Brauchitsch, "Ku Klux," 21–25 (quote, 25).

35. Von Brauchitsch, "Ku Klux," 23–40.

36. On D'Orr, see *Inglewood Raiders*, 9. The city council passed the "anti-mask" ordinance on June 14, 1922, with Klan member Criswell absent; von Brauchitsch, 43–60.

37. Thompson to Robert Bagnall, Dec. 20, 1922, in BF 15: 1920–1922; *NA*, Dec. 2, 1921.

38. "Summary Report," Woolwine Collection, HEH; Woolwine's career in Los Angeles and state politics may be followed in "California Scrapbooks," vols. 1–14, in the Woolwine Collection; C. A. Barlow to Woolwine, June 30, 1922, in ibid., Box 2: folder 1.

39. [Woolwine] to Mr. C. H. Alston, Aug. 9, 1922, Woolwine Collection, Box 2: folder 3, HEH. (Woolwine's lieutenant, Robert F. Herron, probably ghostwrote this letter and suggested that although African Americans could not vote for Woolwine in the primary that August, because most of them were registered Republicans, they could "assist in organization work before the primaries.")

40. E. A. Doran and W. R. Knox to Woolwine, Aug. 8, 1922, Woolwine Collection, Box 2: folder 3, HEH.

41. C. H. Alston to Woolwine, June 14, 1922; [Woolwine] to Alston, June 14, 1922; [Woolwine] to Wood Wilson, July 13, 1922; Alston to Woolwine, Aug. 8, 1922, Woolwine Collection, Box 2: folder 1.

42. Von Brauchitsch, "Ku Klux," 229–36.

43. Tom Sitton, "John Randolph Haynes and the Left Wing of California Progressivism," and Jackson Putnam, "The Progressive Legacy in California: Fifty Years of Politics, 1917–1967," both in *California*, ed. Sitton and Deverell.

44. *SV*, 1922 general election. In the 74th Assembly District, Woolwine won 2,766 votes (50.2 percent) to Richardson's 2,385; a third-party candidate won 355 votes.

45. *CE*, Aug. 19 and 26 (quote), 1922.

46. Calculations from *SV*, 1922 primary election.

47. *CE*, Oct. 7 and 28, Nov. 11 ("regular Republican"), 1922; *SV*, 1922 general election.

48. Ceruti to Walter White, Jan. 11, 1923; White to Ceruti, Jan. 17, 1923; White to Ceruti, Jan. 23, 1923, in BF 15: Correspondence, 1923; Von Brauchitsch, "Ku Klux," 240–42.

49. Thompson to Robert W. Bagnall, Dec. 20, 1922; Thompson to Bagnall, Nov. 28, 1924, in BF 15: 1920–1922, 1924.

50. Thompson to Bagnall, Nov. 28, 1924, in BF 15: 1924.

51. *CE*, June 5, 1925 (reprint of letter originally published April 10, 1925).

52. *CE*, May 8 ("Red"), 15, 22, and 29, June 5, 1925 (publishes suit against *Eagle*).

53. *CE*, May 22, 1925.

54. See, for instance, the officers listed on the local branch's stationary in correspondence dated June 21, 1921, or Feb. 17, 1922. Charlotta Bass was one of five vice presidents; Fred Roberts served on the executive board. During 1921–22, the branch had nine officers and nine more board members; of these eighteen, six were ministers, all of leading churches.

55. "Los Angeles Branch, NAACP, Secretary's Report, November, 1920 . . . November, 1921" in BF 15: 1920–1922; officers list on branch letterhead, June 21, 1921, Feb. 17, 1922; J. C. Banks to James Weldon Johnson, Jan. 5, 1922, in BF 15: 1920–1922; "Bishop Cantwell at Meeting of the N.A.A.C.P.," the *Tidings*, Dec. 9, 29 (text of Cantwell's address to the local branch), 1921.

56. *Cit.*, April 30, 1921. Because people could become members at any time, annual totals were seldom tabulated. A table showing membership from 1919 to 1925 was compiled by the branch; see BF 15: Jan.–June 1926, no date but ca. May 26, 1926 (follows Hudson to Bagnall, May 26). At the end of 1919, the branch had 470 members; in 1920, it had 659 members; in 1921, 1,236; in 1922, 898; in 1923, 879; in 1924, 506; in 1925, 274. Thompson to Bagnall, April 9, 1924 (quote), in BF 15: 1924; Ceruti to James Weldon Johnson, Nov. 29, 1922; Ceruti to Johnson, Jan. 3, 1923 [mistakenly reads 1922], in BF 15: 1923.

57. Lewis, *Du Bois: Fight*, 104–5 (on the Du Bois–Thompson affair); Thompson to Bagnall, April 9, 1924, in BF 15: 1924.

58. Thompson to Bagnall, April 9, 1924, in BF 15: 1924; Douglas Flamming, "The *Star of Ethiopia* and the NAACP: Pageantry, Politics, and the Los Angeles African American Community," in *Metropolis*, ed. Sitton and Deverell. On the pageant, also see chap. 8 in this book.

59. The only detailed account of the meeting is from Thompson to Bagnall, Nov. 28, 1924, in BF 15: 1924.

60. Hawkins oral history (Vasquez); Bagnall to Thompson, May 15, 1924, and Bagnall to Thompson, Dec. 5, 1924, both in BF 15: 1924.

61. *CE,* April 25, 1924, clipping in BF 15: 1924; Thompson to Bagnall, Nov. 28, 1924, in BF 15: 1924; Hudson to Pickins, Feb. 16, 1925, in BF 15: Jan.–July 1925.

62. Thompson to Bagnall, Nov. 28, 1924, in BF 15: 1924.

63. *Cit.,* Jan. 1, 1921.

64. Gutierrez, *Walls;* Sanchez, *Becoming;* Modell, *Economic.*

65. *Cit.,* May 21, 1921; *NA,* June 17, 1921; "Los Angeles Branch, NAACP, Secretary's Report, November, 1920 . . . November, 1921," in BF 15: 1920–1922.

66. *PD,* July 22, 1926, clipping in BF 15: Correspondence, July–Dec. 1926.

67. *WD,* Oct. 6, 1921. For an attempt to segregate the swimming pools of Riverside, California (a policy fought by the NAACP branches in both Riverside and L.A.), see *Cit.,* April 2, 1921. The official name of the Playground Commission was the Board of Playground and Recreation Commissioners.

68. Los Angeles County Superior Court Records, Case No. C180780, *George Cushnie v. City of Los Angeles.* On the buildup, see the letters dated Aug. 20, Oct. 1 and 2, Nov. 9 and 20, 1925, in BF 15: Aug.–Dec. 1925. A summary of the commission's actions and the NAACP case is in "Statement of Geo. Cushnie vs. City of Los Angeles, et al., Rendered by Bert McDonald," in BF 16: Legal Folder, 1927 (hereafter cited as McDonald's statement); press release dated Nov. 27, 1925, in BF 15: Aug.–Dec. 1925. A reorganized Junior Division raised funds for the case; see Bagnall to Dr. Vada J. Somerville, June 8, 1926, in BF 15: Jan.–June 1926. Quote: Hudson to Walter White, July 13, 1926, in BF 15: July–Dec. 1926.

69. McDonald's statement.

70. Ibid.

71. "Report of the Los Angeles Branch, N.A.A.C.P., for 1926," in BF 16: Jan.–May 1927.

72. Bert McDonald to Hudson, Jan. 12, 1927, in BF 16: Jan.–May 1927.

73. Hudson to White, Jan. 14, 1927, in BF 16: Jan.–May 1927. Hudson had voiced similar sentiments to the national director of branches, Robert W. Bagnall, as early as December 1926: "I fear that in a matter so close to the White man we might get a Supreme court decision in California that would open the gates of Jim Crowism." Hudson to Bagnall, Dec. 17, 1926; Bagnall to Hudson, Dec. 31, 1926, in BF 15: July–Dec. 1926. Spingarn quoted in White to Hudson, Jan. 24, 1927, in BF 16: Jan.–May 1927.

74. Hudson to Bagnall, Oct. 1, 1925, in BF 15: Aug.–Dec. 1925.

75. For a useful discussion of *Gary* and its relation to the Long Case, see Ceruti to White, April 25, 1925, in BF 15: Jan.–July 1925.

76. Preusser, "Color," 61. Harrison R. Baker to Harry B. Allen, Feb. 28, 1927, and copy of a deed filed June 1925, both in "Questionnaires from California real estate agents concerning attitudes and practices regarding segregation and housing," ca. 1915, box 2, Survey of Race Relations Collection, Hoover Institution Archives, Stanford, CA (hereafter cited as Survey).

77. McMillan letter (not the standard survey form), March 1, 1927, Survey.

78. Preusser, "Color," 35, 61.

79. Survey.

80. W. H. Fitchmiller to Harry Allen, March 1, 1927, Santa Monica Bay District survey, completed by Fitchmiller, Survey.

81. Responses by Home Protective League, and Incorporated and Federated Home Protective Leagues, Survey.

82. Charles W. Stewart to Harry B. Allen, March 3, 1927, Survey.

83. This paragraph and the two following were pieced together from Ceruti to White, April 25, 1925, in BF 15: 1925; Eunice Long to NAACP, Nov. 3, 1927, in BF 16: Sept.–Dec. 1927; and "Affidavit of Eunice Long" in re Geo. H. Letteau, et al., vs. William H. Long, et al., in BF 16: Legal Folder, 1927.

84. "Affidavit of Eunice Long."

85. Ceruti to White, April 25, 1925, in BF 15: 1925.

86. White to Ceruti, May 7, 1925, in BF 15: 1925; Vose, *Caucasians*, 18, 52–54; Nieman, *Promises*, 129; Herman Belz, "*Corrigan v. Buckley*," in Hall et al., eds., *Oxford*, 199–200.

87. Eunice Long to NAACP, Nov. 3, 1927, in BF 16: Sept.–Dec. 1927.

88. Hudson to Bagnall, Dec. 17, 1926, in BF 15: July–Dec. 1926.

89. *PD*, March 24, 1927; *CE*, March 25, 1927; misc. articles in BF 16: Newspaper Clippings, Jan.–July 1927; Western Union telegraph, Walter White to Mrs. E. Burton Ceruti, March 24, 1927, in BF 16: Telegrams, 1927.

90. The events described in this and the following paragraph are pieced together from Eunice Long to NAACP, Nov. 3, 1927; James Weldon Johnson to Eunice R. Long, Nov. 15, 1927; Johnson to Hudson, Nov. 15, 1927 (all three clipped together); Hudson to Johnson, Dec. 15, 1927; William T. Andrews to Eunice R. Long, Dec. 27, 1927; and from William T. Andrews to Hudson, Dec. 27, 1927 (all three clipped together), all in BF 16: Sept.–Dec. 1927.

91. Hudson to Johnson, Dec. 15, 1927, in BF 16: Sept.–Dec. 1927.

92. Hudson to William Pickens, Feb. 16, 1925, in BF 15: Jan.–July 1925; Lulu Slaughter to Bagnall, Sept. 25, 1925, in BF 15: Jan.–July 1925.

93. Somerville quoted in *PD*, July 15, 1926, in BF 15: Telegrams and Newspapers, 1926.

7. The Business of Race

1. Beavers oral history (UCLA), viii, 1, 47.

2. Beavers oral history (UCLA), 41–44.

3. *CE*, Jan. 7, 1921.

4. *CE*, June 24, 1921.

5. *WD*, Oct. 6, 1921.

6. *CE*, Jan. 14, 1922; *NA*, Jan. 14, June 10, 1921.

7. *Western Progress*, photocopy at HEH.

8. Ibid., "Publishers' Preface."

9. Ibid., 2, 9, 10, 13, 60, 63.

10. *CE*, Feb. 7 ("voluminous Sun") and 14 ("Each month"), 1920; Sept. 10,

1921; June 29, 1928. The Commercial Council directors are listed in James de T. Abajian, *Blacks and Their Contributions to the American West: A Bibliography and Union List of Library Holdings through 1970* (Boston: G. K. Hall, 1970), 88.

11. On tension between black store owners and black consumers in Chicago, see Drake and Cayton, *Black Metropolis*, chap. 16.

12. *CE*, Sept. 3, 1921.

13. *NA*, June 17, 1921.

14. *CE*, June 7, 1921.

15. Lewis, *Du Bois: Fight*, chap. 2; Judith Stein, *The World of Marcus Garvey: Race and Class in Modern Society* (Baton Rouge: Louisiana State University Press, 1986). The standard work on Garveyism in L.A. is Tolbert, *UNIA*.

16. *CE*, Jan. 3, 1920 (an earlier notice about the Black Star Line, in verse, appeared Dec. 13 1919); Tolbert, *UNIA*, 58.

17. Tolbert, *UNIA*, 51–63; *Dir.*, 78; *CE*, Nov. 19, 1919 (rare reference to "Dawson").

18. *CE*, June 7, Nov. 8 and 19, 1919.

19. Anderson, *Development*; Eva Overr-Solomon, "Shall Ethiopia Arise?" *CE*, July 9, 1921.

20. Stimson collection, Scrapbook (Four-Minute Men list); Tolbert, *UNIA*, 54–55; Beasley, *Negro*, 253–55.

21. Lewis, *Du Bois: Fight*, chap. 2.

22. See, for example, *CE*, Jan. 18, 1919, which has an ad suggesting that black women are more likely to get jobs in the colored Red Cross if their skin is lighter.

23. See any issue of *Cit.*, 1920–21, for the Excelento advertisement.

24. Thurman, *The Blacker the Berry*; Arna Bontemps discusses "passing" in chap. 9, *Anyplace*. For a 1920s analysis of passing in L.A., see Juanita Ellsworth, "White Negroes," *Studies in Sociology* 12 (May 1928): 449–54.

25. *CE*, April 22, 1922; John Somerville and Vada Somerville oral history, 8.

26. Tolbert, *UNIA*, 58–59; *NA*, Aug. 26, Sept. 23, 1921.

27. Lewis, *Du Bois: Fight*, 64–74; Tolbert, *UNIA*, 58–63; *NA*, Sept. 23, 1921.

28. *CE*, Sept. 24, 1921; Tolbert, *UNIA*, 64–65, 74.

29. Tolbert, *UNIA*, 58–63, 74–75. John Coleman also stayed with the new version of Division 156. On H. Douglass Greer, see ibid., 72–73; *CE*, Nov. 30, 1918; and *WD*, no date, but ca. 1921. Final quote: *CE*, Nov. 19, 1921.

30. *CE*, Nov. 19, 1921; Thompson quoted in *WD*, issue announcing formation of the PCNIA (no date, but ca. early Nov. 1921); Tolbert, *UNIA*, 66–68.

31. Owen, "From" (emphasis in original); Thompson, "California," 221.

32. Bass quoted in Tolbert, *UNIA*, 73.

33. *CE*, March 11 and 18, 1922, and Tolbert, *UNIA*, 69–71.

34. Tolbert, *UNIA*, 52 (Bontemps), 71, 74.

35. Ibid., 71, 78.

36. Ibid., 78–81 (Bass quoted on 78 and 79).

37. Ibid.

38. Ibid., 72.

39. This quote is from an article in a Race paper [no date, no name of the newspaper] written ca. 1930 and reprinted in George P. Johnson oral history, 87–89 (hereafter cited Article in Johnson).

40. *CE*, Dec. 25, 1925.

41. Article in Johnson. In 1920, homes in West Jefferson cost from $3,000 to $4,000, bungalows along Central Avenue, $2,000 to $3,000. Home prices in the Furlong Tract and Watts varied, with cheaper homes selling for less than $1,000, open lots for even less than that; see *CE*, Jan. 4, April 5, 1919; *NA*, Nov. 12, 1920; *WD*, Oct. 6, 1921.

42. Article in Johnson.

43. O'Melveny Journal, 1926: May 10 (follow-up references, May 11, 18, 19), O'Melveny Papers; Pitt and Pitt, *Los Angeles*, 368.

44. Ibid., May 20, 21.

45. Ibid., June 4, 7, 15; July 6, 8, 9, 13, 26, 27; Aug.–Dec.; Article in Johnson.

46. Article in Johnson.; *CE*, Aug. 26, 1932.

47. BC, *Fifteenth Census*, vol. 4, *Population*, table 16: 212; On the recession, see *WD*, Oct. 6, 1921.

48. Gatewood, *Aristocrats*, 319; Lewis, *Du Bois: Biography*, 513; *WD*, Oct. 6, 1921.

49. Lewis, *Du Bois: Fight*, 155–56.

50. *NA*, June 17, 1921; on Tenette, see *WD*, Oct. 6, 1921.

51. *CE*, July 30, Aug. 5, 1921; *NA*, June 17, Aug. 12, 1921.

52. *WD*, Oct. 6, 1921.

53. Ibid.; *PD*, Oct. 22, 1925.

54. Becky M. Nicolaides, "The Quest for Independence: Workers in the Suburbs," 86–87, and Greg Hise, "Industry and Imaginative Geographies," 22–23, both in *Metropolis*, ed. Sitton and Deverell; Covington, "Color: A Factor in Social Mobility," *Sociology and Social Research* (Nov.–Dec., 1930): 145–52.

55. The local NAACP supported the Urban League's survey; see Report in BF 16: Jan.–May 1927.

56. Here I use the title given to Johnson's summation of the results. See Charles S. Johnson, "Negro Workers in Los Angeles Industries," *Opportunity* 6 (Aug. 1928): 234–40. The project's official name was "Industrial Survey of the Negro Population of Los Angeles, California." The unpublished report (about eighty pages, no date, but ca. 1927) is in Charles S. Johnson Papers, Box 164, folder 10, Fisk University Library, Special Collections (cited hereafter as Johnson, "Industrial Survey").

57. Johnson, "Industrial Survey," 17; Johnson, "Negro Workers," 234.

58. Charles S. Johnson, *The Negro in American Civilization: A Study of Negro Life and Race Relations in the Light of Social Research* (New York: Henry Holt, 1930), 78–79.

59. Ibid., 79; Johnson, "Negro Workers," 238. For a different survey of black employment in Los Angeles in 1926, see Emory S. Bogardus, *The City Boy and His Problems: A Survey of Boy Life in Los Angeles* (Los Angeles: n.p., 1926). A white sociologist, and also social research director at USC, Bogardus conducted

a survey of "Boys' Work" for the L.A. Rotary Club. In it, he encouraged white employers to hire more young black men and boys because "the pall of prejudice" stunted their ambition and might lead them into lives of crime (see esp. 107–8).

60. Calculations from data in Johnson, "Industrial Survey," 70; U.S. Census, 1920 and 1930. See also Stimson, *Rise.*

61. Johnson, "Industrial Survey," 70–82.

62. Ibid., table 70a, 76; Johnson, "Negro Workers," 239–40.

63. Covington, "Union," 208–10.

64. Clarence Johnson oral history, 1–2.

65. Ibid., 3, 11, 14, 19; Covington, "Union," 210.

66. Clarence Johnson oral history, 3, 23.

67. Ibid., 3–4, on origins of union and receiving the union charter "about 1925"; Covington, "Union," gives the correct date, 1926.

68. Clarence Johnson oral history, quotes in order: 282, 7, 9, 29.

69. Ibid., 11–12.

70. Covington, "Union," 209–10.

71. *NA*, Dec. 30, 1921.

72. Bass, *Forty.*

73. Charles Johnson in *Opportunity* 4 (Jan. 1926): 4–5. A. Philip Randolph, "The Negro and Economic Radicalism," *Opportunity* 4 (Feb. 1926): 62–64; William Green, "Why Belong to a Union?" *Opportunity* 4 (Feb. 1926): 61–52, both from a special issue: "The Negro in Industry."

74. Calculations from the data collected in my *Eagle* advertisement survey (1915–1940); see chap. 3, above, as well as chap 3, note 82.

75. Information collected in advertisement survey.

76. List of stores: *CE*, Oct. 3, 1930. Safeway was created in 1926.

77. Herndon established the firm in 1905 as the Atlanta Mutual Insurance Association; the name change came in 1911. See *Africana*, 148; Kenneth Coleman et al., *A History of Georgia*, 2nd ed. (Athens: University of Georgia Press, 1991), 280–81; and *Atlanta Journal-Constitution*, July 11, 2001, sec. B, pp. 1, 6.

78. On Nickerson, see Beavers oral history (UCLA), 42, 79–81; *Dir.*, 81–82.

79. Houston rose quickly in the community. He organized the Benjamin Bowie Post of the American Legion in L.A.—a post for blacks only, named in memory of a black Angeleno who gave his life on the battlefield in France. Houston also worked with Dr. Wilbur Gordon in organizing the Liberty Building and Loan Association. *Dir.*, 83; Beavers oral history (UCLA), 82–87.

80. Beavers oral history (UCLA), 42–43.

81. Ibid., 43–45.

82. Ibid., 45–46.

83. Beavers oral history (CSF), 8; *CE*, May 22, 1925.

84. Beavers oral history (UCLA), 46–47.

85. Ibid., 44–77 (board of directors: 46–47); *Dir.*, 99.

86. Beavers oral history (UCLA), 48–50 ("no doubt," 49).

87. Beavers oral history (UCLA), 50.

88. Beavers oral history (CSF), 4; *Dir.*, 99.

89. *Dir.*, 99.

8. Surging Down Central Avenue

1. This paragraph and those following: Williams oral history, 1–12.

2. Bradley oral history also relates migration from Texas.

3. Gilmore Millen, *Sweet Man* (New York: Viking Press, 1930), 260–61; Bryant et al., *Central*, 29, 25, 198; Hahn oral history.

4. Hudson, *Williams*, 43, 230; Cox, *Central*, 61; Bryant et al., *Central*, 205; *Crisis*, June 1917, 82–84; Williams, "I Am," 59; Williams, "If I Were Young Today," *Ebony* (Aug. 1963): 56.

5. *Dir.*, 99; Cox, *Central*, 30–32, 60; Bryant et al., *Central*, 33.

6. Williams oral history, 14–15.

7. On Watts, the basic work is Adler, "Watts"; see also MaryEllen Bell Ray, *The City of Watts, California: 1907–1926* (Los Angeles: Rising Publishing, 1985); Sides, *L.A.*, 19–20 and passim; Pitt and Pitt, *Los Angeles*, 537; Nicolaides, *Blue*, 159–65.

8. Henry Louis Gates, Jr., and Nellie Y. McKay, eds., *The Norton Anthology of African American Literature* (New York: Norton, 1997), 164–67; Lewis, *Du Bois: Fight*, chap. 5; Lewis, *Portable*, xiii–xli; Nathan Irvin Huggins, *Harlem Renaissance* (London: Oxford University Press, 1971).

9. *LAT*, June 14, 1925, sec. 3, pp. 26–27.

10. *PD*, July 15, 1926.

11. Flamming, "Westerner."

12. Miriam Matthews oral history (CSF); Charles Matthews oral history.

13. *Dir.*, 90; Miriam Matthews oral history (CSF); Charles Matthews oral history.

14. Charles Matthews oral history; Hawkins oral history (Flamming).

15. *CE*, Jan. 16, April 10, 1925.

16. *CE*, Jan. 16 and 30, Feb. 13, April 10, 1925.

17. *Crisis*, Dec. 1915, 91–93; Lewis, *Du Bois: Biography*, 459–60.

18. *CE*, Feb. 6, 13, 20, 1925.

19. Beatrice Thompson to Bagnall, April 4, 1925, in BF 15: Jan.–July 1925.

20. *CE*, May 15, 1925.

21. Du Bois in *Chicago Defender*, May 11, 1946 (pageant date incorrectly stated as 1924); *CE*, May 22, 29, 1925; *LAT*, June 14, 1925, sec. 3, pp. 26–27.

22. *CE*, June 26, 1925.

23. Ceruti to White, July 16, 1925; Bagnall to Hudson, July 27, 1925, in BF 15: Jan.–July 1925.

24. *CE*, June 19, 26, 1925; Bagnall to Hudson, July 27, 1925, in BF 15: Jan–July 1925.

25. See chap. 6, note 56. The branch eventually paid off the debt.

26. Hudson to Bagnall, Aug. 20, 1925; Hudson to Bagnall, Oct. 9, 1925; Hud-

son to Bagnall, Nov. 9, 1925; Bagnall to Hudson, Jan. 5, 1926, all in BF 15: Aug.–Dec. 1925.

27. Hudson to White, July 13, 1926; Hudson to White, July 19, 1926; Vada Somerville to Johnson, Oct. 7, 1926; [William] Pickens to Vada Somerville, Oct. 15, 1926, all in BF 15: July–Dec. 1926; *PD*, July 15, 1926.

28. Information on the beaches is scattered and contradictory. Information for these paragraphs comes from George P. Johnson oral history, 90; Charles Matthews oral history, 27; Willis Tyler editorial, *PD*, Oct. 18, 1927, in BF 16: Newspaper Clippings, 1927; Hudson oral history (draft transcript of tape 1: 4); Smith oral history, 39; Williams oral history, 9; *NA*, July 23, 1937.

29. *LAT*, July 27, 1922, sec. 2, p. 11; *LAT*, July 30, 1922, sec. 5, p. 7; *CE*, Aug. 5, 1922.

30. *LAT*, July 30, 1922, sec. 5, p. 7.

31. Los Angeles Area Chamber of Commerce, Directors' minutes, Carton 14, Aug. 17, 1922, Stenographer's Reports, 3–4, and Carton 15, Feb. 12, 1925, Stenographer's Reports, 2–5, Regional History Collection, Doheny Memorial Library, University of Southern California; George P. Johnson oral history, 91–92; *CE*, May 22, 1922; *PD*, Oct. 22, 1922.

32. *PD*, Aug. 4, Oct. 18, 1927, in BF 16: Newspaper Clippings, 1927; Hudson to Pickens, Aug. 4, 1927, in BF 16: June–Aug. 1927.

33. Hudson oral history, tape 1, transcript 2: 4–5, 15–16 ("didn't mind," 16); Bass, *Forty*, 60–61 (on Cole).

34. Hudson to Pickens, Aug. 4, 1927, in BF 16: June–Aug. 1927.

35. Ibid.; *PD*, Aug. 4, 1927; Hudson's 1967 recollection says four hundred dollars *and ninety* days in jail: Hudson oral history, tape 1, transcript 2: 16.

36. Pickens to Hudson, Aug. 11, 1927, in BF 16: June–Aug. 1927; Hudson oral history, tape 1, transcript 2: 4.

37. Newspaper quotes from *PD*, Aug. 18, 1927, in BF 16: Newspaper Clippings, 1927; "Los Angeles N.A.A.C.P. Wins Against Bathing Beach Segregation," Aug. 20, 1927, in BF 16: June–Aug. 1927.

38. Beach desegregation, recalled matter-of-factly in the Hudson oral history (1967), needs to be researched more thoroughly. On the heels of beach integration at Manhattan Beach, several black homes in the area burned down, with arson not proved but strongly suggested; see *NA*, Oct. 21, 1927, and *PD*, Oct. 18, 1927. In 1937 Fred Roberts and friends were asked to leave Pacific Palisades beach by a man falsely wearing a sheriff's deputy badge; when Roberts refused and the man threatened force, Roberts suggested he "use whatever means he saw fit" to try to remove them, prompting the "officer" to leave. See *NA*, July 23, 1937.

39. Commission of Immigration and Housing, *A Community Survey, Made in Los Angeles City* (San Francisco: n.p. [Commission of Immigration and Housing of California], 1917), 19; *CE*, Sept. 3, 1921.

40. *CE*, May 22, 1925.

41. *CE*, May 8, 15, 29, 1925.

42. Tom Sitton, "Did the Ruling Class Rule at City Hall in 1920s Los Angeles?" in *Metropolis*, ed. Sitton and Deverell.

43. *PD*, Oct. 22, 1925, refers to a Sheffield shooting in 1924, with no reference to Randolph.

44. Smith oral history, 57.

45. Typed copy of Los Angeles Police Department press release, "Wright Act Wins," dated July 27, 1927 (and attached to Hudson to Pickens, Aug. 4, 1927), in BF 16: June–Aug. 1927 (hereinafter cited as "Wright Act").

46. Davis (quoting Hudson) to Hudson, May 14, 1927, in BF 16: Jan.–May 1927.

47. Ibid.

48. Davis to Johnson, May 14, 1927 (letter to Hudson attached), in BF 16: Jan.–May 1927.

49. *PD*, May 26, 1927, in BF 16: Newspaper Clippings, 1927.

50. Ibid.

51. *CE*, June 3, 1927, in BF 16: Newspaper Clippings, 1927. On death threats, see Hudson oral history, tape 1, transcript 2: 6B.

52. Pickens to Hudson, July 6, 1927; Hudson to Dear Old Friend [Pickens], July 14, 1927, in BF 16: June–Aug. 1927.

53. "Wright Act"; Hudson to Pickens, Aug. 4, 1927 ("home raided," italics in the original); "Minutes of [the] Regular Public Meeting of the Los Angeles Branch N.A.A.C.P.," Aug. 14, 1927 ("enough devilment"), all in BF 16: June–Aug. 1927.

54. "Wright Act"; Pickens to Hudson, Aug. 11, 1927, in BF 16: June–Aug. 1927. "Wright Act" copy has handwritten note from Hudson to Pickens.

55. Hudson to Bagnall, Feb. 9, 1926; Pickens to Hudson, Feb. 15, 1926; Bagnall to Hudson, March 4, 1926; Pickens to Flynn, handwritten note attached to Vada Somerville to Pickens, May 23, 1926; Hudson to Bagnall, May 26, 1926; Vada Somerville to Bagnall, n.d., received in New York May 29, 1926; "Report of Baby Contest For N.A.A.C.P.," June 20, 1926; Pickens to Scott, June 23, 1926; White to Hudson, July 19, 1926, all in BF 15: Jan.–June 1926 and July–Dec. 1926.

56. Du Bois in *Chicago Defender*, May 11, 1946, 15; Vada Somerville to Seligmann, Oct. 7, 1926; Vada Somerville to Johnson, Oct. 7, 1926; Hudson to Bagnall, Dec. 17, 1926; Bagnall to Hudson, Dec. 31, 1926; Patton to Bagnall, Dec. 26, 1927; Sayers to Bagnall, Feb. 1, 1927; Bagnall to Hudson, March 9, 1927, all in BF 15: July–Dec. 1926 and BF 16: Jan.–May 1927. Press release, May 11, 1928; [local branch] to [national office], ca. Jan. 20, 1928, in BF 16: Jan.–May 1928.

57. Du Bois in *Chicago Defender*, May 11, 1946, 15; John Somerville oral history. Hudson to Bagnall, May 10, 1927; Hudson to Pickens, May 17, 1927; Bagnall to Hudson, May 19, 1927; Hudson to Pickens, June 10, 1927; Pickens to Hudson, July 6, 1927; Johnson to Sayers, July 18, 1927, all in BF 16: Jan.–May 1927 and June–Aug. 1927.

58. For this paragraph and the one preceding: Hudson to Pickens, Aug. 4,

1927 ("started a *'mess'*"), and Aug. 28, 1927; Banks to Hudson, Sept. 24, 1927; "Minutes of [the] Regular Public Meeting of the Los Angeles Branch N.A.A.C.P.," Aug. 14, 1927 ("loggerheads" and "BRANCH IS BIGGER"), all in BF 16: June–Aug. 1927. See also *PD*, Aug. 18, 1927 ("free-for-all"), in BF 16: Newspaper Clippings, 1927.

59. Sayers to Bagnall, Sept. 19, 1927 (emphasis in the original); Bagnall to Hudson, Sept. 26, 1927, in BF 16: Sept.–Dec. 1927.

60. Bagnall to Sayers, Aug. 26, 1927; Bagnall to "the Officers of the Los Angeles Branch," Oct. 20, 1927; Bagnall to Hudson, Oct. 24, 1927, in BF 16: Sept.–Dec. 1927.

61. Hudson to Pickens, Aug. 28, 1927, in BF 16: June–Aug. 1927; *CE*, Dec. 23, 1927, in BF 16: Newspaper Clippings, 1927. In oral history interviews conducted in the 1960s, each man spoke highly of the other and gave no hint of the 1927 conflict; see John Somerville oral history and Hudson oral history.

62. Vada Somerville to Pickens, Dec. 13, 1927, in BF 16: Sept.–Dec. 1927.

63. Somerville, *Man*, 125.

64. Ibid., 122–25.

65. Photo in Matthews collection, AAHM; Lifton, "Incredible," 38.

66. *CE*, May 4, 11, 25, and June 1, 8, 15, 22 ("Sidewalk" quote), 1928; see also news clippings from other papers in BF 16: Newspaper Clippings, 1928.

67. *CE*, June 15, 22, July 20, 1928, in BF 16: Newspaper Clippings, 1928.

68. *NA*, May 11, 1928; *CE*, June 22, 1928 ("Spirit of Jazz"); and *PD*, June 7, 28 ("demonstrate to the East"), 1928, all in BF 16: Newspaper Clippings, 1928.

69. *CE*, June 15, 22, 1928.

70. *CE*, June 15, 22, 1928; Lifton, "Incredible," 38–39.

71. Somerville, *Man*, 126; *CE*, June 22, 1928.

72. Du Bois quoted in Lifton, "Incredible," 40–41.

73. *CE*, June 22, 29, 1928; these issues inform the following paragraphs as well.

74. *CE*, June 22, 1928.

75. *Crisis*, Sept. 1928, 311–12; *CE*, July 6, 1928, in BF 16: Newspaper Clippings, 1928.

76. Bagnall to Hudson, Jan. 10, 1928, in BF 16: Jan.–May 1928; *CE*, June 29, 1928. Results of the drive are lacking; even Bagnall, who led it, was not sure: Bagnall to Hudson, Aug. 3, 1928, in BF 16: June–Dec. 1928; see also BF 16: Membership Lists, Jan.–Dec. 1928.

77. Bagnall to Hudson, Aug. 3, 1928, in BF 16: June–Dec. 1928; *CE*, July 6, Aug. 10, 1928; *PD*, Aug. 10, 1928, in BF 16: Newspaper Clippings, 1928.

78. On Hill: *Dir.*, 75, 84; "housewife" quote from list of local NAACP officers, ca. Nov. 20 1927, in BF 16: Sept.–Dec. 1927. Quotes in this and following paragraphs from: Branch report prepared for the national convention, June 12, 1931, in BF 17: Jan.–June 1931, and Hudson to Walker Medal Committee, March 5, 1932, in BF 17: Jan.–May 1932.

79. Somerville, *Man*, 127.

80. *Western Progress*, photocopy at HEH, locations mapped by author.

81. *Western Progress* (architectural drawing); Hudson, *Williams*, 230; invitation to opening with photo: BF 16: Jan.–July 1929.

82. *Dir.*, 99.

83. *Western Progress;* Cox, *Central*, 31, 61; Bryant et al., *Central*, 199 ("Brown Broadway").

84. *CE*, Feb. 15, 1929, in BF 16: Newspaper Clippings, 1929.

85. Powell, *Black*, chap. 5; Bass, *Forty*, 62.

9. Responding to the Depression

1. Somerville, *Man*, 127; Patton to Bagnall, Oct. 27, 1929, in BF 16: Aug.–Dec. 1929.

2. Leader, *Los Angeles*, 6, 11, 14; Hawkins oral history (Flamming); Taylor, *Search*, 229.

3. Adams, *Dark*, chaps. 12–13, esp. 180–86.

4. Sides, *L.A.*, 27.

5. Williams oral history; *WW*, entries for "Loggins, Roy L. Sr.," "Loggins, Minnie Lee," and "Golden State"; Hudson, *Williams;* Somerville, *Man*, 127–28.

6. Bagnall to Hudson, Dec. 3, 1929, in BF 16: Aug.–Dec. 1929; Lewis, *Du Bois: Fight*, chaps. 8–9; Hudson to Lampkin, Aug. 4, 1934 (includes Hudson's handwritten note to Pickens: "Glad Du Boise [*sic*] has left organization. Why don't you edit [the *Crisis*]?"), in BF 17: July–Dec. 1934.

7. White, *Man*, chap 16. The mistaken idea that the NAACP refused to support the Scottsboro boys is still presented by historians; see, e.g., the entry for "Scottsboro case" in *Africana*, 1680–81, and Sides, *L.A.*, 31.

8. Griffith to White, June 20, 1935, in BF 17: Jan.–June 1935.

9. Hudson to Pickens, Oct. 28, 1933 (and News Clippings in same file), in BF 17: Sept.–Dec. 1933.

10. Covington, "Color," 146.

11. There is no mention of Mexican repatriation in the *Eagle* during February and March 1931, nor is there evidence that the NAACP's local branch considered the issue. On repatriation, see Ruiz, *From*, 28–31; Sanchez, *Becoming*, chap. 10; Gutierrez, *Walls*, 71–74.

12. Sides, *L.A.*, 63.

13. In her autobiography, Charlotta failed to mention that the council initially urged migrants and unemployed workers to leave L.A. and take up agriculture. Only later, when her politics moved left, would she see salvation in a biracial labor movement; but in *Forty Years*, she described the council as a kind of black-only branch of the American labor movement. Bass, *Forty*, 76–78. See also Sides, *L.A.*, 30.

14. Bryant et al., *Central*, 197–98, 205; *Sentinel*, May 24, 1934 (earliest surviving issue and first-anniversary edition). Bass, *Forty*, 76; *Dir.*, 30; *NA*, Feb. 25, 1938. On national boycott trends, see Greenberg, "*Explode?*" chap. 5.

15. Powell, *Black*, 195–215.

16. *Craftsman Aero News* (two surviving issues, 1937–38, Special Collections, Fisk University Library, Nashville, Tennessee).

17. *WW*, 64; Bass, *Forty*, 77–78; Hudson to Pickens, Oct. 28, 1933, in BF 17: Sept.–Dec. 1933; Lomax oral history, 3.

18. Lomax oral history, 3–4; Sides, *L.A.*, 30.

19. Rampersad, *Life*, 236–41; *CE*, Oct. 9, 1936.

20. *Sentinel*, May 24, 1934; Lomax oral history; *WW*, entry for "Leon Washington"; Rampersad, *Life*, 236.

21. Miller quoted in Sides, *L.A.*, 32.

22. McWilliams, *Southern*, chap. 14, esp. 295–96.

23. Watts, "Shout," chaps. 7–8, esp. 117–28, 138n39.

24. Ibid.

25. Sides, *L.A.*, 31–33; Pettis Perry file, Federal Bureau of Investigation (initial entries are from 1939). Freedom of Information Act censored file in author's possession.

26. "Historical Background of Negro Survey, for Los Angeles," 1935, typed ms., table 3, Index of American Design Collection, Items B 2–6, Box 2, folder 1, HEH. This federally funded survey was conducted by the California State Emergency Relief Administration. There are two drafts of this report: the rough draft is a mess; a final draft, used here, is clearer. On Lomax, see Pitt and Pitt, *Los Angeles*, 124, and Lomax oral history.

27. Bryant et al., *Central*, 25, 29; Otis, *Upside*, 13–23.

28. California legislators were supposed to redraw assembly district boundaries in 1921 based on the 1920 census. But they deadlocked over boundaries, and the lines remained unchanged. Legislators finally revised the districts in 1927, but the new boundaries did not apply until the 1930 elections. On boundary lines, see *The Statutes of California and Amendments to the Code, 1911*, Extra Session, p. 163; *Statutes of California: 1927*, p. 1780; *Statutes of California: 1931*, p. 285. Roberts's obituary (*CE*, July 27, 1952), credited him with maintaining electoral lines that preserved racial representation—meaning his 1927 redistricting plans, which he maintained in the redistricting of 1931.

29. Taylor, *Search*, table on 223; U.S. Bureau of the Census, *Sixteenth Census of the United States, 1940: Population: Internal Migration, 1935–40, Color and Sex of Migration* (Washington, D.C.: Government Printing Office, 1943), tables 16–20.

30. Nugent, *Into*, chap. 7, esp. 234–41; Sanchez, *Becoming*, chap. 10; "Population Change, 1930–1940: Population and Housing Survey," map prepared by the John Randolph Haynes and Dora Haynes Foundation, ca. 1941, copy in author's possession. De Graaf, "City," focusing on the rise in black population, suggests (p. 349) that the district became more crowded in the 1930s; but the data support the conclusions in this paragraph.

31. Bonds quoted in Sides, "Working," 45; Goins, "Ol' Time."

32. *Sentinel*, May 24, July 26, Aug. 2, Aug. 9, 1934. Watts, "Shout," 358. Lomax oral history, tape 1, track 1: 10–11.

33. Hawkins oral history (Flamming).

34. Gregory, *American*, 39–52; Nicolaides, *Blue*, chaps. 1–2.

35. Covington quoted in Sides, "Working," 49.

36. Leuchtenburg, *Roosevelt*; Badger, *New*; Wolfskill, *Happy*—three standards among many.

37. Leader, *Los Angeles*, 143 (county statistics); Crouch et al., *State*, 30 (state-level statistics). In my 2001 essay, "Becoming," 283, I incorrectly presented state-level registration figures as the L.A. County figures.

38. On national voter turnout, see Kirby, *Black*; Sitkoff, *New*; Weiss, *Farewell*. On voter turnout in the West, see Broussard, *Black*, chaps. 5–6; Taylor, *Forging*, chap. 3; *SV*, 1932 general election. The New Deal also mobilized Mexican American voters in L.A. (Sanchez, *Becoming*, 221–22, 250), but that did not foster an immediate interethnic electoral alliance between blacks and Latinos. Roberts quoted from pamphlet in Roberts Family collection, AAMLO, Box 1, folder 16.

39. *CE*, July 15 and 22, Aug. 19 and 26, Oct. 7, Nov. 4, 1932; *SV*, 1932 primary election.

40. Two good accounts of the campaign are Greg Mitchell, *The Campaign of the Century: Upton Sinclair's Race for Governor of California and the Birth of Media Politics* (New York: Random House, 1992), and Sinclair, *Candidate*.

41. *CE*, June 15, 29, Aug. 10, 24, 1934; *Sentinel*, June 14, 28, July 12 ("a new day"), 1934; Somerville, *Man*, 83–84, 86–89; Hawkins oral history (Flamming).

42. *CE*, June 29, 1934; *Sentinel*, June 28, 1934.

43. On Dones, see *CE*, April 6, May 11 ("people's candidate"), June 8, July 13 ("show the boys"), 1934; *Sentinel*, Aug. 2, 1934. The EPIC dropout was John Gold, whose name remained on the ballot and earned 405 votes.

44. On the national patterns of emerging black leadership, see Sitkoff, *Black*; Weiss, *Farewell*.

45. *Sentinel*, Aug. 16, 1934; *CE*, June–Aug., 1934.

46. Hawkins oral histories (Flamming and Vasquez).

47. *Sentinel*, June 21, July 12, Aug. 2 1934, suggested that Hawkins was part of the EPIC bloc, but EPIC actually endorsed no Democrat in the 62nd district primary. They had polled Hawkins about his stand on socialized medicine, and when Hawkins, in deference to his MD brother, had given an ambivalent response, EPIC refused to endorse him. Only after Hawkins won the primary did EPIC place its stamp of approval on him; Hawkins oral history (Vasquez), 48–49, 78; *EPIC News*, all issues July through November 1934, in Upton Sinclair Manuscripts, Lilly Library, University of Indiana, Bloomington.

48. Hawkins oral history (Vasquez), 46–51. Quote from Upton Sinclair editorial in *Upton Sinclair's Paper: End Poverty*, May 1934; anti-McGroarty story in *Upton Sinclair's EPIC News*, May 28, 1934; examples of futile correspondence with Afro-Angelenos: Suzanne Claire Dean to Sinclair, March 19, 1934 (Box 25); Sinclair to Dean, March 21, 1934 (Box 25); Beth Rowland to Sinclair, March 29, 1934 (Box 26); Charlotte Griffey to Sinclair, April 4, 1934 (Box 26); Sinclair to Rowland, April 4, 1934 (Box 26). Sinclair's "Negro Leader," appointed to lead the EPIC charge among Afro-Angelenos, was one "Dr. T. R. M. Howard,

president of the Economic, Commercial and Political League of California" (*EPIC News*, July 16, 1934); in my research I never encountered either Howard or his organization. All Sinclair items in Upton Sinclair Manuscripts, Lilly Library, University of Indiana, Bloomington.

49. Hawkins oral history (Vasquez), 47–51; on railroad brotherhoods for EPIC on the Eastside, see *65th Assembly District Edition of EPIC News*, Aug. 28, 1934, Sinclair Manuscripts, Lilly Library.

50. Whiteman and Lewis, *Glory*, chaps. 3–6, esp. 23, 33–34, 56–59; Leader, *Los Angeles*, 128–29; Hawkins oral history (Flamming).

51. Hawkins oral history (Vasquez); Watts, "Shout."

52. *SV*, 1934 primary election.

53. *CE*, Oct. 5, 1934.

54. Hawkins oral history (Flamming).

55. Ibid.; *CE*, Aug. 17, 1934.

56. *CE*, Nov. 2, 1934.

57. *SV*, 1934 general election; *CE*, Nov. 9, 1934.

58. *Utopian News*, Nov. 15, 1934.

59. *CE*, Nov. 9, 1934.

60. Sides, "Working" (Hawkins's attempt); Hawkins oral history (Flamming).

61. Hans J. Massaquoi, "Gus Hawkins—Fifth Negro Congressman," *Ebony* vol. 18, no. 4 (Feb. 1963): 38–40, 42; Hawkins oral history (Flamming).

62. Robinson, *Jackie*, 20–21; *WW*, 130.

63. Weiss, *Farewell*, 92–94, 200–204, 218.

64. *CE*, June 12, 26 1936; *NA*, full coverage, late July–early Nov., 1936.

65. *CE*, June 26, July 3 ("Just as well"), 1936; *NA*, Aug. 14, 1936.

66. *NA*, July 31, Aug. 7, 1936.

67. *NA*, Aug. 14, 1936; *CE*, July 17, 1936.

68. *NA*, July 24, Aug. 7 (quote), 14, 1936.

69. *CE*, Aug. 14, 1936; Hawkins oral history (Flamming).

70. *NA*, Aug. 21, 1936; *CE*, Aug. 21, 1936.

71. *SV*, 1936 primary election; *NA*, Aug. 28, 1936; *CE*, Sept. 4, 1936. The Oct. 16, 1936, issue of the *Eagle* would concede that "Baumann is giving unstinted support to Hawkins."

72. *CE*, Sept. 18, 1936; *NA*, Sept. 4, 11, 18, Oct. 9, 23, 1936.

73. *NA*, Sept. 25, Oct. 30, 1936; *CE*, Sept. 18, 1936.

74. *CE*, Oct. 9, 30, 1936.

75. *CE*, Aug. 14, 1936; *NA*, Oct. 30, 1936.

76. *SV*, 1936 general election.

77. *NA*, Nov. 6, 1936; *CE*, Nov. 6, 1936.

78. County figures: Leader, *Los Angeles*, 143; assemblymen and their party affiliations listed in California, Secretary of State, *California Blue Book and State Roster* (Sacramento: California State Printing Office) for 1932 and 1938.

79. Unidentified news release, Dec. 2, 1933, in BF 17: Sept.–Dec. 1933; Weiss, *Farewell*, 92–94, 200–205, 293.

80. *NA,* Nov. 6, 1936.

81. *NA,* April 16 (date mistakenly reads 9), 23, 30, 1937, announce the *Talent Hour*'s beginnings; all issues May–Aug. 1937 cover the show; information about the show inexplicably vanished from the *NA* after Aug. 27, 1937.

82. Information from obituaries in *LAT,* July 20, 1952, sec. 1, p. 14; *CE,* July 24, 1952; Logan and Winston, *Encyclopedia,* 526–27.

83. *CE,* June 9, 1938; *SV,* 1938 primary election.

84. Hawkins oral history (Flamming).

10. Race and New Deal Liberalism

1. *NA,* Nov. 6, 1936.

2. Leader, *Los Angeles,* 244–45, 250–53, 228.

3. This is a key theme of Wolfskill, *Happy.*

4. "Historical Background of Negro Survey, for Los Angeles," 1935, typed ms., Index of American Design Collection, Items B 2–6, Box 2, folder 1, HEH; Somerville, *Man,* 86–87.

5. Somerville, *Man,* 87.

6. Covington, "Where," 236–41 (quote 236).

7. Ibid., 239–41.

8. Ibid., 238, 240.

9. Griffith, Jr., to Wilkins, Jan. 22, 1935; Pickens to Griffiths [*sic*], Jan. 29, 1935; Griffith to Pickens, Feb. 4, 1935; Griffith to Wilkins, Feb. 27, 1935; Wilkins to Griffith, March 4, 1935, all in BF 17: Jan.–June 1935.

10. Lampkin to Hudson, Jan. 9, 1934, and see Membership file, 1934, in BF 17.

11. Muse ["Hollywood Representative NAACP"] to Newmark, April 12, 1934; White to Muse, May 1, 1934; Rochester to Muse, May 5, 1934; and "Ann Harding [a Hollywood actress] Joins N.A.A.C.P.," national office press release, May 18, [1934], all in BF 17: Jan.–June 1934.

12. "Report of the Election of Officers of the Los Angeles Branch, December 10, 1933," in BF 17: Membership file, 1934.

13. "'Red' Squad Guards NAACP Election," typed news story, Jan. [1935], in BF 17: Articles and Clippings, 1935.

14. "Souvenir" program, June 22, 1935, in BF 17: Articles and Clippings, 1935.

15. [Wilkins] to Hudson, March 22, 1933; [Hudson] to Walter White, Sept. 21, 1933; White to Hudson, Sept. 28, 1933, all in BF 17: Jan.–Aug. 1933 and Sept.–Dec. 1933. Continued concern in the NAACP about discrimination in the Civil Works Administration is in letters dated Aug. 6, 1935, in BF 17: July–Dec. 1935; Feb. 1, 1936, in BF 18: Jan.–March 1936; and Jan. 25, 1937, in BF 18: Jan.–March 1937.

16. *Federal Civil Works Administration, Rules and Regulations No. 10* (Washington, D.C.: Government Printing Office, 1933), 4, enclosure for Mc-

Clure to Wilkins, Dec. 22, 1933, in BF 17: Sept.–Dec. 1933. Badger, *New,* 191–200; Leuchtenburg, *Franklin,* 120–23.

17. Information and quotations in this and the following paragraphs are from the "Report of Committee on Civil Works Administration, Los Angeles Branch, National Association for the Advancement of Colored People, Los Angeles, California, December 28, 1935," in BF 17: Sept.–Dec. 1933 (hereafter cited as CWA Report).

18. [Wilkins] to Hopkins, Dec. 14, 1933; McClure to Wilkins, Dec. 22, 1933, in BF 17: Sept.–Dec. 1933.

19. CWA Report, 5–6.

20. Ibid., 7.

21. Hudson to Walker, Dec. 26, 1933; Walker to Hudson, Dec. 30, 1933; Scruggs to Walker, Jan. 5, 1934, all in BF 17: Sept.–Dec. 1933 and Jan.–June 1934; Badger, *New,* 197.

22. CWA Report, 9. See also Scruggs to Wilkins, Jan. 12, 1934; Wilkins to Scruggs, Jan. 24, 1934, in BF 17: Jan.–June 1934.

23. Wilkins to Scruggs, Feb. 5, 1934, in BF 17: Jan.–June 1934.

24. Ibid.; Scruggs to Wilkins, Sept. 20, 1934 (Scruggs to Wilkins, June 22, 1934, attached), in BF 17: Jan.–June 1934 and July–Dec. 1934.

25. Badger, *New,* 200; Leuchtenburg, *Roosevelt,* 122–23.

26. Report from California's NYA office to the deputy executive director of NYA in Washington, D.C.: exhibit 1, "Minutes of State Advisory Committee, 28 Sept. 1935," and exhibit 8, Treadwell's description of the NYA and its aims for California, untitled, 1 (quote); Records of the National Youth Administration, National Archives, Washington, D.C. (hereafter cited as NYA Records), Series E62, Box 3, folder "June–December 1935." And see Olen Cole, Jr., "Black Youth in the National Youth Administration in California, 1935–1943," *Southern California Quarterly* 73 (Winter 1991): 385–402.

27. Badger, *New,* 207–8; NA, July 3, 1936. The monthly reports of California's NYA were known as Y-12 reports, Williams having made them mandatory in "Bulletin Y-12." These were superseded by Y-45 reports in 1937. NYA Records, Series E62, Boxes 3 and 5.

28. Treadwell to Corson, Sept. 4, 1935; Treadwell to Williams, Oct. 16, 1935; Treadwell to Brown, Feb. 8, 1936; Jan. Y-12 Report, "Records of the Deputy Exec. Director and the Deputy Admin., Admin. Reports Received from NYA State Offices, 1935–1938," 2; and Y-12 Report for Nov. 1935, 4–5; all in NYA Records, Series E62, Box 3.

29. Y-12 Report for Jan. 1936, 21, NYA Records, Series E62, Box 3.

30. Ibid.; Y-12 Report for Feb. 1936, 18, NYA Records, Series E62, Box 3.

31. Y-12 Report for Feb. 1936, 18, and March 1936, 27, NYA Records, Series E62, Box 3.

32. Tables on the Student Aid program are in Y-12 Reports, Series E62, Box 3; Project Unit figures are in Y-45 Reports, Series E62, Box 5; quote is from "Negro Youth on the National Youth Administration Program in California," 1, E119, Box 2, folder "California 1937–38," all in NYA Records.

33. NYA, State of California, Division of Guidance and Placement, "Comparative Data on Project Personnel as of June, 1937," 3, NYA Records, Series E62, Box 5, no folder title.

34. California state report for Nov. 1936, 4–5, NYA Records, Series E62, Box 4, "California—Reports, Oct thru . . ."

35. Y-45 Report for Aug. 1937; Y-45 Report for June 1938, 7; Y-45 for Oct. 1938, 7–8, all in NYA Records, Series E62, Box 5. Job segregation is apparent in photos of the "Centennial project" attached to the report, NYA Records, Series E62, Box 5. "Negro Youth on the National Youth Administration Program in California," 1938, NYA Records, Series E119, Boxes 2–4.

36. *NA*, April 29, Oct. 21, 1938; "Month Narrative Report for November—1938," 3, 12, NYA Records, Series E62, Box 5; Division of Negro Affairs "Newsletter," Feb. 28, 1938, NYA Records, Series E120, Box 6, Administrative Assistants, folder 1.

37. Table: "Number of Negro Youths on Work Projects in Area #11 (Los Angeles County)" and table on following page for other districts, dated "Dec 29"; Osborne-Marsh report stamped "Received" in Washington June 14, 1939, p. 3; and letter headed "Attention: Mrs. Mary McLeod Bethune" [ca. March 1939], p. 1, all in NYA Records, Series E119, Box 3, folder "California 1938–39."

38. See "California Report for January," NYA Records, Series E119, Box 3, "California 1938–39."

39. Ibid.

40. Osborne-Marsh to Bethune, April 20, 1939, in NYA Records, Series E119, Box 3, "California 1938–39."

41. Information and quote from online Val Verde historical file, Valencia Public Library, Valencia, California.

42. *CE*, May 8, 15, June 5, 19, 1925; Jocelyn Y. Stewart, "Forgotten Oasis of Freedom," *LAT*, March 2, 1994, sec. A, pp. 1, 12–13.

43. *CE*, Nov. 9, 1934, May 4, 25, 1939; *NA*, 1936 (regular column), May 21, 1937 (county park).

44. *CE*, April 20, 1939; Cripps, *Slow*, 361–62. Jocelyn Y. Stewart, "Forgotten Oasis of Freedom," in *LAT*, March 2, 1994, sec. A, pp. 1, 12–13, suggests the county park and the swimming pool were both part of the same project, which contradicts *NA*, May 21, 1937.

45. Cox, *Central*, 45–46.

46. Jackson, *Crabgrass*, 193.

47. Ibid., 362n26.

48. Ibid., 195–203; Nicolaides, *Blue*, 192.

49. U.S. Home Owners Loan Corporation, City Survey Files, Los Angeles, Central Avenue District, Area No. D-52, March 3, 1939, Record Group 195, National Archives, Washington, D.C. For a broader description of HOLC survey results in Los Angeles, see Nicolaides, *Blue*, 192–93.

50. HOLC survey.

51. Jackson, *Crabgrass*, 204–6.

52. Ibid., 207–15, and 365n54. Raymond A. Mohl, "Trouble in Paradise: Race

and Housing in Miami during the New Deal Era," in Mohl, ed., *The Making of Urban America* (Wilmington, DE: SR Books, 1988), 221–25, offers a similar story. See also Greg Hise, "Home Building and Industrial Decentralization in Los Angeles: The Roots of the Postwar Urban Region," *Journal of Urban History* 19 (Feb. 1993): 95–125.

53. *NA*, Oct. 21, 1938.

54. Ibid.

55. Jackson, *Crabgrass*, 224.

56. *CE*, June 11, 1937; Los Angeles County Housing Authority, *A Review of the Activities of the Housing Authority of the County of Los Angeles, 1938–1943* (Los Angeles: n.p., 1944).

57. Hudson, *Williams*, 108–9, 232; Thomas S. Hines, "Housing, Baseball, and Creeping Socialism: The Battle of Chavez Ravine, Los Angeles, 1949–1959," *Journal of Urban History* 8 (Feb. 1982): 123–43; Cuff, *Provisional*.

58. Kirby, *Black*, 206.

59. Kirby, *Black*, 155–70, 202–17; Hawkins oral history (Flamming); Lewis, *Du Bois: Fight*, 199, 466.

60. *NA*, Oct. 21, 1938; Fisher, "History," 235.

61. Sides, "Working," 62 (quote); Bates, *Pullman*, 126–27.

62. Dellums to W. B. Holland, April 5, 1935; Dellums to Holland, April 18, 1935; Dellums to Charles Upton, May 14, 1935, in Dellums papers, Carton 5, folder "Copies, Los Angeles, 1934–38," Bancroft Library, University of California, Berkeley.

63. Dellums to Holland, April 18, 1935; *Dir.*, 92.

64. Dellums to Holland, May 7, 1935; Dellums to Holland, May 14, 1935 (first quote); Dellums to Holland, May 19, 1935 (second quote); Dellums to Holland, July 1, 1935 (results); Dellums to Holland, July 9, 1935, in Dellums papers, Carton 5, "Copies, Los Angeles, 1934–38."

65. Dellums to Holland, Aug. ?, 1935 ("no part"); Dellums to Upton, Aug. 2, 1935 ("petty fights"); Dellums to Holland, Nov. 23, 1935; Dellums to Holland, Dec. 10, 1935 ("not developing"); Dellums to Upton, Jan. 31, 1936; Dellums to Holland, Feb. 7, 1936; Dellums to Holland, March 21, 1936; Dellums to Upton, July 28, 1936 ("Communists frequenting"), all in Dellums papers, Carton 5, "Copies, Los Angeles, 1934–38." Sides, "Working," 61–63 ("crop here").

66. Gutierrez, *Walls*, chap. 3, esp. 107–16 (quote, 112).

67. Leonard, "In," 316.

68. This paragraph and next: Leonard, "Years."

69. Leonard, "Years"; Sides, "Working"; Horne, *Fire*; Gerald Horne, "Black Fire: 'Riot' and 'Revolt' in Los Angeles, 1965 and 1992," in de Graaf et al., eds., *Seeking*.

70. BF 18: early 1937 (state laws); early 1939 (defense program); Badger, *New*, 200–203; Chamberlain, *Victory at Home: Manpower and Race in the American South during World War II* (Athens: University of Georgia Press, 2003), 43–47; Merl Reed, *Seedtime for the Modern Civil Rights Movement: The President's Committee on Fair Employment Practice, 1941–1946* (Baton Rouge:

Louisiana State University Press, 1991); White, *Man*, chap. 23; Bates, *Pullman*, chap. 7 (quote 160).

71. Bates, *Pullman*, 161.

72. Kirby, *Black*, 139–45, 162; Lemann, *Promised*.

Departure

1. Bass, *Forty*, 183; Gottlieb and Wolt, *Thinking Big*, 361; Pitt and Pitt, *Los Angeles*, entry for Jack Tenny, p. 496; *Time*, March 17, 1952, 20.

2. "Acceptance Speech of Mrs. Charlotta Bass, Candidate for Vice President of the United States of the Progressive Party," delivered Saturday, July 5, 1952, C. B. Baldwin Papers, Special Collections Department, University of Iowa Library, Iowa City (hereafter cited as BP). In this speech, Bass suggests that she voted for Roosevelt in 1932 and 1936, but according to a former *Eagle* staffer, she supported Landon in 1936 (Lomax oral history), a claim confirmed by the *Eagle*'s position through 1936.

3. Bass, *Forty*, 121–23, 131.

4. United States War Department, *World War II: Honor List of Dead and Missing, State of California, Los Angeles County*, 31; Bass, *Forty*, 123; various campaign speeches from 1952, BP; and Lomax oral history.

5. Duberman, *Robeson*, chap. 16, esp. 324–25, 334–35; Bass, *Forty*, 141–44.

6. Bass, *Forty*, 157–75; Streitmatter, *Raising*, 102–4.

7. Bass, *Forty*, 173–75.

8. Hall et al., eds., *Oxford*, 781–82; Miller, *Petitioners*, chap. 22; Vose, *Caucasians*, 153, 184–88, 199–202, and chap. 10; Nieman, *Promises*, 144.

9. Undated news clippings from the 1952 campaign in BP; Seth Rosenfield, obituary for Vivian Hallinan, *San Francisco Examiner*, March 17, 1999, reprinted in Floor Statement by Congresswoman Nancy Pelosi, "On the Passing of Three Extraordinary Women," March 25, 1999, online version (Feb. 27, 2003) www.house.gov/pelosi/fltrio.htm.

10. *Time*, March 17, 1952, 20.

11. Photos and *News Release*, issued by the Progressive Party, "Mrs. Bass Goes to Philadelphia," BP; Lewis, *Du Bois: Fight*, 536.

12. Progressive Party, Arnold Perl, Director of Public Relations, . . . For release SATURDAY papers, April 4, 1952, BP.

13. Mrs. Charlotta Bass Acceptance Speech, as Vice Presidential Candidate of the Progressive Party. Made to National Committee of Progressive Party at . . . Chicago . . . March 30, 1952, BP.

14. Address by Mrs. Charlotta Bass, Committee of Women, ALP, Luncheon, Hotel Astor, New York City, April 28, 1952, BP.

15. Progressive Party Convention Hall, Ashland Auditorium, Chicago, Illinois . . . *Acceptance Speech of Mrs. Charlotta Bass* . . . delivered Saturday, July 5, 1952, BP.

16. Gerald R. Gill, "'Win or Lose—We Win': The 1952 Vice Presidential

Campaign of Charlotta A. Bass," in *The Afro-American Woman: Struggles and Images*, ed. Sharon Harley and Rosalyn Tarborg-Penn (Port Washington, NY: Kennikat Press, 1978).

17. Progressive Party Newsletter no. 2, Sept. 4, 1952; "Dr. Du Bois Calls for 'Protest Vote'," undated press release, 2; Illinois Progressive Party, Press Release (Delivered over NBC radio and TV network 12:30 P.M.), Sept. 6, 1952, "Acceptance Speech of Mrs. Charlotta A. Bass," all in BP.

18. Flamming, "Becoming," 297–300; Hawkins oral history (Flamming); Hawkins oral history (Vasquez), 75, 109–12, 121, 133–34, 160–64; Johnson, *Second*, 206; Jackson K. Putnam, *Modern California Politics*, 2nd ed. (San Francisco: Boyd and Fraser, 1984), chap. 4; John Jacobs, *A Rage for Justice: The Passion and Politics of Phillip Burton* (Berkeley and Los Angeles: University of California Press, 1995); Royce Delmatier, *The Rumble of California Politics* (New York: John Wiley, 1970), 349–51, 424–25; Lapp, *Afro-Americans*, 84–85; Raphael J. Sonenshein, *Politics in Black and White: Race and Power in Los Angeles* (Princeton, NJ: Princeton University Press, 1993), chap. 3; and Martin Schiesl, ed., "The California of the Pat Brown Years: Creative Building for the 'Golden State's' Future" (Los Angeles: Edmund "Pat" Brown Institute of Public Affairs, California State University, Los Angeles, 1997).

19. *CE*, Feb. 12, 1916.

20. Carol Tucker and Amy Ko, "Student Preserves Past, Builds Future for Central Avenue," *UCLA Today* online, www.today.ucla.edu/2001/010213future.html, Feb. 23, 2004.

21. Bryant et. al., *Central*, 177, 49–50; Sides, *L.A.*, chap. 4.

22. Sides, *L.A.*, 108–30.

23. Beavers oral history (UCLA), 1.

24. *Atlanta Journal-Constitution*, July 8, 2001, sec. A, pp. 1 ("top magnet"), 7 ("mecca"); Sept. 25, 2002, sec. A, pp. 1 ("No. 1"), 10.

25. Streitmatter, *Raising*, 105.

26. Streitmatter, *Raising*, 106; Bass, *Forty*, 140.

27. Here I join two quotes, twenty pages apart but of a piece: words before the ellipses, 179; words after, 196–97.

28. Hughes, "History," originally in *Opportunity*, reprinted in Hughes, *Panther*, 69.

Selected Bibliography

This bibliography by no means reflects all of the secondary and primary sources consulted for *Bound for Freedom*. It is instead a list of sources cited frequently in the notes, where I have used brief citations to save space. To facilitate finding those references here, I have divided this bibliography into four basic sections—Newspapers, Other Printed Materials, Oral Histories, and Manuscript Collections—and alphabetized the entries within each section. In Oral Histories and Manuscript Collections, I list interviews and manuscript collections alphabetically by subject, instead of by institution. References cited in full in the notes are not listed here.

Newspapers

Black-owned newspapers are indispensable sources for African American history, but they can be difficult to locate. Fortunately, the State Historical Society of Wisconsin's project "African-American Newspapers and Periodicals: A National Bibliography and Union List" has made the task much easier, with its computer index to black-owned newspapers and journals held in archives throughout the United States. You can search for newspapers by place (e.g., Los Angeles) and by name (e.g., *California Eagle*), among other variables, and discover which libraries and archives have what you need. Listed here are the Los Angeles newspapers I cite frequently, for which there are accessible microfilm holdings.

California Eagle (originally *The Eagle*); University of California, Los Angeles, and California Institute of Technology

Citizen Advocate; University of California, Berkeley

Los Angeles Sentinel; California State University, Fullerton

Los Angeles Times; Henry E. Huntington Library, San Marino, California, and Los Angeles Public Library

New Age (later *New Age Dispatch*); University of California, Berkeley

Pacific Defender; University of California, Berkeley

Southern California Guide; State Historical Society of Wisconsin

Weekly Observer; State Historical Society of Wisconsin

Western Dispatch; University of California, Berkeley

Western News; State Historical Society of Wisconsin

Other Printed Materials

Adams, Elizabeth Laura. *Dark Symphony.* New York: Sheed and Ward, 1942.

Adler, Patricia Rae. "Watts: From Suburb to Black Ghetto." Ph.D. diss., University of Southern California, 1977.

Africana: The Encyclopedia of African and African American Experience. Edited by Kwame Anthony Appiah and Henry Louis Gates, Jr. New York: Basic Books, 1999.

Alexander, Carolyn Elayne. *Abbot Kinney's Venice-of-America.* Vol. 1, *The Golden Years: 1905–1920.* Los Angeles: Westside Genealogical Society, 1991.

Anderson, Frederick E. *The Development of Leadership and Organization Building in the Black Community of Los Angeles from 1900 through World War II.* Saratoga, CA: Century Twenty-One Publishing, 1980.

Badger, Anthony J. *The New Deal: The Depression Years, 1933–1940.* New York: Hill and Wang, 1989.

Bass, Charlotta. *Forty Years: Memoirs from the Pages of a Newspaper.* Los Angeles: California Eagle Press, 1960.

Bates, Beth Tompkins. *Pullman Porters and the Rise of Protest Politics in Black America, 1925–1945.* Chapel Hill: University of North Carolina Press, 2001.

Beasley, Delilah L. *The Negro Trail Blazers of California.* Los Angeles: California Eagle Publishing Company, 1919.

Bond, J. Max. "The Negro in Los Angeles." Ph.D. diss., University of Southern California, 1936.

Bontemps, Arna. "The Awakening: A Memoir." In *The Harlem Renaissance Remembered: Essays,* edited by Arna Bentemps. New York: Dodd, Mead, 1972.

———. *Black Thunder.* 1936. Reprinted with an introduction by the author. Boston: Beacon Press, 1968.

———. "Why I Returned." In *The Old South: "A Summer Tragedy" and Other Stories of the Thirties.* New York: Dodd, Mead, 1973.

———, and Jack Conroy. *Anyplace but Here.* 1966. Reprint, Columbia: University of Missouri Press, 1997. A revised and enlarged version of a book first published in 1945 as *They Seek a City.*

Broussard, Albert S. *Black San Francisco: The Struggle for Racial Equality in the West, 1900–1954.* Lawrence: University of Kansas Press, 1993.

Bryant, Clora, et al., eds. *Central Avenue Sounds: Jazz in Los Angeles.* Berkeley and Los Angeles: University of California Press, 1998.

Bunch, Lonnie G., III. "A Past Not Necessarily Prologue: The African American in Los Angeles." In *20th Century Los Angeles: Power, Promotion, and Social*

Conflict, edited by Norman M. Klein and Martin J. Schiesl. Claremont, CA: Regina Books, 1990.

Cairns, Kathleen A. *Front-Page Women Journalists, 1920–1950*. Lincoln: University of Nebraska Press, 2003.

Cole, Olen, Jr. "Black Youth in the National Youth Administration in California, 1935–1943." *Southern California Quarterly* 73, no. 4 (Winter 1991): 385–402.

Cose, Ellis. *The Rage of a Privileged Class*. New York: Harper, 1993.

Covington, Floyd C. "Color: A Factor in Social Mobility." *Sociology and Social Research* (Nov.–Dec. 1930): 145–52.

———. "Greene of Los Angeles." *The Crisis*, March 1933, 57–58.

———. "Union Styles: Black Labor in White Coats." *Opportunity*, July 1931, 208–10.

———. "Where the Color Line Chokes." *Sociology and Social Research* (Jan.–Feb. 1936): 236–41.

Cox, Bette Yarbrough. *Central Avenue: Its Rise and Fall, 1890–c. 1955, Including the Musical Renaissance of Black Los Angeles*. Los Angeles: BEEM Publications, 1996.

Cox, Thomas C. *Blacks in Topeka, Kansas, 1865–1915: A Social History*. Baton Rouge: Louisiana State University Press, 1982.

Cripps, Thomas. *Slow Fade to Black*. New York: Oxford University Press, 1977.

Crouchett, Lawrence P., et al. *The History of the East Bay Afro-American Community, 1852–1977*. Oakland: Northern California Center for Afro-American History and Life, 1989.

Cuff, Dana. *The Provisional City: Los Angeles Stories of Architecture and Urbanism*. Cambridge, MA: MIT Press, 2000.

Daniels, Henry Douglas. *Pioneer Urbanites: A Social and Cultural History of Black San Francisco*. Berkeley and Los Angeles: University of California Press, 1990.

Davis, Clark. *Company Men: White-Collar Life and Corporate Cultures in Los Angeles, 1892–1941*. Baltimore: Johns Hopkins University Press, 2000.

de Graaf, Lawrence B. "The City of Black Angels: Emergence of the Los Angeles Ghetto, 1890–1930." *Pacific Historical Review* 39 (Aug. 1970): 323–52.

———, Kevin Mulroy, and Quintard Taylor, eds. *Seeking El Dorado: African Americans in California*. Los Angeles: Autry Museum of Western Heritage; Seattle and London: University of Washington Press, 2001.

Demaratus, DeEtta. *The Force of a Feather: The Search for a Lost Story of Slavery and Freedom*. Salt Lake City: University of Utah Press, 2002.

Deverell, William. *Whitewashed Adobe: The Rise of Los Angeles and the Remaking of Its Mexican Past*. Berkeley and Los Angeles: University of California Press, 2004.

———, and Douglas Flamming. "Race, Rhetoric, and Regional Identity: Boosting Los Angeles, 1880–1930." In *Power and Place in the North American West*, edited by Richard White and John M. Findlay. Seattle: University of Washington Press, 1999.

————, and Tom Sitton, eds. *California Progressivism Revisited*. Berkeley and Los Angeles: University of California Press, 1994.

Doyle, Don H. *New Men, New Cities, New South: Atlanta, Nashville, Charleston, Mobile, 1860–1910*. Chapel Hill: University of North Carolina Press, 1990.

Drake, St. Clair, and Horace R. Cayton. *Black Metropolis: A Study of Negro Life in a Northern City*. 1945. Rev. ed., Chicago: University of Chicago Press, 1993.

Duberman, Martin. *Paul Robeson: A Biography*. New York: New Press, 1989. First published 1988 by Knopf.

Du Bois, W. E. B. "Colored California." *The Crisis*, August 1913, 192–96.

Dumke, Glenn S. *The Boom of the Eighties in Southern California*. San Marino, CA: Huntington Library, 1944.

Encyclopedia of American Religions. 4th ed. Farmington, MI: Gale, 1994.

Fisher, James A. "A History of the Political and Social Development of the Black Community in California, 1850–1950." Ph.D. diss., State University of New York at Stony Brook, 1971.

————. "The Political Development of the Black Community in California, 1850–1950." *California Historical Quarterly* 50 (Sept. 1971): 256–66.

Flamming, Douglas. "African-Americans and the Politics of Race in Progressive-Era Los Angeles." In *California Progressivism Revisited*, edited by William Deverell and Tom Sitton. Berkeley and Los Angeles: University of California Press, 1994.

————. "Becoming Democrats: African American Politics in Los Angeles, 1920–1965." In *Seeking El Dorado: African Americans in California*, edited by Lawrence B. de Graaf, Kevin Mulroy, and Quintard Taylor. Los Angeles: Autry Museum of Western Heritage; Seattle and London: University of Washington Press, 2001.

————. "*The Star of Ethiopia* and the NAACP: Pageantry, Politics, and the African American Community of Los Angeles in the 1920s." In *Metropolis in the Making: Los Angeles in the 1920s*, edited by Tom Sitton and William Deverell. Berkeley and Los Angeles: University of California Press, 2001.

————. "A Westerner in Search of 'Negro-ness': Region and Race in the Writing of Arna Bontemps." In *Over the Edge: Remapping the American West*, edited by Valerie J. Matsumoto and Blake Allmendinger. Berkeley and Los Angeles: University of California Press, 1999.

Fogelson, Robert M. *Fragmented Metropolis: Los Angeles, 1850–1930*. 1967. Reprinted with a new preface and foreword. Berkeley and Los Angeles: University of California Press, 1993.

Gabler, Neal. *An Empire of Their Own: How the Jews Invented Hollywood*. New York: Anchor Books, 1988.

Garcia, Mikel Hogan. "Adaptation Strategies of the Los Angeles Black Community, 1883–1919." Ph.D. diss., University of California, Irvine, 1985.

Gatewood, Willard B. *Aristocrats of Color: The Black Elite, 1880–1920*. Bloomington: Indiana University Press, 1990.

George, Lynell. *No Crystal Stair: African Americans in the City of Angels.* London: Verso, 1992.

Goins, Edray. "Ol' Time Religion in a Brave New World." Undergraduate research paper, California Institute of Technology, 1994. Copy in author's possession.

Gottlieb, Peter. *Making Their Own Way: Southern Blacks' Migration to Pittsburgh, 1916–1930.* Urbana: University of Illinois Press, 1987.

Gottlieb, Robert, and Irene Wolt. *Thinking Big: The Story of the "Los Angeles Times," Its Publishers, and Their Influence on Southern California.* New York: G. P. Putnam's Sons, 1977.

Greenberg, Cheryl Lynn. *"Or Does It Explode?" Black Harlem in the Great Depression.* New York: Oxford University Press, 1991.

Gregory, James N. *American Exodus: The Dust Bowl Migration and Okie Culture in California.* New York: Oxford University Press, 1989.

Grossman, James. *Land of Hope: Chicago, Black Southerners, and the Great Migration.* Chicago: University of Chicago Press, 1989.

Gutierrez, David G. *Walls and Mirrors: Mexican Americans, Mexican Immigrants, and the Politics of Ethnicity.* Berkeley and Los Angeles: University of California Press, 1995.

Hall, Kermit L., et al., eds. *The Oxford Companion to the Supreme Court of the United States.* New York: Oxford University Press, 1992.

Harris, William. *Keeping the Faith: A. Philip Randolph, Milton P. Webster, and the Brotherhood of Sleeping Car Porters, 1925–1937.* Urbana: University of Illinois Press, 1977.

Horne, Gerald. *Fire This Time: The Watts Uprising and the 1960s.* Charlottesville: University Press of Virginia, 1995.

Hudson, Karen E. *Paul R. Williams, Architect: A Legacy of Style.* New York: Rizzoli, 1993.

———. *The Will and the Way: Paul R. Williams, Architect.* New York: Rizzoli, 1994.

Huggins, Nathan Irvin. *Harlem Renaissance.* New York: Oxford University Press, 1971.

———, ed. *Voices from the Harlem Renaissance.* New York: Oxford University Press, 1976.

Hughes, Langston. *Panther and the Lash: Poems of Our Times.* New York: Alfred A. Knopf, 1969.

Hunter, Burton L. *The Evolution of Municipal Organization and Administrative Practice in the City of Los Angeles.* Los Angeles: Parker, Stone, and Baird, 1933.

Hunter, Tera W. *To 'Joy My Freedom: Southern Black Women's Lives and Labors after the Civil War.* Cambridge, MA: Harvard University Press, 1997.

Jackson, Kenneth T. *Crabgrass Frontier: The Suburbanization of the United States.* New York: Oxford University Press, 1985.

———. *The Ku Klux Klan in the City, 1915–1930.* 1967. Reprint, Chicago: Ivan R. Dee, Inc., 1992.

Johnson, Marilynn S. *The Second Gold Rush: Oakland and the East Bay in World War II*. Berkeley and Los Angeles: University of California Press, 1994.

Jones, Kirkland C. *Renaissance Man from Louisiana: A Biography of Arna Wendell Bontemps*. Westport, CT: Greenwood Press, 1992.

Katzman, David M. *Before the Ghetto: Black Detroit in the Nineteenth Century*. Urbana: University of Illinois Press, 1973.

Keene, Jennifer D. *The United States and the First World War*. Harlow, England: Longman, 2000.

Kirby, John B. *Black Americans in the Roosevelt Era: Liberalism and Race*. Knoxville: University of Tennessee Press, 1980.

Kousser, J. Morgan. *The Shaping of Southern Politics: Suffrage Restriction and the Establishment of the One-Party South*. New Haven, CT: Yale University Press, 1974.

Kusmer, Kenneth L. *A Ghetto Takes Shape: Black Cleveland, 1870–1930*. Urbana: University of Illinois Press, 1978.

Lang, William L. "The Nearly Forgotten Blacks of Last Chance Gulch." *Pacific Northwest Quarterly* 70 (April 1979): 50–57.

Lapp, Rudolph M. *Afro-Americans in California*. 2nd ed. San Francisco: Boyd and Fraser, 1987.

Leader, Leonard. *Los Angeles and the Great Depression*. New York: Garland Publishing, 1991.

Lemann, Nicholas. *The Promised Land: The Great Black Migration and How It Changed America*. New York: Alfred A. Knopf, 1991.

Leonard, Kevin Allen. "In the Interest of All Races: African Americans and Interracial Cooperation in Los Angeles during and after World War II." In *Seeking El Dorado: African Americans in California*, edited by Lawrence B. de Graaf, Kevin Mulroy, and Quintard Taylor. Los Angeles: Autry Museum of Western Heritage; Seattle and London: University of Washington Press, 2001.

———. "Years of Hope, Days of Fear: The Impact of World War II on Race Relations in Los Angeles." Ph.D. diss., University of California, Davis, 1992.

Leuchtenburg, William E. *Franklin D. Roosevelt and the New Deal, 1932–1940*. New York: Harper, 1963.

Lewis, David Levering. *W. E. B. Du Bois: Biography of a Race, 1868–1919*. New York: Henry Holt, 1993.

———. *W. E. B. Du Bois: The Fight for Equality and the American Century, 1919–1963*. New York: Henry Holt, 2000.

———, ed. *The Portable Harlem Renaissance Reader*. New York: Viking, 1994.

Lewis, Earl. *In Their Own Interests: Race, Class, and Power in Twentieth-Century Norfolk, Virginia*. Berkeley and Los Angeles: University of California Press, 1991.

Lifton, Sarah. "The Incredible Life of John Alexander Somerville: Man of Color." *USC Trojan Family* (Summer 1994): 36–41.

Locke, Alain, ed. *The New Negro*. New York: Albert and Charles Boni, Inc., 1925. Reprinted with a new introduction by Arnold Rampersad. New York: Atheneum, 1992.

Logan, Rayford, and Michael R. Winston. *Dictionary of American Negro Biography*. New York: W. W. Norton, 1983.

Los Angeles Negro Directory and Who's Who, 1930–1931. Los Angeles: California Eagle Publishing Company, n.d., ca. 1931. Microfilm reproduction courtesy of the Special Collections Department, Young Research Library, University of California, Los Angeles.

Matsumoto, Valerie J., and Blake Allmendinger, eds. *Over the Edge: Remapping the American West*. Berkeley and Los Angeles: University of California Press, 1999.

McBroome, Delores Nason. "Harvests of Gold: African American Boosterism, Agriculture, and Investment in Allensworth and Little Liberia." In *Seeking El Dorado: African Americans in California*, edited by Lawrence B. de Graaf, Kevin Mulroy, and Quintard Taylor. Los Angeles: Autry Museum of Western Heritage; Seattle and London: University of Washington Press, 2001.

McWilliams, Carey. *Southern California: An Island on the Land*. 1946. Reprint, Salt Lake City: Peregrine Smith, 1973.

Meier, August. *Negro Thought in America*. Ann Arbor: University of Michigan Press, 1963.

———, and Elliott M. Rudwick. *From Plantation to Ghetto*. 3rd ed. New York: Hill and Wang, 1976.

Miller, Loren. *The Petitioners: The Story of the Supreme Court of the United States and the Negro*. New York: Pantheon Books, 1966.

Modell, John. *The Economics and Politics of Racial Accommodation: The Japanese of Los Angeles, 1900–1942*. Urbana: University of Illinois Press, 1977.

Moore, Leonard. *Citizen Clansman: The Ku Klux Klan in Indiana*. Chapel Hill: University of North Carolina Press, 1997.

Murray, Pauli, comp. and ed. *States' Laws on Race and Color*. 1951. Reprinted with a foreword by Davison M. Douglas. Athens: University of Georgia Press, 1997.

Myrdal, Gunnar. *An American Dilemma: The Negro Problem and Modern Democracy*. New York: Harper, 1944.

Negro Who's Who in California, 1948. Los Angeles: Negro Who's Who in California Publishing Company, 1948.

Nicolaides, Becky M. *My Blue Heaven: Life and Politics in the Working-Class Suburbs of Los Angeles, 1920–1965*. Chicago: University of Chicago Press, 2002.

Nieman, Donald G. *Promises to Keep: African Americans and the Constitutional Order, 1776 to the Present*. New York: Oxford University Press, 1991.

Nugent, Walter. *Into the West: The Story of Its People*. New York: Alfred A. Knopf, 1999.

Otis, Johnny. *Upside Your Head! Rhythm and Blues on Central Avenue*. Hanover, NH: Wesleyan University Press, 1993.

Owen, Chandler. "From Coast to Coast." *The Messenger*, May 1922, 407–10.

———. "Through the Northwest and Up the Pacific Coast." *The Messenger*, June 1922, 424–25.

Painter, Nell Irvin. *Exodusters: Black Migration to Kansas after Reconstruction.* 1977. Reprint, New York: W. W. Norton, 1992.

Pitt, Leonard, and Dale Pitt. *Los Angeles A to Z: An Encyclopedia of the City and County.* Berkeley and Los Angeles: University of California Press, 1997.

Powell, Lieutenant William J. *Black Wings.* Los Angeles: Ivan Deach, Jr., 1934.

Preusser, Serena B. "Color Question in California Reveals Many Problems." *California Real Estate,* July 1927, 35, 61.

Rabinowitz, Howard N. *Race Relations in the Urban South, 1865–1890.* New York: Oxford University Press, 1978.

Rampersad, Arnold. *The Life of Langston Hughes.* Vol. 1, *1902–1941, "I, Too, Sing America."* New York: Oxford University Press, 1986.

Ray, Mary Ellen Bell. *The City of Watts, California, 1907 to 1926.* Los Angeles: Rising Publishing, 1985.

Rice, Lawrence D. *The Negro in Texas: 1874–1900.* Baton Rouge: Louisiana State University Press, 1971.

Robinson, Rachel. *Jackie Robinson: An Intimate Portrait.* New York: Harry N. Abrams, 1996.

Rolle, Andrew. *Los Angeles: From Pueblo to City of the Future.* San Francisco: Boyd and Fraser, 1981.

Ruiz, Vicki L. *From Out of the Shadows: Mexican Women in Twentieth-Century America.* Cambridge, MA: Oxford University Press, 1998.

Rydall, E. H. "California for Colored Folks." *The Colored American Magazine* 12 (May 1907): 386–88.

Sanchez, George J. *Becoming Mexican American: Ethnicity, Culture, and Identity in Chicano Los Angeles, 1900–1945.* New York: Oxford University Press, 1993.

Scruggs, Baxter S. *A Man in Our Community: The Biography of L. G. Robinson of Los Angeles, California.* Gardena, CA: Institute Press, 1937.

Sides, Josh. *L.A. City Limits: African American Los Angeles from the Great Depression to the Present.* Berkeley and Los Angeles: University of California Press, 2003.

———. "Working Away: African American Migration and Community in Los Angeles from the Great Depression to 1954." Ph.D. diss., University of California, Los Angeles, 1999.

Sinclair, Upton. *I, Candidate for Governor: And How I Got Licked.* 1934–35. Reprinted with an introduction by James M. Gregory. Berkeley and Los Angeles: University of California Press, 1994.

Sitkoff, Harvard. *A New Deal for Blacks: The Emergence of Civil Rights as a National Issue: The Depression Decade.* New York: Oxford University Press, 1981.

Sitton, Tom, and William Deverell, eds. *Metropolis in the Making: Los Angeles in the 1920s.* Berkeley and Los Angeles: University of California Press, 2001.

Somerville, J. Alexander. *Man of Color: An Autobiography by Dr. J. Alexander*

Somerville: A Factual Report on the Status of the American Negro Today. Los Angeles: Lorrin L. Morrison, 1949.

Spear, Allan H. *Black Chicago: The Making of a Negro Ghetto, 1890–1920.* Chicago: University of Chicago Press, 1967.

Stimson, Grace. *The Rise of the Labor Movement in Los Angeles.* Los Angeles: University of California Press, 1955.

Streitmatter, Rodger. *Raising Her Voice: African American Journalists Who Changed History.* Lexington: University Press of Kentucky, 1994.

Taylor, Quintard. "Black Communities in the Pacific Northwest." *Journal of Negro History* 64 (Fall 1979): 342–54.

———. *The Forging of a Black Community: Seattle's Central District from 1870 through the Civil Rights Era.* Seattle: University of Washington Press, 1994.

———. *In Search of the Racial Frontier: African Americans in the American West, 1528–1990.* New York: Norton, 1998.

Tenette, Louis S., and B. B. Bratton, comps., *Western Progress: A Pictorial Story of Economic and Social Advancement in Los Angeles, California.* Los Angeles: Tenette & Bratton, 1928.

Thompson, Noah D. "California: The Horn of Plenty." *The Messenger* 6 (July 1924): 215–17, 220–21.

Thornbrough, Emma Lou. "The National Afro-American League." *Journal of Southern History* 27 (Nov. 1961): 494–512.

Thurman, Wallace. *The Blacker the Berry . . . A Novel of Negro Life.* 1929. Reprint, New York: Collier Books, Macmillan Publishing Company, 1970.

Tinney, James S. "William J. Seymour: Father of Modern-Day Pentecostalism." In *Black Apostles: Afro-American Clergy Confront the Twentieth Century,* edited by Bos and Randall K. Burkett. Woodbridge, CT: G. K. Hall, 1978.

Tolbert, Emory. *The UNIA and Black Los Angeles: Ideology and Community in the American Garvey Movement.* Los Angeles: CAAS, 1980.

Trotter, Joe William, Jr. *Black Milwaukee: The Making of an Industrial Proletariat, 1915–45.* Urbana: University of Illinois Press, 1985.

———, ed. *The Great Migration in Historical Perspective: New Dimensions of Race, Class, and Gender.* Bloomington: Indiana University Press, 1991.

United States Bureau of the Census. *Fifteenth Census of the United States: 1930.* Vol. 4, *Population.* Washington, D.C.: Government Printing Office, 1933.

———. *Fourteenth Census of the United States, Taken in the Year 1920.* Vol. 4, *Population 1920, Occupations.* Washington, D.C., 1923.

———. *Negroes in the United States, 1920–1932.* Washington, D.C., 1935.

———. *Negro Population in the United States, 1790–1915.* Washington, D.C., 1918.

———. *Occupations at the Twelfth Census, 1900.* Washington, D.C., 1904.

———. *Thirteenth Census of the United States, Taken in the Year 1910.* Vol. 4, *Population, 1910, Occupational Statistics.* Washington, D.C., 1914.

———. *Twelfth Census of the United States, 1900, Population, Part 1.* Washington, D.C., 1901.

Von Brauchitsch, Dennis M. "The Ku Klux Klan in California, 1921–1924." Master's thesis, Sacramento State College, 1967.

Vorspan, Max, and Lloyd P. Gartner. *History of the Jews in Los Angeles.* San Marino, CA: Huntington Library, 1970.

Vose, Clement E. *Caucasians Only: The Supreme Court, the NAACP, and the Restrictive Covenant Cases.* Berkeley and Los Angeles: University of California Press, 1967.

Watts, Jill Marie. "'Shout the Victory': The History of Father Divine and the Peace Mission Movement, 1879–1942." Ph.D. diss., University of California, Los Angeles, 1989.

Weiss, Nancy J. *Farewell to the Party of Lincoln: Black Politics in the Age of FDR.* Princeton, NJ: Princeton University Press, 1983.

Wheeler, B. Gordon. *Black California: The History of African-Americans in the Golden State.* New York: Hippocrene Books, 1993.

White, Richard. "Race Relations in the American West." *American Quarterly* 38 (1986): 396–416.

————, and John M. Findlay, eds. *Power and Place in the North American West.* Seattle: University of Washington Press, 1999.

White, Walter. *A Man Called White: The Autobiography of Walter White.* 1948. Reprint, Athens: University of Georgia Press, 1995.

Whiteman, Luther, and Samuel L. Lewis. *Glory Roads: The Psychological State of California.* New York: Thomas Y. Crowell, 1936.

Williams, Paul R. "I Am a Negro." *American Magazine,* July 1937.

Wolfskill, George. *Happy Days Are Here Again: A Short Interpretive History of the New Deal.* Hinsdale, IL: Dryden Press, 1974.

Oral Histories

Deavers, George [Jr.]. Draft transcript of oral history conducted in 1966 by R. Donald Brown. Oral History Program, California State University, Fullerton.

Beavers, George [Jr.]. "In Quest of Full Citizenship." Transcript of oral history conducted in 1982 by Ranford B. Hopkins. Department of Special Collections, Young Research Library, University of California, Los Angeles.

Bontemps, Arna. Draft transcript of oral history conducted in 1972 by Ann Allen Shockley. Special Collections Library, Fisk University, Nashville.

Bradley, Tom. "The Impossible Dream." Transcript of oral history conducted in 1978 and 1979 by Bernard Galm. Department of Special Collections, Young Research Library, University of California, Los Angeles.

Hahn, Kenneth. Tape-recorded interview conducted in 1994 by Douglas Flamming.

Hawkins, Augustus F. Tape-recorded interview conducted in 1996 by Douglas Flamming.

————. Transcript of oral history conducted in 1988 by Carlos Vasquez. State Government Oral History Program, Young Research Library, University of California, Los Angeles.

Hudson, Dr. H. Claude. Draft transcript of oral history conducted in 1966 and 1967 by R. Donald Brown. Oral History Program, California State University, Fullerton.

Johnson, Clarence. Draft transcript of oral history conducted in 1967 by R. Donald Brown. Oral History Program, California State University, Fullerton.

Johnson, George P. "Collector of Negro Film History." Transcript of oral history conducted in 1967 and 1968 by Elizabeth Dixon and Adelaide Tusler. Department of Special Collections, Young Research Library, University of California, Los Angeles.

Lomax, Almena Davis. Draft transcript of oral history conducted in 1966 and 1967 by R. Donald Brown. Oral History Program, California State University, Fullerton.

Matthews, Charles. "Remembering Ralph Bunche." Transcript of oral history conducted in 1973 by Joel Gardner. Department of Special Collections, Young Research Library, University of California, Los Angeles.

Matthews, Miriam. "Miriam Matthews: An Oral History." Transcript of oral history conducted by Billy Field, n.d. [ca. 1980]. African American Museum and Library of Oakland, California.

Miller, Loren. Draft transcript of oral history conducted in 1967 by Lawrence B. de Graaf. Oral History Program, California State University, Fullerton.

Roberts, Pearl. "Pearl Roberts: An Oral History." Transcript of oral history conducted by Billy Field, n.d. [ca. 1980]. African American Museum and Library of Oakland, California.

Smith, Jimmy [Jimmie]. Draft transcript of oral history conducted in 1974 by Lawrence B. de Graaf. Oral History Program, California State University, Fullerton.

Somerville, Dr. J[ohn] Alexander. Draft transcript of oral history conducted by R. Donald Brown, n.d. [ca. 1966]. Oral History Program, California State University, Fullerton.

Somerville, J[ohn], and Vada Somerville. Draft transcript of oral history conducted in 1967 by Lawrence B. de Graaf. Oral History Program, California State University, Fullerton.

White, Marilyn. Tape-recorded oral history conducted in 2002 by Douglas Flamming.

Williams, Verna Deckard. Transcript of oral history conducted in 1992 by Amy Kitchener. Shades of L.A. Oral History Project, History Department, Los Angeles Public Library.

Manuscript Collections

Baldwin, C. B., papers. Special Collections Department, University of Iowa Libraries, Iowa City.

Bass, Charlotta A., papers. Southern California Library for Social Studies and Research, Los Angeles.

Bowron, Fletcher, papers. Henry E. Huntington Library, San Marino, California.

Dellums, Cottrell Laurence, papers. Bancroft Library, University of California, Berkeley.

Forsythe, Harold Bruce, collection. Henry E. Huntington Library, San Marino, California.

Hawkins, Augustus F., collection. Department of Special Collections, Young Research Library, University of California, Los Angeles.

Lissner, Meyer, papers. Department of Special Collections, Stanford University Libraries, Palo Alto, California.

Matthews, Miriam, collection. African American Museum and Library, Oakland, California.

——, collection. California Afro-American History Museum, Los Angeles.

McGroarty, John Steven, scrapbooks. Archival Center, Archdiocese of Los Angeles, San Fernando Mission, Los Angeles.

National Association for the Advancement of Colored People, Branch Files, Los Angeles, 1913–1939. Photocopied collection courtesy Library of Congress, Washington, D.C.

National Association of Colored Women's Clubs, records, 1895–1992. Part 1: Minutes of National Conventions, Publications, and President's Office Correspondence. Microfilm edition, University Publications of America, Bethesda, Maryland.

O'Melveny, Henry, papers. Henry E. Huntington Library, San Marino, California.

Pardee, George W., papers. Bancroft Library, University of California, Berkeley.

Roberts [Frederick Madison] Family collection. African American Museum and Library, Oakland, California.

Stimson, Marshall, collection. Henry E. Huntington Library, San Marino, California.

Vivian, Octavia. "American Guide: Historical Section—L.A.—263: Important Persons (Negro)." Typed manuscript, Federal Works Program papers, Box 46, "The People," sec. 2, vol. 1, pt. 2. Department of Special Collections, Young Research Library, University of California, Los Angeles.

Index

Compositor: Integrated Composition Systems

Text: 10/13 Aldus

Display: Aldus

Printer and binder: Thomson-Shore